PLAYING WITH PAINTED
A PERFORMANCE WITH C
THE BEACH. STUDYING LC
A COUNTER-HEGEMONIC
MADE MODEL TO CALCULATE HITHERTO INCALCULABLE
SHAPES. FARMING PROCESSES SEEKING TO GROUND
NEW RELATIONSHIPS IN THE LAND. WORKSHOPS
EMPOWERING BLACK TEENAGERS TO RESHAPE THEIR
NEIGHBORHOOD. A DECOMMISSIONED COMPUTER
LAB FINDING A SECOND LIFE. BUILDING A HOUSE FROM
GARBAGE. A ROAD TRIP THROUGH THE VERNACULAR
SETTLEMENTS OF THE MIDDLE EAST. A LABORATORY
FARM TO LEARN FROM INDIGENOUS CONSTRUCTION
TECHNIQUES. A DOUBLE-DECKER BUS STITCHING
DISPERSED SCHOOLS INTO A THINKING MACHINE.
A SERIES OF COMPUTER-GENERATED MAPS ELUCIDATING
URBAN INEQUALITIES. DESIGNING STACKABLE TEACUPS
IN A "MONASTERY" ON A HILL. MURALS TO MATERIALIZE
ANTICOLONIAL SENSITIVITIES IN THE CITY. A SUMMER
SCHOOL GIVING WOMEN A SAFE SPACE TO DEVELOP
ARCHITECTURAL SKILLS.

RAD
PED
GOG

EDITED BY
BEATRIZ COLOMINA
IGNACIO G. GALÁN
EVANGELOS KOTSIORIS
ANNA-MARIA MEISTER

ICAL

A-

IES

THE MIT PRESS

Cambridge, Massachusetts — London, England

CONTENTS

CONTENTS
BY DATE

1930S

1940S

1950S

1960S

CONTENTS
BY LONGITUDE

-120° TO -61°

Urban Planning, University of Lagos—Nigeria

104 **(4,35;50,85)**
Ecole Nationale supérieure d'architecture et des arts visuels-La Cambre; Atelier de Recherche et d'Action Urbaines; Archives d'Architecture Moderne—Belgium

(4,35;52,01)
225 Various schools around the world—The Netherlands, Germany, Austria, USA, Spain, and elsewhere
31 Delft School of Architecture, Delft Institute of Technology—The Netherlands

(4,55;7,49)
207 University of Ife—Nigeria

(5,32;60,39)
162 Extra-institutional, with connections to NTH, Trondheim; Oslo School of Architecture; Warsaw Art Academy—Norway

(7,68;45,06)
36 Politecnico di Torino—Italy

(7,71;11,08)
29 Department of Architecture, Ahmadu Bello University—Nigeria

(8,54;47,37)
374 F+F School of Experimental Design—Switzerland

(9,18;48,78)
318 Institute for Lightweight Structures (Institut für Leichte Flächentragwerke) at University of Stuttgart—Germany
25 University of Stuttgart—Germany

(9,19;45,46)
98 Istituto Universitario di Architettura di Venezia; Politecnico di Milano—Italy

(9,47;51,31)
186 Gesamthochschule Kassel—Germany

(9,99;48,4)
121 Hochschule für Gestaltung—Germany

(11,26;43,77)
93 University of Florence (Università degli Studi di Firenze)—Italy

(11,37;45,84)
80 Global Tools—Italy, Germany, Switzerland

(12,33;45,44)
136 Istituto Universitario di Architettura di Venezia—Italy
48 Istituto Universitario di Architettura di Venezia—Italy

(12,63;43,72)
293 The International Laboratory of Architecture and Urban Design—Italy

(13,38;52,52)
95 TU Berlin—Germany

(14,55;53,42)
282 Szczecin University of Technology—Poland

(15,27;50,67)
165 Sdružení inženýrů a architektů v Liberci (Liberec Association of Engineers and Architects)—Czechoslovakia

(15,97;45,81)
358 State Master Workshop for Architecture—Yugoslavia

(16,37;48,21)
244 Technische Hochschule Wien; Galerie nächst St. Stephan—Austria

(20,46;44,81)
173 Faculty of Architecture, University of Belgrade—Yugoslavia

(21,01;52,22)
110 Warsaw Academy of Fine Arts—Poland

(28,04;-26,2)
86 Department of Architecture, University of the Witwatersrand—South Africa

(31,23;30,04)
297 Department of Architecture, Faculty of Engineering, Cairo University—Egypt

(32,85;39,92)
364 Middle East Technical University—Turkey

(35,22;31,71)
210 Neighborhood Schools—Palestine
77 The Center for the Cultivation of Islamic Art—Israel and the Occupied Palestinian Territories

(35,45;31,85)
334 Alami Farm—Palestine

(35,52;-18,66)
68 Mbari Club; Chemchemi—Mozambique, Nigeria, South Africa, Rhodesia, Kenya

(36,82;-1,29)
119 University of Nairobi—Kenya

(36,98;56,18)
126 Senezh Design Studio—USSR

(37,61;55,75)
379 Experimental Children's Architectural Studio—USSR/Russian Federation

(37,62;55,75)
90 Moscow Institute of Architecture—USSR

(38,75;9,03)
362 Ethio-Swedish Institute of Building Technology—Ethiopia

(44,36;33,31)
65 Department of Architecture, University of Baghdad—Iraq

(54,56;32,64)
75 Faculty of Architecture in the School of Fine Arts at the University of Tehran; Cal-Earth—Iran, USA

60° TO 119°

(67,06;24,97)
278 Middle East Technical University; Karachi University—Turkey, Gambia, Pakistan

(72,57;23,02)
272 National Institute of Design—India

(73,19;22,3)
58 Faculty of Fine Arts (Baroda School), Maharaja Sayajirao University—India

(75,86;22,72)
349 Vastu Shilpa Foundation; The Minimum Cost Housing Group of McGill University School of Architecture—India, Canada

(90,41;23,81)
275 East Pakistan University of Engineering and Technology—East Pakistan (Bangladesh)

(103,82;1,36)
302 Singapore Polytechnic—Singapore

(115,86;-31,95)
160 Australasian Architecture Students Association and other student architecture organizations—Australia, New Zealand

(118,79;32,06)
150 School of Architecture, Nanjing Institute of Technology—China

120° TO 179°

(139,76;35,68)
355 University of Tokyo—Japan
179 University of Tokyo—Japan

38 **(147,32;-42,88)**
Tasmanian College of Advanced Education, University of Tasmania—Australia

212 **(174,76;-36,85)**
University of Auckland—New Zealand

352 **(174,77;-41,29)**
Architectural Centre Inc.—New Zealand

INTRODUCTION

Beatriz Colomina, Ignacio G. Galán,
Evangelos Kotsioris, Anna-Maria Meister

In the 1960s and 1970s architectural education was shaken to the core by a veritable explosion of experimental teaching practices all over the world. It was nothing short of a revolution. *Radical Pedagogies* explores the still-expanding galaxy of these remarkable experiments, which profoundly reshaped architecture by rejecting any normative thinking. The teaching projects had multiple beginnings and endings. They did not follow any existing recipe or method. In fact, it was precisely through their heterogeneous and shifting nature that they destabilized the field. Their effects linger to this day, haunting the conversation.

Etymologically the term "radical" comes from the Latin *radix*, the root. All these teaching experiments were radical in relentlessly shaking disciplinary foundations, disturbing assumptions rather than reinforcing and disseminating them. The field was opened up to new kinds of thinking, practice, and responsibility, along with new modes of perception, solidarity, and communication. *Radical Pedagogies* documents a sustained call to revolutionize architecture, to multiply and magnify its possibilities.

The experiments typically had a short lifespan: some were abandoned or dissolved by the protagonists themselves; others were expelled from, or conversely assimilated into, mainstream education, or terminated due to financial or political constraints.[1] In testing the limits of the discipline, they were by definition precarious. Sometimes it was even their very success that hastened their demise. Conversely, what might have been perceived as failure at the time could historically be categorized as success. Some experiments were even designed to fail. Many were hit-and-run raids, limited strategic interventions, while others were long-term Trojan horses inserted into the system. There were usually multiple afterlives. Despite their often-premature "deaths," these seemingly short-lived projects drastically affected those structures that absorbed them, transforming the discipline for decades to come. Even after their apparent destruction, their ideas linger and the networks persist. After all, in both their rise and fall, they were never isolated but connected and interactive like an extended, ever-shifting but resilient mycelium of fungi.[2] Reading them through their dissolution, absorption, death, and afterlives—rather than solely through their founding myths—is crucial to understanding what they were up against, the threat they posed, and the long-term changes they instigated.

It is important to recognize that the struggle was never simply binary, never simply conservative institution versus radical experiment, fixed administration versus mobile students, new ideas versus old conventions. Rather than just one front, there were multiple shifting battlefields in which the status of all actors was continuously renegotiated. Sometimes the conflict between radical teacher and radical student was the most heated of all.

A remarkable photograph of May 1968, for example, shows Giancarlo De Carlo in a vigorous debate with protesting students who have taken over the Milan Triennale. He leans forward, angry but listening intently as a student lectures him. Both sides, the teacher and the students surrounding him, are radicals. Despite his jacket and tie, Giancarlo De Carlo is a self-professed anarchist and the students are in effect following his call to question institutional authority by refusing to follow him, even as he directs a Triennale ostensibly devoted to the political self-determination of individuals within the "greatest number." The whole ecology of architectural education is destabilized, twisting restlessly around itself in a kind of vortex. The circle of students has become a classroom—a portable, improvised space in which the real teacher is now the streets. The line between urban life and education has dissolved. Protest has become pedagogy.

The pedagogical experiments engaged many dimensions of the politics of the period, either by actively joining political protests or by trying to retreat from and rethink traditional understandings of politics. Pedagogy was conceived as a political arena beyond the confines of architecture teaching. In every case, it was a revolt. But what it means to revolt was constantly questioned—a rest-less project, exacerbated by the fact that a revolution in education is by definition paradoxical, even ultimately a contradiction in terms. Revolt in education can never be satisfied with itself. "Radical pedagogy" might even be an oxymoron.

A sucession of philosophers who were key reference points for radicals in architecture thought through these paradoxes. In 1954 Hannah Arendt had argued that "The problem of education in the modern world lies in the fact that by its very nature it cannot forgo either authority or tradition, and yet must proceed in a world that

Giancarlo de Carlo
debates with Gianemilio
Simonetti as protesting
students take over the
Milan Triennale in May
1968. Photograph by
Cesare Colombo.

is neither structured by authority nor held together by tradition."[3] As she saw it, the crisis in education was bound to a wider crisis in authority. Ivan Illich challenged authority with a project of "deschooling." Focusing on the internal politics of the relations forged inside the classroom, he proposed "educational *webs* which heighten the opportunity for each one to transform each moment of his living into one of learning, sharing, and caring."[4] A central question of the period was how education either sustained social hierarchies or offered the possibility to subvert them. Paulo Freire, the Brazilian philosopher and educator whose "pedagogy of the oppressed" was taken up in the architecture, exhibitions, and teaching of Lina Bo Bardi, argued that a pedagogy encouraging critical thinking was inextricably linked to "the incessant struggle [of the oppressed] to regain their humanity."[5]

In the United States, the liberatory potential of education acquired a deeper significance with the civil rights movement. In his 1963 "Talk to Teachers" James Baldwin decried the default racialization of teaching, observing that societal change was only possible by challenging current education, by releasing rather than entrapping the student: "[T]he paradox of education is precisely—that as one begins to become conscious one begins to examine the society in which he [sic] is being educated. The purpose of education, finally, is to create in a person the ability to look at the world for himself, to make his own decisions."[6] Likewise, writer, teacher, and activist June Jordan mobilized Black and Puerto Rican students to generate knowledge rather than receive it, drawing on their lived experiences in the Harlem community to counter the race, class, and gender power structures embodied and sustained by the university.[7] Activist feminist philosopher Grace Lee Boggs considered education "a great necessity" as well as "a great obsession" and rejected the "myth" that "schools are the best and only place for people to get an education."[8] Boggs demanded a "new system of education" altogether, one that would hand over control to the Black communities that have been "most decisively failed" by the current system. On the other side of the Atlantic, French philosopher Jacques Rancière later echoed this reversal of power dynamics. He described acts of mastery and explication as a form of stultification, since they assume one person's intelligence to be superior to another's. Instead, he proposed a logics of emancipation that challenged traditional hierarchies between faculty and students in modes of knowledge production and dissemination.[9]

While pedagogy was increasingly understood as a political agent, academic institutions became sites of extended intellectual, aesthetic, and often physical battles. As student revolts unfolded around the world from May 1968 they broke down established educational frameworks, demanding student involvement in the curriculum and administration of schools, and greater access to higher education for all, regardless of race, class, disability and gender. Some understood academic institutions as mechanisms for perpetuating existing systems of domination, while others trusted them as necessary hosts or even sources of emancipatory politics.[10] Most intellectuals critiqued the university's privileged position, seeing its claim to independence from political structures as a selective form of freedom complicit with bourgeois liberal ideology.[11] In the US, many institutions of higher education were integral to the development of the military-industrial complex; others were breeding grounds for the civil rights movement. In postcolonial nations, schools were crucial to the project of independence, and yet some served to preserve colonial hierarchies,[12] escaping the ill-fitting frameworks provided by institutionalized education altogether, many experiments happened outside university walls as a form of political resistance.

In architecture education, the political impetus of the 1968 protests was used to set fire to authoritative forces, geopolitical hegemonies, colonial hierarchies, and capitalist structures. New constituencies, techniques, and materials were brought into the gated disciplinary community to transform its social and material ecologies; or education was moved out of schools into different spaces, technologies, media, and forms of countercultural living. In reverse, in postcolonial nations, the very existence of self-determined architectural curricula often constituted a radical political proposition in itself.

Architecture pedagogies, and more particularly schools of architecture, were objects of relentless critique in all these struggles. Within institutional frameworks, authority was challenged from within. And a broad range of newly bred countermovements and unorthodox pedagogical models sought to undermine existing hierarchical structures. There were attempts to institutionalize radicalism, or, alternatively, to abolish institutions altogether. And yet, the question remained regarding the possibility of having any countermovement *within* these educational institutions. "If the implementation of a liberating education requires political power and the oppressed have none, how then is it possible to carry out the pedagogy of the oppressed prior to the revolution?," Freire asked. He proposed a distinction between "*systematic education,* which can only be changed by political power," and "*educational projects,* which should be carried out *with* the oppressed in the process of organizing them."[13] Architecture educators—among them many outspoken political figures and activists—often claimed their "independence" from the systems in which they operated, even if—ironically enough—many of them parasitized, exploited, or simply needed those institutions as contrast for their radical self-definition.[14]

Radical pedagogies sought to break free from conventional definitions of institutions. Often escaping schools or official administrative complexes, they longed to effect direct systematic change in patriarchal, colonial, ableist, or other entrenched discriminatory power structures. But even when deployed inside "traditional" schools, such experiments mobilized institutionalization itself for critical intervention. Institution-building was seen as a form of experimental emancipation; a vehicle toward making visible that which conventionally had been overlooked, such as local building practices, vernacular forms and technologies, or non-academic methods. The emancipatory potential of institutions as recognized parts of society offered paths to recognize disenfranchised groups and communities, validating the needs and sensitivities of non-whites, underprivileged, women, and disabled individuals and communities, among others. Rather than pitting extreme perspectives against conventional structures, this volume identifies a whole spectrum of attempted critiques—from resistance to reinforcement, from undercover activism to outright political protest.[15] It was the very idea of political activism, and of politics more broadly, that was disputed and rethought.

In architecture the "radical" 1960s and 1970s revealed the anxieties caused by the discipline's uncertainty about its identity in a rapidly transforming world. Architecture's evident complicity with the logics of capital and colonial forces, and its implication in sustaining normative hierarchies, prompted questions about its values. As corporations and governments furthered standardization of the building industry, and planning emerged as an independent discipline, the social role of the architect dwindled. Even the bright (white) future that modern architecture had once promised was problematized by anti-colonial sentiments and environmental concerns. Any monolithic illusion of progress had now splintered into a vast array of anti-modern, pre-modern, and postmodern approaches, all of which yearned to define architecture afresh.

No disciplinary protocols could be taken for granted anymore. Architecture was forced to reexamine its foundations. Some forms of radical practice sought to respond to the complicity with power and the market by artificially delimiting disciplinary frameworks, often within an understanding of architecture as a discrete formal language. But most expanded architecture's engagement with larger cultural and environmental milieus. They engaged with different forms of knowledge across disciplines, ranging from anthropology and sociology, all the way to mathematics, statistics, and the "hard" sciences.

As architecture sought to expand its horizons, its focus increasingly moved to the kinds of processes that the built environment mediated, rather than buildings themselves. Turning away from the design of the architectural object, educators redirected the architect's disciplinary tools and protocols toward a whole new set of performances, techniques of analysis, and theoretical frameworks. In parallel to this decentering of building, many teachers and students dismissed the understanding of the architect as singular author, defining new roles for designers, as well as participatory forms of practice in pursuit of new forms of collective agency. Any sense of architecture as a unified, stable field of knowledge was jettisoned by a kaleidoscopic array of challenges to conventional thinking and making.

These shifts sometimes became apparent through the imagery of student designs, studio reviews, thesis projects, and end of year exhibitions. But it was through curricular structures, studio briefs, course descriptions, exercise handouts, reading bibliographies, travel schedules, task lists, and meeting timelines that the essence of the experiments was truly hard-coded. The polemical rejection of previous learning models and the aspiration for new modes of production for architectural knowledge were encapsulated in precisely these pedagogical documents, which allow for the reconstruction of groundbreaking experiments in architecture, but also provide a lucid blueprint of the ethical imperatives—whether elusively implied or explicitly stated—that drove the impulse for change. While commonly perceived as managerial documents that precede learning, curricula and syllabi embody a theory of education and a theory of practice; they impart a particular redefinition of architecture, tell us by whom and for whom it is produced.

Despite calls to hands-on action over institutional bureaucracy, even the most anti-bureaucratic educators of the second half of the twentieth century relied heavily on various modes of inscription. In an age of supposedly increasing dematerialization, the material traces of architecture and its pedagogy became all the more significant. These were no longer precious sketches or skillful drawings by architects, but rather student publications, pamphlets, posters, and an array of new "teaching documents," including travel maps, (pseudo-)scientific diagrams, hand-painted murals, demonstration hand-outs, field research questionnaires, infographics, punch cards, self-governance constitutions, and voting ballots. The more architects agonized over reducing walls to ethereal membranes, the more the thinness of paper was elevated to a surrogate for architecture itself. Architecture was reframed as just one medium among many—inseparable from the profound transformations brought about by a whole new galaxy of new media.

Diverse media did not just probe the limits of the discipline, but became a threat to the gatekeeping of knowledge.[16] Buckminster Fuller prophesied that physical classrooms would soon be deserted and classes would be held electronically, with students connected through two-way TV systems from their own homes.[17] It is symptomatic that the very first mass experiments in remote education were set in motion right after May 1968. As technological innovations—satellite television, early computing networks, and VHS—decisively altered architectural pedagogy, radical groups fantasized about an interplanetary infrastructure for the democratization of educational information, freely distributed through terrestrial computer terminals, orbiting satellites, and even lunar bases. Teachers as a one-way transmitters of knowledge became a target; a relic of hierarchical power structures now undermined by the democratization of photomechanical and electronic technologies. Educational innovation did not solely hinge on new media: even the inherited technique of nineteenth-century art historical education—the Wölfflinian, comparative slide projection—became an instrument for criticism through new means of exchanging content.

Bodies themselves, once understood within the Western humanist tradition as the basis of architectural proportion and harmony, became a medium of radical education:[18] aggregated in well-heated classrooms or sun-drenched outdoor decks; hammering structures together; traveling around the countryside by car, plane, and bus; joined together by the physical exertion of climbing up mountains; coming together in solidarity in homes to self-organize and establish more inclusive learning institutions; gathering in public spaces to protest the gender conformity of domestic space; non-conforming bodies united to question the structures of the past and to start anew.

Radical Pedagogies accepts the unbounded nature of the field of experiments it describes—a body of work whose ever-shifting contours become sharper, but never seek a fixed outline. Embracing this polysemy does not simply provide an opportunity to probe educational experiments that are not easy to categorize, it also allows for the exploration of the breadth of architecture's multiple fields of operation while opening up space for unexpected forms of radicalism. Adopting the open-ended and heterogenous structure of its material, the project still retains certain disciplinary gravitations toward specific geographies and figures, many of which are part of architecture's canon today, even if they tried to work against canonical thinking in their time. But these gravitations are also a reflection of the archives available to build the histories this book aims to record. Many of the case studies included in this volume draw from neatly organized archives in authoritative institutions with a wealth of visual and documentary material. At the same time, many other student initiatives, dissenting faculty, and political activists discussed here were not accidentaly omitted by conventional "archives," but even actively banned from them. Archives are "fundamentally a matter of discrimination and selection, which, in the end, results in the granting of a privileged status to certain written documents, and the refusal of that same status to others," as Achile Mbembe astutely observes.[19] To give space to undocumented experiments, many of the contributions in this volume rely on personal collections, oral histories, and various ephemera—and point to the work yet to be done.

In a moment of global crises, ecological catastrophe, and rapidly increasing inequities, the challenge to inherited disciplinary hierarchies again can, and must, happen in the spaces of education. *Radical Pedagogies* brings to light a panorama of past attempts to subvert the status quo, and reveals work to build upon and ideas waiting to be taken up again. It is a kind of stocktaking of potentials, an invitation to open new paths and formulate an unruly set of new questions for both architects and architecture historians to address—a provocation to challenge conventions, categories, and canons and to collectively reimagine pedagogy toward transformative forms of architecture practice.

1. There is a vast literature on the absorption of radical thought into the institutions that it challenged. A particularly acute parallel to the process of absorption of pedagogical experiments into the disciplinary framework (or the attempt to do so) can be seen with the struggle to absorb subaltern histories into history as a discipline. See, for example, Dipesh Chakrabarty, *Provincializing Europe: Postcolonial Thought and Historical Difference* (Princeton, NJ: Princeton University Press, 2000).

2. Theories of revolution have employed the image of the mycelium of fungi as an invisible connecting tissue between otherwise seemingly disparate moments of resistance. See Abraham DeLeon, "A Schizophrenic Scholar out for a Stroll: Multiplicities, Becomings, Conjurings," in *Taboo: The Journal of Culture and Education* 17, no. 1 (May 2018). For a cultural history of the mushroom as both object and analytic of global economic and political dependencies, see A. L. Tsing, *The Mushroom at the End of the World* (Princeton, NJ: Princeton University Press, 2015).

3. Hannah Arendt, "The Crisis in Education," collected in *Between Past and Future: Six Exercises in Political Thought* (New York: Viking Press, 1961), 195–196.

4. Ivan Illich, *Deschooling Society* (London: Marion Boyars, 1971), 2. Emphasis in the original.

5. See Paulo Freire, *Pedagogy of the Oppressed*, 30th Anniversary Edition, trans. Myra Bergman Ramos (London: Continuum, 2005), 48. Originally published in 1968. Freire's goal has been conceptualized as seeking to "transform what Frantz Fanon terms 'the wretched of the earth' from 'being for others' to 'beings for themselves'." Stanley Aronowitz, "Paulo Freire's Radical Democratic Humanism" in Peter McLaren and Peter Leonard, *Paulo Freire: A Critical Encounter* (London: Routledge, 1993), 13.

6. James Baldwin, "Talk to Teachers," delivered October 16, 1963, as "The Negro Child—His Self-Image"; originally published in *The Saturday Review*, December 21, 1963.

7. On Jordan's pedagogical endeavors, see "'This Class Has Something to Teach America': June Jordan and the Democratization of Poetry and Pedagogy," in Danica Savonick, "Insurgent Knowledge: The Poetics of Pedagogy of Toni Cade Bambara, June Jordan, Audre Lorde, and Adrienne Rich in the Era of Open Admissions," PhD diss. (City University of New York, 2018).

8. Grace Lee Boggs, "Education: The Great Obsession," *Monthly Review* 22, no. 4 (September 1970): 18–39. The essay was originally part of a lecture series entitled "Challenge of the 70s" delivered at the University Center for Adult Education, Wayne State University, in the fall of 1969.

9. Jacques Rancière, *The Ignorant Schoolmaster: Five Lessons in Intellectual Emancipation* (Stanford, CA: Stanford University Press, 1991), 13; original in French, *Le Maître ignorant: Cinq leçons sur l'émancipation intellectuelle* (Paris: Fayard, 1987).

10. German-American philosopher Herbert Marcuse, for example, acknowledged the "subversive" potential of general education but also noted that the expansion of education was driven by the need of industrial societies for a skilled workforce. Herbert Marcuse, "Lecture on Education, Brooklyn College, 1968," in *Marcuse's Challenge to Education*, ed. Douglas Kellner, Tyson Lewis, Clayton Pierce, and K. Daniel Cho (New York: Rowman & Littlefield, 2009), 33–34.

11. Louis Althusser, "Student Problems (1964)," *Radical Philosophy, a Journal of Socialist and Feminist Philosophy*, no. 170 (December 2011): 11–15.

12. On the tension between universities and the project of decolonization in Africa see Achile Mbembe, "Decolonizing the University: New Directions," in Arts and Humanities in Higher Education 15, no. 1 (2016). This period coincides with what Paul Tiyambe Zeleza has called "the golden era" of African universities between 1950 and 1970. See Paul Tiyambe Zeleza, "African Studies and Universities since Independence," *Transition*, no. 101 (2009): 112.

13. Freire, *Pedagogy of the Oppressed*, 54. Emphasis in the original.

14. Some educators shared Althusser's thesis on institutionalized education, criticizing "the school…teaches 'know-how,' but in forms which ensure subjection to the ruling ideology or the mastery of its 'practices'." Louis Althusser, "Ideology and Ideological State Apparatuses (Notes Towards an Investigation)," in *Lenin and Philosophy and Other Essays*, trans. Ben Brewster (London: New Left Books, 1971), 133.

15. This approach builds on feminist methods of critique such as Donna Haraway's argument for diversified approaches rather than oppositional categories in her landmark 1985 essay "A Manifesto for Cyborgs." See Donna Haraway, "A Manifesto for Cyborgs: Science, Technology, and Socialist-Feminism in the Late Twentieth Century," in *Socialist Review* 80 (1985): 65–107. As Chela Sandoval writes, any "global transcultural coalitions for egalitarian social justice" was dependent on the differential as critical practice. See Chela Sandoval, *Methodologies of the Oppressed* (Minneapolis: University of Minnesota Press, 2000).

16. For Canadian media theorist Marshall McLuhan, electric technology represented the very force that would decisively alter "every institution formerly taken for granted." See Marshall McLuhan and Quentin Fiore, *The Medium Is the Massage* (New York: Bantam Books, 1967), 8.

17. R. Buckminster Fuller, Education Automation: *Freeing the Scholar to Return to His Studies* (Carbondale: Southern Illinois University Press, 1962).

18. While McLuhan saw media as "an extension of the central nervous system," German media theorist Kittler famously counterargued that posited that "media determine our situation" by constituting the material basis through which the construction and dissemination of knowledge is made possible. McLuhan and Fiore, *The Medium Is the Massage*, 40–41; Friedrich A. Kittler, *Gramophone, Film, Typewriter*, trans. Geoffrey Winthrop-Young and Michael Wutz (Stanford, CA: Stanford University Press, 1999), xxxix.

19. Achile Mbembe, "The Power of the Archive and Its Limits," in *Refiguring the Archive*, ed. Carolyn Hamilton et al. (Cape Town: David Philip, 2002), 20.

Detail of poster for the *Utopia e/o Rivoluzione* exhibition sponsored by the Cultural Union of Turin and organized by assistants and students at the Faculty of Architecture at Turin University, April 1969. From *Marcatré*, February–July 1969.

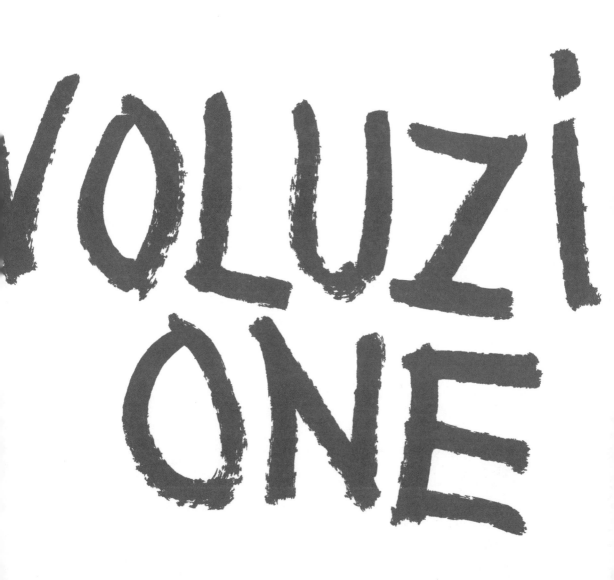

COUNTER HEGEMONIES

THE REVOLT BEFORE THE REVOLT

Caroline Maniaque

Protagonists Georges Candilis (1913–1995),
Bernard Huet (1932–2001), Édouard Albert
(1910–1968), Max Querrien (1921–2019)
Institution Institution ENSBA,
Unités Pédagogiques
Location Paris, France
Dates 1962–1969

It is commonly argued that the significant changes in postwar architectural education in France were brought about by the events of May 68. While it is true that the architectural department of the École des Beaux-Arts was shut down following these major disturbances, the school's administration had been preoccupied with the need for radical reform since the early years of the decade. Student enrollment had increased dramatically, with numbers growing from around two hundred in the interwar period to three thousand by 1968. This not only put pressure on space—with thousands of students squeezed into twenty-three ateliers[1]—but made the process of evaluation more complex and labor-intensive, dependent on a series of competitions and juries. More generally, the Beaux-Arts system was criticized for its emphasis on the question of form at the expense of construction and the practice of architecture. Students complained that design projects were overly abstract, paying little attention to social aspects or the needs of inhabitants. They alleged it was possible to graduate without ever having confronted a real site and its topography or environmental conditions.[2]

< The 1930s building at 1 rue Jacques Callot that housed the Group B ateliers. From *SADG, Bulletin mensuel d'information*, June 1955.

> Entrance of the École des Beaux-Arts, rue Bonaparte, Paris, early 1971. From *Architectural Design*, September 1971. Photographer unknown.

The move to reform was not confined to Paris but extended to other Beaux-Arts schools including those in Strasbourg and Marseilles. It began on a small scale, with the "petite réforme" proposed in 1962. A milestone was reached in 1964, when a committee chaired by Max Querrien, architectural director of the Ministry of Cultural Affairs, agreed to appoint Georges Candilis to lead a new external atelier, bowing to pressure from Philippe Molle, the *grand massier* or president of the student association at the École. Candilis, who had worked with Le Corbusier and was a member of Team 10, focused his atelier on the needs of mass housing. Another external atelier was initiated in 1966: Atelier Collégial no. 1 was led by architect and theoretician Bernard Huet (a former student of Arretche), who had just returned from two years of postgraduate studies at the University of Pennsylvania. His experience in the US had persuaded him of the need to broaden architectural education to encompass urbanism, sociology, history, and philosophy. Huet's atelier was initially based in his office near the Bastille, but soon joined other ateliers in the Grand Palais. A third new atelier was founded by the modernist architect Édouard Albert, who had recently completed the Tour Croulebarbe in Paris.

As a result of the introduction of these three ateliers, the Paris Beaux-Arts was restructured into three groups. In 1967, Group A incorporated the old internal ateliers of the Beaux-Arts (the ateliers of Louis Arretche, Eugène Beaudouin, Guillaume Gillet, Noël Lemaresquier, Michel Marot, Otello Zavaroni). Group B included the older ateliers located near the Beaux-Arts building on Quai Malaquais, either in rue Bonaparte or in a 1930s concrete building on rue Jacques Callot (the ateliers of Xavier Arsène-Henry, Jean Bossu, Alain Bourbonnais, Henri Chappey, Jacques Kalisz, Paul La Mache, Henri Madelain, Jean Niermans, Francis Quénard, André Remondet). Group C was made up of eight reformed and external ateliers (led by Édouard Albert, Georges Candilis and Alexis Josic, Robert Camelot, Jean Faugeron, Paul Nelson, Georges-Henri Pingusson, Pierre Vivien, and Collégial no. 1–Bernard Huet). Each group was now in charge of its own juries and exercises. Despite this relative autonomy, all the ateliers had to accept the same admission process. Similarly, all taught assignments had to be agreed by the school's central administration.

The curriculum was another contentious issue. In 1967 Max Querrien set up four working groups involving a broad range of experts: architects,

urbanists, economists, painters, geographers, sociologists, and administrators. The first of these working groups tackled the question of the social sciences, while the second debated the relationship between architecture and urbanism. The third looked at the teaching of technical, scientific, and mathematical skills, while the fourth investigated artistic education. At the heart of these discussions was the concept "pluridisciplinarity." However, the work of Querrien's committee was overtaken by the events that shook France. Their last meeting was on April 21, 1968, just before the first student protest. By that time, they had managed to sketch out a teaching program based on the guidance of not only the working groups but also the ateliers in Group C. They proposed to replace the old system with a system of autonomous Unités Pédagogiques, both in Paris and in the rest of France. The events of May simply accelerated this movement of reform. On May 8, students went on an unofficial strike, which became official five days later. On May 15, a general meeting signaled the start of a campaign to abolish the Prix de Rome. On August 29, by decree of the Minister of Cultural Affairs, André Malraux, the architectural section of the École des Beaux-Arts was closed and replaced by eighteen Unités Pédagogiques, five of which were to be in Paris and thirteen distributed across France.

All through the summer of 1968, groups of students, administrators, and teachers met to rethink the future of architectural education. A further decree on December 6, 1968 announced the end of the Prix de Rome and assigned the five Unités Pédagogiques in Paris to various locations—Quai Malaquais, the Grand Palais, and the stables of the Chateau de Versailles. Each school had its own teaching focus.

This arrangement did not suit everybody. Around one thousand two hundred students and eighty members of staff signed a petition calling for an additional Unité to absorb students from the Group C ateliers. In February 1969 the administration agreed to the creation of a sixth Unité Pédagogique, to be located in one of the pavilions designed by Victor Baltard on rue de Viarmes. UP6 quickly became the most radical of the Unités, as well as the largest of the Paris schools, with eight hundred and fifty-five students. Two more schools were created as result of the splintering of existing groups: UP7 (out of UP5); and UP8 (out of UP6). The Baltard pavilions on rue de Viarmes—already home to UP6 and UP8—would also become the location for the UERE (Unité d'enseignement et de recherche de l'environnement), financed by the Ministry of Cultural Affairs. With a curriculum consisting of critical analysis of the media, graphic

arts, and furniture, this was a short-lived experiment: created for the 1970–1971 cohort, it lasted for one year.

Between 1969 and 1971 the differences between the Unités Pédagogiques became clearer. From the outset, UP7 was the one most concerned with construction. Substantial changes in teaching methods took place in the more progressive and leftwing Unités: UP1, UP6, and UP8. While maintaining a significant role for the fine arts, the curriculum was opened up to the social sciences and humanities—history, sociology, philosophy, and anthropology—as well as mathematics and computer studies. American schools of architecture, mostly embedded within universities, were one model for these changes. Ultimately, however, French architectural schools remained outside the university.

Establishing the new Unités Pédagogiques was finally an attempt not only to rethink the teaching of architecture and urbanism but also to renew architecture itself. This question was at the core of the debate in the summer of 1968. For those who advocated change, the moment had come to try out new ideas, but many of the professors of the old École, as well as many of the students, resisted radical change. Despite the watershed events of May 68, the most radical educators remained convinced that a socially oriented architectural practice was impossible under capitalism. Traditional teaching threatened to reestablish itself in the new system.

^ UP6 students in the Belleville neighborhood of Paris, 1969.

1. "Registre d'inscription dans les ateliers des élèves architectes 1957–1967." Archives nationales, AJ 52/554.
2. Jean Castex, "De l'atelier Arretche à UP3, Versailles, 1965–1975: la recherche d'une nouvelle pédagogique," in Les années 68 et la formation des architects, ed. Caroline Maniaque (Rouen: Point de vues, 2018), 222–233.
3. Recent scholarship has begun to question some of these judgments. See Des Beaux-Arts à l'université. Enseigner l'architecture à Strasbourg, ed. Anne-Marie Chatelet and Franck Storne, (Strasbourg: Éd. Recherches/ École nationale supérieure d'architecture de Strasbourg, 2014); Paul Quintrand architecte. Une expérimentation entre recherche et projet, ed. Jean-Lucien Bonillo, Éléonore Marantz, and Emmanuelle Reimbold, Colonnes, special issue no. 1 (2014).
4. Éric Lengereau, L'État et l'architecture 1958–1981. Une politique publique? (Paris: Picard, 2001), 259–260; Jean-Louis Violeau, Les architectes et Mai 68 (Paris: Editions Recherches, 2005).
5. Cf. Arrêté du 20 décembre 1965, Journal Officiel du 28 mai 1966.
6. Ibid.
7. Anne Debarre, "Les enseignements d'histoire dans la formation des architectes: des Beaux-Arts aux UP parisiennes, des pédagogies diversifiées (1965–1973)," in Maniaque, Les années 68 et la formation des architectes, 54–67.
8. Jean-Paul Jungmann, "Nos fins d'étude et nos débuts d'enseignement," in Maniaque, Les années 68 et la formation des architectes, 237–241.

FROM STUDY REFORM TO UNIVERSITY WITHOUT PROFESSORS

Nina Gribat

Protagonists Architecture students
at the University of Stuttgart
Institution University of Stuttgart
Location Stuttgart, Germany
Dates 1966–1972

At the beginning of the 1960s there was no sign of change or unrest at the Faculty of Architecture at the University of Stuttgart.[1] Along with the Faculty of Civil Engineering, it was installed in a new building, *Kollegiengebäude 1* (K1), designed by Gutbier, Siegel, and Wilhelm. The university campus was expanding physically to create the necessary preconditions to accommodate growing student numbers. The architecture school was renowned for postwar modernism, attracting students from far beyond the region. Several of the teachers formed the so-called "second Stuttgart School," who had broken free from their own training in the rather conservative tradition of the "first Stuttgart school." In the mid-1960s, however, when the German economic miracle suffered its first setback, the architecture students began to voice discontent. What started at that time as a rather consensual and institutional reform process would become, in the wake of the 1968 student uprisings, a highly politicized period of self-organization and mobilization, before returning to a new normal from 1972 on.[2]

The students' critique centered on the figure of the "artist architect" and their professors' largely unquestioning trust in the far-reaching powers of aesthetics and form in architecture. They began to lose patience with design studios based on outmoded tasks such as a "villa by the lake"—a rather classical trope at the time—and with fickle and self-regarding professors who expressed their opinions with the infamous soft pencil. Rather than the established mode of trusting intuition, experience, and professional reputation, students demanded an architecture pedagogy based on well-founded scientific theories and rational design methodologies. They also called for new teaching formats such as group work, interdisciplinary approaches, and project-oriented study, as well as a stronger orientation of the curriculum toward socially relevant problems. In addition, students requested more say

in the administration of the school—in short, a more democratic university.

At the beginning of the reform movement, architecture students were supported by a broad consensus among professors. They also had formal representation to structure their demands. In 1966 Stuttgart established one of the first Study Reform Commissions at a German university. Made up of two students, two scientific assistants, and two professors, it embodied one of the central demands of the wider reform movement—the one-third parity (*Drittelparität*) that defined the equal participation of all academic groups in the decision-making bodies of the university. Likewise, students' requests for the inclusion of more theory in their education were met with the creation of the IGMA (Institute for the Foundations of Modern Architecture) in 1967, with Jürgen Joedicke as the first chair of architecture theory. Joedicke supported the reform movement of the students and the teaching offers of his chair responded to student demands for instruction in theory and method. Early IGMA publications, such as the *Working Reports on Planning Methods* (*Arbeitsberichte zur Planungsmethodik*) series from 1968 to 1975, clearly show this early focus on rationalization and new methodologies.[3] One of the first issues, for instance, included a report on a conference on design methods in the UK that some of the students had attended. In Joedicke's seminars, students also experimented with systems theory and cybernetics-inspired approaches to design, trying to rationalize the processes of planning and decision-making. They embraced decision-making tools such as the "Zwicky-Box"[4] and complex diagrams that supported the systematization of virtually every design or planning task—even though some recognized the danger of getting too caught up in laborious methods and losing focus. By the mid-1960s Stuttgart's architecture students were also regularly venturing beyond their own faculty for their desired input. The Hochschule für Gestaltung (HfG) in Ulm and its theoreticians, such as Max Bense (who also held a chair at the university's literature department), were important points of reference.

However, Beat music, avantgarde art, and happenings were as important during the reform period at the Faculty of Architecture as the calls for rationalization. Inspired by the emancipatory movements of the 1960s, students combined their demands for more theory and methods with humor and a strong libertarian DIY ethos, resulting in a fertile period of new initiatives. In 1966 a group of

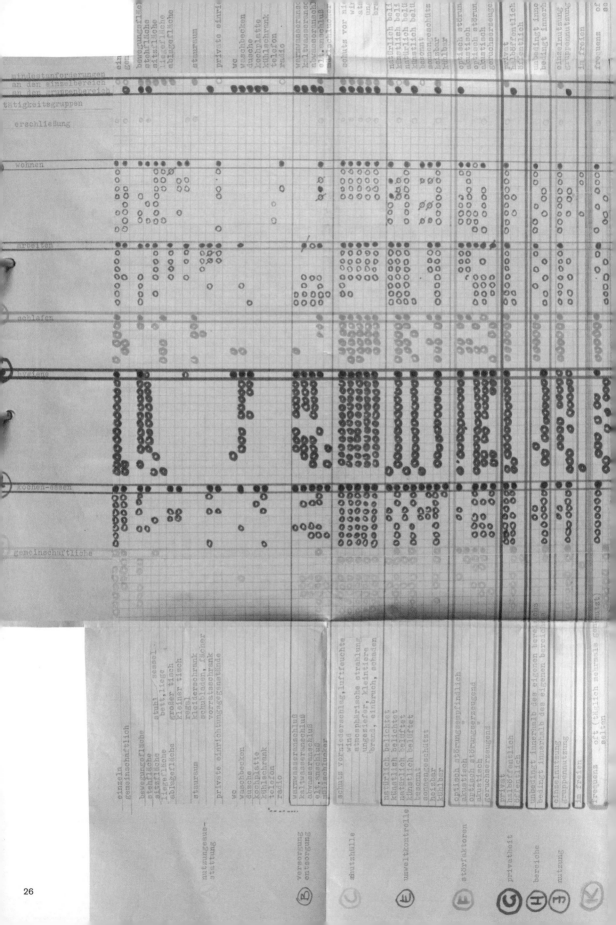

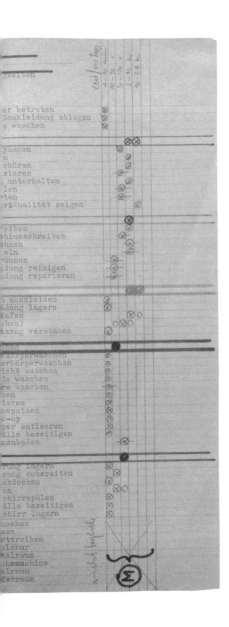

students started organizing exuberant and themed carnival parties. The themes, such as "MATRIarch," fed into diverse narratives and actions, and the elaborate setup and decoration was carried out, over weeks, in the form of happenings. The parties were known well beyond Stuttgart, with thousands of people attending. Students used some of the proceeds to purchase up-to-date equipment (such as a tracing light machine and a darkroom for photography) and to finance a lecture series with an interdisciplinary set of critical scholars.

The magazine *ARCH+* and biweekly flyer *ARCH+informationen* were other examples of an initiative grounded in the same spirit, with a strong commitment to reform and rationalization. Founded in 1967 by three assistants and three students at the Faculty of Architecture, *ARCH+* (subtitle "Study Issues for Architecture-related Environmental Research and Planning") was intended to support the study reform process and to contribute more broadly to a scientific reorientation of the discipline. The layout of the first issues consisted only of texts and diagrams, reflecting the serious commitment to science and institutional and disciplinary reform. The biweekly *ARCH+informationen* was a more humorous and playful outlet, intended to inform students about different events and readings, but also containing diverse collages and general commentaries about the times.

With the increasing politicization and radicalization that accompanied the rise of the student protests in Germany in 1968, the more playful outlets of the study reform movement in Stuttgart came to an end. Students now turned against their professors and against the institution at large. They started aligning themselves with different political groups and proclaiming their demands and beliefs in plenary meetings. Lectures and other conventional teaching formats such as design studios were boycotted. Many professors were challenged to the point where they decided to leave the university. Students began to self-organize their education, in some cases with the support of lecturers or tutors. They also designed experimental study guidelines based on the idea of developing individual curricula in accordance with their own interests.

Without a regular curriculum in place, it became increasingly difficult for students to navigate various self-organized teaching formats and still obtain the required formal study credits. In response, the faculty supported the creation of an Information Centre (IZ) in 1970 to organize increasingly dispersed studies during the period that came to be known as "teaching without professors."[5] IZ aimed to offer students information about courses, the issuing of credits, and general advice. While some students found this period exhilarating and formative, others complained that design had been completely supplanted by text. In addition, autodidactic and grassroots democratic approaches often led to time-consuming and confrontational sessions. Infights between radical leftist splinter groups increased tensions further. In a constant tightrope walk between rationalization and politicization, passionate debates were held about the social relevance of architecture and urban planning. The appointment of a number of new professors around 1972 marked the beginning of a slow return to teaching based on a regular curriculum—albeit one with significant changes. While some of the achievements of the study reform movement (such as one-third parity on all committees) were abolished, other remnants of the radical self-organized pedagogy remained: students could set their own tasks; group work was welcomed; a concern for theory, methods, and interdisciplinary approaches was reflected in the curriculum; and a stronger focus on planning was introduced with the foundation of the SI (Institute of Urban Design). Design studios were reestablished as the main teaching format, but professors could no longer afford to be aloof.

Rather than a clearly demarcated (or even known) radical experiment, the case of Stuttgart represents the sometimes dispersed and messy struggles of different groups of students for innovative or reformed methods of architectural education within the German university system. As intra-institutional cases, such uprisings within the system tend to be erased from history since they are—in hindsight—often considered a disruption from the norm, rather than much-needed moments of reconfiguration, invention, and opening of the discipline at large.

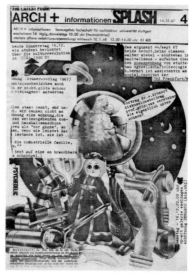

< *ARCH+informationen*, December 14, 1967. Front and back covers.

1. Technical University of Stuttgart [*Technische Hochschule Stuttgart*] up to 1967.
2. See *Vergessene Schulen: Architekturlehre zwischen Reform und Revolte um 1968*, ed. Nina Gribat, Philipp Misselwitz, and Matthias Görlich (Leipzig: Spector Books, 2017).
3. Jesko Fezer, "Jürgen Joedickes Planungsmethodik: Die Funktionalisierung der Architekturtheorie," in *Vergessene Schulen*, 261–279.
4. A multidimensional matrix named after its inventor, the Swiss astrophysicist Fritz Zwicky (1898–1974).
5. *Vergessene Schulen*, 183–192.

WHEN DECOLONIZATION WAS NOT A METAPHOR

Łukasz Stanek

Protagonists Ekundayo A. Adeyemi (1937–),
Zbigniew Dmochowski (1906–1982),
Augustine Egbor (1924–2011)
Institution Department of Architecture,
Ahmadu Bello University
Location Zaria, Nigeria
Dates 1968–1986

In 1968 the Zaria School of Architecture became a vortex of student revolt. Like their counterparts at the École des Beaux-Arts in Paris, students at Nigeria's first school of architecture called for radical change in the way they were taught—a revision of the curriculum to take account of the most pressing issues facing society, with a shift of emphasis from drawing skills to interdisciplinary research. While these demands resembled those voiced in Paris, the Zaria students were responding to conditions specific to Nigeria. What was at stake was a reframing of the architectural profession and its social obligations beyond the path-dependences inherited from the colonial period. This aspiration was formulated in the midst of a civil war seen by many as a disastrous consequence of Nigeria's continuing adherence to the British blueprint of decolonization.

The origins of Zaria's School of Architecture were closely linked to this blueprint. The school had been established in 1952 as a department in the Nigerian College of Arts, Science, and Technology. Before relocating to Zaria in northern Nigeria, it was attached to the University College in Ibadan, Nigeria's first university, founded by the British colonial administration in 1948 to educate the local elites who were expected to take up senior positions in the country and eventually lead it to self-governance. Upon its foundation, the School of Architecture in Zaria was staffed mainly by British lecturers and its curriculum was largely based on British pedagogical models. In 1960, the year of Nigeria's independence, the school secured the accreditation of the Royal Institute of British Architects (RIBA). The RIBA insisted on enforcing its general standards and proved reluctant to extend the curriculum towards context-specific content.

Educational standards were at the center of the revolt in 1968, building on a longer questioning of the school's teaching by students and the handful of Nigerian lecturers on its staff, among them Ekundayo A. Adeyemi, who was himself a graduate of the Zaria school and later its head (1974–1986). In his memoir Adeyemi recalled the alarmingly high attrition rate among students. British lecturers contended that the drawing skills of the majority of students did not match RIBA requirements, which centered on "the ability to observe or think in three dimensions and reproduce this in drawing."[1] William J. Kidd, the British head of school between 1965 and 1969, added that Nigerian students struggled with the curriculum because of their "lack of three-dimensional appreciation."[2] His assertion was easily disproved by Nigerian and foreign educators at Zaria, including the Polish architectural historian Zbigniew Dmochowski, whose surveys of Nigerian vernacular architecture demonstrated the spatial concepts embodied by the various building cultures in the country.[3]

As opposed to the standards set by the RIBA, Adeyemi argued that Zaria's curriculum needed to be aligned with regional and national development goals. Concerned at the high failure rate, Nigerian students, lecturers, and, increasingly, politicians protested against what they saw as an attempt by the British lecturers to block the entry of Nigerians to the British-dominated profession. To counter British economic dominance, which endured despite the country's independence, a series of "indigenization" decrees were issued by the federal government in the course of the 1960s.[4] The decrees restricted foreign control over companies operating in Nigeria, including architectural offices, contractors, and construction material industries. In turn, the newly founded Architects Registration Council of Nigeria (1969) was installed as the supervisory body for architectural education, including the one provided by the Zaria school.

The student revolt in Zaria was part of this antagonistic process of emancipation of Nigerian design and construction from British dominance. The revolt was followed by a revision of the curriculum, instigated by a panel headed by Augustine Egbor, chief architect at the Federal Ministry of Works in Lagos, and inspired by the curriculum of the school of architecture at the University of Science and Technology in Kumasi, Ghana. The panel encouraged the introduction of architectural research in collaboration with the construction industry and other departments of the university, and urged educators to account for social, technological, and environmental conditions of urbanization specific to northern Nigeria. The reorganized school included a project office that oversaw real-life projects by students and staff, and a data room (a repository of technical information). These changes were introduced in the course of the 1970s by an international group of teachers and scholars who filled the void after the departure of many British lecturers. They included a growing group of Nigerians, as well as Americans and Eastern Europeans, among them Czech, Hungarian, and Polish men and women.[5] This cosmopolitan character of Zaria in itself supported a new vision of independent Nigeria which opened the country to multiple worlds of knowledge production and professional experience beyond the former colonial center.

THE TRADITIONAL ARCHITECTURE OF THE CLIMATIC REGIONS

1. Ekundayo A. Adeyemi, *In the Making of an Architect: The Zaria Experience* (Ota: Covenant University Press, 2012), 66–68.
2. W. J. Kidd, "The Faculty of Architecture, Ahmadu Bello University, Zaria," *West African Builder and Architect* 7, no. 3 (1967): 56–59.
3. Zbigniew Dmochowski, *An Introduction to Nigerian Traditional Architecture* (London: Ethnographica / Lagos: National Commission for Museums and Monuments, 1990), 3 vols. See also: Łukasz Stanek, *Architecture in Global Socialism. Eastern Europe, West Africa, and the Middle East in the Cold War* (Princeton NJ: Princeton University Press, 2020), 125–145.
4. For a discussion of the economic imperatives of decolonization, in particular land, compare: Eve Tuck, K. Wayne Yang, "Decolonization Is Not a Metaphor," *Decolonization: Indigeneity, Education and Society* 1, no. 1 (2012): 1–40.
5. *Polacy w Nigerii*, ed. Zygmunt Łazowski et al. (Warsaw: Towarzystwo Polsko-Nigeryjskie/Wydawnictwo Akademickie Dialog, 1996–2000), 4 vols.

> Nick Hollo, "Climatic Comfort Design Guide for Nigeria," 1979. Department of Architecture, Ahmadu Bello University, Zaria.

< Ekundayo A. Adeyemi and a student at the Zaria School of Architecture, 1970s.

A SHORT-LIVED "DEMOCRATIZATION"

Rutger Huiberts

Protagonists Aldo van Eyck (1918–1999)
and the "Stielos" student body
Institution Delft School of Architecture,
Delft Institute of Technology
Location Delft, The Netherlands
Dates 1969–1971

On May 9, 1969 architecture students at the Delft Institute of Technology (now TU Delft) marched to the school of architecture demanding access to the general assembly of the faculty. Eventually acceding to the students' demands, the governing council granted the students equal voting rights in administrative decisions—a "one-man-one-vote" system (the vast majority of students and faculty at the time were male). The students—who held the majority in the room—were instantly able to push through a series of collectively debated motions. Among the changes introduced was the abolition of student-professor hierarchies. Regardless of ranking or year of study, anyone linked to the school could propose, organize, or lead part of the education. The school's existing curriculum was rejected completely. From that point on pedagogy would consist of initiatives formed through a democratic and participatory process.

The "democratization" at Delft echoed student revolts happening throughout Europe, but it was also the culmination of specific tensions that had been gradually building up within the school. Throughout the 1950s and 1960s the school of architecture was increasingly divided along ideological lines: the so-called "modernists" versus the "traditionalists." While student numbers increased fivefold in the postwar boom years between 1945 and 1965, the curriculum and educational debate continued to be dominated by a very small number of faculty split into these two factions. There was little room for dissent, let alone the development of alternative approaches.

One of the few protagonists who did not strictly follow this partisan divide was Aldo van Eyck, who had trained at the ETH in Zurich and initially taught at the Amsterdam Academy of Architecture. When Van Eyck came to Delft in 1966 he introduced a design studio-based education in which brief and method were tailored to match the students' specific interests and abilities. Rather than following preestablished formulas, his pedagogy was structured around the questioning of assumptions, in the form of open debates. In 1968 Van Eyck went further and established "vertical" studios that brought together students from different cohorts, so circumventing the strict hierarchical organization of the school by year.[1]

Following the extremely swift "democratization" of the school of architecture in spring 1969, members of the student association Stylos called for a critical and thorough reconsideration of the school's pedagogy. In their view, student mobilizations at Delft had lacked a clearly defined ideological stance.[2] To redress this, they organized numerous debates and gatherings over the summer and into the fall semester, covering topics that ranged from the detail of the school's future educational approach to the larger role of the architect in society. Some of these debates evolved into self-governed architecture studios. Building on the pedagogical models that Aldo van Eyck had introduced at Delft, these project groups carried out research and case studies that moved away from formal investigations and modernist design studies to focus instead on social and political issues affecting architecture and city planning in the Netherlands.

In March 1970 members of the student association (now going by its phonetic spelling, "Stielos") published a 120-page treatise, *de elite* (The Elite).[3] Entirely written in simplified "communist" spelling, *de elite* provided a Marxist interpretation of architectural practice within capitalist societies, followed by an analysis of the history of education at the Delft school of architecture leading up to the events of May 1969. *de elite* vehemently criticized both the "traditionalist" and the "modernist" faculty, not even sparing educators who were initially regarded as allies of the "democratization" movement. Among others, these included Van Eyck and Herman Hertzberger, who were criticized for being "architect-artists" whose designs distracted society from its real ailments.[4] The authors of *de elite* went on to lament

> Cover of *de elite*, the 120-page manifesto published by members of the student collective "Stielos" in March 1970.

de elite

een analiese van de afdeling bouwkunde van de techniese hogeschool te delft

^ Voting sessions
during the first days of
the "democratization"
at the School of
Architecture at Delft,
May 9, 1969. Photo-
graph by Ad Volker.

< Aldo van Eyck during
the General Assembly.
Van Eyck was among
the more reform-
oriented members of
staff. 1969. Photogra-
pher unknown.

the watered-down outcome of the "democratiza-tion." Whereas the student-led anti-authoritarian actions had successfully steered the teaching away from the "bourgeois" principles of "adaptation and competition," they argued that the liberal leftwing attitudes that emerged after the "democratiza-tion" had focused too much on "self-actualization and cooperation," rather than turning the school of architecture into a true "bastion for the further democratization of society."[5]

de elite's vision of further democratization, however, proved hard to implement. As early as 1970, the once largely united student front had splintered into moderate leftist groups and significantly more radical factions, with the moderates prevailing in terms of numbers. By 1972 the "one-man-one-vote" system was replaced by "one-third parity," with equal representation of students, faculty, and the school's governing body. The recently dismembered curric-ulum was replaced by a hybrid educational system, which offered a baseline curriculum to all, while still allowing students the freedom to self-organize and initiate activities such as "problem-oriented studios" and interdisciplinary seminars. In less than three years, the radical forms of pedagogical self-organization had been reinstitutionalized. Nevertheless, the models of studio-based design education introduced by Van Eyck became the foundation for a redefinition of the curriculum, and these pedagogical models were further expanded by other architects teaching at the school, including Herman Hertzberger, Carel Weeber, Jaap Bakema, and Max Risselada. The "democra-tization" had effected a drastic transformation of pedagogy in the school, though its political outcome was more moderate than some of the more radical factions desired. Any form of true democratization inevitably leads—sooner or later—to some sort of compromise.

1. Dirk van den Heuvel, Madeleine Steigenga, and Jaap van Triest, *Lessons: Tupker/ Risselada: A Double Portrait of Dutch Architectural Education, 1953/2003* (Nijmegen: SUN, 2003), 28.
2. Steef Davidson, *De elite: een analiese van de afdeling bouwkunde van de techniese hogeschool te Delft* (Nijmegen: Stielos, 1970), 5.
3. Ibid.
4. Ibid., 72.
5. Ibid., 5.

UTOPIA E/O RIVOLUZIONE

Alicia Imperiale

Protagonists Giorgio Ceretti (1943–2005), Graziella Derossi, Pietro Derossi (1933–), Adriana Ferroni, Aimaro Oreglia d'Isola (1928–), Riccardo Rosso, Elena Tamagno (1941–2016)
Institution Politecnico di Torino
Location Turin, Italy
Dates April 25–27, 1969

Between April 25 and 27, 1969, following a year that saw massive demonstrations and occupations of universities around the world, the teaching assistants, faculty, and students of the architectural department at the Polytechnic of Turin hosted an exhibition and conference in collaboration with the Unione Culturale Franco Antonicelli.[1] Within the context of the political turmoil of the late 1960s, the participants in *Utopia e/o Rivoluzione* (Utopia and/or Revolution) chose instead to use dialogue, discussion, text, and image to question the role of architectural education and challenge the subservience of the discipline to the logic of capitalism.[2] While the organizers of the meeting were all affiliated with the Polytechnic of Turin, they were careful to emphasize that the initiative was unconnected to the institution. Just as the previous year's student movement had begun outside of the university, the *Utopia e/o Rivoluzione* (Ue/oR) group wanted to have a certain distance when it came to questioning the pedagogy of the school, which they felt was training students to be "product[s] of a cultural machine," with an uncritical approach to the making of the city.

The Ue/oR group saw the tension between utopian thought and revolutionary action as a means to change the discipline of architectural and urban design. In these terms, design could be a social project in which the dialectic between the concrete and the abstract—what they termed the "first dialectical moment"—would bring about the union of theory and practice. Utopia, revolution, urbanism, architecture—all were brought together, simultaneously, in their project for the city. Rather than resorting to the conventional means of urbanism, they proposed random operations that sought to experiment with the elements of chance and surprise. To overcome the social alienation engendered by capitalism (with the aid of architecture),

they focused on the collective dimension of the city, where the social and physical aspects of communities coalesced. This expanded notion of the city was where they believed revolutionary action would find traction and instigate change.

The Ue/oR group (among them, teaching assistants Giorgio Ceretti, Graziella Derossi, Pietro Derossi, Adriana Ferroni, Aimaro Oreglia d'Isola, Riccardo Rosso, and Elena Tamagno) engaged in extensive discussions with faculty from other departments in the university, including the philosopher Gianni Vattimo, the historian Carlo Olmo, and the physicist Arnaldo Ferroni. They also invited other "radical" international architects to present their work and ideas in an exhibition. Romaldo Giurgola and Paolo Soleri, Italians resident in the United States since the 1950s, Architecture Principe (Paul Virilio and Claude Parent), Yona Friedman, and the Utopie Group from France, Archigram from Great Britain, and Archizoom from Italy all contributed to the show. The accompanying discussion raised potent theoretical questions: If there is to be utopia, what utopia? If revolution, where and when? What are the roles of the proletariat and the intellectual in this discussion?

While the organizers had hoped that the participants would approach the *and/or* of the title with subtlety, the meeting quickly split into two camps. Paolo Soleri, Yona Friedman, and Archigram all belonged to the first camp, united by their faith in the possibility (one day in the distant future) of building a utopia where the design of human habitation would be guided by a highly developed system of ethics. The second camp, centered around the Utopie and Archizoom groups, was critical of this realizable utopia. A further split was evident in the different groups' views on technology: the first believed that "an intensive use of technology would save civilization," whereas the second group believed that it would only be saved by revolution. Refusing to assume the professional roles that their university education was preparing them for, the Ue/oR group proposed an alternative pedagogy—one based on concrete revolutionary actions that directly involved the everyday citizen or "user" of the city in the process of creating architecture.

The meeting was important, but even more significant, from a pedagogical point of view, was the afterlife of Ue/oR in publications. *Casabella* published a commentary on the event alongside a full-page reproduction of the broadsheet circulated before the April meeting. The journal *Marcatré* published the full proceedings, including projects from the invited participants, in its final issue.[4] Printed in vibrant red ink throughout, the issue could be seen as a manifesto for the bold super-graphic style of the artist Magdalo Mussio. In 1975 Mussio would republish all of the revolutionary texts related to the Ue/oR meeting in book form, in a testament to their continuing relevance.[5] Architecture's relationship to capitalism is still a pressing concern today. So, too, is the desire for action.

< *Utopia e/o Rivoluzione* graphics, from *Marcatré*, February–July 1969.

1. The Unione Culturale Franco Antonicelli, founded in 1945, is an important center for the discussion of social reform and the intersection of the arts and politics. An earlier French meeting, "Utopie ne s'écrit pas au futur," might have sparked the idea for the Turin event. Other sources say that the event was inspired by the Folkestone festival of 1966.

2. The event was originally announced in "Conferences," *Architectural Design* (March 1969): 128, as "Utopia & experiment in the architecture of today." See Elena Dellapiana, "Architettura e/o Rivoluzione up at the Castle. A Self-Convened Conference in Turin (April 25–27, 1969)," *Histories of Postwar Architecture* 2 (2018), https://doi.org/10.6092/issn.2611-0075/7888 Accessed August 30, 2019.

3. Paolo Nepoti, "Utopia e/o Rivoluzione," *Casabella* 337 (June 1969): n.p. Also Emilio Battisti, "Utopia e/o Rivoluzione. Note sulla mostra-incontro tenutosi a Torino nei giorni 25–26–27 Aprile 1969," in *Controspazio* 2–3 (July–August 1969): 45–47; Pietro Derossi, *Per un'architettura narrative: Architetture e progetti 1959–2000* (Milan: Skira, 2000), 36–38; and Terence Riley, *The Changing of the Avant-garde: Visionary Architectural Drawings from the Howard Gilman Collection* (New York: Museum of Modern Art, 2002), 28.

4. *Marcatré* published the full proceedings of the meetings in its sixth and final issue numbered 50/51/52/53/54/55 (February, March, April, May, June, July 1969).

5. Gruppo Utopia e/o Rivoluzione, *Utopia e/o Rivoluzione: (mostra-incontro, Torino, 25–27 aprile 1969)* (Pollenza, Macerata: Altro/La Nuova Foglio editrice, 1975). The texts were republished without illustrations.

TESTING ENVIRONMENTAL DESIGN

Stuart King, Ceridwen Owen

Protagonist Barry McNeill (1937–2014)
Institution Tasmanian College of Advanced Education, University of Tasmania
Location Hobart, Tasmania, Australia
Dates 1969–1979

Self-directed, self-assessed, and collectively governed, the Environmental Design (ED) program devised in 1969 by Barry McNeill—head of the department of architecture and planning at the Tasmanian College of Advanced Education (TCAE) (now University of Tasmania)—precipitated the most complete and radical transformation of an architecture curriculum in Australia in the 1970s.[1] Launched with an experimental year in 1970, to test its viability, the program then operated under McNeill's leadership until 1980.

The catalysts for McNeill's program—a key juncture in the development of student-centered education in an antipodean context—were both regional and global. From the mid-1960s the annual conferences of the Australasian Architecture Students Association (AASA) had fomented a student-led revolt. The AASA conference in Hobart in 1967 foreshadowed the new directions that architectural education would take in Tasmania. Speakers included Cedric Price, Maurice K. Smith, and Joseph Esherick, as well as Paul Ritter, whose recently published *Educreation: Education for Creation, Growth and Change* (1966) had advocated a sociological model of education in schools of architecture, environmental design, and ekistics. McNeill subsequently spent a year (1968–1969) in North America and Europe, studying at MIT and visiting schools of architecture that were transforming their curricula and establishing ED programs. He was particularly influenced by the student-centered curriculum at the University of Toronto, led by John Andrews and Peter Pragnell, and the students' freedom to choose their own individual direction within the wide-ranging generalist education offered at the Architectural Association (AA) in London under its principal, John Lloyd.

At the heart of McNeill's vision was an emphasis on motivating individuals to "understand or solve problems of intense personal significance" as opposed to teaching factual knowledge, techniques, and "acceptable" solutions.[2] Rather than the curriculum, it was the students who occupied centerstage. Individuals could establish how, where, and when they would acquire the necessary knowledge and skills, and were encouraged to pursue topics of personal interest. However, McNeill also diverged from the models at Toronto and the AA, which were critiqued for allowing individualized studies to fragment the nature of their programs. At Hobart, instead, learning groups on topics of mutual interest were formed across multiple year levels at the start of semester through a cooperative process that unfolded over hours or even days.

As well as defining their own program of study, students established how they would be assessed. With the exception of graduating projects, decisions on whether they had passed or failed were entirely at their discretion. A flat administrative structure also embedded students in all aspects of decision-making, from voting rights in the department's general assemblies, to orientation programs and student admissions. Interview panels for staff appointments were student-led, while the staff themselves were positioned as "academic advisors," providing guidance and facilitating access to diverse learning opportunities. The department's physical facilities were likewise aligned with the fluidity of the program and democratic ideology. Adopting the "kit-of-parts" approach, internal configurations could be continuously built, rebuilt, adapted, and repurposed by staff and students armed with a "meccano-like steel frame and chipboard."[3] A large, centrally located board, named the "Information Exchange," provided a platform for communication where "you could pin your hopes, aspirations, or intended projects."[4]

The radical transformation of architectural education in Tasmania was facilitated by a series of synergistic local conditions aligned with the global project of social justice, student activism, and educational reform. These included a political climate attuned to social and environmental ideals, with the formation of the Green party in Tasmania and the creation of a new progressive model of colleges of advanced education, the resulting institutional flux providing unique opportunities for innovation. Ultimately, however, McNeill's pedagogical approach proved too controversial and in 1980 he resigned in the face of institutional mission creep and further changes in the state's higher education sector, which saw, among other things, the department's relocation from Hobart to regional Launceston. For a few

years, McNeill's anti-institutional agenda for architectural education enjoyed a partial reincarnation as
the Hobart Architectural Cooperative (1981–1985),
an independent alternative for self-regulated,
community-based education.

Though short-lived, the ED program in Tasmania
directly influenced the development of other architecture programs in Australia in the 1970s, including
those of the Canberra College of Advanced Education
(now University of Canberra) and the Royal Melbourne
Institute of Technology (RMIT). Beyond its graduates,
the program's most significant outcome is the internationally practiced interdisciplinary earth science of
permaculture, a system developed by Bill Mollison and
David Holmgren from the initial basis of Holmgren's
undergraduate thesis in the mid-1970s. For McNeill,
architecture and architectural education were, above
all, critical social practices. Environmental Design in
Hobart provided a space for experimentation in a
milieu of exchange, fluidity, and mobility; a laboratory
in which international models from the USA, UK, and
beyond could be channeled, tested, contextualized,
and transformed. It also provided a fertile terrain
for radical thinking from which new seeds of global
transformation could grow.

1. This entry draws upon research and includes excerpts from the following article by the authors: Stuart King and Ceridwen Owen, "A Decade of Radical Pedagogies: Barry McNeill and Environmental Design in Tasmania, 1969–1979," *Fabrications* 29, no. 1 (2018): 303–330.
2. Barry H. McNeill, "Beginnings of a School of Environmental Design," unpublished manuscript, May 4, 1971, 6. NS4638:1:7, Tasmanian Archives and Heritage Office.
3. Barrie Shelton, "A Decade of Student Autonomy in a Design School," in *Student Autonomy in Learning*, ed. David Boud (London/New York: Kogan Page/Nichols Publishing, 1988).
4. Barrie Shelton interviewed by Stuart King and Ceridwen Owen, December 12, 2017.

< General Assembly meeting, Department of Environmental Design, TCAE, Mount Nelson, Hobart, July 1977. Photograph by Leigh Woolley.

A TOTAL STUDY OF ARCHITECTURE

Sebastian Malecki

Protagonists Faculty and students
of the Faculty of Architecture and Urbanism
Institution Facultad de Arquitectura y
Urbanismo, Universidad Nacional de Córdoba
Location Córdoba, Argentina
Dates 1970–1975

Taller Total (Total Study) was the product of a series of long-brewing crises that involved institutions, politics, society, the university, and the discipline of architecture itself. One of the richest and more complex episodes in the history of higher education in Argentina, it entailed a reconfiguration of the whole institutional life of the Faculty of Architecture and Urbanism in Córdoba. First implemented in 1970, Taller Total's roots can be traced back to the debates around the teaching of architecture initiated at the III Latin American Conference of Schools and Faculties of Architecture, which took place in Alta Gracia (Córdoba) in 1964. These debates were initially stalled by the coup d'état in 1966: the military regime's interventions in public universities would lead to the dismissal of some of the most valued teachers in architectural composition. In May 1969, however, with the civil uprising in Córdoba against the dictatorship of Juan Carlos Onganía, the debates were revived in an atmosphere of social and political radicalization. In 1970 a group of young teachers and students at the Faculty of Architecture and Urbanism began to challenge the authority of the dean and the academic council. In an attempt to defuse the situation, Juan Carlos Fontán was appointed as the new faculty dean in

September 1970. To the surprise of many, his first endeavor was to establish the Taller Total.[1]

Taller Total was developed as an alternative to the Talleres Verticales (Vertical Studio) system established in 1955 in Rosario and Buenos Aires.[2] By integrating the second through the fifth years of study, it sought to combine all areas of the study program into a "synthesis" understood as "architecture." Along with this restructuring of the program came a redefinition of the role of the teacher. Academic hierarchies were eliminated as individual professorships gave way to larger disciplinary fields, while tenure procedures were modified—after a six-month probation period, the students were the ones who had the final say on whether a professor could stay or not—and student self-evaluation was instituted.

The military dictatorship had suppressed the tradition of student participation in university governance—established early on with the "University Reform" of 1918[3]—so the Taller Total devised new structures for collective decision-making and political activism. At the base level, there were "work groups" made up of students and professors from the second to the final year. Each of these groups elected a "professor-student coordination group" (with equal representation and revocable mandates), which in turn chose a "general coordination group" that was responsible for all academic, administrative, and political decisions. This created a state of "permanent assembly," in which every issue was discussed by all members.

Taller Total posited a pedagogical model that understood architecture as a social practice in which the "user" played a central role. During this period, the faculty translated into Spanish a great number of theory texts by important foreign authors, among them Pierre Bourdieu, Jean Baudrillard, Lucien Goldman, Christopher Alexander, Geoffrey Broadbent, Henri Lefebvre, and Claude Lévi-Strauss. As a result, the social sciences were integrated into architectural debates, with sociologists, anthropologists, and historians joining the faculty of architecture.

Voiced in a language marked by Marxist theory, dependency theory, and Henri Lefebvre's urban sociology, debates focused on the ideological role of architecture, its relationship to semiotics, and the problem of "habitat." The latter involved a redefinition of disciplinary boundaries, a "dissolution" of theoretical and historiographical conceptions of architecture into the "critical history of the

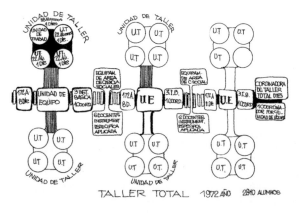

TALLER TOTAL   1972 AÑO   2810 ALUMNOS

habitat," and the consideration of architecture's specific contribution to processes of social transformation.[4] Related to this, there were a number of urban-architectural interventions, such as Taller 9's design of the Chagas disease-resistant house in a village near Córdoba, or the "self-building" national plan to be implemented by the "slum-dwellers movement" developed by the university's Peronista Youth group in collaboration with the Montoneros guerrilla organization.[5]

Endeavors similar to Taller Total began to spread not only to other locations—including Rosario, Buenos Aires, and La Plata—but also to other academic disciplines in Córdoba, such as the School of Arts and the School of Social Work. At the same time, Taller Total began to buckle under the combined weight of its own internal problems—mainly the chaotic situation of the faculty—and the repressive policies enacted by Oscar Ivanissevich, the Minister of Education in Isabel Perón's government. Taller Total would finally be discontinued in 1975. Although most of the professors dismissed for political reasons by the 1976–1983 dictatorship recovered their position with the "democratic return" in 1983, the pedagogical and political experiment of the Taller Total was silenced and practically none of its improvements were taken up again.

∧ Students at the Taller Total.

< Organizational scheme in the "Libro Mostaza" outlining the structure of the Taller Total, early 1970s.

1. J. Sebastian Malecki, "Crisis, radicalización y política en el Taller Total de Córdoba, 1970–1975," *Prohistoria* 25 (2016): 79–103.
2. Federico Deambrosis, *Nuevas visiones* (Buenos Aires: Infinito, 2011); Jorge F. Liernur, *La arquitectura de la Argentina del siglo XX: La construcción de la modernidad* (Buenos Aires: Fondo Nacional de las Artes, 2008).
3. Pablo Buchbinder, *Historia de las universidades argentinas* (Buenos Aires: Sudamericana, 2010).
4. J. Sebastian Malecki, "¿Una arquitectura imposible? Arquitectura y política en el Taller Total de Córdoba, 1970–1975," *Prismas: Revista de historia intelectual* 22 (2018): 95–115.
5. Malecki, "Crisis, radicalización y política."

AUTOGOBIERNO: MILITANT LEARNING

Cristina López Uribe

Protagonists Germinal Pérez Plaja (1943–1978), Juan Manuel Dávila (1940–), Jesús M. Barba Erdmann (1935–2009), Víctor Jiménez (1945–), Ernesto Alva (1940–), Ricardo Flores Villasana (1925–2004), Josefa "Pepita" Saisó Sampere (1929–1997), Carlos González Lobo (1939–2021), Santos E. Ruiz (1935–2009), Héctor Barrena (1945–2020), Alfonso González (1946–), José Luis Rojas Díaz (1945–), Darío Jiménez (1945–), Guillermo Zatarain (1944–)
Institution Escuela Nacional de Arquitectura, ENA, Universidad Nacional Autónoma de México, UNAM
Location Mexico City, Mexico
Dates 1972–1987

During the late 1960s and 1970s, while the Mexican state was presenting itself to the outside world as a left-leaning, peace-loving, and prosperous country, it was busy conducting a dirty war against its own citizens, fueled by Cold War fears of a communist threat. With the involvement of the CIA, Mexican presidents colluded with the secret police and the military in the imprisonment, "disappearance," and murder of many workers, peasants, students, and intellectuals who challenged the regime's systematic repression. Like other countries, Mexico had an active student movement, but it was brutally crushed on October 2, 1968, when military units fired on a peaceful rally, killing a never-determined number. The Tlatelolco massacre, as it would be called, took place just ten days before Mexico was to host the Olympic Games, a showcase for its modernity.[1]

After the Tlatelolco massacre students moved their field of operation from the streets into the classroom:[2] the autonomous status of the universities allowed a measure of protection from state repression. Using the concept of academic self-management (*autogestión*) promoted by José Revueltas, a writer and political activist who was imprisoned after Tlatelolco, they reframed the purpose of university education as a means to critically question all forms of power—to achieve "militant knowledge" as the basis for transforming society.[3]

This was the context in which a crowded plenary assembly of the school of architecture at the National Autonomous University of Mexico (UNAM) voted on April 11, 1972 to dismiss the dean and all his staff and to follow new principles of teaching and learning determined collectively by the assembly. The explosion of student numbers in the 1960s[4] had prompted the university authorities to introduce new courses and reorient the curriculum toward more technical subjects.[5] However, teaching was still largely based on the atelier system. Among students, there was a growing sense that their education simply prepared them to serve the ruling classes and had little connection to reality. Many of the new students were from lower-income backgrounds: not only were they familiar with the living conditions of most of society, they also recognized the contradictions of UNAM's University City campus, originally planned as an idyllic modernist landscape on the outskirts of the city, but now swallowed in a chaotic sprawl of self-built housing.

One week after the plenary assembly, a group of students and teachers occupied the administration offices and forced the authorities out of the school buildings. Over the next few years, they would experiment with new models of learning and teaching of architecture under the terms decided by the assembly. The aims of what came to be known as the Autogobierno movement included: totalization of knowledge (architecture as a means to comprehend, question, and actively transform the human condition), praxis (the linking of theory and practice for a better understanding of society), architecture for the people (the profession as an instrument to answer the needs of society—for mass housing, for example), and teaching in dialogue (teachers and students would collaborate on objectives and goals they had jointly agreed, without imposition).[6] The teachers who agreed to these new terms did so at a personal cost: their salaries were compromised and they risked repression from higher authorities. While the university's governing council had accepted the dismissal of the school's dean, it had refused to recognize the authority of the general assembly and simply appointed a new dean. For two years, the new dean, his staff, and the teachers and students who opposed the movement—around half the population of the school—were forced to continue their activities outside the campus. Autogobierno supporters controlled the buildings while their opposite numbers controlled the school's official records and finances.[7]

A UNAM committee was appointed in March 1973 to study the conflict. After interviewing the self-government community, it declared that the academic goals of "the trend known as Autogobierno" offered a series of possibilities that were worth exploring.[8] A congress was held to craft a new curriculum and, after long negotiations with the UNAM council, this was finally approved in 1976 on the condition that the term "Autogobierno" was replaced with the more neutral "academic unit of numbered workshops." From that point, the school was divided into two academic entities: the numbered workshops, that is, the Autogobierno unit, operated with relative academic, administrative, and political autonomy, while the lettered workshops continued to be guided by the university's existing regulations and its own version of the 1967 curriculum (revised in 1981).

The Autogobierno unit was organized as a federation of architecture studios, each free to interpret the flexible and dynamic curriculum of 1976 in its own way. Design, technical, and theoretical subjects were brought together in the development of the design exercise in the Taller Integral (Integral Workshop), with students participating in only one general evaluation a year.[9] The duration of the degree course was cut from five to four years and complemented by what was known as "university extension," which required students to provide a service to society. Design exercises were preferably real projects spontaneously requested by community groups and developed in dialogue with the users.[10] When real-life projects were thin on the ground, exercises focused mainly on social housing. Participatory design was studied, practiced, and explored in various forms— whereas self-construction was not celebrated, as it was seen as an excuse for the state to neglect its obligation to house the population. The Autogobierno school initiated collaborations with faculty from the departments of economy, geography, and sociology and invited visiting speakers from abroad. Its magazine, *Arquitectura Autogobierno*, published the pedagogical experiments along with (sometimes unauthorized) translations of articles from Italy, the USSR, Cuba, and other countries.

The collaborative and social nature of the Autogobierno unit makes it difficult to critically evaluate their built work. Most of the projects are anonymous, hard to locate, and now radically altered by their users. Nonetheless, it is clear that they succeeded in earning the trust of community-based organizations. They were also instrumental in solving the housing crisis after the 1985 earthquake in Mexico City, when locals were unable to count on the government's involvement.

By 1982, however, the first cracks had started to appear in the organization. The democratic process depended on a strong social commitment. When this started to diminish, it became difficult to reconcile the competing ideologies and affiliations of the various groups.[11] When some workshops dissented

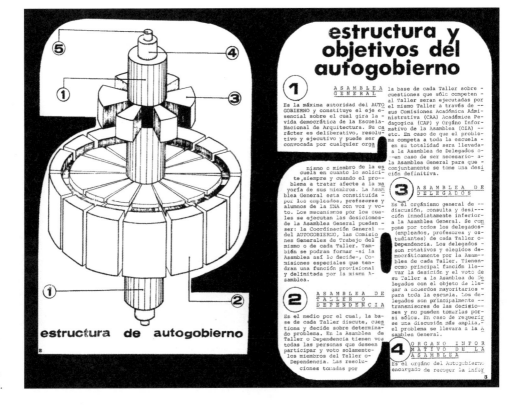

> Fanzine *Basta!*, no. 7 (1974) published by the Comité de Arquitectura en Lucha.

∧ Demonstration on the streets of the University City, UNAM. Mexico City, c. 1973. Photograph by J. Víctor Arias.

∨ Mural on the school of architecture's main façade. Mexico City, c. 1974. Photograph by J. Víctor Arias.

from the general line of the assembly, there were attempts to force them out of the Autogobierno curriculum. Heated debates translated into physical violence. Gradually and strategically, the university authorities reasserted their control. By 1987, with the restoration of full representation at the technical council of the school—the university's own "democratic" system—the Autogobierno unit ceased to work as originally planned.[12] The quality of education it provided was hard to evaluate. Many had begun to feel that they were being used by politicians—the community service they provided was a fig-leaf for the government's neglect of its duty to society. Some teachers ended up working for the government or designing corporate buildings. Others were seen to have betrayed the movement in order to advance themselves academically. In 1992 a new curriculum merged the two options of the lettered and the numbered workshops, marking the official end of the Autogobierno experiment. There are still some remnants of it in the curriculum in use today. Some workshops purportedly apply some of its principles, and some of the protagonists still teach at the postgraduate level or do urban economic research at the school—but the enthusiasm of the 1970s is gone.

1. See Jefferson Morley, "LITEMPO: The CIA's Eyes on Tlatelolco. CIA Spy Operations in Mexico," October 18, 2006, National Security Archive, George Washington University, https://nsarchive2.gwu.edu//NSAEBB/NSAEBB204/index.htm
2. Rafael Reygadas Robles Gil, *Universidad, autogestión y modernidad* (Mexico City: Universidad Nacional Autónoma de México, 1988), 39–53.
3. José Revueltas, *México'68: juventud y revolución* (Mexico City: Era, 1983), 98.
4. In 1955 the brand-new buildings originally planned for 800 students had to accommodate twice this number; by 1964 the number had risen to 3,754, and by 1976 to 6,177. See Ernesto Alva Martínez, "La enseñanza de la Arquitectura en México, en el siglo XX," in *La práctica de la Arquitectura y su enseñanza en México* (*Cuadernos de arquitectura y conservación del patrimonio artístico*), ed. Víctor Jiménez, (Mexico City: Secretaría de Educación Pública, Instituto Nacional de Bellas Artes, 1983).

5. See J. Víctor Arias Montes, "Dame una A…! Una pequeña historia de la emergencia de un movimiento autogestionario," *Cuadernos de arquitectura docencia*, nos. 12–13 (March 1994): 27–43.
6. Leaflet with the April 11, 1972 assembly agreements, document published in J. Víctor Arias Montes, "Pasajes históricos del Autogobierno 1975–1984," in *Publicaciones del Autogobierno* [digital edition], Raíces Digital 4, coord. Carlos Ríos Garza (Mexico City: Facultad de Arquitectura UNAM, 2005). https://arquitectura.unam.mx/raices-digital.html. The historical archives of the Autogobierno are either "lost in a warehouse of the university," as Ernesto Alva claimed in 1983, or were destroyed in 1977 in an unrelated police raid in the campus, as described by some of the protagonists. This text is based on the available documentary evidence and on interviews with Roberto Aguilar, Victor Arias, Ernesto Alva, Ernesto Velasco, and José Manuel Dávila, to whom I owe my gratitude.
7. Germinal Pérez Plaja, "El autogobierno:

breve cronología e interpretación," *Arquitectura Autogobierno. Revista de Material Didáctico* 2 (November 1976): 1–3.
8. "Informe de la comisión del H. Consejo Universitario sobre el problema de Arquitectura," *Gaceta UNAM* (March 28, 1973): 1–3.
9. "Plan de estudios. Escuela Nacional de Arquitectura. Autogobierno UNAM, 1976," in Ríos Garza, *Publicaciones del Autogobierno*.
10. Manuel Castells visited the school in 1977. His lecture and the questions from the public enlist a series of problematics faced by Autogobierno in designing real projects for community-based organizations and practicing participatory design. See Manuel Castells, "Crisis profesional, crisis urbana, crisis escolar," *Arquitectura Autogobierno* 4, 5, 6 (1977).
11. Víctor Jiménez, "La enseñanza de la arquitectura: de los Planes de estudio a la práctica educativa," *Diseño UAM* 3 (November 1984): 48.
12. See Ernesto Velasco León, *Testimonios 1982–1990* (Mexico City: Facultad de Arquitectura UNAM, 1990).

MOLECULAR REVOLUTION IN AULA MAGNA

Alessandra Ponte

Protagonists Massimo Cacciari (1944–), Franco Rella (1944–), Manfredo Tafuri (1935–1995), Georges Teyssot (1946–)
Institution Istituto Universitario di Architettura di Venezia (IUAV)
Location Venice, Italy
Dates 1975–1978

In 1975, to celebrate the thirtieth anniversary of Italy's liberation from fascism, Carlo Aymonino, member of the PCI (Italian Communist Party) and recently appointed director of the Istituto Universitario di Architettura di Venezia (IUAV), inaugurated the newly restored Aula Magna (Great Hall) at the Tolentini in Venice. Supervised by Carlo Scarpa, the renovation included paintings by famous Venetian artists like Emilio Vedova, Vittorio Basaglia, Mario De Luigi, and Armando Pizzinato. The centerpiece of the composition was a panel emblazoned with the first part of the slogan that appeared on the front page of Antonio Gramsci's newspaper *L'Ordine Nuovo* (The New Order): "Educate yourselves because we'll need all your intelligence. Agitate because we'll need all your enthusiasm. Organize yourselves because we'll need all your strength."[1]

CORRI PURE SERPENTE BIANCO CON TE CORRE ORA ANCHE LA MORTE E LA FINE DELLA TUA PISTA È ORMAI VICINA.

∧ Mural by the Indiani Metropolitani in the Aula Magna in Tolentini (IUAV).

> Aula Magna in Tolentini (IUAV).

Photographs taken two years after the inauguration show the word "intelligence" crossed out and substituted with "sharpshooting"—a clear invitation to join the "lotta armata" (armed fight)—while the pristine white walls of the Aula Magna appear insouciantly decorated with images and ironic slogans, the handiwork of the Indiani Metropolitani (Metropolitan Indians), the "creative and libertarian wing" of the political upheaval of the 1977 Movimento (Movement).

Thus, while Venice remained marginal in relation to the real epicenters of the 1977 Movimento (Rome, Milan, and Bologna), IUAV's Aula Magna closely reflected the troubled climate of the time, exposing the growing fracture separating the extreme left extraparliamentary groups from the Italian Communist Party, which, since 1973, under the leadership of Enrico Berlinguer, had been theorizing and negotiating a political accommodation—the "historic compromise"—with the Christian Democrats. The radicalization of the conflict between the far left and the Communist Party corresponded to a profound transformation of the Italian protest movement. Leninist-inspired organizations of 1968, including Potere Operario and Lotta Continua, dissolved to give way to new forms of creative quest or—along a radical diverging trajectory—to terrorism, producing, among other things, an intensification of the actions of the leftwing Red Brigades that would culminate in the 1978 kidnapping and assassination of the Christian Democrat leader Aldo Moro, their riposte to Berlinguer's "historic compromise." What truly characterized the 1977 Movimento, however, was the demand for "autonomy," proclaimed and theorized in various forms: from the structured leftist movement Autonomia Operaia (Workers' Autonomy), led by Oreste Scalzone and Toni Negri, to a heterogeneous assemblage of collectives and groups that systematically refused organization, hierarchy, and any kind of political manipulation. This last area of the movement found inspiration in the writings of Gilles Deleuze and Félix Guattari, whose 1972 book, *Capitalisme et schizophrénie. L'anti-Œdipe,* and the first chapter on the rhizome from their *Mille plateaux* were promptly translated in Italian. Guattari, in fact, was an active and acclaimed participant in the most spectacular demonstration of the 1977 Movimento, the three-day protest against repression held in September in Bologna. There, in the streets of the city, an awestruck Guattari bore witness to the unfolding of his anticipated "molecular revolution."[2]

An echo and a response to these events can be found in a slim volume printed in 1977 by the publishing cooperative of the school of architecture in Venice (CLUVA). Titled *Il dispositivo Foucault* (The Foucault Device), the book collected the papers presented at a crucial seminar by Massimo Cacciari, Franco Rella, Manfredo Tafuri, and Georges Teyssot. The meeting was convened by Rella, quite possibly prompted by Cacciari.[3] Rella had arrived at the IUAV in 1975 after having published a number of texts on Freud,[4] and during the 1977–1978 academic year he taught a seminar on Freud as a complement to Tafuri's course on turn-of-the-century Vienna. Cacciari was an advocate of "negative thought" and professor of aesthetics at the IUAV, affiliated first with Potere Operaio and then with the PCI (of which Tafuri was also a member). Cacciari's 1976 *Krisis. Saggio sulla critica del pensiero negativo da Nietzsche a Wittgenstein* (Crisis: Essay on the crisis of negative thought from Nietzsche to Wittgenstein),[5] was required reading for students enrolled in Tafuri's class on Vienna, along with his 1975 *Oikos: da Loos a Wittgenstein* (Oikos: From Loos to Wittgenstein), written in collaboration with Francesco Amendolagine.

The seminar drew a sizeable audience: after beginning in Aula Gradoni, where Tafuri usually taught

his classes, it had to be moved to Aula Magna at the Tolentini. With the notable exception of Teyssot's contribution, which thoughtfully investigated and tested Foucault's concept of heterotopy, the participants used it as a platform to attack not only Foucault but also Deleuze and Guattari in direct connection with the momentous events that were taking place in Bologna.[6] Cacciari's essay was reprinted, almost untouched, in a special 1977 issue of the philosophy and culture magazine *Aut Aut* titled "Irrazionalismo e nuove forme di razionalità" (Irrationalism and New Forms of Rationality). Cacciari then became the center of a notorious controversy about the notion of power attributed by Italian communist intellectuals to Foucault (and by extension to Deleuze and Guattari). The French philosopher would respond in an essay published in *Aut Aut* and then in a letter addressed to *L'Unità*, the organ of the Italian Communist Party, in December 1978.[7]

In 1976, under the aegis of Aymonino, the Institute for Architectural History at the IUAV—directed by Tafuri since 1968—was given more autonomy and renamed Dipartimento di analisi, critica e storia dell'architettura (Department of Architectural

Analysis, Criticism, and History): the tortuous appellation mirrored Tafuri's appraisal of the state of the discipline. The department offered a new *corso di laurea* (degree program) in history of architecture that attracted numerous students competing for guidance in the development of their master's theses. But the aftermath of the colloquium on Foucault marked a distinct realignment among department members and a certain redistribution of the students. Cacciari gave up teaching at the IUAV to devote himself fulltime to politics, as a member of the PCI, and he began to reflect on Catholicism. Tafuri rather abruptly dissociated himself and his classes from Franco Rella. Ironically, given the substantial presence of students in architecture engaged in Lacanian theory, Rella found himself directing Lacanian theses while Tafuri and Teyssot emerged as leading figures of the department in the following years. Teyssot introduced students not just to Foucault but to the large field of French literature on the history of science and technology, from Michel Serres and François Jacob to Georges Canguilhem and André Leroi-Gourhan. As for Tafuri, he became interested in Carlo Ginzburg's microhistory but slowly and inexorably turned his gaze to the Renaissance, entrenching himself and his students in a sternly philological approach.

Maya carpenter tying the thatch roof of a "pre-classic" Yucatecan house.

1. See *Cronache dai Tolentini: studenti, docenti, luoghi 1964–1975*, IUAV, no. 110 (2012).
2. Félix Guattari, *La révolution moléculaire* (Paris: Les Prairies Ordinaires, 1977), Guattari's book collected previously published essays and articles including a text about the closing of the Radio Alice (a free radio) in Bologna, as examples of the repression ordered by the mayor of the city, the communist Renato Zangari. Guattari's (and Gilles Deleuze's) involvement with the 1977 Movimento and the Italian extreme left are well documented in François Dosse, *Gilles Deleuze et Félix Guattari: Biographie croisée* (Paris: La Découverte, 2007). Interestingly Dosse comments at length about the relation and collaboration between Guattari and Toni Negri, underlining their divergences and questioning Negri's unrepentant Leninism.
3. Massimo Cacciari, Franco Rella, Manfredo Tafuri, and Georges Teyssot, *Il dispositivo Foucault* (Venice: Cluva Libreria Editrice, 1977).
4. Later collected in La critica freudiana (Milan: Feltrinelli Economica, 1977).
5. Massimo Cacciari, *Krisis. Saggio sulla crisi del pensiero negativo da Nietzsche a Wittgenstein* (Milan: Feltrinelli, 1976).

6. See Andrew Leach, Luka Skansi, "The Foucault Device: Forty Years On," in the book of abstracts of The Tools of the Architect, EAHN conference, TU Delft and HNI, The Netherlands, November 2017, 159. Marco Assennato, "Il dispositivo Foucault. Un seminario a Venezia, dentro al lungo Sessantotto italiano," Engramma 156, May–June 2018. http://www.engramma.it/eOS/index.php?id_articolo=%203419. On the vicissitudes of the idea of heterotopy see Daniel Defert, "Postface 'Hétérotopie': Tribulation d'un concept entre Venise, Berlin et Los Angeles," in *Michel Foucault, Le Corps Utopique—Les Hétérotopies* (Paris: Nouvelles Éditions Lignes, 2009), 37–61.
7. Parts of the exchange between Cacciari and Foucault are reprinted in Michel Foucault, *Dits et Écrits*, ed. Daniel Defert and François Ewald, 2 vols. (Paris: Gallimard, 2001). The polemic was exacerbated by an infamous article published in *L'Espresso* in November 1978. The authors arbitrarily collected fragments of an interview with Foucault including an allusion to Cacciari. Hilariously Foucault responded by saying that he never referred to Cacciari for the simple reason that he was unaware of his works.

ALTERNATIVE
MODERNIZATIONS

AN INTERDISCIPLINARY "GALAXY OF TALENT"

Eva Díaz

Protagonists Josef Albers (1888–1976),
Anni Albers (1899–1994), John Cage (1912–1992),
Robert Creeley (1926–2005), Merce Cunningham
(1919–2009), R. Buckminster Fuller (1895–1983),
Clement Greenberg (1909–1994),
Willem de Kooning (1904–1997), and others
Institution Black Mountain College
Location Black Mountain, NC, USA
Dates 1933–1957

With a minimal structure born of both ideological inclination and economic necessity, Black Mountain College's experiment in education was groundbreaking, though relatively brief. Founded in 1933 on the grounds of a YMCA summer camp on the outskirts of the small town of Black Mountain in North Carolina, it closed its doors in 1957. By the end, enrollment had dwindled to fewer than a half a dozen paying students—a little over a thousand had attended since its inception. Notwithstanding its short life and modest size, Black Mountain has assumed a prominent place in widely disparate fields of thought. It has been heralded as one of the influential points of contact for European exiles from Nazi Germany; as a standard-bearer of the legacy of planned or alternative communities such as Brook Farm in Massachusetts; as the bellwether campus of

Southern racial integration; as an important testing ground for proponents of progressive education; and as a seminal site of American postwar art practices. Adding to the college's reputation is the rollcall of famous faculty and students and the breadth of their artistic diversity—Josef and Anni Albers, John Cage, Robert Creeley, Merce Cunningham, R. Buckminster Fuller, Clement Greenberg, Franz Kline, Willem de Kooning, Robert Motherwell, Charles Olson, and Ben Shahn all taught at Black Mountain, while the students included Ray Johnson, Kenneth Noland, Robert Rauschenberg, Dorothea Rockburne, Kenneth Snelson, Cy Twombly, and Ruth Asawa.[1]

If the college was a "galaxy of talent," to use Ray Johnson's semi-ironic phrase, as an institution it also oscillated between moments of bitter dispute and evanescent harmony.[2] Experimentation and its close relative, interdisciplinarity, were key themes of this conversation. Seemingly everyone who attended Black Mountain College shared a desire to experiment, but they did not necessarily agree on what this meant. During the college's heyday from the mid-1940s to early 1950s, competing approaches to experimentation were advanced by its most notable faculty members—visual artists Josef and Anni Albers, composer Cage, and architect-designer Buckminster Fuller.[3] Simultaneously, visual artists such as de Kooning, Kline, and Motherwell, and poets such as Olson and Creeley, were developing the visual and literary rhetorics of expressionism that would soon come to dominate the postwar cultural landscape. In contrast, the vocabulary of experimentation developed at Black Mountain experienced a somewhat deferred reception, coming to prominence only later in the 1960s, in part through responses to the work and pedagogy of figures like the Alberses, Cage, and Fuller.

In spite of its precarious existence, the legacy of Black Mountain College is enormous: the rigorous artistic practices and influential teaching methods that emerged in its brief twenty-three-year existence made it the site of a crucial transatlantic dialogue between European modernist aesthetics and pedagogy and its postwar American counterparts. Still frequently cited as a source in contemporary music, visual arts, and architecture practices that explore what experimentation can mean today, Black Mountain College suggests that working "experimentally" in a cultural practice can foster a shadow venture: using the microcosm of academia to pose models of testing and organizing new forms of political agency and social life.

∧ Josef Albers's Color
Class, Summer 1944.
Photograph by Josef
Breitenbach. Gelatin
silver print.

< Buckminster Fuller
and Merce Cunningham
in *The Ruse of Medusa*,
1948. Photograph by
Clemens Kalischer.
Gelatin silver print.

1. Eva Díaz, *The Experimenters: Chance
and Design at Black Mountain College*
(Chicago: University of Chicago Press,
2015).
2. Ray Johnson, "Norman Soloman's
Doberman Interviews Ray Johnson," n.d.
[c. 1968]. North Carolina State Archives.
3. Competing approaches included
laboratory-like experimentation with
the appearance and construction of
form in the interest of designing
new, though ever contingent, visual

experiences (the Alberses), the organization of aleatory processes (Cage), and
"comprehensive, anticipatory design
science" that propels, teleologically,
current limited understandings towards
a finite totality of universal knowledge
(Fuller). R. Buckminster Fuller, "Bulletin
of the Fuller Research Foundation:
Exhibit 1—Airocean World Plan," June
1955, 4. Buckminster Fuller Papers, Stanford University Special Collections.

"DO NOT TRY TO REMEMBER"

Stephanie Pilat, Angela Person, Hans Butzer

Protagonists Bruce Goff (1904–1982),
Herb Grèene (1929–), E. Fay Jones (1921–2004),
Mendel Glickman (1895–1967), Elizabeth Bauer
Mock Kassler (1911–1998), and others
Institution The University of Oklahoma
School of Architecture
Location Norman, OK, USA
Dates 1947–1960s

"A new school, probably the only indigenous one in the United States" is how architect Donald MacDonald, FAIA, characterized the school of design that took shape at the University of Oklahoma (OU) from the 1940s through the 1960s.[1] Under the leadership of Bruce Goff, Herb Greene, E. Fay Jones, Mendel Glickman, Elizabeth Bauer Mock Kassler, and many others, OU developed a design curriculum that emphasized individual creativity and experimentation, rejecting the rote copying of historical styles as well as the abstract minimalist approach popular elsewhere. Students were taught to look to sources beyond the accepted canon of Western architecture and to find inspiration in everyday objects, the natural landscape, and the designs of non-Western cultures such as Native American tribes (a source of inspiration since childhood for Goff, who led the school from 1947 to 1955).

Dubbing this approach the "American School," Donald MacDonald described the emergence at OU of "a truly American ethic, which is being formulated without the usual influence of the European or Asian architectural forms and methodologies common on the East and West coasts of the United States."[2] At that time, US architecture schools followed a curriculum modelled on either the French École des Beaux-Arts or the German Bauhaus. The University of Oklahoma School of Architecture stood apart from these two trends, cultivating an original and authentically North American approach to architecture and pedagogy.[3] As Susan King explained, "In the minds of the Ivy Leaguers and big city critics, the jump was from Beaux-Arts to Bauhaus because it allowed them to retain their umbilical cord to Europe. The American School cut that umbilical cord."[4] This rejection of existing pedagogical models in favor of experimentation reflected Goff's own training. He was never formally educated in architecture; rather,

he learned architecture by doing it, having started in practice at the age of twelve.

The student work produced at OU provides the strongest argument for the originality and significance of the pedagogical experiment that unfolded under Goff, Greene, and their colleagues. A 1957 publication of the National Association of Architecture Students (NASA) illustrates just how distinctive it was.[5] Whereas boxy, rational, and efficient forms characterize the output of nearly every other school, the OU student work is imaginative and individualistic, marked by wildly organic and otherworldly forms. It often appears as the landscape of fantasies—bizarre, even surreal—yet it is also highly pragmatic and sensitive to the peculiarities of place and people.

In part, the difference in the student work stems from the ways in which architectural history was taught and used. At OU, the relevance of history was grounded in viewing works as exemplary for their own time, rather than as models to be copied in the modern era—mimicry of either historical or contemporary architecture was not allowed. Students were introduced to cultures from around the world and across time, and taught to appreciate the potential of their own surroundings— both the everyday objects and the natural landscape.

While OU students developed a keen awareness of global architectural history, when they arrived in the design studio they were instructed to start afresh. Citing the richness of the world's great architecture, Goff explained, "I believe we should know a great deal about all of them and learn what we can from all of them but forget it all when we need to create an architecture of our own. Do not try to remember."[6] Whereas other schools encouraged students to begin a design with classical columns and temple fronts or with modernist grids and pilotis (or the favorite designs of the instructor), these avenues were forbidden at OU. Students were also discouraged from beginning any design project with an end already in mind. Instead, they had to learn to trust and cultivate their own creative instincts.

The individualistic approach of the American School ran counter to the master-disciple structure employed at contemporary experimental schools such as Taliesin. Imitating Goff's or Greene's work was unthinkable. The faculty were viewed as mentors and guides rather than all-knowing authorities. Goff eschewed academic hierarchies in favor of a more collegial attitude. As Jeffrey Cook described the role of Goff and Greene, "They are not leaders or

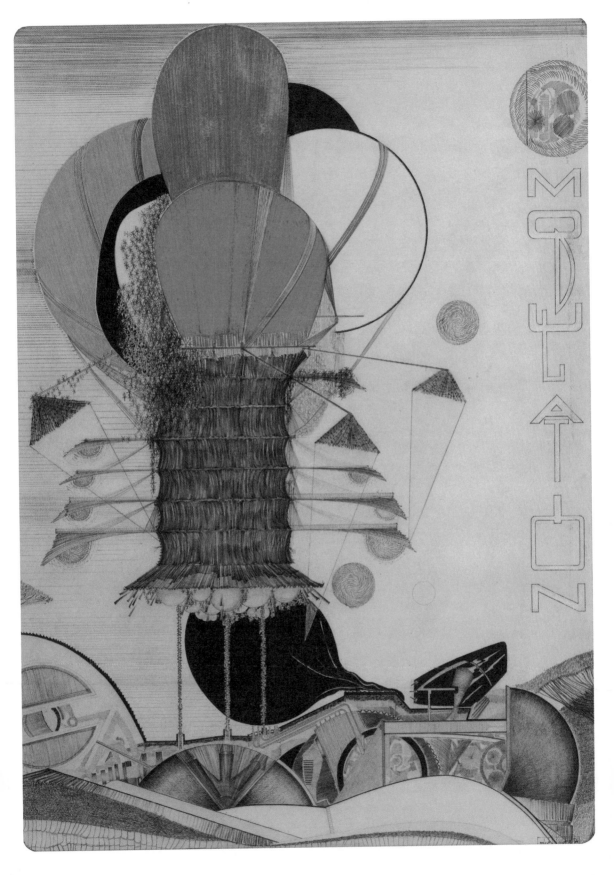

MODULATION

55

godheads in any other way than being fine architects whose work we admire."[7]

In the absence of historical models to appropriate or contemporary masters to imitate, American School students drew inspiration from five key things: "people, place, time, materials, and spirit."[8] The local conditions—landscape, climate, materials—provided a foundation for innovative designs without formal constraints. Project sites and programs were ordinary: students designed service stations, theaters, churches, and schools for Oklahoma and the surrounding region. At the same time, they created original works for each and every project. While the works of the American School relate to their sites and cultural contexts, they never look like the historical buildings in those contexts. Attention to the unique aspects of each project gives rise to a formal experimentation: the fantastic environments imagined on paper and realized in built works are characterized by complex geometries, attention to context, and material resourcefulness.

The University of Oklahoma faculty were not alone in seeking to develop an architecture curriculum that was reflective of the particular time and place—an architecture that was both contemporary and North American. Indeed, at that time, there were a number of other "American Schools," including Berkeley under W. Wurster; North Carolina State under H. Kamphoeffner; and the University of Texas at Austin under H. H. Harris. Among these diverse schools, it was the emphasis on individual creativity that distinguished OU.[9] Here, Goff's own practice was the model. As Charles Jencks put it, "Goff is so extreme that he makes the rest of the avant-garde look like a bunch of prep school conformists wearing the same school tie."[10] In the mid-century, the work garnered international attention, drawing students from Norway, Bolivia, Turkey, Canada, Venezuela, and beyond, who would later help spread the OU legacy around the world. Traveling exhibitions of OU work also inspired students to transfer to Oklahoma from other American universities. Among them were Herb Greene and Robert Faust, who would go on to teach at the University of Kentucky and Auburn University, where they instilled in their students the American School ethos of having confidence in their own unique problem-solving abilities.[11]

≪ Modulation, Fourth Year Studio (Architecture 273) assignment, student Robert L. Faust, with Bruce Goff, instructor, 1954.

< A Study in Proportion, Transparency, Translucency, Opacity, student Ernest Burden, 1955.

> Jerri Hodges and Bruce Goff's Christmas tree, school of architecture at OU, Norman, Oklahoma, c. 1950s.

1. Donald MacDonald, "Preface," *Architecture + Urbanism* 81, no. 11 (November 1981): 18.
2. Ibid., 18.
3. This essay draws on Stephanie Pilat, Angela Person, and Hans Butzer, "Introduction," in *Renegades: Bruce Goff and the American School of Architecture*, ed. Luca Guido, Stephanie Pilat, and Angela Person (Norman: University of Oklahoma Press, 2020), 3–11.
4. Susan King, *The American School of Architecture* (London: RIBA, 1985), 6.
5. National Association of Students of Architecture and American Institute of Architects, *Annual Publication*, 1957.
6. Bruce Goff, "The School of Architecture at the University of Oklahoma, 1947–56," *Architecture and Urbanism*, no. 134 (1981): 13.
7. Jeffrey Cook, "Legacies from an Un-Named School," *Architecture and Urbanism* (1981): 24.
8. Bruce Goff, "Letters to the Editor," *House Beautiful*, no. 97 (June 1953): 29.
9. Despite the originality of the American School approach, it was largely overlooked in histories of pedagogy until recently. Luca Guido, "The American School: Our Shared History," lecture at the University of Oklahoma, November 30, 2016.
10. Charles Jencks, "Bruce Goff: The Michelangelo of Kitsch," *Architectural Design* 48, no. 10 (1978): 13.
11. For more on the American School see Guido, Pilat, and Person, *Renegades*.

THE EDGE OF SCHOOL

Merve Bedir

Protagonists K. G. Subramanyan
(1924–2016), Sankho Chaudhuri (1916–2006),
Jyoti Bhatt (1934–), Ratan Parimoo (1936–),
Gulammohammed Sheikh (1937–),
Kumud Patel (1929–2013), Gyarsilal Verma
(1930–2000), Markand Bhatt (1929–2016),
Nasreen Mohamedi (1937–1990)
Institution Faculty of Fine Arts (Baroda School),
Maharaja Sayajirao University
Location Baroda, India
Dates 1956–1973

Baroda School was a pedagogical experiment—a site, a network, and a creative language—that led a move away from universalist modernism and reinvigorated local traditions and practices in the early years of independent India. These ideas found expression both in the official curricula and in related pedagogical activities such as fairs, periodicals, travel abroad programs, and studios that took place outside regular school hours. Baroda School was an initiative toward recreating lineages of history and theory that would overcome the legacy of the British educational system.

Central to an understanding of the pedagogy of the school is Baroda itself, considered as both a site and a network. As a site, it combined a distinctive experimental approach to teaching with the city's established role as a center for art and culture. As a network, Baroda incubated complex relationships that turned the focus of exploration toward the meanings of nationality and regionalism. Out of this grew the idea of "cultural indigenism"[1]—an attempt "to dig up the soil and make it fertile again, breaking through the parasitic nostalgia that clings onto Indian culture."

Working towards this cultural renewal, the concept of "living tradition" was an essential part of the school's pedagogical position in its early years, according to one of its founding members, the artist Kalpathi Ganpathi (K. G.) Subramanyan.[2] Living tradition referred to the capacity for artists to be individual and innovative without losing touch with the culture they were born into—the basic skills, tools of communication, knowledge, ways of thinking and behaving. By embedding the knowledge of self in the patterns of life, artists as humans continuously shape their society's future between the local and universal, between the individual and the multitude.

Baroda School aimed first to teach the knowledge and skills that had been passed down through the generations in order to avoid the isolation and the alienation of people from their cultural surroundings. But it also wanted to equip its students with instruments of knowledge, enquiry, and communication—to expose them to different kinds of experience that would enrich their work. To do this, the school devised special contact points—"non-permanent institutions"[3]—between different learning methods and areas of study.

One example of these non-permanent institutions, in the first ten years of the school's existence, were the fairs and exhibitions at which the students showed their work, not only in Baroda but in other cities like Bombay, Ahmedabad, and Srinagar.[4] Preparing for the exhibitions provided the opportunity for learning by making, and for experimenting with mediums that were not an established part of the curriculum, such as puppet-making, theater, culinary arts, and other traditional craft forms. The school would be open to the public during the fairs, and the works were sold at affordable prices to help support less privileged students. The same kind of engagement with the outside world was evident in architecture department, which opened its studios outside formal school hours and term-time.

K. G. Subramanyan stated that learning happens only through making the equivalent of something, a process that engages the maker's imagination. For him, the hands and mind were curious composites, allowing human perception to switch from distant suggestion to verisimilitude, from visual make-believe to visual metaphor. Hence, the process of making—the means of gaining knowledge and becoming conscious—defined a pedagogy of indigenous knowledge and bodily sensation. Describing the process of pot-throwing, Subramanyan wrote: "The wheel that makes the clay unit is not only a machine but also a magic tool for the maker. Each unit they make encloses a potent space, and put together…the final object becomes a vibrant power, a dev, a deity. Not pottery, but power." Of the craft of Dhokra, metal casting using the lost-wax technique, he stated, "the core is the most important and powerful; when you take care of the core, the cover takes care of itself."[5]

A similarly immersive learning experience[6] was based on the observation of the growth cycle of trees. Likewise, the landscapes of the Kashmir mountains and Banaras became mediums of exploration. Materials, methods, and techniques derived from nature opened up new effects and possibilities of

< Preparation for
the Fine Arts Fair,
1967. Photograph
by Jyoti Bhatt.

^ Puppets designed
by Jyoti Bhatt for
the Fine Arts Fair,
1969. Photograph
by Jyoti Bhatt.

configuration. Subramanyan claimed that the hands were losing the battle to the machine: making things by hand kept the artist connected with the nature of being, the philosophy of life: "In the operation of a universal education system, the cultivation of hand-skills will have an important place. This will enable the hands and the creativity of people to rise."[7]

From the mid-1960s, teaching in the studio was supported by the resources of the archive set up on the initiative of the head of the department of history of art, Ratan Parimoo.[8] In 1968 Jyoti Bhatt curated the first exhibition from the archive under the title *Living Traditions of India*. The archive was the first in a school in India, and by 1975 its collection had grown to more than eighty thousand transparencies and ten thousand photographs and prints.

From the beginning of the 1970s the Baroda School's pedagogy shifted toward figurative-narrative realism, reflecting political change. Gulammohammed Sheikh's (1937) *Place for People* paintings documented the deadly Hindu-Muslim riots in Gujarat in 1969,[9] bearing witness to the growing communal violence. Other themes developed by artists associated with Baroda included feminism (Nilima Sheikh and Rekha Rodwittiya), trans-discourse (Bhupen Khakhar), communitarian belonging and identity (Jyoti Bhatt).[10]

Articulating the motivations and ideals that underpinned the founding of the Baroda School, Subramanyan referred to how the educational system imposed by the British in India had under-mined the country's artistic traditions, producing artists who "saw the traditional forms as the relics of an obsolete past." The separation of art and craft—and their division into specializations such as architecture, craft, performance art, visual art—was a colonial imposition that limited the teaching of creativity.[11] "In fact," Subramanyan said, "art and craft are continuous in nature, and beauty and usefulness are inseparable."[12] As it worked to restore India's rich cultural traditions, the school's experimental pedagogy would gradually crystallize into an epistemological means to redraw and rewrite historical lineages. Through the school's archive and practice, and through the history of Baroda, which situated and revealed its pedagogy, the canons of history and knowledge around education in India were brought into question.[13]

1. Geeta Kapur, "In Quest of Identity: Art and Indigenism in Post-Colonial Culture," *Vrishchik*, no. 10–11 (1971).
2. K. G. Subramanyan, *The Living Tradi-tion* (Calcutta: Seagull Books, 1987), 8.
3. K. G. Subramanyan, "Bringing Educa-tion to Craftsmen" (originally published in 1971), in *The Magic of Making: Essays on Art and Culture* (Calcutta: Seagull Books, 2007), 341.
4. Ratan Parimoo, "Adventures in Education," in *Baroda: A Cosmopolitan Provenance in Transition*, ed. Priya Maholay Jaradi (Mumbai: Marg Foundation Publication, 2015), 80.
5. Subramanyan, *The Living Tradition*, 10.
6. Parimoo, "Adventures in Education," 73.
7. Subramanyan, "Bringing Education to Craftsmen," 342
8. Rashmimala Devi and Sabih Ahmed, "Archival Imaginaries: Art Practice and Pedagogy in the Early Years of the FFA," in *Baroda: A Cosmopolitan Provenance in Transition*, ed. Priya Maholay Jaradi (Mumbai: Marg Foundation Publication, 2015), 100.
9. Shivaji Panikkar, "In Place of a Conclu-sion: Cosmopolitan and Secular vs. Parochial and Communal," in *Baroda: A Cosmopolitan Provenance in Transi-tion*, 145.
10. Gulammohammed Sheikh, *Contem-porary Art of Baroda* (New Delhi: Tulika, 1996).
11. For the school's attempt over-come this legacy see also Claire Hsu and Chantal Wong, "Building Asia Art Archive," 2018, Asia Art Archive, Ideas, accessed June 15, 2019, https://aaa.org.hk/en/ideas/ ideas/building-asia-art-archive/type/ conversations.
12. Subramanyan, *The Living Tradition*, 11.
13. This work would not have been possible without the support and generous feedback of Özge Ersoy (public program lead at Asia Art Archive) and Sneha Ragavan (New Delhi archives of AAA). My main inspiration was the *Lines of Flight* exhibition they curated in AAA Hong Kong in 2018. The exhibition focused on the archives of Nilima Sheikh, a former student at the Baroda School.

A THEORY OF AN EVERYDAY-LIFE ARCHITECTURE

Vanessa Grossman

Protagonist Lina Bo Bardi (1914–1992)
Institutions Faculdade de Arquitetura e Urbanismo da Universidade de São Paulo (FAU-USP), Museum of Modern Art of Bahia (MAM-BA)
Locations São Paulo and Salvador, Brazil
Dates 1957–1964

In 1957 Italian-born architect Lina Bo Bardi—by then already a naturalized Brazilian émigré along with her husband, art dealer and critic Pietro Maria Bardi—completed a ninety-page essay to submit with her application for the position of Chair of Architecture Theory at the then nine-year-old School of Architecture at the University of São Paulo (FAU-USP). Titled "Propaedeutic Contribution to the Teaching of Architecture Theory," the essay was published as a little book by Habitat, the publisher of the Bardis' magazine, *Habitat—Revista das Artes no Brasil*, launched in São Paulo in 1950.[1]

Conceived as a "contribution to the teaching of architecture," the book not only offered a veritable theory of "everyday-life architecture" but called on Brazilian architects to develop an actualized "theory" of their own. The first part of the book addressed "Problems of Architecture Theory," the second

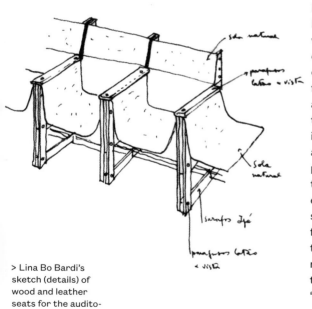

> Lina Bo Bardi's sketch (details) of wood and leather seats for the auditorium of her MAM-BA "museum-school."

"Problems of Method." Together they demonstrated how architectural education could be liberated from the conventional dichotomy of "theory" and "practice." Bo Bardi acknowledged "a certain impatience" on the part of students:

> This impatience is well known: they no longer feel connected to their past; their "roots have been cut," the natural habit of studying calmly and methodically no longer exists, nor the awareness of an acquired and natural cultural inheritance. It is the impatience of those who do not want to know about things that do not produce results immediately, about things that do not provide us with solutions to everyday problems.[2]

Her experience of student impatience was undoubtedly associated with her teaching the Industrial Design course at the Institute of Contemporary Art (1951–1953), which she founded with her husband as a means to underpin, in tandem with *Habitat* magazine, an acute sensibility to modern design in São Paulo.[3]

Responding to this impatience, Bo Bardi proposed her own definition of history, as being "useful only as an old bridge that allows us to cross a river; in other words, man's exigencies have become *suddenly*, rather than *gradually* (an adverb that was well liked by the Science Academies of the eighteenth century) diverse."[4] Rather than a "theory of styles," she looked for more immediate connections between history and practice. Every page of the book was designed as a collage, in the manner of *Habitat* and her own mixed-technique architectural drawings.[5] Text extracts and black-and-white images from various temporalities and sources were freely juxtaposed: Brazilian nineteenth-century writers with Italian Renaissance drawings; North American skyscrapers with the fifteenth-century Filarete column. Drawing on her Italian intellectual background and the work of figures such as Gustavo Giovannoni, who sought a fruitful transition from old to new in cities,[6] Bo Bardi argued that this threshold between history and practice could be even more easily crossed in Brazil. "True innovation," she insisted, is "only slowly accepted and a long time passes before other individuals become proselytes—especially people in countries where tradition dictates a constant conformity to the established aesthetic orders."[7] In order to demonstrate "the difficulties that the new architecture found in the Old World," Bo Bardi stressed the fact that "Le Corbusier himself has been the victim of misunderstandings and hostilities" at the same time as "Brazil kindly offered him" the opportunity "to design one of his best buildings."[8]

In "Propaedeutic Contribution," Bo Bardi established a conversation with different interlocutors,

1. See Lina Bo Bardi's original text, *Contribuição Propedêutica ao Ensino da Teoria da Arquitetura* (São Paulo: Habitat Editora, 1957), republished by the Instituto Lina Bo e Pietro Maria Bardi in 2002. For the English-language version, introduced by a thorough analysis, see Cathrine Veikos's *Lina Bo Bardi: The Theory of Architectural Practice* (London: Routledge, 2014). See also Zeuler R. Lima, "Teorizando uma modernidade humanizada: dois manifestos arquitetônicos de Lina Bo Bardi," in *Leituras em Teoria da Arquitetura*, ed. Laís Bronstein et al. (Rio de Janeiro: Editora Grupo Rio/UFRJ, 2015), 252–279.
2. Bo Bardi, "Propaedeutic Contribution," in Veikos, *Lina Bo Bardi*, 114.
3. See Ethel Leon, "The Instituto de Arte Contemporânea: The First Brazilian Design School, 1951–53," *Design Issues* 27, no. 2 (2011): 111–124.
4. Bo Bardi, "Propaedeutic Contribution," 74.
5. See *Lina Bo Bardi 100: Brazil's Alternative Path to Modernism,* ed. Renato Anelli, Andres Lepik, and Vera Simone Bader (Ostfildern: Hatje Cantz, 2014).
6. See Gustavo Giovannoni, *Vecchie città ed edilizia nuova* (Turin: Unione Tipografico-Editrice Torinese, 1931).
7. Bo Bardi, "Propaedeutic Contribution," 118.
8. Ibid., 120.
9. Ibid., 62, 64.
10. By "things" and "thoughts" Bo Bardi meant theory and practice. See Bo Bardi, "Propaedeutic Contribution," 110.
11. Ibid., 130, 127.
12. See Antônio Risério, *Avant-garde na Bahia* (São Paulo: Instituto Lina Bo e P. M. Bardi, 1995) and Juliana Monteiro, "O período Lina Bo Bardi no MAM-BA (1959–1964): uma análise sobre práticas sinérgicas de gestão," *Revista MUSAS—Revista Brasileira de Museus e Museologia*, no. 4 (2009): 65–78. See also Carla Zollinger, "Lina Bo Bardi and the Bahian Modern Art Museum: museum-school, museum in progress" (2002).
13. Zeuler R. Lima, *Lina Bo Bardi* (New Haven: Yale University Press, 2013), 74. Bo Bardi did not have a copy of her diploma from the Facoltà di Architettura in Rome, which was apparently lost in the bombing of the office she kept with Carlo Pagani in Milan.

from ancient treatise writers like Vitruvius to her contemporaries in America and Europe, particularly in Italy, while at the same time keeping her distance from them. Critical of the "functionalism" already present in Vitruvius's notion of *utilitas*, and of the "scientificism" of the modern movement, she revisited concepts associated with romanticism.[9] For Bo Bardi, "the modernists pose a certain resistance to this conception, perhaps influenced by the old habit of subdividing and separating the parts of the world into things and thoughts. On the contrary, the romantics understood architecture in a cosmic sense."[10] Advocating nature "as the primary source for the study of architecture," she criticized Bruno Zevi's theory of "internal space" as a means of categorizing architecture—a theory refuted by Gillo Dorfles' definition of architecture as typically *spaziale,* making use of both internal and external space.[11] Bo Bardi herself advocated what she called "total-space"—one that participates in everyday life, and for which the human subject is considered to be an "actor" in the world.

Bo Bardi's development of a pedagogical position did not stop with her "Propaedeutic Contribution." The year after its publication, she was invited by architect Diógenes Rebouças to teach at the Federal University of Bahia (UFBA). In April 1958 she traveled to Salvador to give lectures on architecture theory at UFBA's School of Fine Arts, returning in August to set up the School of Architecture with Rebouças. She was then invited by the governor of Bahia to direct the Museum of Modern Art of Bahia (MAM-BA) in Salvador. For four years, from 1960 to 1964, she ran the MAM-BA as a "museum-school," putting into practice the theoretical assumptions outlined in her text by organizing shows, courses, and pedagogical activities that gave material form to her "total-space" for everyday life and past and present cultures.[12] Despite the revolutionary experiment she carried out at the museum-school, Bo Bardi was never awarded the position that inspired her to write "Propaedeutic Contribution" in the first place—she never taught at FAU-USP. She knew that her application would not be well received by some faculty members, who saw her as being "difficult," a derogatory term often applied to women and perhaps complicated further by the bureaucratic obstacle she had to face regarding her Italian diploma.[13] Bo Bardi may very well have been difficult, but this would never have stopped a man—on the contrary. Today one can only imagine the pedagogical projects she might have triggered at the school by radically accessing the relevance of "theory" for architecture practice.

REFLEXIVE ACCELERATION

Ghada Al Slik, Łukasz Stanek

Protagonists Mohammed Makiya (1914–2015), Abdullah Ihsan Kamil (1919–1984), Hisham Munir (1930–), Hazim Al-Tak (1927–2013), Nasir Al-Asedi (1928–2016), Zofia Artymowska (1923–2000), Václav Bašta (1932–1997), Andrzej Basista (1932–2017), Jan Čejka (1933–)
Institution Department of Architecture, University of Baghdad
Location Baghdad, Iraq
Dates 1959–1973

The booklet showing the work of the first cohort of students at Baghdad University's Department of Architecture appears as a riddle. Issued in 1966 by Czech architect Václav Bašta, it juxtaposes Corbusian slabs with a diagram of Mansour's ancient round plan of Baghdad, Miesian-style row housing with survey drawings of ornate Baghdadi houses, and exercises in Bauhaus aesthetics with arabesque patterns. In the context of a rapidly urbanizing Iraq, the booklet conveys the desire to position architecture between the modern movement and the thousands of years of building tradition in Mesopotamia, both Islamic and pre-Islamic.

This was an ambition that had first been formulated seven years before by the department's founders, Iraqi architects Mohammed Makiya, Abdullah Ihsan Kamil, and Hisham Munir. Educated in the United Kingdom and the United States, Makiya, Kamil, and Munir aimed at furnishing a new generation of Iraqi architects with the necessary skills to engage with the accelerated growth of 1950s Baghdad, made possible by the country's reclaiming of a greater share of its oil revenues.[1] The department's curriculum included courses in planning,

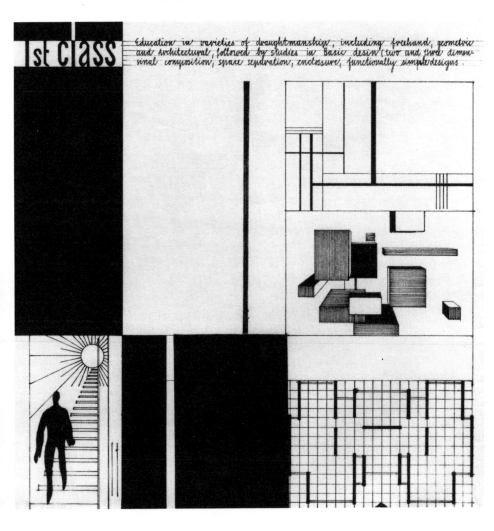

Education in varieties of draughtmanship, including freehand, geometric and architectural, followed by studies in Basic design (two and three dimensional composition, space separation, enclosure, functionally simple designs.

< Booklet presenting work by students in Baghdad University's Department of Architecture, 1966.

architectural design, and interior design, supported by extensive courses in architectural history (including Islamic architecture), building technology, and architectural representation.

Yet political events complicated the familiar trajectory of a post-independence elite learning its tools of cultural emancipation in the colonial metropolis (Makiya recorded Iraqi vernacular buildings using methods of measured drawing learned during his studies at the University of Liverpool in the 1940s). After the 1958 coup led by Abd al-Karim Qasim, which overthrew the Western-leaning monarchy, Iraq turned to the Soviet Union and other Eastern European socialist countries for assistance.

This new orientation resulted in the department's diversification, with Eastern Europeans joining a faculty made up of Iraqi architects educated in the US and the UK and American guest professors, including Robert Mather from the University of Texas. Václav Bašta was joined by other Prague architects, such as Miroslava Baštova and Jan Čejka. A group of at least ten Polish educators taught at the department during the 1960s and early 1970s, among them artist Zofia Artymowska and architects Andrzej Basista and Lech Kłosiewicz.[2] Iraqi architects who taught design studios included Hazim Al-Tak, Nasir Al-Asedi, and Kamal Tal-Eldin. Protagonists of modern architecture in 1960s Baghdad, such as Kahtan Madfai and Rifat Chadirji, served as guest professors.

During the deanship of Makiya (1959–1968), the department addressed the major challenges posed by Iraq's accelerated urbanization, often touching on questions of social-spatial justice, including the persistence of traditional land ownership, urban-rural migration, the acute shortage of housing, and the ongoing dilapidation and destruction of Baghdad's historic neighborhoods. According to Iraqi architect Fuad Uthman, who taught at the department in the 1960s, the curriculum focused on three broad topics: community and regional planning, Islamic architecture, and architectural programs specific to the country.[3]

All three topics were closely related. History courses, taught by Makiya with the support of others, fed into studio assignments focused on heritage areas in Baghdad. Studio teachers insisted on learning from the past, with references ranging from the traditional urban fabric, with alleys and courtyard houses, to Bedouin tents and Madan reed houses. Lorna Salim, in particular, took her students to draw Ottoman-era alleys, historic monuments, and vernacular structures by the River Tigris. Teachers and students studied local materials and construction technologies and explored how they might be modernized. Combined with the daily experience of Baghdad's layered urbanity, these studies supported selective, deliberate, and reflexive readings of the transnational modern architecture represented by the school's cosmopolitan staff.

These lessons would be applied to the new architectural tasks arising from Baghdad's rapid development in the 1960s, including the design of

multistory housing that took account of the country's climate and specific technological conditions and customs, and the insertion of new buildings into historic environments (Kadhemiya and parts of Rusafa and Karkh) designated as conservation areas in the city's new master plan (1967, amended 1973).[4] The plan itself was delivered by architects and planners from the Polish state planning office Miastoprojekt-Kraków, some of whom taught at the Baghdad school.

The teaching of the department during the 1960s provided reference points for a dialogue between modern architecture and building traditions, as envisaged by the 1966 brochure. But it also prepared the way for a new phase in Iraqi architecture. From the early 1970s a fast-growing economy fueled a construction boom that lasted until the First Gulf War in 1990. In that period, just as international architects and construction firms were flocking to Iraq, the Baghdad school was in turn radiating architectural pedagogy out toward the Middle East and the Islamic world at large.

1. Ghada Al-Silk, "Baghdad: Images and Memories," in *City of Mirages, Baghdad, from Wright to Venturi*, ed. Pedro Azara (Barcelona: Universitat Politecnica de Catalunya, 2008), 49–72.
2. Lech Kłosiewicz, "Ucząc w Bagdadzie," *Polska* 7 (1976): 38, 52–53.
3. Fuad Uthman, "Exporting Architectural Education to the Arab World," *Journal of Architectural Education* 31, no. 3 (1978): 26–30.
4. Łukasz Stanek, *Architecture in Global Socialism: Eastern Europe, West Africa, and the Middle East in the Cold War* (Princeton, NJ: Princeton University Press, 2020), 168–210.

∧ Faculty of the Department of Architecture, form the College of Engineering Yearbook, University of Baghdad, 1967

"BASIC DESIGN" TOWARD DECOLONIZATION

Ayala Levin

Protagonists Julian Beinart (1932),
Ulli Beier (1922–2011), Pancho Guedes
(1925–2015), Ezekiel Mphahlele (1919–2008)
Institutions Mbari Club, Ibadan, Nigeria;
Chemchemi, Nairobi, Kenya
Locations Mozambique, Nigeria,
South Africa, Rhodesia, Kenya
Dates 1961–1965

Writing in the late 1980s, the heyday of multicultur-alism, the London-based, Pakistan-born conceptual artist Rasheed Araeen took aim at the pressures exerted on non-Western artists in a polemical essay published in *Third Text*, the journal he coedited. The essay's panning title, "Our Bauhaus, Others' Mudhouse," clearly highlighted the embedded racial-cultural hierarchies of the art world.[1] But it could also be read as a relativizing gesture, one that "provincialized" Europe by drawing an implicit analogy between the revolutionary pedagogies of the Bauhaus and vernacular or "primitive" construction techniques. What seems at first a mere provocation, given the industrial conditions that gave birth to the Bauhaus, merits some further consideration, since the Bauhaus' radical reenvisioning of the relationship between art, crafts, and industry was predicated on a process of "unlearning" formal European traditions in order to reconfigure an imagined premodern state of union between man and his environment.[2]

If the Bauhaus model of "unlearning" was meant to liberate European students from Western preconceptions of art and design, would it be possible to reformulate this approach to address societies in transition to modernity, whose ties with tradition were not yet completely severed? Could a vernacularized Bauhaus pedagogy marrying local arts and crafts with building technology provide a means to manage the industrialization process of decolonizing societies?[3] In other words, could the Bauhaus "go native"?

This is what South African architect Julian Beinart tried to do in 1960s Africa. Returning from his studies at MIT in 1959 to teach at the University of the Witwatersrand in Johannesburg, he devised "basic design" workshops that translated Bauhaus pedagogy—as reformulated in the US by Hungarian

émigrés László Moholy-Nagy and Gyorgy Kepes—to the conditions of decolonization in Africa. Beinart was also an associate of Portuguese-Mozambican architect and Team 10 member Pancho Guedes, who was known for working with African artisans. Beinart's wish to extend the "basic design" course to the African population was made clear in a work-shop the two held in Lorenço Marques (Maputo), Mozambique in January 1961, the first in a series of summer schools. Under a new name, "Basic Courses in Visual Arts," further workshops would be held in Nigeria, South Africa, Rhodesia, and Kenya in the years up to 1965.

In Beinart's workshops the lineage of Bauhaus pedagogy converges with the lineage of the art work-shops set up by missions and colonial educators, which played a significant role in the development of arts education in the African continent.[4] A key figure in the art workshop's transition from colonial to postcolonial form was Ulli (Horst Ulrich) Beier, an Anglo-German Jewish émigré, who took up a post in the department of extra-mural studies at the University College, Ibadan in the 1950s. Responding to the wave of decolonization spreading through the continent, Beier became an influential figure in a golden cultural decade. The founder of *Black Orpheus*, a journal dedicated to contemporary African literature and art, he was also involved—along with a group of young writers including Wole Soyinka and Chinua Achebe—in the creation of the Mbari clubs in Ibadan and Oshogbo. A crucible of Nigerian modernism, the clubs attracted artists, writers, and musicians from across Africa. The Mbari club in Ibadan hosted Beinart's second and third workshops. In the one in Oshogbo, Ulli Beier and his artist wife Georgina Beier facilitated the training of local artists and promoted modern Yoruba dramatic productions.[5] Another key figure who influenced Beinart's educational experiments and research was Ezekiel (from 1977 Es'kia) Mphahlele, an exiled South African intellectual, who also taught in the department of extra-mural studies at the University College, Ibadan. One of the founders of the Mbari club in Ibadan, he would go on to set up Chemchemi, an equivalent cultural center in Nairobi, Kenya, where Beinart would conduct his last workshop.

In the advertisement for their week-long work-shop at the Mbari club, Guedes and Beinart stressed that no qualification or prior experience was required.[6] There would be a series of daily formal exercises, starting with two-dimensional exercises in black and white, gradually adding explorations of color and texture, and moving through collages to the final day's architectural exercise, "the making of space—the ideal house in Ibadan."[7] However, Beinart soon discovered that the students, with their mixed backgrounds and abilities (painters, teenagers, schoolmasters, a forester, a housewife, the club's janitor, and a car salesman, not forgetting the blacksmith who joined on the spur of the moment) found it hard to follow the standard language of instruction. His solution was to resort to action: "And then someone would start—often, I would myself—and then everyone reacted."[8] Significantly, this was not a demonstration, but the setting of the tone for a group improvisation.

To the students' great surprise, Beinart asked them to use readymade materials—bottle tops, leaves, pieces of chalk, mints, sand, and grit—which were combined with old magazines and household paint in primary colors and then poured or fixed onto newsprint or hardboard using what Beier called "blitz techniques."[9] Instead of the "ideal house" exercise, which had originally been envisioned as the culmination of the course, but now appeared

"anti-climactic" after the excitement generated by the collage exercises, they created three-dimensional installations—one tied reinforced rods into a metal tree, another was a mixed-media (mud and cement) sculpture.[10] The use of unexpected formal exercises and readymade materials to break artistic conventions was inspired both by Kepes's Bauhaus techniques and by prominent contemporary American artists. Similar to Jackson Pollock's drip paintings, these practices included dribbling from ordinary household paint tins, stirring them into shapes with sticks and poured sand, or pressing images onto the paint and sand with found objects.[11] In the African context, however, the choice of cheap, readymade materials took on a particular significance, as expensive art materials were scarce. But it was not simply a pragmatic response to conditions of scarcity. Using readymade materials was a deliberate attempt to free the students from the formal precepts of colonial art education and allow for greater access to creative experimentation.[12]

Unlike Beier, who was interested in identifying local talents and then promoting them in the global

art world, Beinart was not looking for unique artistic expressions. The emphasis instead was on dynamic collaboration and elemental explorations of texture and forms. But this did not mean that the works produced by his students remained at the level of formal abstraction. However formal the exercises, the students approached them figuratively,[13] and rather than seeing local conventions of figuration as a pedagogic failure Beinart believed that his "shock" techniques "provided the catharsis which returned the students to the healthy foundations of folk art. This basic teaching merely released what students intuitively could do," but had never done before, "because of inhibitions and misconceptions."[14] In the African context, students did not need to "unlearn" Western artistic conventions to the same degree as their counterparts at the Bauhaus. Nonetheless Beinart believed the basic design course not only effected "a quicker release," but "return[ed] people to the visual roots of their society," enabling them to truly tap into African creative resources.[15] Significantly, this was not a call to "retribalize" urbanized Africans in "homelands"—the official policy at that time in apartheid South Africa. Beinart sought instead to reconnect students to the resources available in their immediate environment, which was already a mix of urban and rural traditions and a space where these various traditions coexisted and changed, not least because of their encounter with Western popular culture.[16]

Beinart privileged visual culture as a pre-literary form of communication that could serve as a substrate for cultural formation even where there was no prevailing written tradition.[17] Drawing on the reformulation of the Bauhaus *Vorkurs* (foundation course) as the basic design course in the USA, his pedagogy was aligned with a liberal arts education that saw the cultivation of visual cognition as a basis for cultivating well-rounded citizens.[18] Referring specifically to the reforming zeal of the German Bauhaus, he explained, "We are not concerned, as the Bauhaus was, with throwing away things, but with making personal decisions as to what is best to retain and what is best to renovate. It is more a problem of fusion than reconstruction."[19] From this perspective, Beinart's references to ethnic visual resources were not driven by an exploitative quest to lock Africans into an immutable "Africanness." No longer tribal, but not modernized according to Western standards either, Africans could judiciously mediate between the two worlds, tapping into their primordial resources.[20]

« Pancho Guedes in
his Lorenço Marques
(Maputo) atelier with
two of his children
(Lonka and Pedro),
friends, collaborators,
and Malangatana
Valente Ngwenya, 1961.

< Jacob Afolabi and
Georgina Beier, Mbari
club, Oshogbo, early
1960s.

1. Rasheed Araeen, "Our Bauhaus,
Others' Mudhouse," *Third Text* 3 (1989):
3–14.
2. Ginger Nolan, "Savage Mind to Savage
Machine: Techniques and Disciplines
of Creativity, c. 1880–1985," PhD diss.
(Columbia University, 2015), 61, 289,
note 90.
3. See, for example, Mark Crinson
and Jules Lubbock, *Architecture, Art
or Profession? Three Hundred Years
of Architectural Education in Britain*
(Manchester: Manchester University
Press, 1994), 119–120.
4. Valentine Y. Mudimbe, *The Idea of
Africa* (Bloomington: Indiana University
Press, 1994), 159–165.
5. Peter Benson, *Black Orpheus, Transition, and Modern Cultural Awakening in
Africa* (Berkeley: University of California
Press, 1986); Wole Ogundele, *Omoluabi:
Ulli Beier, Yoruba Society and Culture*
(Bayreuth: Eckhard Breitinger's Bayreuth
African Studies Series, 2003).
6. Julian Beinart, "Basic Design in
Nigeria," *Athene* 2, no. 1 (Summer 1963):
21.
7. Ibid.
8. Ibid.
9. Dennis Duerden, "School for Painters,"
West African Review (January 1962): 34.
10. Julian Beinart, "Basic Design in
Nigeria," 21.
11. Ibid.
12. Julian Beinart, "Visual Education for
Emerging Cultures: The African Opportunity," in *Education of Vision,* ed. György
Kepes (New York: George Braziller,

1965), 196; Julian Beinart, "Seven African
Summer Schools: 1961–1965," *Cultural
Events in Africa*, no. 3 (February 1965):
1–2.
13. Beinart, "Basic Design in Nigeria," 22.
14. Ibid.
15. Beinart, "Visual Education for
Emerging Cultures," 198.
16. Julian Beinart, "Western Native
Township: The Same and the Change,"
World Architecture, no. 2 (1965), 186.
17. Beinart, "Visual Education for
Emerging Cultures," 184.
18. Anna Vallye, "The Middleman: Kepes's
Instruments," in *A Second Modernism:
MIT, Architecture, and the "Techno-
Social" Moment*, ed. Arindam Dutta
(Cambridge, MA: SA+P Press/MIT
Press, 2013), 144–185; Victor Margolin,
*The Struggle for Utopia: Rodchenko,
Lissitzky, Moholy-Nagy, 1917–1946*
(Chicago: University of Chicago Press,
1997), 215–227.
19. Julian Beinart, "A New Tradition in
African Art and Architecture," *The New
African* (April 1962): 14.
20. The research for this text has
received funding from the European
Research Council under the European
Union's Seventh Framework Programme
(FP/2007-2013) / ERC Grant Agreement
no. 615564. This essay is an abridged and
revised version of Ayala Levin, "Basic
Design and the Semiotics of Citizenship:
Julian Beinart's Educational Experiments
and Research on Wall Decoration in Early
1960s Nigeria and South Africa," *ABE
Journal [online]* 9–10 (2016).

FROM CONSPICUOUS EXPERIMENTATION TO DOING OTHERWISE

Robert J. Kett, Anna Kryczka

Protagonists Jean Lave (1939–),
James G. March (1928–2018), Duane Metzger
(1927–2019), Maya and Samoan craftspeople
Institution The Farm, University
of California, Irvine
Location Irvine, CA, USA
Dates 1967–1969

With its new "California Brutalist" campus inaugurated in 1964, the University of California, Irvine was an early engine in the transformation of Orange County from an agricultural "frontier" into a center for a new form of suburban speculation. While the campus designer, American architect William Pereira (1909–1985), adopted a razed-earth approach to the overall development, he retained a cluster of clapboard houses and barns on the edge of the site, part of the Irvine Ranch built in the nineteenth century and used to house migrant workers. Largely neglected in early visions of the new Orange County and university, this "Farm" soon became the site of an interdisciplinary experiment that linked new thinking in the social sciences with indigenous and countercultural ways of design and life.[1]

Consistent with the radically interdisciplinary and experimental pedagogical philosophy articulated for the new university, the Farm became an appealing site for faculty in the School of Social Science. In 1967 Professor Duane Metzger submitted a proposal to repurpose it as an ethnographic research center, citing the virtues of a "slightly rural" site that could simulate the "primitive" living conditions of visiting indigenous peoples and at the same time be connected to the university's computing infrastructures.[2] Drawing on metaphors of both the scientific laboratory and the artist-in-residence program, the proposal garnered the approval of university administrators interested in fostering an environment of "conspicuous experimentation."[3]

The experimental ethos that guided the new university was particularly strong within the School of Social Sciences. Led by its first dean, James March, a leading figure in the emergent fields of organization theory and design, the school was created without traditional departments.[4] Instead, it encouraged loose formations of interdisciplinary

faculty who would explore the potential of collaborative and computational models of research. As one commentator noted, March approached the design of the school itself as an experiment in organization, seeking to "put about fifty young academics together and then see how they might organize without replicating existing structures."[5] In this regard, the work at the Farm can be seen as an effort to design ideal conditions for anthropological research in keeping with the new vision of social science elaborated through March's broader institutional experiment.

Integrating a belief in the concept of the lab and in the computer as ideal tools for the development of new approaches to ethnography, the project at the Farm was premised on a radical form of decontextualization. Removing expert builders, craftspeople, and intellectuals from their respective cultures was viewed as a route to a systematic and total form of cultural knowledge, free from ethnographic "noise." The site operated as living space, construction site, and classroom, with the pastoral context of the Farm conceived as both a "lab" and as a more "comfortable" context for collaborators from Guatemala, Mexico, and Samoa.

The idea of transporting and housing individuals for the purpose of observing and documenting their expertise shares an affinity with deep and troubling histories of colonial display that structure the origins of anthropology. However, conditions at the Farm evolved in ways that displaced the well-defined positionalities of anthropological research, yielding a series of encounters that prioritized informal collaboration over exploitative observation. Rather than functioning as a noiseless lab, the Farm attracted students interested in learning and living beyond the modalities of the dorm and the classroom.

Introduced to the Farm through this ethnographic experiment, a group of art and social science students worked alongside itinerant counterculturalists to quickly transform the site into a broader project of communal living.[6] They built their own shelters from stolen road signs and in abandoned buses and chicken coops; learned ceramics, "traditional" construction techniques, and tamale-making from visiting Ixil Maya; and took visiting indigenous peoples on tours of Newport Harbor and the grocery store. Part of a much broader "back to the land" movement, the communalists' embrace of anti-establishment, antiwar, and egalitarian discourses introduced alternative frames for engaging with the Farm's other residents. While the experiment at the Farm was not without relations cross-cut by power,

11. "Doing is what the farm is about," says Bruce Green, art major, who exchanges techniques with Yucatec potter. Friend Lisa Endig, sophomore, finds the farm a restful change from books and classes.

12. To other students, the farm is a great place to go to "unscramble your brain. Carolyn Auburn of Rochester, New York.

misunderstanding, and difference, the displacement of the program's original scientist imaginary by these mundane and intimate acts of living together also suggested new methodological possibilities.

While the dream of the Farm as a controlled ethnographic laboratory was short-lived, the emphasis on collaboration and learning through apprenticeship that emerged there proved formative. Jean Lave, a young faculty member involved at the site and initially committed to its computational social scientific program, went on to articulate more contextual models of collaboration and research that have proven influential across education and design. Her work examining the importance of "situated learning" as the co-constructed, culturally and historically specific outcome of "communities of practice" evokes the inseparability of research and practice, learning and living so clearly illustrated through the evolution of the Irvine experiment.[7] Lave's theories are one of many examples from the Farm that illustrate how experimental pedagogical programs, despite their frequent apparent failure, are perhaps most significant as generators of unexpected outcomes.

< Life at the commune was centered on a variety of self-directed creative practices— from throwing pottery and drawing to collaborative building projects—often in partnership with visitors to the Farm.

v Maya carpenter tying the thatch roof of a "pre-classic" Yucatecan house.

1. See Robert Kett and Anna Kryczka, *Learning by Doing at the Farm: Craft, Science, and Counterculture in Modern California* (Chicago: Soberscove Press, 2014).
2. Duane Metzger, "Proposal for a Detached Cross Cultural Teaching/ Research Facility," Special Collections and Archives, University of California, Irvine Libraries.
3. Founding School of Social Science Dean James March, quoted in Donncha Kavanagh, "Reviewing March's Vision," paper submitted to the 28th Standing Conference on Organizational Symbolism (SCOS), Lille, July 2010.
4. For examples of March's early work outlining the fields of organization theory and design, see James G. March and Herbert A. Simon, *Organizations* (New York: Wiley, 1958); Richard M. Cyert and James G. March, *A Behavioral Theory of the Firm* (Englewood Cliffs, NJ: Prentice-Hall, 1963); *Handbook of Organizations,* ed. James G. March (Chicago: Rand McNally, 1965).
5. Kavanagh, "Reviewing March's Vision."
6. Despite Orange County's conservative reputation and strong military presence, it played host to its own brand of countercultural expression, detailed in Nicholas Schou's *Orange Sunshine: The Brotherhood of Eternal Love and Its Quest to Spread Peace, Love, and Acid to the World* (New York: St. Martin's Press, 2011).
7. Jean Lave and Etienne Wenger, *Situated Learning: Legitimate Peripheral Participation* (Cambridge: Cambridge University Press, 1991); Jean Lave, *Apprenticeship in Critical Ethnographic Practice* (Chicago: University of Chicago Press, 2011).

AN IRANIAN "GRAND TOUR": FROM HISTORIC ARCHITECTURE TO FUTURISTIC LUNAR SETTLEMENTS

Pamela Karimi

Protagonists Houchang Seyhoun (1920–2014), Nader Khalili (1936–2008)
Institutions Faculty of Architecture in the School of Fine Arts at the University of Tehran, Cal-Earth
Locations Iran, California (USA)
Dates 1960s–1990s

Iran's first professional program in architectural design was established in the early 1940s under the deanship of the French architect, archaeologist, and art historian André Godard, a graduate of the École des Beaux-Arts in Paris. As part of the School of Fine Arts at the University of Tehran, the architecture department's curriculum was initially modeled on the Beaux-Arts system of ateliers. In 1962, however, the curriculum was radically reshaped by a new dean, architect Houchang Seyhoun, who led the school until 1968. Among many other innovations, Seyhoun initiated a program of field trips exploring Iran's architectural heritage. Architecture majors could earn course credits for documenting historic sites, with a special focus on those monuments where the archival records were either incomplete or missing altogether. This vested interest in the country's rich cultural history, stretching back for thousands of years, was not a symptom of ardent nationalism but rather an attempt to counter the placelessness and absence of identity in the market-driven architecture of the time, which was often a blind imitation of Western styles.

During these field trips—an equivalent of the early modern European "grand tour"—both male and female students created sketches, measured buildings, and crafted blueprints from scratch. They also took photographs and made short documentaries with 8 mm film recorders. Many of the students on these tours would incorporate aspects of regionalism and environmentalism into their later practice. The built work of architect and educator Ali Akbar Saremi, for instance, drew consistently on the formal and functional characteristics of Iran's historic architecture. Another notable graduate, Hussein Amanat, designed the Shahyad Tower as a medley of historical sources, from ancient Zoroastrian fire temples and Sassanian palaces to medieval tomb towers and early modern mosques. While the architecture of the Shahyad (now Azadi) Tower has often been linked to the nationalistic impulses of the early 1970s, Amanat attributes his preference for historical eclecticism to his travels with Seyhoun. Far removed from the fanciful individualism and embellishment of postmodern architecture, this approach aimed to create buildings that were not only culturally attuned and environmentally responsive—like the historical precedents they referred to—but also equal to the demands of modern life.

After the end of Seyhoun's deanship, the Iranian "grand tour" remained an integral constituent of design curricula at the University of Tehran and the other architecture schools that emerged later on. Iranian architects, even if they studied abroad, would still return home to learn about Iran's architectural heritage at first hand. A prime example is Nader Khalili—a graduate of Istanbul's Technical University and a registered architect in California—who in the 1970s abandoned his lucrative design business in Los Angeles and returned home for a five-year exploration of vernacular settlements. Following a long solo research trip in the desert, he embarked on a new design project. Using clay, water, and fire, Khalili invented the Geltaftan process, a renewed approach to kiln firing. After extensive trial and error, he found a way to make the traditional

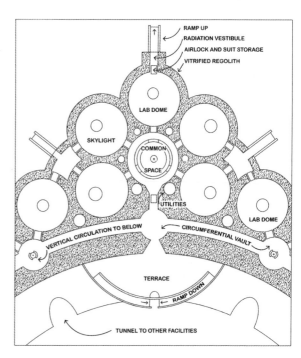

RAMP UP
RADIATION VESTIBULE
AIRLOCK AND SUIT STORAGE
VITRIFIED REGOLITH
LAB DOME
SKYLIGHT
COMMON SPACE
VERTICAL CIRCULATION TO BELOW
UTILITIES
CIRCUMFERENTIAL VAULT
LAB DOME
TERRACE
RAMP DOWN
TUNNEL TO OTHER FACILITIES

adobe architecture more resistant to earthquakes. Cheap to build, and ecologically sustainable, Khalili's system was particularly suited to the construction of emergency accommodation for refugees or the victims of natural disasters. But Khalili also translated his humanitarian "earth architecture" into shelters for the Moon and Mars—as the architect himself noted, the political atmosphere in the late 1970s and early 1980s seemed more attuned to the future than to the problems of the present. In 1984 Khalili was invited to a NASA symposium on lunar bases in the twenty-first century. His presentation, "Lunar Structures Generated and Shielded with On-Site Materials," later published in the *Journal of Aerospace Engineering*, outlined ways of adapting the centuries-old techniques of Iranian adobe architecture for lunar surfaces. In 1991 Khalili would set up Cal-Earth, the California Institute of Earth Art and Architecture, a nonprofit learning center for earth architecture. Based in Hesperia, California, Cal-Earth continues to train hundreds of people each year through on-site, international, and web-based educational programs. Khalili's extensive research and experimentation in the Iranian desert provided the impetus for a design approach that was both humanitarian and futuristic, a trend that has had a lasting impact on other designers, including those who are active in Iran.

Since 2017 the Iranian architect Pouya Khazaeli Parsa has been conducting field trips and engaging young students in experimental design projects in the remote desert regions of Iran. The choice of remote locations aligns with an urge among Iran's creative agents to escape the ideology and mundane routines of life in the urban centers of the Islamic Republic. But while it lies outside the official university curricula, the program remains faithful at its core to the pedagogical trajectories initiated by Khalili and Seyhoun. At Esfahk Mud Center near the northwestern city of Tabas, Khazaeli Parsa and his students not only document old buildings but employ traditional building techniques to generate environmentally friendly designs for the future.

Seyhoun's pedagogical model played a crucial role in shaping an authentic architectural discourse in Iran. Countering Beaux-Arts training and imported canons of architectural education, Seyhoun and his students redefined the field of architecture to make it specific to the needs of the Iranian people, a tradition that endures to this day in both official and alternative educational platforms. Above all, the renewed pedagogical regimes of the 1960s endowed many generations of Iranian architects with a bold imagination. Exploring the rich built heritage of Iran proved to be not a mere excursion into a forgotten past. As Khalili's cutting-edge approach to building in the desert indicates, Iran's arid lands also became a laboratory for envisioning a sustained future life on this planet and beyond.

THE JEWISH SHEPHERD WHO WANTED TO CULTIVATE ISLAMIC ARCHITECTURE

Noam Shoked

Protagonist Simha Yom-Tov (1914–2005)
Institution The Center for the Cultivation of Islamic Art
Locations Israel and the Occupied Palestinian Territories
Dates 1968–1970s

In June 1967 Israel captured the Gaza Strip, the Sinai Peninsula, the West Bank including East Jerusalem, and the Golan Heights from its neighboring countries in what came to be known as the Six-Day War. The conquest of these vast territories, which more than tripled the size of the country, changed the geopolitics of the Middle East. It also changed the practice of architecture in Israel.

In the aftermath of the war a massive building program was launched in East Jerusalem. As the architectural historian Alona Nitzan-Shiftan has shown, many of the Israeli-born architects working in the city were experimenting with a Palestinian vernacular. These architects, however, were often oblivious to the Palestinians' experience.[1] They rarely interacted with the people responsible for that vernacular—residents who now found themselves under Israeli rule.

The architect and educator Simha Yom-Tov was an exception. Born in Romania in 1914, Yom-Tov had emigrated to Mandatory Palestine when he was twenty-one. Soon after, he joined Kibbutz Dalia, where he worked as a shepherd.[2] At the age of forty-five, Yom-Tov audited architecture classes at the Technion, the only accredited architecture school in Israel at the time. Although he never finished his studies, he began taking on design commissions.[3] He was especially interested in planning for Israel's non-Jewish minorities: he planned a village for the Negev Bedouin, organized drafting classes for Druze citizens, and launched a magazine written in Adyghe and Hebrew for the Circassian minority. For a couple of years, he also worked at the Ministry of Interior as a consultant on planning for Arabic-speaking minorities.[4] The conquest of the Palestinian territories marked a new era in his efforts to reach out to non-Jewish people.

In January 1968 Yom-Tov contacted a couple of colleagues and together they founded the Center for the Cultivation of Islamic Art, a research and education agency dedicated to preserving the presumed Islamic identity of buildings and the arts in the Occupied Palestinian Territories and Israel.[5] The center was launched with a festive event in the East Jerusalem YMCA building.[6] In an inaugural speech, Yom-Tov shared its mission: to fight what he perceived as the negative effects of modernization on Islamic culture, and especially on Islamic architecture. The native populations of the region, he explained, had replaced their building traditions with foreign ones. They no longer wanted arches to decorate their facades, nor did they rejoice in the use of their traditional courtyard spaces. The center was designed to mitigate this effect by helping "Arab society" appreciate its own culture. "Perhaps this encounter between people who came here from the West [Ashkenazi Jewish Israelis]," Yom-Tov added, "and those of Eastern culture, whose desire for modernization is strong, is a unique opportunity to create an artistic way for Arab society."[7] Yom-Tov, it seems, wanted that evening to mark the beginning of a new binational movement, perhaps even a new chapter in the fraught relationship between Israel and its neighboring countries.

But a new movement did not come into being that evening. Only 25 people attended the event, most of whom were Jewish Israelis. Palestinians declined Yom-Tov's invitation.[8] "Our [Palestinian] friends have disappointed me," he wrote to an acquaintance. "But since this is not the first time that they have disappointed me…I will continue and refuse to stop developing this matter."[9] And so he did.

In the following months, Yom-Tov contacted Palestinian officials in Israel and the West Bank, inviting them to collaborate on research projects and help develop courses on Islamic art and architecture. He thought these classes should reach the broader Palestinian population.[10] "You know how important it is to spread this idea among the general public, and not just among professional architects and painters," he explained to one of them.[11] But the wider Palestinian population, who probably questioned Yom-Tov's motives, did not show up to his classes. Not even Palestinian students holding Israeli citizenship took interest in the extracurricular course he attempted to organize at the Hebrew and Haifa universities.[12]

Yom-Tov's peers at the Technion were equally suspicious. The dean of research politely refused to fund the center.[13] The faculty were less polite. Architecture professor Aaron Kashtan critiqued

Yom-Tov's focus on symbolism.[14] The architect Michael Kuhn rightly complained that Yom-Tov conflated Islamic with Arabic culture, and that, in any case, neither of the two was a monolith. "I tend to see a mosaic in a place where some see sameness," he noted, not without irony. Equally troubling, Kuhn argued, Yom-Tov was trying to keep these cultures in the past, as if they were museum objects. "I would be the biggest obstacle for anyone drawn to nostalgia," Kuhn warned Yom-Tov.[15] Academia had no space for Yom-Tov's institute.

By the early 1970s Yom-Tov had shifted the center's pedagogical efforts to exhibitions, showcasing drawings and photos of buildings from a number of Middle Eastern countries, including Israel. Among these, he included his own work, such as a tentlike structure made of a thin concrete shell he designed for the Negev Bedouin. Hoping to teach Palestinian visitors about their building traditions, Yom-Tov installed shows in Nablus, Nazareth, and Hebron.[16] These shows, however, were short-lived, lasting for less than a week and rarely reaching a wide public.[17]

Within a few years the center was abandoned. Its demise may seem unremarkable. Yom-Tov's understanding of Islamic and Arab cultures was often paternalistic and reductive, and his classes and exhibitions had little merit. Nevertheless, in light of the ongoing Israeli-Palestinian conflict, Yom-Tov's undertakings remind us that at one point, some believed that a dialogue between the two people was possible, and that architectural education could become a platform for that dialogue.

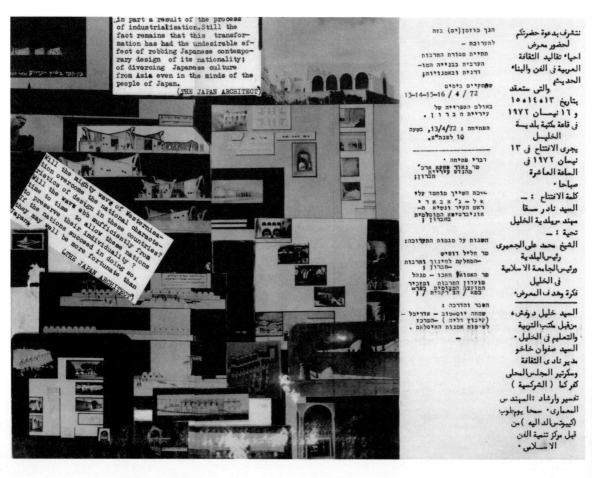

< Invitation to *The Revival of Arab Culture in Modern Building and the Arts* exhibition at the Center for the Cultivation of Islamic Art, Hebron [al-Khalil], 1972.

∨ Simha Yom–Tov showing his design for a Bedouin house to a community representative, 1960. Photographer unknown.

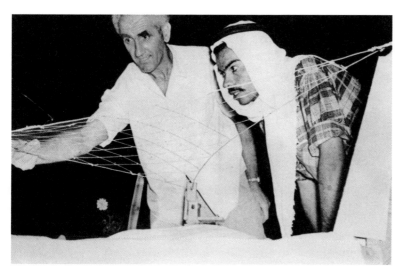

1. Alona Nitzan-Shiftan, *Seizing Jerusalem: The Architectures of Unilateral Unification* (Minneapolis: University of Minnesota Press, 2017), esp. 45–78.
2. Simha Yom-Tov, "Data Sheet," n.d., Kibbutz Dalia Archive; Simha Yom-Tov, "Life Story," 1971, Kibbutz Dalia Archive [KDA].
3. Ada Sa'ar, "Haroeh Ha'adrihal Vesheyodea Lir'ot," *Hashavua Bakibutz Haartzi*, May 10, 1968, 9, KDA.
4. Yom-Tov, "Life Story." On Yom-Tov's plans for a Bedouin village, see Noam Shoked, "Housing Others: Design and Identity in a Bedouin Village," *International Journal of Islamic Architecture* 8, no. 2 (July 1, 2019): 307–335.
5. The center was occasionally referred to as the Center for the Cultivation of Islamic Art—for the Cultivation of the Cultural-Artistic Identity of Arabic Societies. "Tipuah Hayetziratiyut Behavarot Baalot Tarbut Aravit—A"i Sheiva MiMekorot Tarbut Atzmiyim" (Hamerkaz Letipuah Omanut Halslam, n.d.), (3)15.147-95, Yad Yaari Research & Documentation Center [YYRDC]; "Ne'erah Kenes Yeshod Shel 'Hamerkaz Lepituah Tarbut Halslam,'" *Lamerhav*, January 7, 1968, KDA.

6. "Niftah Merkaz Omanut Halslam," *Al Hamishmar*, January 5, 1968, KDA; "E. J'lem, W. Bank Architects Skip Meet with Israelis," *Jerusalem Post*, January 5, 1968, (3)15.147-95, YYRDC.
7. Simha Yom-Tov, "Hamerkaz Lepituah Omanut Halslam Veshtilata Bemisgeret Hahyim Hamoderniyim (Lecture Transcripts)," 1968, (3)15.147-95, YYRDC. Unless otherwise noted, all translations are my own.
8. "E. J'lem, W. Bank Architects Skip Meet with Israelis."
9. Simha Yom-Tov to Hadasah Smuel, January 8, 1968, (4)15.147-95, YYRDC.
10. See, for example, Simha Yom-Tov to Umm El-Fahm municipality, "Kennes Eizori Shel Hamerkaz Lepituah Omanut Halslam—Bkfarhem," January 14, 1968, (3)15.147-95, YYRDC; "Mifgash Amanim 'Letipuah Modernism Aravi,'" *Al Hamishmar*, January 26, 1970, KDA.
11. Simha Yom-Tov to Abed Rahim Haj Yahia, "Kennes Eizori Shel Hamerkaz Lepituah Omanut Halslam," January 14, 1968, (3)15.147-95, YYRDC.
12. Simha Yom-Tov to Eliezer Rephaeli, "Hug Letipuah Omanut Halslam," November 11, 1969, (3)15.147-95, YYRDC. Haifa University was then known as "Haifa Academic Center."
13. See Yosef Hagin (head of the Technion Research and Development Foundation) to Simha Yom-Tov, "Tzevet Mehkar Ltipuah Omanut Halslam," February 27, 1968, (3)15.147-95, YYRDC; Simha Yom-Tov to Yosef Hagin, "Tzevet Mehkar Letipuah Omanut Halslam," February 8, 1968, (3)15.147-95, YYRDC.
14. See Yom-Tov's reaction to Aaron Kashtan's criticism in Simha Yom-Tov to Aharon Kashtan, February 25, 1969, (3)15.147-95, YYRDC.
15. Michael Kohn to Simha Yom-Tov, January 22, 1968, (3)15.147-95, YYRDC.
16. In January 1972 the institute organized an exhibition in Nazareth that included building models from Arab countries. Other exhibitions were installed in Hebron in April 1972 and in Nablus in 1973. See "Taaruhat Bniya Besignon Aravi Nifteha Benatzeret," *Yediot Aharonot*, January 24, 1972, KDA; "Adrihal-Haver Kibbutz Yazam Taaruha Lebniya-Aravit-Modernit Behevron," *Al Hamishmar*, April 14, 1972; Center for the Cultivation of Islamic Art, "Hazmana Letaaruhat Thiyat Masoret Hatarbut Haaravit Babniya Hamodernit Vebaomanuyot," April 13, 1972, (3)15.147-95, YYRDC; "Taaruhat Adrihalut Aravit-Yehudit BeShchem," *Al Hamishmar*, January 14, 1973, KDA.
17. "Taaruhat Adrihalut Aravit-Yehudit BeShchem"; "Adrihal-Haver Kibbutz Yazam Taaruha Lebniya-Aravit-Modernit Behevron."

SURVIVAL AS A CREATIVE PRACTICE FOR SELF-LEARNING

Valerio Borgonuovo, Silvia Franceschini

Protagonists Archizoom, Superstudio, UFO, 9999, Ziggurat, Remo Buti (1938–), Alessandro Mendini (1931–2019), Ugo La Pietra (1938), Gianni Pettena (1940–), Riccardo Dalisi (1931–), Franco Raggi (1945–), Ettore Sottsass (1917–2007), Davide Mosconi (1941–2002), Franco Vaccari (1936–)
Institution Global Tools
Locations Florence and Milan, Italy; River Rhine from Düsseldorf, Germany to Basel, Switzerland; River Ticino between Italy and Switzerland
Dates 1973–1975

"The first Italian counter-school of architecture (or not architecture, or again non-school),"[1] Global Tools was founded in 1973 in the offices of *Casabella* magazine by groups and individuals associated with Italian radical architecture.[2] Defined as "a system of laboratories in Florence for the dissemination of the use of natural materials and techniques, and fitting behavioral models,"[3] it coalesced in opposition to the power structures that had become institutionalized in architecture schools after the failure of the student movements in Italy. At a time when the country's cultural climate was shaped by ongoing generational and political conflict, Global Tools sought to stimulate the free development of individual creativity. Understanding traditional architectural culture as a form of social alienation based on the functional separation between producer and consumer, artist and user, its founders attempted to build a shared heritage of experience and vision consistent with a strategy of "life-long learning," which they considered to be "the only possible objective beyond the end of institutionalized education." This expansion of education was intended to bring closer the "ideal moment at which education coincides with life itself."[4]

Global Tools' research on a "didactic typology" for the future school called for the remodeling of "life as permanent global education"—a nod to *Deschooling Society* (1971), by the Austrian pedagogue and philosopher Ivan Illich, which proposed that young people always learned best in times and situations that were beyond the control of the school. Global Tools rejected the possibility of "teaching by transfusion"[5]—and perhaps even of "teaching" altogether—and instead developed a system of laboratories and seminars designed to stimulate self-learning and the achievement of a new "psychosomatic balance." Rather than inculcating a cultural education, they wanted to engage in a cultural process, "the exaltation of the creative faculties of each individual man," with the goal of "bridging the distance…between the work of the hands and that of the brain."[6] The didactic typologies were to emerge from the dialogue between the participants (or "co-experimenters") in their laboratories, built around the principle of free choice and common interests.

From 1973 to 1975, thanks to the financial support of Franco Castelli (a friend of Ettore Sottsass and owner of the L'Uomo e l'Arte art gallery in Milan), the Global Tools group developed a series of experiments closely related to the "laboratory situations" that Sottsass himself had experienced in the mid-1950s as a participant in the Experimental Laboratory of Alba, part of the International Movement for an Imaginist Bauhaus (IMIB). *Casabella*, then under the direction of Alessandro Mendini, took on the role of promoting the entire program; for several years the magazine had given a platform to the radical vanguard and to the debate on education following the shift from the elite to the mass university.[7] Two official bulletins were published in Italian and English to raise interest in the initiative, which was planned to launch in the summer of 1975. Remo Buti was entrusted with the design of its graphics and branding.

Five autonomous but strictly interconnected research and work groups were formed: Construction, Survival, Communication, Theory, and Body. Experimental musician Davide Mosconi and conceptual photographer Franco Vaccari also took part in these activities and experimentation in the build up to the official launch of the school. A fundamental contribution was made by Riccardo Dalisi, who from 1971 to 1974 undertook a series of experiments in creative participation with the children of Rione Traiano, a postwar district of Naples that had very quickly fallen into decay and illegality. For Dalisi, the children's free creations, made with humble materials and without any previous knowledge, yielded unexpected results, lending form to their imaginative potential and developing both individual and collective creativity through the interpersonal dynamics of the design process. Dalisi framed his teaching within an understanding of its social and political role in urban life. He referred to *The Pedagogy of the Oppressed* (1971), in which the Brazilian educator Paulo Freire defined his pedagogical method as a

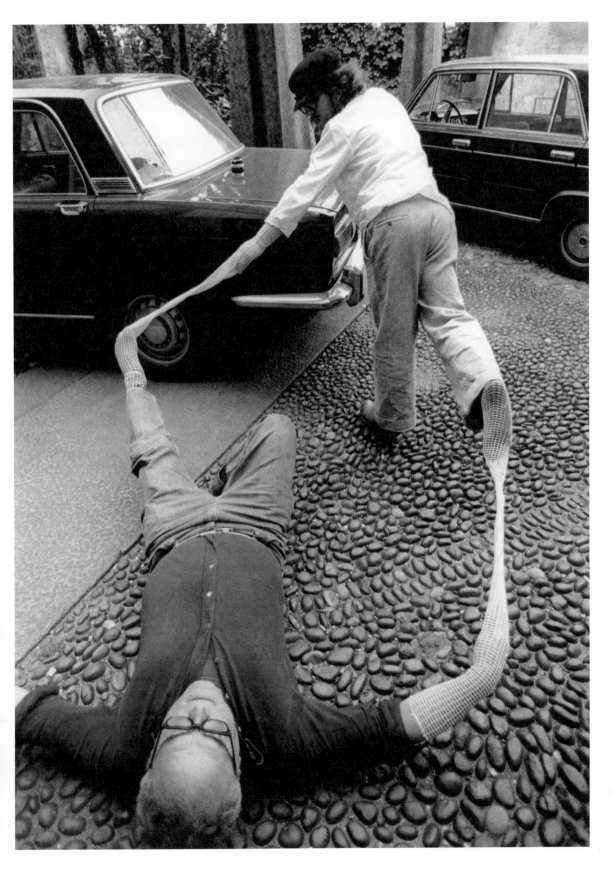

< First Body Group
seminar, "The Body
and Constraints."
Milan, June 5–8, 1975.

v Riccardo Dalisi's
"Architecture of
Animation" workshop
with the children
of Rione Traiano,
Naples, early 1970s.

form of "conscientization": the development of a critical awareness of one's own social reality, activated by the "co-creation" of knowledge in the equal relationship between student and teacher.

Inspired by what Dalisi called "poor technique," the Construction Group proposed "the nullification of every technological filter, of any predetermined instrumental, cultural, methodological, technical-practical, and material medium."[8] Despite its name, the group left only a few built traces. Alongside the overturned hull of a twelve-meter-long "ark" built by 9999 on the initiative of Paolo Galli, there was a polystyrene raft built in the summer of 1975 by Andrea Branzi, Ettore Sottsass, and Japanese designer Masanori Umeda. It sank after just a few seconds after it was launched on the River Ticino.

The Survival Group expressed the most apocalyptic response to the prevailing geopolitical context of the Cold War, conflict in the Middle East, and the first global energy crisis. In 1974 it organized Global Tools' first general seminar in Sambuca Val di Pesa, in the countryside outside of Florence. The seminar—a "survival experiment" focused on cultural deconditioning—was almost like a group therapy session, involving drawing, ceramics with children, cooking and other manual activities such as carpentry, alongside nighttime discussions and debates.

The Communication Group turned their attention to the analysis of the distorting effects of mass media, as a first step toward eliminating every tool of mediation and "filter" that came between reality and the individual. In seeking to overcome the passive role of the spectator, they wanted to encourage a collective participation in the dynamics of communication and, with it, a greater awareness of the environment. In this spirit, the group embarked on a voyage along the River Rhine in September 1974, traveling from Düsseldorf to Basel on a tourist boat—a closed, homogeneous collective space, which allowed for a fairly long period of experimentation without risk of interruption. For their so-called "Global Tour," the group chose a confined situation where isolation and boredom tended to amplify psychic automatism and emotions. Their goal was to gather information produced by passenger communication—voluntary and otherwise. The outcomes of these experiments were to be included in a preliminary report that would inform the basis of future courses.

The Theory Group favored the reversal of semantic relations: between spontaneous production and research, reality and representation, nomadism and stability, rationality and insanity, archaism and

hypermodernity. Adopting an original archaeological method as a metaphor to describe its approach to the relationship between past and future, it sought to revive the role of fantasy and imagination in a design teaching program. Analogies were made, for example, between sporting activities and collective creativity, or between architecture and magic; the group played with science, overturning hierarchies and power relations in the sphere of the production of knowledge. Global Tools set out to promote a different end for creativity—a "non-productive" result—in the process hypothesizing the "abolition of labor." In a document on this theme, the Archizoom group explained how, in the hypothesis of a "society without labor," creativity would correspond to "the release of a liberating energy that is an end in itself (in the sense that it is not productive of values). Therapeutic and deprived of coded meanings." From this perspective, the experiments of Global Tools (and, more broadly speaking, of the entire neo-avant-garde) were intended to favor "a technological destruction of culture, with a view to liberalizing its use."[9]

Finally, the Body Group was developed through an interesting "inventory of the human body" and two seminars held in Milan in 1975. Countering the growing commodification of the body, the performative dimension of these seminars was an act of rebellion. Against an array of optimized bodies, Global Tools proposed a humanity stripped of all tools except those of the body itself. If the science of ergonomics attempted to reconcile labor and health in the light of automation, reinforcing the hypothesis of a union between man and machine, then the exercises and protheses proposed by the Body Group were directed toward a voluntarily anti-ergonomic practice, one that would free man from labor.

The attention paid by Global Tools to the tools of manual work emerged in the context of a renewed cultural, political, and ideological interest in ethnographic studies in Italy.[10] This interest led the shift from the analysis of the city—at the centre of the first visions of Italian radical architecture—to the "habitat." This term, borrowed from biology, was employed in this context to describe a reality in crisis, in which new forms of adaptation required different "cultural references" (or a "destruction of culture"). These references were not to be taken from the Western world, but from territories where alternative forms of modernization seemed to be possible. This is evident, for example, in the second Global Tools bulletin, in the drawings and images taken from study materials dedicated to indigenous populations in the Amazon.

The activities of Global Tools also signaled the shift from an "international" to a "global" vision. While the use of the term "international" by avant-garde artistic movements exalted their political character and supranational solidarity, the term "global" alluded to a broader range of concerns, encompassing processes of integration and cybernetic connectivity. The use of the adjective "global" also referred to Marshall McLuhan's popular text *War and Peace in the Global Village* (1968), which greatly influenced the reflections of the Communication Group, as well as to Stewart Brand's *Whole Earth Catalog: Access to Tools* (1968–1972), the Californian magazine-catalog that collected and promoted do-it-yourself solutions for self-sufficiency, ecology, and self-actualization.

Of all the Global Tools groups, the Body Group was the only one still active at the end of 1975, after more than two years of discussion and experimentation. The educational program as a whole had collapsed before its planned official launch in the summer of that year, partly due to a lack of financial support and disagreements among its promoters in a moment of sudden acceleration of their professional choices. The failure of the program traces the progressive erosion of an artistic and creative community that would soon be swept aside by the individualism that defined the postmodern culture industry of the 1980s.

1. Andrea Branzi, "Tecnologia o eutanasia," *Casabella*, no. 397 (January 1975): 17–19.
2. The term "radical architecture" was introduced by art critic Germano Celant in the essay of the same name in the catalogue of the exhibition *Italy: The New Domestic Landscape* (Museum of Modern Art, New York, May 23–September 11, 1972). It referred to that contradictory and variegated phenomenon of experimentation in the field of architecture and design that arose in Italy in the late 1960s and early 1970s in opposition to twentieth-century rationalism and functionalism.
3. "Global Tools Documento 1," *Casabella*, no. 377 (May 1973): 4.
4. Global Tools document, untitled and undated. Adolfo Natalini Archive.
5. A. Natalini, R. Pecchioli, and R. Buti, "Didactic Typology: Note 2," *Casabella*, no. 379 (July 1973): 45.
6. "Document No. 2," *Global Tools* (June 1974): n.p.
7. See Giancarlo De Carlo, "Order Institution Education Disorder," *Casabella*, nos. 368–369 (August 1972): 12–35.
8. Report of the Construction Group, September 18, 1974. Ugo La Pietra Archive.
9. Archizoom Associati, 1973, unpublished document, Adolfo Natalini Archive.
10. A new edition in 1975 of Gramsci's *Prison Notebooks* gave a new impulse to the social sciences and anthropological studies in Italy.

< Superstudio, "Construction" session during the first Global Tools general seminar, Sambuca Val di Pesa, Florence, November 1–4, 1974.

> Alessandro Mendini, First Body Group seminar, "The Body and Constraints," Milan, June 5–8, 1975.

THE DEPARTMENT OF INVENTION

Hannah le Roux

Protagonist Amancio d'Alpoim Miranda
"Pancho" Guedes (1925–2015)
Institution Department of Architecture,
University of the Witwatersrand ("Wits")
Location Johannesburg, South Africa
Dates 1975–1990

Amancio d'Alpoim Miranda "Pancho" Guedes "was in the middle of a revolution, when the phone rang."[1] The reverberations from the Carnation Revolution in Portugal on April 25, 1974 had reached the Portuguese colony in Mozambique where he had lived since childhood. His fellow Portuguese citizens were leaving in their hundreds of thousands. When he got the call inviting him to head Wits' department of architecture in Johannesburg, Pancho joined them. Exiled from the hybridizing milieu of Lourenço Marques (Maputo) and forced to abandon a prolific architecture practice there, he returned to the South African university where he had studied twenty-five years earlier.[2] He brought with him complex and sometimes competing allegiances to Africa, Europe, and global avant-gardes. This multiplicity of "architectures," or "manners," which had grown out of his fascination for modernism, African arts, and surrealism, as well as his transnational friendships, would push against Wits' largely Anglophile legacy.[3] Within the constraints of the six-year professional degree structure, Pancho was to develop a pedagogy for architects that would gently

> Sketch for a poster advertising a Pancho Guedes talk, "Coming Home," at Wits, 1982. The image depicts the Guedes family's various homes in Lourenço Marques, Johannesburg, and Sintra, seen from the interior of their Citröen Dianne. The sketch would later become a painting, *The Journey.*

< Pancho Guedes fondly inspecting the underside of his "Decadent Temple," 1978.

but fundamentally contest bureaucratic and professional norms and the institution's provincialism. His professorship, which ran until he returned to Portugal in 1990, spanned and negotiated the politically fraught period from late apartheid to the start of the negotiations that would democratize South Africa in 1994.

"The Department of Invention"—Pancho's tongue-in-cheek name for the department of architecture—evolved through a series of pedagogic experiments that reflected the political transitions at the end of apartheid. Initially, Pancho was a relatively itinerant figure, his travels taking him to Sheffield University, the Architectural Association, Rice, Berkeley, and the Escola Superior de Belas Artes in Lisbon. He attended Team 10 meetings,[4] while the Smithsons came to visit him in Johannesburg, as did Cedric Green.

In the first years of Pancho's tenure, the department was concerned with the design of social housing for black communities, reimagining the austere models that dated from the 1950s. After the scholar uprisings in black townships in 1976, reform in housing approaches included owner-building and a transition from rental to freehold ownership. Some of the teaching staff were connected to the Urban Foundation, a business-funded housing think-tank set up in 1977. Thesis projects that year included Franco Frescura's "Housing Strategies for Urbanizing Blacks," "Tokello ya go Ikagela" (Freedom to Build), and housing and urban strategies sited in mixed-race neighborhoods.

This liberal moment was short-lived. As the state became increasingly repressive, an international boycott of academic ties with South Africa took hold and international exchanges became less frequent. The isolation and the relative impossibility of engaging in construction were mirrored in the shift towards utopian and geometrically pure designs produced by both Pancho and his students. Pancho's focus now turned to innovations in the teaching of visual studies and architectural history. Courses previously within the remit of fine arts were absorbed into the department of architecture. "Drawing and Information," for first- and second-year students, was taught by practicing artists who were given free rein to promote experimental work rather than applied techniques.[5]

Much like the personal practice that Pancho had developed in Lourenço Marques, which used drawings and objects produced by untutored artists—including children, workmen, and his self-taught protégé, Malangatana—as imaginative touchstones, the

Drawing and Information course understood artistic experimentation as a form of subversive conceptual work. Its exercises supported the representation of imaginary future forms of architecture, while giving purpose to teaching and learning during the darkly repressive period of late apartheid. Pancho explained its intention: "The other great thing which happens in the school of architecture is the invention of extraordinary and quite absurd works, presented as drawings, paintings, and models, which gives us a tremendous ability to cope with an alternative reality. The first reality is the reality of the drawings and models. Some people feel that you cannot educate people, you can only train them (like you train circus dogs), but I believe you can leave out the idea of training and you can educate people."[6]

A new, four-year history curriculum replaced the longstanding chronological approach with an eclectic set of themes. An engagement with indigenous Southern African architecture, reified in the measurement of rural settlements, expanded into a series of intensive courses with a relatively global reach. Pancho himself taught a course that introduced fourth-year students to individual Renaissance and modernist architects, framing them as their contemporaries, with a common focus on invention dislocated from specific historical forces. Pancho called history "not the dead past but…a source and constant challenge to each and every new invention."[7] The idea of architectural progression was disrupted by the representation of multiple and non-sequential lineages.

These shifts made apparent the department's complicated relationship with politics. The focus on imaginative work and ahistorical production, while defying colonial norms and providing many students with a form of refuge during an increasingly violent period, also suggested a complicity with political power, failing to explicitly confront the clear injustice of apartheid. Apartheid laws meant there were barely any black students on campus, since they had to study in underfunded rural institutions (none of which offered architecture), and young white male graduates often went into exile to avoid being conscripted to the army. When members of the university's staff and student body actively resisted the security forces brought onto campus in the mid-1980s, Pancho and his teaching staff were not visible amongst the protestors. Progressive students began to contest the department's ironic distancing from a directly political position—a challenge brought into focus by the 1985 national student conference, *Metropolis*. By providing a platform for invited representatives of emerging civil movements opposed to apartheid, the event opened up a debate about the potential of architecture to support the aims of social equity, both culturally and technically. In his own address to the conference, Pancho resisted the idea of specific alliances with any formal groups, as he had done on other occasions. Citing his own experience—he had only ever joined a single group, Team 10, that followed principles of informal affiliation and transnational exchange— he explained to students that "if one has a moral responsibility, it is to talk to younger people about the possibility of them becoming citizens of one world and not South Africa."[8] His contribution to *Metropolis* was to install a habitable wooden model of Aldo van Eyck's unbuilt Wheels of Heaven church, inviting students to insert their heads into its chambers from below. Wrapping up his talk, he told the student body:

> Now some of you are very worried for various and different reasons. We've seen people who are very desirous of giving themselves to those who are oppressed who have had a bad deal in this country, for very good intentions. Yet the possibility of doing so is blocked by professionalism. It is something you cannot carry out within the framework of professionalism, but something that you can only carry out as an individual, as a "terrorist."[9]

The general election of 1994, the first to give all citizens the right to vote, marked the symbolic end of apartheid. But well before that, following *Metropolis*, Pancho loosened his tight curation of the department's pedagogy to allow for more explicitly political and, arguably, more Eurocentric content that largely drew on critical theory. The hybridized genres of knowledge that Pancho had curated through staffing, curricular content, and physical objects largely gave way to narratives of spatial oppression and redress that evolved alongside post-apartheid agendas for planning and urban studies. Subsequent decades of restructuring planning frameworks for the city of Johannesburg have yielded little in the way of imaginative public design. But despite the lack of patronage, some of Pancho's former students have followed his example and chosen to work in independent studios, project by project, toward the realization of shared places based in African and transcultural imaginaries. Within this context, the fifteen years of the Department of Invention under Pancho provide a valuable reservoir of pedagogic, conceptual, and material approaches.

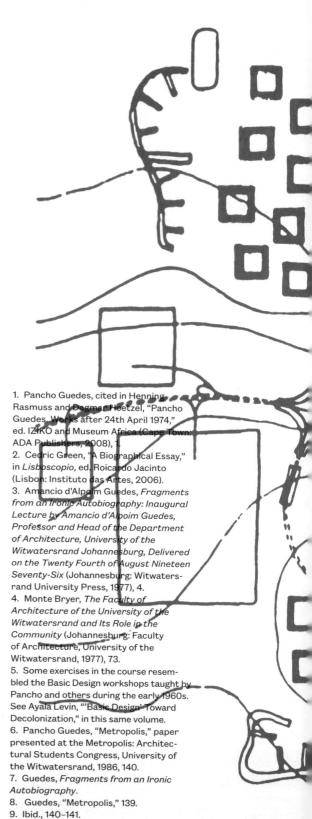

1. Pancho Guedes, cited in Henning Rasmuss and Dagmar Hoetzel, "Pancho Guedes, Works after 24th April 1974," ed. IZIKO and Museum Africa (Cape Town: ADA Publishers, 2008), 1.
2. Cedric Green, "A Biographical Essay," in *Lisboscopio*, ed. Roicardo Jacinto (Lisbon: Instituto das Artes, 2006).
3. Amancio d'Alpoim Guedes, *Fragments from an Ironic Autobiography: Inaugural Lecture by Amancio d'Alpoim Guedes, Professor and Head of the Department of Architecture, University of the Witwatersrand Johannesburg, Delivered on the Twenty Fourth of August Nineteen Seventy-Six* (Johannesburg: Witwatersrand University Press, 1977), 4.
4. Monte Bryer, *The Faculty of Architecture of the University of the Witwatersrand and Its Role in the Community* (Johannesburg: Faculty of Architecture, University of the Witwatersrand, 1977), 73.
5. Some exercises in the course resembled the Basic Design workshops taught by Pancho and others during the early 1960s. See Ayala Levin, "'Basic Design' Toward Decolonization," in this same volume.
6. Pancho Guedes, "Metropolis," paper presented at the Metropolis: Architectural Students Congress, University of the Witwatersrand, 1986, 140.
7. Guedes, *Fragments from an Ironic Autobiography*.
8. Guedes, "Metropolis," 139.
9. Ibid., 140–141.

NER group, detail from the cover of *The Ideal Communist City* (George Braziller, 1969).

CITY AS SITE

FROM COLLECTIVIZATION TO COMMUNICATION

Masha Panteleyeva

Protagonists Alexei Gutnov (1937–1986),
Ilya Lezhava (1935–2018) and the NER Group
Institution Moscow Institute
of Architecture (MARKhI)
Location Moscow, Russia, USSR
Dates 1954–1970

After Stalin's death in 1953, the state of confusion regarding the status of architecture was particularly apparent in the academic setting. Many of the Moscow Architectural Institute's (MARKhI) professors had been leaders of constructivism and later, under Stalin, had achieved high positions and success by adopting the neoclassical style. All that had come to an end with Khrushchev's industrialization of construction speech in December 1954. But for a younger generation of educators, especially the NER (New Element of Settlement) group led by Alexei Gutnov and Ilya Lezhava, this state of uncertainty became an opportunity to explore new directions. Less embedded in the highly institutionalized architectural community, they were more able to respond to the confusion of styles, architectural languages, and methodologies in the teaching of architecture. At a time of rapid political change, they investigated the profession's possible future directions by reestablishing connections with the West—and they developed the tools to do so through their pedagogy. They introduced their students to foreign publications and involved them in international competitions and the close analysis of canonical buildings. In their teaching, the new architectural and urban subject was also built around the close analysis of life in Soviet society—a sociological approach that had been considered controversial in previous decades.

Following the publication of their influential book *NER, On the Way to a New City* (1966), NER was invited by Giancarlo De Carlo to participate in the 1968 Milan Triennial, where their work gained international exposure for the first time.[1] The concepts outlined in the book were first developed in 1957 as part of the group's collective diploma project at MARKhI, an analysis of the elements of the city that ultimately led them to dismiss traditional planning principles and elaborate a new approach to urban development as a dynamic process. NER actively criticized the state of Soviet urban planning, arguing that "today, the city is not fulfilling its primary purpose to be an organic living environment."[2] After defending their diploma, Lezhava and Gutnov were offered teaching positions by MARKhI's dean, Ivan Nikolaev. However, their graduation coincided with a bout of repression against "excessively active youth." Gutnov, NER's ideological leader, was deemed "politically unreliable," and Nikolaev was forced to extend the invitation to Lezhava and two other NER members, Stanislav Sadovsky and Nikita Kostrikin, instead. At first, they refused to accept the appointment, but eventually they yielded, seeing that it would be strategically beneficial for the group to build their professional connections. Gutnov, along with another NER member, Zoya Kharitonova, would go on to accept a position at the Moscow Institute of Planning (MOSPROEKT).

In their radical proposal for a new urbanism, NER attempted to provide a spatial agenda for Marxism, drawing both from the *Communist Manifesto* and the constructivist avantgarde of the 1920s. Rather than being centered around industry, their new city was based on creative communication in a classless society, independent from economic considerations. The major shift introduced by this new urban wave—later implemented within the curriculum of MARKhI—was to see the city as a living organism evolving around the process of socialization among citizens [*obshchenie*]. This in turn led to a change in the status of architectural form, which was conceived as temporary and mobile—its birth already implied the process of its imminent destruction. The NER approach anticipated the future understanding of architecture as an activity or an environment. It emphasized the correspondence between urban structures and social relationships in communism, based on a reading of the urban plan as "simultaneously a symbol of the idea and a program for its realization."[3]

In their writing and teaching Gutnov and Lezhava gravitated toward a symbiosis of the social and the environmental that would become a defining principle not only of their urban design but of the relations within the group itself. Their new collaborative approach became evident in the reduced intellectual distance between students and teachers, which allowed the latter to successfully combine the educational, professional, and theoretical aspects of their work. As mentors, they surrounded themselves with social participatory "ecosystems," both in the form of their own professional collectives

and as part of a new educational model where each participant/designer/student played a unique role.

Ilya Lezhava earned his doctorate in 1967 with a thesis on the subject of *obshchenie* in urban settings. The subject of his thesis, which outlined a new architectural typology of "social centers," led him to collaborate with MARKhI students on entries to the first international competitions that were open to Soviet architects. This included the series of "Theater Architecture" competitions organized by OISTAT,[4] two of which they would go on to win with projects tied to the dynamic nature of social relations in the city. The designs proposed a series of spaces of varying size (calculated according to the social needs of local communities) that sought to promote communication between citizens. Such collective problem-solving and a purely sociological approach to urban planning would be essential elements of many of the students' future careers. The image-based, urban public space proposals that came out of Lezhava's studios presented themselves in a variety of structurally unresolved designs lacking a cohesive architectural form. Such unprogrammed and, to a certain extent, *anarchic* spaces intentionally represented the idea of a new Soviet public sphere that was rapidly becoming autonomous from the state.

1. A. Baburov, A. Gutnov, I. Lezhava, G. Dumenton, et al., *Novyi Element Rasseleniya: na puti k novomu gorodu* [New Element of Settlement: Toward a New City] (Moscow: Stroiizdat, 1966).
2. A. Baburov et al., *The Ideal Communist City*, trans. Renee Neu Watkins (New York: George Braziller, 1971).
3. Ibid., 118.
4. The Organization of Scenographers, Theatre Architects, and Technicians (OISTAT) was founded in Prague, Czech Republic in 1968. Since 1978 it has organized a Theater Architecture Competition every four years.

> NER group, scientific center along a transportation channel (riverbed). Plasticine model created for the Milan Triennale, 1968.

< NER group photograph, 1960. Top to bottom, left to right: S. Sadovsky, A. Baburov, A. Gutnov, A. Zvezdin, N. Gladkova, E. Sukhanova, and I. Lezhava.

IN SEARCH OF A NEW VISUAL VOCABULARY

Federica Vannucchi

Protagonists Gillo Dorfles (1910–2018), Umberto Eco (1932–2016), Giovanni Koenig (1924–1989), Gianni Pettena (1940–), Leonardo Ricci (1918–1994), Leonardo Savioli (1917–1982), 9999, Archizoom Associati, Gruppo Strum, Superstudio, UFO, and Ziggurat
Institution University of Florence (Università degli Studi di Firenze)
Location Florence, Italy
Dates 1964–1969

In the midst of the 1968 protests, the streets of Florence were turned into a pedagogical experiment by students of the university's faculty of architecture. With installations that formed a sharp contrast to the Renaissance backdrop of the city, they challenged the insularity of their design curriculum and its inability to adapt to a rapidly changing urban reality. Among others, Gianni Pettena's *Dialogue with Arnolfo di Cambio*, UFO's *Urboeffimeri*, and 9999's *Design Happening in Ponte Vecchio* set out to disrupt the lives of the city's "bourgeois" inhabitants by adopting the playful and eccentric language of pop art, which had been introduced to the Italian scene by the Venice Biennale four years earlier. Offering new ways of viewing and inhabiting the city, these events were aligned with what art critic Germano Celant would later define as the "radicalization" of architecture.[1] Celant said that architecture could not be reduced to the mere production of objects and buildings, arguing instead for a "radical architecture" that involved a philosophical interrogation of the discipline's meaning and scope, so that the practice of architecture became a way of being-in-the-world and of relating to others. What architecture had to produce, according to Celant, was a recording of these philosophical interrogations in the form of "a text, a photograph, writing, or sound"—the first steps toward constituting a new language of architecture.[2]

Arguably it was the teaching of Leonardo Ricci and Leonardo Savioli at the University of Florence that laid the essential groundwork for the experiments of the Radicals.[3] Following his postwar experience in the commune of Agàpe in Piedmont, Ricci's teaching focused on new urban forms of communal living. For him, the collective experiences of the "contestation years"—from collaborative group work to school occupations—offered an indispensable lesson in nonhierarchical models of organization. In a course called "Elements of Composition," taught from 1964 to 1965, Ricci presented communal living as an essential ingredient in a "non-alienated city."[4] He argued that designing spaces for ever-changing social relationships—rather than for the generic and immutable "man-type" preferred by a certain strand of academicism—could create an "integrated city." If the scope of architecture was "to give form" to a space, this form was in a constant process of becoming.

Savioli, in turn, was the university's professor of interior architecture. In his 1966–1967 course, "Space of Involvement," assisted by Paolo Deganello and Adolfo Natalini, among others,[5] he encouraged his students to design buildings that engaged with their users through the quality of their space and their figurative language. Critical of the modernist injunction that form followed function, he insisted that the task of the architect was to design spaces—not forms—where people could behave freely. Savioli saw form as something dogmatic and typological, giving rise to fixed and uniform urban settings. Conversely, space was flexible, ephemeral, consumable, and, above all, communicative: the inhabitant was its "user and operator." Both Ricci's communal living and Savioli's participatory spaces demanded an architecture whose main purpose was to communicate with its users.

Indeed, at the University of Florence in the 1960s, it could be said that architecture *became* communication. The architect and architectural historian Giovanni Koenig embraced the methods of semiology in courses that laid out his analysis of architectural language, later collected in his book *Architettura e communicazione* (1970). In the fall of 1966, Umberto Eco took over the course on "Decoration" previously taught by the art critic Gillo Dorfles, who had spoken of architecture as mass media. Eco dedicated the course to the semiology of architecture, using the first draft of what would become *The Absent Structure* (1968) as the course text. In his lectures, Eco spoke of architecture as a system of signs enabling communication.

Outside the faculty of architecture, the city of Florence had provided a platform for the discussion of art as communication from the early 1960s on. A series of conferences held at the Forte di Belvedere on themes such as "art and communication" (1963) and "art and technology" (1964) gave rise to the interdisciplinary collective Gruppo 70 and its experiments

< The Linear City,
thesis project by
Ziggurat, 1969.

in "visual poetry" using collages, videos, poetry, prose, and paintings. The architecture students took part in these events while looking beyond the teaching of their professors. As Adolfo Natalini remarked, "at the faculty of architecture in Florence we were taught by Benevolo, Quaroni, Ricci, and Savioli. But, above all, we read *Architectural Design* (with Stirling and Archigram), LC (in those days, it meant Le Corbusier), and we thought that architecture was a means rather than an end."[6] Students and young architects in Florence came to use two-dimensional representation as both a privileged means of communication and a vehicle of inspiration, exploring alternative visions of the city. Architectural magazines such as Alessandro Mendini's *Casabella* brought their work to the attention of a wider audience. Their astonishing collages—*Continuous Monument* by Superstudio, *No Stop City* by Archizoom, *Mediatory City* by Gruppo Strum, *Linear City* by Ziggurat, to name but a few—posed an irreverent critique of contemporary architecture and urbanism, noting its evident inability to fulfill people's basic needs, from emotional and spiritual well-being to social cohesion and equality. In a highly eloquent way, they offered a new visual and discursive vocabulary to debate the urgency of architecture's remaking.

1. Germano Celant, "Radical Architecture," in *Italy: The New Domestic Landscape*, ed. Emilio Ambasz (New York: Museum of Modern Art, 1972), 380–387. A first iteration of the article was published by Celant one year earlier: Germano Celant, "Senza Titolo," *Argomenti ed immagini di Design*, no. 2–3, thematic issue on "La distruzione dell'oggetto" (March–June 1971), 76–81. For a definition of radical architecture in the years of its formation see also *Casabella*, no. 367, thematic issue on "Radical Design" (July 1972); Paola Navone and Bruno Orlandoni, *L'architettura Radicale* (Segrate: G. Milani, 1974); and Andrea Branzi's "Radical Notes" in *Casabella* from October 1972 to April 1976.
2. Celant, "Radical Architecture," 384.
3. Lara Vinca Masini, "Archifirenze," *Domus*, no. 509 (April 1972): 40.
4. Leonardo Ricci, "Ricerca per una città non alienata," *Lineastruttura*, no. 1–2 (1967): 39–51.
5. Leonardo Savioli and Adolfo Natalini, "Spazio di Coinvolgimento," *Casabella*, no. 326 (July 1968): 32–45. The course became the exhibition *Ipotesi di Spazio* (1968) at the Centro Gavinana in Florence in collaboration with the Centro Proposte. See the accompanying catalogue: Leonardo Savioli, Lara Vinca Masina, and Leonardo Ricci, *Ipotesi di spazio* (Florence: Giglio e Garisenda Editori, 1972).
6. Adolfo Natalini, "Com'era ancora bella l'architettura nel 1966...(Superstudio e l'architettura radicale dieci anni dopo)," *Spazioarte*, no. 10–11 (June–October 1977): 6.

DELIRIOUSLY RATIONAL

Daniela Fabricius

Protagonists Oswald Mathias Ungers (1926–2007), Jürgen Sawade (1937–2015), Nikolaus Kuhnert (1939–), Michael Wegener, Peter Neitzke (1938–2015), Hans Kollhoff (1946–), Rem Koolhaas (1944–)
Institution TU Berlin
Location Berlin, Germany
Dates 1963–1969

When Oswald Mathias Ungers began his professorship at the Technical University of Berlin in 1963, one of the first things he did was ask the school to purchase a Rotaprint printing press. The Rotaprint would prove to be instrumental in documenting and disseminating the work of Ungers and his students: between 1965 and 1971, twenty-seven booklets were produced in the series *Veröffentlichungen zur Architektur*, which focused on the city of Berlin as a source of design, using extraordinary graphic clarity and rigor. These little publications would eventually make their way into bookstores and architecture schools around the world and they remain influential today. However, the Rotaprint also had a secondary effect: students used the machine to print political flyers. This was one of many links between Ungers' seminars and the increasingly radical student movement at the TU Berlin.[1]

These publications, together with accounts of Ungers' years in Berlin, sometimes give the impression that Ungers' pedagogical thinking was determined more by his students and teaching assistants than the other way around. Ungers' own practice also changed in Berlin. During his early years in Cologne, he had defended the autonomy of architectural form against social, functional, and economic demands. But already his 1963 candidate lecture at the TU, "Principles of Spatial Design," made it clear that he was turning to more rational systems for producing form.[2] There was a particularly strong push to scientize architecture at the TU Berlin in the 1960s, resulting in a kind of superrationality that merged formalist systems of seriality, typology, and proportion with technologies of mass production, prefabrication, or cybernetics.

Ungers focused his teaching almost exclusively on the study and design of the city of Berlin. An investigation of the city's infrastructure—of traffic and transportation maps, and distinct urban typologies like parks or the River Spree—soon developed into a new excitement around the idea of the megastructure and the possibilities of mass production. Student work was characterized by a highly rational approach using the assemblage of repetitive elements across multiple scales. Even if these proposals were not always utopian, one could say that they were evidence of a deliberate suspension of reality, a way of fantasizing with technology. In a later interview, Ungers reflected on these pedagogical projects as a form of "hypertrophy": "One could not have practically done something like that. I see the danger of these things very clearly, but I said that it has to be possible to expand an idea to the point of absurdity, in order to implement it from that point to gain new perceptions."[3]

If Ungers and his students had enjoyed a productive tension in the first years, this quickly changed after the shooting of Benno Ohnesorg during a protest on June 2, 1967. Ungers, by then dean of the Faculty of Architecture, cautiously endorsed the political activities of the students.[4] But in December 1967 a conference that he had organized was disrupted

by architecture students. Focused on action, the politicized students were uninterested in discussions about form. Over the next three years, there was an increasing radicalization of architecture students at the TU Berlin: seminar and storage rooms were occupied and repurposed as headquarters for leftist groups; the private offices of faculty members were broken into and vandalized; and architecture professors were "put on trial" for their architectural and political principles at spontaneous "tribunals."[5]

Some of Ungers' more politicized students participated in the so-called "critical university" (Kritische Universität), a student-organized series of seminars at the Freie Universität in Berlin.[6] Students who pursued the hypertechnological development of the city in Ungers' seminars were also publishing pamphlets challenging the rationalism of real estate development and urban planning. At the beginning of the fall semester of 1968, architecture students formed a group called "Aktion 507" and organized a critical exhibition on construction and planning in West Berlin: Ungers' own buildings for the Märkisches Viertel housing project were not spared from attack.[7] The students installed the exhibition in the raw concrete structure of Hans Scharoun's building for the architecture school, then still under construction, as a signal of their opposition to what they saw as an obsolete and apolitical culture of artistic architectural design.

To some extent, TU Berlin was a microcosm of West German culture in the late 1960s, with its conflicting attitudes toward utopianism, a new belief in the possibilities of technology, and the emergence of radical leftist politics among the student population. Some of the greatest contradictions were found among the students themselves, who criticized the technocratic tendencies of architecture in their political activities but did not hesitate to appropriate scientific and sociological instruments for their own work.

Largely as a result of the mounting pressure of the student movement, Ungers moved to the US in March 1969 to become the chair of architecture at Cornell University. Initially, he continued working in the techno-utopian vein established at the TU Berlin, but this soon gave way to a new engagement with the historical typologies of the city, resulting in several publications, including the now influential *City in the City: Berlin as Green Archipelago* (1977), coauthored with a young Rem Koolhaas.[8] As he retreated from the political maelstrom of 68, Ungers returned to a purely formal architectural rationalism, as seen in the hermetic gridded geometries of his later work, which coincided with his return to Germany in the late 1970s. For Koolhaas, the teachings of Ungers would have a lasting effect: they laid the foundations for his influential pedagogical research projects in the 1990s, which focused on the city as an incubator of architectural form.

< Graffiti on the Scharoun-designed TU Berlin architecture building: "THE NEW DIFFICULT GRÜNDERZEIT OF BERLIN WILL BE SEEN BY HISTORY AS A VIRTUE BORN OUT OF NECESSITY."

v Posters on the TU Berlin architecture building protesting against the Emergency Acts, May 1968.

≪ Diagnose exhibition poster and book cover showing buildings from the Märkisches Viertel in the background, 1968. Poster designed by Jürgen Holtfreter.

1. See "Lernen von O. M. Ungers," ed. Erika Mühlthaler, special issue, *ARCH+* 181/182 (December 2006); and Jasper Cepl, "Oswald Mathias Ungers und seine Schule," in *Architekturschulen: Programm—Pragmatik—Propaganda*, ed. Klaus Jan Philipp and Kerstin Renz (Tübingen, Berlin: Ernst Wasmuth Verlag, 2012).
2. Ungers was invited to give the candidate lecture on February 11, 1963. Oswald Mathias Ungers, "Berufungsvortrag," *ARCH+ 65* (January 1982): 41–48. The talk was republished in *ARCH+* 181/182 (December 2006). The editor of *ARCH+*, Nikolaus Kuhnert, was a student of Ungers.
3. Thomas Sieverts, Oswald Mathias Ungers, and Georg Wittwer in conversation with Nikolaus Kuhnert, "Das war eine ungeheuer kreative Situation. Die vergessene Reformdiskussion der 60er Jahre," *Stadtbauwelt* 76 (December 24, 1982): 369–392.
4. "Studenten—Unruhen—Ursache oder Indiz sich anbahnender Umwälzungen? Anrisse—Gespräch mit dem Dekan der Fakultät für Architektur, Prof. O. M. Ungers," *Anrisse* 59 (July 1967): 6–10, TU Berlin Universitätsarchiv; reprinted in *Lernen von O. M. Ungers*, 118–121.
5. A chronicle of some of these events is listed in a letter dated July 2, 1970, sent by the faculty members of the school of architecture to Prof. Dr. W. Stein, Senator for Science and Art in Berlin. The subject of the letter is "Documentation of the unacceptable circumstances at the Faculty III." TU Berlin University Archive, 206–221.
6. *Kritische Universität. Freie Studienorganisation der Studenten in den Hoch- und Fachschulen von Westberlin. Programm und Verzeichnis der Studienveranstaltungen im Wintersemester 1967/68* (Berlin: AStA der Freien Universität Berlin, Politische Abteilung), 2. Private archive of Michael Wegener.
7. *Diagnose Zum Bauen in West-Berlin*, TU Berlin, 1968.
8. Oswald Mathias Ungers et al., *Die Stadt in der Stadt: Berlin das grüne Stadtarchipel: ein stadträumliches Planungskonzept für die zukünftige Entwicklung Berlins* (Cologne: Studioverlag für Architektur L. Ungers, 1977).

INTELLECTUALIZING ARCHITECTURE, PROFESSIONALIZING EDUCATION

Roberto Damiani

Protagonists Aldo Rossi (1931–1997), Carlo Aymonino (1926–2010), Giorgio Grassi (1935–), Massimo Scolari (1943–), Antonio Monestiroli (1940–), Gianni Braghieri (1945–), Rosaldo Bonicalzi (1946–), Daniele Vitale (1945–)
Institutions Istituto Universitario di Architettura di Venezia (IUAV), Politecnico di Milano
Locations Venice and Milan, Italy
Dates 1963–1971

During the first ten years of his teaching career the Milanese architect Aldo Rossi played a pivotal role in the transformation of architectural pedagogy in Italian public architecture schools. His teaching introduced an intellectual turn that repositioned academic labor as an autonomous activity with a broader scope than the building-centered professional agenda. This was a time when both students and teachers were demanding changes to the curriculum to replace the remnants of the Fascist public university system. A consensus critical of teaching still considered as a part-time activity and excessive focus on professional training began to emerge from the national conference on architectural education in Rome in 1964.[1] Rossi took the opportunities offered by his early teaching experiences in Venice and Milan to reenvision architecture schools as research institutions led by full-time teachers who instilled in their students a broader understanding of their role as engaged intellectuals.

Rossi had been made acutely aware of the failures of public urban planning in Italy during his collaboration with *Casabella*. After leaving the magazine in 1963, he began his academic career as Carlo Aymonino's teaching assistant at the Istituto Universitario di Architettura di Venezia (IUAV), where the architecture curriculum was taught by full-time practitioners employed as part-time instructors. The result was a professional agenda prioritizing the cultivation of individual artistry, often using as a model the instructor's own personal design style. In the group gathered around Aymonino, however, Rossi met a new generation of teachers who wanted to change what they saw as a naïve and

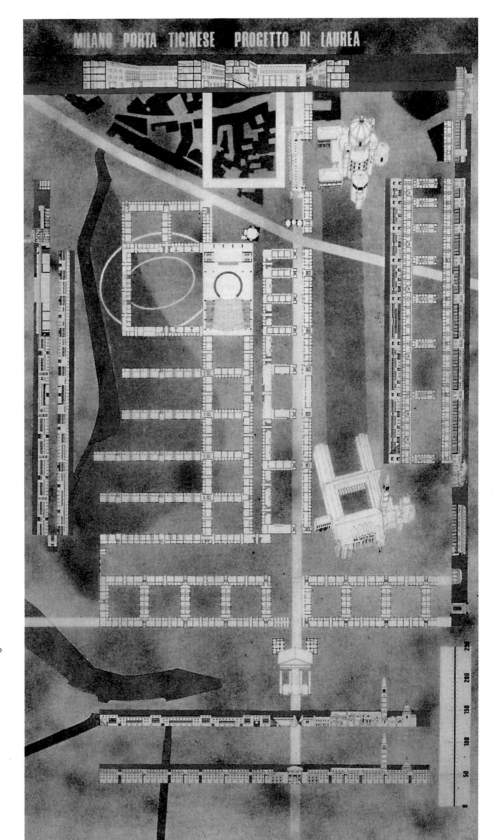

MILANO PORTA TICINESE PROGETTO DI LAUREA

< Daniele Vitale and Massimo Scolari during the student occupation, Politecnico di Milano, November 1967. Photograph by Walter Barbero.

> Porta Ticinese housing complex, thesis project by Daniele Vitale, José Charters Monteiro, Anna Maria Di Marco, Massimo Fortis, Emanuele Levi Montalcini, and Paola Marzoli under the supervision of Aldo Rossi, 1969.

subjective approach to teaching architecture. Over the following two years, they sought to structure what they thought was relevant architectural knowledge through a solid theory that could be taught, discussed, and disseminated.[2] To redress the curriculum's neglect of urbanism, the group conducted their design studio as an urban research unit, using a methodology based on the survey and on formal comparisons between the urban fabrics of different cities to test the principles of a new theory on architecture and the city.

Rossi and his peers saw the analytical techniques of urban morphology and building typology as a fundamental means of not only documenting the city but also of instilling in the students—and future practicing architects—a sensitivity to the city as a cultural artefact. The teaching group placed an emphasis on disseminating their early studies outside the studio. The proceedings of each course were published at the end of the academic year, preparing the way for the publication of Aymonino's *Origini e sviluppo della città moderna* (1965) and Rossi's *L'architettura della città* (1966).[3]

Rossi left Venice in 1965 to take up a post at the Politecnico di Milano. In 1968's escalating climate of political protest the Politecnico appointed a new dean, the young Roman architect Paolo Portoghesi, who encouraged the development of an experimental curriculum. Rossi—along with Guido Canella, Franco Albini, and Vittorio Gregotti—was on the board of teachers and students who addressed the students' demands for a political understanding of architectural design. During this transitional period, dubbed *Sperimentazione*, the conventional course-based curriculum was replaced with a series of integrated option studios taught by "research groups" led by a coordinator. For his own research collective, named La Tendenza,[4] Rossi chose to replace the traditional deliverables of professional drawing sets with research-based urban reports and composite drawings. Dissatisfied with frontal teaching, he invited guest lecturers and involved students in the production of course contents.

The group produced and circulated annotated bibliographies, course syllabi, lectures, and urban reports, all to push forward the project Rossi had started in Venice: the collaborative definition of a research-oriented pedagogical framework to pursue an architectural theory of the city.[5] However, despite Rossi's commitment to teaching, there is very little in the way of documented studio work from those years. The post-68 climate, with its anti-design attitude and resistance to any form of academic examination, along with the vast increase in student numbers,[6] made it very difficult for the Milanese educator to pursue his pedagogical agenda. By November 1971 his experimental approach had become too much for the Ministry of Education, who suspended him from teaching, along with Franco Albini, Piero Bottoni, Guido Canella, and Paolo Portoghesi. Despite his suspension and the changing milieu at the Politecnico, a selection of student projects from schools associated with Rossi were presented at the 1973 Milan Triennale, in the section *Architettura-Città*, which served as an international showcase for the work of the research group.[7]

When Rossi was reintegrated as a full professor at the IUAV in Venice in 1975, he was able to see many of his pedagogical ideas slowly taking shape. The number of full-time teachers had doubled, the new curriculum embodied a pedagogy informed by a systematic method of urban analysis, and schools were playing a more active role as research institutions in envisioning the future of Italian cities.

∧ Dean Paolo
Portoghesi and other
faculty council repre-
sentatives addressing
the riot police. Left to
right: Fredi Drugman,
Guido Canella, Paolo
Portoghesi, Federico
Oliva, Pierluigi Nicolin,
and an undentified
person, Politecnico
di Milano, June 1971.

< Aldo Rossi, Athens,
1971. Photograph by
Gianni Braghieri.

1. See "Dibattito sulle Scuole di Architettura in Italia," *Casabella Continuità*, no.
287 (1964).
2. The teaching team coordinated by Carlo
Aymonino included Carlo Cristofoli,
Constantino Dardi, Gianni Fabbri, Pier Maria
Gaffarini, Emilio Mattioni, and Aldo Rossi.
3. Carlo Aymonino, Aldo Rossi, et al.,
*Aspetti e problemi della tipologia
edilizia. Documenti del corso di caratteri
distributivi degli edifici. Anno accademico
1963–1964* (Venice: Editrice Cluva, 1964);
*La formazione del concetto di tipologia
edilizia. Atti del corso di caratteri
distributivi degli edifici. Anno accademico
1964–1965* (Venice: Editrice Cluva, 1965);
*Rapporti tra la morfologia urbana e la
tipologia edilizia. Documenti del corso
di caratteri distributivi degli edifici.
Anno accademico 1965–1966* (Venice:
Editrice Cluva, 1966).
4. The research group gathered around
Aldo Rossi included Giorgio Grassi,
Antonio Monestiroli, Adriano di Leo,
Giancarlo Motta, Massimo Fortis,
Massimo Scolari, Rosaldo Bonicalzi,
and Daniele Vitale.
5. Aldo Rossi, et al., *L'analisi urbana e la
progettazione architettonica. Contributi
al dibattito e al lavoro di gruppo
dell'anno accademico 1968/69* (Milan:
Facoltà di Architettura del Politecnico di
Milano, 1970).
6. Between 1969 and 1970, Aldo Rossi's
research group enrolled almost seven
hundred students. See *La rivoluzione
culturale: La Facoltà di Architettura del
Politecnico di Milano 1963–1974*, catalogue
of the exhibit curated by Fiorella Vanini
at the Politecnico di Milano in December
2009 (Milan: AgF Stampa, 2009), 51.
7. The exhibit displayed student work
from the universities of Pescara, Rome,
Milan, Naples, Zurich, and Berlin.

LEARNING FROM LAS VEGAS

Martino Stierli

Protagonists Denise Scott Brown (1931–), Robert
Venturi (1925–2018), Steven Izenour (1940–2001)
Institution Yale School of Architecture (YSOA)
Locations New Haven, CT;
Los Angeles, LA; Las Vegas, NV, USA
Date 1968

Learning from Las Vegas (1972) is not only one
of the seminal architectural and urban treatises
of the twentieth century—a foundational text of
postmodernist theory and architectural semiotics
in the age of capitalist consumer culture—it is also
the outcome of an experiment in architectural
education that took place in the fall of 1968 at the
Yale University School of Architecture.[1] "Learning
from Las Vegas" was the first in a series of three
consecutive research studios in which Robert
Venturi and Denise Scott Brown investigated new
methods of architectural education and learning.
Both had been independently involved in instruction
at a number of universities, but at Yale they amalga-
mated their ideas into a coherent approach. Steven
Izenour joined them as their teaching assistant for
the Las Vegas studio and would take on a key role
in the ensuing publication, whose first, large-format
edition for the MIT Press was designed by American
designer and educator Muriel Cooper.[2]

In both content and methodology, the Learning
from Las Vegas studio was unusual, shifting the focus
from formalistic studies of individual objects to the
layout and appearance of the suburban, car-oriented
landscape of "urban sprawl" and the question of how
architecture could communicate meaning in such
an environment.[3] Straddling the disciplinary divide
between architecture and urban planning, the class
sought to analyze and chart the form of the contemporary city while at the same time addressing the
consequences of their findings for architectural
design—which the book famously distilled into the
theory of the "decorated shed." Rather than design,
however, the main focus of the studio was research.
A large part of the semester program was taken up
by library research and a two-week-long field trip
to Los Angeles and Las Vegas.

In their syllabus, Venturi, Scott Brown, and
Izenour particularly stressed the need to devise new
techniques of visual representation for new urban
forms. To this end, the research group experimented
with a variety of visual media. In addition to relatively
conventional forms of representation such as maps
and charts, photography and film played a prominent
role in this investigation. Appropriating a technique
from LA-based artist Ed Ruscha's photography book
project, *Every Building on the Sunset Strip* (1966),
the group mounted a camera on the hood of a car
and drove along the Las Vegas Strip to record a
"deadpan" image of the city.[4] The studio absorbed
not only artistic practices, but also the empirical
methodologies of related disciplines such as sociology and anthropology. Venturi and Scott Brown
introduced the notion of interdisciplinary discourse
into architectural education, situating it at the
intersection of science and the arts. The various
aspects of the emerging proto-urban landscape of
the Las Vegas Strip were documented in hours of
experimental footage and thousands of slides. Many
of these images formed the basis for the analytical
charts that were produced for the final presentation
of the studio's findings.[5]

Particularly in its use of new means of
representation, the Learning from Las Vegas studio
was the prototype for a number of later attempts to
accommodate urban research within architectural
education. However, for Venturi and Scott Brown,
research did not constitute an end in itself. Rather,
the analytical and scholarly approach was intended to
form a basis for architectural design. Their studios
were directed toward designers—even though the
"lessons" from Las Vegas were not easily translat-
able into a design methodology, as the multivalent
and idiosyncratic work of Venturi, Scott Brown, and

< "The Grand
Proletarian
Cultural Loco-
motive" poster
advertising
the final crit of
the Learning
from Las Vegas
Research Studio
at Yale, January
10, 1969. Frontis-
piece of *Learning
from Las Vegas*
(1972).

Associates itself makes clear.[6] As the first of the Venturi, Scott Brown, and Izenour research studios for contemporary architectural education, the impact of the Learning from Las Vegas studio can hardly be overstated. Not only did it provide the blueprint for the integration into architectural education of field trips and on-site research, which has since become a standard in many curricula across the globe; it also established the very notion of research as an indispensable part of design education.

< Participants in the Research Studio arrive in Las Vegas, 1968.

Preparations for Las Vegas Deadpan film shoot, Las Vegas, 1968.

Advertisements on the Las Vegas Strip, 1968.

Robert Venturi and Denise Scott Brown driving on the Las Vegas Strip, 1968.

1. Robert Venturi, Denise Scott Brown, and Steven Izenour, *Learning from Las Vegas* (Cambridge, MA: MIT Press, 1972).
2. Martino Stierli, *Las Vegas in the Rearview Mirror: The City in Theory, Photography, and Film* (Los Angeles: Getty Research Institute, 2013); "Instruction and Provocation, or Relearning from Las Vegas," ed. Michael Golec and Aron Vinegar, special issue, *Visible Language* 37, no. 3 (2003); Aron Vinegar, *I Am a Monument: On Learning from Las Vegas* (Cambridge, MA: MIT Press, 2008).
3. Robert Venturi and Denise Scott Brown, "A Significance for A&P Parking Lots or Learning from Las Vegas," *Architectural Forum* 128, no. 2 (1968): 36–43, 89, 91.
4. Martino Stierli, "Photographic Field Research in 1960s Art and Architecture," in *Experiments: Architecture between Sciences and the Arts*, ed. Ákos Moravánszky and Albert Kirchengast (Berlin: Jovis, 2011), 54–91.
5. *Las Vegas Studio: Images from the Archives of Robert Venturi and Denise Scott Brown*, ed. Hilar Stadler and Martino Stierli (Zurich: Scheidegger & Spiess, 2008/2015).
6. *Eyes That Saw: Architecture after Las Vegas* (Zurich: Scheidegger & Spiess, 2020), ed. Stanislaus von Moos and Martino Stierli; Stanislaus von Moos, *Venturi, Rauch & Scott Brown: Buildings and Projects* (New York: Rizzoli, 1987).

DRAWING AS ACTIVISM

Isabelle Doucet

Protagonists Maurice Culot (1939–), Robert L. Delevoy (1914–1982), René Schoonbrodt (1935–)
Institutions Ecole Nationale supérieure d'architecture et des arts visuels–La Cambre; Atelier de Recherche et d'Action Urbaines (ARAU); Archives d'Architecture Moderne (AAM)
Location Brussels, Belgium
Dates 1969–1979

During the 1970s the École Nationale supérieure d'architecture et des arts visuels de La Cambre—La Cambre, in short—became an important setting for discussions around the social and political role of the architect.[1] Echoing wider calls for architectural education to become more socially and politically engaged, a group of architects and students around Maurice Culot, with the support of the school's director, Robert L. Delevoy, developed a series of "counter-projects"—proposals that would act as manifestos, reinforcing the urban activism of groups such as the Atelier de Recherche et d'Action Urbaines (ARAU), co-founded in Brussels by René Schoonbrodt, who also taught (urban) sociology at La Cambre.[2] This work was situated at the intersection of urban-political action (ARAU and many other grassroots activist groups in Brussels), architectural education (La Cambre), and the intellectual and cultural project of the Archives d'Architecture Moderne (AAM), which was dedicated to the preservation of architects' archives but also promoted architecture and historical research through its *Bulletin* and numerous other publications. Taking aim at functionalist urban planning, which was blamed for the destruction of functionally mixed cities and close-knit neighborhoods, the counter-projects proposed the repair and reconstruction of the historic city—the architecture as well as the traditional urban composition of streets and squares.[3]

Over time, these counter-projects would develop into an aesthetic proving ground for the reconstruction of the European city. In this respect they also resonated to a certain degree with an emerging postmodern urbanism based on European tradition,[4] which found a multitude of outlets in regular contacts with like-minded architects, among them Léon Krier. The international reach of the work was extended through exchanges with other important educational settings like the Architectural Association in London; the editorial work of the AAM; and the La Reconstruction de la Ville Européenne conference held in Brussels in

< Anti-industrialization event organized by La Cambre students and teachers on the occasion of the international conference for the Reconstruction of the European City, November 16, 1978.

v Cover of
*Contreprojets—
Controprogetti—
Counterprojects*
by Léon Krier and
Maurice Culot
(Archives d'Archi-
tecture Moderne,
1980).

1978, which resulted in a manifesto-like publication, *Déclaration de Bruxelles.*[5]

Initially used to stimulate debate around specific sites, the counter-projects produced at La Cambre gradually grew into more spatially articulated projects with more explicit historical referencing. While they may not have been built, counter-projects promoted the conviction that the historical city could be repaired. With ambitions evolving from local sociopolitical activism to the preservation of the built heritage at a time of growing public support for conservation, the urban renovation credo became, simultaneously, a popular route for urban planners and the target of mounting ideological scrutiny from intellectual peers.

1. The architecture school of La Cambre is today integrated into the Faculté d'Architecture la Cambre Horta de l'Université Libre de Bruxelles, which was created in 2009 from the fusion of two "Instituts Supérieur d'Architec-ture": La Cambre and Victor Horta.
2. This short text draws on my earlier publications on the topic. My most detailed writings on counter-projects (in English) can be found in Isabelle Doucet, "Counter-Projects," in *The Practice Turn in Architecture: Brussels after 1968* (London: Routledge, 2015), 39–78. A recent discussion can also be found in Sebastiaan Loosen, "'Le Mono-pole du Passéisme': A Left-Historicist Critique of Late Capitalism in Brussels," in *Re-Framing Identities: Architecture's Turn to History, 1970–1990. East West Central. Rebuilding Europe 1950–1990*, vol. 3, edited by Ákos Moravánszky and Torsten Lange (Basel: Birkhäuser 2017), 261–274.
3. Two collections of counter-projects stand out: Léon Krier and Maurice Culot, *Contreprojets—Controprogetti—Counterprojects* (Brussels: Archives d'architecture moderne, 1980); and *Wonen TA-BK* 15–16 (August 1975), special issue on the ARAU, ed. Francis Strauven.
4. For many, a seminal text is the article by Maurice Culot and Léon Krier, "The Only Path for Architecture" (1978), in *Architecture Theory since 1968*, ed. K. Michael Hays (Cambridge, MA: MIT Press, 2000), 348–355; originally published in English in *Oppositions*, Fall 1978, and in French as "L'unique chemin de l'architecture," *Bulletin des AAM* 14 (1978): 1–5.
5. *Déclaration de Bruxelles*, ed. André Barey (Brussels: Archives d'Architecture Moderne, 1980).

CONTREPROJETS CONTROPROGETTI
COUNTERPROJECTS

PREFACES
PREFAZIONI
FOREWORDS

KRIER · CULOT

CONTRAPLAN

Marta Caldeira

Protagonists Manuel de Solà-Morales
(1939–2012), Juan Busquets (1946–), Miguel
Domingo, Antonio Font, José Luis Goméz Ordóñez
Institution Laboratori d'Urbanisme, Escuela
Técnica Superior de Arquitectura
de Barcelona (ETSAB)
Location Barcelona, Spain
Dates 1971–1974

In 1974 the recently founded Laboratori d'Urbanisme of Barcelona (LUB) published *Barcelona: Remodelación Capitalista o Desarrollo Urbano en el Sector de la Ribera Oriental*, featuring the theoretical "Contraplan" [counterplan] that it had presented in 1971 for Ribera-Poble Nou. More than a rebuttal of the official plan for the area, the Contraplan project epitomized LUB's vision for a structural transformation of Spanish urban planning—a new approach to the city, history, and urban analysis that was waged against the speculative forms of technocratic planning practiced in the final years of General Franco's regime.

In the highly politicized context of early 1970s Spain, the message of founding director Manuel de Solà-Morales and LUB's team members was clear: in order to respond to the needs of society, Spanish urban development needed to be dissociated from the private urban renewal projects supported by the Franco administration. Part urban analysis, part project, and part manifesto, the Contraplan interwove vociferous sociopolitical claims with seemingly objective studies of Barcelona's urban history. Unifying the narrative was a concept of urban morphology, which—together with building typology—connected LUB's approach to the legacy of analytical studies initiated by Saverio Muratori and developed by Carlo Aymonino and Aldo Rossi at the Istituto Universitario di Architettura di Venezia (IUAV). Urban morphology, Solà-Morales argued, was the "fundamental means for urban intervention," a concept that linked the historical analysis of city forms to the social forces behind urban growth, revealing present contradictions in the development process and suggesting directions for future interventions.[1]

From 1971, morphological studies not only guided LUB's research but also structured the study plan of *Las Formas de Crecimiento Urbano,* the textbook for the newly mandatory class on urbanism for architecture students at the Escuela Técnica Superior de Arquitectura de Barcelona (ETSAB), for which LUB was responsible. LUB's strategic translation of urban morphology in architectural education aimed to counter the perceived apolitical apathy of technocratic planning practiced by the state and local municipalities alike. Its mission was to educate the politically conscious "architect-urbanist," with a focus on urban analysis and history. This ideal was posed against the modernist "planner-technician," a role seen as compliant with the private sector and thus denounced by Solà-Morales already in his tenure master class in 1968 and underscored again by LUB's team in the Contraplan.[2]

While Solà-Morales's conception of urban morphology expressly endorsed the intersection of the social, the economic, and the formal, LUB's systematic study of concrete urban realities also tested the limits of the typo-morphological apparatus. If urban morphology explicated land parceling, and typology accounted for buildings, the process of urbanization that unified the two still remained unaddressed. Solà-Morales therefore added a third term, "infrastructure," construing the larger systems that, like transportation or services, also determined the historical development of urban form. Solà-Morales's final formula, proposing "morphology-infrastructure-typology as effect of the processes of land parceling-urbanization-edification,"[3] became the structural core of LUB's urban pedagogy for the last quarter of the century, with educational and professional reverberations that reached beyond Spanish territory.[4]

From the late 1970s on, a series of urban interventions in Barcelona offered Solà-Morales the opportunity to extend his analytical methodology

< Manuel Solà-
Morales, Malaga,
1980. Photograph
by Damián Quero.

—Plano de Barcelona y sus alrededores en 1706.

—Plano de Barcelona levantado por Mayans en 1830.

La observación de la secuencia de mapas muestra cómo la localización de usos, resultado de la competencia por el dominio del espacio, se refleja en organizaciones morfológicas diferenciadas, que se manifiestan de manera unívoca en determinados sectores y se solapan y contradicen en otros.

A la estructura de parcelación agrícola expresada en el plano de 1706, se le suporponen las ordenaciones urbanas periféricas y los trazados del

5. LA RELACION MORFOLOGIA-LOCALIZACION

PUEDE PARTIRSE DE ANALIZAR ESTAS RELACIONES EN LA ORDENACIÓN DE ENSANCHE DE CERDÁ, POR LO SIGNIFICATIVO DEL PAPEL JUGADO EN EL CONDICIONAMIENTO DE LA EVOLUCIÓN DE LA ZONA. HAY, EN ESTE SENTIDO, DOS ASPECTOS A SEÑALAR AL PLAN CERDÁ COMO FUNDAMENTALES PARA NUESTRO TEMA ACTUAL:

1. EL ENSANCHE COMO DEFINICIÓN, RESERVA O IMAGINACIÓN DEL ÁMBITO ESPACIAL DE LA CIUDAD DE LA BURGUESÍA. EN ESTE SENTIDO EL PROYECTO CERDÁ ES, SOBRE TODO, DESMESURADO. SU EXTENSIÓN ESTÁ DEFINIDA SOBRE LA BASE DE LAS DISPONIBILIDADES TOPOGRÁFICAS, Y EN RESPUESTA A LAS EXPECTATIVAS CREADAS SOBRE LAS HUERTAS INTERMEDIAS ENTRE EL CASCO ANTIGUO Y LOS PUEBLOS CIRCUNDANTES, PERO RESULTA TOTALMENTE EXCESIVO PARA LAS POSIBILIDADES DE OCUPACIÓN POR EL TIPO DE ACTIVIDADES Y USOS PREDESTINADOS.

∧ Page from Manuel Solà-Morales, *Barcelona: Remodelación Capitalista o Desarrollo Urbano en el Sector de la Ribera Oriental* (Gustavo Gili, 1974).

to urban practice as Spain transitioned into, and eventually consolidated, a newly democratic political system. Emblematic projects such as Moll de la Fusta (1987) and L'Illa Diagonal (1993) became key interventions in the city's postindustrial planning. If the conversion of the old dock into a promenade at Moll de la Fusta initiated the pre-Olympic renewal of the waterfront by reconnecting it to the city, the Illa Diagonal multipurpose complex constituted in turn the first node in a series of "new centralities" for the underserved peripheries of Barcelona. The projects thus exemplified LUB's idea of the urban project and the shift that the "Contraplan" was intended to signal in urban planning. By integrating historical analysis and the design practice of urban form across the architectural, urban, and metropolitan scales, LUB moved urban pedagogy decisively away from the practices of general master planning. Through what became known as ETSAB's "urbanism for architects," new generations of "architect-urbanists" trained at the Barcelona school were now to see architectural interventions as a tool that, based on an inductive approach to a site's history, needs, and potential, carried the power to impact the broader urban structure.[5]

Model of "Housing with Different Forms of Use" made for a third-year HfG course taught by Peter Sulzer, 1964–1965. Students: Rolf Berner, Mario Forné, Georg Furler, Hans Peter Goeggel, Paul Liner, Christian Merten. Photograph by Herbert W. Kapitzki.

1. M. Solà-Morales with J. Busquets, M. Domingo, A. Font, J. L. Gómez Ordóñez, "La Opción por una Actitud Teórica," *Barcelona: Remodelación Capitalista o Desarrollo Urbano en el Sector de la Ribera Oriental* (Barcelona: Gustavo Gili, 1974), 22.
2. M. Solà-Morales introduced the two terms—"architect-urbanist" and the derogatory "planner-technician"—in the lecture he delivered on the occasion of his tenure at the ETSAB in 1968, *Sobre Metodología Urbanística: Algunas Consideraciones*, which was published that same year by the school.
3. M. Solà-Morales, *Las Formas de Crecimiento Urbano* (Barcelona: Edicions UPC, 1997 [1971]), 76. Translated from Spanish. This was the textbook for the urbanism course that the LUB conducted at ETSAB.

4. Nuno Portas, Portuguese architect, urbanist, and professor of urbanism at Escola Superior de Belas Artes do Porto, Portugal, recognized the impact of what he termed M. Solà-Morales's "process model" in his introduction to the 1997 edition of *Las Formas de Crecimiento Urbano*.
5. On ETSAB's "urbanism for architects" (urbanismo para arquitectos), see M. Ribas Piera, "El Viraje al Paisajismo. Historia de una Docencia," *Ciudades*, no. 2 (1995): 18–19; Victoriano Sainz Gutiérrez, "Un Urbanismo para Arquitectos: La Génesis del 'Urbanismo Urbano'," *El Proyecto Urbano en España: Génesis y Desarrollo de un Urbanismo de los Arquitectos* (Seville: Universidad de Sevilla, 2006), 87–90.

THE VALUE OF FORM

THE PEDAGOGY OF OPEN FORM

Aleksandra Kędziorek,
Soledad Gutiérrez Rodríguez

Protagonist Oskar Hansen (1922–2005)
Institution Warsaw Academy of Fine Arts
Location Warsaw, Poland
Dates 1952–1983

Oskar Hansen, a Polish architect and member of Team 10, first presented his theory of "Open Form" at the CIAM Meeting in Otterlo in 1959. He continued to develop it through projects on various scales: from the design of exhibitions and housing estates created together with his wife Zofia Hansen, to the Linear Continuous System, a project for a network of decentralized cities running through Poland.[1] While the territorial aspirations of Open Form might suggest that it was a model for total planning, its main interest was in developing strategies of indeterminacy, flexibility, and collective participation. For Hansen, architecture was supposed to expose the diversity of events and individuals in a given space. Focusing on the creation of frames for individual expression, architecture was conceived as an instrument that could be used and transformed by its users and easily adapted to their changing needs.

From 1952 Hansen aimed to relate these ideas to his students at the Warsaw Academy of Fine Arts, encouraging them to pursue art practices beyond traditional disciplines. Applying the Open Form ideas of frame composition and subjectivity, he developed a series of didactic methods, first as instructor of the Solids and Planes Composition Studio (1955–70) and then of the Visual Structures Studio (1971–81). What Hansen taught was not "art," but a complete visual language. Students were free to include other mediums to address set exercises, many of them resolved through the use of three-dimensional space. With these approaches, Hansen aimed to stimulate the students' visual imagination, creativity, and intellectual capabilities.

The initial curriculum of the Planes and Solid Figures Composition Studio began with a series of compositional exercises based on dichotomies, such as heavy and light objects, static and dynamic forms, and contrasts of shape and size.[2] These were followed by exercises performed on didactic apparatuses—specially designed devices in wood and plywood dedicated to studying the problems

∧ Students
performing the
"Legibility of a large
number of elements"
exercise, 1960s.

< Students
performing the
"Rhythm" exercise,
1960s.

of "rhythm," "legibility of complex form," and "legibility of a large number of elements." The latter was nicknamed the "Large Number" in reference to the concept of the "greater number," which Hansen and the members of Team 10 used as a way to address the problems of an ever-growing human population and its impact on the built and natural environment. Hansen translated this urban planning concept into a compositional exercise. Another exercise informed by ongoing architectural debates was the "active negative," a sculptural interpretation of spatial sensations experienced by an individual in a given architectural interior. Developed in 1955, parallel to the studies of negative space by Bruno Zevi and

Luigi Moretti and the global interest in Gestalt psychology, it was distinguished by its introduction of a subjective, emotional factor.

In the 1970s the curriculum of Hansen's studio was enriched by the introduction of open-air group exercises. Here, Hansen's theory of Open Form revealed its full potential and subverted the traditional—as well as modernist—elements of artistic communication. Group exercises had begun outside of the academy as an initiative of young graduates and artists. In December 1971 Hansen participated in a meeting of the Young Creative Workshop in Elbląg, where artist Przemysław Kwiek suggested moving the discussion outdoors and replacing words with visual communication—"a performed battle of 'visual tactics'"—that Hansen helped structure.[3] The resulting group action, known as "A Game on Morel's Hill," inspired further exercises performed by Hansen and his students in open-air workshops in Skoki and Dłużew. There, in keeping with the nature of the studio, students were encouraged to collectively construct a visual argument based on existing facts, passing on the baton of words, so that each new voice picked up from where the previous one left off, building up the established dialogue. In this way, the traditional roles of author and audience were eliminated.

One of Hansen's main challenges at the Warsaw Academy of Fine Arts was how to reshape the school's teaching method, a transformation that unfolded in parallel to the architectural transformation of the academy's own premises. The opportunity arose in 1973 when the Faculty of Sculpture moved to another building on the Warsaw riverbank and Hansen, as the only architect on its staff, was invited to redesign it. In the unrealized project, he proposed to introduce an open-space structure that, instead of being based around the figure of the studio master, would encourage a horizontal pedagogical system where students could freely interact with their teachers. When the students elected him as dean of the Faculty of Sculpture in 1981, Hansen made an effort to introduce the Open Form pedagogy as an official teaching system. However, he was forced to abandon the reform after protests from his colleagues and he left his new post soon after, retiring from the academy in 1983.

Thanks to two generations of his students, Hansen's theory played a vital role in the history of Polish art. Open Form constituted an enduring reference point for the further artistic and pedagogical practices of artists including Paweł Althamer, Wiktor Gutt and Waldemar Raniszewski, Grzegorz Kowalski, Zofia Kulik, Przemysław Kwiek, and Artur Żmijewski.[4] The impact of Hansen's work even extended well beyond Poland. Open Form pedagogy became a conceptual basis for the program established in Bergen by Hansen's student, Svein Hatløy, in 1986, and for the summer schools that took place in Hansen's house in Szumin in the early 1990s.[5]

> KwieKulik, Game on Morel's Hill (group action), 1971.

1. For Hansen's architectural oeuvre, see *Oskar Hansen—Opening Modernism: On Architecture, Art and Didactics*, ed. Aleksandra Kędziorek and Łukasz Ronduda (Warsaw: Museum of Modern Art, 2014); *Team 10 East: Revisionist Architecture in Real-Existing Modernism*, ed. Łukasz Stanek (Warsaw: Museum of Modern Art, 2014); *Towards Open Form*, ed. Jola Gola (Frankfurt: Revolver; Warsaw: Foksal Gallery Foundation, 2005).
2. A full curriculum is presented in *30 Years Later: A Look at Oskar Hansen's Studio*, ed. Jola Gola and Grzegorz Kowalski (Warsaw: Academy of Fine Arts in Warsaw, 2013).
3. *KwieKulik: Zofia Kulik & Przemysław Kwiek*, ed. Łukasz Ronduda and Georg Schollhammer (Warsaw: Museum of Modern Art, Wrocław; BWA, Vienna: Kontakt, 2012), 94; KwieKulik, *A Game on Morel's Hill (group action)*, 1971, Filmoteka Muzeum, Museum of Modern Art in Warsaw, https://artmuseum.pl/en/filmoteka/praca/kwiekulik-gra-na-wzgorzu-morela-akcja-grupowa

4. Their practices and their relation to open form are described in detail in *Open Form: Space, Interaction, and the Tradition of Oskar Hansen,* ed. Axel Wieder and Floryan Zeyfang (Berlin: Sternberg Press, 2014); Łukasz Ronduda, "In the Circle of Open Form: Visual Games, Interactions, Participation, Archives, Communities," in *Polish Art of the 70s* (Warsaw: CCA Ujazdowski Castle, 2009), 171–201; Łukasz Ronduda, Michał Woliński, and Axel J. Wieder, "Games, Actions, Interactions: Film and the Tradition of Oskar Hansen's Open Form," in *1 2, 3…Avant-Gardes: Film/Art between Experiment and Archive*, ed. Łukasz Ronduda and Floryan Zeyfang (Berlin: Sternberg Press; Warsaw: CCA Ujazdowski Castle, 2007), 88–103.
5. On Hansen's wider influence, see the other texts in this volume by Masha Panteleyeva, "Designing the Process, Becoming "One with the User,'" and Martin Braathen, "AN-ARK: The Liberated Subject and Coastal Culture."

^ Oskar Hansen presenting the Open Form theory at the AICA congress in Wrocław, 1975. Photograph by S. Stępniewski.

AS THEY WERE TEACHING...

Federica Soletta

Protagonists Bernhard Hoesli (1923–1984), Colin Rowe (1920–1999), John Hejduk (1929–2000), Robert Slutzky (1929–2005), Lee Hodgden (1925–2004), John Shaw (1928–2016), Werner Seligmann (1930–1998)
Institution School of Architecture, University of Texas at Austin
Location Austin, TX, USA
Dates 1951–1958

Between 1951 and 1958, in "the Provençal dimension of the Texas hill country,"[1] a group of young teachers in the University of Texas at Austin developed a pedagogical program that challenged existing models of American architectural education.[2] The newly appointed dean of the School of Architecture, Harwell Hamilton Harris, hired Bernhard Hoesli, Colin Rowe, John Hejduk, Robert Slutzky, Lee Hirsche, Lee Hodgden, John Shaw, and Werner Seligmann[3]—the "Texas Rangers," as they came to be known—who focused their teaching on rethinking the process of architectural design, on the visualization and abstraction of spatial structures, and on what they called the "architectural idea"—the substance of every architectural project.[4]

The curriculum, based on a memorandum drafted by Hoesli and Rowe in 1954, recognized as necessary reference points the work of Frank Lloyd Wright, Le Corbusier, and Mies van der Rohe, as well as Theo van Doesburg's legacy on the construction of space.[5] The program was organized around a series of problems that aimed to help students reason about the experience of architectural space through an analysis of its composition, elements, and history. The exploration of lines formed the core of the first-year studio taught by Hirsche and Slutzky, mostly employing the visual perception methods of Josef Albers, their own teacher at Yale. Here, the technique of drawing, initially a "means of investigation," became an exercise in spatial abstraction, an act of design in itself.[6]

Questions of space, transparency, depth, volumes, and planes defined the studios over the following years, allowing the design process to be explored in multiple phases, from the simple to the more complex. Among the problems proposed in the junior studio, the best known is the nine-square grid, born from a collaboration between Hejduk, Slutzky, and Hirsche. The metaphysical "open-ended" quality of the grid might be seen as a paradigm of the Texas Rangers' curriculum—and is perhaps its most influential contribution to architectural education as a whole.[7] The nine-square grid exercise "enables an in-depth investigation of binary architectonic relationship":[8] without being an end in

< The Texas Rangers. Faculty of the School of Architecture, 1954–1955. Left to right: McMath, Hirsche, Buffler, Goldsmith, Leipziger-Pierce, Hejduk, Harris, Roessner, Slutzky, Rowe, Hoesli, Kermacy, Nuhn, White.

itself, it incorporates any form and dimension; it has no center and yet is still able to provide a frame, a transparent structure; it detaches itself from historical models and nonetheless is ruled by a shape that is central to the history of art and architecture—a square made of squares. The nine-square grid was an attempt at historical abstraction, and may be read through the words of Hejduk: "in retrospect it [my work] has always been an elimination of histories but I had to know history in order to dispense with it. It is an intentional absorbing of all those past things, zooming it, compressing it."[9]

On the other hand, in Rowe's design studio, student projects were interpreted through the study of historical precedents. This should not read as a mimesis of past projects, but rather as the understanding of a principle, the geometry of which was visible in a plan or on a façade, and as the possibility of building a historical vocabulary. Although formally different, the nine-square grid exercise and the use of historical precedents can be seen as complementary approaches within the process of design. If the abstracted nine-square grid worked as a system of coordinates to understand and utilize the elements of architecture and generate an "architectural idea," Rowe's problem considered the reading and interpretation of a historical reference as a "generator of architectural form"[10] that provided the structural and spatial comprehension of a project.

Whether the hills of central Texas functioned as historical nostalgia or as an inspiration evoking the light of Italy or the rocky hills of southern France (as in Palladio or Cézanne), one can only speculate. Nonetheless, the landscape would appear as a recurring theme in the group's work, somehow connecting the solitary vastness of postwar Texas with the European Renaissance and mannerism as well as

modern architecture.[11] Metaphor or trigger, Austin functioned as an empty slate on which this historical legacy was presented as a language and converted into a teaching tool that encompassed Palladio and Mondrian, Le Corbusier and Mies van der Rohe, the simple "American urban type," the urban grid of the nineteenth century, and the boundless desert of the South. Yet Austin itself was not only an experiment but also an incubator, geographically and culturally far removed from the different intellectual backgrounds of the new educators. Perhaps it was precisely this distance that provoked a new vision of teaching that, through the re-examination of the modern movement, challenged the nature of the design process in architectural education.

The methods of the "Rangers" reverberated through the schools of Europe and the United States, finding their way into the curricula of Cornell, Cooper Union, Yale, Pratt Institute, Syracuse, Williams College, Cambridge, and ETH, among others. If the seed of their experiment was born during those few years in Texas, it is probably in the dispersion of its creators, in their continuity and effort as educators, that we can still today identify its global repercussion.

1. Colin Rowe, *As I Was Saying: Texas, Pre-Texas, Cambridge*, vol.1 (Cambridge, MA: MIT Press, 1996), 73.
2. On architectural education in the US see Kenneth Frampton and Alessandra Latour, "Notes on American Architectural Education: From the End of the Nineteenth Century to the 1970s," *Lotus International*, no. 27 (November 1983).
3. Trained by Bernhard Hoesli, Shaw, Hodgden, and Seligmann were the main protagonists of the brief "second School of Texas" and left the school in 1958.
4. Alexander Caragonne, *The Texas Rangers: Notes from an Architectural Underground* (Cambridge, MA: MIT Press, 1995), xix.
5. Rowe and Hoesli, "Memorandum, March 1954," cited in Caragonne, *The Texas Rangers*, 33.
6. As Bernhard Hoesli wrote in the proposed course matrix in 1953, cited in Caragonne, *The Texas Rangers*, 32.
7. "The nine-square grid is metaphysical. It always was and still is for me." John Hejduk, "Frame 2—1954–1963," *The Mask of Medusa: Works, 1947–1983* (New York: Rizzoli International,1989), 35.
8. Slutzky, cited in Hejduk, "Frame 2—1954–1963," 39.
9. Ibid., 36.
10. Caragonne, *The Texas Rangers*, 247.
11. See Rowe's recollection of the Texas landscape and light in *As I Was Saying: Texas, Pre-Texas, Cambridge*, vol. 1, 73.

∧ Bernhard Hoesli in studio, April 1955.

ARCHITECTURAL LANGUAGE AND THE SEARCH FOR SELF-DETERMINACY

José Araguëz

Protagonists John Hejduk (1929–2000), Robert Slutzky (1929–2005), Raimund Abraham (1933–2010), David Shapiro (1947–)
Institution Cooper Union School of Architecture
Location New York, NY, USA
Dates 1964–1985

At a time when schools around the world were experimenting with political activism, computation, new technologies, urban analysis, and ecology, the Cooper Union School of Architecture singled itself out by strictly focusing on the basis of architectural design. Cooper's educational project channeled a rethinking of the inner logics of the language of architecture: of the main architectural elements (for example, columns, façade, walls, ceilings, floor slabs) and the principles by which those elements can be combined into a recognizable architectonic unity through their three-dimensional disposition in space. In other words, the school stimulated a revision of the foundational components of architectural design as well as the spatial relationships that can be established between them.

Two major publications of student work, *Education of an Architect: A Point of View 1964–1971* and *Education of an Architect 1972–1985,* came out under the aegis of John Hejduk, who was head of the department of architecture from 1965 and dean of the school of the architecture from 1975. The former accompanied a 1971 MoMA show of the same name—the first (and, so far, one of only two) devoted

entirely to the work of a single architecture school. In retrospect, it can be seen to have marked a shift between two clearly distinguishable periods at the school: Cooper pre- and post-MoMA. Presenting projects from 1964 to 1971, the exhibition illustrated the various formal problems and drawing exercises conceived to train students in the fundamentals of the language of architecture. The exercises were stylistically neutral enough to facilitate the development of self-determined modes of architectural expression in line with the creative interests of individual students. However, much of the work presented a strong modernist valance, reflecting the presence of instructors who continued to be attached to the modern architectural vocabulary. In my view, Cooper ended up institutionalizing a style—precisely what one would expect its methodological neutrality to avoid.

After the MoMA show, important changes to the faculty brought about a profound interest in disciplinary expansion. With this came a renewed drive to look at fields other than architecture (and other than modernist painting, which had been the primary source of external inspiration in Hejduk's early years at Cooper). No longer bound by the precepts of the modern movement, the work produced at the school began to display a much more varied array of expressive formats. This diversification demonstrated a methodological aptness to cultivating individuality and difference. Explorations of the deepest recesses of the language of architecture, along with an intense exposure to procedural schemes distinctive of practices external to architecture (from poetry to medicine), catalyzed the emergence of each student's independent, highly personal voice. In that regard, the central components of the form-based teaching methods that were put in practice after the MoMA show—some of which arose

> Initial instructions for the nine-square grid exercise. Students were asked to build a model of a sketch simply depicting a 16' by 16' grid of columns, and "to begin to study spatial relationships within that grid." After that, they had to "draw their schemes in plan and in axonometric, and search out the three-dimensional implications in the model."

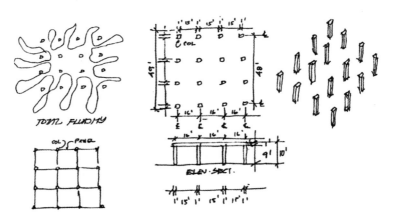

< Sound Struc-
tures project
by Evan Douglis,
1983.

pre-MoMA and were reframed after the exhibition, while others emerged post-MoMA—proved effective at bracketing out the possibility of engendering a linguistically derivative corpus of architectural work. The Cooper methodology—involving different modes of drawing exercises, abstract design techniques such as the nine-square grid problem, and an analytical approach to the study of historical buildings—represented an alternative to the reliance on received formats of architectural expression that was commonplace in the 1970s and 1980s at schools such as Princeton, Columbia, and IIT, to name but a few. *Education of an Architect 1972–1985* documented the work by Cooper students of those years.

Though at times unevenly successful, in terms of the originality of the design results, what could be understood as Cooper's quest for linguistic self-determinacy did yield a sizeable body of student projects possessing an *uncoded* character during that second period. Devoid of clear references, difficult to pin down historically, tending towards the stripping away of recognizable stylistic codes, these projects lived up to the potential for singularity that was written into the school's teaching methods and testified to its capacity to nurture a certain level of disciplinary instability. By becoming a locus of pedagogical idiosyncrasy outside of the prevalent frameworks of academic training, Cooper constituted itself as a point of reference for the disruption of the status quo—"a kind of academia outside of academia, a kind of cloister outside of a cloister."[1]

1. Quote by Peter Eisenman from an unpublished and unedited interview recorded April 20, 1993. Courtesy of the archive at The Cooper Union School of Architecture.

TIME-CONSCIOUSNESS FOR THE POSTCOLONIAL PRESENT

Daniel Magaziner

Protagonists Selby Mvusi (1929–1967)
and Derek Morgan (1925–1997)
Institution University of Nairobi
Location Nairobi, Kenya
Dates 1965–1967

Between 1965 and 1967 two expatriates came together to create the "Faculty of Comprehensive Design" at what was then University College Nairobi, an affiliate of the University of East Africa. Selby Mvusi was born in South Africa; as a Black man, he had chafed against the seeming impossibility of practicing as an artist under apartheid and gone into exile in 1957. He had arrived at University College in late 1964, after studying art education and industrial design in both the US and UK, and teaching art at the Kwame Nkrumah University of Science and Technology in Ghana.[1] His colleague, Derek Morgan, was born in Darjeeling, in colonial India, and had studied at the Architectural Association in London and the Illinois Institute of Technology (with Buckminster Fuller) before taking up a position in Nairobi in the waning days of British rule. The foundation course they developed together was an experiment in social theory and phenomenology, a short-lived laboratory for both living and building in postcolonial Africa.

Though Mvusi had been hired to teach art at University College, he was increasingly convinced that art itself was a dead end, though he retained faith in "plastic form." As far as he was concerned, nothing demonstrated people's time-consciousness—their sense of who they are, here and now—more than the objects they created to suit their needs. But the great tragedy of both the colonial and the dawning postcolonial age was that others—Europeans, Americans—were dictating the terms of African creativity, and in the process assigning limits to it. Mvusi saw the strongest expressions of African time-consciousness in the ways people interacted with contemporary material realities, in both urban and rural settings. Much of the appeal of his Nairobi appointment therefore lay in the opportunity it gave him to address actual urban conditions on the continent through the University College's architecture program—even if that program was nominally under the authority of the Liverpool University school of architecture.

Derek Morgan, who was responsible for training first-year architecture students, objected to the overt premise of the Liverpool-directed syllabus—namely, that East African architectural education was supposed to copy metropolitan antecedents—and early in 1965 he pressed the university

> Selby Mvusi, behind Derek Morgan (third from right), with students in the first year foundation course, Department of Art and Department of Architecture, University of Nairobi, c. 1965.

authorities to allow Mvusi to join him in redesigning the first-year curriculum. Over the next two years, the expatriates collaborated on what they called the "foundation course," a term adapted from both the interwar Bauhaus and its postwar successors in both the US and West Germany, such as the Illinois Institute of Technology and the Ulm School of Design. The foundation course radically revised the practice of architectural education not only at the University College, but in East Africa more widely and, indeed, across the postcolonial world. The syllabus was a mixture of familiar and unfamiliar elements. Relatively typical courses for architectural education were glossed as "form/content appreciation"—and considered, for example, the functions and characteristics of light, or the basic elements of design and color. Recognizing the strand of "tropical architecture" which was then gaining traction in West Africa in particular, there were also courses on climatology in construction and habitation.[2]

Far less conventional lectures paralleled these familiar subjects. Mvusi and Morgan contended that students would only be able to grasp human-material interactions in all their depth if they were familiar with pretty much everything that had brought them to that particular place—Nairobi, in East Africa—at that particular moment in time. This belief translated into broad brushstroke lessons in the histories of art, of urbanization, of capitalism and socialism, of Confucianism and Hinduism, of colonialism and nationalism. Students could only design, Mvusi wrote, once they understood themselves to be "comprehensive" of time. It was only on the basis of this accumulated knowledge that they could formulate truly creative and appropriate responses.

The university authorities grumbled about this unconventional teaching style—and especially about the fact that it left students little time to produce work of their own. The few student projects that survive mostly take the form of photographic experiments or small models—predominantly geodesic domes in the style of Morgan's mentor, Buckminster Fuller. But in the absence of a clear alternative, Morgan and Mvusi were allowed to continue. In the course's second year they planned a new cumulative assignment to capture the essence of the contemporary East African condition—as well as to assuage the university's concerns. Both Morgan and Mvusi were greatly influenced by urban sociology and convinced of the merits of survey research. Over the course of the academic year, they instructed their students to identify research subjects in both Nairobi and the surrounding rural areas and to map their lives—the people they lived alongside, the objects and structures they interacted with, and so on. Students shadowed their research subjects through their daily routines and carefully plotted the worlds that they inhabited. Through this research, they hoped the students would learn to understand themselves as comprehensive of time and gain the necessary knowledge they would allow them to design to meet the needs and conditions of postcolonial East Africans on their own terms.

The foundation course was ambitious and forward-pushing. It was also short-lived. Students produced even less work in 1967 than they had in 1966 and midway through the year the administration canceled the course, judging it impractical. Mvusi was instructed to go back to teaching art. Just a few months later, he was killed in a car crash outside of the city. Morgan retired from teaching soon after.[3] The University of Nairobi architectural program reverted to a syllabus set by supposedly universal standards derived from those that prevailed in better resourced and more politically influential parts of the world.[4]

1. For more on this phase on Mvusi's career, see my "Designing Knowledge in Postcolonial Africa: A South African, Abroad," *Kronos*, no. 41 (2015).
2. For more, see Hannah le Roux, "The Networks of Tropical Architecture," *The Journal of Architecture*, no. 8 (2003): 337–354.
3. For the evolution of the Nairobi program after Mvusi's and Morgan's departure, see my "The Politics of Design in Postcolonial Kenya," in *Flow of Forms / Forms of Flow: Design Histories between Africa and Europe*, eds. K. Pinther and A. Weigand (New York: Columbia University Press, 2018).
4. This piece is adapted from a much longer article, published as "The Foundation: Design, Time and Possibility in 1960s Nairobi," *Comparative Studies in Society and History* 60, no. 3 (2018).

REDEMOCRATIZING THE NATION THROUGH "GOOD DESIGN"

Anna-Maria Meister

Protagonists Tomás Maldonado (1922–2018), Max Bill (1908–1994), Otl Aicher (1922–1991), Inge Aicher-Scholl (1917–1998), students at the HfG
Institution Hochschule für Gestaltung (HfG)
Location Ulm, Germany
Dates 1953–1968

The Hochschule für Gestaltung in Ulm (HfG) is often depicted as the most influential design school in postwar Germany, credited with establishing the profession of the modern product designer—its former student Michael Erlhoff even called it "a milestone in the modern adventure."[1] Founded in 1953 with financial support from the US occupying forces, the school had its roots in the Nazi Resistance: the siblings of one of its founders, Inge Aicher-Scholl, were the White Rose members Sophie and Hans Scholl, who were murdered by the Nazi regime. The school wanted to maintain this spirit of resistance,

seeing itself as a voice of dissent in a country that was myopically rebuilding its cities while failing to engage critically with its horrendous past. Writing in the HfG magazine, *ulm,* Italian art critic Gillo Dorfles confirmed this self-understanding: "it is the fate of every really lively and progressive movement (and educational system) to stand in opposition to the prevailing situation which is accepted by the majority of institutions."[2]

Consequently, the HfG decided early on to move off grid—to Kuhberg (cow's hill)—deliberately going against the conventional German landscape of postwar higher education. The right-angled, minimalist complex occupied the top of the hill next to the ruins of an old fort—a bulwark for a new, modern, and (ostensibly) rational approach to design and architecture. Designed by the Swiss architect and artist Max Bill, and built with the help of students, it was originally conceived as steel construction but took on its concrete form after a local cement producer stepped in with sponsorship.[3] Building on what was first envisaged as an institute of adult learning, the school's founders—graphic designer Otl Aicher, Aicher-Scholl, and Bill—hoped to create a fundamentally different approach to design education. As Bill put it, they were

trying to reshape a nation across all scales "from the teaspoon to the city." In fact, the school's avowed ambition was nothing less than to redemocratize postwar Germany through "good design."

At the HfG, design took on the role of a bearer of moral values that were to be disseminated to the German people. Seeing itself as educating a new democratic elite, the school not only reformed architectural pedagogy but treated architecture as an object of design alongside the spoon, the shelf, or Max Bill's Ulm stool ("Ulmer Hocker"). The HfG created the modern product designer as the successor to the architect: where the Bauhaus had made architecture the center of the curriculum, the school in Ulm made no distinction between shaping buildings and forming teacups—a scalelessness that found its ultimate dissolution in the proposition that a designer should design the design process itself, rather than an object. Under Tomás Maldonado's reign the school's rationalist approach (rooted in a deeply humanist functionalism) soon became the main focus of the curriculum as well as the source of internal debates about form and its validity. With some help from visiting mathematicians, sociologists, writers, and philosophers, this "process design" would become a site of rationalist excess, moving the focus from "good design" in aesthetic terms to "good design" as the desire for total control over production.

The HfG was one of the first institutions to introduce technologies—cybernetics and process design—that heralded the digital turn in architectural education. An interest in what would become the field of systems design was pursued by teachers such as Horst Rittel (a mathematician), Max Bense (a philosopher, and later Anthony Frøshaug (a typographer and designer) and Abraham Moles (a pioneer in information science). And yet the HfG was far from being a "technical school" in the sense of the polytechnic model: students had as many (or more) classes in literature, politics, or sociology as was usual in design training. Conventional representation techniques, however, were now subject to theorization and objectification, with a "good sense for form" being replaced by acts of programming. It appears that the definition of the right parameters for design education was seen as the fundamental basis for producing "good designers," who in turn would make "good design" in the world. The HfG was, if you will, a huge computer processing pedagogical information into a programmed curriculum, all directed toward the humanist ideal of forming a free-thinking adult.[4]

∧ Students working in the plaster workshop of the HfG building, 1955. Photograph by Ernst Hahn.

< Aerial view of Ulm School of Design, 1955. Photograph by Otl Aicher.

The HfG's model of education was reformulated several times during its existence. The school emphasized experimentation and the radical integration of theory as an integral part of design practice, but at the same time it believed that such explorations were best carried out within an institutional framework. So, rather than reinventing the "school" as an institution, the founders took their cues from both the American university and German bureaucracy. At the HfG, experimentation paradoxically created seemingly endless paper trails—the meetings and debates questioning pedagogical formats were transcribed, typed with several carbon copies, disseminated, and filed.[5] These processes, however, were not seen to be at odds with the school's claim to be continually reinventing itself through self-evaluation: in Ulm, radicality was institutionalized, or rather, institutionality was radicalized.

This applied, too, to the life of the students. Looking up at the school, locals saw something like a strange new spaceship stranded on the hill, a curious gaze mirrored by the students on their trips down to town, when they made the locals the subject of photographic essays and briefs. Up on the hill, in the so-called "monastery of rationalism," students and teachers lived and worked together throughout the school year. When winter came, they were often cut off by snow, the only connection to the outside being one (not always reliable) phone line. Elevated high above the city of Ulm, living life at the "right angle" (not coincidentally, the only curved line in the entire building was the bar), nothing escaped the rigorous rule of good taste. Only classical music or jazz was deemed acceptable (definitely not rock), art was mostly considered frivolous, and the walls were kept bare.[6]

When the school with the highest percentage of non-German students in the country was shut down in 1968, it was not simply due to the "termination" of an experiment by conservative forces in the government, as students and teachers claimed.[7] Another factor was perhaps that it had never truly escaped the shadow of that other German design school: the Bauhaus. As Reyner Banham once argued in the school's magazine, "everyone to whom the word modern has any positive meaning has fathered his own dreams on the memory of the Bauhaus, and then transferred their burden on to the HfG at Ulm."[8] Emulating and at the same time resisting the Bauhaus as a model, the school was caught between the politically opportunistic use of its legacy and Gropius's support and the ever stronger impulse to define its own profile as a German design school. Even the final protests against the school's closure in 1968 took place in front of the Bauhaus exhibition in Stuttgart, and featured carefully designed protest posters with well-placed, sans-serif, lower-case lettering.

And yet, rather than being the catastrophe it was made out to be, the end of the school after fifteen contested years might even have been instrumental in establishing its lasting legacy. HfG's "good design" would define Germany's public spaces for decades to come; HfG students would go and teach across the globe; and the "monastery" on the Kuhberg still towers over the city today—a modern monument staking its claim to history.

∨ HfG students demonstrate against the closure of their school during the Bauhaus retrospective in Stuttgart, 1968. Photograph by Herbert W. Kapitzki.

1. See Martin Krampen and Günther Hörmann, *The Ulm School of Design: Beginnings of a Project of Unyielding Modernity* (Berlin: Ernst & Sohn, 2003).
2. Gillo Dorfles in *ulm*, no. 10/11 (1964): 71.
3. René Spitz, *HfG Ulm: The View behind the Foreground* (Stuttgart: Achim Menges, 2002), 107–110.
4. Anna-Maria Meister, "Paper(less) Architecture: Medial and Institutional Superimpositions," in *The Architecture Machine: The Role of Computers in Architecture*, ed. T. Fankhänel and A. Lepik (Boston: Birkhäuser, 2020), 20–27.
5. See Anna-Maria Meister, "Paper Constructions: Ethics & Aesthetics at the HfG Ulm," *Raddar: Design Annual Review*, no. 1 (2019): 70–100.
6. See Bernhard Rübenach, *Der rechte Winkel von Ulm: ein Bericht über die Hochschule für Gestaltung 1958/59* (Darmstadt: Verlag des Georg-Büchner-Buchhandels, 1987); Heiner Jacob, "HfG Ulm: A Personal View of an Experiment in Democracy and Design Education," *Journal of Design History* 1, no. 3/4 (1988): 221–234.
7. Spitz, *HfG Ulm: The View behind the Foreground*, 360–397.
8. Reyner Banham in *ulm*, no. 10/11 (1964): 72.

DESIGNING THE PROCESS, BECOMING "ONE WITH THE USER"

Masha Panteleyeva

Protagonists Karl Kantor (1922–2008),
Evgeny Rosenblum (1919–2000)
Institution Senezh Design Studio
Location Solnechnogorsk at Senezh Lake,
Russia, USSR
Dates 1964–1974

In 1964 Evgeny Rosenblum and Karl Kantor founded the Senezh Experimental Design Studio, which would become one of the most influential design schools in the USSR, educating nearly half of all Soviet design professionals. Conceived as an alternative to the functionalist approach propagated by the state-sponsored Design Research Institute (VNIITE), the Senezh studio's dynamic curriculum emphasized the importance of establishing a connection between "artistic design" and "a way of life." Its members believed in the central role in the design professions of the artist (rather than the engineer), emphasizing an experimental design education over what they perceived as design production. At the same time, the studio successfully combined educational, professional, and theoretical work under the motto "Learn while designing and design while learning."[1] The educational structure followed four main principles: art as

the foundation of all creative production; a "theatri-calization" of design inspired by new developments in theater art (involving, among other things, open communication and collaboration between teacher and student); the products of educational design activities (models, drawings, mock-ups) were seen as artworks in themselves; the creation of work that would bridge the gap between architecture and traditional design.

Although the studio began as a series of seminars and lectures featuring international guests, emulating established schools such as the Bauhaus and the HfG in Ulm, it would soon develop its own independent educational philosophy. Disagreements with the two German schools arose from Senezh's view that capitalist market forces were inimical to the artistic nature of creative design. In an article on Soviet teaching methodologies, Kantor predicted that the bourgeois world's destructive dependence on commercialism would inevitably lead design there to decline into "stylization."[2] He disagreed, too, with the Ulm idea of separating art and design, seeing this artificial divide as the ultimate "evil" impeding design's ability to transform society.

In place of these Western practices, a core technique in the studio was so-called "man-oriented design": in order to fully engage in the creative process, the designer learned to become "one with the user."[3] Departing from the mantra of form follows function, form-giving was based on socio-cultural factors. As Rosenblum put it in his seminal *Artist in Design*, "the personal approach in design

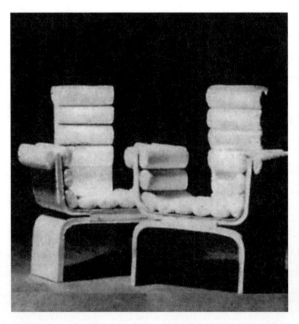

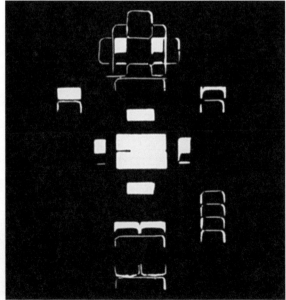

^ At work in the Senezh
Experimental Design Studio.
Evgeny Rosenblum is second
from the right.

< Senezh student projects for
a market hall, including furniture design. L. Abasheva,
V. Vladimirov, V. Stepanov,
A. Yuzenas. From E. Rosenblum,
Artist in Design (Iskusstvo,
1974).

allows the artist to continuously transform design
practices as a field."[4]

This new creative formula of "man-oriented
design" was derived from the concept of Open Form
introduced by Polish architect and educator Oskar
Hansen when he lectured at Senezh in 1967. Hansen's
Open Form approach allowed users to "complete"
the object, adapting it to their own cultural context
through its interactive and dynamic form. This
approach was later formulated into the concept
of *sredovoi dizain* ("context-oriented design")—a
new direction within the profession that would feed
into the *sredovoi* approach in architecture and
urban planning.[5]

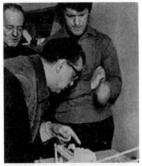

Senezh promoted a multidisciplinary approach: "the designer must not be a narrow specialist: only the universal reproduction of Nature…can create a more human Man."[6] At the core of the curriculum was a course in composition intended to develop knowledge of the *process* of creating artistic form. The course was developed with input from students who were for the most part already established professionals. Although it included some elements of traditional pedagogy (from VKhUTEMAS, for example), its use as a pedagogical tool was consciously denied. The simple exercise of manipulating abstract form was equated with the very *process* of design, in contrast to the conventional understanding of process as something that precedes the final product. Believing that the capitalist "fetishism of objects" could only be truly overcome in the socialist context, Senezh taught design as a new type of artistic production. During late socialism, this approach took on broader resonances, aiming to give material form to Marx's description of communism as "the *genuine* resolution of the conflict between man and nature and between man and man…between existence and essence, between objectification and self-confirmation, between freedom and necessity, between the individual and the species."[7]

The Senezh group ceased its activities in the mid-1990s, a few years before Rosenblum's death. Despite the predominantly experimental nature of its work and the lack of realized projects, the studio developed, in its almost thirty years of existence, a core system of influential design methodologies that renewed academic research and figurative language in a discipline that had continuously struggled with the effects of postwar functionalism and the industrialization of construction.

< Details of the Senezh studio from the cover of *Artist in Design* (Iskusstvo, 1974).

1. Karl Kantor, "The Rebirth of the Bauhaus," *Dekorativnoe Iskusstvo SSSR*, no. 7 (1964): 24.
2. Ibid.
3. Ibid.
4. Evgeny Rosenblum, *Artist in Design* (Moscow: Iskusstvo, 1974).
5. Kantor, "The Rebirth of the Bauhaus," 24.
6. Ibid.
7. Karl Marx and Friedrich Engels, *Iz rannikh proizvedenii* [Selections from Early Works] (Moscow: Gospolitizdat, 1956), 588.

A REFUGE FROM THE DIRTY WAR

Ana María León

Protagonists Tony Díaz (1938–2014), Ernesto Katzenstein (1931–1995), Justo Solsona (1931–), Rafael Viñoly (1944–)
Institution La Escuelita
Location Buenos Aires, Argentina
Dates 1976–1983

La Escuelita ("The Little School") was an underground architecture school conceived and realized in Buenos Aires by architects Tony Díaz, Ernesto Katzenstein, Justo Solsona, and Rafael Viñoly (who later relocated to New York). Banned from teaching at the university during the unstable government of Isabel Perón (1974–1976), the architects came together to organize an institution of their own. However, as the political situation deteriorated and a military junta took over the city in 1976, the project changed. Rather than an official institution, the school was conceived as a marginal entity, legally nonexistent. A lack of official recognition also meant a lack of official control over curricula and content, which allowed the school to operate outside the tighter constraints on architectural education in Argentina at the time. The new dictatorship viewed education activities with permanent suspicion, particularly when they involved the Universidad de Buenos Aires (UBA), where most of the professors and students of La Escuelita came from. Yet it tolerated La Escuelita as long as it dealt "only with architecture"—design, in other words, was considered harmless.

The Universidad de Buenos Aires still is the home of the biggest architecture school in Argentina, and one of the biggest in the world: FADU-UBA. In order to accommodate the huge class sizes, FADU-UBA worked with a hierarchical structure: one professor would supervise a series of assistants, who in turn had students to help carry the load of supervising smaller groups. La Escuelita followed this tradition by incorporating some of its early students into a second roster of teachers, among them Juan Carlos "Yanz" Poli, Edgardo Minond, Ignacio Lopatín, Sandro Borghini, Jorge Sarquis.[1]

Historian Jorge Liernur joined the faculty when he returned from his studies with Manfredo Tafuri at IUAV, reinforcing the school's already strong connection with Italian architecture and theory. As an important destination for Italian migration, Argentina maintained strong links to Italian discourse and production. Italian architects and theorists were important points of reference for La Escuelita,

< Standing from left: Juan Carlos "Yanz" Poli, Raul Lier, Manuel Glass, Eduardo Leston, Justo "Jujo" Solsona, Francisco "Paco" Otaola, Antonio "Tony" Díaz, Edgardo Minond, Hugo Salama, Jorge Grin. Seated from left: Jorge Francisco "Pancho" Liernur, Alejandro "Sandro" Borghini, Luis Ibarlucía. Photograph by Jorge Sarquis.

in particular the work of Aldo Rossi, Manfredo Tafuri, and Giorgio Grassi, whose texts in many instances were translated into Spanish before they were translated into English.[2] Several studio exercises focused on formal and typological experiments on the city, rehearsing some of the positions advanced by Rossi in the mid-1970s. For instance, a joint workshop led by Díaz and Solsona in 1978 took on the Avenida de Mayo—the ceremonial axis that connected the Congress with the Presidential Palace. At the end of the year, the group was even able to invite Rossi to lecture and participate in a studio review. While some students had playfully experimented with the historicist appropriation of forms, Rossi prompted them to return to the city itself in order to comprehend the architectural typologies as historical artifacts. The discussion situated architecture as a discipline beyond purely formal manipulation, informed instead by the historic and cultural context that surrounds it. Tafuri was also in conversation with members of the school during his visit to Argentina in 1981.[3]

With the return to constitutional rule in 1983, La Escuelita was reabsorbed into the FADU-UBA. The compressed intensity and experimental freedom it had established were somewhat curtailed in the process, with the smaller institution being seen by many as a temporary anomaly. And yet, elements of the school's pedagogy lived on, as many of its exercises and conversations continued to inform the curriculum at the bigger institution.

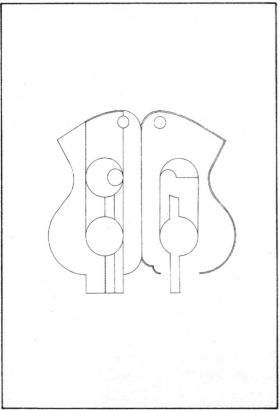

< Student work from the "Exercise on Le Corbusier" taught by Ernesto Katzenstein and Jorge Liernur, 1977.

1. Interviews with members of La Escuelita are available in a documentary sponsored by Moderna Buenos Aires—CPAU. Jorge Gaggero, *La Escuelita: Enseñanza alternativa de arquitectura en la Argentina (1976–1981)* (Buenos Aires: Libido Producciones, 2016), https://vimeo.com/187696866. See Jonas Delecave, "¿Cuál Escuelita?," *Registros: Revista de Investigación Histórica* 16, no. 2 (July–December 2020): 124–150; Delecave, "Uma disciplina em crise: disputas pela arquitetura na escuelita de Buenos Aires (1976–1983)," PhD dissertation, Universidade de São Paulo, 2020.
2. See Ana María León, "Translating Rossi: From Buenos Aires to New York," in *Aldo Rossi, la storia di un libro: L'architettura della città, dal 1966 ad oggi*, ed. Fernanda De Maio, Alberto Ferlenga, and Patrizia Montini Zimolo (Padua: Il Poligrafo, 2014), 177–190.
3. See *Tafuri en Argentina*, ed. Francisco Díaz (Santiago: ARQ Ediciones, 2019).

"Institutions for a Post-Technological Society," typewritten draft with handwritten corrections, c. 1971.

3 1/2"

INSTITUTIONS FOR A POST-TECHNOLOGICAL SOCIETY:

The Future of the Man-Made Environment

Research Project prepared jointly by ~~to Culminate in a Series of Public Presentations~~

The MoMA (Lauls), and
The Institute for Arch + Urban Studies
~~Co-Sponsored by The Museum of Modern Art~~

~~The Institute for Architecture and Urban Studies~~

~~Emilio Ambasz, Director~~

THEORY CONSTRUCTIONS

IMPORTING ARCHITECTURAL HISTORY

Hilde Heynen

Protagonist Sibyl Moholy-Nagy (1903–1971)
Institution Pratt Institute
Location New York, NY, USA
Dates 1951–1969

In an interview in 1967 Sibyl Moholy-Nagy proudly declared herself a "DCT (Devoted Classroom Teacher), the lowest species on the academic ladder."[1] She clarified that she had made it her "life task to scuttle academic stuffiness, to make lecturing as entertaining or better than a variety show." While she found that "college teaching suffers from lack of humor, lack of alertness to the constant shifting of interpretation of historical values, and inflated self-importance," Moholy-Nagy was devoted to countering these traits by offering students up-to-date, visually attractive, and engaging lectures.[2]

Whereas the teaching of architectural history was not seen as crucial in most modernist architectural programs in other schools in the US, Sibyl Moholy-Nagy built an extensive curriculum in the history of art and architecture for the Pratt students. She also taught a course in the graduate program on the "History of Human Settlements." Her undergraduate courses in architectural history were at first mostly conventional survey courses, starting with ancient architecture in Mesopotamia and Egypt and ranging through Greek and Roman antiquity via Romanesque and Gothic to Renaissance and Baroque. Structural systems and developments in city planning were addressed in the last part of the survey, and more contemporary issues were dealt with in "Theory of Architecture," which gave special attention to the works of F. L. Wright, Le Corbusier, Mies van der Rohe, and other modern architects.[3] But gradually she began to experiment with the format and content of her lectures and seminars. Toward the end of the 1960s, she felt "so sure in [her] field that [she could] drop a lot of buildings, architects and even movements which were considered sacrosanct and which [she had] come to consider irrelevant."[4] This allowed the third-year course to expand to include "Non-Western Cultures," "Islamic Architecture," and "Early Settlers' Architecture in North America"—a range that was quite innovative for the time.

In her teaching, Moholy-Nagy relied upon an enormous collection of slides, and had the students make instant sketches while she commented on what they saw. She often used the comparative method of the double-slide projection, showing slides side by side in order to draw out a particular point. She encouraged students to express themselves graphically and comparatively too. Assignments for her courses often asked students to present drawings or models with elaborate captions to answer a specific question. A typical assignment read as follows:

> Consider the following 4 principal criteria for architecture: 1) Exterior form…; 2) Structure…; 3) Plan and space…; 4) Esthetics…Consider each of these 4 overall aspects in the work of a) Frank Lloyd Wright and b) Le Corbusier. …Juxtapose on boards or sheets the solutions most characteristic for Wright and Le Corbusier, and write brief, clear captions which will explain in a few sentences the different approach of each man to the same basic problem.[5]

Moholy-Nagy thus asked students to study the formal vocabulary of specific architects by emulating their design characteristics—and she did this because she was convinced that this kind of knowledge of the history of architecture was a crucial asset for architects.

The role of architectural history was a hotly debated topic in the 1960s, mainly because of modernism's fraught relationship with history. Moholy-Nagy took a clear position in this debate, together with Bruno Zevi, who also advocated for architectural history to be the backbone of an architect's education. The two had met at the History, Theory and Criticism seminar at Cranbrook in 1964, an important moment in the historiography of modern architecture, when a younger generation of architectural historians started to make their mark and lines were drawn as to the how and why of architectural history.[6] The main dividing line was between those who defended a close alliance between architectural history and design education (Zevi, Moholy-Nagy, and others) and those who opted instead for a scholarly and rigorous approach that distanced itself from direct involvement with architectural practice (Henry Millon and his MIT colleague Stanford Anderson).

Moholy-Nagy elaborated on the rationale for her viewpoint in a memorandum drafted in 1970 for Columbia University (she had left Pratt in 1969). Proposing a new history curriculum that firmly positioned architectural history as a crucial hinge in the education of architects, Moholy-Nagy argued that knowledge in architectural history would allow

students and architects to bridge the gap between the longing for continuity (from the general public) on the one hand, and the continuous quest for the new (intrinsic to the profession) on the other.[7] These insights were not met with immediate approval, neither at Pratt and nor at Columbia, but it is fair to say that her insistence on the need for close connections between history and design paved the way for the postmodernist sensibilities that were to gain the day in the 1970s and early 1980s.

1. This text is a much-abbreviated version of chapter 5, "Teaching as Vocation," of my book *Sibyl Moholy-Nagy: Architecture, Modernism and Its Discontents* (London: Bloomsbury, 2019).
2. "Moholy-Nagy: Molder of 'Big City Students' (Interview with Sibyl Moholy-Nagy)," *Prattler* 29, no. 4 (October 30, 1967): 7.
3. Course descriptions in the *Pratt Institute Bulletin* 16, no. 1 (April 1954).
4. Letter to Hattula Moholy-Nagy, December 11, 1968 (Collection HMN).
5. Archives of American Art 948/1162.
6. Donlyn Lyndon, "Cranbrook 1964," *Journal of Architectural Education* 19, no. 2 (September 1964): 26–28; Marcus Whiffen, "History, Theory and Criticism: The 1964 AIA-ACSA Teacher Seminar. Abstracts and Extracts," *AIA Journal* 42, no. 5 (November 1964): 29–40; *The History, Theory and Criticism of Architecture,* ed. Marcus Whiffen (Cambridge, MA: MIT Press, 1965).
7. Sibyl Moholy-Nagy, "Preamble to a History of Architecture design curriculum," Archives of American Art 949/137.

ᴧ Sibyl Moholy-Nagy at the MAS symposium at Columbia in 1962. Around her, from left to right: Edgar Kaufmann Jr., H. Allen Brooks (at rear), James Marston Fitch, Philip Johnson, and an unknown student.

THE METHODS OF "ENVIRONMENTAL DESIGN"

Joaquín Medina Warmburg

Protagonist Tomás Maldonado (1922–2018)
Institutions Hochschule für Gestaltung (HfG),
Princeton University, Università di Bologna,
Politecnico di Milano
Locations Ulm, Germany; Princeton, NJ, USA;
Bologna and Milan, Italy
Dates 1966–1998

In 1966 Tomás Maldonado—artist, teacher, design theorist, and journalist[1]—came to Princeton University's School of Architecture to give a lecture, "How to Fight Complacency in Design Education." He would use the occasion to present one of his most innovative concepts, the "University of Methods."[2] Maldonado wanted new scientific methods in the traditions of logical empiricism and American pragmatism to guide designers in developing solutions for specific concrete problems. And the place to learn these methods, he said, was not a conventional school of architecture but a "school of environmental design." The rise of the term "environment" in the 1960s had brought with it the promise of a greater connection between traditionally distinct design disciplines such as industrial design, architecture, or even city planning. Since it was apparent that the sum of "good design objects" did not in itself add up to a "good design environment," the focus of attention shifted from the design of individual artifacts to an open system of relations that included behavioral environmental design. Here, the structural approaches of systems theory, cybernetics, semiotics, and ecology provided a common basis of operation.

Maldonado's lecture at Princeton had consequences. Later that year, Robert Geddes, dean of the Faculty of Architecture, visited Maldonado in Ulm, where he was director of the School of Design (HfG). Geddes wanted to reorient his own school toward environmental design and hoped to benefit from the teaching experiments in Ulm.[3] But he would end up persuading Maldonado to move to Princeton (a prospect made more appealing by the constant internal struggles at the HfG). The title of Maldonado's first course for the winter semester in 1966 was simply Man and Environment. Its syllabus spoke of diversification, specialization, and a more critical approach to architectural training, culminating in a future vision of a school of human environment and human ecology: "a thoroughly new concept, which will enable us to deal with the new demands of a rising new world."[4]

While Maldonado's teaching in Ulm had incorporated a scientific approach, with practical exercises

in fields such as topology and functional product analysis, his Princeton seminar offered a theoretical, ideological, and critical reflection on problem-oriented design.[5] Maldonado took as a starting point the biologist Jakob von Uexküll's (1864–1944) definition of *Umwelt*, which allowed him to conceptualize the environment as a system of artifacts resulting from a circular causality (*Funktionskreis*) of the utilitarian and the symbolic, of function and meaning. Drawing on the semiotics theory of Charles Morris, which underlined the integral understanding of the semantic, syntactic, and pragmatic values of aesthetic experience, Maldonado worked toward an understanding of function as an integral component of culture at large.[6]

Maldonado's ideas met with some criticism, most notably from Alan Colquhoun, who had attended his first seminar in Princeton (along with Kenneth Frampton). For Colquhoun, Maldonado's approach neglected the communicative, symbolic, and representative aspects of architecture. In place of Maldonado's supposed "biotechnical determinism," he invoked traditional symbols and building types as the real bearers of architectural meaning and culture.[7] Venturi, Scott Brown, and Izenour would refer to Colquhoun's criticism as one of the starting points for their *Learning from Las Vegas* (1972). Indeed, in the years that followed, interest in Maldonado's interdisciplinary methodical openness would decrease in inverse proportion to the rise of postmodern design through typological transformation. However, Maldonado persisted in representing his environmental approach to design education at the Università di Bologna from 1976 to 1984 and the Politecnico di Milano from 1985 to his retirement in 1998. His teaching has become all the more relevant today, as we look for methods for dealing with increasingly complex technical and globally threatened environments that go beyond the rhetorics of sustainability or ecology.

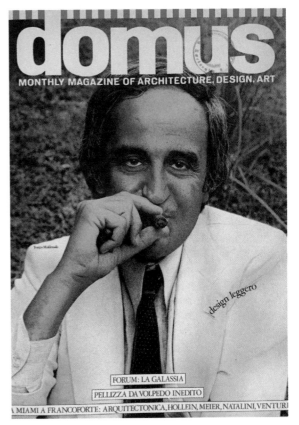

^ Tomás Maldonado featured on the cover of the January 1981 issue of *Domus*.

< Tomás Maldonado teaching at the HfG in Ulm. Photograph by Ernst Scheidegger.

1. Laura Escot, *Tomás Maldonado: The Itinerary of a Technical Intellectual* (New York and Milan: Skira, 2007).
2. Tomás Maldonado, "How to Fight Complacency in Design Education," *Ulm*, no. 17/18 (June 1966): 14–20.
3. Robert Geddes and Bernard Spring, *A Study of Education for Environmental Design: Final Report* (Princeton: Princeton University, 1967), 15.
4. The syllabus consisted of excerpts of a previous article: Tomás Maldonado, "The Emergent World: A Challenge to Architectural and Industrial Design Training," *Ulm*, no. 12/13 (1965): 2–10.
5. Tomás Maldonado, *Design, Nature, and Revolution. Toward a Critical Ecology* (New York: Harper & Row, 1972); Joaquín Medina Warmburg, "Design, Nature, and Revolution: Tomás Maldonado und die Architektur als *environmental design*," in *Zwischen Sputnik und Ölkrise. Kybernetik in Architektur, Planung und Design*, ed. Oliver Sukrow (Berlin: DOM Publishers, 2017), 100–121.
6. Kenneth Frampton, "Apropos Ulm: Curriculum and Critical Theory," *Oppositions*, no. 3 (May 1974): 17–36, 29.
7. Alan Colquhoun, "Typology and Design Method," *Arena. Journal of the Architectural Association*, no. 83 (June 1967): 11–14.

RADICAL EXHAUSTION

Marco De Michelis

Protagonists Manfredo Tafuri (1935–1994),
Giancarlo De Carlo (1919–2005), Francesco Dal Co
(1945–), Marco De Michelis (1945–)
Institution Istituto Universitario di Architettura
di Venezia (IUAV)
Location Venice, Italy
Dates 1967–1969

At the beginning of 1968 the Istituto Universitario di
Architettura di Venezia (IUAV) was a small school of
architecture, unaffiliated with any major university.
Founded in the 1920s as an offshoot of the Venice
Academy of Fine Arts, it was only the second school
of architecture in Italy after the one in Rome. Yet it
had a distinctive character, developed from the end
of World War II, when its director, Giuseppe Samonà,
called on some of the best Italian designers of the time
to teach. Ignazio Gardella, Franco Albini, Lodovico
Belgiojoso, Giancarlo De Carlo, Carlo Aymonino, Carlo
Scarpa, and Luigi Piccinato were among those who
taught at the IUAV, along with historians like Bruno
Zevi and Leonardo Benevolo. By the 1960s all traces
of the old academic system still prevailing in Rome or
Milan had disappeared, as if by magic, and a younger
generation had joined the faculty, among them Aldo
Rossi, Luciano Semerani, Costantino Dardi, and Gino
Valle. Both Zevi and Benevolo departed for Rome in
1967, leaving the chair of architectural history vacant.
Manfredo Tafuri, then little more than thirty years
old, would take over.

When the academic earthquake of 1968 struck,
the IUAV was enmeshed in an open debate concerning
the changes that would be necessary to implement

its new teaching structure. This soon evolved into a
discussion that addressed the very terms of the discipline of architecture and urban planning. De Carlo
saw an opportunity to challenge the idea of urban
planning that Aldo Rossi had formulated a short while
before, in his *Architecture of the City*.[1] Rather than
"significant monuments gathered in a shapeless and
meaningless agglomeration of buildings," he proposed
a critical planning process that would transform the
"act of the project" (*azione progettuale*) into collective action involving the public as protagonists rather
than passive recipients. For Rossi himself, this was a
chance to give life to the Tendenza group and to begin
to develop the tools of typology and morphology that
would further its investigation on the city. Aymonino,
in turn, extended his reflection on the "capitalist
city"—an argument he had been pursuing with
Benevolo, a Catholic, since 1966.

Newly settled at the institute, Tafuri gathered
a small group of young people around him, among
them Francesco Dal Co, Georges Teyssot, Giorgio
Ciucci, Franco Rella, Massimo Cacciari, and Marco
De Michelis. Most were still students at the time.
Together they embarked on an ambitious research
project: the systematic investigation of the ideological values of the modern tradition. This research
would encompass the socialist city in the experiments
of the Soviet avant-gardes, the American city and the
great crisis of capitalism in the late 1920s, reform
policies in Germany and the creation of an "employee
culture," the relationship between plan and utopia
and the visionary work of Le Corbusier, urban form
in the Netherlands and, of course, the modernizing
zeal of Italian fascism. In parallel, the institute worked
to develop the theoretical and critical foundations of
a materialist interpretation of history, partly through
courses dedicated to the collective discussion of
Marx (in particular his *Grundrisse*, which had recently
been translated into Italian) and the reading of crucial
texts by Walter Benjamin, Theodor Adorno, and,
before long, Michel Foucault.

All this took place in the tumultuous context of
the student struggle of 1968, part of a wider social
conflict that literally exposed the limits and imbal-
ances of the Italian "economic miracle" of the previous
decade. 1968 also saw the publication of the first issue
Contropiano, founded by the philosophers Massimo
Cacciari and Toni Negri, and the literary scholar
Alberto Asor Rosa. Other contributors included the
political scientists Mario Tronti, Umberto Coldagelli,
and Rita di Leo. The magazine would become Tafuri's
preferred platform for debating and organizing his

> Manfredo Tafuri and Marco De Michelis, Venice, 1980. Photograph by Odile Seyler.

< Manfredo Tafuri and Carlo Aymonino, 1967. Photograph by Odile Seyler.

1. Aldo Rossi, *L'architettura della città* (Padua: Marsilio, 1966).

reflection on the relationship between architecture and ideology—a reflection complicated by the divergence of his approach from the magazine's established cultural frame of reference. While *Contropiano's* founders developed their ideas through direct confrontation with Marx's texts, Tafuri followed a path that was articulated more through the tradition of German "critical" thought—Adorno above all, and soon Benjamin. As is well known, the drafting of his seminal essay "Toward a Critique of Architectural Ideology" (published at the beginning of 1969) was the direct result of a very tense discussion among the *Contropiano* group.

For Italy, 1968 raised many questions that went unanswered and continued to resonate in the following bloody decade—one characterized by political radicalization and terrorism. The "old" university was reduced to shreds: formerly elite institutions were suddenly open to anyone with a five-year degree. The "mass" university was born, but no provision was made to help institutions absorb much larger numbers. In Venice, the IUAV's student intake multiplied six- or sevenfold, but spaces, programs, contents, and hierarchies remained unchanged. Imposing a radical rethinking of Venice's architecture school would have required a great commitment from those very groups that had observed the events of 1968 so closely. But the season of radical changes in education had been definitively exhausted by the new order.

A NEW DISCIPLINARY APPARATUS

Joseph Bedford

Protagonists Dalibor Vesely (1934–2015),
Joseph Rykwert (1926–), Daniel Libeskind (1946–),
Alberto Pérez-Gómez (1949–),
David Leatherbarrow (1953–)
Institution University of Essex
Locations Colchester and London, UK
Dates 1968–1978

The master's-level course led by Joseph Rykwert at the University of Essex between 1968 and 1978 was the first of its kind—the first research course in the history and theory of architecture that granted a degree. As Rykwert wrote in 1966, "As far as I know, we will be the only university school of architecture in Great Britain offering such a course."[1] And as a contemporary newspaper advertisement put it, "There is at present no mastership course of this nature being offered at any school of architecture or university elsewhere."[2]

Rykwert's innovation was to position graduate studies in architectural history and theory as playing a role equal to technology or design studies in the development of architectural education. From the late 1950s well-known British educators such as Leslie Martin had argued that architecture needed to develop specialized postgraduate research in order to provide the profession "with the higher technical ability and knowledge that it requires,"[3] so that architects could "hold their own in a developing field of technology."[4] New master's-level courses were established in the "white heat"[5] of early-1960s Britain, but they were all in the building sciences, responding to increasing anxiety in the profession about architecture's ability to legitimate its leading role in the construction industry. Architects had traditionally distinguished themselves from other craftsmen by their privileged knowledge of *disegno,* cultivating their skills through Beaux-Arts competitions or evening drawing classes. In the intensive period of reconstruction that followed the Second World War, however, they sought to distinguish themselves from the rest of the construction industry by their advanced technical ability. It was not until Rykwert established the Essex course in 1968 that architects found a new way to signal their unique status—their mastery of history and theory.

Rykwert's seminars offered students a year of immersion in architecture's literary tradition, from Vitruvius, Alberti, Serlio, Perrault, Laugier, and Durand to Le Corbusier and Venturi. Rather than approaching these texts as a source of "timeless knowledge" of proportions and the orders—the way they had been read for centuries in the academies of France and Italy—Rykwert read them hermeneutically with the aim of revealing the historicity of architectural meaning. Students were asked to place the present in a dialogue with the context of the past, as revealed within the text. The "knowledge" produced in this way would then be a knowledge of the present, capable of guiding practice through historical understanding, rather than technical expertise.

To complement his own seminars, Rykwert hired a young Czech philosopher, Dalibor Vesely, whom he had first met in 1965. In the decade that followed his arrival in Britain, Vesely developed a method of teaching that drew from phenomenology. His seminar offered Rykwert's students a parallel training focused on a close reading of philosophical texts such as Edmund Husserl's *Crisis of the European Sciences*, Martin Heidegger's *Being and Time*, Maurice Merleau-Ponty's *Phenomenology of Perception*, and Hans-Georg Gadamer's *Truth and Method*. Similar to Rykwert's approach, Vesely had his students read these texts with an eye to present concerns. Countering the technical and scientific approach of the time, he emphasized modes of thinking that addressed everyday questions through historical and philosophical frameworks so as to instill a deeper understanding of the given—the contemporary.

The two seminars by Rykwert and Vesely constituted the entire course. Combined, they provided the training for a new kind of architectural figure

that they hoped would lead the field, that of the *architect-hermeneuticist*—exemplified by their students Daniel Libeskind, Alberto Pérez-Gómez, and David Leatherbarrow. Such an architect would, they believed, be able to interpret and understand their specific historical moment and so achieve a deeper understanding of architecture. In this way, history and theory would become central to architectural design, as the source of the knowledge required to distinguish "functional design" from "interpretative work."

Rykwert's course lasted just a decade and had a fairly small number of students, but it became an entire school of thought. Over the following decade the methods of the "Essex school"[6] spread throughout North America and Europe, playing a key role in establishing history and theory as central to the disciplinary apparatus that came to distinguish architecture education from the 1970s on.

1. Letter from Joseph Rykwert to John Entenza at the Graham Foundation dated November 15, 1966. Special Collection, Albert Sloman Library, Essex University.
2. See newspaper clipping dated between 1966 and 1968 in Special Collection, Albert Sloman Library, Essex University.
3. Leslie Martin, "RIBA Conference on Architectural Education," *Architects' Journal* 12, no. 3299 (May 22, 1958): 775.
4. Ibid., 774.
5. Harold Wilson, "Labour's Plan for Science," Reprint of Speech by the Rt. Hon. Harold Wilson, MP, Leader of the Labour Party, At the Annual Conference, Scarborough, Tuesday, October 1, 1963, 1.
6. *Architecture Theory since 1968*, ed. K. Michael Hays (Cambridge, MA: MIT Press, 2000), 462.

< Joseph Rykwert, Princeton, 1972. Photographer unknown.

> Diagram by Michael Foster of material covered in Rykwert's seminar, 1969–1970.

A POST-TECHNOLOGICAL UNIVERSITY

Felicity D. Scott

Protagonists Emilio Ambasz (1943–) with Jean
Baudrillard (1929–2007), Manuel Castells (1942–),
Gillo Dorfles (1910–2018), Umberto Eco (1932–2016),
Hans Magnus Enzensberger (1929–), Suzanne Keller
(1927–2010), Henri Lefebvre (1901–1991), Richard
L. Meier (1920–2007), Martin Pawley (1938–2008),
Octavio Paz (1914–1998), Alain Tourraine (1925–),
Sheldon Wolin (1922–2015)
Institution Museum of Modern Art
Location New York, NY, USA
Dates 1968–1972

On January 8 and 9, 1972, New York's Museum of
Modern Art convened a conference titled "Institutions
for a Post-Technological Society: The Universitas
Project." At stake was the redressing of the failure of
design and its institutional frameworks to adequately
respond to the new "technological milieu" and, with
it, the "environmental crisis" brought on with the
emergence of the postindustrial age. As its host,
Emilio Ambasz, then Curator of Design, explained,
the participants had been brought together to
produce a model of a "'synthetic' system of thought
capable of designing the man-made milieu according
to a dynamic notion of order." Sponsored jointly by
MoMA's International Council and the Institute for
Architecture and Urban Studies (IAUS), the event
was conceived as the analytical stage of a larger
project, the ultimate aim of which was "to establish in
New York State an experimental university centered
around the problems of environmental design."

Since 1969 Ambasz had worked with a team of
consultants and research advisors, including architects, legal theorists, art historians, sociologists,
physicists, economists, philosophers, among others,
to prepare a set of *Working Papers*. In July 1971 this
lengthy document was sent to an equally diverse
group of conference participants with disciplinary
backgrounds that ranged far beyond architecture
and design, encompassing general systems theory,
behavioral science, and Anglo-American empirical
philosophy on the one hand, and European philosophy, critical theory, and semiotics on the other.
The line-up included Jean Baudrillard, Manuel
Castells, Gillo Dorfles, Umberto Eco, Hans Magnus
Enzensberger, Suzanne Keller, Henri Lefebvre,
Richard L. Meier, Martin Pawley, Octavio Paz, Alain

Tourraine, Sheldon Wolin, and more, with invitations
also extended to Louis Althusser, Hannah Arendt,
Roland Barthes, Michel Foucault, and others who
were unable to attend. After submitting papers in
advance, which responded to the provocations set
out in the *Working Papers*, participants convened
at the symposia for a multidisciplinary debate on
the future of design and design institutions in the
postindustrial era. With a carefully selected audience of invited architects, academics, and press,
the event took place in the privacy of the Members'
Penthouse and was divided into four sessions: the
first addressed problems of "value" and of how to
establish provisional norms for design; the second
focused on semiotics and urban structures; the
third dealt with planning and forecasting; and the
fourth turned to social and political issues related
to the role of the university in society.

The Universitas Project stands as a little-known
aspect of MoMA's involvement with architectural
pedagogy and alternative institution building—the
museum's relation to the Bauhaus and IAUS being
more widely cited. Ambasz pointed to the Bauhaus,
along with the VKhUTEMAS and the Ulm School of
Design, as precedents for experimental pedagogies,
indicating that one could not implement a new design
paradigm for a postindustrial world within existing
institutional structures. These institutions would
haunt the ensuing intense debates over pedagogical
reform. The partisan exchanges, largely marked
by continental divides, also extended to disagreements about the status of industrial design objects
instigated by Baudrillard's paper, "Design and
Environment or How Political Economy Escalates
into Cyberblitz." Meyer Schapiro launched a lengthy
defense of the importance of the Bauhaus, drawing
further comments from Schorske, Denise Scott
Brown, Lefebvre, and Paz. Refuting readings of functionalism's semantic poverty, let alone of its strictly
industrial epistemology, Baudrillard polemically
argued that the Bauhaus had instituted the "universal
semanticization of the environment." The "revolution
of the object" to which it gave rise was not simply
industrial but sponsored a postdisciplinary semiurgic
logic wherein useful objects functioned primarily as
signifiers within an informatic environment. "The
Bauhaus," he argued, "marks the point of departure
of a veritable *political economy of the sign*."[1]

Charged with fostering a technocratic ideology
and harboring fantasies akin to a "philosopher
king," the experimental institution that was the
ultimate aim of Ambasz's project did not go ahead

The problem of structuring alternative outcomes and of choosing one or more as goals is that both these activities have to be conducted in the light of very incomplete information. This incompleteness stems from two shortcomings. One is that relevant information is, in fact, scarce. The other is that any individual's or group's capacity to absorb, analyze and use large amounts of data is limited.

Thus, it is almost impossible to visualize the alternative future states of a complex system except in a sense so restricted, so superficial and so general that it would be clearly impractical to use such constructs for purposes of action and policy. And when we add to scenarios of this sort qualifiers like "relevant to man", or "imbued with human purpose", etc., we introduce dimensions which range from the biological, through the social, political, economic, to the psychosocial, the psychological and cultural. These are immense bodies of data that have little or no meaning except when they are selected, itemized, interpreted, and restructured into a context of information that is relevant to the ends being considered and to the decisions which will give them reality.

This suggests that ethically meaningful choices concerning ends require large-scale information structures, and that only our ability to multiply and relate such information will permit the widening of our outlook and judgement beyond the inherited ideas which make up our current world view.

Furthermore, there is the difficulty that the resulting construct must embody some "good" or "virtue" which the present lacks. The act of ~~writing~~ designing a desirable future requires, consequently, valuation judgements, and ethical analysis, as an instrument of will and freedom, must enter as an explicitly recognized element of our design methodologies.

The development of the system of thought capable of designing the man-made milieu has been quite neglected until now, both, because it is a difficult approach and because it in some non-trivial way it requires habits of mind and cognition which differ from those favoured in our culture.

^ Emilio Ambasz in MoMA's Sculpture Garden during his exhibition "Italy: The New Domestic Landscape," 1972

> "Institutions for a Post-Technological Society," cut-and-pasted photocopy of text draft with handwritten notes, c. 1971.

but became the topic of one of his "Working Fables," "Univercity."[2] Yet, the symposia and affiliated texts constituted one of the most intellectually ambitious, if politically ambiguous, engagements between the discipline of architecture and technoscientific and theoretical discourses of its time. If MoMA was an unlikely host venue, the lineup was truly remarkable. In retrospect, the unstable, conflictual, at times counterdisciplinary nature of the conversations directed toward environmental design pedagogies marked an event in which architecture recognized its constitutive if uneasy indebtedness to social, technological, political, and economic vicissitudes. Indeed, it situated architectural and design pedagogy as both drivers for and recipients of a complex entanglement of expertise and forms of knowledge, and as a channel through which contemporary forms of life might be radically rethought and potentially transformed according to such technocratic and epistemological dispositions.

1. Jean Baudrillard, "Design and Environment or How Political Economy Escapes into Cyber-blitz," trans. Charles Levin, in *For a Critique of the Political Economy of the Sign* (New York: Telos Press, 1981), 186.
2. Emilio Ambasz, "The Univercity (draft), 1972–74," *Oppositions* 4 (October 1974): 73–74.

PEDAGOGY BEFORE DEMOCRACY

Josep M. Rovira

Protagonists Rafael Moneo (1937–), Ignasi de
Solà-Morales (1942–2001), Josep Quetglas (1946–),
Manuel de Solà-Morales (1939–2012)
Institution Escuela Técnica Superior
de Arquitectura de Barcelona (ETSAB)
Location Barcelona, Spain
Dates 1964–1975

In 1964 the Spanish government—needing new recruits to face the challenges of economic liberalization, industrial consolidation, and the growth in tourism—enacted a set of reforms in the country's schools of architecture and engineering. The duration of study was reduced from seven years to five, making it possible for students from less well-off families, with a different class consciousness, to attend university.[1] But there was no corresponding increase in the numbers of teaching staff or the provision of classroom space, resulting in overcrowding. Nor did old professors modify their teaching or the existing curricula. To make things even worse, there were obvious structural limitations: with a prohibition on associations of any kind, the only body that "represented" university students was the SEU (Union of Spanish Students), a faction of the Vertical Union that Franco had invented to control the working class.

A response to these limitations was not long in coming. Between March 9 and 11, 1966, a group of progressive Catalan students and leftist intellectuals clandestinely created the SDEUB (Sindicat d'Estudiants de l'Universitat de Barcelona) in a Capuchin convent in the city. "We Shall Overcome," a song popularized by Pete Seeger and Joan Baez, began to be sung in student assemblies as a signal of the desire to resist Francoist repression. A rebellious attitude took hold of Spanish universities that year, and it would last until the death of the dictator nine years later, in 1975. Suspensions of professors, demonstrations in the street, closing of faculties, murders—all fed into an environment of conflict.

There was a changing of the guard at ETSAB, the school of architecture in Barcelona, with the arrival of a few new professors who were dedicated to their teaching and determined to bring about change. The first to come were Joan Margarit in structures, Manuel de Solà-Morales in urbanism,

and Jordi Mañà in construction. They modernized the study programs and adapted them to the rigor and work ethic of the architect. But that was only the beginning.

In 1967 students expelled some teachers and brought in new ones. A philosopher arrived, Xavier Rubert de Ventós, with Christopher Alexander's book (*Essay on the Synthesis of Form*) under his arm. Young teachers replaced those who had retired or were absent: Xavier Sust introduced students to a range of contemporary architectural texts, from Christian Norberg-Schulz's *Intentions in Architecture* to Vittorio Gregotti's *Il territorio dell'architettura* and, more importantly, to Robert Venturi's *Complexity and Contradiction in Architecture*.

When the reverberations of May 1968 in Paris reached Barcelona, the situation was further radicalized. It was no longer enough to change the content of the courses; now, the anachronism of the whole system had to be exposed. The government response was to order the ETSAB to close its doors. The streets filled with demonstrations that were repressed by shots or blows, teaching was reduced to compulsory exams, and many students were jailed. In studio projects, design became distinctly secondary to the performance organized around it. Often these performances took on the air of a Dadaist exercise, where a reading of Herbert Marcuse's political texts might alternate with those of an imperialist by the name of Frank Lloyd Wright.

That same year, Manuel de Solà-Morales set up the LUB (Laboratori d'Urbanisme de Barcelona). He was joined in this initiative by recent graduates, all of them more or less left-wing, including Antonio Font, Miquel Domingo, and Joan Busquets. In 1971 Rafael Moneo was appointed to teach the first course on composition. In the program he devised, analysis, history, and culture preceded the action of designing a project. Culture, criticism, and history were considered necessary bases for the production of architecture, while the relevance and centrality of studio projects was reduced. Students were invited to reflect on a significant building and then intervene within it. There was no criticism without knowledge, and no creativity without criticism.[2]

In a similar way, but more problematically, Ignasi de Solà-Morales took over the second course of composition. The traditional focus of the course was abandoned: rather than teaching classical orders and regulating lines, the emphasis shifted to interwar workers' housing in Europe. Again, culture,

criticism, and history were considered paramount while the "project" (in the sense introduced at the IUAV by Massimo Cacciari) became secondary. The teaching of Moneo and Solà-Morales would permeate beyond the school, reaching into the profession and the academic authorities of the state.[3]

Moneo's presence attracted young teachers who would go on to have outstanding careers, both professionally and academically (Albert Viaplana, Elias Torres, José M. Torres, Helio Piñón, Xavier Pouplana, Josep Llinàs). They were the ones to restructure the design studios—the last element of the program to be reformed at the ETSAB. Moneo also encouraged the new professors of urbanism (Josep Quetglas, Miquel Roa, Manuel de Torres Capell) to transmit and develop the thinking of Aldo Rossi and Manfredo Tafuri, among others. Many of the radical Italian texts were translated into Spanish by members of this group, and Rossi, Tafuri, and others from the Venice school were often invited to Barcelona to give lectures. This Italian–Spanish exchange was very well received at that time of reform and renewal, with the death of the dictator—and a new future—in sight.

In the nine years between 1966 and 1975, architectural composition, urbanism, and the history of architecture acquired the status of key subjects.

Before even picking up their pencils, students analyzed architecture and the city. And all this happened while Franco was still in power. It was all achieved thanks to the unrelenting struggle of students and teachers in those difficult times, keeping their eyes fixed on the end of the dictatorship.

∧ Roundtable with Manfredo Tafuri, José Muntañola, Pep Bonet, and Josep Quetglas, ETSAB, February 1983. Photograph by Manuel de Solà-Morales.

> Student assembly, Paranimf Hall, University of Barcelona, 1966. Photographer unknown.

1. For a timeline and evaluation of the resistance against Francoism in the university see https://vientosur.info/spip.php?article569.
2. Moneo's lessons have been collected in *Lessons from Barcelona 1971–1976. Rafael Moneo: A Way to Teach Architecture,* ed. Carolina B. García and Enrique Granell (Barcelona: ETSAB, 2017).
3. These shifts were recorded in the magazine *Cuadernos de Arquitectura y Urbanismo,* the journal of the Colegio de Arquitectos de Cataluña y Baleares, when it was under the editorship of Emili Donato. A section dedicated to "News from the ETSAB," edited by Josep Quetglas and Manuel de Torres, among others, was included in the magazine and served as a bridge between professional and academic interests.

LIFE, IN THEORY

Esther Choi

Protagonists Diana Agrest (1945–),
Mario Gandelsonas (1938–), Peter Eisenman (1932–),
Michael Graves (1934–2015), Kenneth Frampton
(1930–), Anthony Vidler (1941–)
Institution Institute for Architecture
and Urban Studies (IAUS)
Location New York, NY, USA
Dates 1967–1984

The Institute for Architecture and Urban Studies
(IAUS) was imagined by Peter Eisenman as a "halfway
house between a school and office": a space to
develop research and educational material pertaining
to the history, iconography, design, and function of
the public environment.[1] Intended to operate as an
alternative to the architectural education in North
American universities, the IAUS's aims were flexible
and open-ended. Its revolving cast of faculty, visiting
fellows, and students sought to encourage pedagogical experimentation and the constant exchange
of ideas.[2]

For Eisenman, the IAUS's status outside the
academy gave it an advantage in tackling real-world
problems. "The academic environment as it is
presently constituted is not particularly suited to
the introduction of real conditions and practical
constraints which are ultimately a part of the
actual design process," he declared.[3] In his view, the
sequestration of architecture schools from social
institutions and public concerns reflected a wider
divide between theory and practice within the
discourse and profession of architecture. "Ultimately
there is a value in theoretical projections on actual
situations," he suggested, "but [there is] probably a
need to structure this energy in the context of the

urban environment so that the learning process and
the evaluation and the administration of the environment could be part of the same experience."[4] The
IAUS aspired to bridge this impasse between practice
and theory by providing a thinktank educational model
embedded in an urban context.

Yet, within a span of a decade, the IAUS would
be known primarily as an influential hub for the
production of architectural theory, notwithstanding Eisenman's claims that it was better
equipped than academic institutions to address
the everyday problems of the city. Moreover, the
theoretical project advanced by the IAUS focused
nearly exclusively on developing a way of speaking
about the cultural significance of architecture that
was divorced from pragmatic problem-solving—and
unapologetically so. Both formalist preoccupations
and linguistic processes were deployed in the IAUS's
attempt to retether architectural activity to the
legacy of the avantgarde.

There were a number of factors that fueled this
shift. Despite its self-characterization as an educational alternative, the IAUS relied heavily on the
resources of neighboring educational institutions,
where a number of the faculty were also employed. In
1974, one year after the launch of its seminal journal
Oppositions, the IAUS established an undergraduate
program in association with five American colleges.
Aiming to function as an academic research institute,
similar to other affiliate research institutes, the
IAUS's partnership structure enabled students from
Cornell University, Cooper Union, Massachusetts
Institute of Technology, Rice University, Yale
University, and Princeton University to undertake
research assistantships for the IAUS's endeavors.
Graduate students attended seminars led by IAUS
members and regularly conducted "field work" as
part of their course requirements.[5]

Support provided by Princeton University, in
particular, enabled faculty members shared between
both institutions to advance the project of developing a theoretical language specific to architectural
production. As young faculty, Peter Eisenman, Michael
Graves, Kenneth Frampton, and Anthony Vidler
were eager to explore architectural education as an
epistemological endeavor. With the arrival of Robert
Geddes as dean in 1965, a proliferation of new courses
signaled the recognition of architecture as a division
of the humanities, rather than a technical pursuit. By
1967, the same year the IAUS opened, architectural
history and theory appeared in the Princeton curriculum. Architectural criticism was the focus of Vidler's

Values, Concepts, and Methods course (ARC 301). Lectures offered by Frampton explored historical examples of architecture as extensions of European political expression, with a reading list ranging from Marxism and Soviet urbanism to utopianism. In the Analysis and Theory seminar (ARC 519/520), theory was viewed through a historical lens that extended from architect-theorists such as Viollet-le-Duc or Joseph Paxton to the contemporary work of Reyner Banham. By 1968 a new, emergent attitude to cultural theory and production became evident when modernism was referred to as a historical phenomenon in the Princeton curriculum.

Yet the heavy emphasis on theory was not merely a reaction to tradition. The IAUS members' desire to develop a theoretical language to interpret architecture's meaning was also fueled by cultural theory. The arrival of Diana Agrest and Mario Gandelsonas at the IAUS in the early 1970s encouraged a fervor for French structuralism, semiotics, and Marxist perspectives, further evinced through the IAUS's journal, *Oppositions*.[6] At the same time, Agrest's academic appointment as the first female instructor at Princeton's school of architecture provided further opportunities to explore these ideas. Her Values,

Concepts, and Methods course, for instance, featured the subtitle "A semiotic approach to architecture."[7]

In April 1974, a conference organized by Agrest explicitly brought together practitioners, historians, and critics to address the status of architectural theory. The event, "Practice, Theory, and Politics in Architecture," was Manfredo Tafuri's first speaking engagement in the US, and he gave a paper, "L'Architecture dans le Boudoir," that addressed the problematic division between architecture, as a self-contained universe of aesthetic meaning-making, and its responsibility to acknowledge its own relations of production.[8] The drive to "free" architecture from the real—to turn it into an autonomous system of signs and formalist procedures—reduced reality to a world of abstractions devoid of economic and social contexts. The responsibility of architectural criticism, in turn, would be "to begin from within the work only to break out of it as quickly as possible in order not to remain caught in the vicious circle of a language that speaks only of itself, in order to not participate guiltily in the 'infinite entertainment' that it promises."[9]

If, as François Cusset argues, the isolation of the university system in the twentieth century caused intellectual debates to become divorced

< "On Theory" confer-
ence with Manfredo
Tafuri, part of the
"Practice, Theory and
Politics in Architec-
ture" lecture series
organized by Diana
Agrest, Spring 1974.
Left to right: Diana
Agrest, Peter Eisenman,
Rodolfo Machado, Mario
Gandelsonas, Manfredo
Tafuri, Anthony Vidler.
Photographer unknown.

≪ IAUS members
as a soccer team.
Back row from left:
Joseph Rykwert, D.
Cabral de Mello, Mario
Gandelsonas, Kenneth
Frampton, J. Mandel,
G. Gale, T. Schumacher,
Stanford Anderson.
Front row: E. Cromley,
Robert Slutzky,
W. Ellis, B. Spector,
Emilio Ambasz, Peter
Eisenman, V. Caleandro,
Suzanne Frank. Photo-
graph by Dick Frank.

from the stakes of "real life," then what were the ramifications of this?[10] How might we assess the IAUS's lasting influence on how architects choose to engage with—or else ignore—real-world prob-lems today? The divide between the theoretical and the real continues to be an issue for archi-tecture, a design discipline primarily concerned with addressing practicalities. For Eisenman, the answer was not to inundate architects with abstract concepts, formal principles, or imagined circumstances as means to avoid the politics of world-making. Rather, he advocated relativizing the concept of reality altogether. During the conference "Architectural Education USA" (1971), sponsored by the Museum of Modern Art, Eisenman suggested that "rather than something being seen on a scale of more real to less real, it is rather viewed from a central focus with a dual attitude."[11] He ended his paper with a provocation: "In this condition, reality is not a state which is presumed to be known, but rather remains as a continuing potential, informing any given condition of a present awareness."[12] For Eisenman, the social inequalities of life were not givens demanding a moral response; instead, electing to ignore social ills was a blindfold that architecture could actively proffer.

< IAUS fellows and
friends, c. 1974.
Clockwise from
lower left: Bill Ellis,
Rick Wolkowitz,
Peter Eisenman,
Liz Eisenman,
Mario Gandelsonas,
Madelon Vriesendorp,
Rem Koolhaas, Julia
Bloomfield, Randall
Korman, Stuart
Wrede, Andrew
MacNair, Anthony
Vidler, Richard Meier,
Kenneth Frampton,
Diana Agrest,
Caroline Sidnam,
Jane Ellis, Suzanne
Frank, and unknown.
Photograph by
Dick Frank.

^ Anthony Vidler teaching
at Princeton University.
Photographer unknown.

1. Minutes of the Second Regular Meeting of the members and the Board of Trustees of the Institute or Architecture and Urban Studies, April 14, 1969, Box A1-1, Lot 3 061, Institute for Architecture and Urban Studies Archive, Canadian Centre for Architecture.

2. For more on the funding structure and development of the IAUS, see Lucia Allais, "The Real and the Theoretical, 1968," *Perspecta* 42 (2010): 33.

3. Peter Eisenman, Introduction to the IAUS, Undated, Box A1-14, Lot 2 0003, Institute for Architecture and Urban Studies Archive, Canadian Centre for Architecture.

4. Ibid.

5. See Kim Foerster, "Alternative Educational Programs in Architecture: The Institute for Architecture and Urban Studies," in *Explorations in Architecture,* ed. Reto Geiser (Basel: Birkhäuser, 2008), 26.

6. Joan Ockman, "Resurrecting the Avant-Garde: The History and Program of *Oppositions,*" in *Architectureproduction*, ed. Joan Ockman and Beatriz Colomina (New York: Princeton Architectural Press, 1988), 185.

7. Diana Agrest, AUP 301: Values, Concepts, Methods syllabus, 1972, Archives, Princeton University School of Architecture, Princeton, New Jersey.

8. See "Practice, Theory, and Politics in Architecture," audio recording of conference proceedings, 1974, Princeton University School of Architecture Archives. See also K. Michael Hays, introduction to Manfredo Tafuri, "L'Architecture dans le Boudoir: The Language of Criticism and the Criticism of Language," in *Architectural Theory since 1968,* ed. K. Michael Hays (Cambridge, MA: MIT Press, 1998), 147. The talk was published later that year as "L'Architecture dans le Boudoir: The Language of Criticism and the Criticism of Language," *Oppositions* 3 (1974); expanded in Manfredo Tafuri, *The Sphere and the Labyrinth*, trans. Pellegrino d'Acierno and Robert Connolly (Cambridge, MA: MIT Press, 1987).

9. Tafuri, *The Sphere and the Labyrinth*, 282.

10. François Cusset, *French Theory,* trans. Jeff Fort et al. (Minneapolis: University of Minnesota Press, 2008), 36–37.

11. In this dialectic structure, theory and praxis could coexist for Eisenman as "an environment which contains enough reality or practical experience to sustain theory, and equally where theory or obstraction [sic] could be pure enough to inform practice." Peter Eisenman, "The Education of Reality," in *Architectural Education USA: A Conference to Explore Current Alternatives*, papers presented at the Museum of Modern Art, November 12–13, 1971, 7–9.

12. Ibid., 9.

RIDING THE REFORMATIVE WAVE OF POSTMODERN THEORY

Ruo Jia

Protagonists Yungho Chang (1956–), Qian Qiang (1963–), Wang Shu (1963–), Zhang Lei (1964–), Wu Yonghui (1958–), among others
Institution School of Architecture, Nanjing Institute of Technology (NIT)
Location Nanjing, China
Dates 1977–1989

The death of Mao Zedong and the end of the Cultural Revolution in 1976 marked the beginning of far-reaching social reform in China, including a sweeping transformation of architectural practice and education. After a decade-long hiatus, the national college entry exam was reinstated in 1977. Similarly, the graduate school system was restored in 1981. The launch of Deng Xiaoping's "open door" policy in 1978, which loosened China's foreign relations and its ideological embrace of Cold War divisions, also unleashed a flood of translations of Western texts that had been censored for three decades and enabled direct intellectual exchange. Retrospectively, the 1980s would come to be known as modern China's "New Enlightenment Age."[1] The

year of 1985–1986, in particular, was seen as a climax of this "cultural fever," led in part by the first graduating class of master's students.[2]

Chinese architects and educators rode this wave of reform and cultural ecstasy. The focus of this text will be on the cohort of students at the school of architecture at Nanjing Institute of Technology (NIT) who did their BArch in 1981–1986 and MArch in 1986–1988, completing their studies before this exciting era came to an abrupt end with the Student Movement of 1989. The pedagogy of those ten years produced some of the most notable figures of the first generation of experimental architects—among them, Wang Shu [王澍], Zhang Lei [张雷], and Yungho Chang [张永和]—whose work in the late 1990s drew international attention to Chinese modern architecture.

Founded in 1927, the NIT's school of architecture was the first in China. At the beginning of the period of reform, the school was still providing a traditional Beaux-Arts architectural training,[3] but soon new ideas were introduced, often through the department's internal journal *Architectural Translation* [建筑译文], founded in 1977, as well as the student-led journal *Architecture, Student, Thinking* [建筑·学生·思索], founded in 1980. Yungho Chang contributed an article to the latter. In embracing publications as the primary means of disseminating new ideas, the NIT was in line with a wider reforming trend in Chinese architecture. A new journal, *The Architect*

> Sketch by Luo Siwei in the student journal, 1986.

< The class's performance art piece, 1986. First left in red: Jia Beisi. In white, from left to right: Ji Wenbin, Qian Qiang, Wang Shu, Fang Hai.

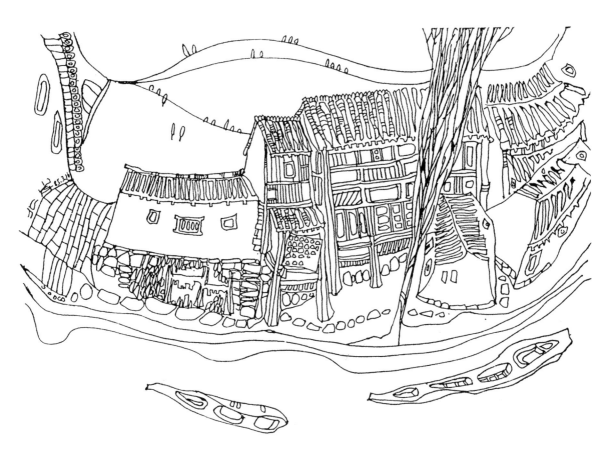

[建筑师], first published in 1979, regularly devoted one of its sections to presentations of international architectural practices and translations of major texts. Right from the start *The Architect* tuned into the foreign discourse around postmodernism. Fredric Jameson's lectures at Peking University in 1985 would make postmodern literary theory and philosophy—and especially French structuralism and poststructuralism—vital strands of the Chinese architectural debate. Deconstruction would make its entry into *The Architect* a year later.

Instead of limiting themselves to the school's curriculum, students followed their own interests, encouraged by the general cultural atmosphere. Wang Shu, perhaps the most internationally renowned student of the class of 1981, recalls: "In the late 1980s, a strong taste for critique pervaded society." For him, "It was an exciting era…coinciding with the new art and new wave of thought, everybody was grasping every opportunity to learn by themselves."[4] The peak of the cultural fever saw an intense engagement with postmodern theory. In the libraries at Nanjing in the summer of 1985 Wang encountered two works first translated into Chinese in 1980—Saussure's *Course in General Linguistics* (1916)[5] and J. M. Broekman's

Structuralism: Moscow-Prague-Paris (1974)[6]—alongside the works of Roland Barthes.[7] As he later recalled: "[the] studying situation was such that at midnight, you could see your classmate on the stairs with a book by Hegel, not returning to the dorm until 3 o'clock."[8]

The students' urge to learn outside of the official curriculum was accompanied by the stimulus of national and international exchange. Wang Tan [汪坦], the foremost Chinese architectural theorist of the time, lectured at NIT in 1983, while French art and architectural historian Hubert Damisch lectured and conducted desk critiques at the school in 1984. In 1984–1985 Wu Yonghui [吴永辉]— then a PhD student at University College London (UCL)—taught a series of courses that encouraged NIT students to ponder the connection between architectural history and theory and postmodern literary theory, film theory, and philosophy. On entering graduate school, the class initiated two student publications. The first of these, *Selected NIT SoA Student Drawings from 85 Salon* [南京工学院建筑系85沙龙画选], published in 1986 and edited by Zhang Lei and Wang Shu, presented sketches of Chinese villages (a choice not unconnected to one of the culture fever's literary movements,

"Root-Finding Literature"). The second, *Space Culture* [空间文化], founded in 1987 by Wang Shu as chief editor, along with Wang Degang [王的刚], Zhang Lei, and Qian Qiang [钱强], was an architectural theory journal centered on the students' papers for Wu Yonghui.[9] The postmodern texts introduced by Wu also inspired the "style" of some master's theses,[10] as demonstrated by Wang Shu's "Notes on the Dead House" [死屋手记] (1988).

Exposure to new theoretical debates and practices also led Chinese artists to respond quickly with their own creations of new art. Robert Rauschenberg's 1985 solo exhibition at the Chinese National Gallery of Art—China's most prestigious setting for art, conferring state approval—coincided with a general cultural phenomenon known as the 85 New Wave Movement. Performance art became widespread in China in the second half of the 1980s. Aside from Xiamen Dada—a key group in Chinese postmodern art, active 1983–1989—the "Three Step Studio" in Taiyuan presented a primitive performance piece in 1986 and expanded it into a "Village Art Activity"; students in Beijing, Shanghai, Xuzhou (Jiangsu Provence, near Nanjing) also engaged in performance art at the time.[11]

With their close connections to the Zhejiang Academy of Art (now the China Academy of Art), the NIT's architectural students did not lag behind.[12] In 1986 they created a performance art piece that simulated a primitive totem ritual. The work, initiated by Qian Qiang, was inspired by a trip to Xin Jiang (a province with a minority ethnicity).[13] Shu Wang directed the show, which ran for around ten to twenty minutes. First, three or four people (including Qian) painted primary colors (red, yellow, blue) on a huge piece of cloth at random, then Wang came in and painted totem patterns on it in Chinese ink. Finally, two people pulled up the fabric with ropes and hung it on the inner façade of the courtyard while the rest got down on their knees as part of the ritual. Because it rained, and the fabric was not absorbent, the paint all merged together and turned into a huge black painting.[14]

All these rich factors from the beginning of China's era of reform provided key foundations for the future architects' thinking and practice in the late 1990s. Two decades before, the sudden arrival in China of experimental thinking and pedagogy from around the world had produced unique effects, enhanced by one crucial complication. Many of the postmodern French intellectuals that were discussed so fervidly by the young Chinese architectural students—among them Barthes, Foucault, Lévi-Strauss, Althusser, and Derrida—had been inspired by China or had visited the country in the 1960s and 1970s. Such connections were underscored by their Chinese audiences in the late 1970s and 1980s as possible pointers for the direction of the country's social and cultural reform. As the work of China's architects in the 1990s makes clear, the new generation's experiments in a kind of self-directed pedagogy sprouted from a rich dialectical soil.

1. The 1919 May Fourth Movement and the "New Cultural Movement" that accompanied it are retrospectively framed as the first age of enlightenment in modern China.
2. A periodic tightening of cultural reception in 1983 would be followed by the "Anti-Spiritual Pollution Campaign" in the second half of the 1980s.
3. Two of the three founding faculty members, Yang Tangbao and Tong Jun, were trained at the University of Pennsylvania in the late 1910s and early 1920s, funded by the US government's share of China's indemnity after the Boxer Rebellion.
4. Wang Shu, preface to *Zao Fangzi* 造房子 [*Building House*] (Changsha: Hunan meishu chubanshe, 2016), 1.
5. As 普通语言学教程, trans. Mingkai Gao (Beijing: shangwu yinshu guan, 1980).
6. The first translation of Broekman's introduction to structuralism, reprinted and widely circulated around 1985. 结构主义: 莫斯科-布拉格-巴黎, trans. Youzheng Li (Beijing: Shangwuyinshuguan, 1980).
7. Shi Jian, Keru Feng, "王澍访谈——回复想象的中国建筑教育传统 (Interview with Wang Shu: Renew the Imagined Tradition of Chinese Architectural Education," August 4, 2006, 世界建筑*World Architecture*, vol. 5, 2012, 24–29, esp. 24.
8. Wang, "Supu wei jia," 1.
9. In an interview with the author on December 17, 2018 Jia Beisi indicated that the journal included essays by Wang Shu, Wu Yonghui, Yue Ziqing, Zhang Lei, Wang Degang; sketches by Luo Siwei and Wang Shu; and a report by the ETH-trained architect Vito Bertin on his architecture studio at NIT.
10. Zhu Jiyi, in an interview with the author, December 23, 2018.
11. Gao Minglu, "Contemporary Chinese Art Movement," in 中国当代文化意识 [*Contemporary Chinese Cultural Awareness*], ed. Gan Yang (Hong Kong: Sanlian Library, 1989), 89–90.
12. Information from author's interviews with Qian Qiang, June 4, 2018 and Wang Shu, June 1, 2018. Other performers included Jia Beisi, Ji Wenbin, Fang Hai.
13. According to Qian, in his interview with author, June 4, 2018, Shanghai.
14. According to Qian, the cloth was made of Dacron and sewn together by Fang.

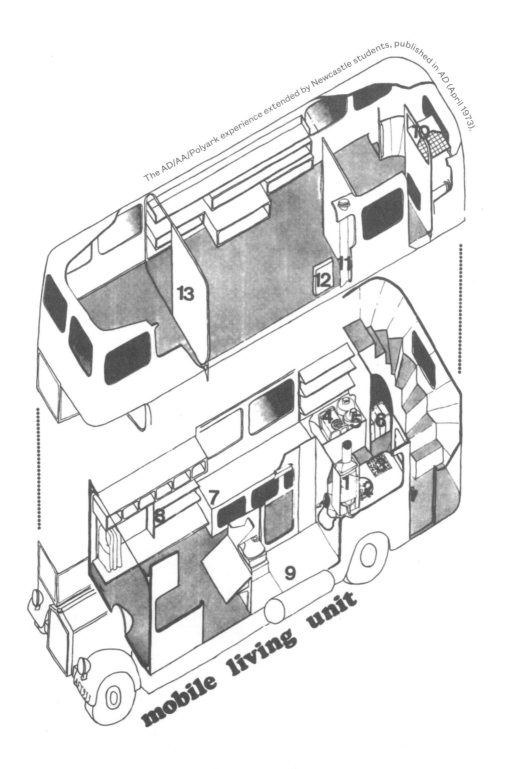

The AD/AA/Polyark experience extended by Newcastle students, published in AD (April 1973).

mobile living unit

BEYOND THE CLASSROOM

"AUTONOMY…TO JOIN LIFE, WORK, AND STUDY"

Ignacio G. Galán

Protagonists Alberto Cruz (1917–2013), Godofredo Iommi (1917–2001), Claudio Girola (1923–1994), Miguel Eyquem (1922–2021), Fabio Cruz P. (1927–2007), José Vial (1926–1983), Arturo Baeza (1927–1981), Jaime Bellalta (1922–2012), Francisco Méndez (1922–)
Institution Escuela e Instituto de Arquitectura, Pontificia Universidad Católica de Valparaíso
Location Valparaíso, Chile
Dates 1952–1973

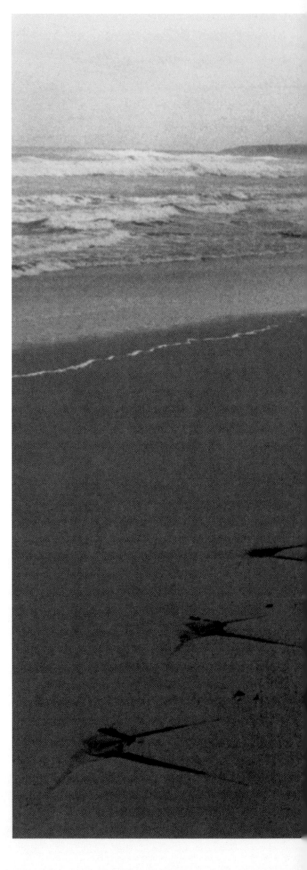

On June 15, 1967 protesting students and faculty took over the School of Architecture at the Catholic University in Valparaíso. A manifesto signed by the group made their reasons clear. For the previous fifteen years, the school had managed to sustain "a real and concrete community of life, by faculty and students fighting…to establish in American lands a place where the freedom to study and the openness to our reality…would be possible."[1] But now that community was under threat, as the university authorities attempted to stifle the pedagogical program the school had developed since the early 1950s. Led by Chilean architect Alberto Cruz and Argentinean poet Godofredo Iommi, the Valparaíso project had consistently sought to destabilize conventional university structures with pedagogical practices that obliterated the boundaries between learning, working, and living.

The origins of the project could be traced back to Cruz's courses on architectural composition at the Pontifical Catholic University in Santiago in the 1940s, which concentrated on the "plastic aspects" of architecture, developing the students' personal artistic language within an eclectic range of references drawn from the avantgardes and the teaching of the Bauhaus.[2] It was an approach that caused friction not only with traditionalist professors but also with the school's new agenda which, under the deanship of Sergio Larraín, started to prioritize the narratives of rationalism and functionalism.

This tension was resolved in 1952, when Cruz was offered a teaching position at the Catholic University in Valparaíso. There, he was able to fully develop his project, and he quickly transformed the young institution by hiring a small group of colleagues and former students.[3] The new cohort of faculty

included, among others, Iommi (with whom Cruz had already been working in Santiago) and Argentinean sculptor Claudio Girola, a former colleague of Tomás Maldonado and a member of the concrete art movement in Buenos Aires. From the outset, their activities expanded beyond the school walls: the group started living a form of communal life and collaborated with students on projects in their newly founded Institute of Architecture. For the group, the continuity between study, work, and life constituted the "erotic" character of the university—a quality not usually associated with academic institutions.[4]

This transgressive agenda was also translated into the pedagogies of the school, with students working outside the classroom to combine Cruz's earlier interest in exploring the formal qualities of architecture with a developing concern with the so-called "lived" experience of the city.[5] The city was analyzed as a set of formal relations discovered through subjective observation, with the resulting analysis informing the creation of a "spatial field" of interventions designed to enhance formal relations between different elements of the city and the territory. Projects were also increasingly influenced by concrete art, whose methods and aesthetics Girola had brought to the school. Concrete art provided a conceptual framework for the students' formal

explorations, which were characterized by a pursuit of architecture's "autonomy" as a language.[6]

The exploration of architecture as language went beyond its relation to the visual arts and unfolded in an alliance with poetry, which was seen as embodying the creative impulse characteristic of modernity.[7] Led by Iommi, this area of inquiry focused primarily on the work of modern French poets, which offered certain qualities—a destabilization of established values and openness to newness—that seemed to be lacking in both modern architecture (as it had been appropriated in Latin America) and Latin American culture. In this regard, the school's pedagogical program was also part of a reconsideration of the subcontinent's cultural project.[8] Grounding this pursuit in European sources was not seen as a contradiction: for the school's faculty, the project of modernity—especially as it was expressed in the work of the French poets—"did not have roots."[9] The school's challenge to modern architecture and its interest in the Latin American context were not conceived in opposition to modernity but, on the contrary, formed part of its pursuit of the "absolutely modern."

The School's faculty used the Institute of Architecture that they had founded to collectively develop this pursuit through a number of projects including the design of a single-family house called

Casa Cruz and the construction of churches to replace the ones destroyed in the earthquakes that shook the south of the country in 1960. While addressing specific material needs, these interventions were characterized by radical formal explorations—including of non-Euclidean geometries—and by an interest in the expressive possibilities of material and construction decisions, many times made on site during the construction process.[10]

And yet, the school's primary means of developing its engagement with language was not the architecture project, but rather the "poetic acts" in which poetry was thought to confront the world around it, its autonomous language entering into friction with the spaces and dynamics of the city. A distinctive form of poetic acts—phalènes—was formulated by Iommi and then fully developed on visits to Europe with other faculty members between 1958 and 1963. Oscillating between public recitation and collective performance, with games and celebratory garments, phalènes usually led to the production of tangible artworks. They imbued spaces and actions with unexpected qualities by generating playing fields in which forms and performances were disengaged from any ulterior goal.[11] The notion of play would become central to the school's practices, entering the curriculum in the form of the Tournaments and Culture of the Body courses. Play was thought to charge spaces with meaning and to open them to new formal possibilities and new subjectivities.[12]

The school's curriculum also increasingly incorporated different kinds of journeys called travesías (drifts or crossings), which extended the poetic appropriation of spaces across larger territories. The first of these trips, in 1965, was a pan-American journey, Amereida, that sought to participate in a symbolic and mythical new origin tale for the continent. Though abruptly interrupted by an encounter with Che Guevara's guerrillas in Bolivia, the trip gave the school an eponymous foundational poem.[13] The poetic emphasis of Amereida, conceived as an extended phalène, and the political confrontation that characterized Che Guevara's activities—each sought in its own distinct way to transform the continent.

The desire to fully develop the school's agenda brought the faculty into conflict with the university in 1967.[14] While some of their demands would resonate with the student movement that shook the world a year later, the school of architecture's leaders rejected the revolutionary political ambitions of the 1968 protests.[15] In fact, as they repeatedly put it, rather than aiming to "change the world,"

they wanted to pursue a "life change."[16] Rather than engaging with their context in sociopolitical terms, they wanted to overcome that context, with the autonomy granted by their poetic explorations allowing them to seek a different kind of productivity for architecture. To achieve this, they insisted that the school had to be autonomous from any institutionalized form of power: "It is necessary to question the existence of the university as such and, especially, as an institution."[17] Iommi argued that students were alienated by the university, estranged "as in a parenthesis" from life. Consequently, in contrast to the 1968 student protests, the school's program did not demand the substitution of one university system for another but instead "question[ed] the whole system as a way of life." This understanding led the school to pursue "a new and deep meaning of autonomy...to join life, work, and study."[18]

This anti-institutional search for autonomy would reach its full expression with the foundation of the Open City (Ciudad Abierta) in 1971. Built by students and faculty in Ritoque, the Open City occupied terrains that the faculty was able to acquire thanks to the agrarian reform of the Allende government.[19] The school's quest for a "life change" was developed through its collective construction, with the continued celebration of poetic acts, tournaments, and journeys, and through its actual inhabitation—hosting some of the school's exercises and providing housing for professors and researchers. This pursuit, originally built in response to the forms of instrumentalization characteristic of the modern world, simultaneously left architecture completely detached from its context, and the school continued to operate relatively untouched by the radical political transformations that followed in the wake of Pinochet's seizure of power in 1973.[20] And yet, for more than twenty years, the members of the school and the institute had developed in Valparaíso a radical way of teaching and inhabiting modernity.

∧ "Giro y relace," Tournaments and Culture of the Body course, Manuel Casanueva and the Valparaíso School, 1975.

< "Edros y Oides," Tournaments and Culture of the Body course, Manuel Casanueva and the Valparaíso School, 1979.

^ "Gran guante
y noctilucas,"
Tournaments
and Culture of
the Body course,
Manuel Casanueva
and the Valparaíso
School, 1978.

1. "Manifiesto del 15 de junio de 1967," facsimile available in Archivo Histórico José Vial Armstrong, 1. Also available in *Fundamentos de la Escuela de Arquitectura de la Universidad Católica de Valparaíso* (Viña del Mar: Escuela de Arquitectura, UCV, 1971).

2. See Alberto Cruz Covarrubias, "Programa del curso de composición pre-arquitectónica," *Plinto* 1 (1947).

3. See the interviews published by Alejandro Crispiani in "La escuela de Valparaíso y sus inicios: Una mirada a través de testimonios orales," *Concurso de proyectos de creación cultural y artística 2001* (Santiago: Pontificia Universidad Católica de Santiago, 2003).

4. See Iommi, quoted in Margarita Serrano, "Godofredo Iommi: La vida peligrosa," *Mundo* 105 (August 1991): 9: "The university must be erotic, if it is not erotic it ceases to be a university."

5. See Alberto Cruz, "Improvisación del Señor Alberto Cruz," presentation of the School of Valparaíso in the pavilion built for the First Conference of Latin American Faculties of Architecture in 1959, in *Desvíos de la deriva: Experiencias, travesías y morfologías* (Madrid: MNCARS, 2010), 158.

6. See G. [Godofredo Iommi], "Primera exposición de arte concreto," *La Unión de Valparaíso*, October 17, 1952. See folder "Carpeta de recopilación arte concreto (primera exposición en Chile), Archivo Histórico José Vial Amstrong. Alberto Cruz insisted on the relevance of considering the "autonomy" of architecture in an interview with the author (August 23, 2012). On the relationship with Concrete art see Alejandro Crispiani, *Objetos para Transformar el Mundo: Trayectorias del Arte Concreto-Invención, Argentina y Chile, 1940-1970. La Escuela de Arquitectura de Valparaíso y las Teorías del Diseño para la Periferia* (Santiago, Chile: Ediciones ARQ, 2011).

7. Godofredo Iommi, "Hay que ser absolutamente moderno," digital version accessible in the Archivo Histórico José Vial Armstrong, http://wiki.ead.pucv.cl/index.php/Biblioteca Con§tel (accessed September 12, 2012), 15: "Toda poiesis es construcción de lo que no se conoce sino al construirlo." Also available in *Cuatro talleres de América* (Valparaíso: Taller de Investigaciones Gráficas, Escuela de Arquitectura, UCV, 1982).

8. Godofredo Iommi et al., *Amereida* (Santiago: Editorial Cooperativa Lambda, 1967), 11.

9. *Amereida II* (Viña del Mar: Taller de Investigaciones Gráficas, Escuela de Arquitectura UCV, 1986), 168.

10. See Rodrigo Pérez de Arce and Fernando Pérez Oyarzún, *Valparaíso School: Open City Group* (Montreal: McGill-Queen's University Press, 2003).

11. See Iommi, "Hay que ser absolutamente moderno," 17, and Claudio Girola, *Reflexiones sobre la representación en las artes plásticas* (Viña del Mar: Taller de Investigaciones Gráficas, Escuela de Arquitectura UCV, 1983).

12. See Claudio Girola Iommi, *Reflexión sobre la representación en las artes plásticas* (Viña del Mar: Taller de Investigaciones Gráficas, Escuela de Arquitectura UCV, 1983). See also Rodrigo Perez del Arce, "Valparaiso Ludens," *Lotus International* 124 (June 2005):18–31 and Manuel Casanueva, *Libro de Torneos* (Valparaíso: Taller de Investigaciones Gráficas, Escuela de Arquitectura, PUCV, 2009).

13. Godofredo Iommi et al., *Amereida* (Santiago: Editorial Cooperativa Lambda, 1967).

14. "Manifiesto del 15 de junio de 1967," 3, and Statement of the Supreme Council, cited in Jaime Rosenblitt, "La reforma universitaria, 1967–73"; consulted in http://www.untechoparamipais.org/chile/cis/images/stories/CATEDRA2010/SESION5/3.pdf.

15. See Iommi, "De la reforma," *Anales de la Universidad de Chile* (Santiago: Editorial Universitaria, 1969), 61–70.

16. See Iommi, "Hay que ser absolutamente moderno," 11.

17. Iommi, "De la reforma," 3–4.

18. Ibid.

19. Alberto Cruz in an interview with the author (August 23, 2012).

20. Ana Maria León has addressed some of the contradictions of the Open City in the changing political context of its time in "Prisoners of Ritoque: The Open City and the Ritoque Concentration Camp," *Journal of Architectural Education* 66, no. 1 (2012): 84–97.

THE STUDENTS' "CONGRESS MOVEMENT"

Barnaby Bennett, Byron Kinnaird

Protagonists Alexis "Lecki" Ord,
Ian Godfrey, Graham Harler, John Byrne,
Kerry Francis, and others
Institution Australasian Architecture
Students Association (AASA) and other
student architecture organizations
Location Australia and New Zealand
Dates 1963–1971

In 1963 architecture students across Australia and New Zealand began organizing a series of large-scale gatherings—congresses, conferences, festivals, even train rides—aimed at critically questioning their education, their profession, and the organization of society as a whole. The movement continues to the present day. To date over twenty of these events have taken place, mostly at two-year intervals. Rather than being developed with consistent organizational oversight, however, the congresses have emerged organically as expressions of student energy, community sovereignty, and the urge to question authority. Together, they constitute a form of experimental self-education that is directed by the students—one that enables them to invite the voices they want to hear and to build the structures they want to inhabit.

The story of the beginnings of the so-called "congress movement" seems to depend on who is telling it—there are many different versions—but what is clear is that it flourished in the 1960s under the strong leadership of the Australasian Architecture Students Association (AASA), headed by Lecki Ord, who would go on to become the first woman Lord Mayor of Melbourne. AASA was largely run from a terrace house in Melbourne, with networks through the country.[1] Between 1963 and 1971 there was a student congress every year in one of Australia's major cities, and two further congresses in New Zealand bookended this consistent run. The organizing committee flew around the country on the cheap, thanks to a contact in the national airline Ansett, and hacked a public telephone to connect with a widespread membership.[2]

In 1966 AASA descended on Perth for its most ambitious conference, "Educreation," with a remarkable array of international guests—among them Buckminster Fuller, Cedric Price, and Team 10 members Jaap Bakema, Aldo van Eyck, and John Voelcker—assembled by its then-president, Graham Harler.[3] "Buckminster Fuller said afterwards it was the most significant and meaningful meeting of students he had seen or heard of," the AASA newsletter *INK* reported. Five hundred delegates came from as far as New Zealand, London, and Singapore and thirty architects, including William Laurie, that year's RAIA Gold Medal winner, "defected from the RAIA convention to ours during the week."[4] More than four decades later, John Byrne would reflect on how he could "still taste the magical contrast of a three-hour (at least) performance by Bucky (my memory says four) about the design of the world, technology, cities, ingenuity, creativity, spaceships, global earth…and a jewel-like one-hour lecture by Aldo van Eyck (with black and white slides), given to us with love and gentleness and insight and logic, about how to design a doorway for people."[5]

Debates on architectural education played a significant role in most congresses. The 1971 congress, held at an abandoned cement works in Warkworth, north of Auckland, set out explicitly to revolutionize the teaching of architecture, taking inspiration from countercultural movements abroad, such as the 1968 student riots in Paris and the Woodstock festival in 1969. A village of idiosyncratic temporary structures was built for the event, including sleeping quarters, toilets, a geodesic dome for meetings, and an impressive hyperbolic paraboloid structure that was spectacularly set alight on the final night of the congress. Looking back, one of the congress organizers, Kerry Francis, recalled: "We wanted an event that was intense, spontaneous, participatory, constructive, and that had a sense of community. We were interested in ideas about education and in particular the notion of the free university.

∧ The 1971 Warkworth Congress concluded in spectacular style with the ceremonial burning of an impressive hyperbolic paraboloid structure made of paper and scaffolding. Structure designed by Richard Wright. Photograph by Julian Feary.

< Cedric Price speaking at the 1968 congress in Hobart, Tasmania. Photograph by Maurice Smith, reproduced in INK, September 1968, with the caption "Seminar at Art School."

1. Barnaby Bennett and Byron Kinnaird, *Congress: Architecture Student Congresses in Australia, New Zealand and PNG from 1963–2011* (Aotearoa: Freerange Press, 2011), 6.
2. Personal communication, Lecki Ord and Ian Godfrey, 2011.
3. *The Architect WA* 9, no. 85 (1966).
4. *INK* 3, no. 1 (1969).
5. Bennett and Kinnaird, *Congress*, 8.
6. K. S. Francis, "The Dream: Being the Theory of an Architectural Congress," Ctrl Shift 07 biennial Pacific Students of Architecture Congress, video, Wellington, NZ, 2007.
7. K. S. Francis, ReCongress 2006 exhibition and symposium, Auckland, NZ.

We were interested in exploring the boundaries of the discipline of architecture, although at the time we would never have used the word discipline."[6]

Student congresses in Australasia have always looked to challenge existing power structures. The Warkworth congress, for instance, would lead to the rewriting of the syllabus of the University of Auckland's architecture school.[7] But beyond this general aim, congresses have evolved significantly over the years, responding to different issues, localities, technologies, pedagogical priorities, and institutional arrangements. There is no legal structure, name, or organizing committee that spans all of the congresses, and perhaps this is precisely what has saved them from institutional fatigue. Instead, what unites them is the extraordinary way in which each one has been a voluntary undertaking—or maybe a calling—on the part of successive generations of students who have used the congress to escape the classroom and build educational structures that respond to their own desires and concerns. This has given the congress an unlikely resilience and a radical impetus that endures in architecture student culture in Australia and New Zealand today.

AN-ARK: THE LIBERATED SUBJECT AND COASTAL CULTURE

Martin Braathen

Protagonist Svein Hatløy (1940–2015)
Institution Extra-institutional, with connections to NTH, Trondheim; Oslo School of Architecture; Warsaw Art Academy
Location Bergen, Norway
Dates 1968–1977

In 1968 Norwegian architect Svein Hatløy set up a nomadic, one-man teaching institution in Bergen. Commuting between there and Warsaw over the next decade, he brought home the gospel of Open Form expounded by his mentor and colleague, the Polish architect and teacher Oskar Hansen, and mixed it with a local, populist regionalism. In Hatløy's own account, he trained nine hundred "students" between 1968 and 1986—the year Norway's third school of architecture was established in Bergen, with Hatløy as its first rector.

Svein Hatløy's one-man school was in strict ideological opposition to Norway's two older schools of architecture in Oslo and in Trondheim. Hatløy himself had trained at Trondheim, and then studied for five years with Hansen at the Art Academy in Warsaw in order to "unlearn" his polytechnic education and relearn architecture as Open Form. Drawing on Hansen's ideology, which placed the subject, the users, at the center of architectural production, Hatløy attacked Norwegian mainstream architecture for being repressive, collectivist, and formalist—an "architecture for architecture's sake."[1] Hatløy's take on Open Form also included a measure of populist and anti-centrist leftwing politics, a specific interest in anonymous architecture, and, not least, an embrace of the specific "coastal culture" of Norway, where he found an architecture shaped by thousands of years of maritime trade and exchange, which he perceived as quite different from the privileged and canonized culture centered on inland Norway and, more specifically, the capital Oslo.

Although he designed a few buildings during his career, Hatløy's adoption of Open Form was first and foremost an educational project, with his teaching taking on several guises. In the first years, from 1968 on, he organized outdoor workshops (he called them "symposia") where practicing architects could begin to relearn architecture. The aim was to learn how to read and make visible the often-hidden forces and qualities of the landscape, from land formations to quirks of geology or climate. He also organized a symposium in Warsaw where Norwegian architects worked on a special iteration of Hansen's Linear Continuous System, with Hansen and several Polish scientists serving as expert advisers.

The architecture schools in Oslo and Trondheim both experienced severe student unrest in the late 1960s. As a result, many students started to program their own studies and temporarily left their schools.

^ First Open Form
plein air workshop in
Norway, 1968. View
toward the Sognefjord
from the study site
near Kaupanger.

Hatløy welcomed these "dropouts" in the studio courses that he taught in Bergen from 1970 on; the studios went by different names, AN-ARK (short for anti- or anarchist architecture) being one of them. A former school building now became the base for a more systematic teaching of Open Form. Again, Hatløy focused on understanding the interplay between culture, landscape, and architecture, and integrated studies of anonymous architecture, excursions to islands and mountainous settlements, and other beginnings of a regionalist architectural approach.

1970 was also the year when Hatløy published a manifesto for Open Form in a guest-edited issue of *Byggekunst,* the Norwegian review of architecture.[2] Introducing the manifesto, *Byggekunst's* editor, Christian Norberg-Schulz, alerted readers to its subversive message—a harsh attack on Norwegian mainstream architecture, aligning it with fascism and suppressive political regimes. Alongside the manifesto, Hatløy provided extensive documentation of Open Form teaching in Poland and in the Norwegian symposia. The special issue launched Hatløy's career as a self-proclaimed radical outsider on the Norwegian scene,[3] and he would continue to use magazines as vehicles for propagating Open Form throughout the 1970s. He commandeered the magazine of the local architecture association, *BAF-nytt,* as both editor and active contributor, and made it a forum for presenting and discussing Open Form and student projects. Other people around him, including his close colleague and coeditor Bertram Brochmann, as well as several of his students, contributed projects and texts in which they tried to come to terms with the concept of Open Form, and also openly challenged it in lively debates.

Understanding Hatløy's endeavor as a "one-man school" does not mean that he was alone. And yet, while others—architects, philosophers, meteorologists, social scientists—were invited into the project, he remained the indisputable ideological center. In the late 1970s he invited some of his students to join him in a teaching-based practice called Gult Felt (Yellow Field)—and in 1986 the teaching project was formally institutionalized as Norway's third school of architecture—and the world's first school of Open Form. With Hatløy as its first rector, and important supporters like the British educator Michael Lloyd, the curriculum of Bergen Arkitekt Skole (BAS) had effectively been two decades in the making, developing through the various teaching experiments in Hatløy's "school under an open sky."

Despite its new institutional status, BAS maintained its opposition to—or even negation of—other schools in Norway, calling itself "the alternative."[4] Led by Hatløy until 2007, the school kept Open Form as its official ideology, integrating elements from the early years into its teaching structures. For instance, all new students were taken out to an island for the first weeks of their studies, so they could build 1:1 in the landscape and learn to live and experience the conditions along the coast. And regular seminars, known in the school as "Oskar Hansen symposia," featured local philosophers, artists, and architects, as well as international figures such as Lucien Kroll. In the last years of his life Hatløy traveled extensively to China to establish new schools of Open Form. At home, the Bergen school of architecture toned down its earlier oppositional rhetoric—without neglecting its roots in Open Form.

< Workshop participants in front of a landscape study, Kaupanger, Norway 1968.

1. See for instance Svein Hatløy's editorial, "Ting og tolkning" [Things and Interpretation], *Byggekunst*, no. 3 (1970): 3.
2. Ibid.
3. He even established a very specific language, using Norway's second written language, called "New Norwegian," which was constructed from diverse dialects in the late 1800s.
4. A publication on the school's history was called the "BAS alternative." See Hatløy et al., *BAS-alternative* (Bergen: Bergen arkitekt skole, 1999).

SIAL'S ŠKOLKA: AN ARCHITECTURAL KINDERGARTEN

Ana Miljački

Protagonists Miroslav Masák (1932–), Mirko Baum (1944–), John Eisler (1946–), Helena Jiskrová (1943–), Milan Körner (1944–), Václav Králíček (1945–), Emil Přikryl (1945–), Martin Rajniš (1944–), Jiří Suchomel (1944–), Jiří Špikla (1943–2017), Stanislav Švec, Miroslav Tůma (1944–), Petr Vaďura (1945–1974), Dalibor Vokáč (1943–2018), Dana Zámenčíková (1945–), Zdeněk Zavřel (1943–), and in limited ways, Tomáš Bezpalec (1952–), Michal Brix (1946–), Karel Doubner (1951–)
Institution Sdružení inženýrů a architektů v Liberci (SIAL) (Liberec Association of Engineers and Architects)
Location Radčice, Czechoslovakia
Dates 1969–1982

Architecture and construction were among the first sectors to be nationalized after the Communist Party came to power in Czechoslovakia in 1948. From that point on, all practicing architects were absorbed into a state-run system of Stavoprojekt offices. Although the terms of their specific operation and regional jurisdiction were adjusted a few times in the following era, they continued to be industrially minded and socialist in their economic organization well into the late 1980s. As the restructuring of the immediate postwar years began to fade from the collective memory, the period from the mid-1960s on was increasingly characterized by experimentation in all spheres of Czechoslovak culture and political thought. A key manifestation of this in architecture was the establishment of bottom-up organizations. In the very north of the country, Stavoprojekt's regional office in Liberec spawned a number of offshoots with the help of the city's mayor. In 1965 the Czech architect Karel Hubáček opened Studio S12, dedicated to the construction of the futuristic Ještěd telecommunications tower.[1] S12 would expand in 1968 to become the Liberec collective of engineers and architects, SIAL (Sdružení inženýrů a architektů Liberce), which in turn supported a pedagogical experiment, Školka (Kindergarten). A playful and productive work environment, Školka would make significant contributions to Czech architecture.

The roots of Školka can be traced back to a request from Helena Jiskrová, a young architecture student from Prague, for a summer internship in the Stavoprojekt office at Liberec. Miroslav Masák, one of the key architects in the office, managed to negotiate a yearly stipend from the mayor to support two interns. SIAL had just been set up, and Masák reckoned that the stipend would allow them to take on a few more interns, who could form something like the SIAL junior team.[2] Jiskrová spread the word around her fellow students at the Czechoslovak Technical University in Prague (ČVUT), and before long a dozen new graduates were seeking participation in this "incubator."[3] An abandoned inn on Jedlová was renovated to serve as both their studio and their home. Located in the village of Radčice, on the bucolic outskirts of Liberec, the studio was both literally and figuratively a space on the periphery of the system, removed from the main Stavoprojekt atelier in an office building in the center of town.

An alternative set of values and behaviors was cultivated in the Školka studio. On a fine day the inhabitants could see the Ještěd tower soaring over the surrounding volcanic landscape from their individual (work-live) rooms, while their doors opened onto the communal studio space, conference room,

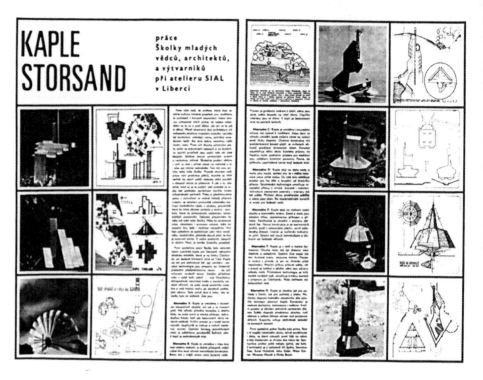

> Designs by Školka members and their mentors for the Storsand Chapel competition, presented in the magazine *Československý architect*; 1969.

< Jedlová Studio, home of SIAL Školka from 1968 to 1982, c. 1970.

kitchen, and bathroom. The young architects spent many of their days and nights together at the studio drafting, playing ping-pong, and dancing. Hubáček and Masák hoped that ambitious and talented young architecture graduates with fresh ideas would help the studio win competitions, as they learned the craft while competing with each other for small commissions and for their mentors' attention. For the first four years of its existence, Školka was supported by the SIAL independent studio. But in the early 1970s, in the aftermath of the summer of 1968 events in Prague, when Warsaw Pact troops crushed Czechoslovakia's brief attempt at liberalization, Stavoprojekt was restructured and SIAL folded back into the state-run system. Against all odds, Hubáček and Masák managed to keep Školka operating for nearly fourteen more years on the spatial and organizational fringes of the Stavoprojekt system. Over those years, the studio was visited by a variety of artists and actors, friends of the young architects, and even Václav Havel, a close friend of Masák.[4]

Masák had imagined Školka as a pedagogical project that would benefit its "mother studio" culturally and, eventually, economically. He had anticipated its pedagogical methods evolving to meet the general needs of the profession, but at the same time he thought it was essential for it to "offer a certain freedom for ideas and work, a space and time for the

total understanding of problems, and most importantly to allow play."[5] Play was "the condition of creation" at Školka. The live-work studio on Jedlová internalized the discourses of both the Czech prewar and the 1960s international avant-garde, while the studio-wide competitions internalized elements of market competition. Motivation for excellence of architectural production was thus internally self-sustained and ran parallel to the official conditions of practice and discourse. Školka's invention of internal competitions outside of the realm of architectural commissions, its involvement in the life of the local community, especially through its design of the annual Liberec fair buildings, and its vital and playful exchange of ideas—all suggest reasons why its operation extended well into the post-1968 era of normalization.

Over the years, participants in Školka took on more central roles in the Liberec Stavoprojekt office. While some emigrated, many would go on to become the Czech Republic's most important architectural educators and practitioners. Masák dated the end of Školka to the literal loss of its space in 1982. Without the studio on Jedlová, much of the atmosphere that defined and embodied Školka was also lost.

1. The most exhaustive collection of essays on SIAL and Školka was produced on the occasion of the SIAL exhibit at the Olomouc Museum of Art in 2010. The catalogue has been reprinted in English. See *SIAL. Liberec Association of Architects and Engineers, 1985–1990: Czech Architecture Against the Stream,* ed. Rostislav Švácha (Prague: Arbor Vitae and Olomouc Museum of Art, 2012). Also important earlier publications: *Architekti SIAL,* ed. Miroslav Masák (Prague: Kant, 2008); Miroslav Masák, *Tak Nějak To Bylo* (Prague: Kant Publishers, 2006); *Mašinistí / Machinists* ed. Miroslav Masák (Prague: Galerie Jaroslava Fragnera, 1996). My own previous research on this work: Ana Miljački, "Na cestě k utopii. Příběh SIALu v obraze a manifestu," in *Architekti SIAL*, 18–25; and *The Optimum Imperative: Czech Architecture for The Socialist Lifestyle, 1938–1968* (Abingdon-New York: Routledge, 2017).

2. This information was relayed to me in a series of conversations with Miroslav Masák from 2004 through 2006, structured through specific questions. The details about the beginning and end of SIAL and Školka are otherwise hard to trace in the literature about them.

3. The list of young architects who worked at Jedlová was presented in the 1982 Czech-Hungarian publication of SIAL's work. The following architects worked in some capacity under the leadership of Miroslav Masák: Mirko Baum, Tomáš Bezpalec, Michal Brix, Karel Doubner, John Eisler, Petr Jakl, Jiří Jauris, Helena Jiskrová, Václav Králiček, Milan Körner, Tomáš Novotný, Josef Patrný, Emil Přikryl, Martin Rajniš, Jiří Suchomel, Jaromir Syrovátko, Jiří Špikla, Stanislav Švec, Miroslav Tůma, Petr Vad'ura, Dalibor Vokáč, Dana Zámenčíková, Zdeněk Zavřel. See *Atelier SIAL* (Budapest: BME Kisz, 1982).

4. Masák claimed that Havel came to visit the Školka studio about three times, thus perhaps not directly influencing the architects who worked there. Masák became Havel's chief advisor on cultural matters and a member of the collegium of the president in 1990. "Masák Master of Arts," interview between Miroslav Masák and Vladimír Šlapeta, *Architects' Journal* 193, no. 10 (March 6, 1991): 50–51.

5. Miroslav Masák, "Námět činnosti 'školky' architektů při SIAL," September 10, 1969, 1, in Miroslav Masák's personal archive.

v Jedlová Studio, the home of SIAL Školka from 1968–1982, c. 1970.

LESSONS FROM RESURRECTION CITY

Mabel O. Wilson

Protagonists John Wiebenson (1935–2003),
Kenneth Jadin (1943–), Tunney Lee (1931–2020),
James Goodell (1941–2014), Anthony Henry
Institutions Poor People's Campaign
and the Structures Committee
Location Washington, DC, USA
Date 1968

Groups of volunteers hoisted four-by-eight-foot panels of plywood and nailed them to an A-frame structure made from two-by-fours. The outcome of their efforts, a plywood tent twenty feet long and eight feet wide, was a test module for a temporary housing structure large enough to shelter a family. A prototype for a smaller module that provided a dormitory for five to six people was also constructed. The various modules could be combined to form compounds housing fifty people, whose daily needs were supported by ancillary amenities such as showers and portable toilets. To facilitate communications and governance in this self-build experiment, the organizers planned that four compounds would make up a civic group headed by an area leader, who would have his/her own living module. Scaling up further, the compounds, arranged in U-shaped clusters, would be distributed on either side of "Main Street," a spine of shared facilities for social and political engagement for the entire encampment. These were the essential elements of Resurrection City, which would function as the base camp for the Poor People's Campaign. For six weeks in late spring 1968, its prefabricated plywood tent structures would house the three thousand civil rights campaigners who descended on Washington, DC. Installed in the nation's symbolic core—south of the Reflecting Pool and the Lincoln Memorial on the National Mall—the temporary city would be built and inhabited by poor people seeking the restoration of their dignity, livelihoods, and housing. Both in its location and its duration, it would bring home more effectively than any single protest march the intractability of poverty in America and the myriad of ways it was underpinned by racism.

Architect and planner John Wiebenson and his collaborators designed the encampment with the express mission to "make the poor 'visible' by bringing representatives to Washington where, during the life of the City, they would be seen by Congressmen and, via the press and TV, by the rest of the country."[1] For them, it was a way to honor the humanitarian appeal of the visionary behind the Poor People's Campaign, Rev. Martin Luther King, Jr., who had been murdered by a white assassin on April 5, 1968, the month before the planned start of the event. The goal of the campaign was to vastly improve the lives of all poor Americans, not just Black Americans. Thus, Resurrection City—whose inhabitants represented a multiracial cross section of America's poor (although the majority were Black Americans)—was conceived to teach the nation about poverty. But could this experiment in prefabricated construction and rapidly deployed urban design also provide a lesson on the future of equitable cities?

Wiebenson—a young white professor who had recently contributed to the formation of the school of architecture at the University of Maryland—spearheaded a small group of planners and urban designers. His dedicated collaborators included Kenneth Jadin, a white architecture professor at a local historically Black university, Howard University;

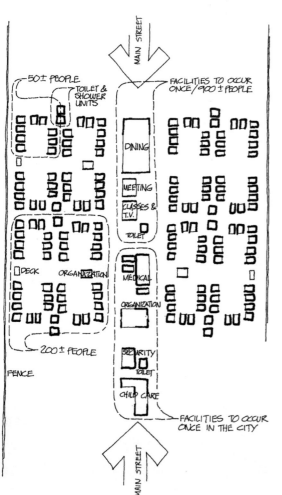

Tunney Lee, a Chinese planner and architect based in Washington, DC, who would later join MIT's planning faculty; and James Goodell, a white architect and planner working at the time for Urban America Inc., a nonprofit headed by architects, planners, bankers, and developers dedicated to urban improvement. They formed the "Structures Committee," a group of educators committed to social change, who worked directly with Anthony Henry, a Chicago-based Black sociologist charged with overseeing the construction of Resurrection City for its sponsor, the Southern Christian Leadership Conference (SCLC).[2] As characterized in a Poor People's Campaign flyer, their task was to provide housing for "several thousand poor people [who] will go to Washington. We will be young and old, jobless fathers, welfare mothers, farmers, and laborers. We are Negroes, American Indians, Puerto Ricans, Mexican Americans, poor white people."[3]

With only a few months to design and implement their ideas, Wiebenson and his collaborators faced several design challenges and constraints. A primary need was to identify affordable materials that could be used strategically. And while affordability was paramount, the structures also needed to be sturdy enough to be occupied by individuals and families for several weeks. Adaptability was another key criterion. Some modules had to accommodate other functions besides inhabitation, including group meetings of various sizes, medical care, food preparation, childcare, education, and a host of impromptu activities.

The designers adapted the psycho-spatial research of planners like Kevin Lynch to anticipate the marchers' behavioral patterns. They prepared diagrams studying communication networks to map how officials, group association leaders, and providers of security and maintenance would coordinate gatherings, medical care, and waste removal. Overall, their approach was functionalist, drawing on their education in architecture and planning programs in schools like the University of Pennsylvania.[4] In other respects, however, they went against their training, which had promoted large-scale modernist urban design projects like the one in Southwest Washington, DC, where the city's Redevelopment Land Agency had overseen the demolition of poor Black neighborhoods to make way for modernist mid- and high-rises housing mostly white middle-class residents. Unlike those projects, Resurrection City was not supervised from above by technocrats, but developed together with the inhabitants, who became agents

^ Resurrection City in the mud, Washington DC, 1968.

< Aerial view of Resurrection City, Washington DC, 1968.

≪ Schematic diagram of Resurrection City, John Wiebenson.

in their own self-help experiment. For the architects and planners involved, direct participation in communities facing social upheaval and urban insecurities replaced the professionalism characteristic of mid-century high modernism.[5]

The Structures Committee brainstormed designs by shifting their research to local universities and engaging in pedagogical experiments. For example, they initiated a design sketch problem with architecture students at Howard University. To test construction methods, materials, and durability, prototypes of some of these designs were developed at full scale in Maryland.[6] Of the various proposals, an A-frame tentlike structure proved to be the most expedient and efficient. However, their ideal plans bumped up against real-life limitations as well as the reality of how systems of racial capitalism deny resources at the same time as they exploit. They had anticipated the donation of construction materials—all they got was a delivery of three hundred gallons of paint.[7] But many people, including students, did volunteer their time and labor, helping to prefabricate parts in Maryland and to assemble the shelters on the National Mall.

On May 13, Rev. Ralph Abernathy, who had taken over the SLCL leadership of the Poor People's Campaign after King's untimely death, drove the first stake into the ground on the designated site south of the Reflecting Pool. Volunteers quickly learned the construction system and efficiently assembled the prefabricated components. The overall organizational grid—a logic adapted from military encampments—was maintained in setting up the shelters, though not all the tents were ready for the first week of the camp, when people arrived from all parts of the United States by whatever means necessary: bus, train, foot, mule train, car caravans.[8] However, the units were arranged in various configurations, departing from the proposed U-shaped template for compounds.[9] The imagined scaled organization of political governance of the various compounds and the larger city failed to materialize, in some ways a casualty of the SCLC's paternalistic top-down organization.[10] The open invitation to participate also meant that more radical groups like Black nationalists brought their confrontational agenda to the discussion. Security proved a challenge, even though the entire compound was surrounded by a chain-link fence—making it an enclave that was neither ghetto nor suburb. The vibrant but often chaotic life of the community was somewhat dampened by weeks of incessant rain, which turned the Mall's lawn into a brown stew that made it difficult to move between the various parts of the settlement. Despite this, many looked forward to Solidarity Day, scheduled for June 19, or Juneteenth, which commemorated the day that enslaved peoples learned of their emancipation in 1865. That day, fifty thousand people rallied at the encampment to join marches to the Capitol demanding funds for better education, social services, employment, and housing.

The backlash to the boldness of the occupation and the persistence of the campaign's agenda for the poor came soon after. On June 24, when the permit of occupation expired after forty-two days, more than one thousand police officers descended on the encampment to remove the residents by force. Those who attempted to remain in the camp were arrested.

Resurrection City certainly gave the issue of poverty a nationwide focus. But its effectiveness as an experiment in self-governance and collective living was harder to gauge. The manner in which people took possession of the modules by transforming arrangements, modifying details, and painting them, was a central part of the self-help ethos the designers hoped to foster. But in a published assessment of their experiment Wiebenson reflected on how an "inability to develop participatory government; inability to encourage growth of group structures among the disorganized; inability to develop rapid response and followthrough to changing needs" had created patterns of spatial territorialization associated with private ownership.[11] From the perspective of the Structures Committee, Resurrection City had "become a demonstration model of the current American community" rather than a model for a future one. One critique that can be made relates to how their self-help solution to housing the poor—beginning with the task of assembling your own unit—was in the tradition of the good old-fashioned "pull yourself up by your bootstraps" liberalism espoused by Booker T. Washington, which had quelled the ambitions to equality of newly emancipated slaves, much to the delight of white Southerners and Northerners.

In the same month that the encampment was cleared, the executive director of the Urban League, Whitney M. Young, Jr., chastised the architecture and planning professions in a speech delivered to the American Institute of Architects (AIA) convention: "When you go to a city—Champaign-Urbana, the University of Illinois is about the only major

institution and within two or three blocks are some of the worse [sic] slums I have seen in the country. It is amazing how within a stone's throw of the School of Architecture you have absolutely complete indifference—unless you have a federal grant for research, and even then it's to study the problem."[12] In many ways, the heuristic agenda of Resurrection City's architectural program sought to address this indifference and restore agency to the poor in determining housing choices. However, self-help without a systemic recalibration of racial inequities meant that what the housing prototypes restored were the already existing sociospatial relations of private property, rather than new forms of community by design.

^ Rev. Ralph Abernathy and two volunteers inside a plywood tent, Resurrection City, Washington DC, 1968.

1. John Wiebenson, "Planning and Using Resurrection City," *Journal of the American Institution of Planners* 35, no. 6 (November 1969): 405.
2. Ibid., 406.
3. Southern Christian Leadership Conference, *The Poor People's Campaign* (Atlanta, 1967). See http://www.crmvet. org/docs/68_sclc_ppc_brochure.pdf. Accessed June 17, 2016.
4. Tunney Lee and Lawrence Vale, "Resurrection City: Washington D.C. 1968," *Thresholds*, no. 41 (Spring 2013): 114. https://www.mitpressjournals.org/doi/ pdf/10.1162/thld_a_00100

5. Citing the head of MIT's School of Architecture and Planning, where Tunney Lee would become faculty in 1970, Felicity Scott observes that the school, like many educational institutions of design and planning, "moved away from 'old-style professionalism' toward the 'catharsis' of direct interaction with people in their environment." Felicity Scott, *Outlaw Territories: Environments of Insecurity/ Architectures of Counterinsurgency* (Cambridge, MA: MIT Press, 2016), 341.
6. Wiebenson, "Planning and Using Resurrection City," 407; Lee and Vale, "Resurrection City," 117.
7. Wiebenson, "Planning and Using Resurrection City," 406.
8. Gordon K. Mantler, *Power to the Poor: Black-Brown Coalition and the Fight for Economic Justice, 1960–1974* (Chapel Hill: University of North Carolina Press Scholarship Online), 137.
9. Ibid., 407. Seven hundred people were accommodated in the first round of tents, but at least eight hundred had to stay elsewhere until their tents were ready.
10. Ibid., 3.
11. Wiebenson, "Planning and Using Resurrection City," 411.
12. Whitney M. Young, "Full Remarks of Whitney M. Young Jr. AIA Convention in Portland, Oregon, June 1968," http://content.aia. org/sites/default/files/2018-04/ WhitneyYoungJr_1968AIAContention_ FulLSpeech.pdf

ARCHITECTURE AS "APPLIED ANTHROPOLOGY"

Vladimir Kulić

Protagonist Bogdan Bogdanović (1922–2010)
Institution Faculty of Architecture,
University of Belgrade
Location Belgrade, Yugoslavia
Dates 1970–1973, 1976–1982

The Yugoslav architect, writer, educator, and politician Bogdan Bogdanović was the charismatic leader of a series of radical pedagogical experiments that helped reshape the architecture curriculum at the University of Belgrade in the 1970s. One of socialist Yugoslavia's most celebrated architects, Bogdanović was best known for his innovative war memorials and for his influential writings on the history of the city. However, he also pursued a much broader agenda: a lifelong surrealist and heterodox communist, he opposed the instrumental rationality that governed postwar modernization under the socialist state, and especially modernist urban planning. As an influential public intellectual and educator, Bogdanović used his considerable authority to sensitize both his students and a wider audience to the cultural and affective bonds between cities and their inhabitants, which he considered the precondition for a meaningful urban life. That larger project also informed his pedagogical experiments, which

opened architecture to a wide variety of disciplinary perspectives, not least to those of anthropology, ethnography, and psychology. These experiments were radical both in method and goal: they dismantled the traditional relationships between teacher and student, and they eventually moved the pedagogical process from the classroom to the countryside, in turn seeking to reconnect architecture to its *radix*—its roots in nature and the archaic depths of human culture.

Bogdanović's pedagogical initiatives came on the heels of the 1968 student revolts. At the University of Belgrade, one of the movement's hotspots in Yugoslavia, students protested against the perceived betrayal of socialism by the new socialist elite, demanding further economic and political democratization. Though the revolt ended in an impasse, it opened the way for a liberalization of the academic system that allowed greater autonomy of the curriculum and included students in the decision-making process. With the support of students, Bogdanović was elected dean of the Faculty of Architecture in Belgrade in 1970, soon after returning from a year-long stay in the United States. The wide-ranging curriculum reform that he led during his brief deanship was undoubtedly informed by the recent push at American architecture schools to dissolve the disciplinary autonomy in the broader field of environmental design (one of his stops in the US was UC Berkeley).

The resulting "New School" in Belgrade replaced the traditional professional education with an

<> Rural School students performing *City of the Rabut Valley* at BITEF (Belgrade International Theater Festival), September 1980.

approach based on research, teamwork, and interdisciplinary collaboration, especially with social sciences and the humanities.[1] In contrast to the ossified old curriculum, the New School introduced a wide variety of elective courses, allowing students to direct their education according to their own interests. Urbanism gained much greater prominence than before, as did the humanities. Interdisciplinarity was encouraged by focusing studies around broad themes that could be explored from many different angles, rather than by learning specific disciplinary methods. The existing classroom space was also thoroughly reorganized through division into "boxes" containing permanent working spaces for groups of ten to fifteen students, who were expected to collaborate under the supervision of a designated faculty member.

Even though it self-consciously resonated with broader international currents of the era, the New School was steeped in the specific conditions of Yugoslav self-managing socialism, which sought to involve the broadest segments of the population in political decision-making. The traditional academic hierarchies between professors and students were to be dissolved in favor of collaboration in the true spirit of self-management. Even the way in which the reform was conceptualized reflected such an ambition: the body in charge of it was named the "Tripartite Committee" as it comprised the representatives of faculty, students, and practicing architects. In order to make the process as transparent as possible, the committee published regular bulletins documenting

their activities.[2] The entire project was widely publicized across Yugoslavia and met with enthusiastic media attention. And while it did not oppose the existing political system, the reform took its proclaimed values seriously—perhaps too seriously, because it ultimately threatened the entrenched positions and methods of the existing faculty.

The New School produced as much opposition as excitement, and its demise was as swift as its rise. Bogdanović's attempt to elevate teaching to the study of the totality of the human environment was resisted by the more conservative teaching cadre, who defined architecture in much narrower terms, as a technical and professionally codified discipline. Already by early 1972 Bogdanović was forced to step down as dean, and by the end of the following year the New School was more or less over. Despite this, the reform produced some lasting effects, such as the greater flexibility of the curriculum and the emphasis on the study of the urban environment, as well as the recurrent attempts to synthesize the teaching of the various disciplines and specializations.

The possibility to teach elective classes, which also survived the demise of the New School, allowed Bogdanović to further develop his own pedagogy unconstrained by institutional compromises. Starting in 1976, he offered an elective spring semester course officially called Symbolic Forms but more widely known as the "Rural School for the Philosophy of Architecture." This high-flown name revealed the endeavor's real ambition to rethink the discipline's very *raison d'être.* For several years, the class met on weekends in the village of Mali Popović outside of Belgrade, at an abandoned school that had been converted into Bogdanović's studio. That modest vernacular building set amidst an idyllic rural landscape was the gathering spot for small groups of students who explored the roots and the nature of urbanity by participating in an unlikely hybrid of urban design workshop, art performance, and community-building exercise.

Similar to the New School, the accent at the Rural School was on teamwork, with Bogdanović acting more as a catalyst of knowledge than as a traditional tutor. What was different was that participants—now relieved of the need to respond to the realities of everyday life—could engage in an open-ended process designed to reveal the deep connections between the natural environment, cultural norms, and the built form. Students worked as a team to invent a fictitious civilization which would then serve as a basis for the design of a city. The fictional scenarios were developed to a remarkable degree of detail and narrative coherence: from topography and climate, which influenced the civilization's foundational myths, to its history, economy, and cultural traits, which sometimes even included such elaborate inventions as alphabet, costumes, and musical instruments. Following Bogdanović's definition of architecture as "applied anthropology," the method in effect simulated *longue durée* processes, but condensed into the time span of a single semester. Anthropological literature—for example, the writings of Lucien Lévy-Bruhl or Claude Lévi-Strauss—served as inspiration, but scholarly rigor was not the goal; Bogdanović soon stopped inviting his anthropologist friends to the workshop because he felt that their focus on real anthropological precedents limited the students' imagination. Rather, the aim was to foster a form of collective creativity that would provide firsthand experience in the creation of culture. After extensive group discussions, each of the students would take on a specific task in the collective effort, but at regular intervals Bogdanović would ask them to rotate their roles so that they did not become too specialized. Students thus had to seamlessly continue what someone else had started before them, not unlike the game of *cadavre exquis* from the repertoire of surrealism, Bogdanović's lifelong source of inspiration.[3]

The process's strong ludic dimension, however, went beyond surrealist games; it was also informed by various later theorizations, such as the French author Roger Caillois' writings on the cultural significance of human play, and contemporaneous developments in game theory. The Rural School was at its most playful in the early fall of 1980, when that year's class was invited to participate in BITEF, the acclaimed Belgrade International Theater Festival that focused on avant-garde and experimental practices. In their performance, students resurrected the civilization they had invented earlier that spring and enacted a fictional ritual dressed in colorful paper costumes and equipped with musical instruments of their own making. The mix of spectators was almost equally colorful: in addition to the regular festival audience, it included international participants at a UNESCO conference taking place in Belgrade at the same time, as well as local villagers dressed in folk costumes. This carnivalesque celebration would mark both the pinnacle, and the swansong, of the Rural School.[4] In 1982 Bogdanović was elected mayor of Belgrade, which placed limits on his pedagogical engagement, and by the summer of 1987 he officially retired from university teaching. Around the same time, he became one of the most vocal opponents of the nationalist policies of Slobodan Milošević. Labeled a pariah by the regime, Bogdanović was soon expelled from his studio in Mali Popović. By 1993 he was forced into exile in Vienna, where he stayed for the rest of his life. His students would never get a chance to put the lessons of the Rural School into practice: as Yugoslavia descended into chaos, its cities were overtaken by forces far more brutal than the subtle webs of meaning that he hoped to cultivate.

1. For the curricular changes under the New School, see Branislav Folić, *Nova škola arhitekture u Beogradu* (Belgrade: Arhitektonski fakultet, 2017).
2. For the bulletins of the Tripartite Committee, see Milorad Mladenović, "Comments on ("Saopštenja") of the New School (of Architecture)," in *Serbian Architecture Journal,* no. 3 (2011): 37–38.
3. For Bogdanović's relationship to surrealism and postmodernism, see Vladimir Kulić, "Bogdan Bogdanović's Surrealist Postmodernism," in *Second World Postmodernisms: Architecture and Society under Late Socialism,* ed. Vladimir Kulić (London: Bloomsbury, 2019), 81–97.
4. On the carnivalesque nature of the workshop, see Igor Marjanović and Katerina Rüedi Ray, "Red Carnivals: The Rebellious Body of Architectural Pedagogy," *Architecture and Culture* 6, no. 3 (2019): 437–455.

"EXPERIENCE" RATHER THAN "PROJECT" IN POSTREVOLUTIONARY ALGIERS

Samia Henni

Protagonist Jean-Jacques Deluz (1930–2009)
Institution École polytechnique d'architecture et d'urbanisme (EPAU)
Location Algiers, Algeria
Dates 1970–1988

In the summer of 1962 Algerians celebrated their independence from 132 years of French colonial rule. Working at the École polytechnique d'architecture et d'urbanisme (EPAU) in the newly liberated country, Swiss architect Jean-Jacques Deluz developed a pedagogical approach to this postrevolutionary reality. His approach was grounded in teaching the discipline of architecture through its practice—through the design and realization of spaces for defined activities in specific locations. The design process was considered an "experiment," while the project itself became a form of direct engagement with the changing reality of independent Algeria.

The end of the Algerian Revolution (1954–1962), or the Algerian War of Independence, marked the beginning of a new era for the country. The Algerian republic's first elected president was the socialist soldier and revolutionary Ahmed Ben Bella, who ruled from September 1963 until June 1965, when he was deposed in a bloodless coup by his Minister of Defense and member of the Algerian National Liberation Army (the armed wing of the Algerian National Liberation Front), Houari Boumediene. Boumediene served as Chairman of the Revolutionary Council from 1965 to 1976, and thereafter as Algeria's second president until his death in 1978.

During his tenure, Boumediene launched colossal construction sites across the country and welcomed a number of internationally renowned male architects to contribute to the recovery of the newly independent country and to redress the issues that the French colonial authorities had purposely disregarded—or, alternatively, dominated—in its colonized territory: education, employment, and land ownership. Some architects were familiar with Algeria's conditions and landscapes: Deluz and the French architect Fernand Pouillon, for example, had both worked in Algeria before it gained its independence. Others, such as the Franco-Russian Anatole Kopp, the Italian Luigi Moretti, the Brazilian Oscar Niemeyer, and the Japanese Kenzo Tange, embarked on a new adventure in a country previously unknown to them.[1] Boumediene and his team commissioned Tange to design the University of Science and Technology of Oran in northwest Algeria. Niemeyer would design the University of Science and Technology of Algiers, the EPAU, also in Algiers, and the University of Constantine in northeast Algeria.

The EPAU, Algeria's national school of architecture and urbanism, was established in 1970, eight years after the end of the revolution. Before that, architecture students were trained at the École des Beaux-Arts of Algiers, which offered three distinct areas of study: architecture; fine arts (painting, sculpture, decoration, perspective, history of art, and anatomy); applied arts (miniatures, illumination, wood painting, ceramics, binding, calligraphy, and mosaics). The creation of the EPAU and, more particularly, its divergence from the French Beaux-Arts model, was

< University of Constantine, Algeria, 1972. Designed by Oscar Niemeyer.

> Sketch by Deluz illustrating the design of his extension to Oscar Niemeyer's EPAU, Algiers.

the cause of debate between the representatives of the Ministry of Education and the newly appointed teaching staff at the EPAU.[2] The Algerian administrators argued for a conventional format that is still used in a number of architecture schools today, namely, a major design project taught in a design studio accompanied by lectures, seminars, and workshops in subjects ranging from technology, structures, and descriptive geometry to the history and theory of architecture. Some of the faculty, however, saw the opportunity for a radically new approach to the teaching of architecture. Among them was Deluz, who called for an education and training based on "experience" rather than "project." By this, Deluz meant knowledge or skill gained from practical observation and contact with the various phases of an architectural project from conception through to realization.

Deluz had emigrated to Algiers in 1956, immediately after graduating from the École polytechnique fédérale de Lausanne (EPFL). Though the war of independence was still raging, he was drawn to a city in the midst of a major transformation under the leadership of its dynamic mayor, Jacques Chevallier, who was committed to planning Algiers' metropolitan area, clearing the slums around it, and building as much new housing as was needed. Deluz worked first for the French architects Alexis Daure and Henri Béri before joining the Agence du plan d'Alger (Planning Agency of Algiers), which had been set up by Chevallier to direct the city's urban development and expansion.[3] The Agence du plan was led at the time by the French architect Gérald Hanning and its multidisciplinary team of professionals included Pierre Dalloz and Robert Hansberger.[4] Deluz would in turn direct the agency between 1959 and 1962, reinforcing and implementing the work of his predecessors: "an urbanism of management, substituting for—or rather superimposed onto—a conventional urbanism of regulation and control."[5] This "organizational" analysis and planning approach, also called "operational urbanism," influenced Deluz's own design methods and pedagogical activities first at the École des Beaux-Arts of Algiers, where he taught from 1964 to 1968, and then at the EPAU, where he remained until 1988.

Once installed at the EPAU, Deluz proposed to "replace the term project with that of the experience at various scales of the elements that make up the project— experience that would have both a long-term and a scientific character."[6] In view of the newly independent nation's desperate need for housing, hospitals, universities, schools, public buildings, and

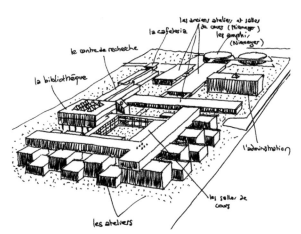

other infrastructure, Deluz was hoping that the government would offer the school the opportunity to study concrete projects and to build without any deadline constraints, effectively providing research laboratories for the students.[7] To educate students and ensure they experienced "reality," Deluz created first the Atelier de recherches et de projets (ARP, or Research and Projects Studio) and then its successor, the Centre de recherches en architecture et en urbanisme (CRAU, or Research Centre in Architecture and Urbanism). Both entities were intended to consider the various stakeholders and complex processes of constructing real buildings through engaged practices rather than detached theories and simulated projects. According to Deluz, "Any architectural intervention occurs in a reality. People are real, their lives, their behaviors, their beliefs are real, the place is real, the climate is real, reality integrates present, past, and future, the urban or natural environment is real, the slope of a terrain is real, the allocated budget, the systems of administration and management, the laws and regulations, the political guidelines—all are realities."[8] Deluz thought it vital for his students in newly independent Algiers to be physically confronted with the various postcolonial "realities" of an architectural project—and not only in the classroom but also, and more importantly, on building sites, dealing with "real people" as well as actual situations. He sought to create what he called an "operative" teaching method that accommodated and learned from the specific conditions of postrevolutionary Algiers. In a report entitled "L'enseignement de l'architecture à l'EPAU: Étude critique et proposition" (The Teaching of Architecture at the EPAU: Critical study and proposal), Deluz criticized the theoretical education of architecture students and the polytechnic system of teaching siloed subjects that had been part of his own training at the EPFL and that was now being perpetuated at the EPAU. In working with "experience" and "reality" rather than with projected simulacra and theoretical future programs, he wanted his students to question the notion of a single solution to a brief.[9] Rather than simply providing a de facto survey, their architectural analysis had to offer an inventory of typological proposals. Each "experience"—the term he used in place of "project"—had to be carried out in the spirit of a scientific experiment and involve an analysis of causal relations. And each research task had to address a specific problem that the student could resolve with reference to the precise directions provided by the instructor. This scientific methodology implied the systematic organization of all fields of research that were strictly related to the subject. The "experiences" had to be varied enough to allow for the study of different levels of intervention, taking into account the varied inter-relations between the many aspects that fed into the work—not just design, construction, and materials, but method, landscape, geography, physiology, psychology, and socio-economic conditions.[10]

Deluz embraced this active "learning-by-doing"[11] method for training architecture and urbanism students at the EPAU, in the building that Niemeyer had designed and that he would later extend. He sought to incorporate his own professional experience at the Agence du plan into architectural education and training, exposing students to his own way of practicing architecture and urbanism. But this radical approach failed to consider either the particular skills and agendas of the EPAU's faculty members or the mindset of his colleagues and superiors at the Ministry of Education, which was not always supportive. Looking back, Deluz described the constraints that had sometimes led to peculiar compromises, claiming that "the engineers pushed for a technical dominance" while a French collaborator wanted to educate "leaders" (the architect as "conductor") and an Italian professor of architectural history wanted to return to the classical teaching of monuments and styles (bypassing traditional vernacular architecture that he deemed unworthy).[12] Conversely, the functionaries at the Algerian Ministry "wanted numbers, success, and homogeneity in the university system."[13] And rather than offering concrete projects and construction sites on which students could learn the profession, the Minister "proposed theoretical studies of standardization that ran counter" to Deluz's intentions.[14] Deluz resigned

from the EPAU in 1988, but he would stay in Algeria, completing a number of commissions including the design of the new town of Sidi Abdellah, about 30km south of Algiers. For Deluz, the pedagogical "experiment" formed "the hyphen"—the connecting element—between the Agence du plan (1957–1962) and the construction, from 1997 on, of this new town, which finally allowed him to implement his "experience" and further test his "operative urbanism."[15]

1. On Niemeyer's projects in Algeria commissioned by Boumediene, see Samia Henni, "Boumedienne, Niemeyer: When Militarism Meets Modernism," preface to *Jason Oddy, Oscar Niemeyer in Algeria* (New York: Columbia Books on Architecture and the City, 2019), 36–49.
2. According to Deluz, Algeria had few architects of its own at the time of independence in 1962, but of these the most prominent was Abderrahmane Bouchama (1910–1985).
3. In 1953 the CIAM-Algiers group, headed by Pierre-André Emery, presented their research on the bidonville Mahieddine in Algiers in an exhibition at CIAM 9 "Habitat" in Aix-en-Provence. See, for example, Zeynep Çelik, "Bidonvilles, CIAM et grands ensembles" in *Alger: paysage urbain et architectures; 1800–2000* (Paris: Les Editions de l'Imprimeur, 2003), 186–227 and "Learning from the Bidonville: CIAM Looks at Algiers," *Harvard Design Magazine*, no. 18 (2003): 70–74.
4. On the Agence du plan, see for example, Jean-Jacques Deluz, *L'urbanisme et l'architecture d'Alger: Aperçu critique* (Alger: Office des publications universitaires, 1988), 63–100; Remi Baudouï, "L'agence du Plan d'Alger" in *André Ravéreau, l'atelier du désert*, eds. R. Baudouï, P. Potier (Marseilles: Parenthèse, 2003), 37–44.
5. Jean-Jacques Deluz, *Le tout et le fragment* (Algiers: Editions barzakh, 2010), 17–18.
6. Jean-Jacques Deluz, *Alger: Chronique urbaine* (Paris: Editions Bouchene, 2001), 174.
7. Jean-Jacques Deluz, *Fantasmes et réalités: Réflexions sur l'architecture* (Algiers: Editions barzakh, 2008), 25.
8. Ibid., 29.
9. Excerpts of this text are published in Deluz, *Le tout et le fragment*, 273–293.
10. Deluz, *Le tout et le fragment*, 280.
11. The theory of education of "learning-by-doing" was first framed by the US philosopher and psychologist John Dewey in his 1916 book *Democracy and Education: An Introduction to the Philosophy of Education*.
12. Deluz, *Fantasmes et réalités*, 25.
13. Ibid.
14. Ibid.
15. Deluz, *Le tout et le fragment*, 25.

LEARNING FROM THE VILLAGE

Lily Zhang

Protagonists Hiroshi Hara (1936–)
and students of the Hara Laboratory
Institution University of Tokyo
Location Tokyo, Japan
Dates 1972–1978

The Hara Laboratory, Hiroshi Hara's research division at the University of Tokyo's Institute of Industrial Science, conducted extensive surveys of villages and vernacular settlements around the world from 1972 to 1978. Among architectural educators in Japan, Hara was one of the first and foremost to shift the focus for spatial investigation beyond the country's borders, using an ethnographic methodology based on field observation, documentation, and interviews. Hara and his students traveled around the globe by car and plane to visit over two hundred villages in nearly forty countries, including areas in the Mediterranean, Central and South America, Eastern Europe, the Middle East, South Asia, and West Africa; they also worked within Japan and some of its remote island settlements. In Hara's view, these communities were not "natural" or arbitrary

formations but manifestations of detailed planning, management, and control.

Hara's team took note of the physical, spatial, and social attributes and configuration of each village, assigning particular importance to the dwelling as the determining organizational unit for the overall settlement. Villages and dwellings were analyzed and categorized into "morphologies," or systems classifying the objects of study into distinct yet related types. Material, form, patterns of spatial organization, and social and geographical context were among the aspects evaluated. The team produced a series of elaborate diagrams examining the range of typologies, along with annotated maps charting their multicountry itineraries. Rather than the typical master-apprentice laboratory model of education, these joint expeditions were collaborations that engaged the students' own inquisitive minds and potential. A female Indian architecture student, Sarayu Ahuja, joined the team for studies of villages in India and Nepal in particular. The lab's cumulative research, titled "Dwelling Group Domain Theory" (*Jūkyo Shūgōron*), was featured in five special issues of *SD Magazine* from 1973 to 1979 and distilled by Hara into the form of his book *100 Lessons: Learning from Villages*, published in 1987.[1]

An architectural pedagogy grounded in the study of villages abroad was unprecedented at a time of

rapidly accelerating urbanization and industrialization in Japan. The more usual architectural response to the country's frenzied postwar economic growth, which peaked in the 1960s, was work of grandiose aspirations and scale. Such impulses were perhaps best represented by the 1970 World Exposition held in Osaka, which was master planned in part by Kenzo Tange. Though he had studied with Tange, Hara was highly critical of Expo 70 and wrote numerous essays attacking both the event—as an overly capitalistic demonstration of corporate interests—and, more generally, what he saw as the oppressive and individualistic tendencies of modernism, epitomized in many ways by Tange and his legacy in architectural education in Japan.

Reasoning that humans are intrinsically social beings who live in groups, Hara condemned Japan's massive postwar program of urban planning, which was based along modernist lines and favored individual lifestyles rather than a connected society. In this context, the investigation of the existing and thriving social orders of village communities became an essential means to address the failures of modern architecture and begin to reconstruct the discipline. Hara would reference the village research

throughout his career and cite formal, conceptual, and planning influences from these studies. While the most intensive concentration of surveys was during the 1970s, he would continue to travel with his students, notably Kengo Kuma, Riken Yamamoto, and Akira Fujii, to areas around the world until he retired from teaching in 1997. For his numerous students and followers, and for architectural pedagogy in Japan, Hara's work would expand institutional focus beyond the classroom, the academic studio, and even the laboratory, to encourage working and learning in the world itself.

∧ Hara lab study trip to the Sahara, 1978.

< Selection of photographs from the Hara lab village research, 1972–1979.

≪ Hara's students, Kengo Kuma at the back, with equipment for village surveys in Africa.

1. *Jūkyo Shūgōron 1–5, SD Magazine* special issues, nos. 4, 6, 8, 10, 12 (1973–79); Hiroshi Hara, *100 Lessons: Learning from Villages* (Tokyo: Shokokusha, 1987).

BUS TOUR ACROSS THE UK

Isabelle Doucet

Protagonists Peter Murray (1944–), Cedric Price
(1934–2003), and Stefan Szczelkun (1948–) and
students at the Architectural Association (AA)
Institutions *Architectural Design*, Architectural
Association
Location UK
Date 1973

On February 14, 1973 a converted double-decker
bus set out on a two-week tour of schools of
architecture in the UK. The "Polyark Bus Tour"
was devised by Peter Murray, technical editor of
Architectural Design (*AD*), together with Cedric
Price, who had argued for a national school of
architecture that would allow students to freely
choose from all the offerings of existing institutions,
and Stefan Szczelkun, tutor at the Architectural
Association (AA) in London. Crewed by students
from the AA, the bus contained living quarters as
well as an array of communication technologies to
support recording and broadcasting.[1] As a "live
project," the mobile unit allowed students to go
beyond the familiar boundaries of their own school
and design studio and to embrace a dialogue with

students from other schools of architecture around
the country—including Cambridge, Nottingham,
Sheffield, Newcastle, Edinburgh, and Kingston.

As an educational experiment, the Polyark Bus
Tour was very much in line with Cedric Price's
ideas for an educational revolution, as developed
through his National School Plan (1964–1966)
and the Potteries Thinkbelt project (1966), which
proposed a flexible network of educational facilities
housed in mobile carriages and other infrastructures connected to the railway system serving the
Potteries of North Staffordshire.[2]

Moreover, Polyark resonated with the intellectual climate of the AA, where students were
experimenting with new forms of learning and
living.[3] The growing fascination with audiovisual
technologies at the AA during the 1970s would
also resonate with the multimedia activities of the
Communications Unit, coordinated by Archigram
member Dennis Crompton.[4] On each stop of their
tour, the crew would video record conversations and
broadcast the recorded material at the next stop,
building up a library of video tapes. Price himself also
seems to have contributed a video message.[5]

Finally, Polyark can be considered a prime illus-
tration of what happens when radical pedagogy
meets the messiness of a real-life experiment.
The project faced all sorts of organizational and
technical challenges on the road and perhaps was
more successful as a technological and pedagogical
experiment (communication technologies/dialogue
between architecture students and educators)
than it was as a means of building connections with
local communities. However, one could speculate
that it was precisely this practical, on-the-road
experience that made the Polyark Bus Tour such
an invaluable learning experience. The project's
mediatized status—notably its extensive coverage
in *AD*—can be seen as an important marker of the
pedagogical value of experimentation, infused with
excitement and success, but equally with challenges
and disappointment.

Airpo
Olivetti   nches
AD/AA/Polyark Bus Tour

< Cover of *AD*,
April 1973,
featuring the AD/
AA/Polyark Bus.

> The AD/AA/Polyark Bus in London. Photograph by Peter Murray.

1. For this short text, I draw from my longer paper, "Architecture Wrestling the Social: The 'Live' Project as a Site of Contestation," *Candide Journal for Architectural Knowledge* 10 [2016]: 12–40 and on Peter Murray's extensive reporting on the project, published as "Cosmorama: AD/AA/Polyark Bus Tour," *Architectural Design*, no. 4 (1973): 201–212. Other recent discussions of the project are found in Samantha Hardingham, *Cedric Price Works 1952–2003: A Forward-Minded Retrospective* (London: AA Publications, 2016); Douglas Moffat, "AD/AA/Polyark: Benevolent Irritants and Distributed Feedback," in *The Other Architect. Another Way of Building Architecture*, ed. Giovanna Borasi (Leipzig/Montreal: Spector Books/ Canadian Centre for Architecture, 2015), 389–390.

2. See also Samantha Hardingham and Kester Rattenbury, *Supercrit 1. Cedric Price Potteries Thinkbelt* (London: Routledge, 2007); and reprints and discussions provided in Hardingham, *Cedric Price Works 1952–2003*.

3. See, for example, the student work collected in *Architectural Association Projects 1946–1971*, ed. James Gowan (London: AA Publications, 1972). On the diverse work produced within the AA design Unit system, see also Irene Sunwoo, "From the 'Well-Laid Table' to the 'Market Place': The Architectural Association Unit System," *Journal of Architectural Education* 65, no. 2 (2012): 24–41; and Igor Marjanovic, "Alvin Boyarsky's Delicatessen," in *Critical Architecture*, ed. Jane Rendell et al. (London: Routledge, 2007), 190–199.

4. See also Irene Sunwoo, "The Static Age," *AA Files*, no. 61 (2010): 118–129.

5. As discussed in Murray, "Cosmorama," 203.

OLD 532

THE SCIENCE OF "STROLLOLOGY"

Philipp Oswalt

Protagonists Lucius Burckhardt (1925–2003),
Bazon Brock (1936–), Paul-Armand Gette (1927–),
Bernhard Lassus (1929–)
Institution Gesamthochschule Kassel (GhK)
Location Kassel, Germany
Dates 1973–1993

In 1973 Swiss sociologist Lucius Burckhardt was appointed Professor of Socio-economics of Urban Systems at the Gesamthochschule Kassel (GhK). With the support of the social democratic government of Hesse, the recently founded university offered unusual freedom in the state education system, taking up many of the reform approaches of the 1968 movement. Burckhardt had previously penned a series of influential writings on urbanism, criticism, and building policy together with Markus Kutter, Max Frisch, and Walter Förderer. After a guest lectureship at the HfG Ulm in 1959, he began teaching in 1961 at the ETH Zurich. There, during the short-lived reformist period between 1969 and 1973, in collaboration with the architects Rolf Gutmann and Rainer Senn, he was able to experiment with a new form of architectural education—the "Lehrcanapé," which replaced the typical introductory formal design exercises with immediate engagement with social issues outside the university.

While the ETH Zurich returned to more conventional forms of teaching at the beginning of the 1970s, Burckhardt would continue to develop his experimental pedagogical approaches at the GhK. Critical of the principle of simplification in classical design education, he resisted the idea of direct problem-solving. Instead, he challenged his students to explore the underlying problems of the task. Rather than immediately addressing the design of an object, he wanted them to think first about themselves and their position in the social fabric.[1] Was a building the right answer to the problem? And if it was, what kind should it be, and what organizational interventions should accompany it?

In dialogue with the French landscape architect Bernard Lassus, Burckhardt later developed the idea of the "smallest possible intervention."[2] With reference to Horst Rittel, he referred to "wicked problems" that cannot be solved in the true sense

of the word. Rather, he argued, the cooperation of various experts is essential to identify, recognize, and define problems in all their complexity. Burckhardt also contended that planning and building were based on value judgments that simply led to a (re) distribution of suffering. What was required instead, in his view, was a methodical transparency in the formulation of the various options for action, which would disclose value questions and make them accessible and open to democratic discussion.[3]

While the teaching experiment at the ETH Zurich, in the spirit of the times, still sought to follow stringent scientific methods, Burckhardt's working methods changed with his move to the GhK. At this small reform university, the courses of study in architecture, urban planning, and landscape planning were not only combined in one department but were also in close exchange with the integrated art academy and other disciplines. Burckhardt turned more and more to artistic and performative working methods. He experimented with different forms of teaching, making the city of Kassel and the surrounding region into his laboratory. From 1976, beginning with excursions to investigate the local conditions—of housing

estates, parks, landscape areas, art galleries—he developed "Strollology" as a scientific-artistic method of "action teaching." Each of his "promenadological" walks followed a specific conceptual script in which the landscape was examined through historical texts, images, and theories. Important impulses were provided by the artists and intellectuals, such as Bazon Brock and Paul-Armand Gette, who were invited to accompany the students. With these walks, Burckhardt sought to overcome the separation of theory and practice and to create a space that dissolved the boundaries and hierarchies between disciplines and between experts and laypersons.

Performatively, the mobile group examined the construction of the landscape (or the built environment), tracing its social conditionality and making visible its aesthetic, moral, practical, legal, and political aspects.[4] The idea was that targeted intellectual and aesthetic interventions could break through everyday stereotypes and reveal new perspectives. For example, the 1987 project "The Journey to Tahiti" transposed Georg Foster's account of James Cook's second voyage to a former military training area and designated nature reserve. At various stations,

∧ Strollology performance titled "The Journey to Tahiti" at the former military training area in Dönche, Kassel, 1987.

< Om stroll in Bergpark Wilhelmshöhe, Kassel, with the artist Paul-Armand Gette, 1985.

an actor recited excerpts from the historical travelogue. The tropical vegetation was ironically and playfully simulated with Turkish flat breads (hung on branches to make bread fruit trees) and borrowed exotic houseplants.

Already during his studies at the University of Basel in 1949, Lucius Burckhardt had turned against the planned car-friendly modernization of his hometown, publishing critical articles and taking a political stand with his fellow students. At Kassel, he would organize the 1992–1993 "car driver's walks" where participants held windscreens in front of them to make a point about the motorist's limited view, only ever directed forward. These and other walks were not only a means of becoming aware of one's own perception, or a tool for investigation and the production of knowledge; they were also a kind of public performance, a pedagogical demonstration.[5]

While some former students still continue Strollology in a rather orthodox way today,[6] others have been inspired to new forms of teaching, one example being Jesko Fezer with his design consultancy at the University of Fine Arts Hamburg.[7] A few years ago, the ETH not only researched the history of Burckhardt's time there but also attempted to reconnect with his teaching format.[8] However, it is perhaps in contemporary art that Burckhardt has the greatest presence. In the late 1980s the curator Hans Ulrich Obrist became aware of Burckhardt's work through Jacques Herzog, one of his former students at the ETH.[9] A friendship developed and Obrist repeatedly invited Burckhardt to collaborate on projects and dedicated a posthumous exhibition to him in the Swiss Pavilion at the 2014 Venice Architecture Biennale. The curator Adam Szymczyk also referred to Burckhardt at documenta 14, which he directed. Obrist appreciated the "questioning of supposed self-evident things";[10] Szymczyk, the "more conscious perception of the environment, which turns mere seeing into cognition."[11]

< Public intervention
on the Friedrichsplatz
in Kassel's inner city at
the end of the sympo-
sium "Denkmalpflege
ist Sozialpolitik"
(Preservation is Social
Policy), November
1975.

∨ Car drivers' walk,
in collaboration with
Helmut Holzapfel,
Kassel 1992–1993.

1. See Lucius Burckhardt, "Vom
Entwurfsakademismus zur Behandlung
bösartiger Probleme," Canapé News
[Zurich], no. 29 (1973): 70; quoted after
Silvan Blumenthal, Das Lehrcanapé:
Lucius Burckhardt und das Architekten-
bild an der ETH Zürich 1970–1973 (Basel:
Standpunkte, 2010), 44–45.
2. See Helmut Aebischer, "Zusammenar-
beit mit vielen," in Raum und Macht: Die
Stadt zwischen Vision und Wirklichkeit.
Leben und Wirken von Lucius und Anne-
marie Burckhardt, ed. Ueli Mäder et al.
(Zurich: Rotpunktverlag, 2014), 101; and
Bernard Lassus, "Zwischen Schichtung
und Tiefe," in Vision offener Grünräume:
GrünGürtel Frankfurt, ed. Tom Koenigs
(Frankfurt Main-New York: Camus

Verlag, 1991), 127–144.
3. Blumenthal, Das Lehrcanapé, 54.
4. See Hannah Stippel, "Nur wo der
Menschen die Natur stört, wird die
Landschaft wirklich schön: Die land-
schaftstheoretischen Aquarelle von
Lucius Burckhardt," PhD diss. (University
of Vienna, 2011), 98; quoted after Mäder
et al., Raum und Macht, 50.
5. Ibid., 108, 52.
6. Especially Bertram Weißhaar, http://
www.atelier-latent.de/.
7. http://gestaltungsberatung.org/, and
Öffentliche Gestaltungsberatung: 2011–
2016 = Public design support / Jesko
Fezer & Studio Experimentelles Design
(Berlin: Sternberg Press, 2016).
8. Silvan Blumenthal, "Das Lehrcanapé.

Lucius Burckhardt und das Architek-
tenbild an der ETH Zürich 1970–1973,"
Standpunkte Dokumente, no. 2 (2010):
44–45. Philipp Ursprung reactivated
the canapé teaching format in the years
2011–2014.
9. "Rendezvous der Fragen: Interview
mit Hans Ulrich Obrist," BauNetz,
May 5, 2014, https://www.baunetz.de/
meldungen/Meldungen-Interview_mit_
Hans_Ulrich_Obrist_3549463.html
10. Ibid.
11. "Was ich immer wollte," Adam
Szymczyk in conversation with
Hanno Rauterberg, Die Zeit, no. 1,
(2014), https://www.zeit.de/2014/01/
documenta-adam-szymczyk-interview.

FIELD OBSERVATIONS

Curt Gambetta, Hadas Steiner

Protagonists Reyner Banham (1922–1988),
Bonnie Foit-Albert (1938–)
Institution University at Buffalo, SUNY
Location Buffalo, NY, USA
Dates 1977–1980

While Reyner Banham taught at the State University of New York, Buffalo from 1976 until 1980, he revisited the industrial architectural typologies that had inspired modernist narratives. As part of that effort, he designed a series of courses in collaboration with the architect Bonnie Foit-Albert, another member of the faculty. Together with students, they measured, photographed, and otherwise documented buildings of the sort typically ignored by architects and historians at that time. For Banham, however, engaged fieldwork required more than firsthand experience. It also entailed an intense corroboration of experience with drawings and photographs, as well as written narratives regarding the construction, use, and significance of buildings. This rigorous method of historical inquiry raised timely questions about the role of observation, reproduction, and narrative in architectural knowledge that still resonate today. Indeed, the practice of fieldwork was leveled as a critique of the kind of "armchair academicism" that Banham repeatedly claimed had overlooked what industrial buildings laid bare: an alternative history of modernism. He implored the students in his classes to experience buildings for themselves and to challenge existing claims, whether those were made in writing or by inclusion or exclusion in images.

During the summer of 1977, Banham and Foit-Albert taught a three-week course entitled "Buffalo: The Industrial Heritage." The objects of study were to be the Larkin Administration Building (1903) by

Frank Lloyd Wright, which had been demolished in 1950, along with the adjacent daylight factories of the Larkin company. Foit-Albert provided an introduction to the requisite survey methods, referred to as "field notes" in the cursory syllabus, as well as a "System of Observation" that organized the analysis of a building from floor plans to site conditions.[1] The field notes would constitute a part of the larger written and photographic narrative, along with architectural plans, sections, and elevations. Field drawings would include details down to building fragments, such as remnants of columns, in addition to sketches of floor plans and elevations—all replete with measurements and notation. The interior and exterior of the Larkin complex were extensively photographed, with particular attention paid to features like stairwells, railings, and columns. Numerous shots also captured Banham and students surrounded by photographic apparatus scrutinizing well-lit gaps in the floor like forensic analysts.

The field notes suggested comparisons with the historic images, drawings, and texts that had set the precedent for how these buildings should be viewed. Banham often remarked that firsthand experience of the grain elevators and daylight factories elicited a sense of déjà-vu that stemmed from the memory of the grainy newsprint reproductions that had illustrated the writings of Walter Gropius and Le Corbusier.[2] For *A Concrete Atlantis*, Banham conducted his own investigations of already well-documented buildings, including the Faguswerke by Gropius (1913), as well as less-known factories. Similarly, Banham, Foit-Albert, and the students peeled away spaces and materials in the effort to uncover what earlier images and polemics had concealed. Course readings reinforced Banham's conviction that present-day images (including mental notes and photographs) were prefigured by the vantage points and conclusions of an earlier generation of architects and historians. References included image-heavy books that contained photographic comparisons of old and new architecture, including J. M. Richards' *The Functional Tradition in Early Industrial Buildings*. Taken together, these pedagogical methods highlighted how firsthand observation of architecture is mediated by its documentation, whether by history, photography, or any other method.

After completing the summer course and displaying its findings, Banham and Foit-Albert developed a curriculum for an interdisciplinary master's program that they called Building Life Cycles. The

proposal submitted to the university was instructive of their pedagogical approach: the objective of the program was to document the "biography" of buildings from their inception through to their construction, use, and decay.[3] Banham and Foit-Albert imagined the building biography as a framework for educating professional students and "average citizens" as to the forces that affected the built environment. They contrasted the study of the lifecycles of buildings with the study of building "types" in architectural history, intending to provide training in the management of the ongoing use of buildings rather than practical or vocational training in their restoration. After conducting research about a building's "biography," students would be asked to propose new uses for usually derelict buildings. The past life of a building, in other words, was integral to its future use. But for Banham, a lifecycle analysis also afforded an ongoing narrative. When students drew the Larkin complex of daylight factories, for example, they deployed notational devices to indicate changes that were made over time. They emphasized alterations, such as bricked-in windows, that signaled duration. Additionally, student letters and photographs from the Larkin seminar document how sensory experience, especially touch, helped to reanimate dormant buildings and histories. Banham would often lecture on the social use of a building while inside it, thus animating an aspect often quarantined to the classroom. In Banham's and Foit-Albert's teaching, even the historian's medium of writing, in the end, was akin to a mental image, made up of an orchestrated series of vantage points, frames, and sequences that recast buildings that had been deemed obsolete within their social and historical context. Rather than being inherited from a static past, history was a project akin to a construction site, generating a cacophony of insights and obfuscations that each generation needed to actively rephrase—not least of which was the revision of teaching itself.

∧ Students Stuart Lacy and Linda Sichel examining a hole in the tongue-and-groove maple ship flooring of the Larkin "O" Building, Buffalo, New York, 1977. Silver gelatin print.

< Reyner Banham discussing a drawing of the Larkin complex with students, Buffalo, New York, 1977.

< Student Stuart Lacy
climbing the smoke-
stack in the Larkin
Complex, Buffalo,
New York, 1977. Silver
gelatin print.

1. "DSN 495/ DSN 595 Tentative Work
Schedule," undated (June and July 1977),
University Archives, University at Buffalo;
"A System of Observation: procedural
notes from Bonnie Albert's Seminar, June
29, 1977," University Archives, University
at Buffalo.
2. Reyner Banham, *A Concrete Atlantis:
U.S. Industrial Building and European
Modern Architecture, 1900–1925*
(Cambridge, MA: MIT Press, 1986).
3. "MAH Program Description" and
"Building Life Cycles" poster, both
undated, private collection of Bonnie
Foit-Albert.

SCHOOLED BY THE BUILDING

CRITICAL UNITY BEYOND PROFESSIONAL REALISM

Horacio Torrent

Protagonists Jorge Vivanco (1912–1987), Eduardo Sacriste (1905–1999), Horacio Caminos (1914–1990), Hilario Zalba (1912–1995), José Le Pera (1913–1990), Rafael Onetto (1915–1967), and Jorge Bruno Borgato (1918–1986), with Enrico Tedeschi (1910–1978), Cino Calcaprina (1911–1977), Guido Oberti (1907–2003), Luigi Piccinato (1899–1983), and Ernesto Nathan Rogers (1909–1969)
Institution Instituto de Arquitectura y Urbanismo, Universidad Nacional de Tucumán
Location Tucumán, Argentina
Dates 1946–1952

In the years immediately after the Second World War, the Institute of Architecture and Urbanism at the Universidad Nacional de Tucumán in northwest Argentina was the setting for one of the most radical attempts to reform the teaching of architecture. Here, a new pedagogy of design was proposed—one that sought a unity between professional practice and architectural design research. Based on a "real-world" approach, this pedagogical project would ultimately be enacted in the design of a new campus for the university.

The institute was created on August 8, 1946, as part of a far-reaching reorganization of the university into research institutes. Its early promoter and first director, from 1946 to 1950, was Jorge Vivanco, who brought together a select group of teachers, including Horacio Caminos, Hilario Zalba, José Le Pera, and Rafael Oneto, along with Jorge Bruno Borgato and Eduardo Sacriste, who directed the institute in 1950 and 1951–1952 respectively. Many were already well known as members of the Grupo Austral, whose founding manifesto in 1939

had denounced the new functionalist academicism and vindicated surrealism and its contribution to modern architecture's critical spirit, while at the same time offering an approach situated in local realities and circumstances.

This group would be joined by a new cohort of Italian teachers, invited to contribute after Vivanco participated in CIAM VI in Bridgwater. Enrico Tedeschi, Cino Calcaprina, and Guido Oberti were appointed in 1947 to teach history of architecture, urban planning, and design of structures respectively. Luigi Piccinato came a year later, to teach an introduction to urbanism and a course in the history of architecture, along with Ernesto Nathan Rogers, who taught architectural theory. The integration of these foreign professors—some of them founding members of APAO (Associazione per l'Architettura Organica) and associated with *Metron* magazine—would introduce the ideas that organicism offered for the reformulation of modern architecture.

For this group of young teachers—aged between twenty-nine and forty-two—knowledge of architecture and urbanism had to be based on a "realistic" approach to design and at the same time incorporate some aspects of a scientific research approach. Their studios effectively became headquarters of professional development: student assignments were directly related to actual commissions and addressed a wide range of scales, accompanying the different learning stages. Thus, students designed buildings including the civic center in Catamarca, a school and hotel in Purmamarca, urban housing developments for Marapa and Ñuñorco, and Villa Alberdi sugar mills. They were tutored closely by their professors and incorporated into their work advice from experts in other fields.

The most significant test and experience for the institute—both professionally and pedagogically—was the project for the university campus, located in the San Javier hills on the outskirts of Tucumán.

The design of the campus was addressed by establishing two distinct areas, one on the brow and the other at the foot of the hill. The structures on the brow of the hill included a community center, educational buildings, and housing, along with an area for sports and recreation. The educational buildings were huge blocks of 105 m by 195 m with a free plan allowing for a flexible organization of the spaces.

The most impressive building was the student housing block, identified by Reyner Banham as the first "megastructure," on account of its immense dimensions—480 m long, 21 m wide, and 30 m high—and its territorial role as the main piece of the complex. The reinforced-concrete core structure, which was able to accommodate four thousand people, was designed to give the impression that the block was floating on the edge of the hill.

The community center in turn was developed as a giant shed of concave and convex cone-shaped shells supported by a reinforced concrete grid of 20 m columns (which were tested at the Politecnico di Milano's structural lab following a typical applied research process). This was the project's centerpiece, with the grand canopy forming the stage for the urban life of the university. Reference images linked the building directly with Piazza San Marco in Venice, conveying the idea of a new monumentality that went beyond the mere fulfillment of function to provide for a cultural and social dimension.

The reorganization of the university into a system of faculties in 1952 increased the division between teaching and research. The institute ceased to exist as such, and at the same time also lost the project for the University City, which would remain unfinished. This was the end of an experiment exploring the relation between research and professional realism, which proposed a critical unity of architectural knowledge. However, as some of the institute's teachers dispersed around the country, they helped to enrich architectural education in

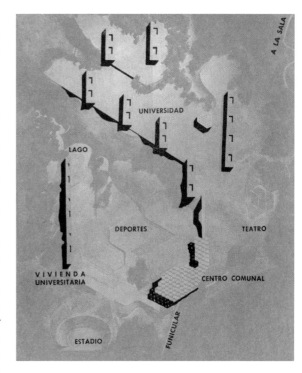

other universities. Beyond its mythical construction, the legacy of the Tucumán institute lives on in the validation of a conceptual unity in the production of knowledge related to professional practice and its leading role in architectural design research.

∧ Plan of the University City of Tucumán.

< Facade of the residential building at the University City of Tucumán.

∨ Model of the University City of Tucumán.

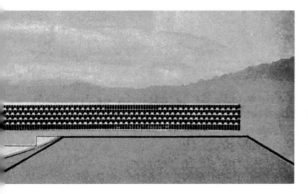

HOW TO TRAIN "POSTREVOLUTIONARY" ARCHITECTS

Martin Cobas

Protagonists Antonio Cravotto
(1925–2000) and others
Institution Facultad de Arquitectura,
Universidad de la República
Location Montevideo, Uruguay
Dates 1952–1965

In 1952, after years of intense—and often belligerent—debate, the architecture faculty of the Universidad de la República enacted the biggest transformation of its curricula since 1918, when French professor J. P. Carré had introduced the Beaux-Arts model. In spite of his academic training—and with the help of a young generation of remarkable students—Carré had resolutely opened the school to avantgarde debates. Already by the early 1920s, its studios were inflected by the language of modern architecture (in different codifications). The so-called Plan 52, then, was as much a political instrument as it was a pedagogic one:[1] it synthesized, in an academic idiom, the revolutionary ideals of an emerging radical socialism. In replacing Beaux-Arts "composition" with "revolutionary organization,"[2] Plan 52 positioned the school alongside the political avantgarde. And it was, paradoxically, the course on "composition" that became the site of the revolution that eventually led to the concept of *building as pedagogy*.

While Carlos Gómez Gavazzo, a disciple of Le Corbusier and noted urban theorist,[3] is generally credited as its intellectual author, Plan 52 grew out of an increasingly politicized milieu where students joined forces with practicing architects. The respective journals of the professional and student associations—*Revista de Arquitectura* and *Revista del CEDA*—would play a crucial role in the discussions that formulated the social rhetoric of the plan. Forged amidst translations of Giedion, Le Corbusier, Candillis, Team X, and discussions on Brutalism, Plan 52 chose political resistance over academic comfort, at a time when Uruguay's economic decline—marked by endemic inflation and unemployment—provoked student militancy and social unrest.

The CEDA (Centro de Estudiantes de Arquitectura/Architecture Student Union) not only published an extensive survey of *rancheríos* (shanty towns) that made visible the country's pressing social needs but also distributed a pamphlet that defined architecture as "a truly social service," with the school being at the intersection of architecture and society, or the "real world."[4] As a sequel—and an important catalyst for the implementation of the plan—CEDA dedicated an issue of the student journal in 1952 to "The University and Society." Facing the biggest student strike in the country's history, its goals were clear. And so was its message:

> Architecture is a vital art: it is neither consolation, nor hobby nor caprice. Like any human activity, it is constrained by temperament, yet what provokes it is external. It must respond with the highest precision to the needs of the community; it must contextualize and interpret social relations; it must contribute to the resolution of problems that no other discipline can solve.[5]

Plan 52 therefore envisioned a postrevolutionary society in which architecture would be ethically bound to respond to the demands of society and centralized planning, but this revolution did not immediately extend to the teaching structure, which consolidated the vertical studio as the most distinctive feature in the education of the architect. It would take more than ten years for Plan 52 to coalesce into an equally radical pedagogy. In 1965 the university commissioned the school of architecture to design a refectory, the Comedor Universitario No. 2.[6] The refectory was part of Montevideo's Medical Center, the core piece of a projected "urban campus" that was intended to connect the university with the city—a project that failed due to a severe lack of funds and political instability.

When the school received the commission, it was assigned by lottery to one of the professors of design, Antonio Cravotto. The small size of the studio, the optimal student-professor ratio, and the postrevolutionary mindset of students, eager to engage with the "real world," favored the creation of a truly collective design laboratory: How do we design, build, and "learn" *in* and *on* a project/building? The project was, as faculty member Thomas Sprechmann put it, an expression of belief in the revolution and its architectural aftermath.[7] It provided the opportunity to train future architects in the specifics of cooperative design and a socially driven program.

The design team of the multiauthored project was made up of three professors, seven students, and eight technical advisers, who were involved in both the design and construction processes.[8] Over the course of a semester, sketches and models, pin up reviews and late-night chats guided the evolution of the teamwork and design decisions in Cravotto's studio. Construction began soon after the project was finalized: a series of oblique and curved brick walls defining a continuous space characterized by expressive structural solutions combined with a meticulous attention to the open areas, a topical gesture evident in the large reflecting pool. The expressionistic nature of the project contrasted with the modern orthodoxy of the adjacent buildings of the Medical Center, projected three decades earlier.[9]

By the time the refectory was inaugurated, Plan 52 had already been revised. Up to then, no other project had rendered its ambitious goals so emphatically, bridging the seemingly discontinuous spheres of the academy and the "real world," of pedagogy and architecture. It was a faithful—if belated—corollary to the plan and to architecture as social reform.

However, another revolution was yet to come. The late 1960s were dominated by an increasing radicalization of the student union amidst generalized social turmoil and the emergence of an urban guerrilla organization (Tupamaros) that foreshadowed a decade-long brutal dictatorship from 1973 to 1985, a time in which unions and academic publications were severely restricted. There was revolution, indeed, and postrevolutionary architects.[10]

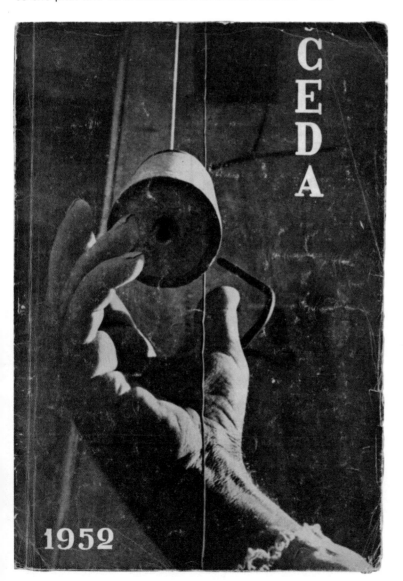

∨ Cover of *Revista del CEDA* (Centro de Estudiantes de Arquitectura), May 1952.

1. See *Plan de estudios y plan de las materias* (Montevideo: Facultad de Arquitectura, Universidad de la República, 1953).
2. See Jorge Nudelman, "1952: Modernidad y Revolución: El Plan de Estudios de 1952 en la Facultad de Arquitectura de Montevideo; una revisión crítica," *Seminario de Crítica*, no. 213 (Buenos Aires: Instituto de Arte Americano e Investigaciones Estéticas, 2017), n.p.
3. This is made evident in the "Exposición de motivos (Introductory Remarks)." See Carlos Gómez Gavazzo et al., "Exposición de motivos," in *Plan de estudios y plan de las materias*, 5–9.
4. Pamphlet published by the Centro de Estudiantes de Aquitectura, CEDA (Montevideo, December 4, 1950). Centro de Documentación del Instituto de Historia de la Arquitectura, FADU-UdelaR, Montevideo. Trans. by the author.
5. *Revista del CEDA*, no. 21 (May 1952): n.p. Trans. by the author.
6. See Antonio Cravotto et al., "Comedor Universitario No. 2," in *Revista del CEDA*, no. 30 (October 1966), 28–31.
7. Thomas Sprechmann, "Programa y revolución," in Juan Carlos Apolo, Laura Alemán, and Pablo Kelbauskas, *Talleres: Trazos y señas* (Montevideo: Facultad de Arquitectura, Universidad de la República, 2006), 126.
8. The eighteen authors were: Antonio Cravotto, Juan Carlos Queiruga, Juan Carlos Vanini (professors); H. E. Benech, E. Chiesa, A. C. Frontini, G. Kohlsdorf, P. Romero, H. Vigliecca, L. Zanzi (students); V. Colom (construction), Tugores and Del Castillo (structure), J. Oliveras, B. Argone, A. Badano, C. Silva, J. Hakas (systems).
9. Notably the Hospital de Clínicas (University Hospital; Carlos Surraco, 1930); and the Instituto de Higiene (Institute of Hygiene; Carlos Surraco, 1933).
10. I wish to thank professors L. Alemán, L. Cesio, M. Fernández, A. Mazzini, colleagues at the Instituto de Historia de la Arquitectura (IHA-FADU-UdelaR), and Pablo Kelbauskas for their advice. Thanks are also due to S. Cebey and L. Saibene for facilitating access to the visual material.

BIG-TIME SENSUALITY

Ivan L. Munuera

Protagonists Ricardo Porro (1925–2014), Roberto Gottardi (1927–2017), Vittorio Garatti (1927–)
Institution National Art Schools (Escuelas Nacionales de Arte, ENA)
Location Havana, Cuba
Dates 1961–1965

One of the most famous photographs of the 1959 Cuban Revolution shows Fidel Castro and Che Guevara playing golf in Havana's Country Club—the symbol of Fulgencio Batista's authoritarian regime and Cuba's aristocracy suddenly appropriated by the bearded revolutionaries of Sierra Maestra.[1] If the

Country Club, situated in the lavish neighborhood of Vedado, represented the old regime, with its exclusionary policies[2] and luxurious leisure architecture, it would become an equally symbolic site for the new socialist order, which built upon its ruins a ground-breaking educational project: the National Art Schools (Escuelas Nacionales de Arte, ENA). If the ambition of the ENA was to transform education in the arts following the principles of the revolution, the construction of its buildings was a de facto school of architecture that gave shape to those goals.

The five buildings of ENA were conceived as a single project designed by three architects:[3] Ricardo Porro (School of Modern Dance and School of Plastic Arts); Roberto Gottardi (School of Dramatic Arts); and Vittorio Garatti (School of Music and School of Ballet), with the supervision on site of José

Mosquera. Built between 1961 and 1965, ENA was defined as much by the political landscape as by the architects' biographies: Porro, who was Cuban, believed in the revolution from the outset and thought that architecture could go hand in hand with the socialist project; Gottardi and Garatti, both from Italy, had first traveled to Venezuela, seeking a milieu where ideas and the built environment could come together, before flying to Cuba once the revolution gained momentum there.

The three architects worked independently, but used three common guiding principles. First, the different buildings were connected materially, as all of them made use of bricks and/or terracotta tiles. Second, they mobilized the same technology, a hybrid solution of thin-tiles covering reinforced concrete structures for the main domes, with *Bóveda Catalana* (Catalan vault) as the primary structural system for the corridors connecting the different buildings.[4] And third, the whole complex established a relationship with the exuberant landscape, one of the most biodiverse in Cuba.[5] The choice of materials and the extremely efficient structure were a direct result of geopolitical circumstances. The imposition of the US economic blockade on October 19, 1960 had led to a steep rise in the cost of imported materials and no steel or Portland cement was produced on the island.

During the development of the projects, a series of regular workshops took place in the Country Club to train not only construction workers but also students from the School of Architecture and Engineering in Havana (Escuela de Arquitectura y Ingenieros de La Habana). ENA turned out to be a theoretical and practical laboratory of architecture, with students and workers learning to build this experimental hybrid structural system at the same time as they studied political and social structures. First mobilized in the building of the school, this knowledge was later applied to the construction of social housing and other projects all over the island during the first decade of the revolution. The pedagogies practiced within ENA were a zealous attempt to supplant old political and social hierarchies through architecture and to challenge the path of academic teaching as well, by bridging the gap between pedagogy and practice.

This pedagogical project was part of a wider literacy campaign, promoted by Castro as a means to renew the country:[6] the whole population of Cuba had to be educated in order to dismantle the ancient distinction between workers and masters.[7] As Che Guevara noted, "we began to feel in our bones the need for a definitive change in the lives of these people. The idea of reform became clear, and communion with the people ceased being theory and became a fundamental part of our being."[8] In this sense, ENA created a horizontal structure that became the emblem of the revolution: if the vertical structures of buildings like the Hotel Riviera (Johnson and Polevitzky and Carrera, 1957) or the American Embassy (Harrison and Abramowitz with Mira and Rosich, 1952) epitomized the old regime, the horizontal forms of ENA—both metaphorical and literal, in their construction techniques, working structures, and forms—inaugurated a new era.[9]

The complex officially opened on July 26, 1965, but work on many of the buildings had been suspended prior to that date.[10] The sexual connotations of some of the structures (including the "Papaya," a fountain in the shape of a vulva) were considered too extravagant and bourgeois by Castro's regime. With the schools in various stages of use and abandonment, Ricardo Porro left Cuba for France in 1966, disillusioned. Vittorio Garatti was accused of espionage and was eventually expelled from the island in 1974. Only Roberto Gottardi stayed in Cuba and tried to secure national landmark status for ENA, something that was finally achieved in 1999, after international recognition led to attempts to finish the original project. In the early 2000s Garatti quipped "Apúrense" (Hurry up), expressing his desire to complete the schools while the original architects were still alive. Since then, his two fellow architects have passed away: Porro in 2014 and Gottardi in 2017.[11]

^ Roberto Gottardi and modelmakers with model of theater, c. 1962.

< Concrete ring base for Catalan vaults, 1962.

≪ School of Ballet under construction, c. 1962. Photograph by Paolo Gasparini.

1. Alberto Korda, author of these famous photographs, declared that the shots were taken in Havana's Country Club in 1959. This information was corroborated in the auction of the originals at Dominic Winter Auction House (UK) in 2010, but others have recently pointed out that the event took place in Colinas de Villa Real in 1962, shortly after the Cuban missile crisis. In any case, the powerful narrative of the revolutionaries in the former Country Club continued.
2. The Country Club was so exclusive that even Fulgencio Batista (the military dictator of Cuba from 1952 to 1959 and honorary club member number 1018) was not allowed to enjoy its facilities. Being biracial, he was barred from entering. See Frank Argote-Freyre, *Fulgencio Batista: From Revolutionary to Strongman* (New Brunswick, NJ: Rutgers University Press, 2006).
3. "A Cluster of Bubbles," *Architectural Forum*, no. 124 (January-February 1966): 80–85.
4. See Isabella Douglas, Rebecca K. Napolitano, Maria Garlock, and Branko Glisic, "Cuba's National School of Ballet: Redefining a structural icon," *Engineering Structures* 204 (2020): 110040.
5. Ricardo Porro, "Écoles d'art à la Havane," *Architecture d'Aujourd'hui*, no. 119 (March 1965): 52–56.

6. For more information on the literacy campaign of 1960: Michelle Chase, "The Country and the City in the Cuban Revolution," *Colombia Internacional*. 73 (January–June 2011): 121–142.
7. Joaquín Chávez, "The Pedagogy of Revolution: Popular Intellectuals and the Origins of the Salvadoran Insurgency, 1960–1980," PhD diss. (New York University).
8. Che Guevara, *Reminiscences of the Cuban Revolutionary War* (New York: Ocean Press, 2006). Originally published in 1963 as *Reminiscencias de Cuba*.
9. Roberto Segre, *Arquitectura y urbanismo de la revolución cubana* (La Habana: Pueblo y Educación, 1989).
10. John Loomis, *Revolution of Forms: Cuba's Forgotten Art Schools* (Princeton: Princeton Architectural Press, 1998).
11. A first draft of this text was published in the booklet of the exhibition *Liquid La Habana: Ice Cream, Rum, Waves, and Spouts* at the School of Architecture in Princeton University (April 9–May 11, 2018). This project grew out of the 2017 seminar Havana: Architecture, Urbanism, and Literature in Transition, taught at Princeton University by professors Beatriz Colomina and Rubén Gallo, with Ivan L. Munuera and Bart-Jan Polman as assistants in instruction.

BUILDING INTEGRATION

Michael Abrahamson, James Graham

Protagonists Gunnar Birkerts (1925–2017),
George A. Owens (1919–2003),
J. Irwin Miller (1909–2004)
Institution Tougaloo College
Location Jackson, MS, USA
Dates 1965–1973

Commissioned at the height of the civil rights era in 1965, Gunnar Birkerts' design for Tougaloo College, a historically Black college near Jackson, Mississippi probes the extent to which architecture itself might operate pedagogically, as a participant in a fraught and ongoing project of integration. Stemming from a $75,000 grant from the Cummins Engine Foundation—a sum that had to cover both a radical restructuring of the curriculum and an architectural master plan—Birkerts' plan for Tougaloo was a latticed concrete megastructure. A model of a kind of urbanity, the building was conceived as a "way station" to prepare students to follow the well-worn paths of the Great Migration that led from the rural South to the increasingly urbanized North and defined the lives of so many African Americans during the twentieth century.[1] At a moment of social foment, countercultural critique, and pedagogical innovations in many US and European schools of architecture, Tougaloo was an on-the-ground experiment that imagined architecture itself as education-through-acclimation by triangulating curriculum and construction with an integrationist corporate philanthropy.

Even before Birkerts began preparing his plan, Tougaloo was a center of civil rights activism. Students were regular participants in sit-ins and boycotts in nearby Jackson, and the campus served as a haven during the Freedom Summer that challenged the segregation of Southern transit systems in 1964. The campus also served as a laboratory of integration where college-sponsored events like Ernst Borinski's "Social Science Forums" regularly brought Black and white Mississippians together to discuss alternatives to the state's segregationist society and develop resistance networks.[2] The master plan was expected to literally concretize this kind of interaction into a new form of campus life where, in the words of college president George A. Owens, a predominantly Black student body and a predominantly white faculty would learn to live together "by doing it."[3]

"Integration" at Tougaloo was simultaneously architectural, pedagogical, and a subject of purposive corporate philanthropy. For Owens, Tougaloo was a site for integrating the students' own histories and perspectives into higher education: the "total life of the campus must be a learning experience," he argued.[4] For J. Irwin Miller, the industrialist behind Cummins Engine and a patron of modern architecture in Columbus, Indiana and elsewhere, integration was both a moral imperative and economic "enlightened self-interest," as he sought out training grounds like Tougaloo for producing able clerical workers.[5] And for Birkerts, the project offered an opportunity to tightly enmesh the functional needs of the college while testing then-current notions of architectural flexibility.

The architecture's materiality was itself thought to perform pedagogically. Concrete was seen as an expedient material integrator—holding together typically disparate elements like door bucks, electrical wiring, plumbing, waterproofing, and insulation while compressing construction timelines—but also as a means of skilling a cadre of workers outside of the segregated Mississippi trade unions. Training workers of color in an integrated system of construction at Tougaloo was meant to free the college from complicity in discriminatory employment practices while building a new class of skilled tradespeople to be hired by Black-owned businesses in the state. In the end, however, the Birkerts design proved to be a challenge for inexperienced fabricators and contractors working with a concrete panel production system imported from West Germany, and ultimately only the library and two dormitories were built as the project became mired in construction difficulties.

The Tougaloo project remained incomplete in other senses as well. The optimism that underpinned the Great Society federal programs of the 1960s were supplanted by Richard Nixon's "Southern strategy," which aimed toward racial polarization rather than the integrations imagined by Owens, Miller, and Birkerts. The Great Migration's promise similarly ran aground as urban protests and uprisings in the late 1960s unmasked the pervasive prejudice and economic disadvantage faced by African Americans in industrial cities across the country. At the same time, the megastructural ambitions of the Birkerts master plan changed their valence. While originally conceived as an integrationist laboratory, the plan came under critique from students radicalized by the Black Power movement. Students felt that the controlled and encompassing

FORUM

< Cover of *Architectural Forum*, April 1966. Design by Peter Bradford based on GBA's Tougaloo College master plan.

> Tougaloo College under construction. Winston A. Burnett Co. set up a precasting plant on campus, next to the water tower, to produce concrete panels for the dormitory.

1. "Designed for Mobility, Both Social and Physical: Three Colleges by Gunnar Birkerts," *Architectural Record* 144, no. 4 (October 1968): 129–144.
2. Maria Lowe, "'Sowing the Seeds of Discontent': Tougaloo College's Social Science Forums as a Prefigurative Movement Free Space, 1952–1964," *Journal of Black Studies* 39, no. 6 (2009): 865–887.
3. George A. Owens, "Inaugural Address," in Inauguration of George A. Owens as President of Tougaloo College, April 21, 1966, Box 3, Folder 8, George A. Owens Papers, Tougaloo College Archives, 32. The inauguration doubled as the first public presentation of Birkerts' master plan.
4. George A. Owens, "An Educational Policy for Tougaloo College" (February 8, 1967), "Speeches, 1964–1967," Box 6, Folder 20, George A. Owens Papers, Tougaloo College Archives.
5. J. Irwin Miller, "Social Responsibilities of the Corporation and the Corporate Executive," Address at Young Presidents' Organization, Columbus, Indiana, September 14, 1970, 2, Box 533, Folder 2, Irwin-Sweeney-Miller Family Papers, Indiana Historical Society.

architecture proposed in the Tougaloo master plan was an emblem of a deeper transition—replacing the local and community-driven mission that the college had pursued for a century with something more like a managerial finishing school to the benefit of self-interested white philanthropists like Miller, no matter how enlightened their intentions.

Its failure to be fully realized notwithstanding, the intervention of Birkerts, Owens, and Miller at Tougaloo recognized that architecture and urbanism are instrumental within a fabric of social relations, racial and otherwise, and like the more critical or utopian propositions of the era, it sought to transform those relations by reinventing construction processes and urban forms. Tougaloo's mobilization of its campus as both a vocational training ground and an apparatus for effecting social change illustrates one among many pedagogical functions to which architecture might be put at a moment of pedagogical radicalism.

DESIGNING DISSENT

Ana María León

Protagonists João Batista Vilanova Artigas
(1915–1985), Carlos Millan (1927–1964),
Lourival Gomes Machado (1917–1967),
Sergio Ferro (1938–), Flávio Império (1935–1985),
Rodrigo Lefèvre (1938–1984)
Institution Faculdade de Arquitetura e Urbanismo
da Universidade de São Paulo (FAU-USP)
Location São Paulo, Brazil
Dates 1962–1969

In 1962 a curriculum reform led by João Batista
Vilanova Artigas, Carlos Millan, and Lourival Gomes
Machado restructured the FAU-USP (Faculdade de
Arquitetura e Urbanismo da Universidade de São
Paulo) into the departments of Projects, History of
Architecture, and Technology of Architecture. For
the first time since the school's founding in 1948,
architecture was treated as an independent course
of study, rather than a subfield of engineering.[1] The
link to engineering—enshrined in a government
decree of 1933—had proved an advantage in the
context of Brazil's rapid industrialization. However,
many architects—Vilanova Artigas among them—
thought it relegated architecture to a secondary
status and gave an unfair advantage to foreign architects, who were already favored by the dominance of
their standards and measurements.[2]

The main consequence of the 1962 reform was
to transform the former polytechnic approach to
composition into an expanded understanding of design
encompassing industrial design, planning, and visual
communication. Artigas had studied this approach
in the United States, which he had visited in 1947
with the express purpose of observing how Bauhaus
pedagogy was being implemented in US architecture
schools. But for Artigas, the reform went beyond
interdisciplinary changes: in his inaugural lecture at
the new FAU-USP building (which he had designed with
Carlos Cascaldi) he played on the multiple meanings of
the word "design," linking it both to form-making and
to intention—to political change. The strengthening
of the design curriculum was conceived to free the
discipline of its lingering dependency on engineering
and to empower local professionals faced with an influx
of foreign architecture firms, whose staff were often
trained at the same schools he had visited in the US.

And yet the curricular reform at FAU-USP was
presented as another continuation of the original

Bauhaus, with no mention of the United States—a
strategy of absorbing the "intruder" that echoed
artist Oswald de Andrade's 1928 "Manifesto
Antropófago," which claimed that Brazil "cannibal-
ized" stronger cultures in order to resist cultural
domination.[3] While participating in modernity, the
FAU-USP sought to resist its totalizing effects:
by promoting a technocratic modernity through
advances in structural engineering and reinforced
concrete, it would contribute to the rise of the
so-called Paulista School. However, this position
was opposed by a younger generation, all of them
former students of Vilanova Artigas, and now
also teaching at FAU-USP—Sergio Ferro, Flávio
Império, and Rodrigo Lefèvre—who argued that
the advanced technological solutions favored by
Vilanova Artigas aligned him and the school with the
developmentalist project of the state.[4] Organized as
Arquitetura Nova, they chose instead to collaborate
with local construction processes and traditions in
ways that allowed them to remain independent from
the pressures of the market and the cannibalizing
strategies of the state. While this relative freedom
gave them some level of control over production,
it also reduced the scale of their interventions.

As the military dictatorship took over the country,
these internal debates at FAU-USP were superseded
by the collective urgency of resistance, protest, and
exile. In this context, Arquitetura Nova eventually
dissolved: Império turned to theater design, Ferro
relocated to France, and Lefèvre died prematurely
in a car accident. Artigas, who had fled the country,
would eventually return and collaborate in the
construction of state-sponsored schools and housing.
Tamed by political compromise, the architecture of
the Paulista school, with its bold structural displays,
would become the perfect symbol of the modern
image the regime wished to promote. However, the
FAU-USP building, with its large open atrium, would
remain an important protagonist in the student
resistance movement. The school continues to be
a site for demonstrations and meetings—a building
designed for dissent.

> Demonstration
in the central hall
of the FAU-USP
building designed
by Vilanova Artigas.
Photograph by Raul
Garcez.

< Central hall of the FAU-USP building designed by Vilanova Artigas. Photographer unknown.

1. Sylvia Ficher, *Os arquitetos da Poli: ensino e profissão em São Paulo* (São Paulo: EdUSP, 2005).

2. For more on this history, see "Designing Dissent: Vilanova Artigas and the São Paulo School of Architecture," in *Architecture and the Paradox of Dissidence*, ed. Ines Weizman (London: Routledge, 2013), 74–88. For more on Artigas, see Ruth Verde Zein, *Tendências atuais da arquitetura brasileira: Vilanova Artigas, 1915–1985* (São Paulo: Projeto, 1985).

3. Oswald de Andrade, "Manifesto Antropofago," *Revista de Antropofagia* 1 (1928): 3, 7.

4. Sergio Ferro, "Arquitetura Nova," *Teoria e Pratica* 37 (1967): 3–15; Roberto Lefèvre, "Uma crise em desemvolvimento," *Acrópole* 333 (1966): 22–23. See also Pedro Fiori Arantes, *Arquitetura Nova* (São Paulo: Editora 34, 2002); Sergio Ferro, "Concrete as Weapon," trans. Silke Kapp, Katie Lloyd Thomas, and João Marcos de Almeida Lopes, *Harvard Design Magazine: No Sweat* 46 (F/W 2018); and Ana Paula Koury, *Arquitetura Moderna Brasileira: Uma Crise em Desemvolvimento* (São Paulo: EdUSP, 2019).

PASSIVE ARCHITECTURE, SOFT PEDAGOGY

Zvi Efrat

Protagonists Arieh Sharon (1900–1984),
Augustine Akhuemokhan Egbor (1924–2011)
Institution University of Ife
Location Ife, Nigeria
Dates 1960–early 1980s

The University of Ife in West Nigeria (now Obafemi Awolowo University) was conceived as part of the initial process of decolonization and nation-building that followed Nigeria's independence in 1960. The story of the making of its campus—revered in a local anthem as "The Most Beautiful Campus in Africa"—is an epic tale of a genuine ambition, shared by politicians, educators, and planners alike, to stage architecture itself as the ultimate pedagogical apparatus. At Ife, a colonial modernism, in its rather transposable structuralist, brutalist, and tropical modes, was effectively reclaimed as a (passive) "well-tempered environment," readily adaptable to the local climate and native habitus. The campus served as the scaffold and casing for a new intellectual agenda, a new curriculum, and new layouts of formal and informal academic activity.

The designer of the campus was Arieh Sharon, a Bauhaus graduate and protégé of Hannes Meyer, who had worked with him on the Trade Union School in Bernau, near Berlin. After returning to Palestine in 1931, Sharon became the leading architect of the local Trade Union Federation. In 1948, the year the State of Israel came into being, he was appointed head of the State Planning Authority and began masterminding what I have framed as the *Israeli Project*.[1] His involvement with the planning and landscaping of the Ife campus and the design of many of its buildings, in collaboration with the Lagos-based architect A. A. Egbor and the Israeli company AMY, was part of Israel's development aid program in sub-Saharan Africa.[2] Sharon considered the Ife campus his last *grand ensemble* and worked on it for over two decades, from 1960 until the early 1980s, a formative period in Nigerian culture and education referred to by some as postcolonial, by others as quasi-colonial.

A cut out in the thick bush land, the Ife campus is a tightly gridded and intricately woven system of ramps, balconies, and covered walkways feeding perpendicular serial buildings and connecting a range of pocket gardens and open patios between and within the buildings. "We agreed with the professors that, in view of the local conditions and customs…the layout of the campus…should be as compact as possible," Sharon writes in his autobiography, elaborating on the thorough preliminary environmental research that guided the design and the scrupulous calculations to maximize air flow, minimize heat gain, and provide protection against the monsoons.[3]

Evidently, several years into the design process, Sharon's radical instrumentality developed into an

> Assembly hall, Ife University, 1960s. Drawing by Harold Rubin.

207

alternative model to what had already been canonized as "tropical architecture." The University of Ife was conceived and designed as a riposte to the British colonial education system, as embodied by the first university in Nigeria, the University of Ibadan, planned by the architects Maxwell Fry and Jane Drew, the main articulators and practitioners of tropical modernism in West Africa.[4] Sharon regarded Fry and Drew's climate-responsive approach, with its fixation on the building's skin, as superficial and often purely decorative.[5] By contrast, the design of the Ife campus did not rely on elements and fixtures such as "concrete canopies and frames around the windows, or louvers and precast ornamental elements around the terraces."[6] Instead, it offered an integrated habitat composed of self-shading inverted ziggurats, perimeter balconies, shafts for "stack-effect" ventilation, open ground floors and a continuous landscape, extending under the buildings and blending natural and architectural surfaces.

The Ife campus performs today as it was initially designed. Its architecture still demonstrates incomparable climatic efficiency and displays remarkable plasticity, porosity, resilience, and artistry. Its efficiency, I would argue, is precisely what produces fluidity and ease, blurs boundaries between formal lecture halls and spontaneously repurposed settings, and allows for a pedagogical eccentricity, as it were.

Much of the academic routine is performed in the open, under buildings, on balconies and staircases, in patios and gardens, shifting according to light, humidity or acoustic conditions.

In filmed interviews conducted in 2018 with architects and scholars teaching at Ife University,[7] the architecture of the campus is rendered as both the staged setting for direct experience and the object of incessant study. Babatunde Jaiyeoba, a former student and now a junior professor at Ife, describes the campus as the core curriculum itself:

> There is almost nothing you want to teach in architecture that will not have precepts on this campus, whether in terms of forms, spaces, decoration, landscape, climate, or even traditional building practices. When we want to explain aspects of architecture to the students, we often tell them: have you passed through this particular area on campus before, have you seen this? I personally always emphasize to the students that just moving around this campus alone is enough of a laboratory for them.

Prof. Bayo Amole, a senior professor at Ife, opens a window onto the allure of animism and the correlation between an architecture-without-doors and the prospect of soft pedagogy:

> The university itself is strange to the Yoruba culture. The very idea of a university, separate from the town, it's like a sacred space. ...
> For many, this collection of buildings seems like a picturesque place, a place where you see the buildings as background. But here, you live with the buildings. You become part of them. ...

Now you see, the open space that we find here, it is formal where it ought to be formal and it is informal. It endeared itself so much that the students call it *motion ground*.... Some people have compared some of the buildings with a train station. They are very long, but you stand at one end and see somebody at the other end. There is something very African about the idea that collectively you can see yourselves. You don't enter the building straight, you go into the building and it creates a small space for you to actually assemble before you begin to take the staircase. And in the original buildings there were no doors. It just means that the external flows into the internal. Some don't like it but the experience is wonderful.

< ∨ Arieh Sharon, Ife University, Nigeria, 1960s.

1. See Zvi Efrat, *The Object of Zionism: The Architecture of Israel* (Leipzig: Spector Books, 2018), 59–87.
2. See Ayala Levin, "Exporting Architectural National Expertise: Arieh Sharon's Ife University Campus in West-Nigeria (1962–1976)," in *Nationalism and Architecture*, ed. Raymond Quek, Darren Deane (Farnham, Surrey and Burlington, VT: Ashgate Publishing, 2012), 53–66; and Zvi Efrat, "Proxy Colonialism: The Export of Israeli Architecture to Africa," in *African Modernism: The Architecture of Independence. Ghana, Senegal, Cote d'Ivoire, Kenya, Zambia*, ed. Manuel Herz (Zurich: Park Books, 2015), 491–501.
3. Arieh Sharon, *Kibbutz+Bauhaus* (Stuttgart: Karl Kramer Verlag, 1976), 125–28. For a detailed description of the architecture of the campus see Abimbola O. Asojo and Babatunde E. Jaiyeobe, "Modernism and the Cultural Expression in University Campus Design: The Nigerian Example," *ArchNet-IJAR: International Journal of Architectural Research* 10, no. 3 (2016): 21–35.
4. Maxwell Fry and Jane Drew, *Tropical Architecture in the Humid Zone* (London: B. T. Batsford, 1956).
5. Tropical architecture's preoccupation with the building's skin was theorized by Hannah le Roux at the symposium *Decolonizing the Campus*, Goethe-Institut Nigeria, Lagos, November 2018.
6. Sharon, *Kibbutz+Bauhaus*.
7. Zvi Efrat, *The Most Beautiful Campus in Africa*, film produced for Bauhaus Imaginista exhibition, HKW, Berlin, 2019.

SELF-ORGANIZATION TOWARD SELF-DETERMINATION

Sandi Hilal

Protagonists Neighbors
Institution Neighborhood Schools
Location Beit Sahour, Palestine
Dates 1987

When the First Intifada broke out in 1987, the Israeli military occupation imposed curfews on Palestinian cities, villages, and refugee camps. The collective punishment was intended to curtail the Palestinians' struggle for the right to self-determination—to make them stop the daily actions of the Intifada, from stone throwing to strikes, and to prevent their collective self-organization, whether in the farming of land or in learning environments.

And yet, neighborhood communities would continue to operate, becoming central to the organization of daily life. They made plans to protect the neighborhood and to feed people by cultivating all unused land. Vitally, they also worked to ensure that schooling would continue, even though schools and universities had been shut down. It took just days for the neighborhood schools to be formed. Every member of the community who had a garage or an empty room in their house cleaned and prepared it to become a classroom. Mothers and fathers became teachers and worked together with groups

of children, teaching whatever they were best at. As part of the school activities, the community was involved in agriculture and in the harvesting of crops. Education was a way of liberating the mind even before bodies, houses, cities, and homelands could be free. But the new neighborhood schools also probed the limits of traditional education, which could be a means to enslave people.

"I feel it's my home.[1] I belong to it and love it. I feel free and independent unlike in my previous school, which has now closed. There, I always felt watched and controlled, in the classroom, the corridor, or at the plaza of the school. I was constantly under surveillance, afraid of being caught doing something I wasn't supposed to be doing. I still remember what happened to my classmates and me during the first weeks of the Intifada by the end of the 1980s, before the schools were shut down by the Israeli military regime. I still remember my engagement in the first school strike. Like the rest of the schools in the West Bank, we had endorsed the request for united Palestinian political leadership. Our plan was to go to our school and announce a general strike. I remember the morning when we refused to enter our classes and we all sat down on the floor, one next to the other, in our wide and long school corridor. A few minutes later, everyone around me was whispering 'She's arrived, she's arrived.' The school headmistress was short and had fat legs. We were all terrified of her. My heart began to beat fast and I could feel the heartbeats of the other students around me. She stood there among us and said

> Children and women protest during the First Intifada, Beit Sahour. Photographer unknown (identification at this time would have meant putting oneself at risk).

< Remnants of a house destroyed by the Israeli military occupation, Beit Sahour, 1987. Photographer unknown.

loudly, 'Everyone go to their classrooms immediately. I don't want to see anyone in the corridor.'

"I was terrified. I looked around and saw that everyone had remained seated. A few seconds passed and no one made a move. I felt very scared but strong; confused and at the same time very determined. It all happened in the blink of an eye. I heard her shouting again, ordering us to move, but as she got angrier, I felt stronger and more determined to stay and to not enter the classroom. I remember saying to myself, 'Don't worry, she doesn't carry a gun like the Israeli soldiers,' and if the kids who confront the soldiers with stones don't fear their guns, why should I fear the voice of the headmistress?

"That was my first encounter with authority. I then realized that authority has different forms and motives, different agendas. I understood that I do not want to learn because my headmistress or my teachers or my family want me to learn. I don't want to learn because I am afraid. I want to learn because I enjoy it."

This joy of learning and of decolonizing would never abandon these students. Education revealed itself as a powerful tool, one that the colonizers deemed dangerous. And still, the project of neighborhood schools was questioned. Some elderly members in the community insisted: "But the neighborhood school can never be a permanent solution."

"Why not? Don't you understand? In the neighborhood school, I learn because I want to, not because I am obliged to. I like to feel that the school belongs to me. We all share this respect for this space. This is the school I dream about. I ask you again, do you think that an architect can contribute to the creation of this type of school?"

1. Quotes in this text refer to author's own recollections of the school.

THE "EXPERIMENTAL BUILDING"

Julia Gatley, Bill McKay

Protagonist Maurice K. Smith (1926–2020)
Institution University of Auckland
Location Auckland, New Zealand
Date 1968

In 1968 the University of Auckland advertised for a new chair and dean of architecture. The New Zealand architect and educator Maurice K. Smith was among those who expressed interest. A graduate of the Auckland School of Architecture, Smith had been teaching at the Massachusetts Institute of Technology (MIT) since 1958. On sabbatical in 1968, he chose to spend the year in the country where he had been born and grown up.[1]

During his sabbatical Smith taught a final-year class at his alma mater. His students were asked to design and build a new studio on a strip of land between two old cottages, both used as architecture studios, on the university's city campus. The Experimental Building, as they called it, was built during the wet winter months from June to August, with a small budget arranged by the school of architecture staff. The studio was used for ten years

before the university demolished it, along with the neighboring structures, to make way for a carpark.

Outwardly the Experimental Building looked two-storied, but in fact it had five floor levels, supported on timber posts. The exterior was clad with weatherboards and fiber-cement sheeting, with an upper-level line of windows of different shapes and sizes, some secondhand, topped by skylights. The interior was even more adventurous, with consecutive platforms spiraling up toward the light. The irregular staircase absorbed at least one salvaged newel post. Each platform was large enough to accommodate drawing boards where students could work.[2]

Smith's own house in Massachusetts, a meandering montage started in 1963, provided something of a precedent for the design. As Mark Jarzombek has shown, the house incorporated student design-build components and reused demolition materials, and its seemingly chaotic appearance belied a "highly conceptual" base, grounded in a particular logic.[3] Besides this, in 1966 and 1967 MIT architecture students had built a series of mezzanines or platforms in their drafting studios, which were published in *Architectural Design* in August 1968.[4] The Auckland students knew this article and quoted excerpts from it in their own student newsletter, observing that with these ad-hoc constructions the MIT students had "rebelled against the constraining

environment" of their two-story drafting rooms.[5] The Aucklanders clearly saw it as a challenge to both the educational institution and to society at large, and took inspiration from it. In 1969 they reflected on the Auckland building:

> When Maurice Smith (who?) hit the scene last year, [the final-year cohort] built its junkyard—woodyard—work-shop—studio experiment in Wynyard St., and minor revolutions rippled the otherwise calm surfaces of [earlier year groups]. Scaffolding and purloined timber appeared and were erected to cause irritation with the staff...[6]

The Experimental Building may well have irritated some of the staff, but others admired it. Faculty member John Hunt described it as "Piranesi, writ small,"[7] while David Mitchell, a leading member of a mid-1970s breakaway group committed to vertical studio teaching, saw it as "a measure of the toler-ance of the times, and of its widespread energy."[8] The Experimental Building also earned a reputation as the site of many great parties.

   The University of Auckland offered Smith a chair of architecture,[9] but not the role of head of school and dean of the faculty. In hindsight, he acknowledged that the Experimental Building had probably been too radical for the decision-makers. He declined the Auckland offer, choosing to stay at MIT, where he remained until 1996, when he retired as professor emeritus.

∨ The Experimental Building, showing its location between two old cottages. Photographs and montage by Tet Shin Choong, reproduced in his BArch building report, "The School of Archi-tecture, University of Auckland," 1970.

1. See Bill McKay, "The Counter-Culture and its Containment: The Loose Years," in *The Auckland School: 100 Years of Architecture and Planning*, ed. Julia Gatley and Lucy Treep (Auckland: School of Architecture and Planning, University of Auckland, 2017), 76–79.

2. For more information, see Ian George, "The 'Experimental Building': Architectural Students Design and Build a Studio," Study paper no. 15, School of Architecture, University of Auckland, 1980; and William Frederick Benfield, "The Experimental Studio by 4th year Students at the School of Architecture: An Experiment in Architecture," BArch building report, University of Auckland, 1969.

3. Mark Jarzombek, "The Alternative *Firmitas* of Maurice Smith," in *A Second Modernism: MIT, Architecture, and the Techno-Social Moment*, ed. Arindam Dutta (Cambridge MA: SA+P Press, 2013), 553–573.

4. Rolf Goetze et al, "Squatters at MIT," *Architectural Design* 38, no. 8 (August 1968): 387–388.

5. "Squatters at MIT," *It* (April 1969): 10.

6. Ibid.

7. John Hunt in an interview with Lucy Treep, Auckland, November 10, 2016.

8. David Mitchell in an interview with Lucy Treep, Auckland, May 16, 2016.

9. "Special Conditions Relating to 4th Chair in Architecture," attachment to J. A. Kirkness, Registrar, "Situations Vacant—General," September 30, 1968. University of Auckland Council Minutes, 1968, vol. 3, 34.

Environmental Communications aerial (blimp) photography session.

MEDIA EXPERIMENTS

ORGANIZING VISUAL EXPERIENCE

Pep Avilés

Protagonist Gyorgy Kepes (1906–2001)
Institution Massachusetts Institute
of Technology (MIT)
Location Cambridge, Massachusetts, USA
Dates 1946–1967

Of the multiple metamorphoses that the famous *Vorkurs* underwent in the post-Bauhaus years, the visual education proposed by the Hungarian-born artist Gyorgy Kepes was one of the most sophisticated and radical installments. In the late 1940s Kepes underscored a crucial difference between his pedagogical approach and that of his former mentor and colleague, László Moholy-Nagy. Whereas the former's interests gravitated toward "organizing" the new findings of visual experience so as to emphasize "the meaning of order in its present social context,"[1] Kepes's postwar pedagogical model aimed at developing new forms of environmental art and public space that were integrated with science and technology. Kepes had emigrated to the United States in 1937, responding to Moholy-Nagy's call to head the Department of Color and Light at the recently founded "New Bauhaus" School of Design in Chicago. His prior knowledge of light-capture techniques—photograms, photography, and "photo-paintings" (paint applied to a glass plate, which he then used as if it were a negative)—informed the development of his visual and graphic pedagogy. His early work and artistic experiments (published in the book *Language of Vision*, 1944) illustrate his efforts to find a new visual grammar to increase meaning and effectiveness in the advertising industry.[2]

The reputation provided by his first book set Kepes up for more ambitious academic challenges. In 1946, a few months before Moholy-Nagy's death, he took up a post at the school of architecture at Massachusetts Institute of Technology. Those years were marked by a blurring of boundaries at MIT, with different departments and colleges being encouraged to engage in multidisciplinary work. Kepes's pedagogical ideas helped to inform the reorganization of the Drawing Fundamentals course, which included visual instruction along with classes on form, light, color, and graphic design.[3] Departing from the material tactility of previous Bauhaus-inspired exercises,

Kepes embedded an increasingly visible scientific and technological culture in an otherwise professionally oriented school. He proposed a curriculum where the entire visual experience was organized and analyzed according to scientific standards.[4] In his classes, art and science became intertwined, producing new expertise in image thinking and image construction. Training the architect's eye to become attuned to the rapid changes affecting postwar culture became a priority.

Kepes's synthesis of art and science drew inspiration from the abstraction of scientific instruments, techniques, and the aesthetics of the technological image. In 1950 he curated the exhibition *Visual Education for Architects* using photographs, charts, models, and diagrams to summarize the ways students assimilated the new principles of design through the four-part structure of the course: the organization of material and scientific data according to issues of balance, rhythm, proportion, and scale; the implementation of formal results from the use of different media; the identification of relations in the human environment; and, finally, the development of individual techniques for communication based on images, signs, and symbols.[5]

A year later MIT hosted another exhibition, *The New Landscape*, that was a landmark in Kepes's ongoing integration of art and science—and the precursor to his visually groundbreaking publication, *The New Landscape in Art and Science* (1956).[6] Kepes saw *The New Landscape* as a teaching instrument, showing students how to combine rational analysis with perceptual enjoyment. Oscillating between aesthetic perception and scientific innovation, it illustrated a radical visual array of the multiple scales and formal patterns of nature—an optical mode of thinking valid for designers, artists, architects, and town planners alike. Largely written by 1952, the book ranged from primitive art to a constellation of scientific and technical images illustrating an aesthetic teleology grounded in technological knowledge. These included more than one hundred images that used scientific means of reproduction (photomicrography, high-speed photography, stroboscopic photography, radiography, radar photography) to document natural phenomena and experiments undertaken in the university's research laboratories and the research departments of commercial corporations. *The New Landscape* also sought to overcome "visual illiteracy in an age increasingly dependent on perceptual awareness."[7] Essays on art and architecture appeared alongside texts by mathematician and

theorist Norbert Wiener, structural engineer Paul Weidlinger, experimental physicist Bruno Rossi—all MIT faculty—as well as crystallographer Kathleen Lonsdale and semiotician Charles Morris, among others. Collaborations with colleagues characterized Kepes's years at MIT. Between 1954 and 1959 he and Kevin Lynch documented the psychological impact of the Boston cityscape in their Rockefeller Foundation-funded research, "Perceptual Form of the City." This collaborative work would form the scientific base for Lynch's influential *The Image of the City*, published in 1960.

Kepes invoked the structural laws of visual experience as a means to inform social meaning and civic engagement in design. From 1956 he offered graduate students at MIT a series of seminars addressing the different topics of his Visual Fundamentals course—scale, proportion, module, rhythm, patterns, signs, symbols, structure. These seminars would result in the *Vision + Value* series of publications edited by Kepes, which included work by his students. They were also one of the spurs for the creation of MIT's

Center for Advanced Visual Studies (CAVS) in 1967. Collaborations with Rudolf Arnheim, John Cage, Marshall McLuhan, Cyril Stanley Smith, and Lancelot L. Whyte, to name just a few, demonstrate the inter-disciplinary nature of these seminars.

However, there was a pragmatism to Kepes's new pedagogical direction that reflected the abandon-ment of the utopianism of the immediate postwar years. Ultimately, his teaching would help to align art, science, and the humanities and to emphasize the cognitive role of design as the integration of knowl-edge became essential to MIT's standing as one of the crucial postwar institutions of education in the US.[8]

∧ *Light as a Creative Medium* exhibition designed by Gyorgy Kepes for the Carpenter Center of Visual Arts, Harvard University, 1965. Photographer unknown.

^ View of *The New Landscape* exhibition, Hayden Gallery, Massachusetts Institute of Technology, 1951.

1. Smithsonian Archives of American Art, TSL from Kepes to Sybil Moholy-Nagy, September 8, 1948 (Reel 5303).
2. Gyorgy Kepes, *Language of Vision: Painting, Photography, Advertisement-Design* (Chicago: Paul Theobald, 1944).
3. Anna Vallye, "The Middleman: Kepes's Instruments," in *A Second Modernism: MIT, Architecture, and the "Techno-Social" Movement*, ed. Arindam Dutta (Cambridge, MA: MIT Press, 2013), 144–185. See also Reinhold Martin, "Pattern-Seeing," in *The Organizational Complex: Architecture, Media, and Corporate Space* (Cambridge; MA: MIT Press, 2003), 42–79.
4. Gyorgy Kepes, *The MIT Years: Painting, Photographic Work, Environmental Pieces, Projects at the Center for Advanced Visual Studies* (Cambridge; MA: MIT Press, 1978).
5. Gyorgy Kepes Papers, Archives of American Art, Smithsonian Institution. [Reel 5316.] See also, "M.I.T. Explores Sight and Structure," *Architectural Forum*, March 1950.
6. Gyorgy Kepes, *The New Landscape in Art and Science* (Chicago: Paul Theobald, 1956).
7. Gyorgy Kepes Papers, Archives of American Art, Smithsonian Institution, Reel 5316. See Robin Watson, "It's Not All Mathematics at the MIT," *Industrial Photography* (November 1961): 39.
8. John R. Blakinger, *Gyorgy Kepes: Undreaming the Bauhaus* (Cambridge, MA: MIT Press, 2019).

PARASITIC PEDAGOGY: THE BUCKMINSTER FULLER TEACHING MACHINE

Mark Wigley

Protagonists R. Buckminster Fuller (1895–1983), John McHale (1922–1978), Harold Cohen (1928–2016), Serge Chermayeff (1900–1996)
Institutions Institute of Design; Black Mountain College; Department of Design, Southern Illinois University and schools around the world
Locations Chicago, IL; Asheville, NC; Carbondale, IL; Raleigh, NC; and around the world
Dates 1948–1983

From 1955 to 1970 the newly founded Department of Design at Southern Illinois University in Carbondale launched a series of overlapping modes of experimental teaching and communication. The industrial designer Harold Cohen had been poached from the Institute of Design (New Bauhaus) in Chicago to be the first director of the school and he immediately took advantage of being off the usual map to challenge normative modes of education. The first exercise, typically, threw students even further off the map. In "Who Are You and What Are You Thinking?" they were asked to design a survival kit for $10 and simply dropped off in the wilderness of a remote peninsula for three days with the kit and an emergency whistle. The idea was to understand, through their absence, the human extensions that they would be designing for the rest of their lives. Back in the school, design projects quickly took the form of applied research tasks on world issues, such as cardboard emergency housing.

A string of global personalities started to visit the seemingly isolated place, including Charles Eames, Sybil Moholy-Nagy, Marshall McLuhan, Paolo Soleri, and Félix Candela. But the biggest noise came from R. Buckminster Fuller, who became the first visiting lecturer in 1956 and a research professor in 1959, his first permanent university position. He built a dome house in town a year later, in a seven-hour performance watched by his students and the media, and it was highly promoted to simulate his residence, but Fuller's presence remained that of a permanent nomad, dropping in for eight-week workshops in between similar workshops he was holding at other schools across the continent and rarely staying more than a few days in a row. His Carbondale contract even required him to keep teaching in other institutions. He had effectively invented a new kind of school made up of his nomadic workshops within multiple institutions as a kind of parallel processing machine.

Fuller had first developed this cross-fertilization of schools the previous decade. After teaching at the Institute of Design in Chicago in the spring of 1948 he brought some of the students and research to Black Mountain College that summer; he then continued the initial work on dome structures back at the institute the following semester and at the new North Carolina State College School of Design in Raleigh during the fall of 1949.[1] His central concept of synergy (the behavior of a whole system that cannot be predicted from the behavior of its parts) was inevitably applied to teaching and the need for collaborative thinking in teams, across institutions, and across disciplines. When Fuller became director of the summer program at Black Mountain in 1949, his prospectus turned teamwork and the rejection of specialization into a polemical manifesto.[2]

Fuller's typical teaching pattern, initiated in 1948, was to give introductory lectures to the students, divide them into research teams to address different aspects of the stated problem and do physical tests before everyone finally collaboratively constructed a single one-to-one structure, usually a dome. These constructions in workshops of a few weeks or a whole semester often represented key innovations that were effectively produced not just by the student team but the net of similar teams working in parallel in different locations. Assignments usually evolved out of the most recent workshops in other schools. Students would prepare final detailed reports documenting the theory, calculations, test models, and resulting structures that became the required reading of subsequent workshops, and often articles, booklets, or books in their own right. With each visit during the workshop, Fuller would give a seminar (like the introductory lectures, this would be recorded, with each workshop typically generating one hundred hours of tape), respond to the ongoing tests, and socialize with the students in an intense flurry of activity. Fuller would be more absent than present but the empowered students would fully identify with the project and host schools would forgo the usual protocols to allow the temporary takeover of space, resources, and emotions. The work usually attracted the media, putting schools on the map. After all, the parasitic teacher was bigger than any of the hosts and vastly

^ Buckminster Fuller and students lifting a necklace dome at Black Mountain College, 1949.

bigger in attaching himself to so many hosts and redirecting flows of ideas between them.

In 1961 Fuller tried to expand and formalize this network, treating Carbondale as the central hub of a global research net. At the UIA congress in London, he called for all design schools in the world to abruptly stop teaching studio for a decade and work together on a definitive image of global resources, based on the research being done at Carbondale. John McHale, the British artist and Independent Group theorist who had been writing about Fuller since the mid-1950s, was recruited to teach and direct the World Resources Inventory at the heart of this global initiative, which was set up in a modest space above a hairdresser and travel agency in the small town. Working with a team of Carbondale students, McHale produced a series of data-intensive reports that became highly influential, as Monica Pidgeon promoted the whole enterprise in the pages of *Architectural Design*, even publishing McHale's account of the school's unique research-centered pedagogy and its aspiration to become an "educational machine" to coincide with the UIA meeting.[3] Just a year before, the school had abandoned the weight of the traditional university by moving the design studios into portable ex-military barracks and building four domes as workshops to support the studios and a flexible "space in between" for events. Some seminars were held in Fuller's dome house and his first visits had already inspired students to build a translucent dome of wood and canvas in the trees for teaching. Domes were understood as machines for gathering, visualizing, extending, and broadcasting information. The school imagined itself turning into a "brain," a giant dome-encased information system sustaining a "world research team"—not just humans assisted by the biggest computer and most advanced visualization devices available, but humans networked as a thinking machine.

A month before the announcement in London, Fuller had delivered a key public lecture at Carbondale suggesting that the whole university should move into a dome without any internal divisions. His model was a circus tent, able to host multiple simultaneous events without barriers and to be dismantled at any moment. The lecture started with Fuller's calculation that he had already been teaching 50,000 students in 106 different universities and ended with his arguing that the classroom of the future would be exponentially larger and electronic, using computers and television.

The basic idea was that all teaching would be done electronically with lifelong education at home based on two-way interactive TV. Abandoning classrooms, classes, and distinct disciplines, universities would become experimental laboratories devoted solely to research and to the crafting of TV programs to convey their discoveries into every home. The central mission was to resist "misconception extension" by stripping away all the traditional patterns of education that steadily erode a child's innate multidimensional intelligence. Students needed to "unlearn everything" and the university had to aspire to be, like any child's room, an open-ended laboratory.

The university published the lecture as the book *Education Automation.*[4] It had already taken the first steps toward "school by television" in 1960, hiring filmmaker Francis Thompson to film fifty-two hours of Fuller lecturing students at the School of Design for a possible educational TV series. The idea was for a whole suite of one-year television courses featuring Fuller aimed at different levels, including series for general education, elementary education, high school, and university, along with more specialized seminars. A twenty-minute, three-screen version was presented in New York to raise financial support.[5] Fuller personally solicited the heads of all architecture schools to commit to buy the TV series. Once again, Carbondale wanted to take advantage of its isolation. The effort was unsuccessful, but the university did generate a series of major publications and appeared at the center of the exhibitions of the decade of interschool research organized by McHale in Paris, London, Prague, and Montreal.

This effective but somewhat mythical image of a school as the hub of a global brain ended when McHale left in 1968 and Fuller a year later. But Fuller still continued to treat the revolution of education as his central mission. More precisely, he believed that traditional design education had to give way to laboratory work since the task was not to teach architecture, but to get rid of it. Architecture as normally understood had to be abandoned in favor of the idea of living within a teaching machine. Unburdened by any architectural training, Fuller was proud to have been twice expelled from Harvard. For him, all design had to be about education. Not only were all the projects of his career done as collaborations with students or ex-students, they all had education literally at their center.

Fuller's first project, the 4D house of 1927–1929, had two-way television at the heart of the plan so children would not have to go to school. The best

^ Buckminster Fuller with group in Africa. Photographer and date unknown.

professors from around the world would visit the house via the TV screen and adults were to remain permanent students. The house was an information-processing machine disconnected physically from all other houses but plugged in electronically to a global network that formed a new kind of posturbanism and a new politics of real-time collaborative decision making. Fuller's first book in 1938 talked about "television education" and the first dome houses of 1948 were already imagined as visualization devices. The idea of the house as physical shelter gave way to the idea of the house as occupiable TV set—a "valve," in Fuller's word, to regulate the mainly invisible flows of energy. The first dome assignment at the Institute of Design, and arguably the assignment of all subsequent teaching workshops, was to test "the 'Private Sky' or 'the house that was not there' idea."[6] Architecture minimizes itself in order to visualize the invisible. The destiny of architecture is information, understood as hidden pattern. From 1952 on, many of the student workshops were dedicated to the development of a Geoscope—a collective data visualization device of planetary resources that Fuller likened to a spherical TV, intended to be installed in all universities and the most public urban sites— and in early 1955 his visiting workshop at the North Carolina State College was even dedicated to the design of the future "network apparatus" of education by television and the "environmental controls" that would house it free of the usual constraints of traditional university architecture.[7]

It is finally hard to imagine the scale and radicality of Fuller's parasitic pedagogy. After fifty-five years of nomadic teaching, his final CV in 1983 lists 1,035 invited visits to 544 educational institutions, not including invitations to give single lectures. The lifelong design goal of education automation seems uncannily close to contemporary thinking about online teaching and transdisciplinarity, but the idea of dissolving architecture itself and heading ever deeper into the televisual still remains too threatening for most schools.

1. Mark Wigley, *Buckminster Fuller Inc: Architecture in the Age of Radio* (Zurich: Lars Müller, 2015).
2. Buckminster Fuller, "The Summer Institute…Black Mountain College, North Carolina 1949…An Outline by R. Buckminster Fuller, Dean of Session," Buckminster Fuller Papers, Stanford University Special Collections.
3. John McHale, "Education in Process," *Architectural Design* 31, no. 6 (July 1961): 320–322.
4. Buckminster Fuller, *Education Automation* (Carbondale: Southern Illinois University, 1962).
5. *An Educational Idea: Comprehensive Documentation of Great Men / prepared cooperatively by the Department of Design and Film Production Unit* (Carbondale: Southern Illinois University, 1960). Canadian Centre for Architecture, Montreal.
6. Buckminster Fuller, letter to Serge Chermayeff, May 26, 1948, Buckminster Fuller Papers, Stanford University Special Collections.
7. Buckminster Fuller, letter to Dean Henry Kamphoefner, School of Design, North Carolina State College, January 11, 1955, Buckminster Fuller Papers, Stanford University Special Collections.

THE GLOBAL WORKSHOP

Dirk van den Heuvel

Protagonist Jaap Bakema (1914–1981)
Institutions Various schools and academies
around the world
Locations St. Louis, MO; Cambridge, MA; Delft,
The Netherlands; Hamburg, Germany; Salzburg,
Austria; Philadelphia, PA; New York, NY: Ithaca, NY;
Barcelona, Spain, and elsewhere
Dates 1959–1981

A prolific teacher and lecturer, Jaap Bakema was like a traveling sales rep of ideas, constantly on the move around the world. Given that he was also the director of one of Europe's largest architecture firms in the second half of the century, the Van den Broek and Bakema office in Rotterdam, the list of teaching posts and guest professorships he accumulated is simply bewildering. The preferred format for these academic engagements was the workshop or design seminar— one that enabled intense study and exchange in a relatively short period of time. The preferred topic

was always a local issue related to the modernization of the city, its public spaces, and infrastructure. For instance, at Washington University, where Bakema was a visiting professor in 1959, the design project involved "The Humane Core: A Civic Center for St. Louis."[1] At Harvard it was a master class about "City Gate Boston" in anticipation of the 1966 competition for Copley Square.[2] In a report from Philadelphia we read "The noise of [the] stencil machine is every-where, multiplying reports about what has to be done waving in ever-wider circles around the problem. … [P]roblems are not solved in campus buildings and saying hello to visiting professors at student parties. Schools for design should be part of high-density areas trying to solve surrounding problems for people who now are not able to solve their problems them-selves."[3] Accordingly, during his time at Columbia University in 1970, Bakema proposed a study into urban renewal around 14th Street against the background of the ongoing national student strike.[4] Urgent societal issues formed the natural context of Bakema's educational interventions.

Bakema's teachings resisted academic ortho-doxy and master-apprentice formats. Continuous dialogue, collaborative work, and workshop-based

design studios were at the heart of his hands-on approach. He derived this working method from the Rotterdam CIAM group Opbouw, and the many Team 10 meetings he oversaw, which combined the workshop ethos with a peer review system of critique. In 1964 this approach culminated in the first International Design Seminar in Delft, where Bakema had just been appointed professor. Bakema fully credited the student association Stylos for organizing the design week "by students for students," where sixty-three students from twelve Western European countries came together to work with a Team 10 cohort of architects: Bakema, Giancarlo De Carlo, José Coderch, Oskar Hansen, Shadrach Woods, and Aldo van Eyck.[5] For Bakema, the various teaching posts and workshops around the world were also opportunities to catch up with older and younger colleagues who would sit on juries or simply drop by when he was around, from Fumihiko Maki in St. Louis, to the old CIAM guard at Harvard, Kenzo Tange in Tokyo, Balkrisna Doshi in Ahmedabad, or Oswald Mathias Ungers in Ithaca and Salzburg.[6]

The workshops were geared to both analysis and synthesis of the group work, and Bakema would not hesitate to join in and summarize the work with his own sketches. While the focus was on the urban context, it was not on morphological or typological definitions of the city. Bakema's crude and diagrammatic sketches aimed at the right organization of flows and spaces, their scale, context and interrelationships.

His talks were overwhelming multimedia events with multiple projectors showing not just slides but, simultaneously, 16mm films that he shot himself on his many travels. Results of workshops in one place would become part of his lectures and teachings elsewhere, thus setting up a kind of global feedback loop between the numerous institutes he frequented.[7]

Bakema sought to convey to his students and colleagues the notion of what he called "total space," "total life," or even "total urbanization." In his view, architectural design had to make people more aware of the larger environment to which they belonged and in which they operated. Architecture could not be uncoupled from urbanism, but had to relate to the deeper structures of society. The central place accorded to social and visual relationships in architecture was in keeping with Team 10 discourse and with structuralism, as voiced in the Dutch journal Forum—which he edited along with Aldo van Eyck and a young Herman Hertzberger,

among others. Bakema's relational understanding of architecture builds on the legacy of the Dutch De Stijl movement and Dutch functionalism. "Growth and change," "habitat," "ascending dimensions," and the "aesthetics of number" were all key terms which Bakema connected to a political program for an egalitarian and open society as embodied (despite its flaws) by the social democratic welfare state. Following Karl Popper's notion of an open society in which criticism of authoritarianism plays a key role, Bakema practiced consistent dialogue. His message to developing countries was not to follow the example of the Western world and make the same mistakes in terms of city planning and overrationalization.

It seems harsh but fair to say that Bakema's globe-trotting lifestyle killed him in the end. In 1975 he narrowly survived a heart attack on a plane from Israel back to Holland. Undaunted, he resumed his travels after his recovery and did not stop until he had completely exhausted himself. After Bakema died in 1981, at the age of sixty-six, Team 10 decided to stop gathering. By that time global architecture had transformed itself into the fashion of postmodernism and the accompanying star system, while academia had become entangled in the web of a new media complex.

^ Studio presentations at the Internationale Sommerakademie für Bildende Kunst, Salzburg, 1975.

v Multiple film and slide projectors used by Bakema and his assistant Frans Hooykaas for an improvised multimedia lecture at the Internationale Sommerakademie für Bildende Kunst, Salzburg, 1975.

<< Cover of Jaap Bakema, Woning en woonomgeving (Delft, 1977).

1. J. B. Bakema, "St.-Louis," Forum 15, no. 2 (1960–1961): 52–60, and "The Human Core—a Civic Centre for St. Louis Mo.," Washington University, School of Architecture (St. Louis, 1961).
2. In the personal archive of Jacob Berend (Jaap) Bakema held at Het Nieuwe Instituut in Rotterdam there is an extensive yet not complete dossier on Bakema's teachings, archive no. BAKE.1 10387138 Onderwijs.
3. Bakema in Team 10 Primer, ed. A. Smithson (Cambridge, MA: MIT Press, 1968), 5.
4. Bakema archive, see note 2.
5. International Week of Design, Delft, April 7th–17th 1964, ed. Stylos (Delft, 1966). Initially called International Week of Design, InDeSem continues as a biannual event.
6. The latter is beautifully documented in J. B. Bakema, Städtebauliche Architektur, Salzburger Studienprojekte erarbeitet im Seminar 1965, Internationale Sommerakademie für Bildende Kunst Salzburg, Zentralvereinigung der Architekten Österreichs, Landesgruppe Salzburg.
7. The most comprehensive compilation of texts, lectures, and projects is the primer Woning en Woonomgeving, ed. J. B. Bakema and O. Das (Delft: Technische Hogeschool Delft, 1977).

ART X: THE DESIGN OF INFORMATION OVERLOAD

Beatriz Colomina

Protagonists George Nelson (1908–1986), Charles Eames (1907–1978), Ray Eames (1912–1988), Alexander Girard (1907–1973)
Institutions Department of Fine Arts, University of Georgia in Athens; University of California, Los Angeles (UCLA)
Locations Athens, GA and Los Angeles, CA, USA
Dates 1952–1953

In 1952 American designer George Nelson was asked to prepare a study for the Department of Fine Arts at the University of Georgia in Athens. Undergraduate students were apparently disinterested in their classes. Nelson brought Ray and Charles Eames and Alexander Girard into a team and, instead of writing a report, they decided to collaborate on a "show for a typical class" of fifty-five minutes to demonstrate a new way of engaging interest. Nelson referred to it as "Art X," and the Eameses called it "Sample Lesson." The subject of the lesson was "communications,"[1] and the stated goals included "the breaking down of barriers between fields of learning, making people a little more intuitive [and] increasing communication between people and things."[2] The performance included a live narrator, multiple images (both still and moving), sound, and even "a collection of bottled synthetic odors that were to be fed into the auditorium during the show through the air-conditioning ducts."[3] Charles Eames later said, "We used a lot of sound, sometimes carried to a very high volume so you would actually feel the vibrations. The idea was to produce an intense sensory environment so as to 'heighten awareness.'"[4] The effect was so convincing

that apparently some people even believed they smelled things when no smell had been introduced, only a suggestion in an image or a sound.[5]

It was a major production. Nelson described the team arriving in Athens "burdened with only slightly less equipment than the Ringling Brothers. This included a movie projector, three slide projectors, three screens, three or four tape recorders, cans of films, boxes of slides, and reels of magnetic tape."[6] The reference to the legendary Ringling Brothers circus was not accidental. Speaking with a reporter for *Vogue*, Charles later argued that "'Sample Lesson' was a blast on all senses, a super-saturated three-ring circus. Simultaneously the students were assaulted by three sets of slides, two tape recorders, a motion picture with sound, and peripheral panels for further distraction."[7]

The circus was one of the Eameses' lifelong fascinations, documented in hundreds and hundreds of photographs from the mid-1940s on. The images were used in many contexts, including *Circus*—their three-screen, 180-slide show accompanied by a soundtrack featuring circus music and other sounds recorded at the circus that Charles presented as part of the Charles Eliot Norton Lectures at Harvard University in 1970—and *Clown Face*, a training film about "the precise and classical art of applying makeup" made in 1971 for Bill Ballentine, director of the Ringling Bros. and Barnum & Bailey Clown College. Charles was on the board of the college, and often referred to the circus as an example of what design and art should be, not self-expression but precise discipline:

Everything in the circus is pushing the possible beyond the limit—bears do not really ride on bicycles, people do not really execute three and a half turn somersaults in the air from a board to a ball, and until recently no one dressed the way fliers do. ... Yet within this apparent freewheeling license, we find a discipline which is almost unbelievable. ... The circus may look like the epitome of pleasure, but the person flying

on a high wire, or executing a balancing act, or being shot from a cannon must take his pleasure very, very seriously. In the same vein, the scientist, in his laboratory, is pushing the possible beyond the limit and he too must take his pleasure very seriously.[8]

The circus, as an event offering a multiplicity of simultaneous experiences that could not be entirely taken in by the viewer, was the Eameses' model for their design of multimedia exhibitions and the fast-cutting technique of their films and slide shows, where the objective was always to communicate the maximum amount of information in a way that was both pleasurable and effective.[9] Likewise, about Art X, the Eameses said they "were trying to cram into a short time, a class hour, the most background material possible."[10] The background becomes the unconscious foreground, a subliminal technique that would only later be used by advertising, as Buckminster Fuller observed.[11]

As part of the "Sample Lesson" they produced *A Communications Primer*, a film explaining Claude Shannon's famous "schematic diagram of a general communication system." The film was subsequently developed in an effort to present current ideas in communication theory to architects and planners, and to encourage them to use these ideas in their work. The basic goal was to integrate architecture and information flow. In fact, for the Eameses, information flow *was* the real architecture. If the great heroes of the Renaissance were "people concerned with ways of modeling/imaging, …not with self-expression or bravura…Brunelleschi, but not Michelangelo,"[12] the great architects of our time would be the ones concerned with the new forms of communication, particularly computers:

> It appeared to us that the real current problems for architects now—the problems that a Brunelleschi, say, would gravitate to—are problems of organization of information. For city planning, for regional planning, the first need is clear, accessible models of current states-of-affairs, drawn from a data base that only a computer can handle for you.[13]

But the issue was now much more than one of efficiency of communication. Instead of asking students to concentrate on a singular message, the idea was to produce sensory overload. As the Eameses suggested to *Vogue*, "Sample Lesson" tried to provide many forms of "distraction," as the audience drifted through a multimedia space that exceeded their capacity to absorb it. The Nelson–Eames team thought that the

< Art X: exhibition/
film/slide show/
lecture/event.
View of lecture
hall at the second
presentation of
Sample Lesson,
UCLA, May 1953.
Photograph by
Don Garber.

v Eames Office,
still from *A
Communications
Primer*, 1953.

most important thing to communicate to under-graduates was a sense of what the Eameses would later call "connections" among seemingly unrelated phenomena. Arguing that awareness of these relation-ships was achieved by "high-speed techniques," Nelson and the Eameses produced an excessive input from different directions that had to be synthesized by the students—anticipating the multimedia sensorium that would captivate Marshall McLuhan.

Art X, or the "Sample Lesson"—for which another test performance was conducted at UCLA in 1953 for business school and engineering students—treated education itself as a medium, or rather multimedium. The idea was to completely transform pedagogy by inventing a kind of performance in which transdisci-plinary ideas were communicated in an unconscious way.

The Eameses did not apply the technique to any other formal classes but honed and perfected it for the multiscreen *Glimpses of the USA* film that Nelson invited them to contribute to the 1959 American National Exhibition in Moscow. Information over-load was once again the key strategy. In a sense, the Eames took their pedagogical technique out of the classroom or, more precisely, turned Buckminster Fuller's dome into a vast classroom for three million visitors. Likewise, in the 1964 IBM pavilion at the New York World's Fair, the classroom literally lifted the public up into the fully enveloping educational space of sensory overload.[14] Pedagogy had become attention design.

1. "Grist for Atlanta paper version," manuscript, box 217, folder 15, The Work of Charles and Ray Eames, Manuscript Division, Library of Congress, Washington, DC.
2. John Neuhart, Marilyn Neuhart, and Ray Eames, *Eames Design: The Work of the Office of Charles and Ray Eames* (New York: Harry N. Abrams, 1989), 177.
3. George Nelson, "The Georgia Experiment: An Industrial Approach to Problems of Education," manuscript, October 1954; quoted in Stanley Abercrombie, *George Nelson: The Design of Modern Design* (Cambridge, MA: MIT Press, 1995), 145.
4. Owen Gingerich, "A Conversation with Charles Eames," *American Scholar* 46, no. 3 (Summer 1977): 331.
5. Ibid.
6. Nelson, "The Georgia Experiment."
7. Allene Talmey, "Eames," *Vogue*, August 15, 1959, 144.
8. Charles Eames, "Language of Vision: The Nuts and Bolts," *Bulletin of the American Academy of Arts and Sciences* 28, no. 1 (October 1974): 17–18.
9. Neuhart, Neuhart, and Eames, *Eames Design*, 91.
10. Gingerich, "A Conversation with Charles Eames," 332.
11. R. Buckminster Fuller to Ms. Camp, November 7, 1973, box 30, The Work of Charles and Ray Eames, Manuscript Division, Library of Congress, Washington, DC.
12. Notes for second Norton lecture, box 217, folder 10, The Work of Charles and Ray Eames, Manuscript Division, Library of Congress, Washington, DC. Eames is referring here to "Professor Lawrence Hill's Renaissance."
13. "'Communications Primer' was a recommendation to architects to recognize the need for more complex information...for new kinds of *models* of information." Eames, "Grist for Atlanta."
14. Beatriz Colomina, "Enclosed by Images: The Eameses' Multimedia Architecture," *Grey Room*, no. 2 (Winter 2001): 6–29.

LEARNING FROM LEVITTOWN

Beatriz Colomina

Protagonists Denise Scott Brown (1931–),
Robert Venturi (1925–2018), Steven Izenour
(1940–2001), Virginia Carroll
Institution Yale School of Architecture (YSOA)
Locations New Haven, CT, and Levittown, PA, USA
Date 1970

Following the Learning from Las Vegas studio at Yale in the fall of 1968—immortalized in the book of the same name published in 1972—Denise Scott Brown and Robert Venturi conducted a less well-known studio in the spring of 1970 called Remedial Housing for Architects. A note in Scott Brown's handwriting on the syllabus in their archives adds, as if it had been an afterthought, an alternative title: "Or Learning from Levittown." The studio brief described the course as follows:

> This is therefore to be a remedial studio (for us and our parents). Its view is not comprehensive but biased; biased in the opposite direction from where we came, in order to reassert balance. We shall be more interested in what people make of their housing than in what architects intended them to make of it. We shall be more interested in the iconography of "Mon (split-level, Cape Cod Rancher) Repos" than in the iconography (or structure) of the Dymaxion house or Falling Water. We shall be more interested in the marketing of industrialized house components than in their design. This is not a course in Housing.[1]

The studio took the research model used to study the symbols in the Las Vegas strip to investigate the domestic symbols of the American suburban house. Scott Brown retroactively explained that they chose Levittown "because it was an archetype in the same way as the strip."[2] It is as if they conceived of these two archetypal vernaculars in tandem—the public and the private, the strip and the suburban house. Toward the end of the Learning from Las Vegas book there is already a hint of Learning from Levittown in the wry observation that "Modern architects, who can embrace vernacular architecture remote in place or time, can contemptuously reject the current vernacular of the United States, that is, the merchant builders' vernacular of Levittown and the commercial vernacular of Route 66."[3] In fact the images of suburbs in the book were taken from the boards of the Learning from Levittown studio, so that Levittown influenced Las Vegas, or rather Las Vegas evolved from Levittown. This late part of

the book, where they refer to Levittown, could also be seen as an anticipation, a preview of something to come, in the same way that, at the very end of *Complexity and Contradiction*, Venturi wrote that "Main Street is almost all right,"[4] already anticipating *Learning from Las Vegas*.

The innovative collaborative "learning from" pedagogy was used again, but now the subject was too profane for even their closest colleagues. If the Learning from Las Vegas studio had already been controversial, Learning from Levittown seemed to have gone too far. Venturi recalled the scandal of the final review, where even their biggest supporters rejected the work: "We forget how much suburbia was despised at the time by the idealists...a whole busload of the students came up from Columbia to be in the audience to 'boo, boo, boo.' Robert Stern was a young student at Yale at the time and Vincent Scully was on the faculty. He had been very friendly and agreeable to us in general, and they walked out. They were against this. We tend to forget that what we were doing was extremely unpopular."[5] Radical pedagogy can be radical simply by virtue of its content. "Learning from" is simultaneously an exercise in modesty, paying attention to what is already there, treating the archetype as the real teacher, and a provocation, a slap in the face.

The studio looked at Levittown houses and the changes that owners had made: "How they have decorated them on the outside and dealt with their lawns in individual ways." Since these changes were external, it can be argued that Venturi and Scott Brown were treating houses as media, as billboards, in a kind of echo of Las Vegas. It's interesting that they also asked students to look at the way in which houses were represented in television commercials, home journals, car advertisements, *New Yorker* cartoons, films, and even soap operas. So, the house is a form of media and the media is full of houses. As Scott Brown put it, they did "lots of content analysis looking at what we called literature, but the literature was Disney cartoons on Daisy Duck, sitcoms, ads on television, articles in *Popular Mechanics* magazine or builders' journals."[6] Another important reference is Pop art. In the readings of the Levittown studio, there are several John McHale articles, including "The Expendable Icon," "The Plastic Parthenon," and "The Fine Arts and the Mass Media," that were pivotal in the development of the concept of Pop in England. One of the exercises in the studio brief asked students to "Do for housing what Oldenburg did for Hamburgers."

STYLING — SPRAWL SPACE & IMAGERY

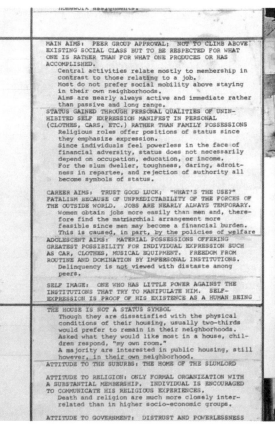

MAIN AIMS: PEER GROUP APPROVAL; NOT TO CLIMB ABOVE
EXISTING SOCIAL CLASS BUT TO BE RESPECTED FOR WHAT
ONE IS RATHER THAN FOR WHAT ONE PRODUCES OR HAS
ACCOMPLISHED.
   Central activities relate mostly to membership in
   contrast to those relating to a job.
   Most do not prefer social mobility above staying
   in their own neighborhoods.
   Aims are nearly always active and immediate rather
   than passive and long range.
STATUS GAINED THROUGH PERSONAL QUALITIES OF UNIN-
HIBITED SELF EXPRESSION MANIFEST IN PERSONAL
(CLOTHES, CARS, ETC.) RATHER THAN FAMILY POSSESSIONS
   Religious roles offer positions of status since
   they emphasize expression.
   Since individuals feel powerless in the face of
   financial adversity, status does not necessarily
   depend on occupation, education, or income.
   For the slum dweller, toughness, daring, adroit-
   ness in repartee, and rejection of authority all
   become symbols of status.

CAREER AIMS: TRUST GOOD LUCK; "WHAT'S THE USE?"
FATALISM BECAUSE OF UNPREDICTABILITY OF THE FORCES OF
THE OUTSIDE WORLD. JOBS ARE NEARLY ALWAYS TEMPORARY.
   Women obtain jobs more easily than men and, there-
   fore find the matriarchial arrangement more
   feasible since men may become a financial burden.
   This is caused, in part, by the policies of welfare
ADOLESCENT AIMS: MATERIAL POSSESSIONS OFFERING
GREATEST POSSIBILITY FOR INDIVIDUAL EXPRESSION SUCH
AS CAR, CLOTHES, MUSICAL EQUIPMENT. FREEDOM FROM
ROUTINE AND DOMINATION BY IMPERSONAL INSTITUTIONS.
   Delinquency is not viewed with distaste among
   peers.

SELF IMAGE: ONE WHO HAS LITTLE POWER AGAINST THE
INSTITUTIONS THAT TRY TO MANIPULATE HIM. SELF-
EXPRESSION IS PROOF OF HIS EXISTENCE AS A HUMAN BEING

THE HOUSE IS NOT A STATUS SYMBOL
   Though they are dissatisfied with the physical
   conditions of their housing, usually two-thirds
   would prefer to remain in their neighborhoods.
   Asked what they would like most in a house, children respond, "my own room."
   A majority are interested in public housing, still
   however, in their own neighborhood.
ATTITUDE TO THE SUBURBS: THE HOME OF THE SLUMLORD

ATTITUDE TO RELIGION: ONLY FORMAL ORGANIZATION WITH
A SUBSTANTIAL MEMBERSHIP. INDIVIDUAL IS ENCOURAGED
TO COMMUNICATE HIS RELIGIOUS EXPERIENCES.
   Death and religion are much more closely inter-
   related than in higher socio-economic groups.

ATTITUDE TO GOVERNMENT: DISTRUST AND POWERLESSNESS

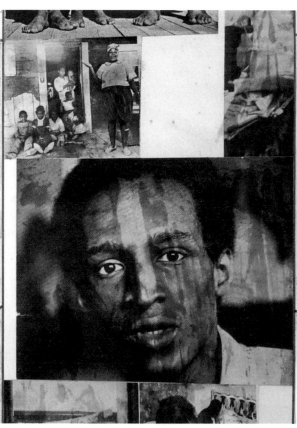

233

It is important to consider the tumultuous context in which the studio took place. In the spring of 1970, there was enormous unrest in New Haven and at Yale. The Black Panther trials were in progress, and there were riots in the city and rallies at Yale. Two bombs went off at the Yale hockey rink. The architecture building burned down the spring before the Levittown studio—a "Free the Panthers" banner appeared on the burned shell. There is a note on the syllabus indicating that the studio and the lecture room would be at 165 York rather than in the school. So somehow, this turn toward housing occurred within a density of urban unrest and challenges to normative architectural education. Not by chance, the Yale student journal *Novum Organum* promoted Venturi and Scott Brown's pedagogical projects alongside devastating criticism of the school and its building. The panels of the Learning from Levittown studio reflected this political context with images of poverty and racial inequity.

After the studio, Venturi and Scott Brown were planning a book called "Learning from Levittown"—and in fact there is a manuscript in the archives written with Virginia Carroll, who had been a student

in the class—but the book was never completed. Perhaps the strong criticism of their studio had an effect. As Venturi recalled during an interview:

> It's interesting that the heads of the schools weren't very happy about what we did. Even Charles Moore was not very happy about what we were doing at Yale, although you think of Charles Moore connecting with the everyday environment. What did he say once at some conference? "I did not learn anything from Las Vegas."[7]

On the other hand, Scott Brown was quick to point out during the same interview that, under Moore's deanship, the Yale School of Architecture allowed them to take all the semester credits for the students, so that the Learning from Levittown studio was the equivalent of four courses relative to all the reading and research it required (which explains the elaborate syllabus and extensive bibliography they had prepared). All the students did during the semester was this studio: design, research, teaching, and communication—all combined into one collaborative experience.

Perhaps not by chance, Venturi gave up teaching right after the Learning from Levittown studio, while Scott Brown remained active in the classroom. Part of the research later materialized in the exhibition *Signs of Life: Symbols in the American City* at the Renwick Gallery at the Smithsonian Art Museum in Washington in 1976, where Venturi, Scott Brown, and Steve Izenour put together the signs and symbols of the commercial strip and the suburban home, in a way reuniting Learning from Las Vegas and Learning from Levittown.

< "Free the Panthers" banner on the burned shell of the Yale School of Art and Architecture building, New Haven, CT, 1970.

<< "Learning from Levittown" presentation panel, 1970.

1. Denise Scott Brown and Robert Venturi, RHA studio brief, University of Pennsylvania Architectural Archives, Philadelphia.
2. Beatriz Colomina, "Learning from Levittown: A Conversation with Robert Venturi and Denise Scott Brown," in *Worlds Away: New Suburban Landscape*, ed. Andrew Blauvelt (Minneapolis: Walker Art Center, 2008), 49–69.
3. Robert Venturi, Denise Scott Brown, and Steven Izenour, "From La Tourette to Levittown," *Learning from Las Vegas* (Cambridge, MA: MIT Press, 1977), 138. Izenour had been a student teaching assistant in the studio.
4. Robert Venturi, *Complexity and Contradiction in Architecture* (New York: Museum of Modern Art, 1966).
5. Colomina, "Learning from Levittown: A Conversation," 49–69.
6. Ibid.
7. Ibid.

ON AIR: LEARNING THROUGH THE WAVES

Joaquim Moreno

Protagonists Tim Benton (1945–),
Charlotte Benton (1944–), Geoffrey Baker (1931–),
Sandra Millikin, Adrian Forty (1948–),
Stephen Bayley (1951–), Dennis Sharp (1933–2010),
Reyner Banham (1922–1988), William Curtis (1948–),
Aaron Scharf (1922–1993), Nick Levinson
Institution Open University, Arts Faculty
Location United Kingdom
Dates 1975–1982

"A305: History of Architecture and Design 1890–1939" was a groundbreaking Open University (OU) arts course broadcast on BBC between 1975 and 1982, with a total enrollment of around two thousand students. Also known as the "University of the Air," the OU was "open to people, to places, to methods and to ideas,"[1] in the inaugural words of its first chancellor, Lord Crowther. Sharing the space opened up by television and radio, it reached well beyond the cloisters of conventional universities, entering the domestic realm of an unseen and unspecified audience—not just young people of student age, but the general population. Academic discourse had to learn how to speak to a much broader audience. Established in 1969—but first proposed by the Labour Party leader Harold Wilson in 1963—this new institution was intended to be a shared public resource that mobilized mass media to make university teaching accessible to less affluent parts of society. This was higher education for the "second machine age," to paraphrase Reyner Banham, conceived to increase

social resilience and literacy to prepare people for the challenges of the age of information.

The new media environment and the new audience demanded a new message—a new way of writing history, with new voices writing new narratives about new protagonists and new themes. Architecture history was on air and the TV set was asking common questions about notable buildings and sometimes debating common problems about the built environment, inviting common audiences to use their own experience to learn from their surroundings, or explaining the symbolic function of design through the very radio or TV set that was broadcasting the program.

Roughly eight hours of film, ten hours of audio, and almost two thousand printed pages were produced and edited by the course team, the BBC's Arts Faculty, and the Open University's Institute of Educational Technology specifically for the A305 curriculum. This mass of pedagogical material was distributed across twenty-four television broadcasts, each one corresponding to a course unit, complemented by thirty-two radio programs, twelve course unit booklets, five supplementary booklets and an anthology of primary source texts called *Form and Function: A Source Book for the History Architecture and Design 1890–1939*. Instead of a syllabus, A305 had a broadcasting schedule prefaced with precise specifications about the different structures of its television and radio programs. TV programs were dedicated to the experience of visiting buildings and inquired about the ways of living they facilitated. Radio programs were, mostly, interviews and presentations by prominent architects, designers, and architectural historians. While television concentrated on objects and object lessons and asked the audience to mobilize their experience to learn, radio offered the opportunity to hear the protagonists of modern architecture address the audience directly. The accompanying *Radiovision Booklet* enriched most of the radio programs with sequences of selected images, while the *Broadcasting Supplements*, with guiding texts, allowed students to experience the broadcasts unencumbered by note taking.

New learning materials and new means of transmission and circulation of information required new means of production. The wider OU project, which effectively dematerialized the transmission of knowledge, required industrial-scale infrastructure. The university's campus had begun to grow in a piecemeal way on a former greenfield site in

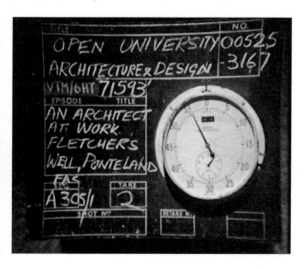

Milton Keynes. A vast machine for the dissemination of knowledge, it relied on room-sized computers, robust logistical networks, and shared telecommunications infrastructure to produce the support materials for the broadcast components and to distribute those materials throughout the country. The entire operation was managed by a new mixture of industrial and academic professionals.

Much like television, this infrastructure was based on the premise of centralized production and domestic reception—the point being that students in this new hybrid educational system should be able to study without leaving home. A web of local and regional centers with libraries of audiovisual recordings ensured that even those living in areas without TV coverage could attend class.

The circulation of knowledge through seemingly immaterial waves had material consequences, in the form of a whole new architecture of production, storage, and distribution. A vast network of tutors, reachable by phone or mail, enabled another feedback loop of personalized support. The OU mobilized, in fact, the biggest printing press of the time and the biggest postal operation in the UK. Both were components of larger networks that distilled the contents of the courses into formats compatible with small mail packages, adjusted broadcast times to the pace of study, and produced supporting material for tutors to ensure uniform grading.

At the same time, the medium of broadcasting transformed the spaces of reception, inventing a new social collective. While education no longer provided a point of physical convergence, the synchronized periods of study produced a shared sense of belonging, countering the loneliness of studying at home. Acquiring a TV set became a form of subsidizing your education, of enabling a private space to respond to a public mandate, much like bringing your own chair to class. The black and white (and soon color) TV set became a means for the state to fulfill the rights to education of each individual. It also offered the tools for emancipation from its own domestic setting—a setting still dominated by hierarchical dynamics and gender discrimination.

Finally, A305 not only spoke to a large and dispersed audience but listened to it. Both tutoring and recordkeeping provided the feedback that sought to make the whole system more effective. The course not only taught through the eyes of modernist architects and historians but also surveyed the impact of modern architecture across Britain from the perspective of its students. Research did not stop with the creation of the syllabus but became a continuous process of recording, editing, and surveying. In other words, listening. A305 added other voices, vectors, and visions to the history of modern architecture. Student feedback configured an alternative map of modern architecture—one in which the voices of its protagonists coincided with their own experiences of the intense transformation of everyday life. The course pursued that relation, seeking to translate the students' experiences into learning opportunities. The course's attention to anonymous objects (and to the flows of energy and information that ran through them) and to contemporary housing debates—addressing both working-class social housing and monotonous middle-class semidetached houses in the suburbs—made the students the real protagonists of their learning and incorporated their voices back into the information loop that A305 set in motion.[2]

< Open University tutor working from home. Telephone tutorials enabled those who could not attend face-to-face tutorials to receive support, 1988.

≪ "What is Architecture: An Architect at Work." Television broadcast 1 of History of Architecture and Design 1890–1939, written by Geoffrey Baker, directed by Edward Hayward, and produced the BBC/Open University. Aired BBC2, February 15, 1975.

1. For the full transcript see: https://www.open.ac.uk/library/digital-archive/pdf/script/script:5747089b4a53f
2. For a fuller discussion of A305: History of Architecture and Design 1890–1939 see my *The University Is Now on Air: Broadcasting Modern Architecture* (Montreal: Canadian Centre for Architecture, 2018).

SYSTEMS FOR PERCEPTION AND SUBVERSION

Mark Wasiuta, Marcos Sánchez

Protagonists David Greenberg (1942–2020),
Bernard Perloff (1942–), Ted Tokio Tanaka (1942–),
and Roger Webster
Institution Environmental Communications (EC)
Dates 1969–1982
Location Venice, CA, USA

Working in Venice, the hub of Southern California's counterculture, the architecture and media collective Environmental Communications (EC) positioned themselves geographically, methodologically, and psychically far from the seminar rooms and lecture halls of LA's schools of architecture. Nonetheless, even from the hazy remove of their Windward Avenue studio, their practice was shaped by a critical assessment of the state of architectural education in America in the late 1960s and 1970s and was directed toward a shrewd pedagogical subversion.

Influenced by the Los Angeles conceptual photography movement and with close ties to experimental groups such as San Francisco's Ant Farm, Environmental Communications saw themselves as a similar exploratory collective devoted to the conception, production, and dissemination of environmental images. Channeling the preoccupations of both environmental design—and its conception of the city as a space of social interaction, behavioral codes, and territories—and the burgeoning ecological movement, the collective assembled a vast inventory of 35mm environmental slides that could serve as the image-kernels of a mediatized counterpedagogy.

Formed by a group of young architects, photographers, and psychologists, Environmental Communications intuited that in an era of accelerating image proliferation the university slide library was the emerging center of institutional and pedagogical power. The group's core members, Roger Webster, David Greenberg, Ted Tokio Tanaka, and Bernard Perloff, theorized that by infiltrating slide libraries with their "environmental photography" they could alter the visual cortex of architectural schools, subvert conventional pedagogy, and spark a revolution in student consciousness.[1]

The term environmental photography referred to the collective's image production as well as the process of attending to a feature of urban space they

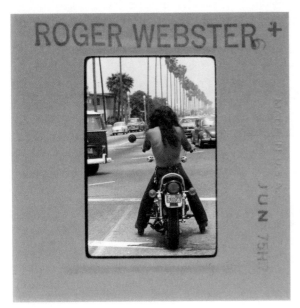
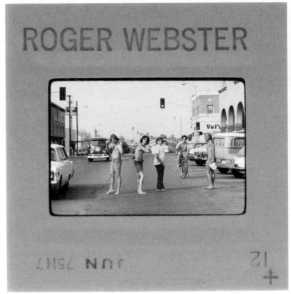
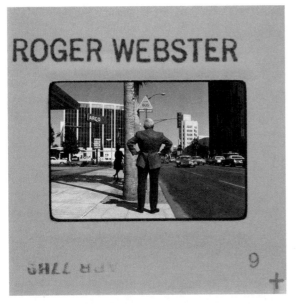
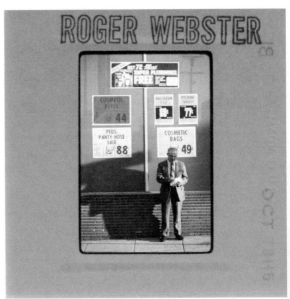

∧ 35 mm slides from
the Environmental
Communications
category "People/
Male."

< Environmental
Communications
aerial (blimp)
photography session.

ROGER WEBSTER

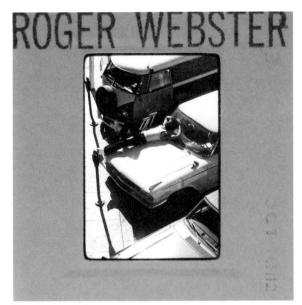

ROGER WEBSTER

ROGER WEBSTER

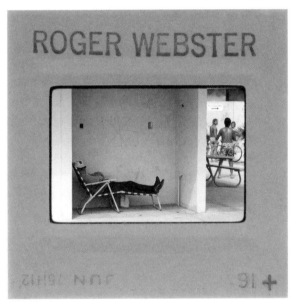

called, somewhat enigmatically, "sense-energy." Through environmental photography, the group members sensitized themselves to the spatial, mediatic, and social conditions they documented in Tokyo, the American Southwest, and, most often, Los Angeles, their primary object of analysis. Hence, with environmental photography, EC pursued their goal of developing (and becoming) "systems for perception" while testing the behavior-altering capacity of images.[2] With scant writing elsewhere, the group consistently attempted to refine the description of their practice through their catalogue texts. "Systems for perception" joined other descriptors including a "matrix," an "experience," and, more directly, a "group" that worked toward "penetrating" and "understanding" the "environmental web."

The group eventually shot tens of thousands of 35mm slides, forming a vast visual taxonomy of Southern California's urban and social geography. Compiled into thematic sets with titles such as "Human Territoriality in the City," "Ultimate Crisis," "Urban Crowd Behavior," and, in a 1979 collaboration with Marshall McLuhan, "The City as Classroom," their slides were sold via the *Environmental Communications* catalogue to museums, cultural institutions, UCLA, Columbia, Princeton, Yale, and Harvard universities and an international network of architecture schools, not to mention the Central Intelligence Agency and *Playboy* magazine. Booklets printed to accompany the slides mimicked the format of audiovisual education, offering instructive descriptions of each slide and brief essays that served as condensed primers on architecture's environmental thought.

The group eventually extended its street-level photographic practices to encompass 16mm film and Sony Portapak video shoots from airplanes, helicopters, and blimps, and they expanded the scope of action at their Windward Avenue studio. Through their film screenings, video festivals, Venice Beach happenings, and slide catalogues EC became interpreters and purveyors of new architectural and environmental trends, mobilizing their environmental images to counter the inert buildings, monuments, and histories that governed architecture and its teaching institutions.

Whether prowling the streets or hovering above them in blimps or helicopters, EC relied on photography as a device to sense, locate, and record diverse environmental patterns. Airborne photography scanned for urban and atmospheric patterns, while serial photographs of people, movement, and objects on the ground chronicled and catalogued patterns of social behavior and interaction. Together these techniques and systems of perception fed EC's massive image accumulation and their project of total environmental documentation and distribution.

While their photography tracked such urban and social patterns, and while their slide sets astutely mapped the domes, inflatables, communes, and media that formed a lineage of alternative architectural practices, the ambiguity of their own role became increasingly evident and potentially troubling to their project. As their catalogues evolved from early rough and striking brochures to slick, professional publications, the group risked evolving, as well, from agents of pedagogical and media subversion to mere image salesmen. This shift in graphic language—less the amateur graininess of the *Whole Earth Catalog* and more the suburban silkiness of a Montgomery Ward department store sales brochure—marked the erosion of EC's radical ambitions, paralleling the fate of the countercultural groups their photography documented. Moreover, this shift also registered the waning impact of behavioral psychology and environmental design on architecture's pedagogy. Similarly, the architectural slide library—which for Environmental Communications seemed full of transformative pedagogical potential in 1969—became more commonly the site of nothing more than institutionalized image administration by the 1980s.

1. Environmental Communications, "Manifesto," unpublished document, n.d.
2. The phrase "systems for perception of urban concepts and human development" appears in Environmental Communications, *Environmental Communications* [slide and media catalogue] (Venice: Environmental Communications, 1971).

Protest organized by the Center for Independent Living. Berkeley, CA, early 1970s. Photograph by Deborah Hoffman.

EVERY BODY NEEDS EQUAL ACCESS

SUBJECT AND
BODY MATTERS

INSTITUTIONAL REFORM AND RUPTURE

Victoria Bugge Øye

Protagonists Karl Schwanzer (1918–1975),
Günther Feuerstein (1925–)
Institutions Technische Hochschule Wien,
Galerie nächst St. Stephan
Location Vienna, Austria
Dates 1961–1969

In the latter half of the 1960s the architecture scene in Vienna was transformed by the rise of several alternative pedagogical venues, both within and outside of traditional institutions. The central hub was the Technische Hochschule (now Technische Universität), which formed the breeding ground for experimental architecture groups such as Haus-Rucker-Co, ZÜND-UP/Salz der Erde, Missing Link, and Coop Himmelblau. Modernist architect Karl Schwanzer was appointed professor in 1959, and two years later he hired the young architect Günther Feuerstein as his teaching assistant. During their tenure, a series of new forums were created that operated fluently across the institutional bounds of the TH, the architectural office, the building site, and the space of the gallery. Their teaching aspired to new and less hierarchical relationships between students and teachers, as well as a reconceptualization of the spaces and formats of design education.

Between 1966 and 1968 Feuerstein organized the "Experimental Design" (*Experimentelles Entwerfen*) workshops at the school, which took place over

< Tensegrity dome under construction at the "Experimental Design" workshop, 1966.

two weeks in the summer. Inspired by French art critic Michel Tapié's theorization of *art informel* as improvisatory and gestural techniques to break from tradition, the workshop was intended as a space for imaginative and "spontaneous" building.[1] Teams of ten to fifteen students worked together to construct tensegrity structures, Bucky Fuller-inspired domes, and concrete shells, in the process gaining hands-on experience with materials ranging from concrete and bricks to lumber and bamboo. This idea of teamwork was central to many of the design studios taught by Schwanzer and Feuerstein, as a way both to test new models of collaboration to replace hierarchical and authoritarian structures still dominant in postwar Vienna and to adapt the field to an increasingly professionalized construction industry. In the design studios, the top-down "desk crit" was replaced by workshop-like conversations (*Entwurfsgespräche*) in small "working groups."[2] For a 1966–1967 studio with a prompt for a national "Austrica 70" expo, Feuerstein even created a block diagram inspired by industrial and organizational psychology to organize and divide responsibilities and tasks across the thirty-three students. The "Austrica 70" studio, which resulted in an underwater city and a "flying balloon" project, among others, also reflected the priorities and interests of a new generation of students who were increasingly aligned with an international network of experimental architects that included Archigram and Superstudio.

For history and theory, Schwanzer introduced the first lecture classes on modern and contemporary architecture in the TH's curriculum, which had previously ended with the Baroque. Students were also introduced for the first time to the city's historical avantgardes, a legacy that had been largely forgotten or, in the case of Jugendstil, seen as kitsch. In April 1969 students from the TH even organized a protest to save Otto Wagner's Karlsplatz metro station from being demolished to make way for a new station right in front of the school's neoclassical main building.[3]

The bureaucratic and hierarchical organization of the TH, originally founded in 1815, made the implementation of curricular changes slow and cumbersome. For this reason, many of the new pedagogical formats happened outside of the school. Between 1963 and 1969 Feuerstein organized the famous *Klubseminars*, which were hosted in the Galerie nächst St. Stephan, an important location for the city's small progressive art scene.[4] The seminars were limited to twenty students, a number

the National Socialists—and called for a new form of sensory awakening outside of established institutions and languages.[7] In 1965 students, former resistance fighters, and union members organized a major protest against a former Nazi professor at the College of World Trade, leading to Vienna's first political fatality since the war. Extensive educational reforms would eventually be implemented with the Kreisky government (1970–1982).

At the TH, design education started slowly to embrace these new ways, although the political potential of experiments with form, material, and program was not always recognized. When the international student congress was held in Vienna in 1968, German students harshly criticized their Viennese colleagues' lack of political engagement. For them, the pavilions and structures, including Coop Himmelblau's Villa Rosa, were "aesthetical nonsense instead of political struggle."[8] While it is true that the TH students may have been less involved in political activism than their colleagues in Germany, France, or Italy, their work on expanding the field of architecture had an immense impact on Austrian architecture culture, still informing the discipline today.

chosen to allow a "face-to-face" connection and the kind of discussion that was impossible in the large lecture halls at the TH.[5] In 1967 the gallery hosted an exhibition, *Urban Fiction*, that showed projects by students in the *Klubseminar*, including Laurids Ortner (Haus-Rucker-Co) and Wolf Prix (Coop Himmelblau), alongside work by Hans Hollein and Walter Pichler.[6] The *Klubseminars* were dissolved in 1969, a year after Feuerstein was fired from the TH for inviting the controversial Viennese actionist Otto Muehl to give a lecture. Feuerstein then began hosting an "Open Office" in his own architecture studio, which became a kind of salon for conversations, lectures, movie screenings, and parties.

While some of the shifts at the TH were part of an international movement against authoritarian structures, the historical and social shifts leading up to May 1968 had a very specific resonance and expression in Austrian society. Criticizing the country's failure to educate conscientious citizens able to resist the barbarism of totalitarianism, authors such as Peter Handke and Thomas Bernhard became vocal critics of the country's educational model— still largely unchanged since the reforms imposed by

∧ Mero-bau under construction at the "Experimental Design" workshop, 1966.

1. Eva Branscome, *Hans Hollein and Postmodernism: Art and Architecture in Austria, 1958–1985* (London: Routledge, 2018), 93.
2. Günther Feuerstein, "TU Wien— Aufbruch Anno '68," *Archithese* 40, no. 3 (June 2010): 32.
3. Christiane Feuerstein and Angelika Fitz, *Wann begann Temporär?: Frühe Stadtinterventionen und sanfte Stadterneuering in Wien* (Vienna: Springer, 2009), 25.
4. See Craig Buckley, "Interview with Günther Feuerstein," in *Clip, Stamp, Fold: The Radical Architecture of Little Magazines, 196X to 197X*, ed. Beatriz Colomina, Craig Buckley, and Urtzi Grau (Barcelona: Actar, 2010); "Séminaire Club d'étudiants en architecture, Vienne, Autriche," *Architecture d'Aujourd'hui* 35, no. 119 (March 1965): 68–69.
5. Feuerstein, "TU Wien—Aufbruch Anno '68," 32.
6. "Urban Fiction: An Architectural Exhibition in Vienna," *Domus*, April 1967.
7. Fatima Naqvi, *How We Learn Where We Live: Thomas Bernhard, Architecture, and Bildung* (Evanston, IL: Northwestern University Press, 2015).
8. Feuerstein, "TU Wien—Aufbruch Anno '68," 33.

PEDAGOGIES OF THE PARTY

Ivan L. Munuera

Protagonists "Gay People at Columbia"
student group
Institution Columbia University
Location New York, NY, USA
Dates 1967–1985

"Who are you? Are you Gay Black, Gay White, man, woman, eighteen or fifty? Who cares! What is important is that you come out, have Gay Pride and leave the dance with a sense of Gay Power. Where else can you attain nirvana than through association with the beautiful people found at the GPC Gay dances?"[1] This was the invitation to one of a series of parties organized by Gay People at Columbia (GPC) in the 1970s. The First Friday Dances challenged the construction of student identities within the university while simultaneously exploring the academic training that could be picked up through festive experiences and the idea of the built environment that was proposed or implied by them. The First Friday Dances enacted the pedagogies of the party.

GPC was founded as the Student Homophile League (SHL) in 1966 by Stephen Donaldson, better known as Donny the Punk. The creation of the organization provoked some furious letters to the university: "Tolerance has its limits. Let the pansies go elsewhere."[2] The dean of Columbia College and several administrators called SHL "quite unnecessary," fearing its potential to promote "deviant behavior" among students.[3] The university chaplain was more understanding, offering Earl Hall, the center of religious life at Columbia, as the base for SHL activities. SHL was a pioneering initiative, being the first campus gay club in the nation. Others soon followed: Cornell University and New York University in 1968, MIT, San Francisco State University, and Rutgers University in 1969.[4] SHL was founded before the Stonewall Riots (1969)—the events that ignited conversations around laws regulating the "homophile" population[5]—at a moment when sodomy was still punishable in New York state.[6] Initially, its members were anonymous, afraid of being pinklisted (blacklisted as queers), but the group's renaming as GPC in 1970 signaled its rebirth as a more activist group.

1970 was the year GPC began to host its famous First Friday Dances, which weaved social fabrics and empowered then marginalized communities, providing visibility for ways of living far removed from the hyperrepresentation of the traditional nuclear family—a heterosexual father and mother with children. The spatial entanglement created by the party was the site where kinships were performed, discussed, learned, and celebrated, and where other centralities and other communities were proposed. The party provided a space to acquire information and knowledge about the environment outside of it.

The built environment played a crucial role in this shift. At a time when "men only" spaces for dancing were still illegal and New York legislation required clubs to have at least one woman for every three men, the First Friday Dances became a place where politics were performed and embodied, reaching their peak during the 1980s.[7] Edgy dress codes, extreme hairstyles and makeup; experimentation with chemical regimes; and the coordination of dancers brought about by DJs—all contributed to a collective bodily regime of social exploration whose genealogy could be traced back to the nightclub scene in New York.

The New York party scene was where new forms of critical consciousness emerged, aided and abetted by an architecture where bodies, music, messages, and technologies were drawn into an extensive urban fabric of political activism. The importance of this scene was recognized by a number of Italian architects and designers who came to the United States with the idea of studying Frank Lloyd Wright and American organicism but soon turned their attention to the *piper* (the Italian word for discos). Theses on the subject launched the careers of Pietro Derossi and the members of Superstudio and Archizoom, among others.[8] The New York party scene was represented at Columbia through the Graduate School of Architecture, Planning, and Preservation (GSAPP) studios led by Paul Marantz, the lighting system designer of famous discos like Studio 54 and The Palladium.

In a period still marked by the Cold War, places like the First Friday Dances agglutinated a different kind of inhabitant—the dancing student—equipped to accommodate through their bodies and their interactions new possibilities for political action. The main inhabitants of the dance floor—what would now be called the LGBTQIA+ community—would develop forms of resistance and empowerment that made the community visible and helped them to achieve representation in the US democracy of the Nixon years. This process gave rise to a collective political intelligence that would later be crucial for

v Cover of the
first issue of
Pride of Lions,
April 1972.

the formation of the coalitions by which LGBTQIA+ communities responded to the emergence of HIV/AIDS. As the *Pride of Lions*, the newspaper published by the GPC, exhorted in 1972: "HOMOSEXUALS: UNITE! ORGANIZE! RESIST!"[9]

PRIDE OF LIONS

The Newspaper of Gay People at Columbia

Volume I, Number 1   April, 1972   COLUMBIANA LIBRARY   FREE

210 LOW LIBRARY
COLUMBIA UNIVERSITY
NEW YORK, NY 10027

GAY
DANCE

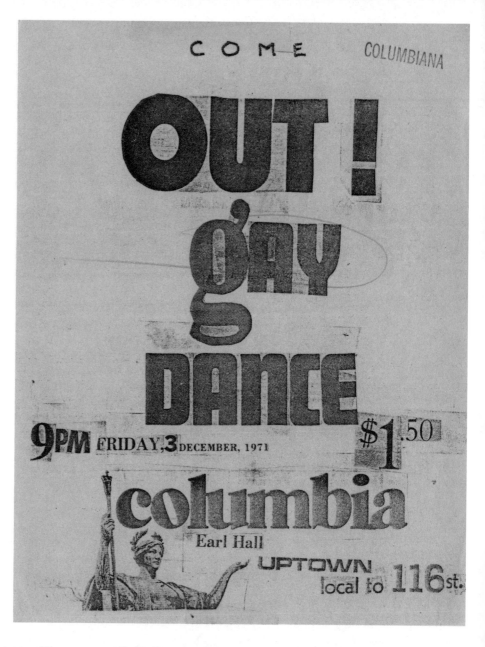

> Ad for a Friday Gay People at Columbia (GPC) dance, December 1971.

1. *Pride of Lions: The Newspaper of Gay People at Columbia* 1, no. 1 (April 1972).
2. Brett Beemyn, "The Silence Is Broken: A History of the First Lesbian, Gay, and Bisexual College Student Groups," *Journal of the History of Sexuality* 12, no. 2 (2003): 205–223.
3. Columbia University Archives, "Gay Students at Columbia," box 224, folders 10–11.
4. Liz Highleyman, "First Student Homophile League Forms," *LGBT History, 1956–1975* (New York: Great Neck Publishing, 2005), 60–63.
5. This policy affected not only gay people, but what we now refer to as LGBTQIA+: lesbian, gay, bisexual, transgender, queer or questioning, intersex, and asexual or allied. The terms used at the time were "homophile" ("homosexual" had negative connotations) and, from the early 1970s, "gay." "Lesbian" was introduced in the 1970s, thanks to the feminist fight. In the 1980s, and facing the HIV/AIDS epidemic, different groups coalesced, forging a common cause, and introducing "queer," "bisexual," and "transgender." In the late 1990s and early 2000s, "intersex," "asexual," and "allied" were added.
6. It remained illegal until 1980. See Carlos A. Ball, *From the Closet to the Courtroom: Five LGBT Rights Lawsuits that Have Changed Our Nation* (Boston: Beacon Press, 2010).
7. On "men only" dance clubs in New York see Martin Duberman, Martha Vinicius, and George Chauncey, eds., *Hidden from History: Reclaiming the Gay and Lesbian Past* (New York: Meridian, 1990).
8. See Sylvia Lavin, "Andy Architect TM," in *Flash in the Pan* (London: Architectural Association, 2014). In later years, GPC was the foundation of research projects and initiatives at GSAPP, such as Ken Lustbader's thesis project "Landscape and Liberation: Preserving Gay and Lesbian History in Greenwich Village" (1993) or Andrew Dolkart's efforts in the LGBT Historic Sites Project (from 1994).
9. *Pride of Lions* I, no. 1 (April 1972): 9.

EXPERIMENTS IN ENVIRONMENT

Mark Wasiuta, Sarah Herda

Protagonists Anna Halprin (1920–2021),
Lawrence Halprin (1916–2009)
Institution The Halprin Workshop
Location Bay Area, CA, USA
Date 1968

Over twenty-four days during the summer of 1968 landscape architect Lawrence Halprin and avantgarde dancer Anna Halprin, founder of the San Francisco Dancer's Workshop, conducted Experiments in Environment—a workshop and teaching exercise devoted to the "ongoingness of collective creativity."[1] A group of thirty-five people from architecture, dance, planning, sociology, growth training, and performance backgrounds drifted from the streets of San Francisco to the woods and outdoor dance deck of the Halprins' home in Marin County, and to the beaches of Sea Ranch, a coastal community developed around Lawrence Halprin & Associates' 1962 masterplan. Conceived in collaboration with psychologist Paul Baum, the Experiments in Environment workshop entailed a range of movement, communication, and notation exercises designed to pursue "ways of learning through exploration and direct experience."[2]

Building a "Driftwood Village," mapping urban circulation, and taking blindfolded walks, the group explored tactility and motion as methods to instigate environmental action and awareness. Participants were instructed to pay attention to their "feelings" as well as their senses, and to encounter the city, nature, and their own bodies, each as environments to be explored. Through such enhanced environmental sensitivity, exercises were conceived as coordinated performances that tested perception and social convention. During the City-Map exercise, for example, workshop members were given daily instruction sheets that orchestrated individual movement and group action. At the sound of the 3:00 chimes all participants finding themselves in Union Square were directed to stand and face the sun. During dinner at Yee Joon, a local Chinese restaurant, participants were told to switch places three times. At the Cable Car Barn they were instructed to imagine themselves in a "place of fantasy" and to act accordingly.

These adjustments to body position, vision, and imagination were meant to also modify behavior and dislodge habits. During the Skyscraper Event participants were asked to wander through local building towers while adopting a personality trait from "Timothy Leary's system" not normally their own.[3] The Halprins and Baum believed that seeing, acting, and moving in space differently would not only trigger a new comprehension of bodies, buildings, and cities, it would also foster new forms of collective creativity. Jim Burns, summer workshop member and senior editor of *Progressive Architecture*, later recalled the spirit of collective environmental engagement: "Young women and men strip on an open-air deck, oil and massage each other's bodies, bathe each other and move together through the mountain woodland. Trying to create its own community, a group of young people lives through the agonies and happiness and involvement that go with environmental creation."[4]

Lawrence Halprin envisioned an escape from the "giving-receiving" format of university teaching.[5] Borrowing techniques from the dance and movement workshops Anna Halprin had been leading at their Marin County home since the early 1960s, Experiments in Environment wagered on the pedagogical potency of the encounter between architecture and dance. The site of this encounter, the Halprins' open-air dance deck—invoked by Burns and designed by Lawrence Halprin in 1954—had already became a West Coast icon and the source of much lore via the dance workshops attended by Simone Forti, Yvonne Rainer, Trisha Brown, and Robert Morris, among others. In New York many of this group were active in the emergence of East Coast postmodern dance, and key figures in the performance experiments at the Judson Church in the 1960s.

Together with an earlier iteration the Halprins had led in 1966, the 1968 Experiments in Environment exerted a similar influence on architecture. Chip Lord, 1968 workshop participant and co-founder of the group Ant Farm, modeled his 1969 University of Houston "educational reform" workshop Time Slice on the Halprins' experiment.[6] Experiments in Environment became the primary reference for Lawrence Halprin & Associates' Taking Part, a workshop approach to community and collective design processes. It was also a proving ground for the RSVP Cycles, Lawrence Halprin's method for combining Resources, Scores, Valuaction, and Performance as tools for collective creativity, and as a system of analysis though which the city would be understood as a space of social action. In Halprin's code, Resources are external facts, figures, and

data, as well as subjective feelings, personal histories, and "life patterns."[7] Scores are instructions that, in his system, stress process and participation, Performance is the enactment and the "style" of the score, and Valuaction—evaluation and action—is a phase of commentary, critique, and conversation and where the Halprins' notion of collective creativity brushes most closely against the therapeutic environment of 1960s encounter group sessions.

For the workshops, scoring and other techniques were corporeal—embedded in the movement of the bodies of participants—but also resolutely informational. Lawrence Halprin identified the punch tape feed of early computer programs as one privileged example of a score. Yet in his argument, the steps and scores of the RSVP Cycles were anything but repetitive automatic procedures. For the Halprins, the 1968 workshop—and those that preceded and followed—formed a bridge linking heightened environmental perception to collective political decision-making. Aimed at "young people disenchanted with educational systems" and buoyed by the hope of countering social alienation, the workshops were committed to free and creative problem-solving.[8] Halprin argued that if conventional scoring—understood broadly as social control mechanisms—were made visible rather than concealed it would "scatter power" and "destroy secrecy."[9] The Halprins postulated that the pedagogical effects reverberating from their scores and simple movement exercises would improve community living, strengthen social interest groups, liberate architecture, and ultimately refresh and renew participatory politics.

> Nakedness session, Experiments in Environment workshop, 1968.

< Driftwood village, Experiments in Environment workshop, 1968.

< Sea Ranch
departure ritual,
Experiments in
Environment
workshop, 1968.

1. Lawrence Halprin and Jim Burns,
*Taking Part: A Workshop Approach to
Collective Creativity* (Cambridge, MA:
MIT Press, 1974), xi.
2. Ibid.
3. The Skyscraper Event score refers to
Timothy Leary's *Interpersonal Diagnosis
of Personality: A Functional Theory and
Methodology for Personality Evaluation*
(Eugene: Resource Publications, 1957).
The book proposes a model for mapping
personality across a combination of
personality types, from the Autocratic
Personality to the Dependent
Personality, etc.
4. Jim Burns, *Arthropods: New Design
Futures* (New York: Praeger Publishers,
1972), 153.
5. Halprin and Burns, *Taking Part*, xi.
6. Ibid., 215.
7. Ibid., 31.
8. Ibid., 11–13.
9. Lawrence Halprin, *The RSVP Cycles:
Creative Processes in the Human
Environment* (New York: George Braziller,
1969), 175.

FEMINIST PEDAGOGY, PARTICIPATORY DESIGN, AND THE BUILT ENVIRONMENT

James Merle Thomas

Protagonists Sheila Levrant de Bretteville
(1940–), Miriam Schapiro (1923–2015),
Judy Chicago (1939–), Arlene Raven (1944–2006),
and Students of the Women's Design Program
Institutions California Institute of the Arts
(CalArts): Feminist Art Program, Women's
Design Program (both 1971–1973); Womanhouse
(1971–1972); Woman's Building: Feminist Studio
Workshop, Women's Graphic Center (1973–1991)
Locations Valencia and Los Angeles, CA, USA
Dates 1971–1991

Conceived in the 1960s and inaugurated at the dawn of the 1970s, the California Institute of the Arts (CalArts) established a reputation for its emphasis on unconventional educational models and experimental artistic practice, serving as an intellectual anchor in the burgeoning Los Angeles art scene. As the school moved to its new location in the foothills of the nearby town of Valencia, a heady (and largely male-centric) posture dominated the institution. Maurice Stein pioneered a new vision for critical theory through his *Blueprint for Counter Education*, while John Baldessari, Michael Asher, Douglas Huebler, and other artists associated with the West Coast American avantgarde led a freewheeling curriculum of studio classes. As art historian Jenni Sorkin notes, "CalArts was a place of intensive masculine bravado; the premier American art school of the 1970s, the place to make a Happening alongside [Allan] Kaprow, the progenitor of the genre."[1] Equally central to the 1970s CalArts scene, however, was a group of female artists and educators who, during a brief but influential period, indelibly shaped the school's history—and whose interests in experimental pedagogy ultimately led them to fully commit to the practice of institution-building, as their efforts eventually eclipsed CalArts and led to the creation of several independent art spaces in Los Angeles.

Central to this history is Sheila Levrant de Bretteville, a graphic designer, artist, and educator who joined the CalArts faculty in 1970, simultaneously teaching in the School of Design and running the institute's graphic design shop while helping to shape the school's visual identity through experimental publications and promotional materials designed to attract forward-thinking students. Channeling the school's emphasis on "ecology, technology, and human need" over "mere taste and style," de Bretteville created a novel recruitment card for potential students in 1970 that included a shrink-wrapped array of small pinecones, toy jacks, and microchips. In its acknowledgment of technology and a broader cultural preoccupation with systems-oriented thinking, de Bretteville's design resonated with the crisp, cheery work of Charles and Ray Eames, whose films and exhibition-based meditations on IBM computers and children's toys encouraged a sense of purposeful experimentation and play—themes central to the newly formed art school's pedagogical stance.

If the CalArts bright yellow recruitment card symbolically linked the new institution to the Los Angeles environment and aspects of its associated aesthetic, a design project created by de Bretteville later that same year explicitly promoted the school's expansive ethos and sense of community.[2] Throughout the spring and summer of 1970, de Bretteville solicited contributions from the school's faculty and administrators for a special edition of the journal *Arts in Society*, which she shaped as both editor and designer. Published in late 1970, "Prologue to a Community"[3] announced CalArts' new experimental direction even through its choice of paper stocks, with alternating folios of heavy card, velum, and newsprint. De Bretteville's bold layout presented the contributions through a kaleidoscopic montage of full-bleed halftone photographic enlargements, captured scans of early video and television screens, juxtaposed swaths of text and image, photocopied maps, and bits of handwriting—a design style she later termed a "tentative, fragmented organization" that emphasized the still-evolving nature of the school and invited readers to imagine themselves as taking part in the conceptualization of a new arts institution, one that had its origins in the tumultuous politics of the late 1960s.

While these visually sophisticated projects signaled the importance of critical thinking and an expansive, interdisciplinary approach—values that were crucial to the school's self-conception at the start of the 1970s—de Bretteville mobilized these aesthetics into a purposeful and highly effective teaching method: a blend of experimental pedagogy, radical and practical feminist activism, and foundational knowledge in graphic and environmental

v Sheila Levrant de
Bretteville, design
for Womanhouse
catalogue, 1971.

Women in Design: The next decade—A conference for women who work with public visual and physical forms, March 20th at the Woman's Building, 172

v Woman's Building,
Los Angeles, Women
in Design poster,
1975.

design that helped to establish the intellectual and institutional reputation of the school during its early years. Working alongside artists Miriam Schapiro and Judy Chicago—who co-founded the Feminist Art Program (FAP) at CalArts in 1971—de Bretteville created the first-ever Women's Design Program, a one-year curriculum featuring design courses, group consciousness-raising sessions, performance workshops, and feminist literature-reading circles. For the two years of the program's existence, de Bretteville's teaching explored the relations between visual material, media design, and gender-normative behavior. At the same time, she continued to shape the visual identity of many of the FAP's most renowned projects.

Although new to teaching, de Bretteville quickly honed an intuitive and empathic pedagogical style at CalArts, drawing on a diverse set of personal influences, from her formalist training in graphic design at the still male-dominated graduate program at Yale in the early 1960s to her interest in Italian Marxism. (After graduating from Yale, she traveled extensively in Europe while working for the Olivetti Corporation in the late 1960s, and briefly lived in Milan before moving to the West Coast.) Also important were the emancipatory writings of Frantz Fanon and Paulo Freire—the latter's book, *Pedagogy of the Oppressed*, could be seen as a catalyst of the sustained effort to align design and teaching at CalArts and elsewhere.[4] De Bretteville effectively yoked these influences to the principles of second-wave feminism and, in particular, to the techniques of consciousness-raising (C-R), which, like aspects of Freire's pedagogy, emphasized group-directed, nonhierarchical power structures in discussion and seminar settings. In both the Women's Design Program and its subsequent iterations, C-R techniques were central to de Bretteville's master class, Feeling to Form, which was structured through an open workshop style, with participants being asked to speak and write through a personal object of their choosing. A second course, Public Announcements/Private Conversations, was devoted to questions of public discourse in spatial and institutional environments, and directly influenced a wave of site-specific artworks created by FAP alumni. Often realized through a purposeful, utilitarian approach to actively designing, constructing, and participating in visual and built environments, de Bretteville's curriculum embraced a wide-ranging approach to new media (the program notably made use of the CalArts video equipment). At the same time, it promoted a sense of artistic production as continuous with other

259

aspects of one's life and encouraged a critical and productive engagement with the politics of domestic labor, housework, and childrearing. No less important were the program's practical workshops, where students gained technical skills in graphic design and typography, mastered various printing and production techniques, and ultimately learned to deploy these skills beyond the traditional confines of the educational institution. Their applied and creative work, as skilled laborers, artists, and activists, would help to establish countless feminist art spaces and collectives in Los Angeles and elsewhere in the years that followed.[5]

An early example of this practical, "built" sensibility can be found in de Bretteville's designs for the exhibition catalog for the Womanhouse, a dilapidated mansion the program occupied from early 1972. Now recognized as a landmark exhibition in the history of second-wave feminist art, the month-long series of site-specific installations, performances, and lectures explored the physical structure of the home as a site of domestic ritual and labor. By rehabilitating an abandoned house, the FAP faculty and students demonstrated that one could transform a historically proscribed "domestic space" into a site of salient cultural critique and art world spectacle. Accordingly, de Bretteville's designs for the format and cover of the Womanhouse catalog—rendered in the shape of a pitched-roof house—creatively framed the contributions of the project's many participants as it drew on experimental graphic design, photocollage, experimental architecture, and even nodded to the influence of conceptual photography—an aesthetic that visually aligned the project with various conceptual art practices unfolding on the West Coast while asserting the importance of (gendered) collective and collaborative modes of production and creative labor.[6]

If the Feminist Art Program and the Women's Design Program were vital elements of CalArts' early embrace of radical pedagogy as a means to align personal politics and aesthetics, the curriculum's spatial, architectural, and institutional dimensions arguably realized their fullest expression after the program's co-founders left the art school and the alumni of the short-lived program began to establish their own spaces in Los Angeles and elsewhere. In 1973 Bretteville and Chicago departed CalArts and joined art historian Arlene Raven to form the Feminist Studio Workshop (FSW), inaugurating the Woman's Building in Los Angeles in November of that year. Part community center, part school, the institution hosted various art galleries, studios, publishing houses, and activist organizations throughout its twenty-two-year existence.[7] Serving as a site for art education, community organization, and, more generally, as a crucial hub in a growing network of feminist activist spaces, the Woman's Building played host to early feminist art historian conferences and sponsored some of the first exhibitions of video and performance art by female artists in the 1970s.[8] While personally overseeing the establishment and direction of the FSW and the Women's Graphic Center (an adjacent printing press and graphic arts facility), de Bretteville continued to teach courses and organized landmark conferences on topics of graphic, visual, and environmental design.

During this period de Bretteville also continued to advocate for a participatory or consensus-based approach to the design of print and visual environments, again drawing on her time in Italy in the late 1960s, and in particular on the work of the radical Superstudio group and the architect Giancarlo De Carlo. Just as de Bretteville's lectures and essays eschewed "simplicity, clarity, and oversimplification," her designs at the time embraced visual unruliness, employing a freewheeling juxtaposition of image and text and a multiple-author mode of production—an approach that accommodated as many different voices and competing aesthetics as possible.[9]

After leaving the Women's Graphic Center in the early 1980s (and after creating a program in Communication Design for the Otis Art Institute), the designer-teacher returned to the East Coast and assumed a position as the first tenured female faculty at the Yale School of Art, extending an influential pedagogical model that continues to inform generations of designers.[10] De Bretteville continues to lead innovative seminars as Director of Graduate Studies in Graphic Design and foster experimental collaborative work by students and teachers.

1. Jenni Sorkin, "Learning from Los Angeles: Pedagogical Predecessors at the Woman's Building," in *Doin' It in Public: Feminism and Art at the Woman's Building*, ed. Meg Linton and Sue Maberry (Los Angeles: Otis College of Art and Design, 2011), 40.

2. *Arts in Society* 7, no. 3 (Research Studies and Development in the Arts University Extension the University of Wisconsin, Fall-Winter, 1970), special issue: "California Institute of the Arts: Prologue to a Community"; and the CalArts institutional history, https://calarts.edu/about/institute/history.

3. *Arts in Society* was published periodically by the University of Wisconsin between 1958 and 1976. For more on the publication's interdisciplinary orientation and political engagement, see the *Arts in Society*, Digital Collections, University of Wisconsin-Madison Libraries, https://uwdc.library.wisc.edu/collections/arts/artssoc/, accessed June 7, 2020.

4. Originally published in 1968, Freire's book was first translated from Portuguese to English in 1970 as *Pedagogy of the Oppressed* (New York: Herder and Herder, 1970).

5. For a representative firsthand account of the feminist programs at CalArts, see the edited transcript of an oral history interview with Suzanne Lacy, conducted by Moira Roth in Berkeley, California, March 16, 1990, Archives of American Art, Smithsonian Institution; excerpted and published online at *East of Borneo*, December 15, 2011, https://eastofborneo.org/articles/suzanne-lacy-on-the-feminist-program-at-fresno-state-and-calarts/ last accessed June 7, 2020.

6. See, for example, Lacy's observation that at CalArts "[John] Baldessari was one pole of the Conceptual world, and [Allan] Kaprow was the other, and then there was Chicago and Schapiro, which was a very strong feminist influence. It turned out that the feminists who were conceptually oriented gravitated toward Kaprow."

7. The FSW was originally headquartered in a building on South Grandview Avenue, near the Los Angeles neighborhood of MacArthur Park. In 1975 it relocated to a 1914 Beaux-Arts building near downtown Los Angeles, where it remained until closing in 1991. For an early firsthand account of the Woman's Building and its organizational history, see Ruth Iskin, "Feminist Education at the Feminist Studio Workshop," in *Learning Our Way: Essays in Feminist Education*, ed. Charlotte Bunch and Sandra Pollack (Trumansburg, NY: Crossing Press, 1983), 169–186; and Woman's Building records, 1970–1992, Archives of American Art, Smithsonian Institution.

8. For a recent assessment of the Woman's Building and its legacy, see the aforementioned *Doin' It in Public* (2011) and *From Site to Vision: The Woman's Building in Contemporary Culture*, ed. Sondra Hale and Terry Wolverton (Los Angeles: Otis College of Art and Design, 2011). Also notable is the Getty Research Institute's two-year initiative to process and preserve a series of media archives related to the Woman's Building; and http://thewomansbuilding.org/, a periodically updated online bibliography and history of the project.

9. Sheila de Bretteville, "Some Aspects of Design from the Perspective of a Woman Designer," *Icographic* 6 (Croydon, England, 1973). For a contemporaneous example of this approach, see de Bretteville's *Pink*, produced the same year.

10 . In addition to training countless designers through teaching at Otis and Yale, de Bretteville's role as an engaged educator is spiritually extended through several recent design-and-arts-oriented collectives; figuring prominently among them is the Los Angeles-based Women's Center for Creative Work (WCCW), co-founded in 2013 by artist Katie Bachler, graphic designer Kate Johnston, and cultural producer Sarah Williams, which facilitates artist residencies and an ongoing graphic design fellowship program (https://womenscenterforcreativework.com/, last accessed June 7, 2020).

^ Feminist studio workshop at de Bretteville's home, September 1973.

"EVERY BODY NEEDS EQUAL ACCESS"

Ignacio G. Galán, Kathleen James-Chakraborty

Protagonists Ray Lifchez (1932–) and members of the Center for Independent Living
Institution College of Environmental Design, University of California, Berkeley
Location Berkeley, CA, USA
Dates 1972–1987

Disability activists founded the Center of Independent Living (CIL) near the University of California Berkeley campus in 1972. One of its early leading figures was Ed Roberts, who in 1962 had been the first student with severe disabilities to attend the university.[1] Following the paradigm of the period, which privileged a medical approach to disabilities, Roberts was housed at the campus's Cowell infirmary, where he was assisted with eating and dressing. He thrived, going on to earn a master's degree in political science. By 1967 he had been joined by twelve other students with major disabilities. While segregated, the "Rolling Quads"—as they called themselves—initiated diverse forms

of activism, operating in the tradition of student protest that had unfolded in Berkeley since the early 1960s and paradigmatically coalesced around the Free Speech demonstrations on campus in 1964. Rejecting their isolation in medical institutions, they demanded greater independence and participation in the community. And with the formation of the CIL, their drive for independent living expanded beyond the campus, to support the wider disabled community of Berkeley.[2] As well as advocating for disability rights, the CIL sought to facilitate spatial transformations and the creation of social networks that would improve access to residential spaces and care. The city had to accommodate diverse bodies, in the same way it did diverse political positions, embracing their differences and the resulting frictions. The slogan, "Every Body Needs Equal Access," summed up the goals of these activists.[3]

Pedagogy at the College for Environmental Design at UC Berkeley was soon to contribute to these goals. Architect Raymond Lifchez joined the faculty of the department of architecture the same year the CIL was founded, arriving from New York City, where he had studied, and later taught, at the Graduate School of Architecture, Planning, and Preservation

in Columbia University, actively participating in the 1968 uprisings. Lifchez's radical concept of equality was informed by his time at Columbia and the idea of *communitas* developed by his professor, urban theorist Percival Goodman.[4] While in New York, Lifchez had already documented the needs of individuals with disabilities in numerous state hospitals, and his work as an architect was closely tied to several advocacy projects.[5] At Berkeley, Lifchez joined ongoing efforts to remove the architectural barriers on the campus. His work—published in an extensive report in 1976—used "performance testing" as its method, giving students in wheelchairs the opportunity and the space to record their observations.[6] Working with architect and lecturer Barbara Winslow, Lifchez went on to develop a larger survey of how and where people with disabilities lived, documented through more than eight hundred interviews and photographs and videos made using ad hoc technologies including wheelchair-mounted cameras—a gadget as sophisticated as many of the customized prosthetic devices invented by CIL members to adapt to their individual needs.

The work of both Lifchez and the CIL stemmed directly from the Berkeley context, which was sometimes called the "crip capital" of America. According to Lifchez, the reputation was "well-deserved," since "the population included an unusually large number of disabled people living in the town, independently, outside custodial care."[7] In the early 1970s the first curb cuts in the US were installed along Telegraph Avenue, one of the main avenues near the UC Berkeley campus. Consequently, Telegraph became a symbolically loaded point of congregation for people with disabilities who, "with the help of electric wheelchairs, prosthetic devices, and good attendant care go everywhere and do everything...and become an integral part of the activities of urban life."[8]

Lifchez introduced the question of access in the seminal undergraduate studio called Social and Behavioral Factors in Design, which he taught until 1987.[9] Doing away with the top-down methodology of the architectural classroom, Lifchez invited students to define "scenarios" involving hypothetical "clients" or "occupants." These subjects were always described in specific ways and situated in complex settings among neighbors and guests. To avoid working with disembodied and generic subjects, Lifchez asked students to write biographies for these occupants as well as incorporate their evolution over time. This specificity introduced students to diverse definitions of architecture's occupants on the basis of age, gender, ethnicity, and ability. One of the exercises, for instance, involved the design of a "House for someone unlike me." Students defined living scenarios in large-scale models that allowed them to discuss concerns collectively. The models acted as mediators of the diverse interests and forms of knowledge that were involved in the design process.[10] Access increasingly became a central concern of the class. Disabled people at Berkeley acted as design consultants, helping students and faculty to develop more nuanced approaches to disability, which were not limited to mobility, but also included sight or hearing. Design teams also increasingly included disabled students, with the classroom itself becoming a context of design to provide the necessary spatial transformations and networks of assistance to allow all students to work together.[11]

Rather than understanding access exclusively as a technical concern, Lifchez's class saw access as a political and environmental concern defined through spatial and social relationships and cultural biases. Many parallel courses at the College of Environmental Design shared the same socio-political emphasis, aiming to bridge the gap between designers and users. Among the most significant of these were Christopher Alexander's and Sim Van der Ryn's courses on environmental design, Robert Sommer's courses on personal space and territoriality, J. B. Jackson's and Amos Rapaport's lectures on vernacular architecture, and the courses taught by Roselyn Lindheim on design for healthcare. Post-occupancy evaluations became a common practice. Case studies explored in studios and seminars considered environments for different disabled communities, such as blind children, while other courses addressed communication theory and behavioral and psychological factors of environmental design. Lifchez showcased the larger intellectual context at Berkeley that supported his work in a special issue of the *Journal of Architectural Education* that he coedited in 1974. The journal featured the research of a number of students in the PhD program, some of whom had served as assistants in his classes.

While Lifchez created a context for his students to learn from disabled individuals, it was the disability community that brought about concrete formations of access (including an increasing number of curb cuts in Berkeley) as well as changes to federal policy. In 1977 a twenty-six-day occupation of the San Francisco Health and Education and Welfare Offices, spearheaded by members of the CIL, marked a major milestone in the disability community's battle

for civil rights, leading to the enforcement of the long-delayed Section 504 of the Rehabilitation Act of 1973, which prohibited discrimination against people with disabilities in programs that receive federal financial assistance.

Lifchez contributed to these efforts as a coauthor of the small guide *Getting There: A Guide to Accessibility for Your Facility* (1979),[12] and with a thorough documentation of the transformations of the built environment led by the disability community, gathered in *Design for Independent Living: The Environment and Physically Disabled People,* which he coedited with Winslow in 1979. Both the CIL and Lifchez's classes treated individuals with disabilities not as objects of needs, but as subjects with the capacity to address their own demands in relation to the built environment. The empowering appropriation of the derogatory term "crip," suggested in Lifchez and Winslow's book, captured the way in which the movement challenged the emphasis on assimilation as a medico-technical concern.[13] As they put it, such an emphasis "can be counterproductive.... It may serve only to obscure the fact that

the disabled person may have a point of view about the design that challenges what the designers would consider good design."[14] The knowledge pursued by Lifchez's classes rejected any technocratic generalization produced from a position of authority. Instead, his teaching sought to acknowledge the particular needs, goals, and expertise of diverse individuals. Along with the leadership of the CIL, Lifchez's pedagogy paradigmatically transformed the location of both technical expertise and invention as characteristics conventionally assigned to the architect, and distributed them among the diversity of users who occupy and transform both architecture and cities.

Full Participation in

^ Center for
Independent
Living, Berkeley,
CA, early 1970s.
Photograph by
Jane Scherr.

< The "Berkeley
scene" in the early
1970s. Photograph
by Jane Scherr.

≪ Studio reviews
of Social and
Behavioral Factors
in Design, College
for Environmental
Design, University
of California,
Berkeley, 1978.

1. On Ed Roberts and the Center for
Independent Living, see Joseph S. P.
Shapiro, *No Pity: People with Disabilities
Forging a New Civil Rights Movement* (New
York: Times Books, 1993), 41–58. Roberts
was paralyzed from the neck down after
contracting polio at the age of fourteen.
2. Aimi Hamraie, *Building Access:
Universal Design and the Politics of
Disability* (Minneapolis: University of
Minnesota Press, 2017), 11–12.
3. See image published in Ray Lifchez and
Barbara Winslow, *Design for Independent
Living: The Environment and Physically
Disabled People* (New York: Whitney
Library of Design, 1979), 10.
4. Paul and Percival Goodman,
*Communitas: Means of Livelihood and
Ways of Life* (Chicago: University of
Chicago Press, 1947).
5. Interview with Raymond Lifchez, June
9, 2018.
6. Office of Programming and
Architectural Services, *Identification
of Architectural Barriers and Other
Environmental Hazards to Physically
Disabled People* (University of California,
Berkeley, 1976).
7. *Design on the Edge: A Century of
Teaching Architecture at the University
of California, Berkeley, 1903–2003*, ed.
Waverly Lowell, Elizabeth Byrne, and Betsy
Frederick-Rothwell (Berkeley, CA: College
of Environmental Design, University of
California, Berkeley, 2009), 156.
8. Lifchez and Winslow, *Design for
Independent Living,* 15.
9. A sensitivity towards questions of
access amongst the CED faculty preceded
Lifchez's courses. In 1954, faculty member
Joseph Esherick designed the James and
Mildred Ackerman House in Greenwood
Commons for wheelchair accessibility.
See https://virtualcollections.
ced.berkeley.edu/exhibits/show/
greenwood-common/ackerman
10. Interview with Raymond Lifchez.
11. Ibid.
12. Raymond Lifchez, Dennis Williams,
Chris Yip, Michael Larson, and Joanna
Taylor, *Getting There: A Guide
to Accessibility for Your Facility*
(Sacramento: California Department
of Rehabilitation, 1979).
13. Lifchez and Winslow, *Design for
Independent Living,* 9.
14. Lifchez and Winslow, *Design for
Independent Living,* 150.

THE PERSONAL IS PROFESSIONAL

Andrea J. Merrett

Protagonists Katrin Adam (1943–), Ellen Perry
Berkeley (1931–), Phyllis Birkby (1932–1994), Bobby
Sue Hood (1940–), Marie Kennedy (1941–), Joan
Sprague (1932–1998), Leslie Kanes Weisman (1945–)
Institution Women's School of Planning
and Architecture (WSPA)
Locations St. Joseph's College in Biddeford, ME;
Stephenson College in Santa Cruz, CA;
Roger Williams College in Bristol, RI; Regis College
in Denver, CO; Washington, DC, USA
Dates 1975–1981

The Women's School of Planning and Architecture
(WSPA) was an experimental summer program
established in 1974. The school's seven founders met
through various feminist organizations in architecture—including the Alliance of Women in Architecture
(AWA) in New York City (launched in 1972 by architect
Regi Goldberg, WSPA founder Ellen Perry Berkeley,
and seven other women) and the first conference
on women in architecture, "Women in Architecture:
A Symposium," held at Washington University, St.
Louis, in March 1974. At a time when women belonged
to a small minority studying and practicing architecture in the United States, WSPA provided a national
support network, open to any woman interested in the
built environment, regardless of academic background
or training.[1]

In 1970, women accounted for less than 4 percent
of practicing architects in the United States (and only
1.2 percent of registered architects). Responding to
the women's liberation movement, women architects
began questioning their professional status and
fighting for greater inclusion. It was period of ener-
getic activism when social change seemed possible.
In a few short years, feminist architects formed
women's professional organizations,[2] organized
conferences and exhibitions,[3] and began researching
the history of women in the profession.[4]

The WSPA founders came from diverse back-
grounds and held various professional positions.
Katrin Adam, who was practicing architecture in
Brooklyn, trained in interior design and carpentry in
Germany before emigrating to the US in the 1960s.
Ellen Perry Berkeley left Harvard's Graduate School
of Design in 1955, before completing her degree.
After working for several architects, she was hired as

a research assistant by Jane Jacobs, who encouraged
her to write. In the early 1970s Berkeley was a senior
editor at *Architectural Forum*. Phyllis Birkby was an
architect, teacher, and lesbian activist in New York
City who had studied at the Cooper Union and Yale.
Bobbie Sue Hood was also a practicing architect,
based in San Francisco. She trained at Carnegie
Mellon and the University of California in Berkeley.
Marie Kennedy received her master's in architecture
from Harvard in 1969. She worked for the Boston
Redevelopment Agency and Urban Planning Aid
before joining the Open Design Office—a Boston-
based feminist architecture practice co-founded by
Joan Sprague—in 1973. Sprague held a bachelor's
degree in architecture from Cornell University and
had been in practice since the early 1950s, including
a decade running a firm in Boston with her husband.
In 1972 she helped initiate the Open Design Office
and its nonprofit research partner, the Women's
Design Center. Leslie Kanes Weisman, the only WSPA
founder teaching architecture full-time, had studied
interior architecture at Wayne State University in
Detroit and was a faculty member at the University
of Detroit.

Although the founders had different ideas about
feminism, they drew on some of the principles of the
women's liberation movement. They set out to create
a nonhierarchical, separatist experience for women
where all participants would be equally valued. To
counter the star system in architecture, they listed
their credentials collectively in the promotional material and acknowledged that teachers had as much to
learn from students as vice versa. All decisions were
made through consensus among the organizers and
scheduling during the first session was conducted
on a wall-sized calendar where any participant could
add an event or meeting. WSPA was conceived as a
learning environment—away from offices and traditional schools of architecture—where women could
explore their roles in a male-dominated profession
and develop a collective identity.

The founders wanted WSPA to retain an experimental quality and designed the school to remain
independent and affordable. Each of the four sessions
(Maine, 1975; California, 1976; Rhode Island, 1978; and
Colorado, 1979) was held at rented college facilities
in different locations across the United States, which
made it possible for women who could only afford to
travel locally to attend from different parts of the
country. The founders also put measures in place
to make WSPA accessible without outside funding.
The cost of running the school was covered through

tuition alone and allowances were made to provide work-study scholarships to some participants. Between fifty to seventy women participated at each session—some at multiple sessions—and two hundred experienced the school in total. Another two hundred and fifty or so women attended the 1981 conference, "A National Symposium: Community Based Alternatives and Women in the 80s," organized by WSPA and nine other groups.

WSPA's pedagogy emphasized both personal transformation and social change. At the first session, the focus was on changing the design professions to make them more inclusive to women. Courses such as woodworking emphasized practical skills, while other courses provoked discussions about the professional and physical environments that women inhabited. The most radical course taught the first year was "Women's Fantasy Environments," initiated as a series of workshops by Phyllis Birkby in 1973. Birkby and Leslie Kanes Weisman used consciousness-raising techniques—a practice of the radical branch of the women's movement—to encourage participants to explore their experiences of the built environment and imagine ideal spatial arrangements, expressed through an open-ended drawing process. Birkby and Weisman believed that, through fantasy, women could escape the patriarchal constraints placed on them: "We

<< Women's School of Planning and Architecture participants forming a woman symbol, 1975. Black and white copy print from color slide. WSPA, St. Francis College. Biddleford, Maine.

v Introductory session of the Women's School of Planning and Architecture, St. Francis College, Biddleford, Maine, August 10, 1975.

encouraged the women to fantasize because we believed in the power of dreams as a force for social and personal change—an important goal of the women's movement."[5] The participants were given a large roll of drawing paper and were prompted to draw their imagined living spaces, responding to questions such as "What does it look like?," "What do you do there?," and "Is there anyone else there?"[6] They then discussed their drawings with the group. The exercise helped the participants make connections between their personal desires and their roles as professionals in providing more adaptive spaces for women.

By the third session of the school in 1978, the focus had moved to the role female professionals could play in changing women's lives. Sharon E. Sutton, Jane McGroarty, and Susan Saegert led a two-and-a-half-day workshop, "The Ecology of Sex Roles," for the entire school. Similar to the fantasy drawing course, they asked the participants to begin by thinking about spaces they found personally significant. They went further than Birkby and Weisman, however, in asking them to make connections between their own experiences and how the environments of local women could be improved. The overall focus of the session brought greater attention to questions of social justice as they pertained to women's access to the built environment. As a result, the session's organizers—Katrin Adam, Susan Aitcheson (a participant in 1975), and Joan Sprague—went on to establish the Women's Development Corporation in Providence, Rhode Island, which continues to build and manage housing for women as well as mentally ill, disabled, and elderly clients.[7]

The school relied on its organizers' energy and enthusiasm. After the first session, several of the founders stepped back to allow interested participants to plan the school for the following year. This strategy was used for each session. It meant that institutional knowledge was not developed and passed on, but it also reinforced some of the founding principles of the school, namely that it was inclusionary, nonhierarchical, and remained flexible. The founders envisioned WSPA to be responsive to the needs of those involved. Feminist activism in architecture over the course of the 1970s helped women overcome isolation and discrimination and encouraged more women to study and practice architecture: by the early 1980s, the number of female architects in the US had quadrupled (from around two thousand in 1970, to more than eight thousand in 1980), and a greater percentage of architecture degrees were awarded to women. It was precisely their own success in a changing political climate that decreased the perceived need for organizations like WSPA.

Despite its short existence, WSPA had several lasting effects. The formal education it provided was somewhat idiosyncratic—based on the skills and interests of those who volunteered to teach—however, it proposed a different set of values for architectural pedagogy. It emphasized empowerment and collective identity over the all-encompassing focus on the design studio and the individual designer typical of conventional schools of architecture. Like other efforts to create feminist learning environments, such as Sheila Levrant de Bretteville's Women's Design Program at CalArts (1971–1973) and the Feminist Studio Workshop at the Woman's Building (1973–1981), WSPA offered participants the opportunity to explore what they had to offer when they were not faced with gendered social expectations and harassment. The school succeeded in promoting social justice through the continued work of many of the participants, especially the Women's Development Corporation—and it provided those who attended with a lifelong network of friends and professional colleagues.

1. The WSPA archive is held at Smith College: Records of the Women's School of Planning and Architecture, Sophia Smith Collection, Smith College, Northampton, MA. See also Andrea J. Merrett, "Feminism in Architecture: The Women's School of Planning and Architecture," in *Histories of American Architectural Education* (provisional title), ed. Peter Laurence et al., forthcoming from Princeton Architectural Press; and Elizabeth Cahn, "Project Space(s) in the Design Professions: An Intersectional Feminist Study of the Women's School of Planning and Architecture (1974–1981)," PhD diss. (University of Massachusetts-Amherst, 2014).

2. Association for Women in Architecture (formerly Alpha, Alpha, Gamma), Los Angeles; Women Architects, Planners, and Landscape Architects (WALAP), Boston, 1972; the Organization of Women Architects in San Francisco, 1973; Chicago Women in Architecture, 1974.

3. "West Coast Women's Design Conference," University of Oregon 1974; "Women in Design: The Next Decade" conference, Woman's Building, LA, 1975; "Women in Design and Planning Conference," Boston Architectural Center, 1975; "Sexual Politics and Design" conference, MIT Department of Architecture, 1975; "Women and Minorites in Environmental Design," ACSA conference, University of Nebraska, 1975.

4. Doris Cole, *From Tipi to Skyscraper* (Boston: i Press, 1973); Susana Torre, ed., *Women in American Architecture* (New York: Whitney, 1977); Gwendolyn Wright, "On the Fringe of the Profession: Women in American Architecture," in *The Architect: Chapters in the History of the Profession*, ed. Spiro Kostof (New York: Oxford University Press, 1977), 280–308; Dolores Hayden, "Two Utopian Feminists and Their Campaigns for Kitchenless Houses," *Signs* 4, no. 2 (Winter 1978): 274–290.

5. Leslie Kanes Weisman, *Discrimination by Design* (Urbana: University of Illinois Press, 1992), 169.

6. Ibid.

7. Women's Development Corporation website: www.wdchoc.org.

Poster for the 1972 IID Summer Session designed by Peter Cook, Dennis Crompton, and Ron Herron.

INTERSECTING GLOBAL AND LOCAL

DESIGN IN THE SERVICE OF NATION-BUILDING

Anthony Acciavatti

Protagonists Charles Eames (1907–1978),
Ray Eames (1913–1988), Gautam Sarabhai
(1917–1995), Gira Sarabhai (1923–), Dashrath Patel
(1927–2010), H. Kumar Vyas (1929–2017)
Institution National Institute of Design (NID)
Location Ahmedabad, India
Dates 1958–1974

For a body with the most quotidian of mandates—improving the quality of consumer goods—India's National Institute of Design (NID) in Ahmedabad was invested with an extraordinary level of expectation. Heralded at its launch in September 1961 as the first of its kind in the developing world, it was based on the recommendations made by the American designers Charles and Ray Eames in their *India Report* (1958), financed by the Ford Foundation.[1] A mere fifteen years later, it had become the ultimate whipping boy of India's failed development in V. S. Naipaul's harshly titled *India: A Wounded Civilization* (1976).[2]

The institute was intended to interface between government and industry as part of India's commitment to a socialist pattern of development.[3] For this reason it was placed within the Ministry of Commerce and Industry, rather than being treated as a scientific association within the Ministry of Education or Community Development. Located in Ahmedabad, a city dubbed the "Manchester of India" because of its large number of textile mills, the newly minted school was overseen by two scions of a local mill-owning family: Gautam and Gira Sarabhai. The initial high hopes for an institute of design in India—and the ultimate dashing of those hopes—owed much to the pedagogical structure built by this brother-and-sister duo and their international connections.

Both Gautam and Gira had an abiding interest in design and handicrafts, no doubt shaped by their upbringing. Like their six siblings, they were home-schooled in the Montessori method. Gautam would graduate from Cambridge University with degrees in mathematics and philosophy, while Gira studied with American architect Frank Lloyd Wright at Taliesin in the 1940s. In 1949 the siblings established, in the grounds of their family mill, the Calico Museum of Textiles, which was credited with launching "Ahmedabad's renaissance in independent India." As the first postcolonial institution devoted to the "interdependence of design and technology" the museum sought to redress shortcomings in art education across the nation by alerting producers and consumers to ways of "integrat[ing] function and materials."[4] Gautam and Gira were expected to bring this set of priorities to the institute.

Before moving into a campus building designed by the sister and brother, the NID spent most of the 1960s in the mezzanine of the still-unfinished Sanskar Kendra, the city museum designed by Le Corbusier in 1951. There, beginning in 1962, Gira and Gautam began to structure the institute's pedagogy along with Dashrath Patel, a photographer and ceramicist, and later H. Kumar Vyas, an industrial designer.[5]

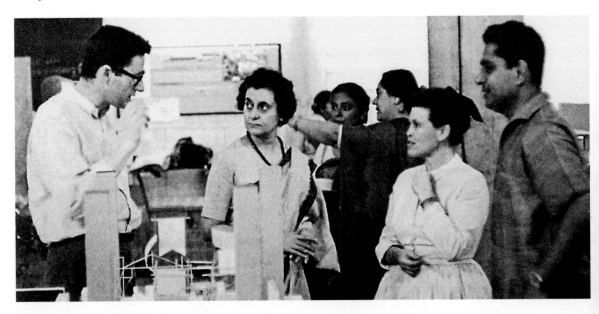

With these two foreign-educated designers, and a growing number of foreign consultants from Europe and the US, the NID began a process of identifying and training future faculty members to instruct postgraduate students.

As the faculty recruitment process developed, the administrative and pedagogical structure of the school took shape. The organizational diagram of the school grouped disciplines in one of two departments: visual communication or product design. Architecture, or "industrial architecture" as it was known at the NID, was part of the product design division, along with textiles and ceramics. Over the first decade, design projects at the NID generally proceeded on three overlapping fronts: exercises, research, and work for clients. Architecture was the exception. Since students on the program were already graduates from professional schools of architecture, they immediately began working on live commissions, collaborating for example with Louis Kahn on the Indian Institute of Management in Ahmedabad, or with Frei Otto on a new student dormitory at the NID. As Peter Scriver and Amit Srivastava have noted, the NID functioned "effectively as the architect of record for a number of significant projects" in India.[6] And these international collaborations extended beyond architecture to include projects with industrial designers, engineers, painters, musicians, and ethnographers.

Throughout their tenure at the NID, Gautam and Gira struggled with the direction of the curriculum. They drew on their background in the Montessori method and time at Taliesin, but they also came to rely on foreign expertise and institutions to frame the pedagogy of the institute. As Alexander Keefe has written, with Ford Foundation dollars and the Sarabhais' international connections, Ahmedabad in the 1960s "became a kind of outpost of the New York downtown scene."[7] Composers John Cage and David Tudor, designers George Nakashima and Enrico Peressutti, and dancer Yvonne Rainer were among those who led short workshops at the institute in the 1960s.

Alongside this "downtown scene" another strong influence was the Hochschule für Gestaltung (HfG) in Ulm, West Germany, where both Vyas and design faculty member Sudhakar Nadkarni had studied in the early 1960s. The Ulm school—created on the initiative of the brother-and-sister Scholl Foundation—inspired the two-part division of the curriculum at the NID. Faculty from the two schools also collaborated on design projects ranging from an

electric-powered tangential fan with Hans Gugelot and Ernst Reichl to photography projects with Christian Staub. Not only did these projects mirror HfG's method of instruction, but the work of the NID was increasingly seen as derivative of Western design. J. S. Sandhu, a designer and professor at the Royal College of Art in London, delivered a damning verdict on the NID's potential to be a catalyst for change in an unsolicited report sent to Charles and Ray Eames in 1970: "A Bauhaus or [HfG] Ulm or Charles Eames Associates can only flourish in a particular place and period, and are often the result of the general development of the country rather than the cause."[8]

While the NID did achieve some notable successes, such as its collaboration with the Eames office on the design of the exhibition *Nehru: His Life and His India*, which opened at the Union Carbide Building in New York in 1965, the majority of its work fell short of the expectations of both government officials and the Ford Foundation. In the words of Ford Foundation representative Douglas Ensminger, it did not look like the NID was "evolving as an indigenous Indian institution"[9]—a somewhat ironic assertion, given that it was the foundation that had hired American designers to advise on the NID's creation, and kept it alive with regular injections of cash: $1.1 million in grants during its first ten years.[10]

Gautam's and Gira's solution to mounting criticism from the Ford Foundation and the government was to hire former Vice Admiral A. B. Soman as the institute's administrative director in November 1970. A decorated veteran and one-time Chief of Staff of the Indian Navy, Soman had no special expertise in education but was selected on the basis of his supposedly "excellent connections in Delhi." Unsurprisingly, Soman and Gautam failed to agree on the boundaries of their respective positions and butted heads over pedagogy and administrative duties.[11]

The Ford Foundation had asked the Eameses in 1969 to assess whether or not the NID had lived up to the ideals of the *India Report*. The couple did not submit their report until May 1971, perhaps because they were awaiting the outcome of the national elections in India, or mulling over Sandhu's reservations. Whatever the case, the report's tepid tone seems to have sealed the Ford Foundation's decision to cut off all funding.[12] In private correspondence with officials in New Delhi the following year, Charles Eames voiced his concern over the fact that the institute seemed to tackle "so few simple-homely-down-to-earth-Indian design problems."[13]

At the NID itself, the situation was going from bad to worse. The Sarabhais and the institute's board of directors terminated Admiral Soman's contract at the beginning of July 1972, after less than two years.[14] A public scandal followed the decorated navy veteran's dismissal. Days later, on July 5, the Bombay edition of the *Economic Times* ran the headline "Soman Flays NID." Refusing to go quietly, Soman wasted no time in denouncing the institute's leadership. He accused Gautam and Gira of nepotism and of misusing taxpayer and Ford Foundation funds. And in his most stinging rebuke, he attributed the institute's few high-profile successes to foreign consultants.[15] Opposition parties seized on the scandal, using it to criticize the policies of Prime Minister Indira Gandhi's government. In 1972 a commission led by retired senior civil servant Niranjan Nath Wanchoo was appointed to investigate the allegations.[16] While they were ultimately absolved of all wrongdoing, the Sarabhais decided to leave the institute in 1974 and devote themselves to their family businesses and the Calico Museum of Textiles.

The NID remained open and major reforms ensued. In the mid-1970s, the institute gained its own degree-awarding powers. Over time, the NID became a recognizably more conventional school of design, counting some of India's most celebrated designers among its alumni. What was singular about the first institute of design in the "Third World," as it matured in the Cold War hothouse of India, was the country's willingness to attempt to address some of its most pressing economic and social problems through design and the sciences, a synthesis never before attempted in the service of nation-building in a postcolonial context.

< *Nehru: His Life and His India* exhibition designed by the Eames Office and the National Institute of Design and first shown at Union Carbide in New York City, 1965.

<< Foreground from left: Glen Fleck, Indira Gandhi, Ray Eames, and Dashrath Patel. Background: I. Kamalini Sarabhai (pointing) with Usha Bhagat, Personal Secretary to Indira Gandhi, 1964. Photographer unknown.

1. For more on this, see Anthony Acciavatti, "Towards a Communication Oriented Society: The Eameses' India Report," in *The World of Charles and Ray Eames*, ed. Catherine Ince and Lotte Johnson (London: Barbican Museum and Thames and Hudson, 2015), 242–247, 311–312.
2. V. S. Naipaul, *India: A Wounded Civilization* (New York: Vintage, 1976), 129.
3. R. K. Bannerjee, "40 Years of NID," unpublished manuscript, Ahmedabad, c.1999, 9.
4. "The Calico Museum of Textiles Ahmedabad," *Journal of Indian Museums* 4 (Museums Association of India, 1948): 120.
5. Patel studied at the College of Art, Madras (1949–1953), before taking up postgraduate studies in painting, sculpture, and ceramics at the École des Beaux-Arts in Paris. Vyas, born and raised in Uganda, studied industrial design in the early 1950s at the Central School of Art and Design in London.
6. Peter Scriver and Amit Srivastava, *India: Modern Architectures in History* (London: Reaktion Books, 2015), 212.
7. Alexander Keefe, "Subcontinental Synth: David Tudor and the First Moog in India," *East of Borneo* (April 30, 2013), http://www.eastofborneo.org/articles/subcontinental-synth-david-tudor-and-the-first-moog-in-india.
8. Report from J. S. Sandhu to Charles Eames dated September 16, 1970. Eames Papers, Library of Congress, Washington, DC, Box 44, Folder 2.
9. Letter from Douglas Ensminger to Gautam Sarabhai dated November 8, 1968. Eames Papers, Box 44, Folder 33.
10. *Report 63/69* (Ahmedabad: National Institute of Design, 1969), 39.
11. See Bannerjee, "40 Years of NID," 43.
12. Eames Papers, Box 44, Folder 2.
13. See letter from Charles Eames to Sharada Prasad dated November 6, 1972. Eames Papers, Box 44, Folder 4.
14. See letter from Gira Sarabhai to Ray and Charles Eames dated January 10, 1972. Eames Papers, Box 45, Folder 2.
15. "Soman Flays NID," *Economic Times* 12, no. 123 (July 5, 1972): 1.
16. "Charges Against the Chairman of the National Institute of Design, Ahmedabad," in *Rajya Sabha Official Debates*, Session 82, November 16, 1972 (New Delhi: Government of India, 1972), 95.

AGAINST BLANKET MODERNIZATION

Farhan Karim

Protagonists Richard E. Vrooman (1920–2002),
Daniel C. Dunham (1929–2000)
Institution East Pakistan University
of Engineering and Technology
Location Dacca, East Pakistan (Dhaka,
Bangladesh)
Dates 1964–1971

During the 1940s potential engineering students in the British colonial province of Bengal had to conform to specific physical requirements: they could be no shorter than 5 ft. 3 in. and weigh no less than 105 lbs., while the circumference of their chest had to be a minimum of 30 in. with an expiration of at least 2 in.[1] The insistence on regulating these bodily measurements was not intended to mandate a certain aesthetic appearance for future "technicians"; rather, it was to ensure that students had the necessary physical ability to carry out menial labor as subjects of an "underdeveloped" colony. This pedagogical approach, rooted in the colonial conception of underdevelopment, would be recycled in different ways in post-partition Pakistan.

In 1958 the United States Agency for International Development (USAID) partnered with the military junta of Ayub Khan to initiate a massive program of educational reform in West and East Pakistan. Defined by a blend of the American social theory of modernization with Ayub Khan's theory of basic democracy, the program's subtext was that Pakistan did not deserve a full democracy since the majority of its population was uneducated. In order to create its coveted new "citizens," the country had to develop a new educational infrastructure.[2] Under the authoritarian rule of Ayub Khan—who served as Pakistan's president between 1959 and 1968—a number of new universities, polytechnics, and training centers were established to revamp the country's tertiary level technical education.

The setting up of a full architecture program in West and East Pakistan was also part of this effort. In 1962 charters were granted to the MacLagan Engineering College in Lahore and Ahsanullah Engineering College in Dacca (now Dhaka), which were renamed the West Pakistan University of Engineering and Technology (WPUET) and East Pakistan University of Engineering and Technology (EPUET)

respectively. Through the USAID and American Technical Assistance Program, three professors from Texas A&M University—Richard Edward Vrooman, James C. Walden, Jr., and Samuel T. Lanford—arrived in Dhaka to establish a new architecture department and to train the first generations of local educators at EPUET.[3] Vrooman, the new school's first dean, designed a building for the architecture department that instantly became the symbol of a creative, technology-oriented future for Pakistan. The iconic precast concrete louver panels attached on the north and south facades served both as *brise-soleils* and as the railings of the verandahs that wrapped around the building. The brutalist tone of the structure—characterized by solid curved walls at the east and west ends, sculptural rainspouts, hidden glazed surfaces, a completely free ground floor, and a web of diagonal beams—underscored Vrooman's disillusion with a homogenizing modernism and his trust in a reenvisioned regionalism—an attitude that resonated with the postcolonial aspirations of East Pakistan.[4] The building itself served as an educational device; up to the present day, numerous student assignments are based on the building—on the observation and analysis of its use of passive climate control, its structural expression, its "honesty" of materials, its human scale, and more.

The curriculum devised by Vrooman and his team took the Texas A&M's MArch program as its template. Their approach was pragmatic and aimed at training young architects who could assume leadership in "nation-building" endeavors. Among the part-time instructors was the American architect and city planner Daniel C. Dunham, who was then working as the chief architect at the Dhaka office of Louis Berger Group (LBG), a global engineering behemoth involved with major postconflict reconstruction projects, building dams and roads across Africa, the Middle East, Latin America, and Asia. Before LBG, Dunham had worked as a UN consultant, developing an economic prototype for a solar stove in Africa. His pedagogical approach differed from his colleagues at EPUET, as he was the only one of the expat teaching staff actively engaged in the design and construction of several large-scale architectural projects in East Pakistan. Dunham's ideas of development and modernism did not come from a paternalistic mindset, but had their roots in several sources, among them his personal experience during the American Depression.[5] Dunham was nevertheless was influenced by LBG's approach to development: first, adopt local technology, then train the locals in modern technology and leave behind a permanent trail that can be followed and sustained.

Dunham and his colleagues faced a formidable challenge in East Pakistan, working with economic scarcity while at the same time attempting to define an "appropriate" architectural expression for a new country whose "authentic" cultural roots were claimed by several competing groups: secular Bengalis, Muslim nationalists, and rural and "tribal" subalterns. Dunham developed a studio that was critical of formalism and social utopia.[6] Inspired by New Deal ideas of economy and hands-on practice, he applied the principle of "austerity" in his teaching, blending his work experience with his academic training at Harvard and the Department of Tropical Architecture at the Architectural Association in London. During his seven-year stay in East Pakistan, he developed an intense interest in the country's history, often taking journeys to its remote corners. Dunham's travels were his personal means of discovering a newly decolonized country's past, of delving into its precolonial condition—its uncontaminated cultural heritage. He would eventually incorporate the experience of these journeys into his teaching.

Although the beginnings of East Pakistan's first architecture school were driven by the impulse of modernization, and in many ways continued the colonial legacy of underdevelopment, Dunham and his colleagues developed a pedagogy that sought to resist authoritarian rule, colonial stereotypes, and blanket modernization. Dunham's insistence on reconsidering the Depression era and the New Deal presented America as a model for thinking about poverty rather than as a self-satisfied exporter of wisdom.

For a brief period, against the backdrop of growing Bengali nationalism—which would lead the state to break away from Pakistan in 1971 to become Bangladesh—it was possible for Dunham and his colleagues to imagine a new future for the profession that was pragmatic and at the same time moral; a model for architectural education free from real-estate speculation and structural coercion. Following independence, EPUET was renamed Bangladesh University of Engineering and Technology (BUET). Vrooman's building remains fully functional and continues to inspire the imagination and creativity of educators and students alike. The moral-pragmatic trend of architectural pedagogy set by Dunham and others has evolved in multiple dimensions through interventions by educators such as Shayer Ghafur (professor at BUET) and Hasibul Kabir (graduate of BUET and professor at the university of BRAC, Dhaka).

∧ Daniel C. Dunham
and Wajeda J. Rab
during a studio crit
at EPUET.

< Students building
models at EPUET.

1. Prospectus, Bengal Engineering College, Civil, Mechanical, Electrical, Metallurgical and Architectural Engineering Degree Courses, 1946.
2. Farhan Karim, "Interpreting Rural: Doxiadis vis-à-vis East Pakistan," *South Asia Chronicle* 9 (2019): 243–280.
3. "Laying the Foundation for Bangladesh's Architectural Future: An Interview with James Walden," USAID *Frontlines*, November/December 2012 online edition, https://2012-2017.usaid.gov/news-information/frontlines/new-players-and-graduation/laying-foundation-bangladesh%E2%80%99s-architectural.
4. Rafique Islam, "The First Faculty of Architecture in Dhaka," unpublished manuscript; Adnan Morshed, "A Symbol of Architectural Education," *Daily Star,* February 24, 2020.
5. Conversation with Katherine Dunham, daughter of Daniel and Mary Dunham, 2017. A personal archive of Daniel and Mary Dunham's time in Dhaka can be found at https://dunham-family.com/dhaka-memoirs/
6. Rafique Islam and Mary Frances Dunham, "Contribution of Daniel C. Dunham to the Profession and Practice of Architecture in Bangladesh," paper presented in ARCHASIA; Rafique Islam, "Daniel Dunham Pioneer of Modern Architecture in Bangladesh, 2014," self-published, printed by The Book Patch, Scottsdale, AZ.

COUNTING QUALITY, SEEING PATTERNS

Ijlal Muzaffar

Protagonists Charles Abrams (1901–1970),
Jaqueline Tyrwhitt (1905–1983),
Michel Écochard (1905–1985)
Institutions Middle East Technical University
(METU); Karachi University
Locations Ankara, Turkey; Bathurst and
Kombo St. Mary, Gambia; Karachi, Pakistan
Date 1953–1963

In July 1954 the US housing finance expert Charles Abrams landed in Turkey on yet another consulting job for the United Nations.[1] His mandate was complicated; he had to write a report on the prevailing land use and zoning as well as propose planning legislation and housing finance structures for the future. A seasoned observer of bureaucracies, Abrams quickly realized that his contribution would simply be submerged in the pile of reports that bore witness to the Turkish Ministry of Public Works' long dealings with international institutions. Unable

to cut through the red tape of mid-level officials, he decided to take matters into his own hands. Enlisting a translator to join him, Abrams acquired a jeep and a driver to take a "four thousand-mile" whirlwind tour around the country.

The trip was hasty, zooming through villages and towns, conducting ad-hoc interviews with unsuspecting officials, from provincial governors and mayors to "private architects, businessmen, directors of factories, village officials, and villagers," with most destinations not even meriting an overnight stay.[2] Still Abrams was satisfied with his findings, concluding that the trip gave him "a fairly comprehensive idea of the country and its conditions."[3] He was not the first expert to have taken such a trip and come to such a definitive conclusion. But, as Burak Erdim has outlined in detail, he was the first to propose a university of engineering and planning— one that would later be named Middle East Technical University (METU) and go on to become one of Turkey's premier higher education institutions—as a solution to Turkey's planning woes.

But what *did* Abrams find during his expedition in Turkey? How were random samples able to "elicit the nature of the principal problems" facing a country?

Abrams' claims to expertise were asserted through a coupling of planning and pedagogy. His self-educating stance was meant to educate everyone else as well. But if the end result of his efforts, the creation of the METU, was an exception arising from the confluence of national and international agendas,[4] the same could not be said of his cavalier attitude, which substituted personal findings for quantitative statistics. In this respect, Abrams had plenty of company.

A decade after Abrams landed in Turkey, Jaqueline Tyrwhitt, planner and CIAM secretary, arrived in the small colonial twin towns of Bathurst and Kombo St. Mary, Gambia on a UN mission to design a master plan.[5] Just like Abrams, she was dissatisfied with the information available to her and, adopting a no less derring-do attitude, she ordered eight men to stand in pairs with a register in hand at the four main roads into the town. Their task was to record, from dawn to dusk, whatever traveled in and out on those roads: buses, lorries, cycles, pedestrians, animals. The resulting tally, Tyrwhitt claimed, was a better indicator of the pressures of urbanization than any previously collected data.

The authors of these (to us) patently absurd exercises seem to have been immunized against the concept of overreach by the particular self-pedagogical mode they adopted—one in which gaps in quantitative data could be circumvented by staking a claim to the discovery of qualitative essences. The same logic of substitution permeates the postwar meetings of CIAM. At CIAM 8 in Hoddesdon (1951), for example, the so-called "younger generation" led a charge to imbue CIAM's previous quantitative approach to planning with intangible "humanist" values, while the 1952 meeting in Sigtuna declared: "The Habitat is not a human shelter. It is a cell of a socially organized body. The cell depends on the body of which it is part. Conversely, the cell without a body loses all meaning in the sense that we understand it."[6] In the West, the small cell, the quantifiable supplement, made the bigness of the whole body available to the qualitative imagination.

But when the focus shifted to "primitive civilizations," or "technically underdeveloped" areas,[7] the relationship between smallness and bigness was flipped. What was supposed to be the supplement became the premise, the origin. The big, the infrastructure, the long-term—where planning depended on countable aspects of capital and money and state apparatuses—was displaced, delayed, erased, turned into a bigness beyond counting. The small, the immediate, the short-term came to stand by itself, as testimony to a new uncountable bigness, a qualitative bigness beyond history.

This flip is evident in the most celebrated example of the CIAM idea of "Habitat" in a non-Western context, Michel Écochard's proposal for "housing for the greatest number" in Morocco.[8] It was only by dispensing with precise quantification—and with it, the long but calculable history of colonial land grabs that had "flooded" Casablanca with economic migrants who needed to be housed—that Écochard was able to ask: Where do the rules of the Habitat begin? What is the minimum space people can live in? Can we allow slums and compounds to be shelters?[9] Écochard, too, invoked the small. But this small was not the habitable "cell" that lent a qualitative shock to the quantitative body of urbanism assembled by the Athens Charter. This smallness was the small *as such*—a pure quality that did not need to be understood in relation to quantity, or history, but could be freely imagined.

Écochard would take this idea of smallness to Karachi in 1953. The purpose of his visit was a UN mission to propose a refugee housing scheme based on the Casablanca model.[10] But while there, and in breach of UN protocol, he took on a private commission to master plan and design Karachi University. Duly reprimanded by the UN, Écochard undertook the work without any financial compensation, seeking to use the pedagogical program to define a stance towards future patterns of urban development. "These plans and reports I have made, Écochard insisted, "can be considered as a whole…it will be seen that [in them] I have laid the foundations of all plans and recommendations."[11] Accordingly, his proposal for a refugee settlement in Karachi imagined the occupants moving through a series of plans that unfolded over time, from single-story units to high-rises, with each phase, astonishingly, razed to the ground to make room for the next. To make these hard changes appear less severe, each transformation remained within the same qualitative "framework."

We can thus trace a line connecting Écochard's Karachi premonition to Abrams' Turkish adventure and Tyrwhitt's Gambian counting exercise. But this trajectory also extends into the present day: "The twentieth century has been a losing battle against quantity," Rem Koolhaas declared in *S,M,L,XL* in 1995. Teaching at Harvard a few years later, however, he claimed that he had found a cure for this "bigness" in Lagos.[12] Flying over the city, he had seen the new future of global modernism taking shape on the ground below. Defending this experience against the suggestion that he was glamorizing poverty, he would argue that Lagos had restored his belief in planning.[13] What he had seen there was a new kind of creative modernity that did not respect the rigid boundaries of traditional planning—of new and old, original or copy, finished or unfinished.

A Western vanguard discovers unfettered creativity outside the West: we have heard this story before. When accused of erasing historical complexity, Koolhaas fires back at his critics, lamenting "how political correctness defines the limits of what you can do."[14] Without stepping further into this debate, I would like to highlight one particular aspect of this maneuvering: that this framing of "Africa" and the non-West more generally happens in a pedagogical mode. Unlike Écochard, Koolhaas does not want to bulldoze everything that stands in the way of his perceived patterns. Yet, his celebration of ubiquitous creativity in Lagos is just as destructive. Lagos becomes a looking glass, its historical complexity turns into something effervescent, as the expert himself seeks to learn from the ground up, and to teach others, through reading formal patterns as a substitute for history. The quantitative bigness that is imagined to have eclipsed modernism in the West is now replaced with a qualitative bigness that is projected onto the non-West—the quantitative

bigness of master planning is replaced with the qualitative bigness of creative patterns.

These modes of substituting specific problems of quantity with a generalized discussion of quality follow a particular template. All of them claim to count quality, not quantity, to see patterns, not numbers, through a pedagogical lens. The arrow is always already beyond any number. "Bigness" becomes an essence without a measure, historical or economic.

In highlighting this substitution, the point is not to ask for more quantitative analysis but rather to stress that what passes as "quality" serves to delay—to displace—the question of a just quantity. Why are the inhabitants of Lagos deprived, struggling for survival, why has city's governance been inadequate? These are not just isolated national problems. They are historical problems, where centuries of colonial theft in collaboration with native elites overlap with patriarchal power, Cold War politics, and structural inequalities consolidated by the GATT and Bretton Woods regimes. These are quantitative questions. Their debt can be counted. Yet architecture and planning continually fill this quantitative hole with qualitative appendages. "Build your own house and gain prosperity," the discourse goes, "Overcome planning limitations and restore

< Middle Eastern Technical University (METU), Ankara, Turkey, 1956. Main pedestrian access.

> Charles Abrams visiting an Indian village while attending a UN seminar on "housing and community improvement" in New Delhi in 1954, a few months before his visit to Turkey.

the ingenuity lost in the West's quest for modernity and progress." When experts are not speeding around in jeeps to map qualitative patterns, they are sitting in a plane, marveling at the scene down below. In these claims, value and quantity do not emerge from quantitative analysis, from a historically informed discussion of presence or absence of capital, but from chasing a qualitative essence that promises to one day imminently generate quantity out of nothing.

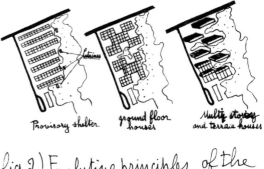

Provisory shelter | ground floor houses | multy storey and terrace houses

fig 2) *Evolutive principles of the proposed city*

The 3 stages possible according to the rise of the standard of living, but always with the same framework

1. Abrams was on his way back from New Delhi, where he had just co-headed the United Nations Seminar on Housing and Community Improvement in Asia and the Far East, New Delhi, India, January 21–February 17, 1954 (see UN Technical Assistance Program, UN document no. TAA/NS/AFE/1). After Turkey, his itinerary continued to the Gold Coast (now Ghana).
2. United Nations Technical Assistance Program, "The Need for Training and Education for Housing and Planning," prepared for the Government of Turkey by Charles Abrams, August 23, 1955 (UN Archives, New York: file no. TAA 173/57/018; report no. TAA/TUR/13). Abrams also recalls the trip in the memoir of his professional life, *Man's Struggle for Shelter in an Urbanizing World* (Cambridge MA: Joint Center for Urban Studies, MIT and Harvard, 1964), 42–47.
3. Abrams, "The Need for Training," 2.
4. Burak Erdim, "Policy Regionalism and the Limits of Translation in Land Economics," in *Systems and the South: Architecture and Development*, ed. A. Dutta, A. Khorakiwala, F. López-Duran, A. Levin, and I. Muzaffar (Abingdon: Routledge, 2021).
5. Jaqueline Tyrwhitt, "Report on Town Planning for Bathurst and Kombo St. Mary, Gambia, West Africa" (New York: Bureau of Technical Assistance Operations, United Nations, 1963).
6. CIAM, 1952. "Note sur le projet de Charte de l'Habitat. Réunion de Stockholm," unpublished transcript, Bakema Archive, NAi, Rotterdam, quoted by Elisa Dainese in "The Concept of 'Habitat': The Cellular Design Reformulation of the Post-War Modern Movement," in *Landscape and Imagination: Towards a New Baseline for Education in a Changing World*, ed. C. Newman, Y. Nussaume, B. Pedroli (Pontedra: Bandecchi & Vivaldi Editori, 2013).
7. Ibid.
8. See Michel Écochard, "Housing for the Greater Number," originally addressed to the United Nations and European Economic Commission (1951), cited in Jean-Louis Cohen, "The Moroccan Group and the Theme of the Habitat," in "The Last CIAMs," *Rassegna*, no. 52 (December 1992): 59–60.
9. Ibid.
10. For a more detailed analysis of Écochard's Karachi proposal, see my "Boundary Games: Écochard, Doxiadis, and the Refugee Housing Projects under Military Rule in Pakistan, 1953–1959," in *Aggregate: Governing by Design,* ed. A. Dutta, T. Hyde, D. Abramson (Pittsburgh: University of Pittsburgh Press, 2012).
11. Michel Écochard, in a letter to M. Qureshi, Joint Secretary of Ministry of Health and Labor, Government of Pakistan, Karachi, 26 June, 1954. UN Archives, New York. File TAA 173/70/027, Rag 2/173–Box 256.
12. Rem Koolhaas, "Harvard Project on the City," in *Mutations (*Barcelona: ACTAR, 2001).
13. Rem Koolhaas in conversation with Kunlé Adeyemi, *The Guardian*, February 26, 2016: https://www.theguardian.com/cities/2016/feb/26/lagos-rem-koolhaas-kunle-adeyemi
14. Ibid.

> Michel Écochard, proposal for a refugee settlement in Karachi, 1954.

FROM PRODUCER TO MEDIATOR OF PLANNING KNOWLEDGE

Piotr Bujas, Alicja Gzowska, Łukasz Stanek

Protagonist Piotr Zaremba (1910–1993)
Institution Szczecin University of Technology
Location Szczecin, Poland
Dates 1965–1989

In 1965 the Polish Ministry of Higher Education set up the International Postgraduate Course in Urban and Regional Planning for Developing Countries at the University of Technology in Szczecin.[1] Offered to professionals with at least two years' experience, the course attracted participants from Asia, Africa, and Latin America, with a total of 492 graduates during its thirty-year existence. Scholarships were funded by the Polish government, travel by the home institutions. From 1979 on, classes in Szczecin were complemented by training provided by the Szczecin faculty abroad and coordinated by UNESCO.

The course in Szczecin was conceived and led by the Polish planner Piotr Zaremba. Based on his experience in Poland, as well as in North Korea and the People's Republic of China in the late 1950s, Zaremba was an authority in urban planning, with a particular focus on the integration of urban and regional plans, urban ecology, and port cities.[2] Reflecting on the role of foreign experts, Zaremba argued that they should not "elaborate the whole plan of the city or a region, as this job must be carried out by nationals."[3] Rather than following foreign planning models, urban and regional development had to be guided by "local town planners familiar with the traditions, ways of living, and needs of the inhabitants."[4] In this context, the role of foreign advisers was to provide training in methodology, to present case studies of selected problems, and to support local planners in developing alternative plans of spatial development and establishing criteria for evaluating them. These recommendations defined the general principles of Zaremba's teaching, whether in Thailand, Iraq, Libya, Mexico, China, or in the framework of the course in Szczecin.

Zaremba stressed the need for interdisciplinary teamwork in planning, and this was reflected in the curriculum in Szczecin. While the majority of participants were architects and town planners, the course also attracted civil engineers, geographers, sociologists, and economists working in administration, planning, and research institutions.[5] The six-month training started with the design of structural units for a medium-size town—an exercise that established the disciplinary competences of the participants and informed the make-up of the teams that then worked on the general plan of a medium-size town. This interdisciplinary and collaborative approach was also a theme of the lecture series and, in particular, of the individual thesis, which focused on a design task in the participant's home country.

The specific Polish experience of postwar planning—including state-led industrialization, the integration of economic, social, and spatial planning, as well as attention to the conservation of cultural and ecological values—was conveyed not only in the lectures of Polish planners but also by study trips focusing, among others, on the linear urbanization of Gdynia, Gdańsk, and Sopot; on Warsaw, with its UNESCO-listed reconstruction of the Old Town; and on the continuous urbanization of Silesia. While these examples reflected the large-scale planning pursued by the Polish state, the discourse on socialism was virtually absent from the texts published by the course's teachers and affiliated scholars. Similarly, references to inequalities in the global redistribution of wealth or to the structural dependence of postcolonial countries on the former colonial metropolises were kept general—particularly in English-language publications—in an evident attempt to bypass Cold War polarization.

Indeed, during the heyday of the Cold War, the political significance of the course lay not in the promotion of the socialist path of development, but in its very existence.[6] The Postgraduate Course in Szczecin constituted an alternative center of knowledge production to those in Western Europe and the United States, along with the research at the Institute

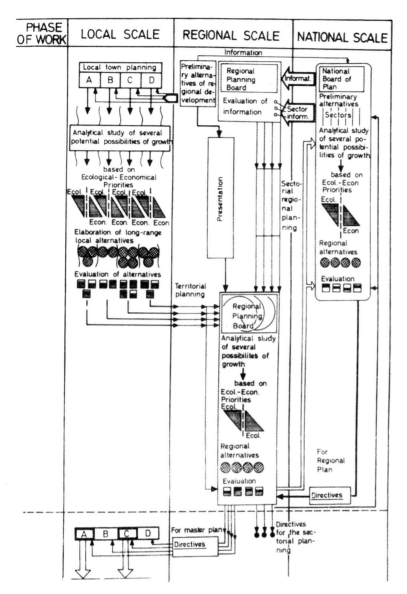

PHASE OF WORK	LOCAL SCALE	REGIONAL SCALE	NATIONAL SCALE

< Planning method-
ology diagram from
Piotr Zaremba, *Urban
Ecology in Planning*
(Ossolineum, 1986)

≪ Piotr Zaremba
and collaborators in
North Korea, winter
1954–1955.

1. This contribution is a result of
the research project no. 2015/19/N/
HS2/03406 financed by the National
Science Centre (Poland).
2. Piotr Zaremba, *Urban Ecology in
Planning* (Wrocław: Ossolineum, 1986).
3. Piotr Zaremba, "Proposal for Training
in Coastal Urban and Regional Planning,"
November 15, 1983, 2. Piotr Zaremba
Legacy, Loose Files, no. 1019, National
Archives, Szczecin.
4. Zaremba, "Proposal," 2. Cf. Krystyna
Mieszkowska, "Podyplomowe studium
urbanistyki i planowania regionalnego
dla krajów rozwijających się 1966–
1990," *Przestrzeń i Forma* 22-23 (2014):
189–200.
5. Alicja Gzowska, "Szczeciński produkt
eksportowy, czyli jak zrobić miasto?,"
Szczeciner, no. 3 (2013): 104–109.
6. Łukasz Stanek, *Architecture in Global
Socialism: Eastern Europe, West Africa,
and the Middle East in the Cold War*
(Princeton, NJ: Princeton University
Press, 2020), 25.
7. Piotr Bujas, Alicja Gzowska, Hou Li,
and Łukasz Stanek, "Planning Transition
beyond Socialism: From Poland to China
and Back," paper presented at the
International Planning History Society
Conference, Yokohama, July 17, 2018.

of Tropical Architecture in Gdańsk, the research in tropical construction at the Architecture and Civil Engineering University in Weimar (East Germany), and, in particular, the teaching and research at the Patrice Lumumba Peoples' Friendship University in Moscow (Soviet Union). Together with the technical assistance offered by socialist countries, they provided developing countries such as Nehru's India or Nkrumah's Ghana not only with expertise but also with leverage in their negotiations with the West.

By the end of the Cold War this dynamic had been recalibrated, with the Postgraduate Course in Szczecin becoming less an alternative source of knowledge and more a mediator of international planning culture. This mediation was multilateral, as evidenced by the exchanges of Zaremba and his collaborators in China during the 1980s. Learning from his contribution to the planning of port cities in Guangdong province and the PRC's Special Economic Zones in that period, Zaremba attempted to use the experience of post-Mao economic reforms to plan Poland's transition beyond socialism.[7] The Special Economic Zone that Zaremba proposed for Szczecin, created in 1992, was the first in postsocialist Poland. By that time, however, the country had embarked on a course of shock therapy that left no place for either the gradual transition envisaged by Zaremba or the Postgraduate Course, which was dissolved in 1994.

ARCHITECTURAL EDUCATION AS MANIFESTO

Irene Sunwoo

Protagonist Alvin Boyarsky (1928–1990)
Institution Architectural Association (AA)
Location London, UK
Dates 1971–1983

As chairman of the Architectural Association (AA) in London from 1971 to 1990, Canadian-born educator Alvin Boyarsky presided over a seminal episode in the history of Britain's first school of architecture. Established in 1847 by students as an educational alternative to apprenticeship, the AA had maintained its progressive ethos, institutional autonomy, and democratic foundations. Throughout the 1960s, however, an impending merger with the Imperial College of Science and Technology—part of the Royal Institute of British Architects' postwar push to consolidate architectural schools in polytechnics and universities—threatened the AA's independence and its tradition of radical activity. After several tumultuous years of intense debate about the school's future, in 1971 AA students and staff elected Boyarsky as chairman of the school, with a mandate to restore its institutional stability and steer its reinvention.

In his previous role as director of the IID Summer Sessions, which launched in 1970, Boyarsky had already demonstrated his vision of an architectural school as a global platform for experiment, fueled by the energy and ideas of an international network. Eclipsed by the increasing responsibilities of his new position, the Summer Sessions concluded in 1972. Yet, in various ways, Boyarsky formalized the nimbleness and pluralism of its institutional model at the AA through a series of curricular and extra-curricular innovations.

One of Boyarsky's most revolutionary and enduring pedagogical contributions at the AA was his reconceptualization of the architecture studio curriculum. In an abrupt departure from the horizontal, technocratic curriculum that had shaped the school's postwar teaching, in 1973 Boyarsky relaunched the undergraduate studio program, known as the "unit system," as a competitive framework of vertical studios.[1] In place of shared briefs and teaching objectives, this revised "unit system" provided tutors with an autonomous pedagogical and intellectual territory in which to develop intensely focused, individualized yearlong investigations. Structured to support a multiplicity of arguments and design methods hosted by the different studios, or "units," the new system thus signaled a broader shift in the education of architects: from a system of professional training that codified the architect's responsibility to design and build for the needs of society, to an educational model premised on the continuous production of theoretical and critical inquiry.

As they progressed through the Intermediate School (second and third years of study) and the Diploma School (fourth and fifth years of study), AA students could now select from a broad range of units, each with different teaching methodologies and polemics. For example, in 1973 Intermediate Unit 1 approached architecture through community action. Organized by the renegade planner Brian Anson, the unit spearheaded a campaign to educate Scottish communities on the effects of North Sea offshore oil drilling, which had recently spurred numerous speculative planning proposals.[2] That same year the "Rational Technology Unit" (Intermediate Unit 4), formed by tutors Gerry Foley and George Kasabov, responded to the energy crisis through seminars and research on resource consumption, population growth, and the conservation of materials and energy in an effort to understand how to design "with nature" rather than "against it."[3] Meanwhile, Intermediate Unit 6 harnessed technologies and techniques from television production. The unit tutors, Archigram member David Greene and filmmaker Mike Myers, argued that "the imaginative communications skills needed to make a good film or a good television programme are the same in principle as those needed to make good buildings."[4]

Advanced students encountered an equally diverse menu of Diploma School units, each a unique microcosm of architectural study. A comparison of three of the Diploma units that helped launch the unit system in the 1970s, when the contemporary city preoccupied several young tutors at the AA, illustrates how this shared interest was taught through distinctive theoretical filters. In Diploma Unit 2, for example, Bernard Tschumi led an exploration of "urban politics." The unit experimented with different forms of representation—including photography, literature, performance, and film—in its analyses of the city as "subjective spaces and social playgrounds" and in which the possibility of revolution was explicitly linked to "everyday life."[5] In contrast, Diploma Unit 1, taught by the Czech émigré Dalibor Vesely, positioned the city as an "institution" that was "deeply rooted in the nature of our civilization." Student projects examined "the problem of urban dwelling and elementary patterns of urban fabric, such as street patterns, urban blocks, [and] clusters" from historical and contemporary perspectives. To nourish design investigations, Vesely organized a lecture series that presented an alternative history of urbanism through the work of expressionist and surrealist artists and architects.[6] The study of early twentieth-century avantgardes also informed Diploma Unit 9, taught by Elia Zenghelis, which explored the ideological potential of urban density. In its own reevaluation of the history and conditions of the modern metropolis, the unit mined the history of Russian constructivism, and in particular speculative projects by Malevich.[7]

Borrowing the language of contemporary political and economic discourse, Boyarsky began to identify and promote the AA unit system as a competitive "marketplace" that could accommodate divergent architectural positions and nurture emerging theoretical arguments and design methods. After a decade in operation, the unit system continued to support experimental thinking and design, though it also supported traditions. Some of the "first generation" of tutors who taught in the unit system in the 1970s—including Tschumi, Vesely, and Zenghelis—left behind a legacy of pedagogy and architectural investigations that were reinterpreted and advanced in the 1980s by a "second generation" of tutors who had studied under them—such as Nigel Coates, Mohsen Mostafavi, and Zaha Hadid, respectively.

By the early 1980s the AA had also institutionalized an abundance of extracurricular activities that Boyarsky initiated in the early years of his chairmanship in concert with the heightened productivity of the new unit system. In the mid-1970s the school began to produce an intense program of events, exhibitions, and publications. A television studio was installed at the AA, where interviews with invited guests such as John Habraken and Peter Eisenman were recorded and later screened on monitors placed throughout the school. The short-lived broadsheet *Ghost Dance Times* (1974–1975), edited by Martin Pawley, then an AA tutor, provided scurrilous and often scathing accounts of juries and the school's densely packed lecture series. Established in 1975, the annual publication *AA Projects Review* systematically documented student work, while a curatorial counterpart of the same name exuberantly displayed that work throughout the AA's premises at the end of each academic year. Building renovations at the AA in 1978 included the

introduction of a gallery, making it possible to stage exhibitions there and in other spaces throughout the school simultaneously. These exhibitions focused on both historical and contemporary topics, as well as the design investigations pursued by units, and frequently resulted in the production of books. Nowhere was the intertwined relationship between exhibitions and publications more deftly handled than in the lavish *Folios* series, introduced in 1983. Packaging essays and reproductions of drawings in twelve-by-twelve-inch boxes, the *Folios* were not just exhibition catalogues; they were portable exhibitions in and of themselves. In the spirit of critical exchange, the journal *AA Files*, founded in 1981 and steered by inaugural editor Mary Wall, published reviews of AA exhibitions as well as its lectures, publications, and even unit work.

In these ways the school operated as the nexus of a remarkable constellation of protagonists during the 1970s and 1980s. But importantly, in tandem with the studio pedagogy of the revised unit system, which emphasized the interrogation of disciplinary norms over the transference of skills, the expanded program of the AA established a hybrid institutional model with a broader goal for architectural education. The new task of the school of architecture, Boyarsky stated, was to "be a critic of society," rather than merely its

provider or form giver.[8] To be sure, Boyarsky was not alone in his call for architectural education to embrace a more critical stance. The capacity of the studio, atelier, and other pedagogical spaces to adopt a manifesto had already become apparent, for example, in Denise Scott Brown, Robert Venturi, and Steven Izenour's 1969 studio at Yale, which culminated in the publication of *Learning from Las Vegas* (1972), or even the radical formation of Unité Pédagogique no. 6 (UP6) in France. For Boyarsky, however, architectural education as a polemical mechanism presented itself at an institutional scale and in the shape of the AA. If a school of architecture was to function as a critical thermometer of contemporary architectural production, then it should be fueled by "the energies and interests of a lot of people, so that the school community is bubbling with dozens of sometimes contradictory interests and activities." The "so-called curriculum," Boyarsky argued, must therefore be "conditioned daily, weekly, and annually."[9]

Boyarsky's redesign of the AA was not simply one amongst many post-68 efforts to initiate educational reform through a new institutional model. Instead, one could argue that it became the model for late-twentieth-century architectural education—emulated widely and exporting tutors across the world to lead other major schools of architecture,

while at the same time having cultivated a generation of architects. In the long view, it belongs within
a lineage of institutions such as the Bauhaus and the
École des Beaux-Arts. If the AA's model of architectural education had crystallized through critiques
of the standardization and professionalization of
pedagogy, it had also reclaimed a role for the school
of architecture as the crux of architectural culture
and the site of disciplinary reinvention.

1. On the postwar AA unit system and
Boyarsky's transformation of it, see Irene
Sunwoo, "From the 'Well-laid Table' to
the 'Marketplace': The AA Unit System,"
Journal of Architectural Education 65,
no. 2 (2012): 24–41.
2. "Unit 1," Intermediate School,
AA Prospectus (1973–1974), 2.
3. "Unit 4, Rational Technology Unit,"
Intermediate School, *AA Prospectus*
(1973–1974), 6.
4. "Unit 6," Intermediate School,
AA Prospectus (1973–1974), 9.
5. Bernard Tschumi, "A Chronicle
of Urban Politics" in *Chronicle of
Urban Politics* (London: Architectural
Association, 1974), unpaginated.
6. "Unit 1, City of Continuity, towards
Urban Resurrection," Diploma School,
AA Prospectus (1973–1974), 2–3.
7. "Unit 9," Diploma School, *AA
Prospectus* (1973–1974), 18–20.
8. Alvin Boyarsky, "Participants Forum,"
International Institute of Design Summer
Session, London, audio recording, 31 July
1972, Alvin Boyarsky Archive.
9. Ibid.

SUMMER SCHOOL AS A "WELL-LAID TABLE"

Irene Sunwoo

Protagonist Alvin Boyarsky (1928–1990)
Institution International Institute of Design (IID)
Summer Sessions
Location London, UK
Dates 1970–1972

In the midst of widespread social unrest during the late 1960s, schools of architecture in Berlin, New York, Paris, Rome, and other cities became the stages for student occupations and protests that challenged the legitimacy of high modernist ideals and architecture's complicity in political and economic power structures. Sizing up the ongoing institutional shifts and debates during this time, Alvin Boyarsky—then a young professor at the University of Illinois at Chicago (UIC), with strong ties to London—identified a broader crisis in architectural education looming on the cusp of the 1970s. His diagnosis was twofold: on the one hand, the narrow professional concerns of schools of architecture impeded the discipline's ability to fully engage with the ever-changing, heterogeneous conditions of contemporary life. On the other hand, the insularity of schools—isolation that was both geographic and intellectual—reinforced parochialism, stalling advancements in the field at large. Rather than craft a new repertoire of design exercises or resituate architecture's disciplinary coordinates within the sphere of the university, Boyarsky sought to reinvent the institutional typology of the school of architecture as an instrument that could continuously disrupt and recalibrate architectural practice and thinking at an international scale. Or, as he explained, invoking the cybernetic terminology *du jour* to describe the ambition of his own educational experiment, the International Institute of Design (IID), was to "put noise into the system."[1]

The IID's main preoccupation was the organization of three Summer Sessions, which took place in London at the Bartlett School of Architecture (1970), the Architectural Association (1971), and the Institute of Contemporary Arts (1972). For each six-week event, architects, educators, historians, planners, and students from over forty countries convened to participate in a dense program of workshops, lectures, and seminars led by a remarkable ensemble of provocateurs. With Boyarsky at the helm, contributors included Archigram, Archizoom, Superstudio, Coop Himmelb(l)au, Reyner Banham, Aldo van Eyck, Yona Friedman, Antoine Grumbach, John Habraken, Hans Hollein, Arata Isozaki, Charles Jencks, Anatole Kopp, Stanislaus von Moos, Gordon Pask, Martin Pawley, Cedric Price, Colin Rowe, and Bernard Tschumi, among many others. The resulting pluralism of the Summer Sessions—billed as a "well-laid table" of ideas from around the world—challenged the localized, professionalized curricula that had come to dominate schools of architecture in the postwar decades. By refusing a predetermined curriculum, the Summer Sessions encouraged attendees to navigate the program according to their own interests and objectives. In addition, by promoting a multitude of arguments and experiments in place of an overarching agenda, the IID offered a platform in which divergent architectural positions could coexist and theoretical enquiry could flourish. The breadth of intellectual concerns, design methods, and regional perspectives supported by the Summer Sessions was staggering: from the redevelopment of London to resettlement initiatives in Ghana, from new histories of Russian constructivism to the polemics of the Italian Radicals, from semiological readings of the city to proposals for "garbage housing."[2]

from schools in Canada, Cuba, Denmark, Hungary, Italy, Japan, Nigeria, South Africa, and Yugoslavia to discuss newly implemented pedagogical methods and contemporary institutional conflicts.[3]

Accordingly, the graphic identity of Boyarsky's independent school consistently alluded to the idea of mobility. Images of buses, subway lines, boats, and jetliners were screen printed onto letterheads, posters, and participant goodie bags. Specially designed postcards were produced and mailed out in packets alongside those from Boyarsky's own collection, touting the Summer Sessions as a new and exotic institutional destination. But if Boyarsky embraced international travel as a means to liberate architectural pedagogy from the hermetic agendas of isolated schools, he pushed his colleagues' proposals further by actually convening a network of individuals in London. For one of the key outcomes of the IID's ether of communication was the initiation of extended contact on the ground, between architects, educators, and students from around the world. Emphatically cross-cultural in its scope, predicated on the continuous circulation of information and individuals around the world, and invested in the state of architectural education across institutions and at an international scale, the IID was a global school of architecture—and indeed, the first of its kind. If the IID was a testing ground for Boyarsky's experimental model of teaching and learning, he would hone and institutionalize that model at the Architectural Association in London, where he became chairman in 1971. Though his duties there soon eclipsed the IID, which held its final Summer Session in 1972, the ethos and strategies of his short-lived summer school nevertheless laid the foundations for his enduring and groundbreaking institutional reinvention of the AA.

Certainly, Boyarsky's call for a model of architectural education unfettered by local conditions and issues was not an entirely unique proposition. Other programs with an international purview were introduced, for example, by Harold Cohen at the University of Southern Illinois, by Giancarlo De Carlo at the International Laboratory of Architecture and Urban Design (ILA&UD) in Rome, and at the AA's Department of Tropical Architecture—although in those instances the scale of enquiry was tailored to specific fields of research, whether world resources, urban case studies, or climatic issues. Cedric Price was a crucial sounding board for Boyarsky in the realization of the IID, but his architectural proposals for alternative, mobile institutions—such as Potteries Thinkbelt and the Polyark bus, a mobile architecture school that relied on video technology—were also an important point of reference. What set the IID apart from emerging institutional models was its concerted effort to aggregate disparate disciplinary interests and approaches as well as its insistence on an internationally diverse group of contributors and students. The IID Summer Sessions also delved into anthropology, planning, politics, history, media, housing, energy studies, building technologies, and even architectural education. Forums were held for students and teachers

∧ Cover of *AD*, April 1971. Caricatures of IID participants (clockwise from back row, left): Brian Richards, Reyner Banham, Peter Cook, Warren Chalk, Sam Stevens, N. John Habraken, Alvin Boyarsky, Robert Maxwell, Cedric Price.

starring Alvin Boya

Hans Hollein   Nicholas

co starring   Brian Richards   Colin Rowe   g

Fred Scott   Martin Pawley   Archigram

Special character portrayal   Cedric Price   Reyner

Settings by Archigram   Fred Scott trained by AA stables

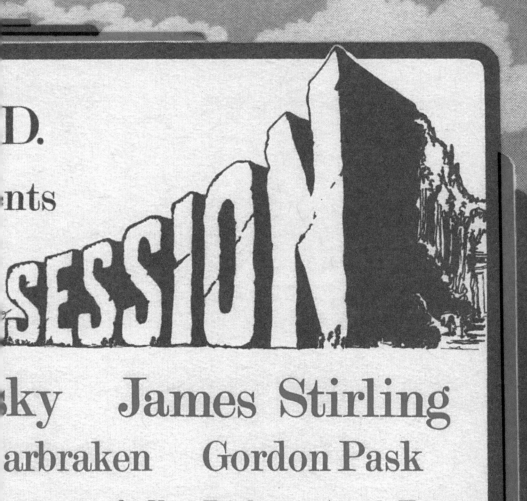

D.

nts

SESSION

ky   James Stirling

arbraken   Gordon Pask

appearances by Yona Friedman   Anatole Kopp

olas Morgamthaler   Robin 'Agripper' Middleton

ham   At the Organ   plus a cast of thousands

Written Produced Directed   A Boyarsky

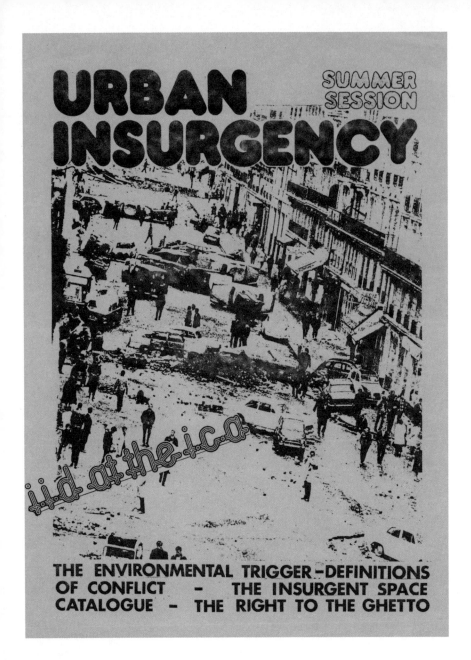

The poster contains the following text:

URBAN INSURGENCY

SUMMER SESSION

iid at the i.c.a

THE ENVIRONMENTAL TRIGGER – DEFINITIONS
OF CONFLICT – THE INSURGENT SPACE
CATALOGUE – THE RIGHT TO THE GHETTO

∧ Poster for the Urban Insurgency workshop organized by Bernard Tschumi and Brian Anson, 1972 IID Summer Session.

< Postcard for the 1971 IID Summer Session. Graphic design by Sampson Fether Morgan.

1. Alvin Boyarsky, "In Progress IV: Summer Session 70," *Architectural Design* (April 1971): 220.
2. For event transcripts, itineraries, and reflections on the 1970 IID Summer Sessions see *Architectural Design* (April 1971): 219–238; on the 1971 IID Summer Sessions, see *Architectural Design* (April 1972), 220–243; on the 1972 IID Summer Sessions, see *Architectural Design* (May 1973), 284–308. On the history of the IID Summer Sessions, see *In Progress: The IID Summer Sessions*, ed. Irene Sunwoo (London: Architectural Association; Chicago: Graham Foundation for Advanced Studies in the Fine Arts, 2016).
3. For transcripts of three forums from the 1972 Summer Sessions, see "Participants Forum: Toronto Curriculum," "Participants Forum: Education in Italy," and "Participants Forum: South Africa," in Sunwoo, *In Progress: The IID Summer Sessions*, 245–258.

HOPE AND CONFLICT

Britt Eversole

Protagonist Giancarlo De Carlo (1919–2005)
Institution The International Laboratory of
Architecture and Urban Design (ILA&UD)
Location Urbino, Italy
Dates 1976–2003

On the cusp of neoliberalism and still nursing
the hangover from the blunted exuberance of
1960s student and working-class movements,
the International Laboratory of Architecture and
Urban Design (ILA&UD) was conceived in 1974 and
hosted its first students two years later.[1] ILA&UD
was the vision of Milanese architect Giancarlo De
Carlo and Carlo Bo, a senator and literary critic
who was rector of the Università di Urbino (home
to ILA&UD) and an occasional critic of urban policy.
Their relationship dated to the Resistance and
the postwar era. Along with Ludovico Quaroni and
others, Bo had collaborated with De Carlo on the
exhibition on urbanism at the 1954 Triennale di
Milano, a controversial installation that advocated
for popular participation in planning in opposition
to elitist aesthetic, bureaucratic, and technocratic
approaches. Architect Connie Occhialini, who was

also instrumental in ILA&UD's inception, oversaw
the laboratory's daily activities over its nearly three
decades of existence. De Carlo and ILA&UD's faculty
viewed their approach as a pedagogy of resistance:
architectural education in a pluralistic, postideolog-
ical world required a third way beyond autonomous,
negative utopias or postmodern complicity with the
market's alienating effects and hunger for nostalgic,
eclectic pabulum. ILA&UD's agonistic approach to
learning—its practical idealism—wagered on experimenting with collaborative and conflictual design
methods developed through international debate
and collective research.

ILA&UD's precedent was the CIAM summer
school, which from 1952 to 1956 was directed by
Franco Albini, Ignazio Gardella, Ernesto Rogers,
and Giuseppe Samonà and was based at the Istituto
Universitario di Architettura di Venezia (IUAV). De
Carlo organized the final session in the wake of the
intergenerational crises that erupted at the 1956
Dubrovnik conference. While the program fulfilled
CIAM's agenda of using education to spread its
message, its impact was most felt in Italy, where
the emphasis on research, regional planning, and
student-faculty collaboration changed the IUAV
curriculum.[2] De Carlo recalled that the international
students "worked day and night…[and] opened a
window, letting fresh air…into old architectural
schools that were provincial, suspicious, jealous, and
afraid to look into their own hearts."[3]

ILA&UD shared a similar aspiration for creative
international collaboration, taking up the study of
global problems at a local scale, and learning from
the existing environment and from users destined
to occupy an architectural or urban design—a clear
nod to Team 10's critique of heroic modernism.
Rejecting the institutional authority of a school as
well as the one-off nature of a summer course, the
faculty described ILA&UD as a laboratory "where
continuous research is performed, led by architects
and non-architects from different countries who
meet, compare their ideas and their work, explore
theoretical themes, and draw up projects based
on common interests."[4] Faculty and students from
schools around the world came to the isolated,
fog-bound town of Urbino each year. Taking Urbino
as a case study (or in later years Siena, Venice, and
San Marino), the students analyzed local urban and
architectural problems, and then speculated on solutions. During their residency they attended lectures
on architectural history and contemporary topics,
including science, technology, politics, economics,

and ecology. Students returned to their home countries—America, Argentina, Belgium, Brazil, Canada, Chile, Croatia, France, India, Italy, the Netherlands, Norway, Scotland, South Africa, Spain, Sweden, Switzerland—and reconsidered each year's theme by investigating local manifestations of the same issues, which ILA&UD then collected and published.[5]

The diversity of ILA&UD's participants characterized what De Carlo called its "heteronomy." Cultural and political differences among the students presented problems and opportunities for the laboratory, generating irreconcilable battles as well as unexpected design proposals. On the other hand, among the recurring faculty and visiting lecturers—Denys Lasdun, Donlyn Lyndon, John McKean, Christian Norberg-Schulz, Renzo Piano, and Alison and Peter Smithson—there were common interests: place and memory, politics and community engagement, and the language of architectural and urban form as a matter of civic discourse. The research efforts arising from these interests tackled an array of built expressions and lived experiences of architecture: typology, the street, public space, the town as an architectural nucleus, adaptive reuse, the vernacular, and landscape.

It was the pedagogical focus on conflict that set ILA&UD apart from other educational environments. The curricular committee grounded their position as a response to century-old challenges confronting architecture and society at the twentieth century's close: industrialization, consumerism, wealth inequity, radical technological change, the destruction of the environment, and a host of attendant social conflicts, especially demands by minorities and the oppressed for civil rights and social justice. The promises of Enlightenment "progress" had failed to extend modernity's benefits to all citizenry, which exacerbated feelings of "cultural dislocation, alienation, and rootlessness" amidst the "loss of personal liberties through manipulation by bureaucratic and state machineries."[6] The committee further argued that whereas the architects of the modern movement overturned the aesthetic, material, and technical backwardness of nineteenth-century architecture, they never repudiated that century's "social-cultural values." Modernism transformed architecture into a "neutral discipline" that aimed at providing total solutions for a universal society but ultimately only produced a "model of harmony" that served the privileged, "preserved social and

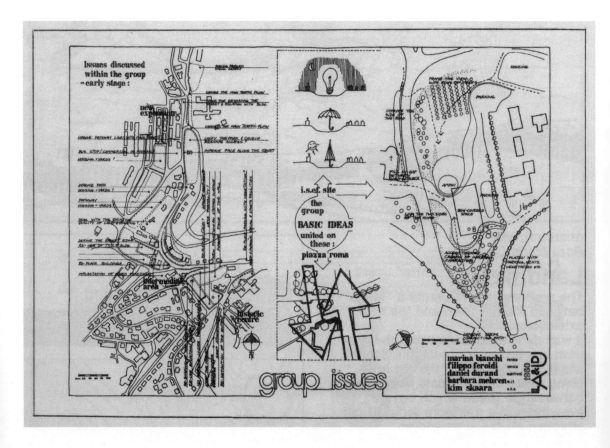

economic inequality," and reinforced human behaviors that "inhibit self-realization and fundamental social change." Modernism's "unified language [was] insensitive to cultural inheritance and regional differences, [and] replaced popular expression."[7] The reconsideration of modernism had been underway for three decades and was fundamental to Team 10 discourse and De Carlo's critical writings; however, ILA&UD's faculty found few answers in late-twentieth-century architecture and education, which tended toward formalism, rationalism, and technocracy, often on behalf of those in power. In a pluralist society, and at a moment when the dominant pedagogical methods reinforced the narcissistic production of "objects" that satiate architects' egos and encourage the formulation of hermetic, career-making projects, ILA&UD sought a humbler, bottom-up, antiheroic approach.[8]

The pedagogy during ILA&UD's first decade revolved around methods and effects of "participation," which reflected De Carlo's intellectual stewardship.[9] However, rather than a method that was embraced for its sociopolitical *bona fides*, they considered participation to be in crisis. De Carlo argued that participation as idea and practice had morphed into techniques of power-sharing and co-management that were exploited by entrenched bureaucracies, corporations, and those with political power as "a deterrent to all kinds of conflict." Equally problematic were forms of participation that aimed only at increasing an architect's understanding of a population, which they argued "usually ends in a position of [the architect being] patronizing" toward users by using research as leverage.[10]

ILA&UD reconsidered participation along two methodological lines: "talking" and "reading."[11] The former took the familiar form of debate, especially in the studios: dialogues across nationalities cut a cross-section through design techniques, pedagogical approaches, cultural biases and values, aesthetic preferences, and even political ideologies. Talking and arguing, as a means of learning how to negotiate conflict, were crucial for marginalizing doctrinarism from the outset, and for emphasizing differences over similarities.[12] "Reading" was defined as the "critical interpretation of a physical environment from the peculiarity of physical fabrics and their use." Reading as communicative drawing and analysis had a practical orientation: getting around the language difficulties that students would face when speaking with the Italian public and one another. It also had a political and cognitive outlet: learning

to read "architectural signs"—physical manifestations of architecture as well as how people behave in public space—was another way of developing design abilities as a form of communication skills. Recognizing that "there is no behavior that lacks conflict" required students to reconsider matters of form and language beyond the simple act of addressing users' basic need for shelter. Similarly, reading gave a political orientation to the theme of "reuse"—a recurring concern that asked students to study and intervene in dense urban fabrics and to adapt existing architectures to new purposes. Rather than merely recycling existing structures, reuse introduced a wide field of references including "reconsideration of discarded values, recovery of abandoned technologies, readoption [*sic*] of signs and messages that do not meet institutional codes, etc."[13] Taken together, participation and reuse underlined ILA&UD's pedagogy of resistance to the architect as specialist, problem-solver, and form-giver: "[Architects] deal with problems but not always just to solve them; sometimes architects have to raise problems."[14] Lastly, reading as a design skill was a means of looking to context in order to evolve a "multiplicity of architectural languages." De Carlo defined the term as a "healthy" diversity of architectural expressions that are at once legible, specific, rooted in their time and place, and result from popular decision-making amidst a culture of irreconcilable conflict, rather than the "disease" of anachronistic citations in what they called architecture's new "eclecticism"—their term for what would soon be labeled "postmodernism."[15]

ILA&UD rooted its investigations in historical places whose patrimony and existence were threatened by a globalized world. Its enclave-like setting allowed students and educators to escape their institutions and collectively experiment on a more sensitive yet still international approach to teaching design. Its pedagogical method eschewed any one perspective, project, or ideology, and embraced an ethics of practice rather than a moralism of a singular method or theory.[16] Projects and ideologies breed moralisms: lists of dos and don'ts that insist upon the repeatable integrity of the method as the most important matter but make no promises to anyone other than architects and their discipline, much less to the future. Ethics arise from a constant questioning that is verbal, historical, social, political, technical, and self-critical, all of which take the future effects and consequences of architecture as the most important concern. It was in conflict and in an insistence that architecture is a "process of changing" the present and future that ILA&UD wagered on its pedagogy of resistance, one that insisted on a practice of hope for a different world and profession as a means of refounding architectural education.

1. This essay benefited from access to the ILA&UD archives at the Biblioteca Civica d'arte e architettura Luigi Poletti in Modena, and to De Carlo's papers at the Fondo Giancarlo De Carlo in the Archivio Progetti at the Istituto Universitario di Architettura di Venezia. Special thanks to Jessica Pagani at the Biblioteca Poletti for her accommodation and generosity. Architect William Rawn, who attended the first residential course at ILA&UD in 1976, provided valuable insight from a student's perspective. The most comprehensive study of the history of ILA&UD is Mirko Zardini, "From Team X to Team x," Lotus International 95 (1997): 76–97. See also Giovanna Borasi, The Other Architect: Another Way of Building Architecture (Montréal: Canadian Centre for Architecture, 2015).
2. Regarding CIAM's educational agenda see Ernesto Rogers and Jane Drew, "Rapport de la IIIème Commission: Réforme de l'enseignement de l'Architecture et de l'Urbanisme," in CIAM 7, Bergamo 1949 Documents (Nendeln: Kraus Reprint, 1979). See also Britt Eversole, "CIAM Summer School," Radical Pedagogies: Architectural Education in a Time of Disciplinary Instability, https://radical-pedagogies.com/search-cases/v01-ciam-summer-school/.
3. Giancarlo De Carlo, "I miei incontri ravvicinati con Giuseppe Samonà," as quoted in Giancarlo De Carlo: Immagini e frammenti (Milan: Electa, 1995), 40–41.
4. No author listed, Untitled Promotional Literature for ILA&UD (Urbino, 1980s). Fondo International Laboratory of Architecture and Urban Design, Biblioteca Civica d'arte e architettura Luigi Poletti.
5. The large body of discursive and scholarly publications that resulted from ILA&UD's efforts—annual "yearbooks" of student work and faculty lectures, bulletins, books, exhibitions and catalogs,

public conferences and funded research documents—paralleled that of the New York-based Institute for Architecture and Urban Studies (IAUS), even if ILA&UD's antiheroic agenda was diametrical to the IAUS.
6. Marcel Smets, Tijl Eickerman, Daniele Pini, Julian Beinart, Peter Butenschøn, Giancarlo De Carlo, and Connie Occhialini, "The Future of ILA&UD: First Draft of the Platform," International Laboratory of Architecture and Urban Design 1st Residential Course, Urbino 1976 (Urbino: ILAUD, 1977), 58–60.
7. Ibid. See also: No author, "Extracts from the Discussion at the International Permanent Staff Meeting" (Zurich, January 19–21, 1977), 1, Fondo International Laboratory of Architecture and Urban Design, Biblioteca Civica d'arte e architettura Luigi Poletti. ILA&UD's critique of modernism reflected De Carlo's broadside delivered at the 1959 CIAM Otterlo conference. See Giancarlo De Carlo, "Talk on the Situation of Contemporary Architecture," in New Frontiers in Architecture: CIAM '59 in Otterlo, ed. Oscar Newman (New York: Universe Books, 1961), 80–88.
8. Giancarlo De Carlo, "Introduction," International Laboratory of Architecture and Urban Design 2nd Residential Course, Urbino 1977 (Urbino: ILAUD, 1978), 5–8.
9. De Carlo's writings on politics, participation, and education are too numerous to list here. Major examples include the following: Giancarlo De Carlo, La piramide rovesciata (Bari: De Donato Editore, 1968); Giancarlo De Carlo, "How/Why to Build School Buildings," Harvard Educational Review: Architecture and Education 4 (1969): 12–34, republished as Giancarlo De Carlo, "Ordine–Istituzione, Educazione–Disordine," Casabella, nos. 368–369 (August/September 1972): 65–71, 112–114; Giancarlo De Carlo, An

Architecture of Participation (South Melbourne: Royal Australian Institute of Architects, 1972).
10. Giancarlo De Carlo, "Further Notes on Participation with Reference to a Sector of Architecture Where it Would Seem Most Obvious," ILA&UD Bulletin 1 (1977): 1–2. Fondo International Laboratory of Architecture and Urban Design, Biblioteca Civica d'arte e architettura Luigi Poletti.
11. De Carlo, "Introduction," International Laboratory of Architecture and Urban Design 2nd Residential Course, Urbino 1977, 5, 7. See also multiple authors, International Laboratory of Architecture and Urban Design Annual Report Urbino 1978, Participation and Reuse (Urbino: ILAUD, 1979).
12. "Extracts from the Discussion at the International Permanent Staff Meeting," 2.
13. No author, "Minutes of the Meeting of the International Permanent Staff held in Zurich, January 19–21, 1977," 5.
14. Ibid.
15. Although the term "postmodernism" does not appear in ILA&UD publications and internal documents until after the 1980 Biennale di Venezia, the laboratory's educators launched a sustained critique of architectural eclecticism in the late 1970s. See Giancarlo De Carlo, "Multiplicity of Language vs. Eclecticism," International Laboratory of Architecture and Urban Design 1982 Year Book, Multiplicity of Language vs. Eclecticism (Urbino: ILAUD, 1983), 120–126. Eclecticism was also the theme of ILA&UD Bulletins 2, 3, and 4 in 1982.
16. See the unpublished manuscript, Giancarlo De Carlo, "About the method, first of all it should be said that ILAUD never intended to found or follow a theory" (1989), Fondo International Laboratory of Architecture and Urban Design, Biblioteca Civica d'arte e architettura Luigi Poletti.

ENGINEERING ARCHITECTURE EDUCATION

Shaimaa Ashour, Zeinab Shafik

Protagonist Yousef Shafik (1921–1990)
Institution Department of Architecture, Faculty of Engineering, Cairo University
Location Cairo, Egypt
Dates 1965–1981

In the first half of the twentieth century architecture education in Egypt was shaped by a proliferation of government missions and scholarships to Western countries—mainly to Europe (particularly England, France, Germany) but also, to a lesser degree, to the US. Yousef Shafik was one of those who went to America, to pursue his graduate studies at Illinois Institute of Technology in 1948. After completing his studies, he worked in Mies van der Rohe's Chicago office from 1952 till 1954 before returning to teach at Cairo University. There, he would subvert the established architectural discourse, based on a foundation of the history and theories of Western classical architecture, and introduce the then-revolutionary ideas of modernist theory and practice. Other professors brought influences from Western European universities and imported international debates: the latest developments in Switzerland and England were absorbed alongside Beaux-Arts pedagogies from Paris. All of them ultimately transformed the Architecture Department in Cairo University into a "melting pot," a crucible for change.[1] What is striking is that established professors did not resist the challenge to the existing order. Ready for change, some even aimed to learn from the younger generation.[2] In the years that followed, the department cultivated "the creative ideas, the debates, and the challenges of modern international architectural trends that the returnees from the missions brought home."[3]

The dean of the faculty of engineering supported the new orientation of the architecture department as it aligned with the general impetus of the country under the leadership of Gamal Abdel Naser. The period was broadly characterized by the demand for social justice, the unfolding of nationalism (with the denial of individualism), and a call for industrialization and technological development. This political program overlapped with that of modern architecture, then dominant in some major schools of architecture in the West but completely new to Egypt. The displacement of local cultures by standardized, supposedly international types seemingly matched the prevailing political will.

Shafik's pedagogy addressed these changes with an approach that situated the discipline of architecture as a form of engineering to be addressed technically, technologically, and rationally. In this context, he maintained architecture as a department within the faculty of engineering and pushed to have architecture students work together with the engineering disciplines in the preparatory year. In addition, he introduced two main streams into architectural studies: Science and Technology, with new courses emphasizing construction and technology, new building materials, scientific thinking, and programming.[4]

Where Cairo University led, others followed.[5] The new paradigms introduced there would be introduced at Ein Shams University, the second largest architectural program in Cairo, by Shafik's students and colleagues. A unified jury was formed to review graduation projects from architectural programs in different Egyptian universities, further consolidating the influence of Shafik, who defined the criteria used to evaluate them.

All throughout his teaching career, Shafik remained a practicing architect and pursued links between the two spheres, introducing practical standards for quality control for design projects within the academy.[6] Rather than Beaux-Arts renderings, he privileged simple black and white line drawings, which were more consistent with the principles of his teaching—with its emphasis on logical processes, clarity in the definition and analysis of design problems, and a search for simplicity and efficiency.[7] Studios were supported by a series of lectures in design philosophy which provided a forum for discussion and triggered design ideas. Shafik's emphasis on scientific thinking led him to advocate for the use of computer-aided design as early as the mid-1970s.[8]

Pedagogical changes were introduced at different levels and in three different phases. In the early years of his tenure as department chair in 1966, Shafik used to send teaching assistants and young graduates to complete their education abroad through the government missions. Many of them never returned to Egypt, particularly after the 1967 war, when the country started to lose talented young students and teachers due to political and economic pressures. Others returned with new ideas but initially found no place to implement them.[9] Shafik found a solution, initiating new courses—in subjects such as scientific methods, operations research, humanities and project management—that would be taught by this younger generation. Housing became an independent subject for the first time during those years, and urban design emerged as an area of focus—both were also taught by the young faculty.[10]

Egypt's defeat of Israeli forces in October 1973 opened the door to a new period both in the country (with Anwar Sadat's postnationalist policies) and in the academy. At the architecture department at Cairo University, the basis for scientific research was reinforced through a partnership with MIT.[11] A gift from the US to Egypt in the wake the Camp David agreements,[12] the joint project initially focused on materials research, with Shafik heading three working groups: building industrialization and prefabrication; economic studies; and incremental development. The project ran for four years from 1976 till 1980, producing fieldwork in Egypt, annual progress reports, and a number of published papers. With the opening of these channels of cooperation, many teaching assistants and graduate students participated in the project, with some of them being awarded grants to complete their PhD studies in the US.[13]

Following this new impetus, graduate courses were developed at both the master of science and PhD levels, and professional diplomas were established. Shafik's goal was to develop research that responded directly to the demands of the Egyptian market and addressed the needs of local employers through a professional degree—ultimately pursuing, in the academic institution, the closest alignment of teaching and practice. By carefully recalibrating existing international channels, Shafik acted as the catalyst for a far-reaching transformation of pedagogy, ideology, and professional networks in Egypt.

1. El Sharkawy in an interview with the authors, 2019.
2. Ibid.
3. Interview with Abdel Kader, 2019.
4. Sawsan Helmy, "My Mentor Yousef Shafik," Cairobserver: The University, 2015, https://cairobserver.com/print#.W8s2mqeB1o4)
5. Interview with El Sharkawy, 2019.
6. Ibid.
7. Interview with Serag Eldin, 2019.
8. Helmy, "My Mentor Yousef Shafik."
9. Interview with Abdel Kader, 2019.
10. Ibid.
11. See The Joint Research Team on the Housing and Construction Industry, Cairo University and MIT, "The Housing and Construction Industry in Egypt Interim Report Working Papers 1977"; "The Housing and Construction Industry in Egypt; Summary of Working Papers 1978"; "The Housing and Construction Industry in Egypt. Interim Report Working Papers 1978," sponsored by United States Agency for International Development, Massachusetts Institute of Technology, Cambridge MA. Also: "Extracts from Working Papers. The Housing and Construction Industry in Egypt for the Seminar on Development of New Approaches to Housing Policy and Production in Egypt," co-sponsored by Cairo University and Massachusetts Institute of Technology; Technology Planning Program; Ministry of Housing and Reconstruction, Cairo, Egypt (January 21–24, 1978).
12. Ibid.
13. Interview with El Sharkawy, 2019.

DESIGNS ON TRADITION: DECOLONIZING CONTEMPORARY AFRICAN ARCHITECTURE

Ikem Stanley Okoye

Protagonists David Aradeon (1933–) and a small group of students including Olusoji Dosekun (1951–) and Chijiokeh Iloputaifeh (1954–)
Institution Faculty of Environmental Design, Department of Architecture and Urban Planning, University of Lagos
Location Akoka, Lagos, Nigeria
Dates 1978–1998

As the Department of Architecture at the University of Lagos (UNILAG) expanded during the 1970s, the notion of architecture as a kind of applied science—the equivalent to medicine, say—was tested to near breaking point.[1] A move to include in the curriculum newly produced *academic* knowledge about both the building technologies and the spatial and formal cultures that were considered specifically African provoked a serious debate about the kind of architectural and urban design knowledge that should be transmitted to students. A large part in instigating this debate was played by the young architect David Aradeon, who had joined the architecture faculty of UNILAG's School of Environmental Design a few years after returning to Lagos from New York, where he had trained at Columbia University and subsequently practiced. From the start Aradeon took a stand against the particularly egregious views held by influential British architects such as Maxwell Fry and Jane Drew, who justified their own practices in the decades around Nigeria's independence by insisting that local traditions of art and architecture had *nothing* worthy of a modern architect's attention; nothing worthy of emulation.[2] Aradeon took aim at what they "pontifically" called "tropical architecture"—but which was, in effect, the simple application of the international style to a warmer climate—arguing instead for the cultural significance of local traditions of organizing space and housing. Inspired by his post-1968 travels in West Africa, he was also able to find precedents in the built and polemical work of two Lagos-based professional colleagues—the UK-born, naturalized Nigerian Alan Vaughan-Richards and Demas Nwoko, who was an artist and writer (and member of the Mbari club of Ibadan) as well as an architect. Fusing new techniques with the historical spatial forms of African art and sculpture, the two men explored what African traditions could offer modern architecture in Nigeria.

Lagos at that time was already hyper-modern. With the civil war at an end, the city was buoyed first by the flush of enthusiasm that came with the reunion of long-separated friends, and then by the even greater optimism and related excesses of the emerging oil-boom economy. Once again, Nigerians could imagine their future as the leaders of the continent, a role that implied also being in the vanguard in matters of architecture and urbanism too. Talk of a new capital city was brewing, while parts of old Lagos were increasingly subjected to neglect or to the wrecking ball.

This was the scenario when Aradeon began teaching at the University of Lagos. Given UNILAG's status as federal university, his students, both young men and women, came from all over Nigeria, and not only from towns but even rural villages. A few also came from elite European (mainly British) high schools, at a time when Nigerian youngsters often returned home with their parents since emigration abroad, especially to the former colonial metropole, was not yet conceivable. They all had something in common: an imagined future as equally skilled competitors in a contemporary globalized architecture based very much on American and European models. In the minds of these young students Mies van der Rohe, Le Corbusier, Buckminster Fuller—and, later, the likes of Norman Foster or SOM—occupied a status not far removed from that of rock stars. A few architectural magazines such as *The Architectural Review* and *Architectural Record*, circulated and discussed in unsupervised settings, played a role in these familiarizations. In fact, in the architecture schools competing with UNILAG, students were as likely to encounter visiting teachers such as Buckminster Fuller, Jane Drew, or Julian Beinart as they were to engage with traditional architecture (at Zaria or Ife, say) or the interest in tropical modernism among local architects (Enugu).

But David Aradeon was sensitized to a different set of ideas. In his graduate studies in New York he had encountered both the preservationist James Fitch and the Columbia GSAPP Historic Preservation Program, as well as Bernard Rudofsky, shortly before his iconic 1964 MoMA exhibition on *Architecture without Architects*. Following his New York years, Aradeon traveled through sub-Saharan Africa between 1968 and 1972 on a research grant from the Ford Foundation, developing his interest in a range of phenomena with origins in local African worlds. These included traditional adobe architecture, with its complex spatial meanings, and informal urban settlements. Back in Lagos, these interests would pit him against the current that constructed European modernism and its climatological rhetoric as exemplary, if not liberating, not least because of the rather ironic identification of European modernism with the nationalism that ended colonialism.

What Aradeon developed an argument for—if not exactly an alternative kind of nationalist architecture—was certainly an approach that paid attention to local architectural traditions. Radical in this particular context, it emphasized a contemporary architecture sensitive to the particularities of its cultural, economic, and ecological situation. In the late 1970s, by then a senior lecturer some five years into his second stint on the faculty, Aradeon encouraged his students to learn from the sophistication and complexity of the architectures of their heritage: earthen architecture, the brick buildings of the "Brazilian" quarter, and the spatially sophisticated logics of informal urban settlements. And he fought to have these subjects included in the curriculum, not just within the framework of architectural and urban history but as new modes of architectural knowledge-making central to any legitimate African studio practice.

Aradeon had his students discover, explore, and formalize the concepts inherent in traditional settlements and buildings. A set of ideas that in Europe might have been regarded as vernacularist regionalism were justified, perhaps ironically, by an intellectual appeal to a notion of functionalism embedded in the logics of historical African spatial practice. Experimental assignments encouraged students to explore physical and spatial forms, structural knowledge, and the histories and aesthetics of traditional architecture. Especially in studio, this involved the use of models to play with traditional forms—a modernist analytical approach that would not have been out of place in the canonical modernist workshops of Russian architect Iakov Chernikov, say, or of Walter Gropius. Unusually for the time, Aradeon asked students to apply the spatial relationships, forms, shapes, and materials found in traditional environments to the design of contemporary spaces that responded to the functional demands of the present. Typically, these projects were explored through drawings that were intentionally rough and rapidly produced (more sketches than the pristine, perfected, technical drawings conventionally preferred at architecture schools). Students were also expected to develop their projects through scaled models of what were typically complex-form buildings. Construction materials had to be locally sourced, which inevitably meant clay or adobe, modified into bricks. Roofs tended to be timber, with a steep pitch, resisting the modernist aesthetics of the day (though flat roofs were welcomed where they made sense—for example, in the Sahelian universe). Always, however, the projects were inarguably forward-looking.

Students were initially resistant to Aradeon's ideas—something that says less about them than it does about the architectural culture they inhabited. Not least, they were under the sway of notions of the architect as genius, with the self-actualization that implied. Their idea of design was not inclined towards the deliberate, unassuming, but self-assured arguments about appropriateness, history, and tradition preferred by Aradeon. In many ways, their response also anticipated the negotiations among the faculty over the department's future direction, which continued for several years.

Aradeon's approach was given a boost when he was invited (most likely in 1976, the year he returned to Lagos after his travels in West Africa) to curate an architectural exhibition as part of FESTAC, the Second International Festival of Black and African Arts and Culture. Held mainly in Lagos, this vast exposition drew on a lineage that could be traced back to the *négritude* philosophy of the African diaspora in the 1920s and 1930s, which was developed initially by francophone intellectuals such as Aimé Césaire, Leopold Senghor, and Leon Damas, and which also fed into the Harlem Renaissance. Aradeon's exhibition was themed around seven typologies, organized by medium (building material), spatiality, and structure, and depicted in more than 200 large-format photographs and drawings as well as scale models built by 13 of his students. The examples were drawn from almost every single African country and included everything from the archaeological "pit circles" of Zimbabwe to the traditional settlements of the Algerian Mzab.[3] The exhibition was remarkable in anticipating something like a Black architecture. As well as educating a Lagosian—and wider global diaspora audience—about Africa's architectural heritage and the possibilities it held for the future, it attempted to embed the study of historical African architecture at the heart of the curriculum.

Ironically, after FESTAC, Aradeon and his dean at UNILAG (left-leaning, Cornell-trained American John S. Myers, previously of the University of Minnesota) found that the more the school made courses in historical and regionalist architecture a requirement, the more the students rebelled. For a while, Aradeon's methods prevailed, not least because an explosion of student numbers meant that his studio and lectures became central experiences for those who were too slow off the starting blocks to get places on the more popular courses. By the late 1980s, however, student opposition to Aradeon had taken the form of barely veiled physical threats, as some feared that their readiness for the professional examination was being undermined by a brewing stand-off between Aradeon and the Nigerian Institute of Architects (NIA) over the transferability of foreign registrations by waiver. Some also mistakenly believed that Aradeon's dispute with the professional body was somehow related to his regionalist penchant. Such rebellions were a frequent occurrence at the university, which has a historically well-organized student body marshaled both through the student union and the somewhat notorious, even feared, local equivalents of American college fraternities. "Architecture: The Search for Identity and Continuity"—a lecture Aradeon gave in 1998, when he was close to retirement—reflects on the lessons from this period, and could be seen as his insistent swan song.[4]

In the absence of influential Aradeon protégés— Nigerian forerunners, perhaps, of Francis Keré or Mariam Kamara today—it could be tempting to see his call for a repositioning as a failure. But this is hardly the case. It is more accurate to say that Aradeon's teachings were subverted by oil-boom optimism and by his former students' exposure to the commercial success of architects such as Alex Ekwueme, Lanre Coker, and Olufemi Majekudunmi. The remarkably farsighted nature of Aradeon's approach becomes evident when we realize that many of the major architecture and urban design projects that are driving the contemporary transformation of Lagos are in locations chosen by Aradeon and his students as sites for their thesis projects.

1. This idea was engaged in a preliminary manner as early as in 1971 but reached a kind of crisis in 1978.
2. See David Aradeon, "Space and House Form: Teaching Cultural Significance to Nigerian Students," JAE 35, no. 1 (Autumn 1981): 25–27.
3. David Aradeon, Festac '77: African Architectural Technology Exhibition (Lagos: Nigeria, The International Secretariat, 1977).
4. The lecture was later published: David Aradeon, The Search for Identity and Continuity: An Inaugural Lecture Delivered at the University of Lagos on Wednesday, 11th February, 1998 (Lagos: University of Lagos Press, 1998).

AN INSTITUTION FOR INDEPENDENCE

Eunice Seng

Protagonists Lim Chong Keat (1930–)
Institution Singapore Polytechnic
Location Singapore
Dates 1959–1961

Singapore Polytechnic (SP) officially opened in February 1959, three months before the city-state attained full internal self-governance—and almost eight years after the idea of a technical institute for Singapore had first been mooted.[1] In its first year of operation, some two thousand and eight hundred students were enrolled across fifty-eight courses in five departments: Engineering; Architecture, Town Planning, and Building; Science and Technology; General Education; and Commerce.

Penang-born architect, urban designer, and botanical researcher Lim Chong Keat taught in the polytechnic's architectural program between 1959 and 1961.[2] As one of a small number of foreign-trained Malayan architects, his teaching embodied an emerging consciousness of practice and discourse-building that learned from and responded to Southeast Asian vernacular traditions and climatic conditions in the context of decolonization.

Lim had only returned from the US the year before. After his initial training at the University of Manchester, he had studied at the Massachusetts Institute of Technology (MIT), specializing in architectural acoustics under Robert Newman. Once back in Malaya, Lim applied to teach in the new diploma program in architecture at the Technical College in Kuala Lumpur, set up in 1956 by the German architect-historian Julius Posener.[3] But rather than going to Kuala Lumpur, he would become the first senior lecturer in the Singapore Polytechnic's architecture department, which was headed by David Vickery. Within a curriculum based on polytechnic programs in the UK, Lim was tasked with devising the course of studies for the first year and given the freedom to develop his own design studio and courses in subjects such as visual fundamentals and theory of design. Responding to the nation-building context, Vickery emphasized the importance of building in a "distinctly Malayan" manner, recognizing the integral relationship between climate and architecture.[4]

Lim's own pedagogy of architectural integrity was based on attitudes formed while at MIT, where he had absorbed the intellectual underpinnings of the Bauhaus via Gyorgy Kepes and Walter Gropius, and had been introduced to other influential thinkers such as George Santayana, José Ortega y Gasset, Sigfried Giedion, Sergei Chermayeff, and Bernard Rudofsky. Alongside these influences, his teaching combined

< The first cohort of architecture and town planning students at Singapore Polytechnic, 1959.

> Kampong House prototype by second year student, Tay Kheng Soon, 1960–1961.

the principles of urban planning with tropical environmental design and an awareness of vernacular traditions.[5] The integration of the universal and the regional was intrinsic to Lim's pedagogy and architectural practice. Acknowledging "the prodigious architectonic integrity of Frank Lloyd Wright, espoused in the nature of materials," and the Sullivan precepts of "form following function…and function following form," Lim absorbed all of these elements into his first-year courses through "ex tempore" lectures and studio teaching, imparting architectural ideas from Europe and America while articulating their confrontation with the cultural and climatic contexts of colonized Malaya. In a context where the education of architects was mostly focused on technical training, Lim's "holistic" approach was refreshing.

Just a few months into Lim's teaching, there was an abrupt change in the direction of the polytechnic, signaled by the replacement of the first board of governors in August 1959 and followed by Vickery's resignation a month later. The new board, chaired by the Deputy Prime Minister, immediately worked to realign the polytechnic's teaching with the government's policy of industrialization. Non-technical subjects—such as English literature, history, geography, embroidery work, secretarial skills, and general education—were dropped from the syllabus. The number of departments was reduced to four— Engineering, Building and Construction, Accountancy, Nautical Studies—with courses grouped into three levels—craft, technician, and professional. In late 1959 Penang-born architect Kee Yeap—trained at the University of Sydney and Harvard GSD—replaced Vickery as department head. His first task was to "tighten the curriculum…based on the standards of universities in the Commonwealth, the United States, and other countries, with special emphasis on climatic conditions, cultural background, and local building conditions."[6] Although this vision sounds similar to Vickery's goals, the institution's shift from a comprehensive to a technical bureaucratic mode of education had already been set in motion. Significantly, the original plan of preparing students for examinations set by overseas institutions was abandoned. Instead, the polytechnic began to set its own internal examinations and award its own diplomas. The first professional diploma students graduated in August 1961.

Lim's influence on the polytechnic's pioneering class was profound.[7] Among others, architect Lee Seng Loong has mentioned the importance for his own thinking and practice of Lim's introduction to architecture in Malaysia and his "holistic" teaching approach. Planner-architect Ong Teong Pin has reflected on the continuing relevance of Lim's teaching of the architectural principles of "form and function" and "commodity, firmness, and delight." Each has described the formative impact of a field trip that Lim led to West Malaysia (from Malacca to Penang) at a time when the region was going through tremendous social and political change.

After two years at SP, however, Lim felt there was no integrated teaching team, and he left the polytechnic for the "realities of practice" in 1961. He had set up the Malayan Architects Co-Partnership (MAC), modeled after Gropius's TAC, the year before, along with two other foreign-trained architects, William Lim Siew Wai (AA and Harvard GSD) and Chen Voon Fee (University of Manchester and AA). Keen to participate in the social and cultural affairs of the city-state, he joined the inaugural boards of the Singapore Institute of Architects (SIA) and the Housing Development Board (HDB).

Tay Kheng Soon joined MAC in 1963. One of the first cohort of SP architecture students, he saw in Lim Chong Keat an intellectual architect who "exuded the Bauhaus" and was completely different from the predominant figure of the businessman architect. Tay would return to SP in 1966 to co-teach a studio with William Lim. The studio focused on developing new theories and means of renewing high-density Asian cities that did not involve destroying the historic urban fabric—a deliberate counterpoint to the US-style urban renewal that brought great hardship to the urban poor without land tenure. Both were leaders of the Singapore Planning and Urban Research (SPUR) group, and this studio was generally known as the SPUR studio.[8]

Lim Chong Keat would continue to play a formative role in advancing architectural education and professionalization and shaping Singapore's urban development. Between 1959 and 1971 he held a number of important posts: Chairman of the Commonwealth Association of Architects Board of Architectural Education, President of the Singapore Institute of Architects, founding Chairman of Architects Regional Council Asia (ARCASIA), board member of the HDB and the United Nations Review Panel for State and City Planning of Singapore. In the early 1980s he would direct the South East Asian Cultural Research Program on Folk Habitat at the Institute of Southeast Asian Studies (ISEAS).

At SP itself, the pedagogical emphasis on tropical building and construction continued into the 1960s under Kee Yeap's headship. In 1969, four years after Singapore separated from Malaya as an independent nation, the architectural program was transferred to the faculty of architecture at the University of Singapore (now the National University of Singapore). All that remained of the architecture program at SP was a three-year diploma course that focused on technical training for the building industry.

Secondary school students visit the CCUM computer room as part of the seminar "Computers in Secondary Education," c. 1970.

1. Singapore Polytechnic, *Singapore Polytechnic Official Opening, 24th February 1959* (Singapore: The Polytechnic, 1959).
2. See Lim Chong Keat, "Architectural Education at the Singapore Polytechnic," *Journal of the Malayan Society of Architects* 2, no. 1 (September 1959): 28–33.
3. Julius Posener, "A Letter from Julius Posener: Views on Architectural Education," *Singapore Institute of Architects Journal* 4 (September 1961): 13–16. Posener remained at the Technical College from 1956 to 1961.
4. "Architects urged: 'Build Malayan,'" *Straits Times*, August 6, 1959, 7.
5. Lim Chong Keat in an interview with Eunice Seng, September 29, 2019.
6. "Poly Building Chief Tightens Syllabus," *Singapore Free Press*, December 18, 1959, 7.
7. See Robert Powell, "Unlearning," in *Line, Edge & Shade: The Search for a Design Language in Tropical Asia: Tay Kheng Soon & Akitek Tenggara*, ed. Robert Powell, Albert K. S. Lim, and Tay Kheng Soon (Australia; Singapore: Page One, 1997), 14; and *In Their Own Words: Pioneer Architects on Singapore Polytechnic*, ed. Wong Yunn Chii (National University of Singapore, 2019), 154–155.
8. Students from the studio revealed that they were directly involved in devising and producing the imagery used in SPUR's 1966 manifesto "Our Cities Tomorrow: Sky High Structures May Solve Population Problems," first published in *Asia Magazine*. Chan Swee Him, interview with Eunice Seng and H. Koon Wee, August 4, 2016.

TECHNOLOGY AND
ITS COMPLEXES

EDUCATIONAL BOMBSHELL

Mark Wasiuta

Protagonists Buckminster Fuller (1895–1983),
Herbert Matter (1907–1984), Mercedes Matter
(1913–2001), Ed Schlossberg (1945–)
Institution The 1969 World Game Seminar
Location New York, NY, USA
Date 1969

"To start with, here is an educational bombshell."[1] This is Buckminster Fuller bracing his audience for the claim that the perilous antagonisms of the Cold War proved that the political theories of the late 1960s were obsolete. Fuller argued that nation-states—along with sovereign control of goods, populations, and militarized economies—had to give way to an egalitarian allocation of resources guided by the impartial logic of computers. From the debris of Cold War politics an ecologically oriented global consciousness would arise. The mind-blowing blast of this educational bombshell was the World Game—Fuller's computationally inspired, decades-long, global teaching project.

Initially proposed for the US Pavilion at Expo 67 in Montreal, the World Game was played for the first time in 1969 at the New York Studio School for Drawing, Painting, and Sculpture. Over the next fourteen years, the World Game evolved and expanded through workshops, seminars, strategy papers, and designs for the perpetually unrealized World Game Simulation Center. Emerging from Fuller's and John McHale's World Resources Inventory, the World Design Science Decade enterprise, and Fuller's Geoscope, the World Game was at the heart of Fuller's research at the Southern Illinois University Carbondale and the University of Pennsylvania. Across its different conceptualizations and manifestations, the World Game remained fixated on the goals of overcoming energy scarcity and altering conventional territorial politics by learning how to conceive, map, and advocate new networks of resource distribution.

Mirroring Cold War command and control infrastructures, proposals for World Game centers described colossal subterranean computer systems that could process and visualize environmental information drawn from, among other sources, Russian and American spy satellites. The World Game was meant to neutralize Cold War frictions by reconceiving and redirecting the tools and techniques of a dangerously

∨ The World Game, visualized with a dymaxion map and rolls of acetate.

militarized world. According to Fuller the stakes were dire. Utopia or oblivion. The World Game was not only a mode of learning but a "process of discovery taking place on the frontier of man's future."[2]

Against this epic background of planetary survival and the vast scale of global communications, the 1969 World Game seminar was a surprisingly modest event. Mercedes Matter, dean of the Studio School, had squeezed some dollars from the Rockefeller Brothers Fund to lure Fuller to New York for the six weeks of the seminar.[3] The most sophisticated piece of equipment in the room was the 16mm film camera that Mercedes' husband, Herbert Matter, used to document the happenings. "The eyes of the camera focus ours," announced Ed Schlossberg—a doctoral student in physics at Columbia University, Fuller's teaching partner for the 1969 game, and an early, fervent World Game collaborator.[4]

World Game vision was the underlying motif. Participants watched films on everything from ecology to gravity, cell duplication, computer analysis, systems research, and the moon shot. They tracked global resources, collected data, and envisioned design scenarios—such as how to provide plastic housing for all humanity by 1980. The most active scene of visualization was on the spools of acetate sheeting covering the twenty-foot-wide metal dymaxion maps. Onto the acetate participants plotted population concentrations, energy grids, temperature gradients, mineral deposits, communication networks, and other world resource information. Sheets were lowered and raised to allow the World Gamers to make spatial and visual correlations between different layers of global data. This layered, shuffling, collocational vision became the methodological basis for subsequent World Game events and served as the analog alternate to the interactive, cybernetic, global information display of the much-anticipated World Game Center to come.

Along with the publication of the *World Game Report*, the release of Herbert Matter's film helped publicize the World Game and contributed to its popularity among environmentally aware college students in the 1970s.[5] Through the ten relentless reels of Matter's film and the grayscale probity of the report, the World Game was framed as urgent and serious. But the World Game was perhaps less monochrome and leaned more toward the trippy visual culture of its era—and toward a softer ethos of 1960s participation—than those documents would suggest. Ed Schlossberg's World Game diary recounts the first days of the game: "Those who demonstrate concern and openness…are asked to participate. Energy begins to flow immediately. We will proceed to grow with no definite goal in mind. We would like students to learn to think and act comprehensively."[6] The World Game was not only a demonstration of Fuller's "Design Science," and a "necessary tool of human evolution," it was also a vast playing field of self-realization won through global problem-solving. Fuller's own language veered from the scientific into a kind of hippy nomadism. He explained the objective of the game was to allow global citizens to "travel independently, or in groups, either to and fro locally or continuing intermittently on or around the world, dwelling from time to time here or there, finding everywhere facilities to accommodate their needs in an uncompromising manner."[7]

At the end of the 1969 game Fuller was astonished by the results. "I feel I have seen what has been going on in my head for years, but it is more beautiful than I imagined."[8] The game had blown Fuller's mind open for all to view. For Ed Schlossberg the enduring questions were related to the formation of World Man and World Game subjectivity: "What is the world game? It isn't. We are."[9]

1. R. Buckminster Fuller, "The World Game—How to Make the World Work," manuscript. R. Buckminster Fuller Collection, M1090:S18:28, Stanford University Libraries.
2. Mercedes Matter, "Statement on the World Game Seminar," 1969. R. Buckminster Fuller Collection, M1090:S18:31 Stanford University Libraries.
3. In the end, Fuller attended the seminar only intermittently and for far less than the full six weeks.
4. Edwin Schlossberg, "World Game Diary," 1969. R. Buckminster Fuller Collection, M1090:S18:24, Stanford University Libraries.
5. R. Buckminster Fuller, *World Game Report* (New York: New York Studio School of Painting and Sculpture, in association with GOOD NEWS, 1969).
6. Schlossberg, "World Game Diary."
7. R. Buckminster Fuller, "Testimony of R. Buckminster Fuller Before the Senate Sub-Committee, March 4, 1969," in *Inventory of World Resources Human Trends and Needs. Document 1. The World Game* (Carbondale: World Resources Inventory, Southern Illinois University, 1971).
8. Schlossberg, "World Game Diary."
9. Ibid.

THE ANTI-PEDAGOGICAL LESSON OF CEDRIC PRICE

Mark Wigley

Protagonist Cedric Price (1934–2003)
Institution Architectural Association (AA)
Location London, UK and elsewhere
Date May 1968

Cedric Price was first appointed to the Architectural Association in London as a part-time visiting tutor in 1958, the AA's youngest tutor ever, at the age of twenty-four. Without ever having a permanent appointment—he was visiting tutor for just six years—he would become one of the AA's most influential teachers over the next half-century, haunting the school's design reviews, lecture room, and bar after opening his office a stone's throw away in 1960. Much, if not most, of his design work and research was devoted to the question of education and yet he was ultimately anti-education for the same reason that he was a self-anointed "anti-architect." Traditional norms of teaching and the institutions housing them had to be resisted along with traditional architecture. The two gestures were linked. The withdrawal of architecture enabled "learning," understood as self-directed research rather than education conveying established knowledge. Price's endless search for a post-architecture of mobility, flexibility, and interactivity was all about identifying technological systems that could foster learning. Price rejected the idea of making any level of education compulsory but thought it should be a lifelong choice—a common resource as available as fresh water and air. Indeed, new forms of learning were seen to be the dominant activity of future domestic life—organizing the spaces, systems, rhythms, and interconnection of houses—and the main social industry that would liberate new kinds of building and urbanism. Architecture needed to learn how to depower itself in favor of learning.

Most of Price's design projects rethink education. Computer networks, cybernetic feedback, and television systems were the key. Buildings gave way to open-ended learning nets facilitated by dense "nerve center" structures that fed compact mobile interfaces installed in houses, factories, and civic structures or dispersed throughout the landscape of the city. National and international computer nets promised equal access to the latest and most complete information as the new ground for undoing architecture. Design for Price was self-directed learning about systems that facilitate self-directed learning. Whether the projects were built or not was never the test; anything built needed to have an expiry date anyway, and its unbuilding needed to be designed with the same precision. The architect's greatest responsibility was learning, which might mean the responsibility to abandon or demolish architecture, or to refuse to offer it in the first place.

> ATOM: interior of bus showing seats equipped with electronic display devices, Cedric Price, c. 1968. Negative with translucent red tape affixed to edges.

Price's projects were manifestos of learning. Consider just a few examples: the Fun Palace of 1964 was a "university of the streets" in which almost all the substance of architecture was removed in favor of a scaffolding system in which multiple spaces and atmospheres could be assembled, adjusted, moved, and dismantled in response to the changing desires of the public—enabling citizens normally excluded from higher education to educate themselves; the Potteries Thinkbelt of 1966 reimagined the university as a set of temporary buildings linked by a transportation network into a "learning industry" with "cities caused by learning"; the INFORMATION HIVE of 1966 fostered self-paced learning through dense arrays of televisual consoles, shared screens, and computers; the ATOM of 1967 imagined an "educationally integrated community" with learning technologies installed in houses, factories, buses, and parks coordinated by a "town brain" communication distribution center; the THINK GRID of 1968 proposed a community learning network for Oakland, near Detroit with a grid of one hundred information pods, new classroom experiments, and domestic equipment—with the conclusions published in the report "An Investigation Into New Forms of Learning, 1968."[1]

Price guest-edited a special issue of *Architectural Design* in May 1968 on the question "What is Learning?" as distinct from education.[2] His series of supplements to the magazine in 1970–1972 continued the theme of continuous access to learning, proposing the transfer of electronic learning equipment from university-school to the home, using empty houses as small schools for adults, and so on.

If design was all about rethinking education, design education had to doubly rethink itself. Price rejected the idea of the architectural profession shaping and policing educational standards. Each school should specialize in something different and be networked to the other schools to share the results of their thinking—as was tested when Price instigated the Polyark idea of students moving ideas between schools in a 1970 issue of *Archigram*:

While students are at present one of the most mobile social groups of technologically advanced societies the nature of their own particular production plants—schools, colleges and universities, is static, introspective, parochial, inflexible and not very useful.[3]

Price's own teaching was not about a particular pedagogy or even a class, but an anti-pedagogical multiplicity of research projects with precisely constructed systems charts of each ongoing investigation and documentation, supported by imagined information and interaction servicing systems lightly housed by anti-buildings. If pedagogy is the method and practice of teaching, then Price was even anti-teaching, except for the idea of children teaching their parents. The patronizing and disciplining idea that knowledge comes down from on high was rejected in favor of bottom up, or even sideways:

I personally think that architectural education would be involved in making learning available. There was some talk about education from above. In fact, the education is far better sideways, i.e., you know, students, staff, practitioners, clients or whatever order you want—and is a lifelong process anyhow.[4]

The question was always: what can the teacher learn? A few weeks before his death, Price described his obsessive research for Fun Palace as "reducing my range of ignorance."[5] The ultimate test was always the reduction of stupidity. Price described himself as "an outsider not involved with formal architectural education,"[6] yet his persistent anti-pedagogical presence as a resolute and canny critic of the discipline of architecture continues to demand that architecture schools undo their habits and pretensions in the name of what might be thought of as an anti-architectural right to learning which might even entail a refusal to educate.

1. Cedric Price, "Oakland Community College, an Investigation into New Forms of Learning," Canadian Centre for Architecture, Montreal, Cedric Price fonds, DR2004:0280-3.
2. "What Is Learning?," special issue guest-edited by Cedric Price, *Architectural Design* 38, no. 5 (May 1968).
3. Cedric Price, "The Cedric Price Column," *Archigram*, no. 9 (1970).
4. Cedric Price, "Has the Architectural Profession a Future? Presented at the Conference on 'The Architect's Future,' Architectural Association, 6 March 1975," in *Cedric Price Works 1952-2003*, vol. 2: *Articles and Talks*, ed. Samantha Hardingham (London: Architectural Association, 2016), 239.
5. Cedric Price, interview with author, RIBA, 66 Portland Place, London, June 17, 2003.
6. Cedric Price, "Monochromatic Observations on a Polychromatic Occasion: AA Projects Review," *AAQ: Architectural Association Quarterly* 9, no. 1 (1977): 3–11.

THE AUTOMATION
OF KNOWLEDGE

Georg Vrachliotis

Protagonist Konrad Wachsmann (1901–1980)
Institutions University of Southern California (USC);
Hochschule für Gestaltung (HfG), Ulm;
TH Karlsruhe; Sommerakademie Salzburg;
Illinois Institute of Technology (IIT)
Location Los Angeles, CA, USA and elsewhere
Dates 1952–1957

"Automation is nothing more than the work process brought under perfect control,"[1] argued Konrad Wachsmann in his 1959 book *Wendepunkt im Bauen* (Turning Point of Building). To illustrate the point, a photograph of the interior of a machine hall showed countless machines linearly interconnected as modules in a seemingly endless chain. Wachsmann was so fascinated by the idea of the transfer line—a synchronized organism formed of an "arbitrary number of special machines," each regulated by "self-control and feedback"—that he briefly elevated it to a "symbol of the concept of automation" at large.[2] This tying of the new space of possibilities of automation to a global view of modularization also made apparent the pedagogical claim inherent in the ambitious project of industrial construction.

In an unpublished lecture manuscript, "The Pedagogic Impact of Automation," Wachsmann differentiated between "automation as social philosophy of production" and "automation as method

of production."[3] That he was more interested in unifying than separating these areas, however, is evident from his attempts to transfer the form of group work and teamwork into the technical sphere of automation—and vice versa. In Wachsmann's conception, the modular structure of the transfer line corresponded to the organization of teamwork, in which a certain number of students were interconnected like independently working machines to form a large apparatus. *Wendepunkt im Bauen* soberly defined automation as a completely controlled work process, regardless of whether it was performed by a machine or a human. For him, the modularization of the building process went hand in hand with the modularization of knowledge: as in a factory production line, learning processes could be broken down into individual interconnected steps.

Wachsmann first experimented with group work at the Institute of Design in Chicago in the early 1950s. From the experience gained there, he concluded that the number of participants should not exceed the "ideal number" of twenty-one. As if planning on a drawing board, he designed every single step of the group work, which was also reflected in the language he used. Subsequent seminars at the Technical University in Karlsruhe with Egon Eiermann (1954), the University of Tokyo with Kenzo Tange (1955), and the Summer Academy in Salzburg (1956–1959) were planned with the utmost precision, with Wachsmann assuming

that this team, divided into seven working groups, consists of twenty-one participants and that seven individual problems of the study program have been selected accordingly,

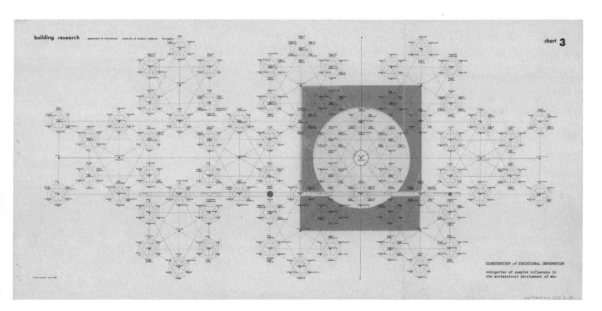

part of the total working time available must be divided into seven equal working periods. These seven working periods are separated by seven discussion periods. Each of these discussion periods shall be divided into seven equal time intervals so that the same time is available for discussion of each individual problem.[4]

For Wachsmann, the design process was not like a circuit diagram—it *was* a circuit diagram.

Wachsmann's goal was nothing less than the development and implementation of an extensive electronic database for industrial construction, to be stored on punch cards and made available to universities.[5] In order to ensure the completeness of this stored knowledge, he proposed radical measures, again painstakingly prescribed:

The groups work best on four drawing boards that are pushed together, with a large folder on every fourth drawing board containing all the sketches and other data that are produced during the work. The folders must be accessible to all team members at all times and also appear during discussions so that they can always go back to earlier stages of development. Therefore, there should be no wastepaper baskets, because every sketch, drawing or calculation or every written thought must be preserved, as one of the essential principles of this working technique lies in the later reconstruction of the entire development process of the seminar paper.[6]

Wachsmann's aim was to produce buildings that looked as if they were "products of industrialization, of automation, i.e., that these buildings were no longer designed, but really the results of scientific research."[7] With descriptions of this kind Wachsmann clarified what was for him the most radical impact of automation on the education of architecture: the rationalization, modularization, and finally the mechanical reproduction of architectural knowledge itself. In such an advanced technoscientific world, nothing less than the authorship of the architect was up for reassessment.

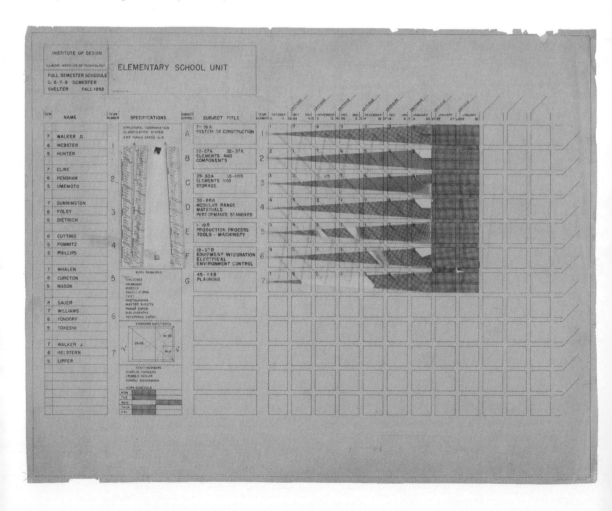

∧ Konrad Wachsmann
with a group of
students, Konrad
Wachsmann Archive
no. 205. Photograph
by F. Solmus
Pressephoto.

< Diagram for an
"elementary school
unit," Konrad
Wachsmann Archive
no. 314 Bl.1.

≪ Diagram of the
"coordination
of educational
information," Konrad
Wachsmann Archive
no. 353 Bl.34.

1. Konrad Wachsmann, *Wendepunkt im Bauen* (Wiesbaden: Krausskopf Verlag, 1959), 104.
2. Ibid., 66.
3. Konrad Wachsmann, "The Pedagogic Impact of Automation," unpublished manuscript, undated, c.1959. Konrad Wachsmann Archive, Akademie der Künste Berlin.
4. Ibid., 207.
5. Cf. Peter Rodemeier, "Konrad Wachsmann—oder die Liebe zur Geometrie," in *Vom Sinn des Details. Zum Gesamtwerk von Konrad Wachsmann*, ed. Konrad Wachsmann (Cologne: Rudolf Müller Verlag, 1988), 65–69, especially the chapter "Das Studium im Team," 60.
6. Wachsmann, *Wendepunkt im Bauen*, 207.
7. Wachsmann, "Das Studium im Team," 61.

THE COMPUTER MISFITS

Evangelos Kotsioris

Protagonists Howard T. Fisher (1903–1979), William Warntz (1922–1988), Carl Steinitz (1938–), Eric Teicholz (1940–), and other faculty and students
Institution Laboratory for Computer Graphics and Spatial Analysis (LCGSA) at Harvard Graduate School of Design (GSD)
Location Cambridge, MA, USA
Dates 1964–1974

The Laboratory for Computer Graphics (LCG) was proposed in 1964, and officially established a year later, as part of the Graduate School of Design (GSD) at Harvard University. Initially affiliated with the school's department of Regional and City Planning, the so-called "Harvard lab" was founded by architect and mathematical cartographer Howard T. Fisher with the active support of Dean Josep Lluís Sert as an experimental venue for the use of computers in the automated creation of thematic maps; essentially maps that used lines, shapes, and symbols to visually communicate s and other measurable data. During its twenty-six-year lifespan, the LCG was an epicenter for the development of "systems for the analysis and graphic representation of spatial factors in man's physical and social environment."[1] These included new software on mapping and cartography developed by faculty and students, including SYMAP and ODYSSEY, two of the programs that would ultimately contribute to the development of GIS (graphic information systems).[2] Often overshadowed by the technical advances it made possible, the lab was also a significant educational

experiment, training one of the first generations of designers in computers and new media.

The LCG was a true product of the 1960s, a decade in which the problems faced by American cities—including urban decay, inner-city poverty, and racial segregation—became fundable research topics for Ivy League design schools. The formation of the lab was only made possible by an initial grant of $249,000 from the Ford Foundation. Louis Winnick, an economist and former director of research of the New York City Planning Commission, who handled the Foundation's investments in housing and community development, had supported Fisher's proposal to make computer mapping accessible to large numbers of practicing planners.[3] The LCG came at the heels of the Harvard–MIT Joint Center for Housing Studies, which had been established in 1959, and preceded the founding of the Urban Systems Laboratory (USL) at MIT in 1968.[4] Like the LCG, these other Cambridge-based "labs" had been proposed as interdepartmental, multidisciplinary entities dedicated to the study of urban issues. Most importantly, both had received substantial financial support from the Ford Foundation, during a period in which the self-proclaimed "private, nonprofit institution whose purpose is to serve the public welfare" was accused of also indirectly supporting the Cold War (cultural) "development" agenda of the CIA.[5]

From its inception, the LCG was an interdisciplinary endeavor. Its diverse cast of members comprised architects, geographers, cartographers, mathematicians, computer scientists, and artists invested in the idea that the introduction of the computer could profoundly alter the ways in which the design disciplines operated in both education and practice. The lab's first courses focused solely on the creation of maps through the use of SYMAP (short for "SYnagraphic computer MAPping"), the

< Looking over a map produced with the SYMAP program. Harvard Graduate School of Design Association, "The Laboratory for Computer Graphics," Supplement, Summer 1967.

computer program that Fisher had started developing at Northwestern University before getting hired by Harvard. In the mid-1960s this involved manually keypunching data on cards, taking them to the Harvard Computer Center for processing, and picking up the printed results hours, if not days, later. While the lab's early courses on the theory and application of computer graphics initially attracted mainly planning students, the involvement of Carl Steinitz (at the time assistant professor in city planning and landscape) as a research associate in 1966 started to pique the interest of landscape and other students. After Fisher's retirement in 1968, the scope and research directives of the LCG gradually broadened to include architectural representation and design, prompting the lab's new director, professor of theoretical geography and regional planning William Warntz, to append the words "and Spatial Analysis" to the lab's name (LCGSA).

Some of the most groundbreaking courses taught at the LCGSA were initiated by Eric Teicholz, a young GSD-trained architect and fellow of the Harvard Computing Center supported by "an IBM donation."[6] As a joint fellow at the LCGSA in 1967, Teicholz developed OTOTROL, one of the first computer programs capable of producing three-dimensional perspective drawings. Through a series of experimental workshops and seminars in computer-aided design (CAD), he aimed to reposition the use of the computer—previously confined to the periphery of the architectural profession (essentially engineering, contracting, and cartography)—at the very center of the design process.[7] Convinced of the potential of the new media as both objects and tools of the architect's education, Teicholz encouraged the use of video tape recording (VTR) and all means of "photomation," including television, still photography, moving picture photography,

lasers, and holography. Long before the formation of the Media Lab at MIT, and other similar research enclaves across US universities, the LCGSA reimagined design as a digital, multimedia endeavor.

By the early 1970s, however, the LCGSA needed to find new sources of funding. Little remained of the initial Ford Foundation grant that had made it palatable to Harvard, or of the large fund secured from the National Science Foundation (NSF) soon after. Under yet another executive director, the chemist-turned-geographer Allan H. Schmidt, the LCGSA turned to software sales to external parties and continuing education workshops for design professionals, both for a steep fee. What became increasingly evident, much to the dismay of GSD's new dean, Maurice D. Kilbridge, was that the LCGSA often relied for its funding on big governmental and institutional sponsors, such as the Defense Intelligence Agency, the Office of Naval Research, the National Air Pollution Administration, the Federal Housing Administration, and the Office of Planning and Coordination of the State of New York. Since its formation, the Harvard lab had solicited contracts from agencies involved with controversial issues of urban and territorial management, including the mapping of low-income populations in major urban centers like New York, daytime/nighttime activities and their intensities in urban settings, racial imbalance in public schools, the use of computers in the processing of mortgage insurance applications, air pollution studies, planning studies for hospitals, welfare facilities, shopping centers, and highways, as well as studies for minimizing overland sonic booms, among others.[8] For many of the lab's faculty, the opportunity to work on "real-life," if contentious, projects such as these constituted the most meaningful training students could receive.

During the same period, a series of mapping commissions for high-circulation newspapers and magazines provided much-needed income for the lab's operation while at the same time communicating its capabilities to a wider audience. In 1972 the LCGSA produced a three-dimensional map charting population growth for a *Life* magazine article on rising US birth rates and Nixon's attacks on the legalization of abortion.[9] The year after, in 1973, the *New York Times* ordered a series of maps that portrayed the "geographical movement of black Americans from 1960 and 1970"—the tail end of the so-called Second Great Migration, when an estimated 1,380,000 African Americans left the South "in search of jobs and new opportunities" in the industrial centers of the northeastern and western parts of the US.[10] Three years later, on the occasion of its thematic issue on the US bicentennial in 1976, the *National Geographic* commissioned the lab to produce a series of maps depicting the "vast population shifts" in North America since 1790—essentially representing the result of European settler colonization and the westward expansion of the nineteenth century.[11] While seemingly objective, the maps produced by the LCGSA were loaded with the politics implicit in data selection and visualization. While such commissions raised its profile, Kilbridge feared that the LCGSA risked becoming a freelancing operation that used the resources of Harvard primarily to service the agendas of governmental agencies, private institutions, or even popular publications, rather than catering for the educational needs of GSD students.

After the antiwar student demonstrations that shook Cambridge between 1967 and 1972, especially the so-called "November Actions" of 1969, when MIT students protested against the complicity of the Ivy League institution in defense-related research, labs like the LCGSA came under a new level of scrutiny. Although it had moved from its former location in the basement of Harvard's Memorial Hall to the GSD's newly completed Gund Hall in 1972, the LCGSA continued to give the impression of a semiautonomous appendage to the school. As a result, in early 1974, Kilbridge appointed a committee to probe the nature of these working relationships and evaluate the LCGSA's educational contribution to the GSD. Among the eight members of the committee that would debate the lab's fate was architect Nicholas Negroponte, co-founder of the Architecture Machine Group (AMG) at MIT, which competed for funding from some of the very same sources as the Harvard lab.[12] The committee's reproachful conclusion was that the LCGSA was "not central to the operations

of the GSD or any department" and that its "focus has been too narrow," essentially leaving out newer strands of research, including the potential use of artificial intelligence and robotics in design.[13]

Largely through Fisher's intervention, the LCGSA was spared on the condition that the lab moved away from commercial software development and recentered its activities on its educational mission.[14] In the years that followed, the LCGSA's faculty and students produced some of its most pioneering research on computer graphics and real-time CAD, allowing users to actively shape and manipulate designs on a computer screen, rather than having to go through the cumbersome and time-consuming process of punching and processing data before printing out. Yet the lab's largely technocratic approach and the fittingness of its activity within a design school would continue to be contested by the GSD leadership, which often found it hard to see the immediate need to teach computing skills to students of design.

The Harvard lab undoubtedly paved the way for what is currently known as design computation. But, like other American "computer labs" of the 1960s and 1970s, it cannot be disentangled from the ethical questions arising from its enmeshment with the military-industrial complex, conspicuous funding, and commercialization. By 1982 the LCGSA was not only being accused of using Harvard's name to promote its annual user conference, known as "Computer Graphics Week," but was also running a growing deficit. This time, GSD dean Gerald McCue decided to take drastic action and significantly reduced the staffing of the lab, which continued to operate but only under a limited scope until its final dissolution in 1991. Whether due to financial or ethical concerns, this deprived the GSD of one of the most historically significant experiments in computing, right at the beginning of a decade during which architectural pedagogy would become unthinkable outside of the "digital."

> Computer-generated population distribution maps of the United States created by the Lab for Life, May 19, 1972.

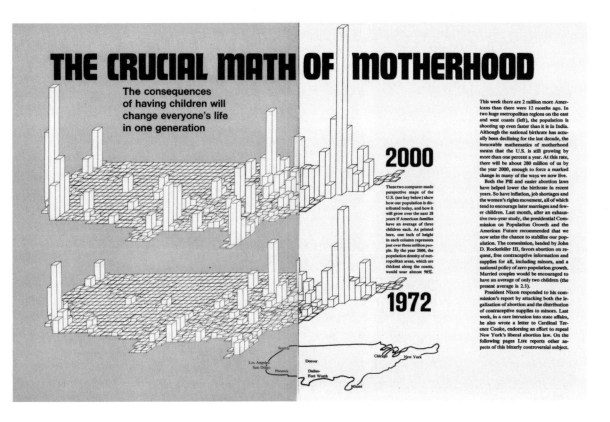

THE CRUCIAL MATH OF MOTHERHOOD

The consequences of having children will change everyone's life in one generation

2000

These two computer-made perspective maps of the U.S. (see key below) show how our population is distributed today, and how it will grow over the next 28 years if American families have an average of three children each. As printed here, one inch of height in each column represents just over three million people. By the year 2000, the population density of metropolitan areas, which are thickest along the coasts, would soar almost 90%.

1972

This week there are 2 million more Americans than there were 12 months ago. In two huge metropolitan regions on the east and west coasts (left), the population is shooting up even faster than it is in India. Although the national birthrate has actually been declining for the last decade, the inexorable mathematics of motherhood means that the U.S. is still growing by more than one percent a year. At this rate, there will be about 280 million of us by the year 2000, enough to force a marked change in many of the ways we now live.

Both the Pill and easier abortion laws have helped lower the birthrate in recent years. So have inflation, job shortages and the women's rights movement, all of which tend to encourage later marriages and fewer children. Last month, after an exhaustive two-year study, the presidential Commission on Population Growth and the American Future recommended that we now seize the chance to stabilize our population. The commission, headed by John D. Rockefeller III, favors abortion on request, free contraceptive information and supplies for all, including minors, and a national policy of zero population growth. Married couples would be encouraged to have an average of only two children (the present average is 2.3).

President Nixon responded to his commission's report by attacking both the legalization of abortion and the distribution of contraceptive supplies to minors. Last week, in a rare intrusion into state affairs, he also wrote a letter to Cardinal Terence Cooke, endorsing an effort to repeal New York's liberal abortion law. On the following pages LIFE reports other aspects of this bitterly controversial subject.

Seattle

Los Angeles
San Diego   Phoenix

Denver

Dallas-Fort Worth

Chicago   New York

Miami

1. Harvard University, Laboratory for Computer Graphics and Spatial Analysis, *Context, the Newsletter for the Laboratory for Computer Graphics and Spatial Analysis*, no. 1 (February 1968): 1.
2. Nicholas R. Chrisman, *Charting the Unknown: How Computer Mapping at Harvard Became GIS* (Redlands, CA: ESRI Press, 2006).
3. Ibid., 3.
4. For LCGCA's assessment of the Joint Center, see "The Joint Center for Urban Studies of the Massachusetts Institute of Technology and Harvard University" (Cambridge, MA, September 1968), D000 Series D, Folder DB026, Loeb Library Special Collections; on the USL's funding by the Ford Foundation, see Felicity D. Scott, "Discourse, Seek, Interact: Urban Systems at MIT," in *A Second Modernism: MIT, Architecture, and the "Techno-Social" Moment*, ed. Arindam Dutta (Cambridge,

MA: MIT Press, 2013), 342–393.
5. *The Ford Foundation Annual Report*, 1964 (New York: Ford Foundation, 1964), n.p.
6. *Red Book: Projects of the Laboratory for Computer Graphics and Spatial Analysis*, ed. William Warntz, Allan H. Schmidt, and Carl Steinitz (Cambridge, MA: Harvard University LCGSA, 1969), III, Loeb Library Special Collections.
7. *Context*, no. 2 (September 1972): 2.
8. For multiple documented examples, see Warntz, Schmidt, and Steinitz, *Red Book*.
9. "The Crucial Math of Motherhood," *Life*, May 19, 1972.
10. "The New York Times," *Context, the Newsletter for the Laboratory for Computer Graphics and Spatial Analysis*, no. 5 (November 1973): 1; Paul Delaney, "Civil Rights Unity Gone in Redirected Movement," *New York Times*, August 29,

1973, 16.
11. "'This Land of Ours': Thematic Issue with Supplement," *National Geographic* 150, no. 1 (July 1976): 40–41.
12. On AMG's own problematic relationships with funding structures at MIT see Molly Wright Steenson's contribution "Demo or Die: A Lab for Deployed Research" in this volume.
13. Konrad Kalba et al., "Memorandum from the Committee to Review the Laboratory for Computer Graphics and Spatial Analysis (LCGSA)," Harvard Graduate School of Design, May 22, 1974, 2–3, B000 Series B, Folder BB022, Loeb Library, Special Collections.
14. Howard T. Fisher, "Comment on the 'Final Report of the Committee to Review the Laboratory for Computer Graphics and Spatial Analysis,'" September 20, 1974, B000 Series B, Folder BB022, Loeb Library, Special Collections.

A SPINNER
IN HIS WEB

Daniela Fabricius

Protagonists Frei Otto (1925–2015),
Ewald Bubner (1932–), Berthold Burkhardt (1941–)
Institution Institute for Lightweight Structures
(Institut für Leichte Flächentragwerke) at
the University of Stuttgart
Location Stuttgart, Germany
Dates 1964–1991

When asked to describe the Institute for Lightweight Structures (IL, later ILEK) Frei Otto affectionately referred to it as a *Spinnerzentrum*, playing off the double meaning of "Spinner" in German: one who is crazy and one who spins connections and webs. Based at the University of Stuttgart (earlier, Technische Hochschule Stuttgart) and housed under the roof of one of his tent structures, the IL was led by Otto from 1964 until the early 1990s. With an initial intake of just six students, the institute aimed to abandon any restrictive assumptions about pedagogy to develop new ways of thinking and new ways of building. It was here that Otto's famous models for the groundbreaking pavilion at Expo 67 in Montreal and the 1972 Munich Olympics stadium were designed.

The IL's free-form philosophy appealed to a generation eager for alternative methods of pedagogy. By 1971 there were seventy students as the institute's growing reputation attracted young architects from all over the world. A description by Berthold Burkhardt, a central member of the research team, evokes the fluidity of this community:

[Students] made the pilgrimage from the city centre to the IL tent on the Vaihingen campus not primarily to gain subject credits, but to be there a few weeks and be able to experiment, discover, discuss, and listen. ... It quickly became clear outside Germany that an unusual place in an unusual tent had come into being here in Stuttgart, an open experimental workshop.[1]

The unusual tentlike structure that housed the IL was built in 1966 in a secluded, wooded area on the new campus of the university, "among scientific neighbors, who view it as a curiosity, a thorn in the side of exact sciences."[2] Based on the minimal form of a soap-film model, it initially served as a full-scale test structure for the Expo 67 pavilion before it was donated by the government to house the IL after 1968, refurbished with a sheathed roof and glass sides. The building was designed without a definite

interior layout so that groups could assemble and disperse as needed. The interior was equipped with mobile, heated benches that could be plugged into a pipe system, and on warm days classes were frequently held outdoors. According to Burkhardt, "bureaucratic, formal, or rigidly fixed behavior structures simply could not develop in this tent." He continues: "experiments are not restricted to models and architectural ideas—the human beings involved here…experiment with themselves…the methods of cooperation and the attendant personal and psychological effects belong…to the IL's own…structure."[3]

Otto's *Spinnerzentrum* was in effect an interdisciplinary architectural thinktank that had the capacity to address a wide range of new critical themes, among them "buildings in cold regions and deserts," "cities on and under water," "living in outer space," "old and new nomadic architecture," "tent and trailer cities," "chemical architecture," and "erotic architecture."[4] Rather than insisting on the figure of the architect, Otto described how:

Methodical inventors are the real avant-gardists of today. …For the inventor in such manifold fields like architecture and environmental design one coined the lovingly disrespectful yet appreciative expression "Spinner." Spinners produce new threads and nets. Spinners try to find new syntheses in all fields of science, technology, and art.[5]

In accordance with this vision of interdisciplinary cooperation, Otto facilitated collaboration between architects, engineers, biologists, anthropologists, and historians. The IL's insistence on large-scale orchestrated research and experimentation as a form of architectural practice remains almost unparalleled in architectural culture.

Belying first impressions, Otto was not a guru-like "mad scientist" working in isolation, but a "spinner" at the center of a web. The IL was set up as a series of networks, not only within Stuttgart University, but also between research and industry. The student researchers occupied a key position in this network of scientific and alternative modes of research. Otto encouraged new forms of social interaction; in lieu of a formal teaching plan there were open discussions and interdisciplinary research groups. The laboratory environment at the IL encouraged direct experience and playfulness, and student work was largely focused on making and documenting physical models.

These models were of two types: measurement models that were used to simulate and document structural conditions in buildings; and more playful

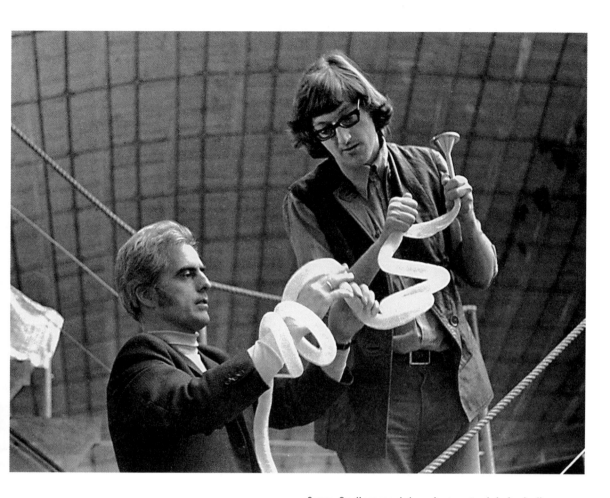

form-finding models using materials including soap film, eggs, shaving cream, rubber, and balloons. The experiments all ultimately shared the larger goal of the institute: to find an architecture of unprecedented lightness. Scientific precision allowed for the creation of soap-film structures in ideal conditions, with special instruments that could measure the diameter and tension of the soap film. Measurement models, like those used for the Expo 67 pavilion, the 1972 Olympics roofs, and the 1977 Multihalle Mannheim, were designed to produce data objectively. Made with metal wires loaded with weights and springs to create strain, they were fitted with stereophotographic cameras and tiny gauges that could register even the smallest movements. An enormous amount of information was produced by the sheer intricacy of the models, made possible by the "cheap labor" of the students.

Alongside these carefully constructed models, there were experiments with unknown and immeasurable geometries. Most were inspired by natural forms: in IL publications, model experiments and even completed projects were often shown next

∧ Frei Otto (left) with Eberhard Haug, 1973. Pneumatic experiment with inflated animal intestines.

> "Multimedia" test of simultaneous measurements of the Olympic stadium model using 6 × 6 cameras, miniature cameras, and gauges.

< Frei Otto at the Institute for Lightweight Structures, University of Stuttgart, 1969. The first models for the Munich Olympic stadium can be seen in the foreground.

to photographic images taken from nature. After the completion of the Olympic tents, the IL would shift its focus almost exclusively to the topic of "Biology and Building." In 1984 it was awarded a new DFG (German Research Foundation) grant for a vast project, "Natural Constructions—Light Constructions in Architecture and Nature," that involved a large number of outside researchers who specialized in the static calculation and measurement of objects of the natural world, whether grasses, birds' nests, or diatoms.

Otto eventually had students experiment directly with biological "building materials"—the tensile strength of spider silk, or the compressive strength of animal bones. Cameras were put inside animal intestines, and students were sent to zoos and slaughterhouses. The ILEK still has a large library of photographs and slides showing the results of a decades-long project of discovering and inventing new possibilities for structural forms.

While the IL was almost synonymous with the figure of Otto, it also drew prominent visitors and collaborators such as Buckminster Fuller and Kenzo Tange. Most figures associated with the institute came from the realm of biology, in particular Otto's longtime collaborator and friend Johann-Gerhard Helmcke. The IL was the site of a several conferences and published numerous large volumes of research on topics including pneumatic structures, bones, "ancient architects," and solar architecture,

as well as more modest newsletters and booklets. The main IL series of forty-one volumes published between 1969 and 1995 became a crucial resource for students and teachers at schools around the world. The intensity and volume of research was so great that already by 1975 the IL was debating how to manage this "information explosion," and proposed sharing its own fifty thousand+ files via a documentation center and automated information network.[6] This research was perhaps the most intricate, and unique, web woven by these "Spinners."

1. Berthold Burkhardt, "The Institute for Lightweight Structures: University Institute and Spinners' Centre," in *Frei Otto. Complete Works* (Basel: Birkhäuser, 2001), 97.
2. Berthold Burkhardt, "Frei Otto at Work," *Architectural Design*, no. 3 (1971): 140.
3. Ibid.
4. "Ein Interbau und ein Spinnerzentrum," in *Frei Otto: Schriften und Reden 1951–1983*, ed. Berthold Burkhardt (Braunschweig: Vieweg, 1984), 91–92. This text was originally published in *Allgemeine Bauzeitung* 40 (1970): 36–37. All translations from this text are mine.
5. Ibid., 93.
6. *IL8: Nets in Nature and Technics*, Information of the Institute for Lightweight Structures (Stuttgart: Institute for Lightweight Structures, 1975).

THE ALGORITHMIZATION OF CREATIVITY

Diana Cristóbal Olave

Protagonists Ernesto Garcia Camarero (1932–), Ignacio Gomez de Liaño (1946–), Juan Navarro Baldeweg (1939–), José Miguel de Prada Poole (1938–), Jorge Alberto Sarquis Jaule (1940–), Javier Seguí de la Riva (1940–2021)
Institution Centro de Cálculo de la Universidad de Madrid (CCUM), Seminario de Análisis y Generación Automática de Formas Arquitectónicas (SAGAF-A)
Location Madrid, Spain
Dates 1966–1975

In 1966 the European Council for Nuclear Research (CERN) in Geneva decommissioned an IBM 7090 computer because it could no longer perform its original task—high-energy physics research.[1] Obsolete at CERN, the computer was donated to the University of Madrid by IBM, with the promise of annual research grants if the Spanish Ministry of Education funded the construction of a new building to house the machine and auxiliary spaces for research. This would be the nucleus of the Calculation Center at the University of Madrid (CCUM), a research institution devoted to the application of computer techniques in "fields where automation [had] not yet penetrated"[2]—one of which was deemed to be architecture.

CCUM was the first building in Spain constructed specifically to house a computer—one of the first computers in the country, in fact, to be used exclusively for education and research. The focus on the computer as an instrument of investigation rather than management paved the way for an unconventional and unprecedented interdisciplinary setting. The directors of the center looked for areas of research beyond the sciences and organized a series of courses where professors, students, and technicians worked together to link the computer with disciplines as diverse as art, architecture, linguistics, and music.

Despite this broad disciplinary heterogeneity, the objective of all CCUM courses was essentially the same: the "algorithmization of creativity,"[3] to use the expression coined by one of the center's directors, the mathematician Ernesto García Camarero. To do this, it was necessary to resolve the difference between two terms that had hitherto been considered antagonistic: "algorithmia" and "creativity." The former denoted "the possibility of solving problems

and reducing processes through a finite set of well-defined and simple rules," whereas the latter invoked "a human activity that is not well defined…and always comes up surrounded by a mysterious halo."[4] CCUM participants saw in the computer and its associated mathematical techniques the means of overcoming these apparently irreconcilable differences. They equated the notion of algorithmic creativity with the capacity to produce an unlimited number of combinatorial arrangements through a limited number of well-defined and simple rules, and embarked together on projects that reframed "creative" disciplines such as architecture as iterative decision-making sequences—that is, as algorithms.

To frame architecture as a series of mechanical step-by-step rules was not new in the history of the discipline. In the computational context of the 1960s, the architects of the CCUM looked for ways to describe sequential instructions through certain mathematical properties that moved away from mere quantification, following a mathematical shift that was also taking place elsewhere.[5] While this algorithmic turn was found in other computation centers that the CCUM sporadically collaborated with (for example, the Design Methods researchers in the UK), it had singular valences in the Spanish context. Many proponents of computing at the time used algorithmic techniques to "correct" architecture's methodological deficiencies by shifting the goal of design from the control of an outcome to the creation of a machinic decision-making process. In Madrid, however, the displacement of personal agency by externalized algorithmic processes was framed as a means to "liberate" design from the prevailing cultural norms and authoritarian rule. "Algorithmic creativity," at the CCUM, invoked the idea of developing exhaustive sets of possibilities—as opposed to a result focused on optimization or economic efficiency. This in turn had ethical implications. Even if they appeared more abstract and inscrutable than conventional means of architectural representation, algorithmic techniques fostered visual culture and paradoxically fused computation with the idea of rendering information "transparent," "visible," and "exposed."

In the wake of the major institutional reforms that took place at the end of the dictatorship, the CCUM courses gradually disappeared and mutated into other institutions and spaces, such as the courses led by Javier Seguí de la Riva and José Miguel de Prada Poole at the ETSAM (Escuela Técnica Superior de Arquitectura de Madrid). Yet, the legacy of the

center should be understood in terms of the peda-gogical approach it pioneered. During its brief but intense life, the CCUM encouraged experimentation across formats (workshops, festivals, exhibitions), permeability between creative and technoscien-tific fields, and collaborative and polyphonic work. In a context that did not yet guarantee freedoms of speech, press, or assembly, the immunity provided by the seemingly nonideological IBM technology—which echoed the technocratic narrative embraced by the Franco regime—evaded censorship and provided a space for collective experimentation.

1. Secretary of the Department of Mathematics of the University of Madrid, typescript, 1965. General Archives, UCM.
2. Ernesto García Camarero, "Presentación," in *Seminarios y Conferencias* (Madrid: CCUM, 1968), 1.
3. Ernesto García Camarero, "L'art cybernétique," in *SIGMA 9, Contact II, art et ordinateur* (Bordeaux: SIGMA, 1973).

4. Ernesto García Camarero, "L'ordinateur et la créativité," in *L'ordinateur et la créativité*, ed. J. Segui de la Riva et al. (Madrid: CCUM, 1970), 5.
5. See Theodora Vardouli, "Graphing Theory: New Mathematics, Design, and the Participatory Turn," PhD diss. (MIT, 2017).

∧ Secondary school students visit the CCUM computer room as part of the seminar "Computers in Secondary Education," c. 1970.

NATURE AS TECHNOLOGY

John R. Blakinger

Protagonists Gyorgy Kepes (1906–2001)
Institution Center for Advanced Visual
Studies (CAVS), Massachusetts Institute
of Technology (MIT)
Location Cambridge, MA, USA
Dates 1967–1974

In the late 1960s and early 1970s Gyorgy Kepes and the fellows he invited to his Center for Advanced Visual Studies (CAVS)—the art-and-science think-tank he founded at MIT in 1967—designed unusual civic-scale environmental art: massive light towers illuminating Boston Harbor, tiered platforms suspended over the Charles River, and dazzling optical displays reflected from floating buoys.[1] These projects were intended to transform technology into a simulation of natural phenomena by evoking the sun, moon, and stars through lasers, sensors, and lighting equipment. They used advanced technologies but also put into practice the unique techniques and technocratic pedagogical models that had become pervasive across scientific disciplines in the postwar period, like the interdisciplinary thinking fundamental to cybernetics, systems theory, and emerging ecological discourses. Kepes generalized these approaches as "idioms of collaboration," or what he described, using the words of sociologist Daniel Bell, as a new "intellectual technology."[2] He believed the center's proposals would transform technology's destructive power by stimulating creative experience. "The uncharted space is within ourselves, in our still unfathomed ethical potentials, in our still untapped imaginative power."[3]

Kepes attracted an eclectic group of artists, architects, and critics to MIT to participate in these collaborations. The inaugural cohort of visiting fellows included Otto Piene, the artist who had previously cofounded the neo-avantgarde collective Group ZERO; Jack Burnham, the critic who would curate the landmark art and technology exhibition *Software* and elaborate what he called "systems esthetics"; Stan VanDerBeek, the experimental film-maker who pioneered immersive forms of expanded cinema; and emerging international figures in the arts, from Spanish architect Juan Navarro Baldeweg to Greek kinetic sculptor Takis Vassilakis and Ecuadorean installation artist Mauricio Bueno.

The fellows organized conferences, symposia, and workshops, but also designed elaborate collaborative projects. The first such project, a group exhibition planned by Kepes and the CAVS fellows as the official US representation at the 1969 São Paulo Biennial, was a disaster: the show was canceled after it was boycotted by artists (including some from the CAVS) protesting against Brazil's military dictatorship and the Vietnam War. Kepes's nuanced position on the controversy—he was adamantly opposed to the war but wanted to participate in São Paulo nonetheless—left him exposed to attacks. He was caricatured as a naïve technocrat. Following the failed exhibition, the center shifted its activities to large-scale environmental interventions in the natural and urban landscape, or what Kepes called civic art. Light towers, illuminated projections, and spaces for participatory events would, Kepes hoped, create a new environmental consciousness.

None of these proposals were actually realized, but they were visualized through models and abstract studies of lighting effects, as captured in photographs by Kepes's longtime darkroom assistant, Nishan Bichajian. Reports, descriptions, and proposals accompanying these images reflected systems concepts like environmental homeostasis. These ideas drew loosely from Burnham's systems esthetics as well as Kepes's own cybernetics-inflected

≪ Juan Navarro
Baldeweg, proposal
for "increasing ecolog-
ical experiences," 1972.

< Gyorgy Kepes, 1967.
Photograph by Ivan
Massar.

v Inside the Center
for Advanced Visual
Studies, c. 1969.
Photograph by Nishan
Bichajian.

discourse, as anticipated in his 1942 book *Language of Vision* and articulated in *The New Landscape in Art and Science* from 1956 and his *Vision + Value* series. One key text in his 1972 *Vision + Value* volume, *Arts of the Environment*, contrasted the utopian potential of advanced technology—"bioengineering, genetic engineering, the pill, distant sensors, cyborgs, and an ever-increasing communications network"—with the dystopian reality of technological society in the twentieth century.[4]

The politics of the center's pedagogy were therefore contradictory; the CAVS was radical in the sense that it aimed to rival advanced research in science and technology through advanced research in architecture and design. Its interdisciplinary approaches mimicked experimental methods used at MIT's other research institutes, and the designed environments produced at the center were wildly imaginative. But the center was also institutionally compromised. Many of its key collaborators were affiliated with MIT's two weapons centers, the Lincoln Laboratory and the Instrumentation Laboratory. Kepes worked directly with scientists whose primary research had applications in the Vietnam War, and whose labs were funded through defense contracts. Even the center's foundational pedagogical model, the "intellectual technology" of collaboration, was itself indebted to warfare: Daniel Bell formulated the concept in reference to militaristic fields like game theory and operations research.

A backlash against military power at MIT exploded across campus in 1969, when the March 4 movement—named to evoke the act of demonstrating, or marching forth—targeted the role of defense contracts on campus.[5] The key concept that emerged from the protests was "conversion": the idea that research with destructive applications might be converted to more peaceful ends.[6] The center's environmental projects were intended, both literally and metaphorically, to convert technologies and techniques through their humanistic application in the creation of aesthetic spectacles. Conversion was profoundly paradoxical: did these proposals reflect an authentic transformation of military power, or a superficial embellishment that only legitimated MIT's existing research agenda? The CAVS's own participants became cynical; Jack Burnham later denounced the center's projects, specifically Kepes's beloved light tower, as extravagant, indulgent, and ultimately pointless: "What was the civic purpose of the light monument? *No one really knew.*"[7]

After Kepes's retirement in 1974, Otto Piene was appointed CAVS director and the center's agenda was more carefully calibrated to avoid the ideological entanglements that defined its early years under Kepes. But despite its initial failures, the center had a lasting impact on academic culture. Kepes's pedagogical experiments anticipated the interdisciplinary approaches to art and architecture that have since proliferated across the university. The CAVS was perhaps the single most significant precedent for the institutionalized exploration of new media in laboratory settings—a phenomenon that is now ubiquitous.

1. For a complete study of Kepes and the CAVS, see my *Gyorgy Kepes: Undreaming the Bauhaus* (Cambridge, MA: MIT Press, 2019), especially chapters 5 and 6.
2. Kepes uses the phrase "idioms of collaboration" in a report titled "A Collaborative Approach at the Center for Advanced Visual Studies: Prepared for the Old Dominion Foundation" and dated April 1966. A copy of the report is in the Institute Archives and Special Collections at MIT in AC 8, box 193, folder "Center for Advanced Visual Studies 3 / 3." Kepes uses the phrase "intellectual technology" in Gyorgy Kepes, interviewed by Douglas M. Davis, "Art & Technology—Conversations," *Art in America* 56, no. 1 (January–February 1968): 40. Daniel Bell discusses intellectual technologies in multiple writings from the 1960s.
3. Gyorgy Kepes, "Art and Ecological Consciousness," in *Arts of the Environment*, ed. Gyorgy Kepes (New York: George Braziller, 1972), 12.
4. Ibid.
5. See Jonathan Allen's edited volume *March 4: Scientists, Students, and Society* (Cambridge, MA: MIT Press, 1970) for the primary documents relating to the March 4 movement. The volume was republished in 2019.
6. This is put forth in the Review Panel on Special Laboratories, "Final Report" [Pounds Panel Report] (October 1969). A copy of the report is available in the Institute Archives and Special Collections at MIT. The Pounds panel, which included Noam Chomsky, was tasked with evaluating questions raised by the March 4 movement.
7. Jack Burnham, "Art and Technology: The Panacea that Failed," in *The Myths of Information: Technology and Post-Industrial Culture*, ed. Kathleen Woodward (Madison, WI: Coda Press, 1980), 209.

DEMO OR DIE: A LAB FOR DEPLOYED RESEARCH

Molly Wright Steenson

Protagonists Nicholas Negroponte (1943–)
and dozens of faculty and student collaborators
Institution MIT Architecture Machine Group
(as MIT Media Lab 1985–)
Location Cambridge, MA, USA
Dates 1967–1985

MIT's Architecture Machine Group (AMG), founded by Nicholas Negroponte and Leon Groisser in 1967, was a laboratory that meshed architecture, engineering, and computing into a new vision of architectural research and teaching. Better known for what it grew into in 1985—the MIT Media Lab—it became quite likely *the* most influential model for creative computational research and practice.

AMG was intentionally multidisciplinary: while located in the Department of Architecture, half of its student researchers came from the Department of Electrical Engineering. MIT's Undergraduate Research Opportunities Program (UROP), founded in 1969, encouraged undergraduates to work in a research capacity at MIT, which is how the mix of student researchers came to AMG. In 1971 AMG supported eight students a semester, growing to fifteen per semester, and by 1975 there were roughly one hundred AMG "enthusiasts."[1] While it might be assumed that a research lab would be the realm of graduate students and faculty, Negroponte noted that the UROP students were the ones who were most fully devoted to the lab, many continuing on to master's and doctoral degrees, joining the faculty, and becoming a part of the Media Lab after its founding in 1985; some are still there.[2]

Negroponte believed that as architecture students worked with both the tangible and the representational, they needed different teaching methods than the abstract, symbolic techniques taught in computer science thus far.[3] "The student of architecture is an inherently tactile person," he wrote in *Soft Architecture Machines*, "accustomed not only to working with his hands but also to physical and graphical manifestations; and he is accustomed to playing with those." Learning to program and experiment with various input/output devices like tablets, light pens, CRTs, and plotters provided students with "a way of thinking about thinking."[4] Technological experimentation produced the method and the material for

further exploration. This concept undergirded the "demo or die" ethos of the lab, where students continually demonstrated their projects to lab visitors (who included politicians, CEOs, cultural figures, and potential sponsors), ensuring that the technology worked at least well enough to grant an idea of the project, even if it was just smoke and mirrors.[5]

Projects such as the URBAN 5 computing system, designed by Negroponte and Groisser, grew out of the Computer-Aided Urban Design class they began teaching in 1968. Projects from the late 1970s onward, such as the Spatial Data Management System and the Media Room, spawned master's theses and dissertations like the Aspen Movie Map, a proto-Google Map and Street View application that allowed its user to "drive" down streets in Aspen, Colorado from an Eames chair equipped with joysticks in its armrests.

Early on, Negroponte explored possibilities for funding architectural research. In the preface to his 1966 master's thesis he raised many of the questions that would resurface when he started the Media Lab almost twenty years later—and that many architecture and design schools still grapple with today:

> as a profession we have made few preparations and have done little research. All this work must take place within the academic world as we have no General Motors or NASA to sponsor philanthropic research. However, schools of architecture are still trade schools by nature and not compatible, at this moment, with the process of research. The design process for the student is usually not a serious synthesis or analysis process, rather it is the execution of disjointed ideas and feelings.[6]

During Negroponte's time as student, professor, and lab founder at MIT, this would change dramatically: the $256 that counted as research funding in the

< URBAN 5 system, showing the blocks onscreen and the user making selections with the light pen in dialogue with the system.

v Aspen Movie Map, as driven from the Eames chair in the Media Room. To the left, a street map showing precise location; to the right, an aerial view. Photograph by Robert Mohl.

entire Department of Architecture in 1965 became $198,255 in 1970 and $1,000,000 in 1980, due in large part to AI and computer-related research funded by the Department of Defense.

Similar to the MIT AI Lab, the majority of AMG's funding came from defense research contracts with the Advanced Research Projects Agency (ARPA— later DARPA) and the Office of Naval Research (ONR), among others; the contribution from non-defense sources, such as the National Science Foundation and private corporations, was much smaller. For most of AMG's lifespan, this meant that the majority of its projects needed to demonstrate a tactical military application, as a consequence of the Mansfield Amendment of 1969, which prohibited the use of defense funding for basic research. As research funding for AI and other advanced computing topics began to wane in the early 1970s, Negroponte and AMG followed the lead of Patrick Winston, director of the MIT AI Lab from 1972 to 1997, who encouraged researchers to explain their work in tactical military terms.[7] This seemed to present no conflict for Negroponte. When asked whether Vietnam had any impact on AMG's milieu—massive anti-war protests shook the MIT campus for years—he admitted that

he had attended a couple of large rallies but otherwise had remained all but "oblivious."[8]

In 1985 AMG folded into the MIT Media Lab following a seven-year, $40 million fundraising effort by Negroponte and former MIT President, Jerome Wiesner, in which forty corporations pledged their precommercial research budget to the lab. The commercial funding allowed the Media Lab to grow much larger than the Architecture Machine Group could ever have become. In 2019 its annual operating budget was approximately $75 million—still primarily corporate-funded.[9] When the Media Lab became embroiled in a scandal around financial support from the convicted sex trafficker Jeffrey Epstein in 2019,[10] Negroponte publicly stated in a town hall meeting at the Media Lab that he would have supported the donations even if he had known Epstein's crimes (a statement he later walked back).

How should we tally the history of AMG? Negroponte built new models of research in architecture that still shape the technical imaginary. Indeed, the Media Lab made tech sexy, expanding the possibilities for its creative development and use in ways that changed the cultural status of technology. And yet, while its impact is undeniably important, there are still important questions to ask about the history of AMG and the Media Lab. Why did Vietnam have no impact on AMG? What are the ethics of the Media Lab's fundraising, and why did it exist in a state of exception? What happens when sponsors, be they defense or commercial, so heavily shape the terms of research? What happens when research is only what can be demonstrated or deployed? And, most importantly, who benefits and who is harmed?

< Individuals gather in the offices of the MIT Science Action Coordinating Committee in 1969.

Syllabus for "Making a Place in the Country," James Campe and Sim Van der Ryn, College of Environmental Design, University of California, Berkeley, Fall 1971.

1. Rosters and official counts were not kept by AMG in Negroponte's personal papers or AMG's archives at MIT; there are fifty-four bachelor's and master's theses on file at MIT from the Architecture Machine Group years.
2. Molly Wright Steenson, *Architectural Intelligence: How Designers and Architects Created the Digital Landscape* (Cambridge, MA: MIT Press, 2017), 262.
3. Nicholas Negroponte, *Soft Architecture Machines* (Cambridge, MA: MIT Press, 1975), 191.
4. Ibid.
5. Stewart Brand, *The Media Lab: Inventing the Future at MIT* (New York: Viking, 1987), 15.
6. Nicholas Negroponte, "The Computer Simulation of Perception During Motion in the Urban Environment," master's thesis (MIT, 1966), 2.
7. Steenson, *Architectural Intelligence*, 197.
8. Nicholas Negroponte, interviewed by Molly Steenson, Princeton, NJ, December 4, 2010.
9. MIT Media Lab, "About the Lab: Funding and Support," https://www.media.mit.edu/about/funding-and-support/.
10. Ronan Farrow, "How an Élite University Research Center Concealed Its Relationship with Jeffrey Epstein," *New Yorker*, September 6, 2019, https://www.newyorker.com/news/news-desk/how-an-elite-university-research-center-concealed-its-relationship-with-jeffrey-epstein.

architecture 102ABC   15 units (full-time)

making a place
in the country

fall 1971   mon-fri 8-5   J. campe, S. VanderRyn

MATERIAL ECOLOGIES

AN AGRICULTURAL SCHOOL AS A PEDAGOGICAL EXPERIMENT

Pelin Tan

Protagonist Musa Alami (1897–1984)
Institution Alami Farm
Location Jericho, Palestine
Dates 1949–1967

In 1949 Palestinian politician Musa Alami established an agricultural school in Jericho with the mission of hosting and educating refugee children displaced by the 1948 war that followed the Israeli declaration of independence.[1] For many, including the Lebanese writer Cecil A. Hourani, the school would soon be seen as "perhaps the most interesting agricultural, social, and educational experiment being conducted in the Middle East."[2]

Born into a prominent Jerusalem family, Alami studied law at Cambridge University. On his return home he became involved in nationalist politics and represented Palestine at a number of important negotiations, including the London Conference in 1939, which was called to plan an end to the British Mandate.[3] Anticipating this end, Alami founded the Arab Development Society (ADS) in 1945 "to assure the welfare of Arab refugees following the British withdrawal from Palestine in 1948."[4]

What Alami did not anticipate was the 1948 war or the seizure by Israel of his property in Jerusalem and agricultural land in the Baysan and Jaffa districts. Himself displaced, Alami moved to Jericho and, continuing the project of the ADS, founded the experimental farm and school on an initially unpromising site—two thousand acres of arid land on the West Bank of the Jordan valley, alongside the Jerusalem–Amman road, and seven miles north of the Dead Sea.[5]

Initially housing eighteen refugee families, the settlement that Alami founded was not only a farm but a self-sustaining habitat—a model town in which schooling and collective care of the land became, simultaneously, an experiment in new relations with the territory and a praxis and a tool for decolonization.[6]

The settlement would grow to encompass forty-five architectural structures including not only houses but a school, clinic, conference room, swimming pool, and fishing pools. All living quarters included a kitchen, lavatory, shower, and a small verandah; larger homes would have two living rooms, smaller ones just one.[7] The construction was in mud brick baked in the sun, which, as Alami pointed out, "provides excellent insulation against the heat." Even though "cement, timber, and plumbing materials all had to be purchased at high prices," the average cost of each house was just 280 Jordan dinars ($784).[8] Construction was partly funded by a grant to the ADS from the Arab League Economic Committee.[9] With the discovery of springs on the site, the farm was fully productive by 1951 and capable of large-scale cultivation by 1955.[10] Simultaneously, the farm engaged in the education and vocational training of the refugee children, teaching a range of skills that were in high demand in the Arab world, from electrical engineering to weaving, from carpentry to metalwork.[11]

The settlement endured several violent attacks. The farm was destroyed in Arab riots against the British in 1958 but rebuilt with funds from the Ford Foundation and World Bank. It was then attacked a number of times by Zionists, who damaged the irrigation infrastructure. But according to David Gilmour, who interviewed Alami in Jericho in February 1979, both the farm and the school survived, and continued to be highly successful, until the Israeli invasion in 1967, which laid waste to two thirds of the land and destroyed all but one of the twenty-seven wells.[12] Alami was not allowed to rebuild or restore the irrigation system.[13]

If the approach of the project—modernist, nationalist, and developmentalist—was very much in line with the impetuses of its time, the farm nevertheless built an alternative utopian pedagogy, working through education (knowledge production) and cultivation (rooting in the earth/land). In this respect, its experimental condition was in dialogue with other projects in the Jordan valley that sought to provide urgent solutions and housing for Palestinian communities during the 1940 and 1950s—including the refugee housing built in the West Bank by the Egyptian architect Hassan Fathy.[14]

The activities of Musa Alami's farm school—cultivation, agricultural production, caring for clean soil and crops, protecting seeds, sustaining livestock—could be seen as an anticolonial structure, a praxis and a tool of decolonization. In relation to Kathryn Yusoff's claims that the Anthropocene exhibits a colonial geology and the racialized territorialization of the earth,[15] Alami Farm took on a particularly relevant role in the occupied Palestinian lands,

which are still subject to extreme environmental exploitation and degradation as a result of the settler colonization process. And yet, as sociologist Salim Tamari has indicated, the farm and school project received some criticism from local activists in the initial period of its establishment because they felt the agricultural project would "normalize" the status of Palestinian refugees in the Jordan Valley and thereby defuse the issue of their return to their original homes.

Today, Musa Alami Farm functions as a dairy producer and most of the 1950s buildings (a significant modernist legacy) are still standing. With the exception of the conference room, however, they are unused, almost ruins—but they still bear witness to an important pedagogical project and anticolonial structure.[16]

< Musa Alami Farm in Jericho, Palestine. Frames from video footage by the Arab Development Society, c. 1955. Included in the video installation by Susanne Bosch, Alter Nationality, 2018.

1. The displacement of the Palestinian population is commemorated annually on 15 May, Nakba Day—the "Day of the Catastrophe."
2. Cecil A. Hourani, "Experimental Village in the Jordan Valley," *Middle East Journal* 5, no. 4 (Autumn 1951): 497–501.
3. https://en.m.wikipedia.org/wiki/Musa_Alami
4. The description is included in the archives of Musa Alami Farm held at the ADS Archives in Jerusalem and the ADS Collection at the Middle East Centre Archive, St. Antony's College, University of Oxford. The archives include flyers, moving images of the farm activities, the first design plan, photos.
5. Kennett Love, "Mr. Alami's Oasis," *New York Times* (1953).
6. I am using the term decolonization as describing the praxis of the project.
7. Love, "Mr. Alami's Oasis."
8. Hourani, "Experimental Village in the Jordan Valley."
9. From the description included in the archives of Musa Alami Farm. Further source: Sir Geoffrey Furlonge, *Palestine Is My Country: The Story of Musa Alami* (New York, Washington: Praeger, 1969), 167–211.
10. Ibid.
11. Ibid.
12. David Gilmour, *Dispossessed: The Ordeal of the Palestinians, 1917–1980* (1982), 128–129.
13. Ibid. "The Israeli army systematically smashed the irrigation system, the buildings and the well-boring machinery. Most of the land quickly reverted to desert. ...A chunk of land was predictably wired off for 'security reasons' and turned into a military camp. It is now deserted, ...the Israelis refused to allow him to buy the necessary equipment either to restore the damaged wells or to drill new ones. So he made some manual repairs to four of the least damaged wells and with these he was able to salvage a fraction of the land and keep the farm and the school functioning. ...[The Israelis] are now telling him that he has too much water—though he has less than a fifth of what he used to have—and have warned him that they will be fixing a limit on his consumption and will be taking away the surplus for their own 'projects' (i.e. their expanding settlements near Jericho)."
14. Susanne Bosch and Salim Tamari, "The Miracle of Holy Land?" Public talk (January 5, 2013) hosted by Birzeit University Museum and International Academy of Art, Palestine.
15. Kathryn Yusoff, *A Billion Black Anthropocenes or None* (Minneapolis: University of Minnesota, 2018), page loc. 1676 (Kindle format).
16. I would like to thank artist Susanne Bosch, architect Jens Haendeler, the Arab Development Society members, and Alami Farm workers for their help with archival and field research on the Alami Farm (March–October 2019). German artist Susanne Bosch has focused on the archive of the Alami Farm and assembled an archival installation. I conducted a teaching workshop for Al-Quds University art and spatial practice students on geontology and the Anthropocene in the seminar building at Alami Farm in March 2019.

CLIMATE AND ARCHITECTURAL REGIONALISM

Daniel A. Barber

Protagonists Victor Olgyay (1910–1970),
Aladar Olgyay (1910–1963)
Institution Princeton Architectural Laboratory,
Princeton University
Location Princeton, NJ, USA
Dates 1952–1963

In 1952 the twin brothers Victor and Aladar Olgyay took over the Princeton Architectural Laboratory (PAL), a converted stable building that operated as a woodshop and modelmaking space, with a new extension—a glass cube—for daylight testing and other activities.[1] Hungarian émigrés, the brothers had previously worked at Notre Dame and MIT, in each case promoting methods of integrating new knowledge about climate patterns into the design process. Over the next decade at the PAL, they would work through the ways architects could integrate climate data into modern design techniques.

The Olgyays were employed primarily as research professors, their salaries partly paid by grants from the Rockefeller Foundation and the National Science Foundation. Working with a number of students and faculty in the PAL, they developed a precise method to consider regional climatic conditions that was first summarized in a 1953 article in *Architectural Forum*, "The Temperate House," then further clarified and updated in *Solar Control and Shading Devices* (1957) and the more prominent *Design with Climate* (1963).[2] The diagram they used

to communicate the method was first drawn in 1952, and repeated in numerous iterations over the subsequent decade.[2] Though opaque to the uninitiated, it laid out steps to consider climate early in the design process, and was intended for both students and practitioners.

The Olgyays' research was in the service of a broader pedagogical program: to inflect and reconfigure design methods to take environmental factors into account. Victor Olgyay's course, Architectural Research 516: Climate and Architectural Regionalism, set out the basic premise. "The primary task of architecture," Olgyay wrote, "is to act in man's favor"—evidence of both the brothers' approach to design and their deep investment in a consistent concept of "man" amidst all the tumult of the postwar period. The work of architecture, they believed, was to provide a comfortable space for maintaining a set of persistent values: both in terms of data that could be measured (consistent thermal interior) and as a social foundation for evaluating design (traditional social patterns).

Architecture Research 516 was premised on two essential ideas. The first was that "the shelter which works with, not against, the forces of nature and which makes use of its potentialities to create better living conditions, may be called 'climate balanced.'" The imperative for *balance* was a central aspect of the radical conservatism of the Olgyays' approach: for them, the promise of modern architecture lay in the capacity to use design tools to offset disrupting factors in the thermal interior, in any region. The second premise was that this balanced design would articulate a new formal disposition that reflected a specific *regional* condition: "As architecture a structure then expresses regional character." Their subsequent research clarifying the parameters of the user's "comfort zone" also aimed to find forms and explore materials so as to produce a consistent thermal space for a building's inhabitants.[3]

Parallel to the Olgyays' work at the PAL, new research was providing a greater understanding of geophysical patterns and their effects on human life. Just down the road at the Institute of Advanced Studies in Princeton, the mathematician John von Neumann was, from the late 1940s, using an early mainframe computer to model and predict weather patterns.[4] Through this research, biologists, physicists, and ecologists were beginning to adjust models of "nature" away from the concepts of balance, harmony, and peak conditions, and toward an understanding of the chaos and unpredictability

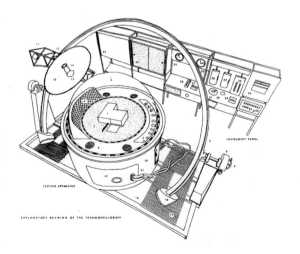

EXPLANATORY DRAWING OF THE THERMOHELIODON

of the biosphere.[5] Such conceptions developed into complex models aiming to capture the vagaries of global weather patterns; into theories of chaos and interconnection; and into the rapid increase in climate knowledge that eventually led to the climate models of the present.

In this context, the consistency and reliability the Olgyays were invested in could be seen as a desperate attempt to maintain a measure of predictability in the midst of increasing knowledge about the contingencies of human life. Theirs was a conservative, almost nostalgic approach at a time of changing conditions for knowledge production. But the radicality of their pedagogy derives not from this conservative aspect, but from its unintended effects: they pioneered methods to use design, rather than mechanical systems, to produce a thermally consistent space. The data, parameters, and techniques they used were later absorbed by ASHRAE and other regulatory bodies. In effect, they constructed a framework for architecture that placed the thermal experience in the center.

The broader architectural appeal of the Olgyays' discourse revolved around the development of devices to model and test climate conditions in a laboratory setting, so as to predict performance in the real world. In 1957, working with a group of students in the lab, they built the Thermoheliodon. The device simulated solar path, humidity, wind, soil conditions, and other climatic factors. Though never fully functional and frustratingly analog, it was nonetheless a vast improvement on the heliodons and other devices intended to help architects make choices related to site, region, and climate. Other researchers developed similar devices—at the University of Sydney, the University of Kansas, and later Arizona State University—and also pursued pedagogical models for climate engagement. The programming of the first climate-focused environmental performance software programs, Eco-tect, would be based on the Olgyays' 1952 diagram. Their work helped to bring climate issues to the foreground of architectural forms of social articulation, in a moment just before fossil-fuel-based HVAC systems assumed command over the thermal interior.

∧ Victor and Aladar Olgyay, method of climatic interpretation in buildings, 1952.

∨ Jean Labatut, et al., Princeton Architectural Laboratory, view of the building with student experiments, 1948.

< Victor and Aladar Olgyay, "Explanatory Drawing of the Thermoheliodon Device," from the Report on the Thermoheliodon, 1957.

1. The glass cube was added in 1947 by Jean Labatut, director of the architecture program at Princeton. On the PAL before the Olgyays arrived, see Matthew F. Clarke, "Jean Labatut and Éducation à pied d'oeuvre: The Princeton Architectural Laboratory" in Princeton University Library Chronicle (2008).
2. Victor Olgyay, "The Temperate House," Architectural Forum 94, no. 3 (March 1951): 180–189; Aladar Olgyay and Victor Olgyay, Solar Control and Shading Devices (New York: Reinhold, 1957); Victor Olgyay, Design with Climate: Bioclimatic Approach to Architectural Regionalism (Princeton, NJ: Princeton University Press, 2016). A longer discussion of their work and its effects, as well as a more complete list of their published work, can be found in Daniel A. Barber, Modern Architecture and Climate: Design before Air Conditioning (Princeton, NJ: Princeton University Press, 2020).
3. See Daniel A. Barber, "The Nature of the Image: Olgyay and Olgyay's Architectural-Climatic Drawings in the 1950s," Public Culture 29, no. 1 (January 2017): 129–164.
4. See, for example, The Dynamics of Climate: Conference on the Application of Numerical Integration Techniques to the Problem of General Circulation, ed. John von Neumann et al. (Princeton, NJ: Institute for Advanced Study, 1955). The ENIAC computer Neumann used was located at the Aberdeen Proving Grounds, an Army base in Maryland, but the research was centered at the IAS.
5. Michael G. Barbour, "Ecological Fragmentation in the Fifties," in Uncommon Ground: Rethinking the Human Place in Nature, ed. William Cronon (New York: Norton, 1996), 233–255.

SOFT MACHINES, CELLULAR SYNTHETIC ENVIRONMENTS

Lydia Kallipoliti

Protagonists Wolf Hilbertz (1938-2007)
(Responsive Environments Laboratory) and
Charles Harker (1945-) (Tao Design Group)
Institution University of Texas at Austin
Location Austin, TX, USA
Dates 1968-1973

Horror, as Virginia Woolf once suggested in "The Cinema," is all in all the anticipation of formlessness: constant change and indeterminacy.[1] Sprayed with a gun, or grown on a mesh, the design-build experiments of Charles Harker and Wolf Hilbertz at the University of Texas at Austin exhibited this fear: material behaviors that resisted premeditated design intent. A further unsettling effect of their pedagogical experiments was instilled in the increased proximity between the architect and the object, as the mediation of representation was firmly rejected. Even though Harker and Hilbertz never worked together while contemporaries at the same institution in the 1970s, they were both dogmatic in their opposition to the canon of plan, section, elevation; no T-squares were anywhere near their studios. Instead, they used lists of processes in the form of manuals and codes to be followed, then observed vigilantly, in order for rules to be overridden.

Considering the earlier constellation of instructors at UT Austin during the 1950s, famously known as the Texas Rangers, the convergence of Harker and Hilbertz under the deanship of Alan Y. Taniguchi proposed an entirely different pedagogical agenda than that of the Rangers, who descended from Josef Albers' teaching at the Bauhaus. Harker asked his students to spray polyurethane, while Hilbertz deployed photo-polymerizable polymers, yet both were committed to an evolutionary design logic based on material phase changes. They also understood the architect's agency as dynamically editing data and physical phenomena, rather than proposing a formal vision of a new reality. In determining undercuts, complex extrusions and intersections of space, the learning process was based on the direction of parameters, some of which depended on deep knowledge of material properties as well as chemical interactions.

Each in their own ways, Hilbertz and Harker advocated for "soft machines," evoking an authorship ethos on the fragile line between architecture and "nonarchitecture." This objective was in alliance with other

significant pedagogical initiatives at the time, such as Nicholas Negroponte's and the MIT Architecture Machine Group's outlook of the computer as the "anti-architect" in the landmark book *Soft Architecture Machines* in 1975,[2] or Robin Evans's evocation of "anarchitecture" or the "tectonics of non-control" in his thesis on piezoelectrics at the Architectural Association in London in 1969.[3] Like Negroponte and Evans, Hilbertz and Harker endorsed user participation in the design process and turned their design-build studios into open-source educational platforms bringing together different authors and mediums. Hilbertz and Evans introduced the concept of "interference" as an external environmental occurrence of creative disruption to the expected turn of events. For both these authors, interference was not blocking the course of actions, but revealing a path that would otherwise have been invisible in the design process.

In 1971, as a research associate and adjunct instructor at UT Austin, Harker founded a private nonprofit organization, the Tao Design Group Inc., to pursue the work he had begun in his thesis, "Supramorphics."[4] On a six-acre site in Hill County, west of Austin, Harker and his group explored the creative potential of plastic materials in pedagogical design-build experiments. The first realized project, Earth House, was made possible with a $25,000 grant for plastics applications in the Development of Habitable Sculptures; it was exhibited at the Pompidou Centre in Paris in 1975 and in the exhibition *Transformations in Modern Architecture*, curated by Arthur Drexler at the Museum of Modern Art in New York in 1979. Beyond a material property, the term plastic indicated for the group a construction process where the original intention was continually reinvented through the act of building itself. Harker was quite assertive in dismissing architectural

blueprints on site. His denial, nevertheless, was founded on less prescriptive rule-based systems that allowed the collective group of authors to visualize a constantly evolving form. In this light, Harker juxtaposed Le Corbusier's "machine for living" with a concept for habitation that he termed a "soft machine": *form as the articulation of a set of interacting forces* and of matter as patterns of energy that come to be solidified in time. For Harker the "soft machine" would actively modify the individual's psychological effects of buildings to the individual, through the effective use of form, space, and color. As he argued, "we have little idea of the effects of our environment on the human animal."[5]

Hilbertz moved to UT Austin in 1970 from the Southern University in Baton Rouge, Louisiana, where he was an assistant professor. An architect and marine scientist from Germany, Hilbertz was for different reasons also contemptuous of architectural representation. Upon his arrival, and at the initiative of Dean Taniguchi, Hilbertz founded the Responsive Environments Laboratory, where he developed his research on the automated creation of the built environment. With his students, Hilbertz produced forms using computer-controlled light configuration interference patterns and photo-polymerizable materials, exploring flexible working systems of structural erection and reclamation around computer-controlled devices for extruding or spraying inorganic plastic construction materials. In his lab, light configuration interference patterns outlined the contour of the desired structures,[6] while plastic monomers mixed with light-sensitive catalysts were introduced into the light pattern and accreted as polymerized plastics on the surface described by the pattern.

Hilbertz was largely interested in navigating material evolution as a partially controlled design process to create patterns and forces that would eventually result in a built form. While this line of thinking was closely allied to Harker's experiments, Hilbertz showed a greater dedication to technological mediation and instrumentation through analysis, monitoring, and testing. He viewed the environment as an evolutionary code and the interfacing of information and form-generating systems. In the later years of his tenure at Austin, Hilbertz investigated processes of electro-accretion as a means of growing shelters from sea minerals (coral reefs) and developed the electro-accumulated substance now called *biorock*, later patented along with Thomas J. Goreau.[7] Still, Hilbertz was committed to using the discipline of architecture, coining the term "cybertecture" (CYBERnetics+ archiTECTURE) to outline a conceptual, as well as a technical framework for an evolutionary environmental system organized ecosystematically, analogous to open living systems.[8]

Both Hilbertz and Harker searched for systems and codes of underlying patterns, a type of analog computation that would allow for variable pattern reproduction. In their minds, the fields of ecology and cybernetics converged in their reflection with the architectural discipline. Environmental concerns did not equate to a list of responsibilities and pragmatic liabilities, but to the gestation of environments as new types of natures that triggered environmental cognition and required a dialectical reassessment of subject and milieu. Such concerns necessitated relentless experimentation with matter, as well as a theorization of the design process that originated from the study of living systems. Controlling the growth of materials and directing the evolution of material interactions prescribed a design practice of semi-control, which allowed contingent parameters from the expanded environment to be directly integrated into the process of making.

The same willingness to relinquish complete control that defined the "soft machine" also extended to pedagogical matters. Most of Hilbertz's and Harker's workshops were short-lived intense assignments, producing living prototypes or inhabitable installations. They were also social experiments, requiring participants to work together as a collective force. Rather than a studio guided and controlled by the professor, these events were more about collective production, exhaustion, and the process of how a small community of authors and piles of materials form and reform. The concept of "softness" therefore applied not only to the articulation of formal elements but also to a renewed sense of collective agency and authorship that called for the dissolution of the designer's ego.

These architectural experiments unfolded as part of a critical disciplinary shift arising from the epistemological intersection of ecology and cybernetics: rather than the materialization of substances into form and objects, their focus was on the examination of matter as patterns of crystallized energy.[9] The experiments also called into question conventional means of representing disciplinary knowledge and the language of the design process. Pictorial environmental representations became less relevant, giving way to performance equations and statistical information. The enduring legacy of the pedagogy of Harker and Hilbertz remains the conflict of image versus code and the idealization of "softness" as a type of authorship that leaves space for external interference, indicating the end of the natural world as a passive, conceptualized, and historicized context of observation within which architecture is placed.

« Derrick Hilbertz with Wolf Hilbertz's catenary formation by accretion, Port Aransas, Texas, c. 1978.

< Charles Harker & the Tao Design Group, Earth House, Austin, Texas, 1972.

1. Virginia Woolf, *Selected Essays,* ed. David Bradshaw (Oxford: Oxford University Press, 2008), 172–177. Woolf's essay "The Cinema" was originally published in *Arts* (June 1926).
2. Nicholas Negroponte, *Soft Architecture Machines* (Cambridge, MA: MIT Press, 1975), 1.
3. See Robin Evans, *Translations from Drawing to Building* (Cambridge, MA: MIT Press, 1997), 11.
4. Charles Harker, "Supramorphics: Beyond the Specified Form" (self-published in blurb.com, 2009). "Supramorphics" was based on Harker's thesis and theories written at the University of Texas at Austin written between 1968 and 1972.
5. Harker, "Supramorphics," 2009. At Charles Harker, "Tao Design Group," http://web.mac.com/charker/TAO_Design_Group/, accessed November 2006.
6. Wolf Hilbertz and Joseph Mathis, "Space Form Manipulation," *Architectural Design* 53, no. 11 (November 1973): 683.
7. Patented with Thomas J. Goreau. See Wolf Hilbertz, "Electrodeposition of Minerals in Sea Water: Experiments and Applications," *IEEE Journal of Oceanic Engineering* 4, no. 3 (July 1979): 94–113.
8. Wolf Hilbertz, "Toward Cybertecture," *Progressive Architecture* (May 1970): 98.
9. Gregory Bateson describes this dialectic as a primordial philosophical debate in his paper "Form, Substance and Difference" in the Nineteenth Annual Korzynski Memorial Lecture, delivered on January 9, 1970 under the auspices of the Institute of General Semantics. It was originally published in the *General Semantics Bulletin,* no. 37 (1970). With the permission of the institute, Bateson republished the lecture in his book *Steps to an Ecology of Mind: Collected Essays in Anthropology, Psychiatry, Evolution, and Epistemology* (San Francisco: Chandler Publications, 1972), 455ff.

THE "OUTLAW BUILDERS" STUDIO

Anna Goodman

Protagonists Sym Van der Ryn (1935–)
and James (Jim) Campe (1942–)
Institutions University of California,
Berkeley, Farallones Designs
Locations Inverness, CA, and Berkeley, CA, USA
Dates 1971–1972

Architectural education has long been a place to experiment with notions of individual and collective production. Less explored have been the lines between designer, builder, and user, which Sim Van der Ryn's and James Campe's "Making a Place in the Country" studio took as its subject matter. They obliterated the lines between those agents, both in the embodied experience of the studio itself and, importantly, in its documentation and circulation via new approaches to print media. Their radical approach located human and material inputs within a broad understanding of the total social and ecological environment.

American architect Sim Van der Ryn moved to Berkeley, California in the early 1960s from the University of Michigan without any clear mission other than to distance himself from the strictures of functionalism. After working in a number of local offices he found himself in 1964 teaching at UC Berkeley alongside Christopher Alexander, just as the soon-to-be famous "pattern language" author pivoted his interest in computer networks to an affinity for the vernacular. In several of his early courses at Berkeley, Van der Ryn asked students to analyze common tools such as hammers, can openers, and lathes and then to break them into a series of related and unrelated characteristics. These analyses resulted in elaborate matrixes of qualities, processes, and outcomes.[1] In the budding milieu of postwar developments in computer science, the disaggregation of material and social properties fitted into a new approach to part and whole within architecture.

At the same time, Van der Ryn became interested in material reuse, hands-on learning, and behavioral

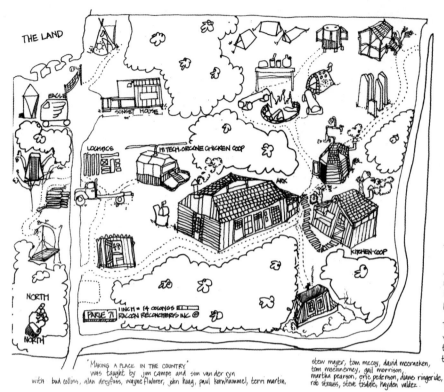

THE LAND

EAGLE
SUNSET HOUSE
LOGISTICS
HI TECH-ORGONE CHICKEN COOP
ARK
KITCHEN-COOP
NORTH
NORTH
1 INCH = 14 COLONGS
PARK 71 RACOON RECRUITERS INC @

This is a record of a TEN week SECOND year university class in architecture which took place THREE consecutive days a week on a FIVE acre wilderness site

The class was designed to give some actual experience in how to make a place in the country – learning something of the process of building a livable situation in harmony with the setting and ourselves. A learning situation directly connected to life's flow, survival, sharing skills.

There was no place within the university where we could live together, prepare food together, build structures.... so we chose the country. A place where the awareness of change in ourselves, in our place, is too great not to be recognized.

We grew under the sky rather than under a ceiling. We worked to the sounds of nature, rather than the hum of flourescent lights. We came together in a time and place that was right for us as a group.

This publication is about our coming together; what we built, how we lived, and what we thought about the process that determined the form of "our place in the country."

"MAKING A PLACE IN THE COUNTRY" was taught by jim campe and sim van der ryn with bud collins, alan dreyfuss, wayne fluhrer, john haag, paul kornhummel, terri martin,

stew mayer, tom mccoy, david mccracken, tom mcinerney, gail morrison, martha pearson, eric pederson, diane ringeride, rob strauss, steve tisdale, hayden valdez.

observation methods within learning environments. As Timothy Stott has demonstrated, Van der Ryn joined other Berkeley faculty in engaging school children to elaborate and test new notions of "human ecologies,"[2] focusing on process, creative collaboration, and iteration in response to user behaviors. With James Campe and other students, Van der Ryn organized a practice—Farallones Designs—to promote reuse and hands-on engagement with the physical world. One of their first efforts was to help young children reconstruct their school environments using found materials. This would be the start of a series of studios in which architecture students tested how deep learning might result from a combination of play and collaboration in the production of the built environment.

Soon after, fleeing Berkeley's fraught political environment in 1969, Van der Ryn took his family out of the city to Inverness, California, a rugged and isolated piece of land pushed against the sea.[3] In this context, the presence of "place" in the title of the course he taught with Campe, "Making a Place in the Country" (Fall 1971), can be seen to refer more to events happening on and around Berkeley's campus than to the term "placemaking" engaged by thinkers with phenomenological commitments during this

period. Both Van der Ryn's study of the lack of communal facilities in campus dorms (1967) and his advocacy on behalf of activists during the People's Park protests (May 1969) indicate that he was interested in supporting citizens' efforts to claim the built environment for their own uses.

The Making a Place in the Country studio brought architectural education back to the simplest acts of human–environment exchange—from subsistence agriculture to basic carpentry—and asked students to experiment via hard physical labor and serious play with the boundaries between their individual and collective identities. Operating within the undergraduate curriculum, the course substituted for fifteen units of integrative design credit for Berkeley architecture students. Participants built rudimentary shelters and camps on site but also kept their bases in Berkeley. In a collectively constructed workshop named "The Arc," they used found and recycled materials to build small structures that served both communal needs and personal development, including a kitchen, sauna, chicken coop, and various structures for resting and individual contemplation. The goal of these communal forms of work and living was to free the participants from the rigidity of existing architectural forms and the institutional control they represented and enforced. Like other contemporary groups—such as Ant Farm, operating nearby in San Francisco—the studio sought an alternative to the prevailing forms of living, even if the bricolage of the Inverness constructions was very distant from the futuristic aesthetics of Ant Farm's inflatables.

While the experiment only lasted ten weeks, it produced several important outcomes for students and faculty. First, it rearticulated the meaning of practice away from notions of expertise. In Inverness, students learned skills as they performed them and became teachers in turn, an approach shared with the contemporary advocacy planning and community design movements. Those groups, however, saw the built environment as a realm for power struggles, whereas Van der Ryn and his crew focused on a holistic vision of human–environmental relations. Second, the studio reshaped its participants' view of technology as an acting agent within the architectural process. Rather than a means toward a specific end, the studio integrated systems thinking and advanced materials with intuitive processes and vernacular knowledge. Their focus on the cyclical process of harvesting and recycling energy and other resources responded not just to countercultural environmentalism but also to the work of Christopher Alexander and the contemporaneous rise of studies of "traditional" environments.

Upon returning to Berkeley, Campe ran a four-credit course in which students evaluated and communicated their experience in Inverness, supplementing the photographic documentation and drawing required by the studio with self-reflective writing exercises. The result was the *Outlaw Builders News,* which was distributed on the streets of Berkeley. In the do-it-yourself spirit of the *Whole Earth Catalog,* it described the students' approach to living in dialogue with the natural environment and how this related more broadly to ecological and human systems.[4] From their first experiments in elementary schools, the loose group circulating around Van der Ryn and Campe had used the term *outlaw* to signal a shared anti-institutional attitude.[5] In various guises, they slipped in and out of the university curriculum, making use of its resources while offering alternative visions of design production.

In 1974 Van der Ryn and Campe left the university to found their own teaching and research center, the Farallones Institute (1974), which had a rural campus in Occidental, California and an urban base at Berkeley's Integral Urban House.[6]

They continued to undertake technological experiments that grappled with the problems of energy and waste recycling and, within a few years, Van der Ryn's appointment as State Architect of California helped bring ecological design to the forefront of the field.[7] Commentators have pointed out the paradox of an "outlaw builder" in the heart of government bureaucracy.[8] Yet it is hard to see how Van der Ryn could have passed on the opportunity to supervise and design government projects and to organize policy toward what soon became known as "sustainable" ends. Ultimately, his systems approach found an easy fit with the technological developments of later twentieth-century architecture and governmental culture. The radical reorganization of the human–ecological relationship, however, remained much more elusive.

< Site plan for "Making a Place in the Country," 1971. From The Outlaw Building News, Farallones Institute, Spring 1972.

≪ The Arc, Inverness, California, 1971.

1. Sim Van der Ryn Archives, College of Environmental Design, University of California, Berkeley, Folder: Architecture 6 1961–65 II.1.
2. Timothy Stott, "Ludic Pedagogies at the College of Environmental Design, UC Berkeley, 1966 to 1972," in *The Culture of Nature in the History of Design*, ed. Kjetil Fallan (London: Routledge, 2019), 58–72.
3. Sim Van der Ryn, "Making a Place in the Country," in *Design on the Edge: A Century of Teaching Architecture at the University of California, Berkeley, 1903-2003*, ed. Waverly Lowell, Elizabeth Byrne, and Betsy Frederick-Rothwell (Berkeley: College of Environmental Design, University of California, Berkeley, 2009), 189–191.
4. Simon Sadler, "An Architecture of the Whole," *Journal of Architectural Education* 61, no. 4 (May 2008): 108–129.
5. "Making a Place in the Country," *Outlaw Building News*, Spring 1972.
6. Greg Castillo, "Counterculture Terroir: California's Hippie Enterprise Zone," in *Hippie Modernism: The Struggle for Utopia*, ed. Andrew Blauvelt et al. (Minneapolis: Walker Art Center, 2015), 87–101.
7. Richard Ingersoll, "The Ecology Question and Architecture," in *The SAGE Handbook of Architectural Theory*, ed. C. G. Crysler, S. Cairns, and H. Heynen (London: SAGE, 2012), 573–589.
8. Simon Sadler, "The Bateson Building, Sacramento, California, 1977-81, and the Design of a New Age State," *Journal of the Society of Architectural Historians* 75, no. 4 (December 1, 2016): 469–489.

GARBAGE BUILDING

Curt Gambetta

Protagonist Martin Pawley (1938–2008)
Institutions Cornell University, Rensselaer
Polytechnic Institute (RPI), Florida A&M University
(FAMU), University of California, Los Angeles (UCLA)
Locations Ithaca, NY; Troy, NY; Tallahassee, FL;
Los Angeles, CA, USA
Dates 1973–1979

Garbage Housing—a series of university research
programs and studios led by British architect and
critic Martin Pawley in the United States during
the 1970s—aimed to build cultural sensibility and
technical knowledge about the reuse of garbage as a
building material for low-cost housing. Allying studio
research with development work in the global South
and economically disadvantaged communities in the
North, the program experimented with construction
systems and emergency housing prototypes made
out of garbage, a process of cultural alchemy that
Pawley called "secondary use."[1] While his research
bears some resemblance to contemporary studies

of product lifecycles and sustainability more broadly,
what makes it distinct is its unabashed cultural
critique of property ownership in late-twentieth-
century consumer societies.

Pawley undertook Garbage Housing research at
four universities in the US after serving as a fifth-
year tutor at the AA in London from 1969 to 1972.
He started at Cornell University in 1973, before
moving on to Rensselaer Polytechnic Institute (RPI),
Florida A&M University (FAMU), and the University of
California, Los Angeles (UCLA). Hands-on research
focused on nuts-and-bolts problem-solving, using
physical constructions to prove the viability of
whether a particular housing problem could be
solved at little or no cost with garbage materials.
Typically, Pawley first provided students with a
brief for a housing project and directed them to
identify waste materials that were suitable for the
construction of 1:1 scale studies. According to former
students and collaborators, he favored a "put up or
shut up" approach emphasizing full-scale mockups
and hands-on work. Between hands-on experiments,
he assigned "sketch projects," which were carried out
at speed, rather than developed through protracted
architectural drawing, and supplemented with blocks

< Dora Crouch House, RPI, Troy, New York, 1975–1976. The house frame was made of paper tubes (from rolls of newsprint) and metal catering cans, sealed for use as jointing and spacing. Student pictured: Larry Birch.

v Students installing "roof tiles" made of neoprene discards from a local automobile parts manufacturer, Dora Crouch House, RPI, Troy, New York, 1975–1976.

of textual information about material flows and sources. Prototypes included designs for joinery, wall components, and self-supporting enclosure systems. For example, students at RPI studied the use of soup cans as prefabricated wall blocks and joinery for trusses made out of commercial paper tubes. Studio and thesis research would culminate in the construction of a full-scale house prototype. Though many of the house designs resulted in generic shells and familiar types, others were heretical send ups, including a Frei Otto-like net of tires constructed at FAMU and the cardboard substitute for a Corbusian weekend created by students at Cornell.

Design experiments were informed by Pawley's criticism of housing. In essays and books such as *Architecture versus Housing* (1971) and *Home Ownership* (1978), Pawley condemned the uniformity and permanence of both public housing and private, owner-occupied dwellings and outlined his ideas for an alternative approach to housing in a series of texts published under the rubric "Garbage Housing," including essays in *Architectural Design* in 1971 and 1973 and a book-length manifesto of 1975. Inspired by music festivals, cars, and nomadic architecture projects such as Archigram's *Instant City* (1969),

GARBAGE HOUSING
MARTIN PAWLEY

and social welfare during the 1970s. His studio at Cornell University proceeded from an agreement of support from the socialist government in Chile, but was disrupted by the military coup in 1973, midway through the semester. By the end of the 1970s, funding sources yoked Garbage Housing research to neoliberal housing policies and modes of governance. Research at FAMU was funded by modest state grants for the improvement of existing housing stock for economically disadvantaged, largely African American communities in rural north Florida. Besides studios and thesis projects, FAMU research included training workshops for potential users, anticipating that renters and house owners could improve their own housing by using free or low-cost waste materials for heating, ventilation, and other passive environmental systems. Growing emphasis on skills and self-driven building solutions showed that governance was not limited to the activities of the state, to paraphrase political theorist Wendy Brown.[2] Rather, governance extended to modes of personal conduct and self-calculation that were cultivated in the space of university research. Ultimately, though Pawley intended for students and house occupants to gain a sense of self-reliance by learning how to build with waste, the ephemerality of wasted objects seemed to reinforce the precarity of their life conditions. Like the waste that was used to construct it, Garbage Housing risked becoming a one-off use.

Pawley imagined Garbage Housing as cheap, mobile, and easily adaptable, allowing users to swap out disused waste components with great ease.

The Garbage Housing process conflated hands-on construction and maintenance, assigning responsibility for the housing to its occupants. In his AA diploma project, "The Time House" (1970), Pawley argued that ownership stemmed from an individual's acquisition and use of objects over time. Just as the students had sourced and adapted cans and bottles for walls, the imagined occupants of a Garbage House would gradually appropriate otherwise impersonal consumer products and in the process forge a unique and tactile relationship with their domestic environment. For Pawley, the ideal starting point for the large-scale application of Garbage Housing was housing for architecture students. As he observed in his 1975 book, architecture students were primed to build for themselves and were inherently transient. In youth culture, Pawley saw the glimmer of a new culture of fleeting ownership and itinerant living.

Over the course of their research, Pawley and his students were forced to confront the changing political dynamics of state support for housing

∧ Cover of Martin Pawley's book-length manifesto, *Garbage Housing*, 1975.

1. Martin Pawley, *Garbage Housing* (London: Architectural Press, 1975).
2. Wendy Brown, "Neoliberalism and the End of Liberal Democracy," in *Edgework: Critical Essays on Knowledge and Politics* (Princeton: Princeton University Press, 2005), 37.

HOW THE OTHER HALF BUILDS

Bushra Nayeem

Protagonists Balkrishna Vithaldas Doshi,
Witold Rybczynski, Vikram Bhatt
Institutions Vastu Shilpa Foundation (VSF),
Ahmedabad, India; The Minimum Cost Housing
Group (MCHG) of McGill University School of
Architecture, Montreal, Quebec, Canada
Locations Indore, Madhya Pradesh, India;
Montreal, Quebec, Canada
Dates 1983–1986

The Low-cost Urban Shelter (LUS) project was
established in 1982 as a North-South collaboration between the Minimum Cost Housing Group
(MCHG) at McGill University in Canada and the
Vastushilpa Foundation (VSF) in India. Its protagonists researched an overlooked area—the informal
housing sector—as a way to gain better understanding of the demand for low-income urban
shelters. For many urban planners and architects,
looking at slums as a source of solutions rather
than problems was a radical notion. But as this

pedagogical experiment showed, squatter settlements could provide an alternative method of
learning what people needed to build a shelter and
what could be achieved without planners or an elitist
education system that perpetuated structural
inequalities in the name of a universalizing discipline.

The MCHG had been set up in 1970 by the
Colombian architect Alvaro Ortega to conduct
research in the field of human settlements, specifically focused on housing problems in developing
countries. The VSF was formed by the architect
Balkrishna Vithaldas Doshi in 1978 as an association
where academic and professional architects could
develop research into means of improving local
construction techniques and materials and the
environmental qualities of housing in urban and rural
India. With financial support from the World Bank, the
VSF was able to plan sites and services projects for
a 128-ha. area on behalf of the Indore development
authority. The site had 7,000 plots, including 4,200
for low-income households.

The idea of the LUS went back to 1976, when
Doshi had visited McGill University and raised the
possibility of collaboration with faculty members
Witold Rybczynski and Vikram Bhatt. It would be
another seven years before the project got off the

ground, with funds from the Canadian International Development Agency (CIDA). The main purpose of the LUS was to develop innovative planning methods within the limitations of current Indian sites and services projects. The findings of its research into existing slums would be used as the basis to design demonstration projects featuring new technologies and nonconventional planning methods in 200 of the low-income plots in Indore.

The empirical method of the LUS research included surveys of informal structures in India. Participants interviewed the inhabitants and documented their use of space, preparing drawings of the selected locations, with observational notes and in most cases photographs. An analysis of these materials would then inform the development of new design methods through a design/build simulation exercise.

This project could be seen as facilitating an exchange of knowledge between North and South. Two VSF staff participated in the graduate diploma in MCHG—there were no equivalent programs in India at that time. In return, four graduate students from McGill spent the summer in Indore, where they got the chance to develop a demonstration project and acquire valuable field experience. The project played a significant role in stimulating interest in what had been a neglected field for professionals in developing countries. Its pedagogy was directly connected to practice. As a real, ongoing project, it benefited 200 families.

A further objective of the LUS was to disseminate the results of the research both in India and abroad through publications, public lectures, and workshops for students and professionals in planning, architecture, and related fields. "How the Other Half Builds" was the title of one series of reports on the results of the collaborative project,[1] which were distributed to the World Bank, International Development Agency, Ministry of Housing and Public Works (INDIA), and Indore Development Authority, among others. Another example was the paper describing the collaborative project presented at the Annual Meeting of the Association of Collegiate Schools of Architecture (ACSA) in New Orleans in March 1986. Rybczynski was also invited to the United Nations Habitat Center at Vancouver to share the VSF-MCHG exchange experience.

Beyond trying to present slums as solutions rather than problems, the project was a radical example of the production of architectural and urban planning knowledge as part of North-South interactions during the late twentieth century.

Collage of the stands of some of the countries participating in the UIA Congress in Paris in 1965. From *Deutsche Bauzeitung*, October 1965.

< Design/build simulation exercise, Minimum Cost Housing Group and Vastushilpa Foundation.

1. Vikram Bhatt et al., *How the Other Half Builds*, vol. 3: *The Self-Selection Process* (Montreal: Centre for Minimum Cost Housing, 1990).

Türkei

Kuba

Tschechoslowakei

Italien

UdSSR

USA

Polen

UdSSR

Frankreich

RETOOLING
THE PRACTICE

MODERNIZATION AND ADVOCACY

Julia Gatley, Paul Walker

Protagonists John Cox (1902–1984), Gordon Wilson (1900–1959), George Porter (1921–1998), and Al Gabites (1919–2004)
Institution Architectural Centre Inc.
Location Wellington, New Zealand
Dates 1946–1953

The Architectural Centre was established in Wellington in 1946 to promote good (modern) design to the public and raise awareness of its potential to transform the urban environment.[1] It also aimed to provide support for local architecture students at a time when New Zealand's capital did not have its own architecture school and students had either to move some 500 miles north to study at Auckland University College (now the University of Auckland) or pass the examinations set by the Auckland institution while serving an apprenticeship in Wellington. Centre members, including some of the city's best-known architects such as Gordon Wilson and Ernst Plischke, ran annual summer schools of design for the first six years of its existence. Two of these, *Te Aro Replanned* of 1947–1948, and *Demonstration House* of 1948–1949, captured the public imagination. Some 20,000 visitors—ten percent of the city's population at the time—came to see the *Te Aro Replanned* exhibition, while *Demonstration House* was inaugurated by the New Zealand Prime Minister, Peter Fraser. This level of public engagement with architectural pedagogy was remarkable, especially since the initiatives were independent, rather than institutional, and also overtly modern, in contrast to the notably conservative flavor of the Auckland curriculum.

Te Aro Replanned proposed clearing the Te Aro district—half of downtown Wellington—and transforming it into a landscape of medium- and high-rise buildings in park-like settings.[2] Fears of inner-city dilapidation and decay were coupled with concerns about unfettered suburban sprawl. A future city with a dead heart and a population of ten million sprawling across its hinterland was the nightmarish scenario envisaged by the Centre's president, John Cox, a senior planning advisor to the New Zealand government, at the launch of the *Te Aro Replanned* project. The solution was to be densification. Students presented their vision of the future city in drawings

and a clean, abstract model. Equally modern was their effective use of mass media to promote their ideas, initially to Wellington readers but ultimately also in several magazines with a national circulation. The exhibition's tremendous success gave the Centre the impetus and the authority to become an important critical voice. This extended to direct political action, when members determined that one of their own— the then-president, architect George Porter—would stand in the 1959 local elections. As a city councilor, and chair of the city's housing committee in the 1960s, Porter oversaw a program of public housing that included projects in the Te Aro area with a strong likeness to the student work of 1947–1948.

The summer school of 1948–1949, *Demonstration House*, involved the design and construction of a detached modern house.[3] Students worked in groups to produce possible designs, and then the participants came together to build the selected scheme. The design itself was important in demonstrating the potential of the modern house as a desirable, as well as economically viable, option for typical middle-income New Zealand families. The timber-framed house was U-shaped to capitalize on the sun while sheltering a private courtyard from the wind. Again, the project was widely publicized— the prime minister's presence at the opening helped to secure media interest—and a standalone booklet on the house complemented the Centre's own quarterly journal, *Design Review*, while reinforcing its promotion of modern design. Centre members understood the persuasive power of print.

However, subsequent summer schools met with dwindling enthusiasm. By this time the Centre had established its own course in architecture, which ran throughout the academic year. The course would be gradually taken over during the 1950s by Wellington Technical College, which in 1962 split in two, forming Wellington High School and Wellington Polytechnic. That same year, the New Zealand Institute of Architects (NZIA) ruled that architects needed to have a university degree qualification, something the polytechnic could not provide. Now redundant, the Wellington Polytechnic's School of Architecture closed in 1964.[4]

Meanwhile, the NZIA lobbied the New Zealand government to approve the establishment of the country's second university school of architecture. Victoria University of Wellington and the University of Canterbury in the South Island city of Christchurch vied for the role. Canterbury had

ᵛ "Something different in the way of a home," claimed the *New Zealand Free Lance* when it published this photograph of the Demonstration House in September 1949.

the allied disciplines of fine arts and engineering, while Wellington had more architecture students, more architects, and more building activity.[5] In addition, the initiatives of the Architectural Centre and Wellington Technical College showed that Wellington had both the demand for such a school and the skills-base necessary to build it, in the form of architects with teaching experience. These factors would prove decisive. In 1966 the university grants committee approved the establishment of the Victoria University of Wellington School of Architecture. The new school was set up in 1974 and taught its first courses in 1975. For its first ten years it had a particularly technocratic flavor that contrasted with the publicly engaged character of the Centre: its focus was on educating architects rather than the wider population. Some of the early Centre members taught there on a part-time basis, while the Centre itself was revitalized by a younger generation who engaged with the city as a protest and lobby group.

∧ Before construction could begin, the sloping site had to be excavated. Photograph by Tom McArthur.

1. Julia Gatley and Paul Walker, *Vertical Living: The Architectural Centre and the Remaking of Wellington* (Auckland: Auckland University Press, 2014).
2. Paul Walker, "Order from Chaos: Replanning Te Aro," in *Zeal and Crusade: The Modern Movement in Wellington*, ed. John Wilson (Christchurch: Te Waihora Press, 1996), 79–87.
3. Julia Gatley, "A Contemporary Dwelling: The Demonstration House," in *Zeal and Crusade*, 88–95.
4. "Wellington Polytechnic School of Architecture," *NZIA Journal* 31, no. 2 (March 1964): 52. See also A. C. Light, "Intermediate Examination," *NZIA Journal* 31, no. 4 (May 1964): 139.
5. Rachel Barrowman, *Victoria University of Wellington, 1899–1999: A History* (Wellington: Victoria University Press, 1999), 190.

THE LAB AND
THE NATION

Matthew Mullane

Protagonist Kenzo Tange (1913–2005)
Institution University of Tokyo
Location Tokyo, Japan
Dates 1946–1974

Most architecture students beginning their education in Japan today will choose not only a university and a department but also a "laboratory," or "*kenkyūshitsu*." Labs are tightknit spaces of instruction centered around a senior designer-educator who teaches the discipline through their own particular design philosophy using a mixture of individual classroom exercises, form-finding experiments, "desk crits," and collaborative group projects like pavilion design or community outreach. The lab leader acts as an interface between academia and the so-called "real world" of architecture, using their practice to introduce students to pragmatic issues of commission, contracts, design, and fabrication. The model has even influenced the field of architecture history in Japan, where both undergraduate and graduate research is organized by senior scholars around tangible projects like a book translation, field study, or the creation of new archives.

One of the most important precursors to this pedagogical model was the eponymous "Tange Lab" *(Tange kenkyūshitsu)*, which Kenzo Tange oversaw as a professor at the University of Tokyo from 1946 to 1974.[1] The lab was effectively a teaching extension of his architecture office where commissions, competition entries, and governmental collaboration met historical and theoretical research on topics spanning from Japanese shrines to contemporary

demographic analysis. Its alumni include some of Japan's most famous architects, among them Kisho Kurokawa, Fumihiko Maki, and Arata Isozaki. The Tange Lab also incubated the Metabolist group, which extended many of the lab's core ideas into avant-garde provocations.[2] Considering the lab's mixture of theory and design, it is no coincidence that these figures became some of the most prolific writers of their generation as well. The lab was as much a zone of history and theory as it was about design, fostering speculation on both fronts.

While Tange embraced speculation, the lab was not a space of freewheeling experimentation.[3] Student activity was guided by a set of very specific theoretical concepts and research directives. Tange foregrounded biological metaphors of growth, metamorphosis, and flexible adaptation to describe how cities could manage massive urban expansion, population growth, technological change, and an economic shift from industry to mass communication. Practically speaking, the lab's methodological hallmarks drew on statistical analysis, management, cybernetics, and information theory.[4] Rendering social data like transportation, mobility, and media consumption into form became a key component of some of the lab's most notable projects, including the 1960 Tokyo Bay project and pavilions at the 1970 Osaka World Exposition. In addition to studying media, Tange and his students also used an expanded array of media to distribute the lab's work, choosing newspapers, magazines, and television broadcasts to promote projects at a popular level, and reports, models, graphs, charts, and diagrams to communicate their work to businesspeople and politicians.

The lab's postwar approach represents a double take on "radicality": trying to shape the future of education while also reanimating rooted traditions of the architecture profession in Japan. First, the structure of Tange's classrooms established a new pedagogical model that, in the words of one its most famous students, Fumihiko Maki, was "part atelier, part laboratory."[5] This hybrid structure resolved an ongoing struggle between engineering and art-based design that had influenced both teaching strategies and institutional makeup since the discipline's modern inception in the 1870s. The lab also recentered Japanese architectural education on and in Japan, reversing prewar trends that saw students traveling either to large European firms in the late nineteenth century or to the offices of leading modern architects in the 1920s and 1930s.[6] Following efforts by the government to situate Japan as a

global partner after the war, students were encouraged to contribute to international competitions. In a new Cold War landscape of international collaboration, the lab packaged "Japanese architecture" to a non-Japanese audience as a distinct aesthetic and historical object, a phenomenon that continues to influence the way Japanese architecture is historicized and presented in exhibitions.

The second layer of "radicality" active at the lab follows the word's second meaning, related to the "roots" of the architecture profession in modern Japan—as nation-builder. The lab's emphasis on the managerial control of postwar growth recapitulated technocratic planning strategies first implemented by the Japanese empire in places like Korea, Taiwan, and Manchuria from the 1910s through the 1940s. Tange had actively contributed to wartime architectural projects and competitions and helped carry popular design strategies of population control back home from the colonies after the war and the collapse of the empire. The continuity of design philosophy between these two periods was augmented by new tools like computers and frameworks like cybernetics, but the emphasis was nonetheless the same: to control national growth at an urban scale.

The lab's commitment to strong government, nation-building, and a new media-based capitalism is illustrated by its relationship to the popular protests that broke out at various points of its operation, namely the 1960 protests against the Treaty of Mutual Cooperation and Security between the United States and Japan, the 1968–1969 protests at the University of Tokyo, and a series of protests staged at Osaka Expo '70 inside and on top of pavilions designed by Tange and his students.[7] The spontaneity of the protestors overtaking and stalling the normal systolic rhythm of the city offered a different model of transformation and proved the lab wanted urban change controlled by bureaucrats and businesses, not citizens alone. The conflicted radicality of the lab represents a broader paradox of postwar architectural experimentation beyond Japan that saw new architectural media and technology perpetuating older modes of state control in new computerized and corporatized ways.

1. For an extensive overview of Tange's career through interviews with his students and colleagues during this time, see *Tange Kenzō to Kenzo Tange*, ed. Toyokawa Saikaku (Tokyo: Ohmsha, 2013). In English, see *Kenzō Tange: Architecture for the World*, ed. Seng Kuan and Yukio Lippit (Zurich: Lars Müller, 2012), and Zhongjie Lin, *Kenzo Tange and the Metabolist Movement: Urban Utopias of Modern Japan* (New York: Routledge, 2010).

2. For more on Metabolism in English, see Rem Koolhaas and Hans-Ulrich Obrist, *Project Japan: Metabolism Talks*, ed. Kayoko Ota and James Westcott (Cologne: Taschen, 2011). In Japanese, see Yatsuka Hajime and Yoshimatsu Hideki, *Metaborizumu: 1960 nen dai Nihon no kenchiku abuangyarudo* (Tokyo: INAX, 1997), Ōtaka Masato and Kawazoe Noboru, *Metaborizumu to metaborisutotachi* (Tokyo: Bijustsu Shuppansha, 2005), and Mori Art Museum's *Metaborizumu no mirai toshi—sengo nihon, ima yomigaeru fukkō no yume to bijiyon* (Tokyo: Shinkenchikusha, 2011).

3. For the most extensive documentation of the Tange Lab in Japanese, see *Gunzǒ toshite Tange kenkyūshitsu: sengo Nihon kenchiku, toshi shi no meinsutorīmu*, ed. Toyokawa Saikaku (Tokyo: Ohmsha, 2012).

4. For more on the Tange Lab as a hub for cybernetics research and information theory, see Yuriko Furuhata, "Architecture as Atmospheric Media: Tange Lab and Cybernetics," in *Media Theory in Japan*, ed. Marc Steinberg and Alexander Zahlten (Durham, NC: Duke University Press, 2017), 52–79.

5. Fumihiko Maki, *Nurturing Dreams: Collected Essays on Architecture and the City* (Cambridge, MA: MIT Press, 2008), 12.

6. For more on architecture education and practice in Japan before World War Two, see Jonathan M. Reynolds, *Maekawa Kunio and the Emergence of Japanese Modernist Architecture* (Berkeley: University of California Press, 2001), and Ken Tadashi Oshima, *International Architecture in Interwar Japan: Constructing Kokusai Kenchiku* (Seattle: University of Washington Press, 2010).

7. For more on Expo '70 as an experiment in crowd control and critical responses to it, see Yuriko Furuhata, "Multimedia Environments and Security Operations: Expo '70 as a Laboratory of Governance," *Grey Room*, no. 54 (Winter 2014): 56–79, and *Review of Japanese Culture of Society* 23 (2011), a special issue dedicated to "Expo '70 and Japanese Art: Dissonant Voices."

< Tange and his student Nagashima Masamitsu in the lab's studio. In front of them are early models of the Yoyogi National Museum constructed by another student, Kamiya Koji.

> The lab's "Regional Structure of the Japanese Archipelago" project from 1965–1967 visualizes the "flow of marine freight" in and out of Japan for the year 1961, broken down by prefecture. The national basis of data visualization in this case has broader connotations, showing how prefectures are comparatively connected to global trade.

≪ Tange pointing at the site of the Yoyogi National Gymnasium constructed for the 1964 Summer Olympics. Maps were a constant feature of both lessons and student projects, as theorizing the relationship between architecture and urban space was an important component of the lab's education.

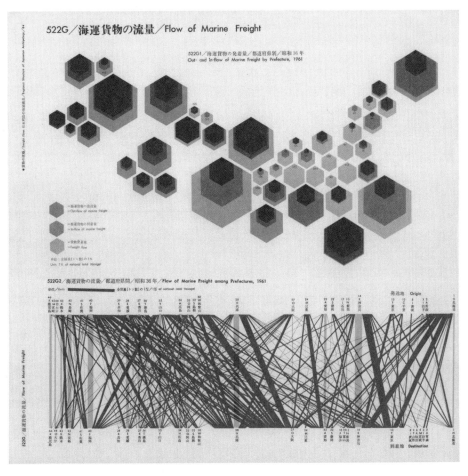

SHAPING THE "ZAGREB SCHOOL": EDUCATION IN THE GUISE OF PRACTICE

Igor Marjanović, Katerina Rüedi Ray

Protagonists Dragutin (Drago) Ibler
(1894–1964) and Drago Galić (1907–1992)
Institution State Master Workshop
for Architecture
Location Zagreb, Yugoslavia
Dates 1952–1984

In the decades immediately after World War II ambitious young architects would assemble in a neoclassical villa on a hill above Zagreb to further their studies in Yugoslavia's State Master Workshop for Architecture.[1] A combination of apprenticeship and postgraduate study, the master workshops were set up by the government in 1949 to provide art and architecture graduates in Belgrade, Ljubljana, and Zagreb with advanced skills in neoclassical socialist realist aesthetics—this was the height of Eastern Bloc communist orthodoxy. Resembling the Beaux-Arts atelier model acceptable to Stalinism, and inspired by similar enterprises in the Soviet Union, the workshops were intended to support talented participants with government bursaries for three years after graduation while they worked in the studios of experienced artists and architects. However, by the time the decree inaugurating the workshops went into effect, Yugoslavia had reached the end of its short-lived Stalinist period and was already exiting the Soviet sphere of influence. The master workshops were soon abandoned—except in Zagreb, where they unfolded, over a span of more than thirty years, as unusually independent and hybrid experiments integrating academia and practice, art and architecture.

The Zagreb master workshops were led by major figures such as the painter Krsto Hegedušić, sculptor Frano Kršinić, and architect Dragutin (Drago) Ibler. While Hegedušić's folk pictorial style and Kršinić's classicism fitted the Soviet-inspired model, Ibler, who ran the workshop for architecture between 1952 and 1964, was a less obvious choice. An early modernist with significant prewar commissions throughout Yugoslavia, he quickly shifted the focus away from socialist realism. He was also no stranger to integrating architecture with fine arts. A student of Hans Poelzig at the Berlin Art Academy, Ibler had returned home in 1926 to set up the department of architecture at the Royal Academy of Fine Arts in Zagreb. He was also the president of the radical art group Zemlja (Earth).[2] The school of architecture

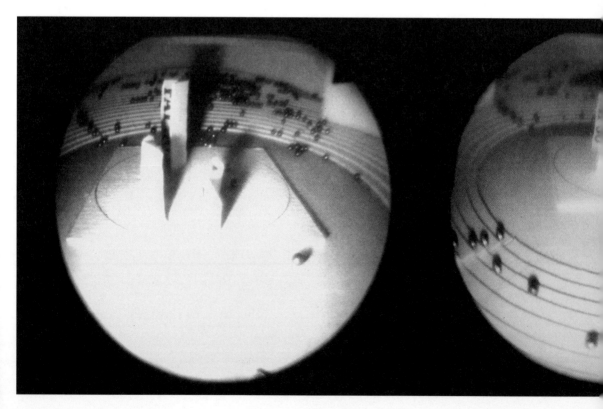

at the Royal Academy—which came to be known as the Ibler School—would continue to operate until Ibler was forced to emigrate to Switzerland by the Croatian Nazi "Ustashe" regime in the early 1940s. Despite being much smaller than the University of Zagreb's department of architecture modeled on the Germanic polytechnic tradition, it produced some of the most significant modernist practitioners in prewar Yugoslavia.

When Ibler returned to Zagreb in 1952, he immediately began renewing his prewar connections to both practice and modernist design. Appointed director of the State Master Workshop for Architecture, he took advantage of the authority and independence of the Beaux-Arts atelier "master" role to sidestep communist technocratic orthodoxy, instead promoting modernism as a symbol of cultural progress and global connectivity—an aspiration also reflected in his key role in organizing the 1956 CIAM X meeting in Dubrovnik.[3] This aesthetic was further explored in the master workshop, where participants worked on Ibler's prominent state commissions throughout the 1950s and early 1960s, including the "Wooden Skyscraper"—a Corbusian concrete tower with wooden façade elements—in the center of Zagreb, as well as the Yugoslav embassy in Moscow and state residences in Belgrade and beyond.

In addition to serving as Ibler's private office, the master workshop was also his home. He slept on a modest metal bed on the upper floor of the villa, looking in from time to time on the work on the drafting boards in the former salon below. Nested within an elite neighborhood, the villa's ample spaces were a rarity at a time of postwar communist austerity: its elegant bourgeois rooms provided generous studio space, while the lush landscape reinforced a feeling of "being apart." This sense of separation was further amplified by the workshop's privileged position outside tight political control, with funding coming from different sources—federal, state, and local authorities—as it moved from the Academy of Fine Arts to the Academy of Arts and Sciences. This constant flux, combined with the intimacy of scale and single-person leadership, meant that the workshop remained beyond the grasp of the powerful academic factions of state-run education, allowing its projects to be more artistic, progressive—and, ultimately, built.

After Ibler's death, the workshop continued to evolve between 1964 and 1984 under the leadership of Drago Galić, himself a graduate of the Ibler School and Ibler's close associate on major prewar projects, such as the workers' insurance office building in Skopje.[4] Galić maintained the workshop's

independence but at the same time also extended its influence by building bridges to the University of Zagreb, where he served as dean of the faculty of architecture from 1962 to 1966. While the university curriculum focused on the postwar socialist rebuilding of the country, it also emphasized the local vernacular tradition, as elucidated in the influential textbooks on architectural design by Zdenko Strižić, a member of the teaching staff who, like Ibler, was a former student and colleague of Poelzig.[5] However, it was in the workshop that Galić mentored a select group of architects who would become influential in Croatian academia, among them Hildegard Auf-Franić, later dean of architecture at the University of Zagreb (1997–2001). Galić's impact on practice was also substantial. Unlike Ibler, he encouraged participants to pursue their own built projects and design competitions that often served as incubators for their own professional offices. This increased the workshop's impact further; what began as artistic drawings and models in the atelier often materialized as socially engaged projects characterized by abstract modular forms with touches of vernacular materials—a regional variant of modernism that we can call the "Zagreb School of Architecture." Rather than a single entity, this school of thought operated across several institutional frameworks: the university, the academy, and the workshop. Within this constellation, it was the master workshop that provided the most enterprising and productive—yet still ideologically acceptable—bridge between academia and practice.[6] Its volume of built work was certainly radical for a Yugoslav educational enterprise, ensuring the survival and ultimate ascendancy of modernism as the mainstream building practice in postwar socialist Croatia and in Yugoslavia more widely.

< Wooden skyscraper in Zagreb, workshop of Drago Ibler, 1955–1958.

< Competition entry for the Opera, Belgrade, workshop of Drago Galić, 1970–1971. Design team: Boško Budisavljević and Marijan Uzelac.

« Competition entry for the House of Culture, Bitola, North Macedonia, workshop of Drago Galić, 1970. Design team: Dino Bakulić, Stijepo Ganzelja, Zdravko Mahmet, and Melita Rački.

1. The villa is now the Croatian Museum of Architecture; see *Croatian Museum of Architecture,* ed. Andrija Mutnjaković (Zagreb: Croatian Academy of Arts and Sciences, 2018), 58–75.
2. On the Ibler School, see Željka Čorak, *U funkciji znaka: Drago Ibler i hrvatska arhitektura izmedju dva rata* [In the Function of a Sign: Drago Ibler and the Croatian architecture between the World Wars] (Zagreb: Centar za povijesne znanosti, 1981), 70–74. See also Ariana Novina, "Škola za arhitekturu na Akademiji likovnih umjetnosti u Zagrebu—Iblerova škola arhitekture" [School of Architecture at the Academy of Fine Arts in Zagreb—the Ibler School of Architecture], *Peristil* 47 (2004): 135–144.
3. Ibler served as President of the Society of Yugoslav Architects (1956–58). On his involvement with CIAM and other international networks, see Tamara Bjažić Klarin, "CIAM networking—Međunarodni kongres moderne arhitekture i hrvatski arhitekti 1950-ih godina / CIAM Networking—International Congress of Modern Architecture and Croatian Architects in the 1950s," *Život umjetnosti* 99, no. 2 (2017): 40–57.
4. Goran Mickovski and Vladan Djokić, "Okružni ured za osiguranje radnika u Skopju arhitekta Drage Iblera, 1934 / Social Security District Office in Skopje Designed by the Architect Drago Ibler, 1934," *Prostor* 23 (2015): 83–95.
5. Zdenko Strižić, *Arhitektonsko Projektiranje I* [Architectural Design I] (Zagreb: Školska Knjiga, 1952), and Zdenko Strižić, *O Stanovanju: Arhitektonsko Projektiranje II* [On Housing: Architectural Design II] (Zagreb: Školska Knjiga, 1956).
6. As in other Yugoslav republics, Croatian art, architecture and design after World War II would be increasingly absorbed into the larger project of industrialization and socialist self-management. See Fedja Vukić, *The Other Design History* (Zagreb: Upi2M Books, 2015) and *Project Zagreb: Transition as Condition, Strategy, Practice*, ed. Eve Blau and Ivan Rupnik (Barcelona: Actar, 2007).

TECHNICAL DIPLOMACY

David Rifkind

Protagonist V. H. Ingvar Eknor (1918–2012)
Institution Ethio-Swedish Institute of Building
Technology
Location Addis Ababa, Ethiopia
Dates 1954–1974

The history of the Ethio-Swedish Institute of Building Technology is intricately bound up with Ethiopia's political transformations since the Second World War. Founded in 1954, the institute was created to train building professionals to support the modernizing agenda of Emperor Haile Selassie's government, which was engaged in numerous public works projects across Ethiopia and Eritrea.[1] Given the ambitious scope of the program—which encompassed administrative, educational, and healthcare facilities, as well as communication, transport, and sanitation infrastructure projects—the government recognized the need to develop local technical expertise to complement the foreign-trained professionals hired to direct those ventures. Subsequent changes in the institute's curriculum and organizational structure paralleled changes in the country's governance over the next six decades.

Popularly known as the Building College, the coeducational Ethio-Swedish Institute of Building Technology was a joint initiative of the Ethiopian Ministry of Education and the Swedish government, and the first architecture program in Ethiopia. The importance of its role in the state's ambitious modernization project is reflected in the fact that it was inaugurated just four years after the country's first higher education institution, the University College of Addis Ababa. The institute's founding director, in the years up to 1960, was the Swedish architect V. H. Ingvar Eknor, who had trained at Chalmers University of Technology (under a predominantly technical curriculum) and served as the ministry's Chief Architect in Ethiopia since 1946.[2] The institute had three administrative divisions—the Building College, Testing, and Building Research[3]—and initially employed Swedish faculty, assisted by Ethiopian graduates of the Technical School in Addis Ababa.[4] This transnational educational experiment was supported by Sweden's International Assistance Committee (a government agency for development projects abroad) and

was among the plethora of knowledge networks enmeshed with economic and political interests in postcolonial Africa.

The Building College organized its curriculum around the range of technical skills that were considered necessary to design and manage large-scale building and infrastructural projects. European construction technologies, materials, and methods had been employed in the country for half a century, but until then they had not been incorporated into Ethiopian technical training. Initially the program offered a three-year diploma in building engineering and sent students overseas to complete their undergraduate degrees.[5] Within two years the curriculum had evolved into a four-year Bachelor of Science in building engineering, and the institute conferred its first undergraduate degrees in July 1958. The following year, the curriculum was extended to a five-year bachelor's degree, making it possible for the first time to complete the whole program without a period of study abroad.[6]

The five-year degree program in architecture and town planning was initially based at the campus of the College of Engineering in Arat Kilo, a charter member of Haile Selassie I University, founded in February 1961 as part of a series of social reforms in response to the attempted coup of 1960. It began with a freshman year of introductory studies, followed by two years of professional education. Students then undertook one year of compulsory university service, which offered a chance to gain professional experience by working in a design practice, before returning for two more years of professional education. The three-year diploma in building technology prepared students to work in a variety of trades in the construction industry—as building engineers, contractors, construction supervisors, quantity surveyors, technical assistants in architects' offices, and building maintenance engineers, among others.[7] While the terminology and structure of the educational system mirrored those of Western countries, students and faculty engaged with building projects around the capital (by architects such as Arturo Mezzedimi, Henri Chomette, and the partnership of Zalman Enav and Michael Tedros) that critically examined those structures through an architecture that was self-consciously specific to place and culture.

There were two major changes during the 1968–1969 academic year: the Department of Architecture and Town Planning relocated to the Building College campus near the old airport in

Lideta, while the Building College itself merged with the College of Engineering and formed the Faculty of Technology of Haile Selassie I University.

After the 1974 revolution, which deposed Emperor Haile Selassie and installed the Derg regime, the university was renamed Addis Ababa University. Classes were interrupted for several years as students and faculty undertook compulsory national service. While classes would resume and the Faculty of Technology would continue to train architects and building professionals, a number of talented students left the country during the 1980s to pursue their architectural education in Europe.[8] Nonetheless, Ethiopia still had enough of its own Building College-educated architects and allied professionals to manage the new regime's ambitious public works program, which included significant numbers of public housing developments, markets, educational facilities, and transportation projects. The transnational transfers of knowledge that the Building College had facilitated, along with traveling faculty and mobilized resources, had provided an opportunity for the country to formalize architectural education and rapidly educate a new generation of designers and builders.

1. *Ethio-Swedish Institute of Building Technology General Catalogue* (Addis Ababa: Ethio-Swedish Institute of Building Technology, 1957), 5. Institute for Ethiopian Studies collection.
2. Ingvar Eknor, *Nittiofyra års minnen* (Örkelljunga: Vulkan, 2015). See also Ingvar Eknor, *Building Construction Parts 1 & 2* (Addis Ababa: Ethio-Swedish Institute of Building Technology, 1958).
3. "Programme for the Inauguration of the Ethio-Swedish Institute of Building Technology," Institute for Ethiopian Studies collection. The head of the Testing section was Thure Alvemark, and the head of the Research section was Bernhard Lindahl.
4. *Ethio-Swedish Institute of Building Technology General Catalogue*, 7–8.
5. "Haile Sellassie [sic] I University, Dedication of the New Faculty of Technology," brochure (1971). Institute for Ethiopian Studies collection.
6. Ibid.
7. Ibid.
8. In 2010 the institution was reorganized as the Ethiopian Institute of Architecture, Building Construction and City Development, an autonomous body within Addis Ababa University.

CONSTRUCTING PRACTICE

Onur Yüncü, Berin F. Gür

Protagonists Charles Abrams (1901–1970), G. Holmes Perkins (1904–2004), Thomas B. A. Godfrey (1920–), Marvin Sevely (1919–1973), Jaakko Kaikkonen (1887–1971), Kemal Kurdaş (1920–2011), Apdullah Kuran (1927–2001), Ekmel Derya (1925–2003)
Institution Middle East Technical University (METU)
Location Ankara, Turkey
Dates 1958–1974

Every summer from 1958 until 1974, the Middle East Technical University (METU) department of architecture organized two months of construction practice for its students as a requirement of a course called "Summer Practice in Construction and Surveying." During those years, students built nearly twenty small-scale structures in various parts of Anatolia under the supervision of their teachers. The functions of the buildings were defined in response to local requirements, and alongside faculty members and students, local craftsmen also played a significant role. When the course started in 1958 (only two years after METU's architecture department was set up), it had multidimensional objectives: to instill a knowledge of construction materials and construction

activity; to familiarize students with the rural regions where a large percentage of Turkey's population lived; to generate a social contract with the future inhabitants of the buildings; to contribute to communities by providing facilities for public use; to introduce local people to new construction techniques.[1] These objectives were set in accordance to the educational ideals pursued by METU's faculty of architecture in its founding years, which sought not only to prepare students for the profession but also to help them to develop as responsible and creative individuals.

METU was established in 1956 as part of a United Nations initiative to promote a modern approach to architecture and urban planning in Turkey. Charles Abrams and G. Holmes Perkins were the UN consultants who were instrumental in its creation. They envisaged a research institute that would support the wider Middle East region in the preparation of planning laws and housing legislation.[2] Through the influence of the UN, METU was also founded with a distinct local mission: to serve the surrounding communities through its educational facilities. It was in this spirit that the course in construction practice was initiated by the first acting dean of METU's department of architecture, Thomas B. A. Godfrey, together with Marvin Sevely.[3] The first construction practice in 1958 was a pilot project for model village—Ağla—selected by the International Mediterranean Countries Development Organization. The course was conducted by a visiting professor, the Finnish architect Jaakko Kaikkonen.[4] The idea of the work

where intellectual training was integrated with empirical experience—with "learning by doing."

Construction practice was on a scale of 1:1, but it was neither a simulation of professional practice nor an application of theoretical knowledge to a "real-life" building site. Rather than bridging a gap between theory and practice, the course introduced a specific component to Turkish architectural education with its own objectives and tools of learning.[8] By giving students more responsibility and encouraging them to continuously reflect on the social and practical processes of design and construction, it opened up new possibilities for generating knowledge.

Over the years of its existence, this model of learning proposed an alternative, progressive architectural pedagogy that not only engaged with experimentation through construction, and integrated thinking and doing, but also cultivated a broad understanding of the architect's social responsibility. And yet, this mode of construction practice ended in 1974, a victim of internal political tensions between opposing student groups. The tradition of constructing small-scale buildings in rural regions would enjoy a brief revival, from the summer of 1999 to 2006, thanks to the efforts of Selahattin Önür, then head of the department of architecture.

being in the service of the community was supported and successfully maintained by Kemal Kurdaş, president of METU (1961–1969), and the subsequent deans of the department of architecture, Apdullah Kuran (1960–1968) and Ekmel Derya (1969–1970).

The roots of this ethos could be traced back to the early 1950s, when architectural education in the US underwent significant changes in response to social and political challenges and new conceptions of individuality and society.[5] From his experience at the School of Fine Arts at Penn and, before that, Harvard GSD, Perkins understood that an architect's responsibility extended beyond the construction of a single building. Rather than being limited to a design exercise, a project had to take into account people's social, cultural, and physical requirements. Consequently, architectural education had to equip students with an insight into the inherently social character of architecture—an understanding of culture had to be developed alongside design skills and knowledge of technical, economic, and aesthetic issues.[6] This cultural understanding, integrated with the mission of serving the local community, was a founding principle of METU's department of architecture.

The initial draft of the architecture curriculum underlined the importance of hands-on field experience directed by the faculty.[7] Accordingly, the Practice in Construction course placed emphasis on process rather than product, encouraging students to continually reflect on and learn from what they were doing. It enacted an integrated pedagogy

∧ Students and faculty on a lunch break during the construction of the coffee house in Gölevi, Ordu, Summer 1965. Designed and coordinated by Sümer Gürel.

< Faculty on the terrace of the coffee house in Güneyköy, Elazığ, Summer 1966. Designed and coordinated by Nejat Erem.

1. *ODTÜ Mimarlık Fakültesi Yaz Uygulamaları*, ODTÜ Mimarlık Bölümü Öğrenci Yayını 2, ed. Suha Özkan (Ankara: ARP Yayınevi, 1974), 3–4; Selahattin Önür, "Önsöz," in *1/1 Yaz Uygulaması*, ed. Berin F. Gür and Onur Yüncü (Istanbul: 124/3, 2004), 5.

2. Derya Yorgancıoğlu, "Reconstructing the Political and Educational Contexts of the METU Project," PhD diss. (METU, 2010), 103.

3. Ibid., 98–99

4. Özkan, *ODTÜ Mimarlık*, 6.

5. *Architecture School: Three Centuries of Educating Architects in North America,* ed. Joan Ockman (Cambridge, MA: MIT Press, 2012).

6. *METU Catalog 1957–1958*, Ankara, 24.

7. Yorgancıoğlu, "Reconstructing the Political and Educational Contexts of the METU Project," 108.

8. Berin F. Gür and Onur Yüncü, "An Integrated Pedagogy for 1/1 Learning," *METU Journal of the Faculty of Architecture* 27, no. 2 (December 2010): 83–94.

COSMOPOLITAN PEDAGOGY IN THE POST-COLONY

Łukasz Stanek, Ola Uduku

Protagonists Max Bond (1935–2009), Niksa Ciko (1930–2005), Lutz Christians (1926–), Sylvia Crowe (1901–1997), Jane Drew (1911–1996), Zbigniew Dmochowski (1906–1982), Buckminster Fuller (1895–1983), Berislav Kalogjera (1923–1999), Samuel Opare Larbi (1959–2015), John Lloyd (1927–2017) Miro Marasović (1914–2004), Kamil Khan Mumtaz (1939–), John Owusu-Addo (1928–), Charles Polónyi (1928–2002), Wiktor Richert, Kenneth Scott (1918–1982), Austin Tetteh, Patrick Wakely (1929–), Nebojša Weiner (1934–), Zvonimir Žagar (1931–)
Institution School of Architecture, Town Planning and Building in Kumasi, Kwame Nkrumah University of Science and Technology
Location Kumasi, Ashanti Region, Ghana
Dates 1958–1979

The first school of architecture in sub-Saharan Africa was created within the Kumasi College of Technology in 1958, a year after Ghana's independence from Britain.

By the time the college became the Kwame Nkrumah University of Science and Technology (KNUST) in 1961, it had three departments—Architecture, Building Technology, and Planning—to which the Department of Housing and Planning Research was added in 1964.[1] The Kumasi school remained preeminent well into the 1970s, delivering a comprehensive architecture and planning program that straddled economic and physical planning, community development, urban and rural architectural design, and construction management.

After an aborted attempt at founding a US-style institution, the Architectural Association (AA) in London was approached to help set up the school and John Lloyd became its first dean. The curriculum was based on AA's tropical studies program, and British academics were given a leading role in developing a postcolonial educational program with a view toward a gradual transition to Ghanaian leadership. After 1963 the curriculum was redesigned to take better account of the needs of Ghana, and in 1965 Lloyd argued that "A Faculty of Architecture…, if it is to truly contribute to the future of the [African] continent, must drastically define anew the task of an 'architect'."[2]

By that time, with Ghana's membership in the Non-Aligned movement and increasing links with

socialic countries and black America, the Kumasi school—far from being simply an outpost of British architectural education—had become a node of various global networks intersecting in Ghana under its first president, Kwame Nkrumah (1960–1966).³ During KNUST's initial years, its staff included the African-American architect Max Bond, the Hungarian Team 10 member Charles Polónyi, architects from Britain (Patrick Wakely), West Germany (Lutz Christians), Pakistan (Kamil Khan Mumtaz), Poland (Stanisław Sikorski), and a significant group of Yugoslav (Croatian) architects and engineers (Niksa Ciko, Miro Marasović, Berislav Kalogjera, Nebojša Weiner, Zvonimir Žagar). High-profile visitors gave talks on a number of topics: Sylvia Crowe on landscape design, Jane Drew on tropical architecture, Zbigniew Dmochowski on vernacular building cultures in West Africa, Paul Oliver on vernacular architecture and music, Buckminster Fuller on structural design, and Eustaquio Toledo on thermal comfort.⁴

In the course of the 1960s Ghanaian architects began to join the faculty, among them John Owusu-Addo and Samuel Opare Larbi. Owusu-Addo and other faculty members also worked at the university's Development Office, which transformed the campus, originally designed by British architects following a master plan by James Cubitt and Kenneth Scott, into one of the most remarkable modernist ensembles in West Africa. Other architects practicing in Kumasi and Ghana's capital and economic and cultural center, Accra, also contributed to the teaching at the school.

This close connection to architectural and planning practices was reflected in the curriculum, which addressed urgent challenges of post-independence, such as Ghana's rapid population growth, fast-track urbanization, scarce industrial and technological resources, meager building industry, and insufficient number of professionally qualified Ghanaians. Students and staff contributed to the planning of the Volta River Resettlement project, rehousing 80,000 people after the construction of the Akosombo Dam.⁵ Studio projects addressed tasks assigned to graduates by the Volta River Authority, including the design of new townships, low-cost housing type designs, and self-help construction systems. Polónyi drafted planning strategies that matched the government's provision of plots of land and infrastructure with self-help construction initiatives. Žagar and his students developed prototypes of self-built social centers made of tensegrity

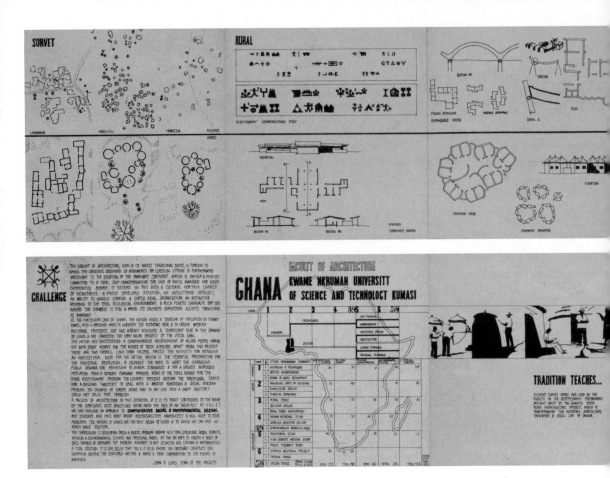

structures. Wakely developed school designs for different climate types in Ghana in the framework of an internationally funded program.[6] The teaching of history was overhauled as well, shifting from the routine Eurocentrism toward a "comparative study of world cultures" that linked architecture to questions of economic and social development.[7]

The curriculum looked to redefine the architectural profession, in line with Max Bond's and John Owusu-Addo's call for Ghanaian architects to "assume a broader place in society as consolidators, innovators, propagandists, activists, as well as designers."[8] This redefinition was facilitated by the cosmopolitan faculty, with their multiplicity of experiences. For instance, the methods of community planning developed in Britain by the sociologist Ruth Glass and the planner Max Lock were combined with Polónyi's previous experience of resettlement projects in Hungary. In turn, the postgraduate course in regional planning, taught by Ghanaian sociologist and urban planner Austin Tetteh with Polish planner Wiktor Richert, confronted Eastern European, state-socialist regional planning with the Anglo-American

tradition.[9] Likewise, Kamil Khan Mumtaz's teaching drew both on his training at the AA and his experience in South Asia. In this way, the curriculum of the Kumasi school reflected and benefited from the short-lived cosmopolitanism of Nkrumah's Ghana during the "Africa decade" of the 1960s.

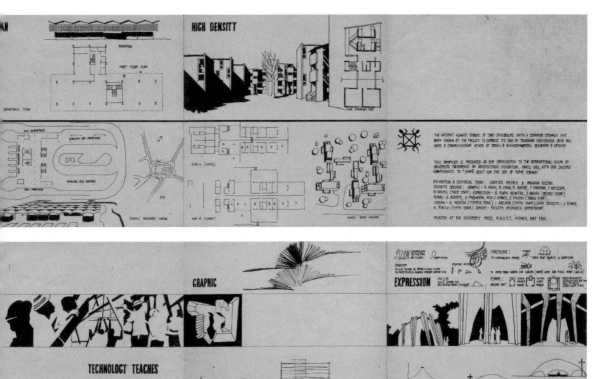

∧ Leaflet for
the Faculty of
Architecture, Kwame
Nkrumah University
of Science and
Technology, May 1965.

< Students
participating in the
course "Structures
and Structural Design"
taught by Zvonimir
Žagar at the Kumasi
School of Architecture,
1965. Photograph by
Zvonimir Žagar.

1. Hannah le Roux, "Modern Architecture in Post-Colonial Ghana and Nigeria," *Architectural History* 47 (2004): 361–392.
2. Faculty of Architecture, Kwame Nkrumah University of Science and Technology, Kumasi, 1965. J. Max Bond, Jr. papers, 1955-2009, Department of Drawings & Archives, Avery Architectural and Fine Arts Library, Columbia University, New York (USA).
3. Łukasz Stanek, "Architects from Socialist Countries in Ghana (1957–1967): Architecture and Mondialization," *Journal of the Society of Architectural Historians* 74, no. 4 (December 2015): 416–442.
4. *Arena: Architectural Association Journal* 82, no. 904 (July–August 1966), "Kumasi Special Issue." See also Ola Uduku, "Bolgatanga Library: Adaptive Modernism in Ghana 40 Years On," in *The Challenge of Change: Dealing with the Legacy of the Modern Movement: Proceedings of the 10th International DOCOMOMO Conference,* ed. Dirk van den Heuvel, Maarten Mesman, Wido Quist, and Bert Lemmens (Amsterdam: IOS Press, 2008), 265–272.
5. Irene Appeaning Addo, Iain Jackson, Rexford Assasie Opong, and Ola Uduku, "The Volta River Project: Planning, Housing and Resettlement in Ghana, 1950–1965," *The Journal of Architecture* 24, no. 4 (2019): 512–548.
6. Ola Uduku, *Learning Spaces in Africa: Critical Histories to 21st Century Challenges and Change* (London: Routledge, 2018), 82–83.
7. John Lloyd, "Intentions," *Arena, the Architectural Association Journal* (July–August 1966): 40.
8. Max Bond and John Owusu-Addo, "Aspirations," *Arena, the Architectural Association Journal* (July–August 1966): 62.
9. Łukasz Stanek, *Architecture in Global Socialism: Eastern Europe, West Africa, and the Middle East in the Cold War* (Princeton, NJ: Princeton University Press, 2020), 106–108.

PROFESSIONAL EDUCATION AND ITS DISCONTENTS

Andreas Kalpakci

Protagonists Zahir-ud Deen Khwaja
(1922–2006), Mourad Ben Embarek (1929–2011),
Jane Hawkins, and other delegates and students
Institution Union Internationale
des Architectes (UIA)
Location Paris, France
Date 1965

From July 5 to 9, 1965 the Union Internationale des Architectes (UIA) gathered in Paris for its eighth congress. Responding to what it saw as an assault by young architects on the very foundations of the profession, it took as its theme the "Education of the Architect." Sigfried Giedion had sounded the alarm in the pages of the UIA's journal the year before: "The future of the architect's vocation rests for the most part in the hands of the coming generation. The chances they have of defending the integrity of their professional ethics appear to us to constitute a very important problem."[1] The abrupt death of Le Corbusier less than two months after the meeting in Paris seemed to give concrete form to the UIA's fears. Dispatches about the congress were appended to obituaries of the modern master in the architectural press—as if to exorcise the death of modernist practice itself.

The UIA delegates—1,746 of them, plus 490 students—discussed the before, during, and after of architectural training. Supporting materials from twenty-eight national delegations were displayed on the ground floor of the École des Beaux-Arts as a comparative exhibition of architecture schools, their methods and results. Architectural training was further divided into three broader fields: general studies, technical education, and design. If the architect achieved a balance between all three—so the theory went—they would be capable of blending into complex postwar bureaucracies while still retaining their individual powers of creativity and expression. Rather than attempting to resolve the arguments for different pedagogical methods, congress delegates looked for common ground, anticipating a future state-led reform of architectural education that would be coordinated internationally by UNESCO.[2]

The UIA had "noble ideas, but little power," one commentator from Canada reported.[3] Others took a dimmer view of UIA's technocratic internationalism. Delegates from the Global South criticized the self-absorbed nature of the discussions, pointing out a deep disparity. In industrialized societies, architectural education could afford to focus on technical and aesthetic training because it was supported by preexisting institutions of general education. In nonindustrial societies, by contrast, such specialization was an unattainable luxury, as architecture had to respond to more basic needs. It was clear that there was an urgent need to devise new systems of education from scratch.[4] Quite unexpectedly, the congress had become a platform for new actors to make their voices heard.

Pakistani architect Zahir-ud Deen Khwaja called out the congress's false assumption: technical training in any country, he argued, could not forgo its stage of industrialization.[5] Moroccan architect Mourad Ben Embarek, speaking on behalf of the "Working Group of Architects of the Third World"— with delegates from Ethiopia, Ghana, Lebanon, Madagascar, Morocco, Nigeria, Pakistan, Peru, and Syria, among others—offered three precise recommendations. Industrialized countries had to give "Third World" countries more technical assistance to allow them to set up new schools to train local architects. There was an urgent need for new methods of teaching oriented toward real-world concerns, rather than architectural display. And, in relation to this, architectural education had to take account of questions of sociology, urbanism, and ecology in order to counter the effects of rapid urbanization and industrialization.[6]

Some of the most scathing criticism, however, came from the architecture students, who found the congress lifeless, despite the UIA's efforts to provide opportunities to connect with the delegates—from meeting with R. Buckminster Fuller to visiting an exhibition of the works of Robert Le Ricolais.[7] Jane Hawkins, a British student, "pointed out that the views of the students seemed to have been overlooked by the congress," adding that her peers "found the meetings singularly uninspiring."[8] The disconnect between established practice and students was further underlined by that year's Athens Awards, an international competition in which students were invited to design an architecture school. Assessing the 106 entries exhibited on the upper floor of the École, the jury, chaired by Josep Lluís Sert, lamented the absence of "outstanding projects."[9]

A major point of contention was the growing demand for self-actualization among the students.

10 ARCHITECTURAL DESIGN

October 1965 Price 5/-

They wanted to be able to participate in and shape their own education, and they believed that the fact they had created their own dedicated organizations, comparable to their professional counterparts, showed they had the maturity to do it.[10] The Peruvian delegation enthusiastically seconded this motion, adding that they hoped to establish more frequent exchanges outside of UIA congresses.[11] Representatives of the Union Internationale des Étudiants d'Architecture (UIEA) piped up from the audience (several times) to remind delegates that the theme of the congress had been resolved by their own Stockholm conference one month

earlier.[12] But perhaps the most forceful advocate of the students' position was Philippe Molle, a Beaux-Arts student who had just finished his tenure as the first General Secretary of the UIEA,[13] and who would later submit the first teamwork diploma project at the École.[14] "On behalf of 4,000 French architecture students," Molle addressed a letter to all UIA delegates requesting reform and protesting against the inertia of professional architects.[15]

The rumblings of discontent could not have come as a total surprise. The UIEA conference in Stockholm had given students the opportunity to define a common position on issues that were already

< The space-frame tower in Place du Trocadéro, Paris, was designed by Jean Ginsberg and displayed the flags of the countries participating in the UIA congress. From the *Architects' Journal*, July 14, 1965.

≪ Cover of *AD*, October 1965, dedicated to the International Year of Cooperation.

in the air—issues raised, among other things, by the seventh UIA congress in Havana two years earlier, which had discussed "architecture in countries in the process of development."[16] The Stockholm conference resolved "that pedagogical institutions must be pressed to set up an interchange of ideas so that students of developed and developing countries may be able to help and learn from each other."[17] For the students, aligning architecture with the socioeconomic conditions of each country was an essential aim of architectural education: their demand for participation in defining their course of studies also envisaged an increased exchange across the North–South divide.

In retrospect, it seems clear that the student dissent at the UIA congress in Paris in July 1965 anticipated the revolt of May 1968.[18] There, participants from the Global South voiced, loud and clear, the need for radical institutional reforms. Even if their scathing criticism had no direct impact on the UIA's resolutions at the time, it was extensively documented in the official report of the congress, signaling a gathering of discontent that the profession could no longer ignore.

1. Sigfried Giedion, "Continuity and Evolution of the Vocation of the Architect," *Revue d'informations de l'Union internationale des architectes*, no. 25 (February 1964): 21.
2. UIA, *La formation de l'architecte: Huitième congrès mondial de l'Union internationale des architectes: Exposition des sections*, exhibition catalogue (Paris: Centre de recherche d'urbanisme, 1965).
3. Thomas Howarth, "Architectural Education: UIA in Paris," *Journal of Architectural Education* 20, no. 3/4 (February–May 1966): 42–44.
4. Ibid.
5. Zahir-ud Deen Khwaja, "Formation technique des architectes dans les pays en voie de développement," in *Huitième congrès de l'Union internationale des architectes: Rapport général*, by UIA (Paris: Imprimerie CIRNOV, 1965), 208–209.
6. Mourad Ben Embarek, "Formation des architectes dans les pays en voie de développement," in *Huitième congrès de l'Union internationale des architectes*, 156–159.

7. "Conference in Paris: Student Section," *Architects' Journal* 142, no. 29 (July 28, 1965): 190–193.
8. Howarth, "Architectural Education," 44.
9. "Proclamation des Prix d'Athènes," in *Huitième congrès de l'Union internationale des architectes*, 395–397.
10. William Moffett, "Participation des étudiants à leur propre enseignement," in ibid., 237–238; Jane Hawkins, "Organisation de l'Union des étudiants en architecture de Grande-Bretagne," in ibid., 318–320.
11. Oswaldo Jimeno Aguilar, "Méthodes d'enseignement et échange d'étudiants de pays en voie de développement," in ibid., 337–338.
12. Eduardo Leira, "Conclusions de la 9e Conférence des étudiants en architecture (Stockholm)," in ibid., 167–168.
13. José María Gómez Santander, "Breve historia de la UIEA," *Nueva Forma*, no. 36 (January 1969): 99–100. I thank Lucía Carmen Pérez-Moreno for this reference.
14. Claude Feuillet, "Evry-Petit-Bourg, ville de l'an 2000," *L'Express* (December 28, 1966), AR-10-07-17-03, Fonds Georges

Candilis, Cité de l'architecture et du patrimoine.
15. Philippe Molle, "4,000 étudiants français protestent dans une lettre remise à tous les congressistes," *Logement CIL* (August 1965), Archives de la Grande Masse des Beaux-Arts. I thank Christophe Samoyault for this reference. Molle played a key part as student leader (*grand massier*) in the reform of the École, which in 1965 was already under way. See Jean-Louis Violeau, *Les architectes et Mai 68* (Paris: Éditions Recherches, 2005), 29–31.
16. UIA, *L'architecture dans les pays en voie de développement: Septième congrès de l'Union internationale des architectes* (Havana, 1963).
17. Bengt Ahlqvist and Antonio Velez Catrin, "Rapport de la 9e Conférence internationale des étudiants en architecture à Stockholm, Suède, 1965" (Stockholm: 1965). Personal archive of Nuno Portas. I thank Bruno Gil for this document.
18. *Les années 68 et la formation des architectes*, ed. Caroline Maniaque (Rouen: Éditions Point de vues, 2018).

ON THE EDGE OF AVANTGARDE

Michael Hiltbrunner

Protagonists Peter Jenny (1942–),
Hans-Rudolf Lutz (1939–1998), Hansjörg
Mattmüller (1923–2006), Doris Stauffer (1934–
2017), Serge Stauffer (1929–1989)
Institution F+F School of Experimental Design
Location Zurich, Switzerland
Dates 1971–1981

In 1977 a group of students went hiking with the typographer and publisher Hans-Rudolf Lutz in a forest close to Zurich.[1] It was a pleasant setting but tough-going, rather muddy and steep. They didn't know the sense of their walk, just that it was experimental practice. Two of the students secretly taped all their conversations and later used the recordings as the screenplay for a fictional movie. The script still exists, but there's no trace of a movie. Doubtless it would have been very much avantgarde, with everyday chitchat and adolescent wordplay staged by the filmmakers themselves. Learning creative practices beyond disciplines and restrictions was how the F+F School of Experimental Design in Zurich operated in the 1970s, and it was also what the students expected from the school.

The first "F+F courses in experimental design" were held in early 1971 at the home of architect Lisbeth Sachs in Rämistrasse in Zurich. At the time the school was led by the artist Hansjörg Mattmüller and the art researcher and photographer Serge Stauffer. Artist Bendicht Fivian, architect Peter Gygax, graphic designer Peter Jenny, and activist, artist, and photographer Doris Stauffer were cofounders of the school. Along with Hans-Rudolf Lutz, filmmaker Georg Radanowicz and artist Verena Voiret were also closely involved. The first official education program was introduced in 1972—and after a number of changes the school is still active today as F+F School of Art and Design.

The school had its origins in the F+F program offered at the former Zurich School of Arts and Crafts (now Zurich University of the Arts) between 1965 and 1970. The initials F+F—standing for "Form und Farbe" (Shape and Color)—was a reference to the Bauhaus preparatory course introduced in Zurich by Johannes Itten in 1939. A group of teachers proposed to evolve this preparatory course into a design program that went beyond the standard technical and vocational models. Mattmüller, who taught in the preparatory course, and Stauffer, who was the photography instructor, were charged with heading the new F+F program. Breaking with Bauhaus practices, they moved the focus beyond formal aspects and color theory, seeking to introduce social issues, critical thinking, and an awareness of contemporary problems in design studies. They required students to adopt cross-disciplinary practices, hoping to open the way for design research and experimental methodologies of high artistic merit.

The booming advertising industry was expressly interested in graduates with skills in creative solutions and modern design. In this context the new F+F program at the Zurich School of Arts and Crafts was particularly welcome. Not only did it provide "creative" training for both industrial design and the fine arts, it also allowed for cross-disciplinary work and free experimentation, as it shifted the focus from crafts toward modern design.

Two years into the new program, in 1967, tensions erupted when an expert committee proposed to reform the School of Arts and Crafts into an "Institute and Forum for Design" that excluded the fine arts and had a strong commercial orientation in order to drive the "production of consumer goods and means of communication."[2] This proposal—which was strongly opposed by the F+F program—followed on the heels of a 1961 report by Max Bill which envisioned a radical restructuring of the school to create an "Institute for Design" that would carry forward the work he had begun at the Ulm School of Design.[3] Both Bill's report and the 1967 proposal were rejected.

The F+F program soon got more radical. In early 1969 students initiated a self-taught collaborative course that Doris Stauffer developed into a "teamwork" course during the spring semester. Once a week, students created a joint happening or a design-oriented field test. Taking Alexander Sutherland Neill's anti-authoritarian Summerhill School as a model, Stauffer introduced a class council. The realization of group projects, rather than awarding of individual grades, became the measure of progress. The teamwork strengthened the class's political awareness and antihierarchical activism. Stauffer had co-founded the Zurich women's liberation movement (Frauenbefreiungsbewegung or FBB) in 1969 and she invited her students to actively contribute to FFB events such as "Misswa(h)l" (loosely, "mis(s)takes"), where, among others, Verena Voiret auctioned off the clothing she had won in a beauty contest. Also in early 1969, Peter Jenny started teaching on the preparatory course and explored radical approaches beyond the limits of art and design with his students—the spirit of the F+F program now permeated the whole school.

In late 1969 students and teachers, many of them from F+F, formed a committee calling for a radical democratization of the Zurich School of Arts and Crafts.[4] Rather than vocational training, they wanted the focus to be on design-oriented research. They envisioned open ateliers and specially equipped studios for various areas of design. Students would be able to arrange their own schedules, with instructors holding the role of advisors, rather than teachers. Students could begin and end their studies at any time. There would be no specific disciplines. The school would be an independent institution—its governing body would be a charitable foundation, and a plenary assembly would constitute the legislative body in which all members (students, staff, instructors) would have a vote. Reaching into the wider community, the school would also be a cultural center, with adult education courses taught by students as a way of promoting intergenerational dialogue. When it was circulated internally in February 1970, the proposal caused a scandal.

The governing body of the Zurich School of Arts and Crafts decided that the F+F program had gone too far— it had become too anti-authoritarian, too radicalized, too much of an influence on other parts of the school. They determined that it could continue to operate only under strict conditions: it had to revert to the initial program, with none of the new courses and interests introduced in the interim. The response of the F+F student council was to pass a resolution in mid-March 1970 to withdraw from the school. They also organized a protest against the blocking of democratic reform that was widely reported in the media, including Swiss television. In the summer of 1970 the former class members presented an exhibition, *Experiment F+F,* at the Kunsthalle Bern. The show was a major success, paving the way for the creation of the independent F+F School of Experimental Design the following year.[5]

The foundation of the F+F School was driven by ideology, not commercial interests. Teachers had to make do with a small salary. The school was to function as a kind of open laboratory where ideas could flow freely, underscoring the relevance of creative work in an evolving society. The school offered evening, weekend, and summer classes to

participants of all ages and backgrounds, who came not only from all around Switzerland but from neighboring countries. Teachers designed experimental lessons, documented the processes, and continually refined their teaching formats into an alternative pedagogy of design that took account of the latest developments in the arts.

The F+F curriculum was unconventional. In a "witches' course" taught by Doris Stauffer in 1977, women photographed parts of their bodies they were unhappy with and then discussed the images.[6] In one of his classes in 1971 Hans-Rudolf Lutz and his students sowed letter formations and, later in the year, harvested a word.[7] In 1974 Serge Stauffer set his students the task of creating pornography, obscene texts, paintings, or sculptures, with the rationale, "the provocation of pornography confronts us with our own, individual artifice."[8] In another experiment, Peter Jenny asked his students to use lights to create illusory spaces in a windowless corridor.[9] Team spirit was valued as highly as individualism. Outright idleness was as important as creative activity, and the art of imitation was cultivated alongside the encouragement to think outside the box.

The school was successful with this approach. In 1976 the F+F participated in the Venice Biennale and exhibited its work at Kunsthaus Zürich, where Serge Stauffer published sixteen theses that framed art as a specialist vocation to "serve societal research."[10] Rather than artistic production—that is, artworks—the key issue was "knowledge about design, about shaping various kinds of *information*."[11] For Stauffer, the development of an individual methodology had to include criticism against all kinds of repressive measures.

By 1977 there had already been three program cycles. At the same time tensions in the team became visible: co-founder Peter Jenny left the school and became professor of visual design at the department of architecture at ETH Zurich. Doris Stauffer's "witches' course" for women was quite successful, but it was attacked by Hansjörg Mattmüller, who saw it as discriminatory and insisted it had to be made available to men, too. To avoid further confrontation, Stauffer offered the course independently at the "Frauenwerkstatt" (women's studio) in 1978, before finally leaving the F+F school under protest in 1981. Serge Stauffer, in solidarity with Doris Stauffer, organized a "men's course" for emancipation and creativity in 1978. He also stepped back from his role as the F+F's co-leader and, after a final "art lab for advanced learners" in 1979, retired from the school.

The achievements of the school's founders were crucial for its further development, and are still influential today. By the 1980s, however, the F+F school had gradually shed its experimental character, with the focus shifting to the teaching of the preparatory course and vocational training. At the same time, internationally recognized philosophers such as Jean Baudrillard were invited to lecture, and the school worked with the Berlin publishing house Merve. Thus, research-based art, the actual language of artists, gave way to a poststructuralist, philosopher's art. In the 1990s the school's director, Hansjörg Mattmüller, became increasingly isolated, and a new director could only be found after the City of Zurich intervened. A restructuring of the school ensued. Today, the—still independent—F+F School of Art and Design offers accredited Swiss vocational diplomas in photography, graphic design, fashion design, fine arts, and film.

< Forest happening, teamwork course by Doris Stauffer, 1969.

<< "Miss-Wahl" (loosely, "mis(s) takes") Frauenbefreiungsbewegung FBB (women liberation movement) happening with a contribution by the F+F class, Zurich, 1969.

1. This text evolved out of Michael Hiltbrunner, "Drop Out of Art School: 'Research Meant Trying New Things.' The F+F School in Zurich around 1970 and Artistic Research Today," trans. Mary Carozza, in *Fucking Good Art*, no. 38 (2018): 102–130, and a series of talks by the author.
2. Mark Buchmann, Lucius Burckhardt, and Victor N. Cohen, *Institut für Forum für Gestaltung IFG, Bericht der Experten-Kommission zur Prüfung einer Reform der Kunstgewerbeschule der Stadt Zürich* (Zurich: Stadt Zürich, 1967), 10.
3. Max Bill envisioned a new campus with two hundred design students living and working on site; see Max Bill, "Bericht an den Schulvorstand der Stadt Zürich über das Projekt 'Institut für Gestaltung,'" 1961.
4. Studiengruppe Demokratisierung der Kunstgewerbeschule, "Vorschlag für eine demokratische Schule für Gestaltung," 1970, Archive ZHdK, Klasse F+F, 1965–1970.
5. Cf. *Experiment F+F, 1965–1970*, ed. Hans-Rudolf Lutz et al. (Zurich: Verlag H. R. Lutz, [1970]).
6. Cf. *Doris Stauffer. A Monograph*, ed. Simone Koller and Mara Züst (Zurich: Scheidegger & Spiess, 2015).
7. Cf. Hans-Rudolf Lutz, *Typoundso* (Zurich: Verlag H. R. Lutz, 1996), 62.
8. Serge Stauffer, *Kunst als Forschung. Essays, Gespräche, Übersetzungen, Studien*, ed. Michael Hiltbrunner (Zurich: Scheidegger & Spiess, 2013), 105.
9. Cf. Peter Jenny, *Sign and Design. Zeichnen und Bezeichnen* (Zurich: ETH, 1981), 63.
10. Stauffer, *Kunst als Forschung*, 179.
11. Ibid., 199.

A PROTEST ADDRESSED TO THE FUTURE

Anna Bokov

Protagonists Vladislav Kirpichev (1948–),
Lyudmila Kirpicheva (1959–)
Institution Experimental Children's
Architectural Studio (EDAS)
Location Moscow, USSR/Russian Federation
Dates 1977–1993 (still in operation)

EDAS, standing for *Experimentalnaya detskaya architekturnaya studiya* (Experimental Children's Architectural Studio), was founded by architect and educator Vladislav Kirpichev in Moscow in 1977. It was conceived as an extracurricular activity for local kids of different ages, from kindergarteners to high school seniors. While art schools for young people were popular in the Soviet Union at the time, EDAS set itself apart by establishing architecture as its primary focus—playfully critiquing rigid institutional norms. The studio's architectural framework defined a type of spatial production, from models to various three-dimensional constructions and projection drawings, traditionally reserved for professionals, forming new ways of communication and ensuring unbounded visionary ambition.

While still a student at MARKhI (Moscow Architectural Institute), Kirpichev had won first prize in the UNESCO Center of Creative Activity competition, held as part of the XI Congress of the International Union of Architects (1972)—the first Russian architect to win an international competition since the 1930s. For the insular Soviet Union, this was an act of unprecedented significance.[1] Kirpichev's success in this and other international competitions made him an instant cult figure and triggered an avalanche of competitions that paved the way for the formation of the famous "paper architecture" movement of the 1980s. Kirpichev was joined in 1982 by a MARKhI student, Lyudmila Ban'ko, whom he would soon marry. The Kirpichevs have continued ever since to work together "organically" and remain, to borrow Peter Cook's phrase, "a couple that is rarely seen apart."[2]

Kirpichev participated in competitions throughout the 1980s and 1990s, in parallel with his work at one of the large state-run design institutions, Mosproekt, which he had joined immediately after graduating from MARKhI. At the time, Mosproekt focused on "standardized" (*tipovoye*) construction and did not provide outlets for individual creativity. Working on competitions was, no doubt, a way to channel his own ideas, but the "conceptual" realm was still only the sublimation of a real practice. Kirpichev understood that if he could not change the present, he could at least create a new type of design school to educate the next generation of like-minded individuals. EDAS was a protest addressed to the future.

Kenneth Frampton visited the studio in 1990 and drafted an essay on EDAS, "Transform the World: Poetry Must Be Made by All," in which he lamented the end of the "brief but exhilarating golden age" of the Soviet avantgarde of the 1920s and wrote that EDAS

> surely has to be seen as a categorical attempt to redress this loss, by tapping into the ever-vital source of youth as it rises up so to speak in one "unspoilt" generation after another. Part Svengali, part pedagogue of exceptional talent and conviction, the architect Kirpichev guides this never-ending flow of energy into the lost avantgarde traces, to recover from the still unworked seams of the moment, the elixir of a seemingly inevasible exuberance and fantasy.[3]

The choice to work with children was not accidental. Despite the USSR's concerted efforts at indoctrination, they were the one group in the totalitarian society who had a chance of being uncontaminated by the system. According to the Kirpichevs, children are far more "anarchistic" than adults, "anything is still possible…young people are less limited by obligations; they don't know the correct answers to the questions."[4] At EDAS, then, the potential for radicality lies in the students themselves, as political agents outside the system. Kirpichev's "therapeutic enterprise"—far removed from the inflexible structures of Soviet-style education—transforms the processes of learning and creating into an "explosive expressivity of [the school's] tidal production."[5]

During the 1980s, arguably the studio's most formative period, EDAS's young students were steeped in the Russian avantgarde tradition that had reemerged from oblivion after the "thaw" period of the 1950s. In fact, Kirpichev himself had been taught by Ivan Lamtsov, one of the original disciples of the revolutionary Higher Art and Technical Studios in Moscow, known as VKhUTEMAS. Lyudmila also studied with the son of the avantgardist Grigory Barkhin, the architect Boris Barkhin, who praised her draftsmanship. With her arrival at EDAS, the studio's pedagogy evolved from what could be described as an expressive painterly approach to a honed architectonic rigor, with a kind of attention to craftsmanship and precision that imparted an almost transcendental quality to the creative process— something that was noted by Kenneth Frampton and others. Western architects, among them Peter Eisenman, Bernard Tschumi, Rem Koolhaas, and Zaha Hadid, were also looking back to the Russian avantgarde for inspiration, with the emergence of the deconstructivist approach—a movement that developed in parallel with the dramatic political developments that preceded the collapse of the Soviet Union. As their own inspiration for EDAS, the Kirpichevs cite the work of both Russian and international luminaries, ranging from Andrey Tarkovsky and Konstantin Melnikov, to John Cage, Ryūnosuke Akutagawa, and Hermann Hesse.

Almost miraculously, EDAS survived not only the dissolution of the Soviet Union but also the extensive economic reforms of Russia during the 1990s. After spending over a decade in Western Europe, between 1993 and 2004, the Kirpichevs returned to Moscow. Today the studio continues to function almost in its original format, still led by the couple. EDAS students are integrated vertically, with ages ranging from one to twenty-one, and enrollment from ten students up to one hundred in a given period of time. Housed in a converted apartment in a prerevolutionary residential building in the center of the city, the studio is an afterschool activity—some students spend one afternoon a week, while others come almost daily.

Activities range from drawing and modelmaking to writing and going on fieldtrips. They can be short, one-minute exercises or extend over several hours, exploring materiality, media, or methods of making. Experimental studies and research on a particular topic—brainstorming sessions—may be combined with the development of models and drawings over several months. An important aspect of studio assignments is iteration and seriality—students produce many different versions of a task and learn how to develop an idea from a simple sketch to a complex project. Design topics include vertical and horizontal structures (towers and bridges), movement structures (stairs and ramps), spaces (small-large, open-closed, shallow-deep), as well as light, sound, and tactility. Typically, assignments start with abstract spatial categories, evolving later, if at all, into articulate architectonic elements.

What sets the Kirpichev teaching approach apart from other educational models is that it is not driven by the end product, despite the impeccable craftsmanship of the student work. Instead, a drawing or a model embodies the state of working in itself—a concentrated, focused effort only possible when one is completely immersed

in the process of discovery. In that respect, EDAS could be compared to a miniature Black Mountain College, the legendary experimental school that combined the rigor of the Bauhaus pedagogy with the fluidity of holistic learning.[6] For EDAS students, the craftsmanship is not a goal but a communicating vessel, to paraphrase André Breton. The work is the pedagogy itself—Kirpichev's mystique and influential legacy have been perpetuated by several generations of disciples, including myself, who have in turn embedded and cultivated the EDAS approach into their teaching and practice.[7] EDAS's models, constructions, drawings, and paintings are not only inspired by the works of legendary VKhUTEMAS and UNOVIS teachers—Kazimir Malevich, El Lissitzky, Lyubov Popova, Nikolay Ladovsky, Ivan Leonidov, and other pioneers of the avant-garde—they are tapping into the seemingly inexhaustible creativity, energy, and anarchy of youth.

The Kirpichevs' two-part mantra is simple:

1. "No one knows what is right" (*Nikto ne znaet, chto takoe pravil'noe*). It does not exist, just as there is no horizon and no perspective.

2. "Everything is possible!" (*Mozhno vse!*)[8]
As the Kirpichevs say, "We do not select children; we do not test their creativity; we work with any child; in our forty-three years of practice there is not a single case where we did not achieve [great] results."[9]

Sample questionnaire that guided Planning for Change students who interviewed family members and neighbors about the reasons for their migration to the city as well as the satisfactions and disappointments they found there.

1. "Debut—1973," *Soviet Union*, no. 280 (July 1973): 51.
2. Vladislav and Lyudmila Kirpichev in conversation with Anna Bokov, June 4, 2020. The Kirpichevs referred to the architect Peter Cook, who said of them, "There are couples who are rarely seen together. This is a couple that is rarely seen apart."
3. Kenneth Frampton, "Transform the World: Poetry Must Be Made by All," manuscript, June 12, 1990, Zurich. Vladislav and Lyudmila Kirpichev Archive.
4. Fred A. Bernstein, "Avant-Garde School: Two Teachers Have Been Bringing Out the Inner Architects in Moscow Children since the Soviet Era," *Architectural Record* 204, no. 5 (May 2016): 130–131.
5. Frampton, "Transform the World."
6. Steven Holl, quoted in Bernstein, "Avant-Grade School," 130–131.
7. The author of this piece was a student at EDAS between 1988 and 1991.
8. Vladislav and Lyudmila Kirpichev in conversation with Anna Bokov, June 4, 2020.
9. Ibid.

< Vladislav and Lyudmila Kirpichev (standing, left) with EDAS students, 1988. Photograph by Igor Palmin.

```
┌─────────────────────────────────────────────────────────┐
│                                                           │
│              SAMPLE QUESTIONNAIRE                         │
│                                                           │
│   Name_____  │
│                                                           │
│   Address_____ Date_____  │
│                                                           │
│   1. Did you always live in this city?    Yes_____ No____│
│   FOR PEOPLE WHO ANSWER NO TO QUESTION 1:                │
│      2. If not, where do you come from?                  │
│                                                           │
│   _____ │
│                                                           │
│      3. Why did you come to this city?                   │
│                                                           │
│   _____ │
│                                                           │
│   _____ │
│                                                           │
│                                                           │
│   FOR ALL PEOPLE INTERVIEWED:                            │
│   4. Has the city met your expectations?                 │
│                                                           │
│   _____ │
│                                                           │
│   5. If not, why do you think it hasn't?                 │
│                                                           │
│   _____ │
│                                                           │
│   _____ │
│                                                           │
│                                                           │
│   6. What do you like about life in this city?           │
│                                                           │
│   _____ │
│                                                           │
│   7. What don't you like?                                │
│                                                           │
│   _____ │
│                                                           │
└─────────────────────────────────────────────────────────┘
```

ACTIVATING THE SOCIAL

ARCHITECTURAL ANALYSIS AS A TOOL FOR REFORM

Daniel Talesnik

Protagonists Tibor Weiner (1906–1965),
Abraham Schapira (1922–2016), Gastón Etcheverry
(1923–2016), Hernán Behm (1923–2019),
Dr. José Garcíatello (1898–1966)
Institution Escuela de Arquitectura,
Universidad de Chile
Location Santiago, Chile
Dates 1946–1963

In 1946 students at the University of Chile's school of architecture proposed a major curricular reform that would remain in place until 1963. Two previous student-led reform movements in 1933 and 1939 had attempted—without success—to modernize the Beaux-Arts training offered by the school, calling for a new approach tied to the social reality and needs of Chile. While the students had a clear idea of what they wanted, they had lacked the support of someone with firsthand experience of implementing this kind of change. This time around, however, student leaders Abraham Schapira, Gastón Etcheverry, and Hernán Behm were assisted by the Hungarian architect Tibor Weiner, who had trained at the Technical University of Budapest, undertaken postgraduate studies at Hannes Meyer's Bauhaus, and practiced in the Soviet Union in the 1930s before moving to Chile. Together with Weiner, they introduced a class called Architecture Analysis, a theory-based course

with design exercises that developed into a method for facing any given architectural problem.

The new study plan, implemented in the first semester of 1946, was simpler and more straight-forward than Meyer's Bauhaus study plan—but freely based on it. Studies were organized in two cycles, analysis and synthesis, coinciding with the "Elemental Studio" (two years) and the "Core Studio" (three years). The final stage comprised a research seminar and diploma (one year). Similarly, the curriculum's classes were structured in four families: Techniques, Plasticity, Sociology, and Philosophy. The overlaps with Meyer's final Bauhaus curriculum of 1930 are clear, but it should be noted that parts of this curriculum were not actually implemented due to Meyer's short-lived tenure at Dessau. The parallels are at times on a subject-to-subject basis, as in the classes of hygiene, sociology, or technology of materials. Several of the science and social science courses of Meyer's Bauhaus were also replicated—but there was one essential differ-ence: Meyer's plan had not included history classes.

In the reform curriculum in Santiago, on the other hand, *architectural analysis* became both a method and the name of the main class for all first- and second-year students. This class, a combination of theory and studio, was taught by Weiner in 1946–1947 before his return to Hungary the following year. As a research strategy and a tool for exploration, *architectural analysis* would become Weiner's main educational legacy in Chile. Analysis in this context meant scrutinizing an existing living environment or a site for a new project using a variety of methods,

< Students and colleagues bid Tibor Weiner farewell at Los Cerrillos Airport, Santiago, Chile, March 1948. From left to right: Miguel Lawner, Ana María Barrenechea, Tibor Weiner, Simón Perelman, and Jorge González.

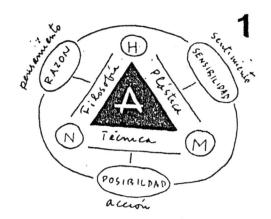

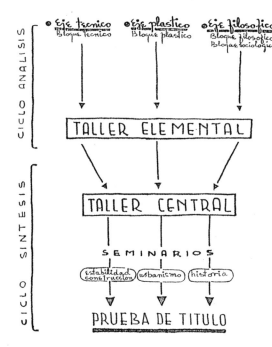

^ Diagram by Tibor Wiener showing the reform program's triangulation of nature, man and material. From *Arquitectura y Construcción*, no. 11, 1947.

v Scheme of the reform study plan taken from an exhibition catalogue prepared by the student council of the University of Chile in 1946.

such as: written descriptions, architectural drawings, and sketches for formulating a problem; time charts and isotypes for surveying daily activities; bubble diagrams for studying circulation and social relationships; scientific measurements and diagrams for recording meteorological conditions.

This analytical approach went hand in hand with a socially committed disciplinary impulse, evident in the designs of the post-reform graduates and demonstrated further by the high-profile roles of several of Weiner's former students in the fields of state-led architecture and urbanism. There were wider repercussions, too, extending beyond Chile. Following a presentation of the core ideas of the reform at the Sixth Pan-American Architectural Congress in Lima in 1947, many architecture schools in the region reformed their study plans, with the school of architecture at the National University of Engineering in Lima modeling its new study plan directly on the Chilean initiative. Other exchanges were established with schools in Tucumán, Buenos Aires, Montevideo, Panama City, and Mexico City. Published in book form, the syllabus of the biology and hygiene course taught by José Garcíatello also inspired similar classes in the region. By 1963, when the reform study plan of the University of Chile's architecture school was abandoned, most of its original advocates had resigned from the university, including many of the students who had been taught by Weiner and had become teachers themselves.

Although the Chilean educational project developed sixteen years after Meyer's dismissal from the Bauhaus, the proposal was not a mere copy of Meyer's curriculum, but rather an innovation within the Latin American context: in institutionalizing a systematized analysis of architecture, it instilled a technological impulse, an aesthetic shift, and a social awareness in architectural education. The school's graphic language was science-infused, as evident in the Bauhaus-inspired diagrams and charts made by the Chilean students. Most importantly, the design objectives of the exercises changed the way architecture was taught in Chile more generally, with texts and analyses showing a greater sociopolitical consciousness. The 1946 reform consolidated the analytical approach that had filtered into Chilean discourse, turning it into the basis of a full-fledged study plan. It can be read as an effort to reconnect the architecture of the modern movement, as it had been imported into Latin America, with a sociopolitical agenda. The reform attempted to correlate image and project—method and purpose.

A PLAN
FOR CHANGE

Brian D. Goldstein

Protagonists C. Richard Hatch (1933–), J. Max
Bond, Jr. (1935–2009), Arthur L. Symes (1935–)
Institutions Planning for Change, Architecture
in the Neighborhoods, Architects' Renewal
Committee in Harlem (ARCH)
Location New York, NY, USA
Dates 1964–1974

As participatory planning efforts grew in the United
States in the 1960s they typically focused on adults.
But architect C. Richard Hatch recognized that the
long-term efficacy and equity of planning in predominantly low-income, majority-minority communities
required engaging their full range of residents,
including children as young as the fourth grade. In
this context, Planning for Change and Architecture
in the Neighborhoods represented two efforts to
create a pipeline of diverse New Yorkers who understood how cities worked and how, through planning
and architecture, these citizens might work to
change them. In the city's public schools and among
young people in their late teens and early twenties—
especially those who had left high school before
graduating—Hatch envisioned creating a "knowl-
edgeable citizenry" with the "social and technical
skills…increasingly important to adult performance
in a largely urban world."[1]

Both Planning for Change and Architecture in the
Neighborhoods grew out of the Architects' Renewal
Committee in Harlem, or ARCH, which Hatch,
who was white, launched in 1964 as the nation's
first community design center. Harlem, New York
City's most prominent majority African American
community, suffered at mid-century from acute
poverty, discrimination, overcrowded housing, and
constant—and disruptive—large-scale redevelopment. In this context, ARCH offered free design
services to Harlemites, seeking to provide neighbors
with the expertise and control over their built environment that they had lacked. This took form over
the next decade in a series of efforts intended to
help Harlemites bend public redevelopment to their
will. While community-derived alternate plans for
Harlem neighborhoods targeted for urban renewal
were the most visible of these initiatives, from
ARCH's first years Hatch determined that education
was equally important. In guides that supported

beleaguered tenants or pointed neighbors to government resources, the community design center set
out to remedy information gaps that had often left
Harlemites vulnerable to the decisions of outsiders.

Efforts to teach younger residents architecture and planning involved a longer time horizon
but a more radical ideal: that control over one's
built environment would come through developing
an understanding of the means of urban development from early in one's education. As Hatch later
explained, "[p]lanning and programming for community development require social and technical skills
which are not now taught in our schools."[2] In an era
when planners and architects were increasingly
looking to open their professional doors to more
voices, ARCH sought to build a foundation for
enlarged and diversified participation, beginning in
elementary school.

Planning for Change was the first such example,
an effort to teach students in city public schools
"about New York City, and how to change it."[3] From
1965, ARCH staff began to develop a planning curriculum for junior high students. Amid the experimental
and participatory culture of the Great Society era,
this effort gained federal government sanction in
1966.[4] That year, ARCH tested Planning for Change
in the social studies curriculum for eighth graders
in four public schools, in West and North Harlem;
Bedford-Stuyvesant, Brooklyn; and the South Bronx.
Each community claimed high poverty rates and
predominantly minority populations who had experienced official and landlord neglect and disruptive
redevelopment. By 1968 Hatch had left ARCH as
the organization transitioned to African American
leadership but remained at the helm of Planning for
Change through his own firm. The program was then
active in nine schools across the city, now focused on
fourth- and fifth-grade students.[5]

Whether teaching younger or older students,
Planning for Change emphasized common pedagogical goals, each centered around the idea that
students could comprehend the complexity of their
neighborhoods and then reshape them "by planning
together."[6] Students pursued a curriculum that
introduced the recent history of migration and
demographic change, different urban housing types,
the workings of city government, and neighborhood
organizations, but also left open ends in both lessons
and outcomes, to let students "do things for themselves," as Hatch explained.[7] Thus, lessons asked
students to draw from their own experiences, incorporated memoirs by authors like Piri Thomas and

386

What Is in PLANNING FOR CHANGE?

Planning is one way of working for change. It is a way of trying to make life better in cities. Not that change comes easily! To bring about change, you need power and money. Planning can't give you these. But it can help you get them. With a good plan for change, people are more willing to listen to you. And they are also more likely to give your neighborhood money for solving problems.

PLANNING FOR CHANGE is a guide to action. It is for students who want to do something about their neighborhood. It shows how to find out why problems exist:

    why some landlords don't make repairs;
    why streets are so congested;
    why some people can't get jobs;
    why there are so few parks and playgrounds; and
    why city life is often noisy, dirty, and uncomfortable.

It helps you figure out the way the city works—how decisions are made and how you can have a say in them. It shows you how to get information that will help you solve problems.

1. Unit 1 tells you why and how people come together in cities. It describes how city plans are made. It helps you find out how the city government works and how to make it work for you.

2. Unit 2 shows how to find out who lives and works in your city— and your neighborhood—and why.

3. Unit 3 will help you to learn about the music, art, and literature of the city and of your neighborhood.

4. Unit 4 will help you investigate the buildings, parks, streets, people, and politics of your area.

5. Unit 5 will help you gather ideas about other ways of living from new kinds of communities here and in other countries. And it will show you designs by famous architects for city neighborhoods.

6. Unit 6 will help you to make your own plan for the future, for improving your neighborhood and the lives of the people in it.

∧ Introduction to the 1970 edition of the Planning for Change workbook, making clear the program's emphasis on teaching young students to approach planning from many angles, both political and cultural, before shaping their own visionary schemes.

Malcolm X, poems, and folk songs to prompt reflections about urban life, and brought students into the city through field trips. In one exercise, students listened to the sea shanty "Leave Her, Johnny, Leave Her," discussed the singer's laments as a way into a bigger conversation about why people flee their homes or jobs, and then wrote new verses reflecting frustrations with their own communities.[8]

Despite emphasizing everyday realities, utopia was a common theme across versions of Planning for Change, with work by figures like Ebenezer Howard and Frank Lloyd Wright intended to inspire "radical new schemes" for students' neighborhoods. The goal was not to turn such neighborhoods into garden cities or Broadacre City, but to teach the value of imaginative thinking in places of frequent difficulty and frustration. In one lesson, they viewed slides of iconic utopian schemes like Moshe Safdie's Habitat 67, then—using shoe boxes—constructed a community of their own "box-apartments," each tailored by a student to their own design. As the 1968 teacher's manual said of fourth-grade students, "It is our intention here to broaden the range of their vision in every way possible."[9]

With this in mind, students' lessons culminated in planning exercises focused on reimagining familiar places. These embodied the self-determination, collaboration, and local knowledge that suffused participatory design more broadly in the late 1960s. The concluding exercise for fourth graders, for example, was to build a model of a nearby block over several weeks, using materials like cereal boxes, paper cups, and straws. Beyond an aesthetic or formal exercise, however, they were to also take photographs, analyze maps, make firsthand observations, interview block inhabitants including tenants and police officers, and assess land use patterns. "As each piece of the model goes into place," teachers were told, "the children will have developed an understanding of the complex division of labor and the inter-dependencies required to sustain just one block." Based on that research, they were to propose new designs for the block ("their own utopia") including interventions like playgrounds, and present these to city officials.[10]

Fifth graders—as well as students in later versions of Planning for Change—were to extend this to a "plan for change" for their entire neighborhood, an exercise as much about opening up possibilities in students' minds as the plan itself. As the 1970 workbook, seemingly the last edition, told students, "Even if some of what you plan never becomes reality, you will end up with an idea of the way life should be." Participatory planning was about giving more residents a voice in their built environment; Planning for Change worked to include young children, convincing them that in neighborhoods that officials had shaped from the top down, such bottom-up involvement was as essential as math or reading.

Architecture in the Neighborhoods extended this idea to an older group of young residents, at a time when ARCH and its leaders were becoming involved with young adults more broadly, including through teaching and advocacy in higher education institutions such as Yale University and Columbia University.[11] Like Planning for Change, Architecture in the Neighborhoods followed the ambition that better, more equitable built environments would result from ensuring broader, more representative participation in shaping them. This program, too, had roots in ARCH's early history, with the organization discussing a "technical training school" in Harlem within its first months; this was to instruct students in their late teens and twenties in drafting, surveying, and graphic design, all seen as readily employable skills, and prepare interested students

for college-level training in architecture.[12] With the transition in ARCH's leadership from Hatch to African American architect J. Max Bond, Jr. in 1967, this unrealized program gained new life but also a new edge amid the era's politics. ARCH's racial transition channeled broader shifts from gradual, integration-oriented approaches to civil rights to the nationalistic, often militant approaches of the Black Power movement. In this context of racial self-determination, early emphasis on job training became an effort to put architecture and planning under the control of people of color.

Thus, Architecture in the Neighborhoods sought to address what its director, architect Arthur Symes, also African American, called the "dearth of Black and Puerto Rican talent in the fields of Architecture and City Planning."[13] It did so through a curriculum (described below) that would teach skills in architecture, urbanism, and art to students ranging from eighteen to twenty-five, so that they could complete high school degrees and continue their formal training in accredited undergraduate programs. If simple in premise, this was radical both demographically—in a field with a scant percentage of professionals of color—and ideologically, as an effort to put design in the hands of minority professionals, with the ambition that they would bring those skills back to their neighborhoods.

With the sponsorship of ARCH, Cooper Union, and the New York Chapter of the American Institute of Architects, and funding especially from the Ford Foundation, twenty-five students began in Architecture in the Neighborhoods in summer 1968. Depending on their results on standardized test scores, they received instruction in math, reading, and English; attended workshops on engineering and computing; went on field trips; and, most centrally, took studio courses that taught drawing, three-dimensional exercises, and architectural design. While many studio assignments were simply to develop skills and familiarize students with spatial thinking, design prompts emphasized more substantial projects. Two such assignments focused on a small vacation home and brownstone rehabilitation. Suggesting the program's interest in skills relevant to students' real lives, leaders concluded that the latter was "a more meaningful experience" for them. Those who completed the summer program—nineteen in this first class—continued evening classes while entering full-time professional placements, especially in architectural offices, where employers were required to commit to providing meaningful design work—not menial positions that would reinforce racial and social hierarchies already present in the profession.[14]

Twelve students remained by the spring of 1969, eight of whom continued in architecture schools including Michigan, Howard, Kansas, and City College of New York, with some financial support from the program. One graduate, Kenneth Knuckles, would go on to a long career in New York urban development. Ford Foundation funding concluded in 1970, yet Architecture in the Neighborhoods held on until at least late 1972. It ceased soon after, however; Planning for Change likewise ended in the early 1970s. ARCH closed its doors around the end of 1974, scrambling for money as the federal government withdrew from urban commitments. "Architecture and planning are just too important to be omitted from the lives of people who happen to be poor," Symes had argued in the *New York Times* in 1969. These efforts to empower young, typically low-income New Yorkers of color offered pedagogical models for diversifying design fields whose exclusivity had surely contributed to their racially disparate effects at mid-century. As the optimism of the Great Society and utopianism of Black Power tipped to the retrenchment and cynicism of the Nixon and Ford years, however, those experiments and their ambitions left the scene.[15]

1. C. Richard Hatch Associates, *Planning for Change: A Course in Urban Politics and Neighborhood Planning for the Fourth and Fifth Grades in New York City's Public Schools: Teacher's Manual* (New York: Center for Urban Education, 1968), ii.
2. Richard Hatch, "Planning for Change: Towards Neighborhood Design and Urban Politics in the Public Schools," *Perspecta* 12 (1969): 43.
3. C. Richard Hatch Associates, Inc., *Planning for Change* (New York: Center for Urban Education, 1968), n.p.
4. The effort gained the support of the Center for Urban Education (CUE), a laboratory under the oversight of the US Department of Health, Education, and Welfare that focused on creative pedagogical approaches in urban schools. On CUE, see Robert A. Dentler, "Eulogy on a Laboratory: The Center for Urban Education," *Urban Review* 6, no. 5–6 (September 1973): 3–7.

5. C. Richard Hatch, "Children as Urban Planners: A Center Report," *Urban Review* 2, no. 3 (December 1967): 24; Hatch, *Planning for Change: Teacher's Manual*, C-O 8.
6. Hatch, *Planning for Change: Teacher's Manual*, S-B 3.
7. Hatch, "Planning for Change," *Perspecta*, 44.
8. Hatch, *Planning for Change: Teacher's Manual*, L-II 9.
9. Ibid., L-VI 2–3.
10. Hatch, *Planning for Change: Teacher's Manual*, L-III 14–17, L-VI 7–9.
11. For example, in 1968–1969, Hatch taught in the Department of City Planning at Yale University as well as in the architecture studio curriculum at Columbia University; his successor at ARCH, J. Max Bond, Jr., likewise taught in the Division of Architecture at Columbia beginning in spring 1968, a period when ARCH became deeply involved in Harlemites' activism against the university's plans to build a gymnasium in Morningside Park. See Brian D. Goldstein, *The Roots of Urban Renaissance: Gentrification and the Struggle over Harlem* (Cambridge, MA: Harvard University Press, 2017), 68–70; Sharon Sutton, *When Ivory Towers Were Black: A Story about Race in America's Cities and Universities* (New York: Fordham University Press, 2017), 87–88; Hatch, "Planning for Change," *Perspecta*, 43.
12. "ARCH Notes for Neighborhood Projects," February 25, 1965, box 8, folder 34, Nelam L. Hill Papers, Schomburg Center for Research in Black Culture, New York Public Library, New York; ARCH, "Curriculum Advisory Committee for a Technical Training School," June 10, 1965, Walter Thabit Private Collection (in possession of Marci Reaven).
13. Arthur L. Symes and Rae Banks, *Architecture in the Neighborhoods* (New York: ARCH, Cooper Union School of Art and Architecture, and New York Chapter of the American Institute of Architects, 1968), 4.
14. Symes and Banks, *Architecture in the Neighborhoods*, 10–15, 19.
15. "Negro Architects Helping Harlem Plan Its Future," *New York Times*, March 16, 1969, 57; Lynn Haney, "Training of Blacks as Architects Increasing," *New York Times*, March 15, 1970, 354; "New York Chapter, the American Institute of Architects, Equal Opportunities Committee, "Minutes of Meeting," February 5, 1970, John L. Wilson Papers, Schomburg Center for Research in Black Culture, New York Public Library, New York; "Architects in the Neighborhood," *Partisan Planning*, November 1972, 8–11; Goldstein, *The Roots of Urban Renaissance*, 147.

THE BLACK WORKSHOP

Jessica Varner

Protagonists Charles Brewer, Richard Dozier,
Reginald L. Jackson, Joseph Middlebrooks, E.
Donald van Purnell, Charles H. Taylor Jr.
Institution Yale University
Location New Haven, CT, USA
Dates 1968–late 1970s

In 1968 ten Yale University students from architecture, city planning, and graphic design joined together to found the "Black Workshop" activist group. Though Yale had awarded an honorary doctorate to Martin Luther King Jr. in 1964 and admitted a record number of African American students—fourteen in all—that same year, racial tensions remained apparent in the seams and cracks of the university. Yale still had no African American professors and offered little support to African American students. The Black Workshop came together to redress both the university's inadequate response to its newly admitted students and its longstanding neglect of the greater New Haven community. Through operations extending from fieldwork in the Dwight neighborhood to admissions counseling for prospective students and faculty hiring measures, it fought to bring community engagement, new methods, and diverse faces to Yale University.

Yale's failure to address the "urban crisis" or the "Black experience" in New Haven—a city violently torn apart by urban renewal practices—was fundamental to the group's mission.[1] From the beginning,

it set up outside the walls of Yale, as an "extension school" or "outside school within the university," [2] a deliberate counterpoint to the institution's policy of disengagement: "[T]oo often has the university ignored its responsibility to the community in which it found itself."[3]

To invert New Haven's bulldozer-and-megastructure past, the Black Workshop led a range of community projects from 1968 to 1969. Besides planning the Hill neighborhood model cities program and rehabilitating eight units within the Portsea Street row houses, it advocated for the Dwight neighborhood schools and designed and set criteria for the Newark Day-Care Council for the New Jersey Department of Community Affairs. As noted by Richard Dozier, one of the Black Workshop's founders, "Architects need not always build a building. In some communities building a building might be the worst option."[4]

The workshop also resisted Yale's pedagogical conventions and proposed new structures for architectural education by redefining expertise, developing new methods for teaching, and formulating alternative ways to evaluate work and give course credits for community design projects (which did not fit into the limited academic schedule, and did not stop when the semester ended). The Black Workshop conducted local fieldwork studios that were redesigned each term; open-ended results were encouraged. In the absence of set texts on community design, students were free to develop self-directed research programs in law, health, federal programs, cultural methods, and design. A similar freedom extended to collaborations beyond the university. For example, in February 1970, workshop members traveled to raise interest in organization among Black architects, planners, and students. From this outreach, architects Donald L. Stull (Boston), J. Max Bond Jr. (New York), and Arthur Symes (Harlem) were asked to volunteer as teachers in the workshop on weekends. Funds were short. Black Workshop students paid tuition to Yale, and were granted degrees from Yale, but the program ran outside the university.

Praise and support for the Black Workshop came from places of power, but the university's central administration was mostly unsupportive. In 1970 Charles Moore, Dean of the Faculties of Design and Planning, appealed to Yale President Kingman Brewster, Jr. for assistance. "The Black Workshop is a most important part of the School,"[5] he wrote, requesting funding from Yale's Davenport Fund, which paid the salaries of professors such as James

Stirling and Robert Venturi. Moore also proposed that the Black Workshop should be granted its own space and autonomy to run its community internship program and project-based curriculum. After two years of continuous lobbying, Yale University gave the workshop a storefront space on Chapel Street and a meager $2,000 operating budget to support its "social" aims.[6]

The Black Workshop continued to fight on various fronts for over a decade, but without full institutional support or financial backing it petered out in the late 1970s. Richard Dozier, by then an assistant professor at Yale, reconceived the actions of the workshop within a less revolutionary program. Renamed the Black Environmental Studies Team, the workshop was effectively absorbed into the university and its radical intentions were diluted.[7]

1. Richard Dozier, "The Black Architect at Yale," *Design Quarterly*, no. 82/83 (1971): 16.
2. Letter to Howard Weaver from Black Workshop, May 12, 1969, cited in Brian Goldstein, "Planning's End? Urban Renewal in New Haven, the Yale School of Art and Architecture, and the Fall of the New Deal Spatial Order," *Journal of Urban History* 37, no. 3 (2011): 410.
3. Letter to the Admissions Committee (City Planning) from the Black Workshop, Inc., April 10, 1970, Yale Manuscripts and Archives, New Haven, CT.
4. Ibid.
5. Letter to Kingman Brewster, Jr. from Dean Charles Moore, June 22, 1970, Yale Manuscripts and Archives, New Haven, CT.
6. Dozier, "The Black Architect at Yale," 16.
7. Robert A. M. Stern and Jimmy Stamp, *Pedagogy and Place: 100 Years of Architecture Education at Yale* (New Haven: Yale University Press, 2016), 318.

< Poster from the Equality Protests that the Black Workshop helped to organize. From Yale Daily News, 1969.

RESEARCH, PUBLICIZE, PROTEST

Christopher Barker

Protagonist The Architects' Resistance (TAR)
Institutions Columbia University, Massachusetts Institute of Technology (MIT), Yale University
Locations New York, NY; Cambridge, MA; New Haven, CT, USA
Dates 1968–1970

The Architects' Resistance (TAR) was a network of architecture students and faculty from Columbia, MIT, Yale, and other schools in the US that emerged from the protests, occupations, and shutdowns of the 1968–1969 academic year. TAR described itself as "an action group, a communications network, and a research organization."[1] Like SDS and other student organizations of the period, it was mostly comprised of local campus chapters that mobilized together on issues of national significance. TAR was angered by the architectural profession's complicity with the social and political crises of the late 1960s. It argued that the profession was dominated by corporate and governmental interests; that architects had neglected their moral responsibility to society; and that architecture had been reduced to a purely technical and aesthetic undertaking. "Architecture is not an abstract art existing in a moral void," declared TAR, "Because it is part of a larger process we must also be concerned with such larger issues as ending the war in Vietnam, ending imperialistic exploitation, supporting black liberation, and achieving a more equal distribution of economic power."[2]

TAR's message was conveyed through press releases, position papers, protests, and conferences that politicized current events in architectural education and practice. These elements were coordinated in a series of "radical action projects" (a term in circulation among activist circles at the time)—short campaigns that were equal parts research, agit-prop, and activism. In its "Architecture and Racism" campaign (March 1969), TAR condemned Skidmore, Owings and Merrill's lucrative contract with the Anglo-American Corporation to design the Carlton Centre in Johannesburg, South Africa (completed 1974). Architecture for racists, TAR argued, was racist architecture. After SOM declined an invitation from MIT students to speak in Cambridge about the project, TAR rolled out protests in Boston, New York,

and Washington DC. Seeking maximum symbolic impact, it organized the protests to coincide with the anniversary of the Sharpeville massacre, both a symbol of the brutality of apartheid, and the beginning of a period when new streams of foreign investment enriched South Africa after its forced withdrawal from the British Commonwealth.

Another radical action project called "Architects and the Nuclear Arms Race" was launched later that spring. TAR opposed a new fallout shelter design program directed by the Office of Civil Defense and endorsed by the AIA. In Boston, TAR circulated a petition to architecture schools and private firms. "The American Institute of Architects, the architecture schools, and individual architects are receiving thousands of dollars from the Office of Civil Defense in return for helping the OCD foist a large and dangerous hoax on the American people," TAR

argued.[3] TAR's "counter-conference" at the Boston Architecture Center proved far more popular than the official OCD-AIA lecture taking place in the same venue.

TAR gained national attention at the 1969 AIA convention in Chicago, where the architectural press eagerly reported on the actions of radical students. In alliance with Students Associated for Responsible Architecture (SARA) and the AIA Association of Student Chapters (AIA/ASC), TAR prevailed on the AIA to adopt a resolution inspired by its "Architecture and Racism" campaign, "that AIA members not accept commissions which tend to support racial discrimination."[4] A second resolution established an AIA/ASC joint task force to raise and manage a $15m fund for new initiatives in community design. (A third resolution proposed by TAR—that the AIA immediately disassociate

itself from the OCD's fallout shelter program—was defeated.) In the following weeks, the AIA took out advertisements in national newspapers to proclaim its social commitment, but the ambitious new $15m program remained vaguely defined, and only a fraction of the amount was ever raised.

The Architects' Resistance was a vocal critic of mainstream American architecture during the twilight of the 1960s. TAR censured the insensitivity and greed of the profession, but also promoted community design as a better alternative to conventional private practice. "All people must have the right and power to control their own lives," declared TAR in its first internal group statement, collectively signed by fifty students and faculty at the Yale School of Art and Architecture, the day after staging a walkout at the American Institute of Architects' New England Regional Conference in November 1968.[5] For TAR, architecture needed to become "[a] less cumbersome, mysterious, expensive, and elite process and a more routine service available to anyone."[6]

v The Architects' Resistance, "Architecture and Racism" handbill, March 1969.

WE ARE MEMBERS OF THE ARCHITECTS' RESISTANCE - WE ARE HERE TODAY TO CHARGE SKIDMORE, OWINGS AND MERRILL WITH RACISM AND HYPOCRISY. ON MARCH 21, 1960 THE GOVERNMENT OF SOUTH AFRICA OPENED FIRE ON A PEACEFUL DEMONSTRATION IN SHARPEVILLE - KILLING 67 PEOPLE - ONE ACT IN AN ENDLESS SERIES OF ATROCITIES COMMITTED AGAINST THE BLACK PEOPLE OF SOUTH AFRICA.
TODAY MARCH 21, 1969, SKIDMORE, OWINGS AND MERRILL, THE MOST PRESTIGIOUS ARCHITECTURAL FIRM IN THE UNITED STATES, IS BUILDING THE 50 MILLION DOLLAR, 51 STORY CONCRETE BUILDING, CARLTON CENTER, IN JOHANNESURG, IN THE HEART OF RACIST SOUTH AFRICA.
THIS PROJECT CLEARLY DEMONSTRATES SOM'S ALLIANCE FOR PROFIT WITH AN IMPRESSIVE LIST OF CORPORATIONS WHOSE HUGE INVESTMENTS IN SOUTH AFRICA ARE RESPONSIBLE FOR MAINTAINING THE OPPRESSIVE APARTHEID SYSTEM. THIS ALLIANCE HAS ALSO BROUGHT OVER 20 MILLION DOLLAR COMMISSIONS TO SOM'S DRAWING BOARDS. THE ARCHITECTS' RESISTANCE BELIEVES THAT THE PROFESSION OF ARCHITECTURE HAS A RESPONSIBILITY GREATER THAN THE PURSUIT OF PROFIT.
WE ARE A GROUP OF ARCHITECTS, ARCHITECTURE STUDENTS, PLANNERS AND DRAFTSMEN WHO BELIEVE THAT ARCHITECTURE, LIKE OTHER PROFESSIONS, IS NOT AN END IN ITSELF, BUT PART OF A POLITICAL PROCESS, A PROCESS THAT SHOULD GRANT ALL PEOPLE THE RIGHT TO CONTROL THEIR OWN LIVES AND BE GOVERNED BY HUMAN VALUES, NOT MATERIAL ONES.
WE ARE HERE TODAY TO DEMAND THAT SKIDMORE, OWINGS AND MERRILL AND PAUL WEIDLINGER ASSOC. (ENGINEERS) IMMEDIATELY DISSOCIATE THEMSELVES FROM THE CARLTON PROJECT AND REMIT ALL PROFITS ACCRUED THERE TO BLACK ORGANIZATIONS IN SOUTH AFRICA. WE ALSO DEMAND THAT THE AMERICAN INSTITUTE OF ARCHITECTS PUBLICLY CENSOR SOM AND ANY OTHER FIRMS BUILDING IN SOUTH AFRICA AND THAT THEY IMMEDIATELY DROP THESE FIRMS FROM MEMBERSHIP IF THEY REFUSE TO HALT THEIR OPERATIONS IN SOUTH AFRICA.

1. The Architects' Resistance, "Architecture and Racism," Position Paper no. 1 (March 1969), n.p.; collected in Art Workers Coalition, Open Hearing (New York: Art Workers Coalition, 1969), 101-103.
2. TAR, "Architects and the Nuclear Arms Race," Position Paper no. 2 (May 1969), n.p.
3. Ibid.
4. "So Ordered," AIA Journal (September 1969): 85.
5. "Meeting of Architects and Planners Concerned with Community-Run Communities and Environments for Users," Meeting minutes, November 9, 1968, private collection of Robert Goodman.
6. TAR, "Architects and Registration," Position Paper no. 4 (May 1970), 3.

FROM *COURS SAUVAGE* TO ARCHITECTURAL ACTIVISM

Jean-Louis Violeau

Protagonists Students and faculty
Institutions Unité Pédagogique No. 6 (UP6) and
Unité Pédagogique d'Architecture Nantes (UPAN)
Location Paris and Nantes, France
Dates 1969–1974

If we could retain some of the events that made May 1968 possible, they would—for the generation that was born in the 1980s and is nostalgic for the 1960s—certainly be as follows: the decision to speak out ("la prise de parole"), which Michel de Certeau has described so well for those who did not experience May 68;[1] the meetings held beyond the atomized times of everyday life; and, finally, the comeback of utopia. Regarding architecture and its pedagogy, the Unité Pédagogique no. 6 (UP6) in Paris was the school that most pushed forward the lessons of May 1968. But UP6 also had a smaller, more provincial ally in Nantes: the Unité Pédagogique d'Architecture (UPAN), which

was influenced by the so-called "Mao-spontex," a spontaneous political current that avoided the characteristic seriousness of the proletarian left and advocated instead for a return to the grassroots, and for listening to the masses.

Both schools became a site of activism beyond the confines of architecture education, as the place of origin, and first meeting place, for various political groups. The group VLR (Vive la Révolution!) founded not only the magazine *Tout! Ce que nous voulons: TOUT!*, the one leftwing periodical truly interested in urban struggles, but also two other major post-1968 movements: FHAR (Front Homosexuel d'Action Révolutionnaire), which sought the social recognition of homosexuality, and the feminist MLF (Mouvement de Libération des Femmes), which published its first dossiers in *Tout!*

To understand the numerous "pedagogic experiences" that emerged in France between 1969 and 1975, one has to go back to November 18, 1969, the date of the first so-called "wild course" (*cours sauvage*). Organized less than a year after the founding of the Unités Pédagogiques, it marked the beginning of a series of protests against the educational reforms promoted by the Ministry of

Culture. At the Louvre, in front of the politically charged sculpture *Winged Victory of Samothrace*, the sociologist Bruno Queysanne staged a public intervention titled "Le Capital dans la Construction et les Travaux Publics." The two hundred students who attended the event appropriated the slogans of the nascent strike: "Urbanisme = spéculation," "Pas de prof de construction," and "3 morts par jour sur les chantiers."[2]

In Nantes, until the opening of a formal school in 1974, architectural education revolved first around the question of program and, later, around the construction of new buildings, a process which was then understood as "theoretical practice." In this context, the Nouvelle École (New School) group was constituted in 1971 as the Centre d'Étude et de Recherche Opérationnelle en Architecture (Center for Operational Study and Research in Architecture). Over the next three years, the entire faculty worked with students on proposals for functional distributions of space and program. This led to the development of a complex space defined by metal girders: the beams featured a geometry typical of the early 1970s, a framework with forty-five-degree angles, creating sections of twenty-five square meters—each intended for work groups of twenty-five students. These liberalized and labyrinthine spaces represented a rupture with the ideal type of the immense Beaux-Arts atelier. Despite functional flaws in the construction, everyone was allowed to work in isolation or in small groups in a way that allowed radical changes of atmosphere within the space of a few meters. In line with the spirit of the time, the building was never officially inaugurated, but rather was inhabited and appropriated by the students.

Simultaneously, during the summer of 1972, two issues of *Les Temps Modernes* (nos. 313 and 314–315)

were edited collectively, providing active support to the struggles of agricultural labor in the surrounding areas of Nantes. Indeed, the public figure of Bernard Lambert, as well as the movement of "worker peasants," were born in the region at that time.

In all these instances, architectural interventions became the vehicle for defiant political activism in the public sphere. In 1971, when the design process for the new school at Nantes had just begun, there was even a suggestion to simply build a huge garage, as a hub for trucks which would go forth to spread architects' wisdom to the surrounding cities. It is necessary to remember this period, as—at least in France—the human sciences landed with a crash in architectural teaching, changing the field forever. To quote one of the Maoist slogans so popular at the time: "The one who has not done research has no right to speak out!"

∧ Plastic arts workshop, UPAN new school site of Mulotière, 1975. Georges Evano and Jean-Luc Pellerin, with Bernard Barto. Photograph by Gilbert Champenois.

< UP6 Villeneuve la Garenne students give shape to a new "Maison du Peuple," May 1972.

1. See Michel de Certeau, *La Prise de parole et autres écrits politiques*, ed. Luce Giard (Paris: Seuil, 1994). Certeau's analysis was first published as *La Prise de parole. Pour une nouvelle culture* (Paris: Desclée De Brouwer, 1968).
2. "Urbanism = speculation," "No professor of construction," "Three deaths every day on building sites."

REVOLUTIONARY LEARNING IN THE NEIGHBORHOOD

Joaquim Moreno

Protagonists Álvaro Siza Vieira (1933–), Francisco Guedes (1945–2013), Eduardo Souto de Moura (1952–), Adalberto Dias (1953–), Domingos Tavares (1939–), Manuela Sambade, Graça Nieto, Paula Cabral
Institution Architecture Section, Escola de Belas Artes do Porto (ESBAP), Universidade de Porto
Location Porto, Portugal
Dates 1974–1976

In August 1974, four months after the Carnation Revolution that brought it to power, Portugal's new socialist government issued a decree creating the SAAL (Mobile Local Support Service) program. Matching financial and technical support with grassroots politics and community organization, SAAL was arguably the most intense moment of "social architecture" in Portugal in recent times.

For architecture students at ESBAP, Porto's School of Fine Arts, which had been practically paralyzed by an "experimental" pedagogy and student protests, SAAL was both an extension and an alternative: an extension because it offered the opportunity to work closely with local populations; an alternative because it opened up a mode of experimental practice focused on new conditions for urban life. Architect Álvaro Siza Vieira, who was teaching in Porto at the time, captured well the paradoxical nature of this collaborative work: "Architecture represents compromise transformed into radical expression; the capacity to reconcile opposites and overcome contradictions. To learn this requires an education that looks for otherness within each one."[1] For architecture students, the SAAL program offered a radical new perspective on the relations between architecture and society—and also between design and building, often involving a bottom-up approach to construction.

Before SAAL, faculty and students at the Porto school had engaged with the city through surveys of specific neighborhoods and studio assignments focused on the design of social facilities. But institutional stasis—the "impossibility of designing without knowing"[2] (an analytical position that deferred action)—meant their efforts were of no use to impoverished neighborhoods that were fighting for their survival, under threat from a totalitarian regime that wanted to raze the housing and decant the inhabitants to the periphery of the city. Nonetheless, this prior experience helped to establish a shared sense of belonging that was fundamental for SAAL's principal means of operation: grassroots political organization and the formation of residents' committees to steer the process.

< Meeting of residents and architects in the Leal neighborhood of Porto, 1975. Photograph by Sergio Fernandez.

Eduardo Souto de Moura and Adalberto Dias, then fourth-year students, recalled the earlier investigations undertaken by the school in the São Victor area. They had traced the nuclei of the so-called "proletarian islands"—rowhouses packed behind a street façade—and established basic criteria such as the number of people living in each house, or the number of families that had to share a single toilet.[3] These studies would allow them to jumpstart the SAAL process, which opened up the opportunity not only for active political engagement, helping local communities, but also for professional practice.

Both Dias and Souto de Moura thought it imperative to seize this opportunity but also understood that their education had not prepared them well for the task. For help in designing the housing, they turned to Siza, who they considered the best architect on the faculty. Siza has recalled the experience as one of intense dialogue, encounter, and confrontation.

Rather than supporting an approach that hovered between a reticent "architecture by the people" and a paternalistic "architecture for the people," Siza proposed a design-based alternative. In conditions of scarcity—of building materials, space, time—form

had to be discovered through a consideration of the architectural issues. Only a collaborative design process could foster Siza's alternative: "architecture *with* the people." The design was therefore guided by a number of pressing questions: How to start immediately but also have a plan? How to construct in dialogue instead of manipulating the dialogue? How to learn construction and also learn how to build things with others? How to articulate the right to housing and the right to the city? How to resolve the lack of space without losing the feeling of solidarity in the community? How to transform compromise into radical expression?

These questions all came into play in the construction of new social housing on the empty site of Senhora das Dores, where the neighborhood committee drove the process forward with a sense of urgency. In this context, where it was almost necessary to build before designing, Siza's transmission of the accumulated knowledge of modern housing projects proved vital. While the experiments of Bruno Taut or J. J. P. Oud were not technically replicable in Porto's inner city, given the scarcity of resources, these well-tested projects were useful references for a very delicate design experiment. Developed by a "technical brigade" led by Siza and mostly made up of architecture students engaged in an intense dialogue with the community, the Senhora das Dores housing remains an intense and fragile memento of the experimental application of SAAL's revolutionary ideals.

For those who lived this experiment from within, as students, drafting through the night and visiting the building the next morning, it was a dramatic introduction to both the role of architects in society and the role of participation in the discipline. The stagnation of the Porto school became an opportunity—an event where architecture overlapped with violence and reality; a juncture bringing together different scales, from the small islands of housing in the inner-city neighborhoods to the dreams and disappointments of the revolution; an occasion when architects were asked to face the growing complexities and contradictions of participating in changing social paradigms and to turn those challenges into a postinstitutional method.

∧ Álvaro Siza on site at SAAL's São Victor social housing, Porto, 1974.

> Residents demanding "total autonomy for the residents' commissions," Porto, 1975. Photograph by Alexandre Alves Costa.

1. Álvaro Siza, "Sobre pedagogia," in *01 Textos* (Porto: Civilização Editora, 2009), 167–169. Original in *Jornadas Pedagógicas*, FAUP, 1995.
2. See José António Bandeirinha, *O Processo SAAL e a Arquitectura no 25 de Abril de 1974* (Coimbra: Imprensa da Universidade, 2007).
3. Information based on unpublished interviews with the protagonists of this process.

CONTRIBUTORS

Michael Abrahamson is an architectural historian and critic whose work explores the systems of creativity, subordination, and legitimation that undergird architectural practice. He is currently career-line faculty at the University of Utah.

Anthony Acciavatti is a historian who focuses on overlaps between the histories of science and architecture in Asia and the Americas. He is the Daniel Rose Visiting Assistant Professor in Urban Studies at Yale University.

Ghada Al Slik is Professor of Architecture at the University of Baghdad. Her work focuses on Iraqi contemporary architecture and heritage preservation. She is the Chair of Docomomo Iraq.

José Aragüez is an architect, writer, and Adjunct Assistant Professor of Architecture at Columbia University. He is the editor of *The Building* (Lars Müller Publishers, 2016), and his work focuses on architectural thinking as a form of knowledge.

Shaimaa S. Ashour is an architect with multidisciplinary interests ranging from Egyptian nineteenth- and twentieth-century architecture to cultural heritage, architectural advertising and urban history. She is an Associate Professor at the Arab Academy for Science, Technology, and Maritime Transport.

Pep Avilés is Assistant Professor at the Department of Architecture at Penn State University and editor of the journal *Faktur: Documents and Architecture.*

Daniel A. Barber is Associate Professor of Architecture and Chair of the PhD Program in Architecture at the University of Pennsylvania Weitzman School of Design.

Christopher Barker is a PhD candidate at the Graduate School of Architecture, Planning, and Preservation, Columbia University.

Joseph Bedford is Assistant Professor of History and Theory at Virginia Tech and the founding director of the Architecture Exchange, a platform for theoretical exchange in architecture.

Merve Bedir is an architect whose practice focuses on collaborative design and alternative learning processes. She is an Adjunct Assistant Professor at Hong Kong University.

Barnaby Bennett is a designer, researcher, and publisher. He holds a practice-based PhD from the University of Technology Sydney and is the founder of Freerange Press.

Anna Bokov is an architect and historian. Her book *Avant-Garde as Method: Vkhutemas and the Pedagogy of Space, 1920–1930* (2020) focuses on the Russian counterpart of the Bauhaus and its groundbreaking educational experiments.

John R. Blakinger is Endowed Associate Professor of Contemporary Art and Director of the Art History Program at the University of Arkansas. He is the author of *Gyorgy Kepes: Undreaming the Bauhaus* (MIT Press, 2019).

Valerio Borgonuovo is an independent curator, researcher, educator, and teacher with a post-degree specialization in neuroscience, art, and culture management. He is the coauthor of *Global Tools 1973–1975. When Education Coincides with Life* (Nero Editions, 2019).

Martin Braathen, PhD, is an architect and curator at the National Museum, Oslo, Norway.

Victoria Bugge Øye is an architectural critic and historian based in New York. She is a PhD candidate at Princeton University School of Architecture, where her work focuses on architecture post-1945 and its intersections with discourses of science, medicine, and the environment.

Piotr Bujas is an architect, designer, researcher, curator, and founder of Bureau of Architecture, Design-Research (BADR) and of TRACE: Central European Architectural Research Network.

Hans Butzer is Dean of the Gibbs College of Architecture at the University of Oklahoma. Butzer is an award-winning architect and educator and cofounder of Butzer Architects and Urbanism (BAU).

Marta Caldeira is an architect and historian. Her research investigates transnational discourses of architecture and the city, with a particular focus on historical contexts of political transition. She is a Senior Lecturer at Yale School of Architecture and Director of Research at Yale Urban Design Workshop.

Esther Choi is the coeditor of *Architecture at the Edge of Everything Else* (MIT, 2010) and *Architecture Is All Over* (Columbia, 2017; with Marrikka Trotter). She holds a PhD from Princeton University.

Martín Cobas is Professor of Architectural History and Design at Universidad de la República, Montevideo, and editor of the journal *Vitruvia*. His work focuses on the histories and theories of modernization in Brazil and the New World.

Beatriz Colomina is the Howard Crosby Butler Professor of the History of Architecture and the founding director of the program in Media and Modernity at Princeton University. Her books include *X-Ray Architecture* (2019), *Are We Human?* (2016), *The Century of the Bed* (2015), *Manifesto Architecture* (2014), *Clip/Stamp/Fold* (2010), *Domesticity at War* (2007), *Privacy and Publicity* (1994), and *Sexuality and Space* (1992).

Diana Cristóbal is an architect and PhD candidate in Architectural History at Princeton University. Her work bridges histories of science and technology with modern architecture and urban design. She is an Adjunct Assistant Professor at Barnard College.

Roberto Damiani is an Assistant Professor—Teaching Stream at the John H. Daniels in Toronto and editor of *The Architect and the Public: On George Baird's Contribution to Architecture* (2020).

Eva Díaz is Associate Professor of Contemporary Art History at Pratt and author of *The Experimenters: Chance and Design at Black Mountain College* (University of Chicago Press, 2015). She recently completed the manuscript of her new book, *After Spaceship Earth*, analyzing the influence of R. Buckminster Fuller in contemporary art.

Isabelle Doucet is Professor of Theory and History of Architecture at Chalmers University of Technology, Sweden. Through a focus on resistant practices and conceptual-methodological inquiries, she studies the relationship between architecture, (urban) politics, and social/environmental responsibility.

Zvi Efrat, architect and architectural historian, is partner at Efrat-Kowalsky Architects (EKA) and was formerly Head of the Department of Architecture at the Bezalel Academy of Arts and Design. His book, *The Object of Zionism, The Architecture of Israel,* was published by Spector Books, Leipzig, in 2018.

Britt Eversole is Assistant Professor of Architecture at the Syracuse University School of Architecture, where he teaches architectural theory, research, and design. His research examines intersections of politics, technology, and architecture.

Daniela Fabricius is a historian and theorist of architecture and urbanism, and Adjunct Assistant Professor at the Pratt Institute.

Silvia Franceschini is a curator, editor, and researcher whose work deals with postcolonialism, comparative modernities, and globalization in contemporary art and design. She is associate curator at Z33 House for Contemporary Art in Hasselt and coauthor of *Global Tools 1973–1975. When Education Coincides with Life* (Nero Editions, 2019).

Ignacio G. Galán is an architect, historian, and Assistant Professor at Barnard College, Columbia University. His work studies the relation between architecture, politics, and media with a focus on nationalism, colonialism, and migration.

Curt Gambetta is a designer and historian whose work focuses on postcolonial India, histories of fieldwork in architecture, and waste infrastructure. He is a PhD candidate at Princeton University.

Julia Gatley is an Associate Professor at the University of Auckland School of Architecture and Planning. Her research focuses on twentieth-century New Zealand architecture.

Brian D. Goldstein is an Assistant Professor at Swarthmore College. His research focuses on the history of the built environment, race and class, and social movements in the US. He is the author of *The Roots of Urban Renaissance* (Harvard University Press, 2017).

Anna Goodman is an Assistant Professor at Portland State University. She studies architectural politics, including how discourses and aesthetics of labor organize architectural education.

James Graham is an architect and historian. He teaches at the California College of the Arts.

Nina Gribat is professor of urban planning at B-TU Cottbus-Senftenberg, Germany. Her work mainly focuses on urban restructuring processes in East Germany and study reforms at architecture faculties in West Germany in the 1960s and 1970s.

Vanessa Grossman is an architect, a historian, and a curator whose research focuses on architecture's intersections with ideology, power, and governance, with a special focus on global practices in Cold War era Europe and Latin America. She is an Assistant Professor at Delft University of Technology.

Berin F. Gür is an architectural scholar whose studies focus on design, politics of space, theory and criticism of contemporary architecture. She is a Professor at TED University Department of Architecture.

Alicja Gzowska is an art historian collaborating with Polish National Institute of Architecture and Urban Planning and University of Warsaw, specializing in postwar Polish architecture.

Soledad Gutiérrez Rodríguez is a curator and researcher, part of the curatorial team of Thyssen-Bornemisza Art Contemporary. Her practice deals with cooperative practices and the immaterial potential of art realized through performance and collective processes.

Samia Henni is an architectural historian and theorist whose work focuses on the intersection of architecture, urbanism, colonial practices, and military measures. She is an Assistant Professor at Cornell University and the author of *Architecture of Counterrevolution* (2017) and the editor of *War Zones* (2018).

Sarah Herda is director of the Graham Foundation for Advanced Studies in the Fine Arts, where she oversees international grantmaking, exhibitions, and public programs.

Dirk van den Heuvel is an Associate Professor at TU Delft and heads the Jaap Bakema Study Centre, Het Nieuwe Instituut in Rotterdam. He is coauthor of *Habitat: Ecology Thinking in Architecture* (2020), *Jaap Bakema and the Open Society* (2018), and *Team 10: In Search of a Utopia of the Present 1953–1981* (2005).

Hilde Heynen is a Professor of Architectural Theory at the University of Leuven, Belgium. Her research focuses on issues of modernity, modernism, and gender.

Sandi Hilal is an architect and researcher, founding member and codirector of DAAR–Decolonizing Architecture Art and residency. She is among the founders of Campus in Camps, an educational program established in Dheisheh Refugee Camp, Bethlehem, and coauthor of *Architecture after Revolution, Permanent Temporariness*, and *Refugee Heritage*.

Michael Hiltbrunner is a cultural anthropologist and art scholar at the Institute for Contemporary Art Research at Zurich University of the Arts. His recent research focuses on personal archives of research-based art and the F+F School in Zurich as a lab for experimental design. He also works as an independent curator and lectures on art theory and cultural analysis.

Rutger Huiberts is an architect (TU Delft '11, *cum laude*) with a background in urbanism. His writing has appeared in *Manifest, Volume, MONU, CLOG, Conditions, OnSite Magazine*, and elsewhere.

Alicia Imperiale is an architect and historian whose research focuses on the interplay between technology and art, architecture, representation, and fabrication in postwar Italy. She teaches at Yale University and Pratt Institute.

Kathleen James-Chakraborty is a historian of early modern and modern architecture. She is a Professor of Art History at University College Dublin. Her books include *Modernism as Memory: Building Identity in the Federal Republic of Germany* (University of Minnesota Press, 2018).

Ruo Jia is a PhD Candidate in History and Theory of Architecture at Princeton University School of Architecture. Her current research focuses on the theorization of the productive gap opened through cross-cultural, translingual, and interdisciplinary translations in the case of French poststructuralist theory of the 1960–1970s and Chinese experimental architecture of the 1990s–2000s.

Lydia Kallipoliti is an architect, engineer, and scholar. She is an Assistant Professor at the Cooper Union and the author of *The Architecture of Closed Worlds*.

Andreas Kalpakci is an architectural historian at ETH Zurich researching international organizations. His dissertation *Making CIAM* (2017, with distinction) reassessed modernism from an institutional perspective.

Farhan Karim's work focuses on architecture in post-independence Bangladesh, Pakistan, and India. He is an architect and Associate Professor at the University of Kansas.

Pamela Karimi is an Associate Professor at the University of Massachusetts Dartmouth and the author of *Domesticity and Consumer Culture in Iran: Interior Revolutions of the Modern Era* (2013) and *Alternative Iran: Contemporary Art and Critical Spatial Practice* (2022). Her current work engages with the US quest for outer space settlements in light of the oil crisis of the 1970s and the geopolitical importance of the Middle East.

Aleksandra Kędziorek is an architecture historian and curator. She co-curated a touring exhibition *Oskar Hansen: Open Form* (2014–2017) and co-edited *Oskar Hansen—Opening Modernism: On Open Form Architecture, Art and Didactics* (2014).

Robert J. Kett is a curator and anthropologist of design and Assistant Professor at ArtCenter College of Design.

Stuart King is a Senior Lecturer in architectural design and history at the University of Melbourne, where he researches in Australian architectural history.

Byron Kinnaird is the Research and Education Officer of the New South Wales (NSW) Architects Registration Board and a codirector of Freerange Press.

Evangelos Kotsioris is a New York-based architectural historian, educator, and curator. His work investigates the intersections of architecture with science, technology, and media.

Vladimir Kulić is an architectural historian whose work focuses on Yugoslavia, Eastern Europe, and the former socialist world. He is an Associate Professor at Iowa State University in Ames.

Anna Kryczka holds a doctorate in Visual Studies from University of California, Irvine and is currently a full-time Humanities Professor at Pasadena City College.

Ana María León is an architect and historian, and teaches at the University of Michigan. Her work examines how spatial practices and discourses of power and resistance produce modernities in the Americas.

Ayala Levin is an architectural historian specialized in architecture and urban planning in postcolonial African states. A particular concern is the production of architectural knowledge as part of north–south or south–south exchanges. She is an Associate Professor at UCLA.

Cristina López Uribe is an architectural historian who specializes in twentieth-century Mexican architecture. She teaches at the National Autonomous University of Mexico and is a member of the Laboratorio Editorial de Arquitectura.

Daniel Magaziner is Professor of History at Yale University, where he teaches nineteenth- and twentieth-century African history. He is the author of two books on South African history and numerous articles on the history of art and design in postcolonial Africa.

Sebastian Malecki holds a PhD in history. He is a researcher at Conicet and Assistant Professor of Architectural History and Argentinean History at the Universidad Nacional de Córdoba. His research focuses on twentieth-century Argentinean architectural history.

Caroline Maniaque is the author of *French Encounters with the American Counterculture 1960–1980* (2011). She co-curated the exhibition *Mai 68. L'architecture aussi!* (Cité de l'architecture et du patrimoine, Paris), edited *Les années 68 et la formation des architectes* (2018), and coedited *Architecture 68. International Panorama of the Renewal of Education* (Geneva: Métis Presses, 2020).

Igor Marjanović is the William Ward Watkin Dean of Rice Architecture. An architect, scholar and curator, he has written extensively on the history of design pedagogy, ideology, and identity.

Bill McKay is a Senior Lecturer at the University of Auckland School of Architecture and Planning. His interests include alternative models of design practice and construction.

Anna-Maria Meister is an architect, historian, critic, and Professor for Architecture Theory and Science at TU Darmstadt. Her work investigates the interdependencies of bureaucratization of design and the design of bureaucracies, focusing on societal projections and social consequences.

James Merle Thomas is an interdisciplinary scholar whose research examines the art, technology, and media cultures of the twentieth and twenty-first centuries. He is an Assistant Professor of Art History at Temple University, and curator at the Philadelphia-based Slought.

Andrea J. Merrett is an architect and historian and holds a PhD from Columbia University, New York. Her work focuses on women, gender, and feminism in the history of architecture. She is a founding member of ArchiteXX.

Marco De Michelis is Professor of Architectural History at the Institute of Architecture, University of Venice. He has authored several books on architectural history and is the former editor of *Ottagono* and former director of the Architecture Gallery of the Triennale, Milan.

Ana Miljački is a critic, curator, and Associate Professor of Architecture at Massachusetts Institute of Technology, where she teaches history, theory, and design. She is the author of *The Optimum Imperative: Czech Architecture for the Socialist Lifestyle 1938–1968* (2017).

Joaquim Moreno is an architect, historian and curator whose current work focuses on the architecture of television. He is Assistant Professor of Architecture History and Theory at the Architecture School of Oporto University.

Matthew Mullane is a postdoctoral fellow at Tokyo College, The University of Tokyo, completing a book on architecture and observation in Japan.

Ivan L. Munuera is a New York-based scholar, critic, and curator working at the intersection of culture, technology, politics, and bodily practices in the modern period and on the global stage. He is currently developing his dissertation on the architecture of HIV/AIDS at Princeton University.

Ijlal Muzaffar is an Associate Professor of Architectural History at the Rhode Island School of Design. His forthcoming book, *The Periphery Within*, explores how modern architects and planners shaped new temporalities and spaces of intervention in the Third World development discourse.

Bushra Nayeem is a PhD candidate at the University of Kansas. Her work is focused on architecture, development, and postcolonial viewpoints.

Ikem Stanley Okoye studied and practiced architecture in the UK (Bartlett, UCL and trained in the history of art and architecture in the US (MIT). He teaches at the University of Delaware and his widely published scholarship focuses on African and Diaspora architecture, art, and landscapes.

Philipp Oswalt has been Professor for Architecture Theory and Design at Kassel University since 2006. He directed the "Urban Catalyst" (2001–2003) and "Shrinking Cities" (2002–2008) projects and was director of the Bauhaus Dessau Foundation (2009–2014).

Ceridwen Owen is Associate Professor in architecture and design at the University of Tasmania, where she explores ecologically sustainable and socially inclusive design practices.

Masha Panteleyeva is an architectural historian whose work focuses on the politics of architectural production during late socialism. She is a lecturer in architecture at Cornell University.

Angela Person is a cultural geographer whose research centers on postwar American architecture, and is Director of Research Initiatives and Strategic Planning in the Gibbs College of Architecture at the University of Oklahoma.

Stephanie Pilat is a designer and architectural historian whose teaching and research examines points of intersection between politics and architecture. Pilat is a Professor and Director of the Division of Architecture at the University of Oklahoma.

Alessandra Ponte is an architectural historian. In recent years she has been researching mining processes and information technologies. She is Full Professor at the Université de Montréal.

David Rifkind is an architectural historian whose research examines modern architecture and urbanism in Italy and the Horn of Africa. He is Director of the School of Architecture at the University of Florida and the author of *The Battle for Modernism:* Quadrante *and the Politicization of Architectural Discourse in Fascist Italy* (2013).

Hannah le Roux is an architect, educator, and curator. Her work revisits the modernist project and its transformation through the design agency of Africans. She is Associate Professor at the University of the Witwatersrand.

Josep M. Rovira is Professor of History of Art and Architecture at the ETSAB, UPC. He was one of the editors of the architectural magazine *Carrer de la Ciutat* and the founder and editor of the art and architecture magazine *3ZU.*

Katerina Rüedi Ray is an architectural historian writing on architectural education, identity formation, and globalization. She is Director Emerita of the School of Art at Bowling Green State University, Ohio.

Marcos Sánchez is on faculty at the University of Southern California and the Southern California Institute of Architecture (SCI-Arc) in Los Angeles.

Eunice Seng is Associate Professor and PhD Program Director in Architecture at the University of Hong Kong and Founding Principal of SKEW Collaborative. Her work explores interdisciplinary intersections and agency in architecture, housing, domesticity, and public space.

Felicity D. Scott is Professor of Architecture at Columbia University. Her books include *Architecture or Techno-Utopia: Politics after Modernism* (MIT Press, 2007), *Ant Farm* (ACTAR, 2008), *Outlaw Territories: Environments of Insecurity/Architectures of Counter-Insurgency* (Zone Books, 2016), and *Disorientations: Bernard Rudofsky in the Empire of Signs* (Sternberg Press, 2016).

Zeinab Y. Shafik is Professor of Architecture at Cairo University. Her work focuses on the areas of human sciences in architecture and urban design; preservation and conservation of sites of heritage value; user participation and community development.

Noam Shoked is an assistant professor at Tel Aviv University. His work focuses on the relationship between architecture and politics in Israel and the occupied West Bank.

Federica Soletta is a PhD candidate in architectural history and theory at Princeton University. Her research focuses on nineteenth-century historiography and the intersection between photography, natural science, and architectural history.

Łukasz Stanek is Senior Lecturer at the University of Manchester, UK. He authored *Henri Lefebvre on Space* (2011) and *Architecture in Global Socialism* (2020).

Molly Wright Steenson is Vice Provost for Faculty at Carnegie Mellon University. She is the author of *Architectural Intelligence: How Designers & Architects Created the Digital Landscape* (MIT Press, 2017) and co-editor of *Bauhaus Futures* (MIT Press, 2019).

Hadas A. Steiner teaches architectural history and theory at the University at Buffalo, SUNY. She is at work on a manuscript, *The Accidental Visitant*, which studies the interactions between the modern fields of ornithology and architecture.

Martino Stierli is The Philip Johnson Chief Curator of Architecture and Design at The Museum of Modern Art, New York.

Irene Sunwoo is the John H. Bryan Chair and Curator of Architecture and Design at the Art Institute of Chicago.

Pelin Tan is an art historian/sociologist whose work focuses on conflict territories, conditions of labor, and transversal research methodologies in art and architecture.

Daniel Talesnik is an architect and architectural historian. He is a curator at the Architekturmuseum of the Technische Universität München.

Horacio Torrent is an architect and architectural historian whose research focuses on the relationship between modern architecture and the city. He is Professor of Architecture at the School of Architecture at Pontificia Universidad Católica de Chile.

Federica Vannucchi holds a PhD in Architecture from Princeton, a master's in Environmental Design from Yale, and an MArch from the University of Florence. She teaches global history and theory of architecture at Pratt School of Architecture in New York.

Jessica Varner is an architect and architectural historian whose work focuses on environmental, material, and legal histories of synthetic chemical use in buildings. She holds a PhD from the Massachusetts Institute of Technology and is currently a Fellow in the USC Society of Fellows.

Jean-Louis Violeau is a French sociologist and professor at l'École nationale supérieure d'architecture de Nantes. He published his PhD, *Les architectes et mai 68,* in 2005, then his HDR, *Les architectes et mai 81,* in 2011, with Éditions Recherches.

Georg Vrachliotis is Professor of Theory of Architecture and Digital Culture at TU Delft.

Paul Walker researches colonial and postcolonial architecture in Australia and New Zealand. He is a Professor at the University of Melbourne.

Joaquín Medina Warmburg is an architectural historian whose approach focuses on phenomena of cultural internationalization in the context of modernity, including technical and environmental issues. He is Full Professor at Karlsruhe Institute of Technology.

Mark Wasiuta is an architect, curator, and writer, and codirector of the Critical, Curatorial, and Conceptual Practices in Architecture Program at Columbia University's Graduate School of Architecture, Planning, and Preservation.

Mark Wigley is Professor and Dean Emeritus at Columbia GSAPP. His books include *Derrida's Haunt* (1993), *White Walls, Designer Dresses* (1995), *Constant's New Babylon* (1998), *Buckminster Fuller Inc.* (2015), *Cutting Matta-Clark* (2018), and *Konrad Wachsmann's Television* (2020).

Mabel O. Wilson is a professor of Architecture and Black Studies at Columbia University. Her books include *Negro Building: Black Americans in the World of Fairs and Museums* (2012) and the co-edited volume *Race and Modern Architecture: From the Enlightenment to Today* (2020).

Onur Yüncü is a practicing architect and design studio critic whose work focuses on research by design and architectural education. He is an Assistant Professor at TED University Department of Architecture.

Lily Zhang is the James Harrison Steedman Memorial Research Fellow in Architecture at Washington University in St. Louis. She studied architecture at Princeton University and the University of California, Berkeley.

ACKNOWLEDGMENTS

Radical Pedagogies is a multi-year collaborative research project that started in 2010 as a series of PhD seminars led by Beatriz Colomina at Princeton University. We would like to thank all the students, scholars, and protagonists who have been vital to this ongoing project.

The project developed through a multitude of media including symposia, lectures, essays, exhibitions, and an online database of case studies—all offering opportunities to test arguments and incorporate new voices. *Radical Pedagogies* was first exhibited at the 3rd Lisbon Architecture Triennale of 2013. It was then developed in a major installation in the Arsenale at the 14th Venice Architecture Biennale of 2014 directed by Rem Koolhaas. An expanded version was shown at the 7th Warsaw Under Construction Festival of 2015, organized by the Museum of Modern Art in Warsaw. We want to thank Federica Vannucchi and Britt Eversole for their crucial contribution as co-curators of the Venice Biennale installation, and Cristóbal Amunátegui and Alejandro Valdés for the design of the installations in both Venice and Warsaw. We also thank the organizers who invited us to share the project in these exhibitions: Beatrice Galilee and José Esparza in Lisbon; Ippolito Pestellini Laparelli and Rem Koolhaas in Venice; and Aleksandra Kędziorek in Warsaw.

We are grateful to the editors of several publications who over the years invited us to present the project in written form. These include: Will Hunter at *The Architectural Review*; Nicholas Risteen at *Pidgin*; Nick Axel at *Volume*; Sony Devabhaktuni, Patricia Guaita, and Cornelia Tapparelli, editors of *Building Cultures Valparaíso: Pedagogy, Practice and Poetry at the Valparaíso School of Architecture and Design*; Ernesto Silva at *Materia Arquitectura*; Ethel Baraona, Guillermo López, Anna Puigjaner, and José Zabala at *Quaderns*. We have also benefited from various invitations to present this project in lectures around the world, and greatly appreciate the opportunity to show the ongoing work and learn from the audience's invaluable responses.

This ever-expanding project has always actively resisted the sense of completeness or linear narrative that the book format may suggest. Rather, it has evolved through the contributions of a diverse and ever-changing group of scholars, educators, and architects from around the world. *Radical Pedagogies* was treated as an open question with so many possible responses. We want to thank all the contributors to the exhibitions and to this volume for sharing their perspectives, research, and expertise. We also want to thank the archivists, librarians, witnesses, and informants, former students or teachers, who have been instrumental to this work.

Radical Pedagogies is part of a wider set of collaborative projects undertaken by the PhD proseminar at Princeton which have culminated in events, exhibitions, and publications over the last twenty years. All the students and participating scholars have to be thanked here because the projects overlap and contaminate each other. In fact, the whole initiative can be seen as an exercise in radical pedagogy—displacing singular, hierarchical, top-down, monolithic disciplinary doctrine with multiplicities, interactivities, and nonhierarchical collaborations.

To bring such a large volume to life is no small feat. We are most grateful to Thomas Weaver at MIT Press for so thoughtfully shepherding the material from draft to book, to Rosa Nussbaum for her inspiring design, to Pamela Johnston for her sensitive copyediting, and to Emma Leigh Macdonald for guiding the image permissions. We also want to express our deep gratitude to Barry Bergdoll, Hal Foster, Sarah Herda, Sylvia Lavin, and Monica Ponce de Leon for their sustained input and support for the project.

The publication of this book has been made possible by the generous support of the Barr Ferree Foundation Fund for Publications at Princeton University, Elise Jaffe and Jeffrey Brown, the Graham Foundation Fund to Individuals, and the Princeton School of Architecture. Over the years, the project has also been the recipient of financial support from Princeton University's Humanities Council, Department of Art and Archeology, Princeton Institute for International and Regional Studies (PIIRS), Department of French and Italian, Program in Latin American Studies (PLAS), Program in Media and Modernity (M+M), and Interdisciplinary Doctoral Program in the Humanities (IHUM).

Lastly, and most importantly, this book is meant to be a beginning rather than an end. While the voluminous tome seems to assert a certain degree of comprehensiveness and finitude, it hints just as much at the many histories of bold, daring experiments in architectural education from the second half of the twentieth century that are yet to be told and shared. Our objective is to offer a resource for further inquiry, interpretation, and invention.

RADICAL PEDAGOGIES EXHIBITIONS

Radical Pedagogies: Action, Reaction, Interaction at the 3rd Lisbon Architecture Triennale: "Close, Closer" in Lisbon, Portugal, from September 12 to December 15, 2013

Curated by Beatriz Colomina, Ignacio G. Galán, Evangelos Kotsioris, Anna-Maria Meister with other PhD students of the School of Architecture at Princeton University. Exhibition design by Ignacio G. Galán, Evangelos Kotsioris, Anna-Maria Meister with Dorit Aviv and Loren Yu. Construction by Dorit Aviv, Ignacio G. Galán, Evangelos Kotsioris, Anna-Maria Meister with John Hunter, Rui Morais e Castro, and POLIGONO.

Radical Pedagogies: Action, Reaction, Interaction at the 14th International Architecture Exhibition of the Venice Biennale "Fundamentals" in Venice, Italy, from June 7 to November 23, 2014

Curated by Beatriz Colomina, Britt Eversole, Ignacio G. Galán, Evangelos Kotsioris, Anna-Maria Meister, Federica Vannucchi with other PhD students of the School of Architecture at Princeton University. Exhibition design by Cristóbal Amunátegui and Alejandro Valdés (Amunátegui Valdés architects). Graphic design by Pablo González (Smog). Installation management by Inmaterial. Multiplatform publishing concept and augmented reality by Ethel Baraona and César Reyes (dpr-barcelona). Web design by Anne-Sophie de Vargas.

Radical Pedagogies: Reconstructing Architectural Education at the Warsaw Under Construction 7 Festival, Warsaw University of Technology, Faculty of Architecture, Warsaw, Poland, from October 12 to November 10, 2015

Curated by Beatriz Colomina, Evangelos Kotsioris with Britt Eversole, Ignacio G. Galán, Anna-Maria Meister, Federica Vannucchi, and other PhD students of the School of Architecture at Princeton University. Curatorial cooperation on behalf of the festival by Aleksandra Kędziorek. Exhibition design by Cristóbal Amunátegui and Alejandro Valdés (Amunátegui Valdés architects). Graphic design by Pablo González (Smog). Facsimiles and website support by Lily J. Zhang.

PREVIOUS PUBLICATIONS

Beatriz Colomina, Esther Choi, Ignacio G. Galán, Anna-Maria Meister, "Radical Pedagogies in Architectural Education," *The Architectural Review* 233, no. 1388 (October 2012): 78–83.

Beatriz Colomina, Ignacio G. Galán, Evangelos Kotsioris, Anna-Maria Meister, "Radical Pedagogies: Lisbon Architecture Triennale," *Pidgin,* no. 17 (Spring 2014): 116–127.

Beatriz Colomina, Ignacio G. Galán, Evangelos Kotsioris, Anna-Maria Meister, "The Radical Pedagogies Project," "The Warsaw Experiment," *Volume,* no. 45: "Learning" (September 2015), 34–37 and special insert.

Beatriz Colomina, Ignacio G. Galán, Evangelos Kotsioris, Anna-Maria Meister, "Radical Pedagogies: Notes Towards a Taxonomy of Global Experiments," in *Building Cultures Valparaíso: Pedagogy, Practice and Poetry at the Valparaíso School of Architecture and Design,* ed. Sony Devabhaktuni, Patricia Guaita, Cornelia Tapparelli (Lausanne: EPFL Press/ Routledge, 2015), 58–79.

Beatriz Colomina, Ignacio G. Galán, Evangelos Kotsioris, Anna-Maria Meister, "Radical Pedagogies," *Quaderns d'Arquitectura i Urbanisme,* Publicació del Collegi d'arquitectes de Catalunya, no. 266–267 (2015): 81–86.

Beatriz Colomina, Ignacio G. Galán, Evangelos Kotsioris, Anna-Maria Meister, "Pedagogías Radicales: Reimaginando los Protocolos Disciplinares de la Arquitectura = Radical Pedagogies: Re-imagining Architecture's Disciplinary Protocols," *Materia Arquitectura,* no. 14 (December 2016): 32–45, 102–107.

IMAGE CREDITS

INDEX